The Child of the Covenant

Being the Child of the Covenant – the Heir of both the Originator and the Interpreter of the Law of God – the Will and Testament of 'Abdu'l-Bahá can no more be divorced from Him Who supplied the original and motivating impulse than from the One Who ultimately conceived it. Bahá'u-'lláh's inscrutable purpose, we must ever bear in mind, has been so thoroughly infused into the conduct of 'Abdu'l-Bahá, and their motives have been so closely wedded together, that the mere attempt to dissociate the teachings of the former from any system which the ideal Exemplar of those same teachings has established would amount to a repudiation of one of the most sacred and basic truths of the Faith.[1]

By the same author

TRUSTEES OF THE MERCIFUL
(Bahá'í Publishing Trust, London 1972)

THE REVELATION OF BAHÁ'U'LLÁH
1. Baghdád 1853–63
2. Adrianople 1863–68
3. 'Akká, The Early Years 1868–77
4. Mazra'ih and Bahjí 1877–92

THE COVENANT OF BAHÁ'U'LLÁH

The Child of the Covenant

A Study Guide to the Will and Testament of 'Abdu'l-Bahá

by

Adib Taherzadeh

GR

George Ronald
Oxford

George Ronald, *Publisher*

A catalogue record for this book is available from the British Library

ISBN 0-85398-439-5

Typeset by Stonehaven Press LLP, Knoxville, Tennessee

Contents

A Note from the Publisher

The numbers identifying passages of the Will and Testament of 'Abdu'l-Bahá refer to paragraphs rather than pages. Thus a passage identified as 4–WT refers to paragraph four of the Will and Testament. Numbering begins with the paragraph 'All-Praise to Him . . .' and continues throughout the book to the final paragraph, number 56. The passage in parentheses following paragraph 29 and beginning 'This written paper . . .' is unnumbered, as are the headings at the start of each section.

Preface

The Will and Testament of 'Abdu'l-Bahá constitutes a fundamental document of the Covenant of Bahá'u'lláh. It is described by Shoghi Effendi as 'the Child of the Covenant'[2] and 'the Charter of a future world civilization, which may be regarded in some of its features as supplementary to no less weighty a Book than the Kitáb-i-Aqdas'.[3] The necessity of a deeper study of this momentous document becomes obvious when we note that Shoghi Effendi has stipulated that one of the qualifications of a true believer is 'loyal and steadfast adherence to every clause of our Beloved's sacred Will'.[4]

With these statements in mind, the author of this book, having previously published *The Covenant of Bahá'u'lláh*, decided to prepare a detailed study guide for the Will and Testament itself. The organizational principle behind this guide is the relationship of various aspects of the Covenant and its verities to almost every subject mentioned by 'Abdu'l-Bahá in His Will and Testament. In some instances a study is made of a full paragraph, in many cases of a sentence, and sometimes of certain words. Parts of this book are extracted from my earlier volume *The Covenant of Bahá'u'lláh* and the reader will therefore find some materials familiar but will appreciate each subject in a different light in the context of the Will and Testament.

To deepen one's knowledge of the Faith is a personal obligation, achieved through the study of the holy writings in a spirit of humility and in a prayerful attitude. This is especially true for an in-depth study of the Will and Testament, of which steadfastness in the Covenant is the major component. Another factor to be borne in mind is the following warning uttered by Shoghi Effendi in a letter written on his behalf on 25 March 1930:

> The contents of the Will of the Master are far too much for the present generation to comprehend. It needs at least a century of actual working before the treasures of wisdom hidden in it can be revealed . . .[5]

It is the hope of the author of this book that this study guide, however inadequate in scope and depth, will stimulate the believers in their own study of this weighty document. To facilitate this, apart from the Table of Contents, a special table has been provided at the end of the book linking each paragraph of the Will and Testament to the corresponding chapters of the book.

Excerpts from the Bahá'í holy writings are either from translations by Shoghi Effendi or those authorized by the Universal House of Justice. Quotations from memoirs of Persian believers are all translated by the author. Persian and Arabic names are transliterated in accordance with the system adopted for books on the Bahá'í Faith.

I am deeply indebted to Dr Ann Boyles for her skilful editing of this book as well as her valuable suggestions to improve its syntax. My grateful thanks to Miss Alda Rendina for excellent typing of the manuscript from my scribbled and often illegible handwriting. My warmest thanks to Miss Breda Nagle for her meticulous checking of the manuscript. I also wish to extend my thanks to Miss Golara Khayltash, Miss Orkideh Mohajeri and Miss Mahsa Vossugh who have assisted in typing certain sections of the book. I am grateful to Wendi Momen for the skilful production of the index. I am also grateful to the Bahá'í Publishing Trust of the United States for permission to quote their booklet *A Tribute to Shoghi Effendi* by Amelia Collins and to the Bahá'í Publishing Trust of the United Kingdom for permission to quote passages from *The Priceless Pearl* by Rúḥíyyih Rabbaní. And last, but not least, my deepest appreciation is offered to my dear wife, Lesley, for her loving support and encouragement, which she has showered upon me throughout.

Adib Taherzadeh
Haifa, July 1999

Introduction

The Revelation of Bahá'u'lláh has given birth to the institution of the Covenant, which endows the human race with undreamt-of potentialities and provides the means for man's infinite progress and spiritual development in this Dispensation.

The terms of this Covenant were revealed by Bahá'u'lláh's pen in the Kitáb-i-Aqdas, followed by His Will and Testament, known as the Kitáb-i-'Ahd. Through these writings Bahá'u'lláh established a mighty and irrefutable Covenant with His followers, a Covenant unprecedented in the annals of past religions. Never before has a Manifestation of God left behind an authoritative statement in which He has explicitly directed His people to turn, after Him, to a successor with the authority to promote the interests of His Faith, to interpret His words, to unravel the significance of His teachings and to expound the aim and purpose of His Revelation. Nor has a Manifestation previously devised a system of administration for governing the religious affairs of the community.

The Gospels are silent on the question of successorship. Only a vague and inconclusive statement, 'And I say also unto thee, That thou art Peter, and upon this rock I will build my church'[6] has led a section of the followers of Christ to consider Peter as His successor. Such a claim, which is not upheld by a clear and unequivocal declaration in the Gospels, has caused bitter conflicts throughout the chequered history of Christianity. As a result, the religion founded by Christ has been divided into major sects which have multiplied through time.

A similar situation arose in Islam. The story of Muḥammad and the statement He is reported to have made concerning 'Alí, His cousin and son-in-law, at G͟hadír-i-K͟humm* may be regarded merely as an allusion to the Prophet's successor and not an explicit and unequivocal appointment. This episode, recounted by both the S͟hí'ah and Sunní sects of Islam, is interpreted differently by each. The story is as follows:

Having completed the rites of pilgrimage to Mecca in the last year of His life, Muḥammad, on His way back to Medina, ordered the large concourse of His followers to stop at a place known as G͟hadír-i-K͟humm. In that vast plain a number of saddles were stacked up,

---

* See also chapter 4

making an improvised pulpit from which Muḥammad delivered an important address to the congregation. There, He is reported to have taken 'Alí by the hand and said, 'Whoever considers Me as his Lord, then 'Alí is also his Lord.'

The Shí'ahs consider this verbal statement to be authoritative and on its basis believe 'Alí to be the lawful successor to the Prophet. The Báb and Bahá'u'lláh also confirm this belief. But the majority of the Muslims, the Sunnís, reject this view. Almost immediately after Muḥammad's passing, His followers were divided into these two major sects which multiplied with the passage of time.

In contrast, one of the distinguishing features of the Revelation of Bahá'u'lláh is that its Author has established a mighty Covenant with His followers concerning His successor, a Covenant whose characteristics are delineated by Bahá'u'lláh Himself in His 'Book of My Covenant', written in His own hand, unequivocal in the provisions it makes for the future of His Cause and acknowledged as an authentic document even by those who violated it. It is through this divinely-ordained instrument alone that the unity of the Bahá'í community has been preserved, the purity of its teachings safeguarded and the incorruptibility of its institutions guaranteed. This is 'the Day which shall not be followed by night'[7] is Bahá'u'lláh's own testimony in this regard.

Revelation of the Word of God by His Manifestation resembles the down-pouring of rain. In the same way that showers in the spring season vivify the world of nature, the Word of God is creative and a source of life to human souls. It penetrates people's hearts and imparts to them the spirit of faith. This process continues throughout the Revelation of the Prophet but the vernal showers of the divine springtime cease with His passing.

During the rainy season pastures become verdant and the rain also creates pools of reviving waters. Likewise, when the Manifestation of God is no longer with man, the words He has left behind become the source of spiritual life for His believers. For the Christians the Gospels and for the Muslims the Qur'án have acted as the spiritual reservoir of the water of life and the repository of God's teachings.

However, the water that flows to all the people, who have free access to it, soon loses its purity, being mixed with the mud and pollution of man-made ideas. In older Dispensations, the Manifestations of God left their words to posterity, with no clear provision made for further guidance. Their followers had to interpret their utterances as best they could. As a result, people disagreed in their understanding of the teachings. The followers interfered with the Word of God: they compromised the laws and precepts which were promulgated by the Prophet. Man-made dogmas and rituals were added, human innovations and practices were introduced and the purity of the teachings was lost. Schisms occurred and sects and denominations were created within a religion. The unity and love which had existed among the followers during the lifetime of the founder of the religion disappeared after Him and in the course of time were replaced by enmity and contention.

In the Dispensation of Bahá'u'lláh the revelation of the Word of God has taken a different form altogether. Whereas in former times, with the exception of the Qur'án and the writings of the Báb, the words of the Prophets, in most cases, were recorded years after their revelation, the words of Bahá'u'lláh were taken down by His amanuensis the moment they were uttered. In some cases He Himself inscribed the verses revealed to Him. These writings, usually referred to as sacred text, or Tablets, are preserved and safeguarded and their authenticity is assured. The words of God in this Dispensation have been revealed with such profusion that – as Bahá'u'lláh Himself testifies – were His writings to be compiled, they would produce no less than one hundred volumes of holy scripture for mankind in this age. The analogy of the pool is no longer apt. More appropriate is the analogy of an ocean created when the words of God were sent down as copious rain.

The Qur'án consists of over six thousand verses and was revealed by Muḥammad in 23 years. The speed of the revelation of the words of Bahá'u'lláh was about one thousand verses in an hour![8] For example, the Kitáb-i-Íqán (Book of Certitude), one of the most important of Bahá'u'lláh's works, was revealed in the course of two days and two nights. During the 40–year ministry of Bahá'u'lláh the world of humanity was immersed in an ocean of divine revelation whose latent energies are destined to revitalize the whole of humankind.

A distinguishing feature of the Revelation of Bahá'u'lláh is that, unlike the Dispensations of the past, the Word of God, sent down for the spiritualization and guidance of man, has not been simply handed over to him freely. To no one is given the right to interpret His words, to add even a dot or to take one away. Bahá'u'lláh has preserved the purity of the water of His Revelation against all pollution. On the one hand, He has revealed the Word of God for the benefit of all mankind; on the other, He has not allowed anyone to interfere with it. He resolved these two contrasting features through the institution of the Covenant, firmly established in the Kitáb-i-Aqdas and His Will and Testament which was written in His own hand and designated as 'The Book of My Covenant'.

Instead of leaving His Revelation freely to man and allowing him to interpret His writings and act upon them as he likes, Bahá'u'lláh has created, in the person of 'Abdu'l-Bahá, a pure channel for the interpretation of His Revelation and the guidance of the community. As the primary recipient of the Revelation of Bahá'u'lláh, He is the authorized interpreter of the sacred words. His soul embraced every virtue and power which that Revelation conferred upon Him, virtues and powers which, through the operation of the institution of the Covenant, are to be vouchsafed progressively to humanity in the course of this Dispensation and which are the cause of the social, the intellectual and spiritual development of man on this planet until the advent of the next Manifestation of God.

'Abdu'l-Bahá acts in this analogy as a receptacle. Before a receptacle is filled, it must first be empty. The person of 'Abdu'l-Bahá had so surrendered His will to that of Bahá'u'lláh that He was utterly empty of self and had nothing to express or manifest in His being except self-effacement and absolute servitude. His whole being became the incarnation of every goodly virtue, a stainless mirror reflecting the light of glory cast upon Him by Bahá'u'lláh.

'Abdu'l-Bahá states that there are three stations in this vast creation: the station of God, which is unapproachable; the station of the Manifestations of God, which is equally inaccessible; and the station of man. The only station befitting man is that of servitude. To the extent that the individual believer abides on the plane of servitude, he will grow closer to God and become the recipient of His power, grace and bounties. As 'Abdu'l-Bahá reached the lowest depths of servitude, hence He became the embodiment of all divine qualities and attributes. Although He genuinely considered Himself a servant of the servants of Bahá'u'lláh, He manifested a majesty and grandeur which no human being could ever hope to possess. 'Abdu'l-Bahá was not a Manifestation of God but by virtue of His being the repository of Bahá'u'lláh's Revelation, 'the incompatible characteristics of a human nature and superhuman knowledge and perfection have been blended and are completely harmonized' in His person.[9] He knew the secrets of the hearts of men and His words were creative.

The Most Great Infallibility mentioned by Bahá'u'lláh is inherent in the Manifestation of God and no one can share in it.[10] 'Abdu'l-Bahá did not possess this but Bahá'u'lláh conferred infallibility upon Him. The Manifestation of God is like a sun which generates its own heat and light; the moon does not possess its own light but receives it from the sun and reflects it towards the earth. Similarly, Bahá'u'lláh acts as the Sun of Truth and 'Abdu'l-Bahá as the Moon of this Dispensation.

'Abdu'l-Bahá should not be viewed as an ordinary human being who persevered in His efforts until He emptied Himself of selfish desire and consequently was appointed by Bahá'u'lláh as His successor. Rather, He should be seen as having been created by God for the purpose of becoming the recipient of God's Revelation in this age. We shall never know His real station because He was 'the Mystery of God', a title conferred upon Him by Bahá'u'lláh. He was the priceless gift of Bahá'u'lláh to mankind. In many of His Tablets Bahá'u'lláh has extolled the station of 'Abdu'l-Bahá in laudatory terms. To cite an example, in the Súriy-i-Ghuṣn Bahá'u'lláh testifies to this truth:

> We have sent Him down in the form of a human temple. Blest and sanctified be God Who createth whatsoever He willeth through His inviolable, His infallible decree. They who deprive themselves of the shadow of the Branch, are lost in the wilderness of error, are consumed by the heat of worldly desires, and are of those who will assuredly perish.[11]

When 'Abdu'l-Bahá was in His early teens in Baghdád, Bahá'u'lláh designated Him 'the Master'. Other titles conferred upon Him in His youth are all indicative of a mysterious being who is the Centre of Bahá'u'lláh's Covenant.

Every Covenant has two sides, each with its own obligations. Bahá'u'lláh has fulfilled His side of the Covenant by bequeathing to humanity two precious gifts: one, the outpouring of His Revelation; and the other, His Covenant with its centre in the person of 'Abdu'l-Bahá. To revert to our analogy: Bahá'u'lláh vouchsafed to mankind the ocean of His Revelation. He also created an unbreachable reservoir for it in the Covenant, in the person of 'Abdu'l-Bahá, to provide an unfailing supply of pure water, no matter how much pollution men may try to introduce into the life-giving waters of that Revelation. Having identified the part that Bahá'u'lláh fulfils in this Covenant, we note that the followers of Bahá'u'lláh, who constitute the other side of the Covenant, have the obligation to draw the life-giving waters of His Revelation from that reservoir, to become revived, to live in accordance with His teachings and be transformed into a new creation.

During the ministry of Bahá'u'lláh, the believers had the inestimable privilege of turning to Him in person; many were honoured to attain His presence. These believers received the bounties of God directly from Bahá'u'lláh and were guided by Him in numerous Tablets revealed for them. Consequently they were enabled to conduct their lives according to His good-pleasure. Those souls who acquired spiritual qualities through their direct contact with the Supreme Manifestation of God were magnetized by Him and were transformed into spiritual giants of this Dispensation.

After the passing of Bahá'u'lláh, it was 'Abdu'l-Bahá who, by virtue of the Covenant of Bahá'u'lláh as revealed in His Will and Testament (the Kitáb-i-'Ahd), possessed the authority and infallibility to guide the friends to the spiritual potencies of the Revelation of Bahá'u'lláh. Thus the believers turned to 'Abdu'l-Bahá for guidance and He imparted to them the soul-stirring truths which were enshrined in the teachings of Bahá'u'lláh and shared with them the inestimable gems of spirit which were hidden in the depths of the ocean of His Revelation.

Also during this period a number of faithless relatives of 'Abdu'l-Bahá joined hands with some unscrupulous individuals in both the East and the West in an assault on the mighty wall of the Covenant which the hand of omnipotence had placed around the sanctuary of His Cause. These persons asserted that their objections were founded on the Revelation of Bahá'u'lláh but, although they had access to the writings of Bahá'u'lláh, they distorted their meaning and betrayed their purpose. Turning away from 'Abdu'l-Bahá and denying the authority with which Bahá'u'lláh had invested Him, they deprived themselves of the centre of infallible interpretation and guidance and thus they extinguished the spirit of the Faith within their hearts.

In a Tablet emphasizing the importance of steadfastness in the Covenant, 'Abdu'l-Bahá states that in this day the confirmations of Bahá'u'lláh will reach only those who are firm in the Covenant.[12] The Master affirms that even should one who was an embodiment of the Holy Spirit fail to turn to the Centre of the Covenant, he would become a dead body. For a period of 29 years 'Abdu'l-Bahá guided the Bahá'ís of the world to fulfil their part of the Covenant and at His passing He bequeathed an undivided Faith and the pure, life-giving water of the teachings to future generations.

With the passing of 'Abdu'l-Bahá, the Apostolic Age of the Faith came to an end and the Faith entered the Formative Age. The forces of the Revelation of Bahá'u'lláh, which streamed forth from the person of 'Abdu'l-Bahá during His ministry, had now ceased. But 'Abdu'l-Bahá had a plan for the believers. He did not abandon them to their own devices. He delineated in His Will and Testament the outline of a marvellous scheme to enable the believers to raise up the institutions created by Bahá'u'lláh for the governance of society in His Dispensation. Thus the believers in the Formative Age were given the opportunity to play their part, as bidden by 'Abdu'l-Bahá, in the building up of the institutions of the Faith which are to act as channels for carrying the spiritual energies released by Bahá'u'lláh to every part of the planet. Central to this design was the institution of the Guardianship, which continued the essential task of preserving the purity of the water of the revelation after 'Abdu'l-Bahá, interpreted its provisions and guided the believers in erecting the administrative order of the Faith.

Shoghi Effendi has singled out the Will and Testament of 'Abdu'l-Bahá from among all His writings as being specially invested with divine authority capable of shaping the destiny of the Community of the Most Great Name during the Formative and Golden Ages of the Faith, saying:

> It was 'Abdu'l-Bahá Who, through the provisions of His weighty Will and Testament, has forged the vital link which must for ever connect the age that has just expired with the one we now live in – the Transitional and Formative period of the Faith – a stage that must in the fullness of time reach its blossom and yield its fruit in the exploits and triumphs that are to herald the Golden Age of the Revelation of Bahá'u'lláh.[13]

The Will and Testament, described by Shoghi Effendi as the Charter of the New World Order, was written in 'Abdu'l-Bahá's own hand and is signed and sealed by Him. It consists of three parts, written at different times during the darkest days of 'Abdu'l-Bahá's life, when He was living in the house of 'Abdu'lláh Pá<u>sh</u>á. 'Abdu'l-Bahá was incarcerated in the fortress city of 'Akká through the machinations and intrigues of Mírzá Muḥammad-'Alí, the arch-breaker of the Covenant, who was ably assisted by his brothers and other Covenant-breakers. The date on which each part was written is not given but the first part of the Will is likely to have been written sometime in 1906 or later.*

The dangers surrounding 'Abdu'l-Bahá were great. Every day was fraught with perils and tribulations and 'Abdu'l-Bahá took great care for the protection of this historic document, placing it under ground. These are His own words:

> This written paper hath for a long time been preserved under ground, damp having affected it. When brought forth to the light it was observed that certain parts of it were injured by the damp, and the Holy Land being sorely agitated it was left untouched.[14]

Concerning the significance of the Will and Testament of 'Abdu'l-Bahá, Shoghi Effendi writes:

---

* One clue to the date of the Will's completion is that <u>Sh</u>u'á'u'lláh, a son of Mírzá Muḥammad-'Alí, sent a letter from the United States to Majdu'd-Dín, the arch-enemy of 'Abdu'l-Bahá, dated 27 Tashrín 2nd (27 November) 1905. Somehow this letter came into the possession of 'Abdu'l-Bahá. He refers to this letter in the first part of the Will and Testament (see Will and Testament para. 9). Bearing in mind the time it took for the letter to reach the Holy Land by surface post, and not knowing when or how it fell into 'Abdu'l-Bahá's hands, it is reasonable to assume that the first part of the Will was written sometime in 1906 or later.

We stand indeed too close to so monumental a document to claim for ourselves a complete understanding of all its implications, or to presume to have grasped the manifold mysteries it undoubtedly contains. Only future generations can comprehend the value and the significance attached to this Divine Masterpiece, which the hand of the Master-builder of the world has designed for the unification and the triumph of the world-wide Faith of Bahá'u'lláh.[15]

He also states:

. . . the full meaning of the Will and Testament of 'Abdu'l-Bahá, as well as an understanding of the implications of the World Order ushered in by that remarkable Document, can be revealed only gradually to men's eyes, and after the Universal House of Justice has come into being. The friends are called upon to trust to time and to await the guidance of the Universal House of Justice, which, as circumstances require, will make pronouncements that will resolve and clarify obscure matters.[16]

Of the genesis of the Will and Testament Shoghi Effendi writes:

The creative energies released by the Law of Bahá'u'lláh, permeating and evolving within the mind of 'Abdu'l-Bahá, have, by their very impact and close interaction, given birth to an Instrument which may be viewed as the Charter of the New World Order which is at once the glory and the promise of this most great Dispensation. The Will may thus be acclaimed as the inevitable offspring resulting from that mystic intercourse between Him Who communicated the generating influence of His divine Purpose and the One Who was its vehicle and chosen recipient. Being the Child of the Covenant – the Heir of both the Originator and the Interpreter of the Law of God – the Will and Testament of 'Abdu'l-Bahá can no more be divorced from Him Who supplied the original and motivating impulse than from the One Who ultimately conceived it. Bahá'u'lláh's inscrutable purpose, we must ever bear in mind, has been so thoroughly infused into the conduct of 'Abdu'l-Bahá, and their motives have been so closely wedded together, that the mere attempt to dissociate the teachings of the former from any system which the ideal Exemplar of those same teachings has established would amount to a repudiation of one of the most sacred and basic truths of the Faith.[17]

The Will and Testament of 'Abdu'l-Bahá has been described by Shoghi Effendi as the document which has fulfilled the prophecy of the Báb concerning the establishment of the World Order of Bahá'u'lláh, of which the Will and Testament is a charter. Shoghi Effendi further identifies the Will and Testament as 'the Charter of a future world civilization, which may be regarded in some of its features as supplementary to no less weighty a Book than the Kitáb-i-Aqdas'.[18]

A careful study of the relationship between the Will and Testament of 'Abdu'l-Bahá and the Kitáb-i-Aqdas may bring to light the workings of a process of organic evolution in the realm of divine revelation. It appears that instead of revealing in detail every aspect of His laws and teachings, Bahá'u'lláh intentionally left certain aspects of His Revelation to mature and then be revealed during the ministry of 'Abdu'l-Bahá. Thus 'Abdu'l-Bahá's contribution to the Cause of Bahá'u-'lláh may be described as the supreme act of enriching the vast ocean of Bahá'u'lláh's Revelation. Shoghi Effendi describes this process in these words:

> In fact, he who reads the Aqdas with care and diligence will not find it hard to discover that the Most Holy Book itself anticipates in a number of passages the institutions which 'Abdu'l-Bahá ordains in His Will. By leaving certain matters unspecified and unregulated in His Book of Laws, Bahá'u'lláh seems to have deliberately left a gap in the general scheme of Bahá'í Dispensation, which the unequivocal provisions of the Master's Will have filled. To attempt to divorce the one from the other, to insinuate that the Teachings of Bahá'u'lláh have not been upheld, in their entirety and with absolute integrity, by what 'Abdu'l-Bahá has revealed in His Will, is an unpardonable affront to the unswerving fidelity that has characterized the life and labours of our beloved Master.[19]

When the provisions of the Kitáb-i-Aqdas and those of the Will and Testament of 'Abdu'l-Bahá are realized at their appointed time, the World Order of Bahá'u'lláh will come into being, unveiling to mankind the glory and majesty of the Revelation of Bahá'u'lláh. As we have already stated, 'Abdu'l-Bahá, through His Will and Testament, left for the Bahá'ís of the Formative Age a master plan for the building of the institutions of the Administrative Order and it was Shoghi Effendi, whom 'Abdu'l-Bahá extolled as a pearl, unique and priceless, the Sign of God, the Guardian of the Cause of God and the Expounder and Interpreter of His Word, who guided the believers in the execution of this task. In the course of his 36 years as Guardian, Shoghi Effendi, in addition to all his other achievements, expounded the relationship between the two divinely-ordained, uniquely guided institutions of the Faith: the Guardianship and the Universal House of Justice. In his letter addressed on 21 March 1930 to the members of the National Spiritual Assembly of the United States and Canada he wrote, referring to the unique nature of the Administrative Order created by Bahá'u'lláh and 'Abdu'l-Bahá:

> Not only have they revealed all the directions required for the practical realization of those ideals which the Prophets of God have visualized, and which from time immemorial have inflamed the imagination of seers and poets in every age. They have also, in unequivocal and emphatic language, appointed those twin institutions of the House of Justice and of the Guardianship as their chosen Successors, destined to apply the principles, promulgate the laws, protect the institutions, adapt loyally and intelligently the Faith to the requirements of progressive society, and consummate the incorruptible inheritance which the Founders of the Faith have bequeathed to the world.[20]

Now, since the passing of Shoghi Effendi, it is the Universal House of Justice, the other of the two 'chosen successors' of Bahá'u'lláh and 'Abdu'l-Bahá, which performs the function of protecting the purity of the Revelation. It ensures that no one may infringe the exclusive prerogative of the Guardian by attempting to assert authoritative interpretations of the writings. At the same time, it performs the various functions conferred upon it in the writings of Bahá'u'lláh and 'Abdu'l-Bahá and, through its legislative actions, provides that element of elasticity which enables the Faith to meet the challenging needs of a fast-evolving human society.

The world-vivifying forces of the Faith stream out from this divinely-ordained institution into a vast network of Assemblies, bestowing spiritual life upon multitudes in every part of the world. Concerning the significance of these divinely-ordained channels, Shoghi Effendi makes this remarkable statement:

> The moment had now arrived for that undying, that world-vitalizing Spirit that was born in Shíráz, that had been rekindled in Ṭihrán, that had been fanned into flame in Baghdád and Adrianople, that had been carried to the West, and was now illuminating the fringes of five continents, to incarnate itself in institutions designed to canalize its outspreading energies and stimulate its growth.[21]

A deeper study of the writings of Shoghi Effendi makes it abundantly clear that the Will and Testament of 'Abdu'l-Bahá is a momentous document endowed with undreamt-of potentialities whose import only the passage of time can reveal. Its provisions are designed not only to guide the believers in the erection of the divinely-ordained institutions but it also provides, like the Kitáb-i-'Ahd, rigorous tests of faith to every follower of Bahá'u'lláh. As we study the following pages of this book, we will observe that many believers, including some outstanding but egotistical and ambitious teachers of the Cause, were severely tested.

They failed to abide by the sacred provisions of these vital documents and consequently the flame of their faith was extinguished and they spiritually perished.

1

Prerequisites for the Study of the Covenant of Bahá'u'lláh

A true understanding of the Covenant of Bahá'u'lláh gained by focusing on the Kitáb-i-'Ahd and the Will and Testament of 'Abdu'l-Bahá is dependent upon one's wholehearted faith in the Revelation of Bahá'u'lláh. To comprehend, however inadequately, the manifold mysteries contained in these two great documents and to appreciate the provisions enshrined in them, one must first and foremost recognize the station of Bahá'u'lláh as a Manifestation of God whose sublime and momentous Revelation has many unique features. In the person of its Author, transcendental in His majesty, in the intensity of its glory, in the prolific outpouring of its holy writ, in the unifying power of its Covenant, in the revolutionizing influence of its teachings, in the release of its world-vitalizing forces, in the strength and vitality of its institutions, the Revelation of Bahá'u'lláh 'stands unparalleled in the annals of the past, nor will future ages witness its like'.[22] It endows the human race with undreamt-of potentialities and provides the means for its progress and spiritual development in this Dispensation. Bahá'u'lláh has extolled His Revelation in glowing terms. His writings are replete with passages such as these:

> None among the Manifestations of old, except to a prescribed degree, hath ever completely apprehended the nature of this Revelation.[23]

> I testify before God to the greatness, the inconceivable greatness of this Revelation.[24]

> The purpose underlying all creation is the revelation of this most sublime, this most holy Day, the Day known as the Day of God, in His Books and Scriptures – the Day which all the Prophets, and the Chosen Ones, and the holy ones, have wished to witness.[25]

> This is the Day whereon the unseen world crieth out, 'Great is thy blessedness, O earth, for thou hast been made the footstool of thy God, and been chosen as the seat of His mighty throne.'[26]

Belief in the authenticity of such a momentous Revelation and firmness in the Covenant of Bahá'u'lláh are the first requirements for the successful study and understanding of the Will and Testament of 'Abdu'l-Bahá. The next step is to recognize the limitations of the human mind in unravelling the divine mysteries concealed within the revealed Word and in appreciating the true station of its Author.

Although God has endowed every human being of sound mind with the capacity to recognize and to know the Manifestation of God, this capacity has its limitations. We observe that in this material world God has not given creatures of the lower kingdoms the capacity to comprehend the qualities and powers of the higher ones. In each kingdom there are barriers which the creatures cannot overstep. Thus an animal, no matter how intelligent, cannot understand human intellectual and spiritual powers. It can perceive people only as creatures similar to itself and judge their actions from its own limited outlook.

The same is true when we examine the relationship between the Manifestation of God and human beings. One is on a level far above the other. Although a Manifestation of God is physically human, to regard Him as being one with humanity is inadmissible. To view man as an equal with Him is similar to the animal observing a human and considering itself to be his equal.

In one of His Tablets[27] Bahá'u'lláh mentions that a disease has afflicted many of those who, in their own estimation, have acquired a measure of knowledge and learning. The disease is that such people consider themselves to be the equal of the Manifestation of God and on the same level. He states that a great many people suffer from this disease and consequently they have deprived themselves of the bounties of God's Revelation.

If we recognize that the Manifestation of God abides in a realm far above that of man, it becomes evident to us that the human intellect, when freed from self and ego, will admit its inability to appreciate fully the inner realities of the Word of God and His Covenant. Expatiating on this theme, Shoghi Effendi writes:

> To strive to obtain a more adequate understanding of the significance of Bahá'u'lláh's stupendous Revelation must, it is my unalterable conviction, remain the first obligation and the object of the constant endeavour of each one of its loyal adherents. An exact and thorough comprehension of so vast a system, so sublime a revelation, so sacred a trust, is for obvious reasons beyond the reach and ken of our finite minds.[28]

Although the human mind, with its limitations, is unable to apprehend fully the unique significance of the Word of God, it has the capacity to reach great heights of understanding. Indeed, the power of the intellect is one of the greatest gifts bestowed by God upon man. Through it man is enabled to discover many mysteries of creation, both spiritual and material. Humanity is therefore indebted to men of learning, those souls endowed with high intellectual powers and who open the doors of knowledge to the face of mankind. When this knowledge born of human intellect combines with faith in Bahá'u'lláh as the Supreme Manifestation of God, the individual can reach the pinnacle of true knowledge and understanding. To such people, Bahá'u'lláh addresses these words in the Kitáb-i-Aqdas:

> Happy are ye, O ye the learned ones in Bahá. By the Lord! Ye are the billows of the Most Mighty Ocean, the stars of the firmament of Glory, the standards of triumph waving betwixt earth and heaven. Ye are the manifestations of steadfastness amidst men and the daysprings of Divine Utterance to all that dwell on earth. Well is it with him that turneth unto you, and woe betide the froward. This day, it behoveth whoso hath quaffed the Mystic Wine of everlasting life from the Hands of the loving-kindness of the Lord his God, the Merciful, to pulsate even as the throbbing artery in the body of mankind, that through him may be quickened the world and every crumbling bone.[29]

However, human reason, if not assisted by the spirit of faith, is insufficient as a tool by which a mortal being can comprehend the potentialities of the Covenant of Bahá'u'lláh or grasp the many divine mysteries hidden within the Kitáb-i-'Ahd and the Will and Testament of 'Abdu'l-Bahá. The history of the Faith confirms this. Many believers of proven ability, keen intelligence and deep knowledge, relying entirely on their own interpretations of these two momentous documents, failed to comprehend the true significance of their contents; they became deluded, were severely tested and lost their faith altogether.*

Although the human intellect has its limitations, through the power of prayer, the assistance of the Holy Spirit and reliance on the interpretations of 'Abdu'l-Bahá and Shoghi Effendi, it is possible to acquire a profound understanding of the Kitáb-i-'Ahd and the Will and Testament of 'Abdu'l-Bahá. The words of God are revealed for man to comprehend and to become revived by their life-giving influence. How, then, should he approach the holy writings in order to fathom the inner reality of the Word of God and become exhilarated by its transforming power? Bahá'u'lláh has shown the way by laying down certain conditions through which a soul can immerse itself in the

---

* See the stories of the Covenant-breakers in later chapters.

ocean of His words and obtain the pearls of wisdom and knowledge hidden in its depths.

The criteria Bahá'u'lláh has established for understanding His Revelation and His Covenant are different from those usually advocated by men of learning and knowledge untouched by the light of His Faith. Their criteria are generally based on the premise that to master any subject in depth, the individual must acquire academic knowledge and become an accomplished scholar.

Although Bahá'u'lláh has enjoined His followers to acquire knowledge and has praised the station of men of learning, He has not made recognition of His Cause, the true understanding of His words and the comprehension of the inner realities of His Revelation dependent upon acquired knowledge. The opening paragraph of the Kitáb-i-Íqán states:

> No man shall attain the shores of the ocean of true understanding except he be detached from all that is in heaven and on earth.[30]

Bahá'u'lláh continues:

> The understanding of His words and the comprehension of the utterances of the Birds of Heaven are in no wise dependent upon human learning. They depend solely upon purity of heart, chastity of soul, and freedom of spirit. This is evidenced by those who, today, though without a single letter of the accepted standards of learning, are occupying the loftiest seats of knowledge; and the garden of their hearts is adorned, through the showers of divine grace, with the roses of wisdom and the tulips of understanding. Well is it with the sincere in heart for their share of the light of a mighty Day![31]

The writings of Bahá'u'lláh are replete with similar passages in which He states that man can acquire the knowledge of God and come to understand the significance of His words only through purity of heart, detachment from earthly things and humility and meekness before His servants. These qualities, together with a staunch faith in the Revelation of Bahá'u'lláh and the guidance of 'Abdu'l-Bahá and Shoghi Effendi, constitute the two essential prerequisites for a deeper understanding of the provisions of the Will and Testament of 'Abdu'l-Bahá.

Apart from these two requirements, the study of the Will and Testament and of the Kitáb-i-'Ahd calls for some general knowledge of the history of the Covenant and of the family of Bahá'u'lláh, particularly those who violated His Covenant. Therefore, a brief history of the personal life of Bahá'u'lláh and of some who rose up against the Centre of the Covenant is provided here.

2
The Family of Bahá'u'lláh

The Covenant established by Bahá'u'lláh may be said to embody two contrasting features. One facilitates the individual's integration and consolidation in the community of the Most Great Name, enabling believers to rise to the loftiest heights of heroism and self-sacrifice and of loyalty and devotion. This process imparts a new life and vigour to the body of the Cause, thereby releasing progressively a world-vitalizing spirit that propels the onward march of the Faith towards its ultimate goal of the unification of the human race. The other feature of the Covenant protects the stronghold of the Cause from all attacks by the unfaithful and, through the power inherent within the institution of the Covenant, defeats their evil doings. The result is their expulsion from the Faith and their spiritual extinction.

This second feature can best be observed through the study of the fierce opposition of most members of Bahá'u'lláh's family to the Centre of the Covenant. It created an unprecedented tempest which raged furiously within the community for several decades and threatened to disrupt its unity and shake its divinely-ordained but young and vulnerable institutions. The onslaught of the family members and other Covenant-breakers upon the Cause of God, on the one hand, and their eventual extinction, on the other, constitute the most dramatic episodes in the ministries of 'Abdu'l-Bahá and Shoghi Effendi. These are some of the darkest pages in the history of the Faith yet they cast light upon the mysterious forces operating within the Cause of God – forces that tear down every obstacle as the Cause marches towards its ultimate victory. They clearly demonstrate the vitality and the indestructibility of the Faith and serve to delineate the pattern of crisis and victory that characterizes its worldwide growth and development.

Rebellion against the Covenant originated from the immediate family of Bahá'u'lláh – His sons, daughters, wives and close relatives. Since the Will and Testament of 'Abdu'l-Bahá refers to their manifold betrayals and evil doings, it is necessary to become informed about their relationship to Bahá'u'lláh and the manner in which He conducted His personal life.

To attempt to study the life of Bahá'u'lláh purely from the human point of view is an unhelpful exercise. Whereas man is motivated by the human spirit and lives his life as dictated by the laws of nature and his environment, Bahá'u'lláh, the Manifestation of God, lived His life in conformity with the standards of the Divine Realm and regulated His conduct in accordance with the dictates of the Most Great Spirit, which animated Him.

While the Manifestations of God all shine with the splendours of God's Revelation, they can reveal themselves in only two ways. The first is to appear in their naked glory. Should this happen, all human beings would witness their awesome power, would bow before their majesty and would submit their will entirely to God's Viceregent on earth. People would thus become puppets of God and lose their free will; all would follow the path of truth, not by their own volition but by capitulating to the irresistible power of the Manifestation of God. By the force of God's command, all would obey His teachings and would live a goodly life; no one would have the choice to be different. The Covenant of God would become meaningless because if there were no free will, how could human beings observe the laws of the Covenant? Should the Manifestation of God appear in this way and expose His august attributes to the generality of mankind, people would be devoid of the power of creativity, becoming creatures whose actions were controlled from a higher realm. The principles of justice and of reward and punishment would then become inoperative in society.

The only other way that the Manifestations of God can reveal themselves, which ensures the preservation of human free will, is to conceal their divine power behind the veil of human characteristics. Although they possess majestic, divine qualities, it is, according to Bahá'u'lláh, against the law of God for them to reveal these to the generality of mankind.

For instance, we observe with amazement that Bahá'u'lláh, the Supreme Manifestation of God, who held the powers of earth and heaven in His hands, and who, through the utterance of one word, as testified by Himself in His Tablets, could have conquered the hearts of His enemies, did not exercise His God-given spiritual powers to stay the hands of His oppressors. Thus He appeared to the generality of mankind to be an ordinary human being devoid of any superhuman powers; only those who have spiritual eyes can see a glimpse of His radiant light and recognize His station, while the great majority of the people fail to discover His inner spiritual reality. Through this method people can exercise their free will to accept or to reject the Message of God, to live in accordance with His teachings or to disobey Him.

A Manifestation of God has two sides: human and divine. The human side performs a special role, veiling the splendours of the divine light that shines within His person. Therefore, a Manifestation of God is bound to regulate His life so as to express all His human characteristics. He has to eat, sleep and carry on His life like any other person. These limitations of human nature can become barriers for people in recognizing Him as the Manifestation of God. One of these is the marriage of the Manifestation – an especially great obstacle for many of Christian background, who have been brought up to believe that celibacy befits a holy person and that marriage is inappropriate for a Manifestation of God. On the other hand, the Manifestations of God are perfect in body as in spirit and attributing a lack of sexual urge to a holy person would amount to physical deficiency rather than a virtue. Perhaps the Christian view stems from the fact that Christ seems not to have been married when He declared His mission. However, Christ did not speak against marriage. That He Himself did not marry may be because His ministry was short and for most of it He was homeless, going from place to place until He was crucified.

Since the Manifestations of God share with the people all characteristics of human nature, it follows that they may live a normal life, engage in a profession, have a home, marry and raise a family. They also possess all human emotions. They are sensitive beings who experience feelings of joy and sadness, of pain and comfort, of likes and dislikes. What distinguishes them from the rest of mankind is that their spiritual side completely dominates their physical nature and they are absolutely detached from the material world.

Another feature of the life of a Manifestation of God which is essential for hiding His glory is that He lives in accordance with the laws and conventions of the society to which He belongs. He eats the same type of food, wears the same type of clothes and carries out the same customs as the rest of the people of His culture and background. He does not live in the pattern of the future society that will emerge centuries later as a result of His teachings and about which He has full knowledge. For example, during the ministry of Jesus two thousand years ago, Christ lived in a manner similar to the Israelites of the time. By following the customs of the people of His own land, the Manifestation of God does not appear conspicuously different from the rest of the people and this is how His glory is hidden behind His human facade. Thus His contemporaries look upon Him as an ordinary man.

Bahá'u'lláh belonged to a noble family of Ṭihrán. His father, Mírzá 'Abbás-i-Núrí, known as Mírzá Buzurg, held a very important ministerial position in the court of the Sháh and was highly regarded by the dignitaries of the realm. Circumstances of family life in Islamic countries were totally different from those of present-day Western society. The law of Islam concerning polygamy prevailed, allowing men to have a maximum of four wives at the same time. Mírzá Buzurg married four wives and had three concubines and 15 children – five daughters and ten sons. Bahá'u'lláh was born on 12 November 1817 in Ṭihrán. His mother, Khadíjih Khánum, the second wife of Mírzá Buzurg, had a son and two daughters from a previous marriage. As a result, Bahá'u'lláh had ten brothers and seven sisters. Some of them became steadfast believers, some followed Mírzá Yaḥyá and others remained indifferent or died before Bahá'u'lláh's declaration in the Garden of Riḍván.

Bahá'u'lláh received an elementary education during His childhood in Ṭihrán. The nobility of those days usually employed the services of a teacher at home to tutor their children. The main subjects were calligraphy, the study of the Qur'án and the works of the Persian poets. This type of schooling ended after only a few years when the child was in his early teens. Bahá'u'lláh's education did not go further than this. He Himself testifies in His Tablet to Náṣiri'd-Dín Sháh that He did not attend any school in His life:

> O King! I was but a man like others, asleep upon My couch, when lo, the breezes of the All-Glorious were wafted over Me, and taught Me the knowledge of all that hath been. This thing is not from Me, but from One Who is Almighty and All-Knowing. And He bade Me lift up My voice between earth and heaven, and for this there befell Me what hath caused the tears of every man of understanding to flow. The learning current amongst men I studied not; their schools I entered not. Ask of the city wherein I dwelt, that thou mayest be well assured that I am not of them who speak falsely. This is but a leaf which the winds of the will of thy Lord, the Almighty, the All-Praised, have stirred. Can it be still when the tempestuous winds are blowing? Nay, by Him Who is the Lord of all Names and Attributes! They move it as they list.[32]

It is necessary for the purpose of studying the Covenant to become informed of Bahá'u'lláh's marriages and His children. Bahá'u'lláh had married three wives before the declaration of His mission in 1863. As has already been stated, the Manifestation of God conducts His personal life according to the customs of the time. Polygamy was a normal practice in those days; indeed, it would have been abnormal for a man who belonged to the nobility to be monogamous in that society.

In order to appreciate this subject, it is essential to become familiar with some aspects of the Islamic world of the 19th century. Among the Muslim communities of the Middle East, women lived entirely under the domination of men and were not allowed to take part in public affairs. Girls grew up in the home of their parents, lived most of their time indoors and had no contact with the public. When they were given in marriage to their husbands (an event over which they had no control), they moved into a different house and spent most of their time in complete seclusion until they died. No man, except a very close relative, was ever allowed to see the face of a woman. She had to wear a *chadur** and veil her face. It was considered a sin for a woman to show her face to any man. When a male guest arrived at a home, all the women had to retire into the inner apartment, their sanctuary where no strange man would ever be admitted.

Another restriction was that women, especially unmarried girls, were not to talk to men. Neither would they be permitted to go out for shopping or other services; these were the exclusive preserve of men. Such acts would have necessitated women taking part in public affairs and coming into contact with men. So strong was this restriction that if ever a woman was seen talking to a strange man she would receive very severe punishment from her parents or husband. The stigma attached to this behaviour was so repugnant that sometimes the poor victim would commit suicide. Some Muslim clergy in Persia are known to have inflicted torturous chastisements upon a man who was accused of talking to a woman. Usually a much more severe punishment awaited a non-Muslim man if he was found speaking to a Muslim woman.

Women in those days had no status in the community. They were treated like objects. Some members of the clergy went so far as to claim that women had no souls, much as Christian theologians had done seven hundred years earlier. Within such a society a woman's life was spent almost entirely within the four walls of a house, caring for her family and the menfolk who lived there. It was very rare for a young girl to receive any education. The great majority of women were illiterate and were therefore left out of the mainstream of human progress and civilization. Even the few who received some education were circumscribed in their activities. Parents were responsible for providing a son with his livelihood, his home and all his needs – including a wife, who would be given to him as a matter of routine. Parents arranged their children's marriages and usually the parties most concerned had no say in the matter.

In the Western world today, a couple meet and get to know one another, fall in love and get married. But in the time of Bahá'u'lláh

---

* A large piece of cloth which covers the entire body from top to toe and is wrapped around one's clothes.

this was not the case in the East and often not in the West either. 'Love' took second place to family duty, appropriate social ties and questions of inheritance.

It was customary to betroth a boy and a girl soon after they were born and when the boy reached his late teens he had to marry; the couple had no choice. There was no question of the partners loving each other before their marriage; the boy was not even allowed to see the face of his bride until after the wedding. If the two parties were not betrothed so young, the parents would usually seek a bride for their son once he was in his teens. This was done by a female member of the family, his mother or a sister. Once the choice was made, the marriage could take place. All the young man saw of his future wife was a figure wrapped in a *chadur* and heavily veiled. If he was fortunate, his female relatives had perhaps described to him what his bride really looked like.

Although couples were not in a position to choose their partners in marriage and had no possibility of knowing and loving each other, not all marriages were devoid of love and unity. It is not difficult to visualize the case of a couple, unacquainted with each other initially, who develop a bond of friendship, love and harmony after marriage. Yet within such an environment, the dominant position of the husband was noticeably upheld as he exercised unquestioned authority over his wife.

In these circumstances all the responsibility of running the home – which entailed hard labour in those days – was left to the wife, who would be lucky if there were other female members of the family to help her in her duties. It was considered improper to employ a maid to assist in the work, since only a woman who was a close relative could be admitted into the household. However, since polygamy was commonly practised, a man could usually marry up to four wives and they were expected to assist each other in managing the family home. This often became a necessity where the husband was wealthy and influential and had to maintain a large household and conduct a lifestyle befitting his station in society. It was usually the first wife who would seek out, or give her consent for, the second wife.

It is clear that marriage customs in Persia during the 19th century are not comparable to those now current in most parts of the world. The mere mention of polygamy today will raise in people's minds associations of sex, lust and corruption. But this was not true in the case of people who contracted marriages according to Islamic law over a hundred years ago. Men practised polygamy not necessarily from lust but because they were conducting their lives within a society that had established certain customs and conventions to which all had to conform. Thus a young man happily submitted his will to that of his parents and carried out their wish in marrying someone of their choosing; thereafter he contracted further marriages as a routine matter.

Bahá'u'lláh married Ásíyih Khánum in Ṭihrán in 1251 AH (1835) when He was over 18 years of age. Ásíyih Khánum, later surnamed Navváb by Bahá'u'lláh, was a daughter of a nobleman, Mírzá Ismá'íl-i-Vazír. Her date of birth is not known. She was a most noble and faithful follower of Bahá'u'lláh who served her Lord until the end of her life in 1886. There were seven children of the marriage, four of whom died in childhood. The other three were 'Abbás, entitled the 'Most Great Branch', 'Abdu'l-Bahá; Fáṭimih, entitled Bahíyyih Khánum, the Greatest Holy Leaf; and Mihdí, entitled 'the Purest Branch'.

The second wife of Bahá'u'lláh, whom He married in Ṭihrán in 1849, was Fáṭimih Khánum, usually referred to as Mahd-i-'Ulyá. She was a cousin of Bahá'u'lláh and gave birth to six children, of whom four survived. They were one daughter, Ṣamadíyyih, and three sons, Muḥammad-'Álí, Ḍíyá'u'lláh and Badí'u'lláh. These four, along with their mother, violated the Covenant of Bahá'u'lláh. Mahd-i-'Ulyá died in 1904.

The third wife, Gawhar Khánum, was not known by any other title. The dates of her birth, marriage and death are not known. Her marriage took place some time in Baghdád before the declaration of Bahá'u'lláh's mission. While Navváb and Mahd-i-'Ulyá travelled with Him in all His exiles, Gawhar Khánum remained in Baghdád with her brother, Mírzá Mihdíy-i-Káshání.[33] For some years she was among the Bahá'í refugees in Mosul[34] and later went to 'Akká at Bahá'u'lláh's instruction. She gave birth to one daughter, Furúghíyyih; mother and daughter both became Covenant-breakers after the passing of Bahá'u'lláh.

It is appropriate at this juncture to clarify a point that has puzzled many, namely the lack of detailed information about the wives of Bahá'u'lláh. Here, again, one has to consider the social circumstances of the time. As already stated, women in those days took no part in public affairs; their entire lives were spent at home in private life. To enquire into the life of a woman was considered unethical, even insulting. It was discourteous even to ask the name of someone's wife. She would usually be referred to as 'the person in the house' or, if she had a son, as the 'mother of so and so'. Within such a society historians (always male) usually could not invade the privacy of women by delving into their lives. To do so would highly offend the men of the household.

Although one would not find such practices in the household of Bahá'u'lláh and those believers who were close to Him did come into contact with the female members of His family, nevertheless, owing to the customs of the time and the privacy to which women in general were entitled, very little has been recorded about their lives by oriental historians of the Faith.

Navváb, honoured by Bahá'u'lláh with the designation 'the Most Exalted Leaf', was the embodiment of true nobility. She was utterly detached from the things of the world and was faithful to the Cause of God. Her deep attachment to the Cause of Bahá'u'lláh was one of her great distinguishing features. She had a compassionate and loving nature, was patient, humble and utterly resigned to the will of Bahá'u'lláh. Navváb suffered a great deal at the hands of those in the family who later broke the Covenant. Her faith in Bahá'u'lláh, whom she knew as the Supreme Manifestation of God, was resolute and unshakable. She served her Lord with exemplary devotion and complete self-effacement. Her daughter, the Greatest Holy Leaf, has described her in these words:

> I wish you could have seen her as I first remember her, tall, slender, graceful, eyes of a dark blue – a pearl, a flower amongst women.
>
> I have been told that even when very young, her wisdom and intelligence were remarkable. I always think of her in those earliest days of my memory as queenly in her dignity and loveliness, full of consideration for everybody, gentle, of a marvellous unselfishness, no action of hers ever failed to show the loving-kindness of her pure heart; her very presence seemed to make an atmosphere of love and happiness wherever she came, enfolding all comers in the fragrance of gentle courtesy.[35]

In one of His Tablets Bahá'u'lláh bestows upon Navváb the unique distinction of being His perpetual consort in all the worlds of God. 'Abdu'l-Bahá in a Tablet states that the 54th chapter of Isaiah refers to Navváb, the Most Exalted Leaf, whose 'seed shall inherit the Gentiles' and whose husband is the 'Lord of Hosts'. 'Abdu'l-Bahá also refers to the verse, 'for more [are] the children of the desolate than the children of the married wife' and states that this refers to Navváb.

The three members of the family of Navváb occupy the highest rank in the Faith. 'Abdu'l-Bahá is, of course, the Centre of the Covenant of Bahá'u'lláh, the Perfect Exemplar and the embodiment of all divine virtues. His sister, the Greatest Holy Leaf, is regarded as the noblest woman of this Dispensation and its outstanding heroine. Her life was laden with unbearable sufferings in the path of Bahá'u'lláh and dedicated to the service of His Cause.

The third child of Navváb was her noble and long-suffering son, the Purest Branch. He was the one who, in the prime of youth, offered up his life in the path of his Lord when he fell through a skylight in the prison of 'Akká onto the floor below. In a prayer revealed after the martyrdom of the Purest Branch, Bahá'u'lláh makes the following statement, which Shoghi Effendi describes as astounding:

> I have, O my Lord, offered up that which Thou hast given Me, that Thy servants may be quickened, and all that dwell on earth be united.[36]

It has already been stated that all the children of Mahd-i-'Ulyá and Gawhar Khánum became Covenant-breakers. It is appropriate here to define the term Covenant-breaker. A believer who recognizes Bahá'u-'lláh as the Manifestation of God for this age will wholeheartedly obey His teachings and commandments. One of these commandments is to turn to 'Abdu'l-Bahá as the Centre of the Covenant, to be submissive to Him and abide by His bidding. The same is true in relation to Shoghi Effendi and the Universal House of Justice. A true believer, therefore, is one who believes in Bahá'u'lláh and follows those upon whom He has placed the mantle of authority. A Covenant-breaker is one who, while professing to believe in Bahá'u'lláh, arises in active opposition to Him or to the Centre of the Covenant, 'Abdu'l-Bahá, or to Shoghi Effendi or today to the Universal House of Justice.

Bahá'u'lláh has described those who break the Covenant as 'birds of the night'[37] that dislike the rays of the sun and flee from light, preferring the darkness. The nature of a Covenant-breaker is to perceive the spiritual power and ascendancy of the Centre of the Covenant but not to bring himself to submit to His authority. Instead he rises in opposition against the one he knows to be invested with the potency of Bahá'u'lláh's Revelation.

The Arch-breaker of the Covenant of Bahá'u'lláh was Mírzá Muḥammad-'Alí, the eldest son of Bahá'u'lláh's second wife, Mahd-i-'Ulyá. He was born in Baghdád in the first year after Bahá'u'lláh's arrival there. From the early days of his youth he found that he could not rise to the level of 'Abdu'l-Bahá, who was nine years his senior. He lacked the spiritual qualities that distinguished his eldest brother, who became known as 'the Master' from the early days in Baghdád.

The most essential prerequisites for the spiritual survival of all those who were close to Bahá'u'lláh were humility, self-effacement and utter nothingness in His presence. If these qualities were missing in an individual, he would be in great danger of spiritual downfall and eventual extinction. While 'Abdu'l-Bahá, the Greatest Holy Leaf, the Purest Branch and their illustrious mother were all embodiments of servitude and selflessness, Muḥammad-'Alí, his brothers, his sister and their mother were the opposite. Although the latter were all sheltered beneath Bahá'u'lláh's protection and flourished through the outpouring of His favours, they were the victims of selfish desires and worldly ambitions. During Bahá'u'lláh's lifetime they were subdued by His authority and kept under control through His admonitions. At the same time, Mírzá Muḥammad-'Alí and his brothers were the recipients of a great many favours from the believers who, because of their love for Bahá'u'lláh, honoured and revered them too. Thus these three sons acquired an undeserved prestige and basked in the sunshine of their father's glory and majesty.

Inwardly Mírzá Muḥammad-'Alí was faithless and led his two younger brothers in the same direction, while outwardly he used the power of the Faith and the resources of the community to bolster his own image in the eyes of Bahá'u'lláh's followers. He emerged as an important person in the service of his father by transcribing some of His Tablets and by the use of calligraphy, of which he was a master. From the days of his youth he entertained the ambition to occupy a position of eminence within the Faith, similar to that of 'Abdu'l-Bahá, who, from early on, had distinguished Himself among the entire family.

Another Covenant-breaker was Mahd-i-'Ulyá's daughter Ṣamadíyyih. With her husband Majdu'd-Dín she joined hands with the arch-breaker of the Covenant and inflicted great sufferings upon 'Abdu'l-Bahá. The second son of Mahd-i-'Ulyá, Mírzá Ḍíyá'u'lláh, was a vacillating person who wavered in his allegiance to the Centre of the Covenant. He was easily manipulated and became a willing tool in the hands of Mírzá Muḥammad-'Alí. He died six years after the passing of Bahá'u'lláh and therefore did not live long enough to take part in the act of opposition to the Master.

The youngest son, Badí'u'lláh, was the closest ally of the Arch-breaker of the Covenant. He died at an advanced age in 1950, leaving behind bitter memories of acts of treachery, deceit and arrogance. His venomous attacks on 'Abdu'l-Bahá and Shoghi Effendi stained the annals of the glorious Faith his own father had founded.

Mahd-i-'Ulyá herself, from the early days of Baghdád, harboured a great enmity towards 'Abdu'l-Bahá and was a motivating force behind Mírzá Muḥammad-'Alí, causing great suffering for the Master, whom she bitterly despised.

Gawhar Khánum, the third wife of Bahá'u'lláh, had only one daughter, Furúghíyyih, who was married to Siyyid 'Alí Afnán,[38] a bitter enemy of 'Abdu'l-Bahá. Led by Mírzá Muḥammad-'Alí, both mother and daughter rebelled against the Centre of the Covenant. Furúghíyyih's children, especially her eldest son Nayyir, described by Shoghi Effendi as the 'pivot of machinations',[39] spread the virus of Covenant-breaking in the family of 'Abdu'l-Bahá and caused all of its members to succumb to this deadly disease.

It is clear from the foregoing that the history of Bahá'u'lláh's family has two contrasting features: one, glory and faithfulness; the other, dishonour and treachery. Navváb, her two sons 'Abdu'l-Bahá and the Purest Branch, and her daughter the Greatest Holy Leaf, shine brilliantly above the horizon of Bahá'u'lláh's Revelation and occupy immeasurably exalted positions within His Cause. The rest of the family, including Mahd-i-'Ulyá, Gawhar Khánum and their sons and daughters, all became darkened and perished spiritually, sinking miserably into ignominy and oblivion. This contrast of light and darkness, of good and evil in Bahá'u'lláh's own family is one of the most thought-provoking and mysterious features of His ministry. His eldest Son was the perfect mirror reflecting His light and the Centre of His mighty Covenant while another son turned into the 'centre of sedition' and the arch-breaker of that same Covenant.

Many people are puzzled by the fact that almost the entire family of Bahá'u'lláh defected. Why is it that those who were nearest to Him, who were members of His household, His sons and daughters, should be foremost among the violators of His Covenant? In normal circumstances, when a person attains a prominent position in the community, it is often the family members who rally around him and lend their whole-hearted support. But in the case of Bahá'u'lláh it was the reverse and a similar situation was created within the family of 'Abdu'l-Bahá after His passing. To appreciate the reasons for this, we observe once again that the proper attitude of a believer towards the Manifestation of God should be a true demonstration of servitude, self-effacement and complete obedience. Whenever these qualities are absent, a barrier will be created between man and God. In such a case the believer may be associating with the Manifestation of God in person, yet because of this barrier he will not be able to appreciate His glory or become enchanted with His Revelation.

One might, by way of analogy, compare such believers to those who, with no knowledge of mathematics, hear an eminent mathematician expound his theories. They can see him in no other light than that of an ordinary human being whose words are incomprehensible to them. They judge the scientist by their own standards and consequently remain unmoved by his intellectual powers. The closer they are to him, the better they can see his human nature, which acts as a barrier and hides his greatness from them. Only those who understand mathematics can appreciate the real genius of the scientist. In their view, his scientific knowledge outweighs his human characteristics and therefore they do not focus their attention on his outward appearance and human limitations.

This analogy sheds light on the Covenant-breaking by most of the members of Bahá'u'lláh's family and on the reasons for their unfaithfulness to Him. Mírzá Muḥammad-'Alí and his kinsfolk who followed him did not possess that spiritual quality which makes a man humble and enables him to recognize the splendours of God's Revelation in this day. Because of their ambitious nature and their lack of spirituality and self-effacement, their inner eyes were blinded – unable to discern Bahá'u'lláh's spiritual powers. They could see Him only with their outward eyes, and because they were closest to Him they saw Him as an ordinary human being. They found Him to be, in their estimation, just a great man and nothing more. In reality, they had not recognized Bahá'u'lláh as a Manifestation of God. As long as Bahá'u'lláh was among them, they were subdued by His authority, basked in the light of His favours and were accorded honours and privileges by His followers. But after His ascension, these same family members turned their backs on Him and broke the Covenant.

3
Tests of Faith

One of the common features of the ministries of Bahá'u'lláh and 'Abdu'l-Bahá is that during their lifetimes neither of them identified their successors to the believers in general. In many of His Tablets Bahá'u'lláh extolled the station of 'Abdu'l-Bahá and praised His outstanding qualities. But at no time during His ministry did Bahá'u-'lláh disclose to His followers the position of 'Abdu'l-Bahá as His successor and the Centre of His Covenant. He kept this a well-guarded secret and did not intimate to His followers in general that 'Abdu'l-Bahá would be administering the affairs of the Cause after Him. The same is true of 'Abdu'l-Bahá; he did not disclose the identity of Shoghi Effendi to the believers. In the case of Bahá'u'lláh, the only two references in His writings on the question of successorship are found in the Kitáb-i-Aqdas. In these passages He alludes in meaningful, profound and eloquent language to the one who will become the Centre of the Cause after Him but He does not explicitly mention His successor's name, only indicating that He has issued from Him.

> When the ocean of My presence hath ebbed and the Book of My Revelation is ended, turn your faces toward Him Whom God hath purposed, Who hath branched from this Ancient Root.[40]

> When the Mystic Dove will have winged its flight from its Sanctuary of Praise and sought its far-off goal, its hidden habitation, refer ye whatsoever ye understand not in the Book to Him Who hath branched from this mighty Stock.[41]

It is known that 'Alí-Muḥammad Varqá, the renowned Apostle of Bahá'u'lláh, asked Him about the identity of the person alluded to in the above verses. In a Tablet addressed to Varqá,[42] Bahá'u'lláh indicated that the intended person was the Most Great Branch and after Him the Greater Branch. However, this disclosure was not shared with the Bahá'í community.

The passages cited above were revealed in the Kitáb-i-Aqdas 19 years before the ascension of Bahá'u'lláh. During the intervening years, no one who read them had any doubt as to the identity of the one 'Whom God had purposed, Who hath branched from this Ancient

Root'. It was obvious to all, especially to every member of Bahá'u'lláh's family, that this was a reference to 'Abdu'l-Bahá and no one else.

The only document that explicitly announced 'Abdu'l-Bahá as the Centre of the Covenant of Bahá'u'lláh and the one to whom all must turn after His ascension was the Kitáb-i-'Ahd (The Book of the Covenant), which was published among the believers only after Bahá'u'lláh's passing. This historic document was probably written at least one year before His ascension, for it is alluded to in the Epistle to the Son of the Wolf as the 'Crimson Book'. Bahá'u'lláh kept His Will and Testament secret, retained it in His own possession and did not share its contents with anyone during His lifetime. But there is evidence to suggest that He had intimated its contents to 'Abdu'l-Bahá.

Bahá'u'lláh entrusted the Kitáb-i-'Ahd to 'Abdu'l-Bahá during His last illness before His ascension and informed the members of His family a few days before He departed from this world that in a document entrusted by Him to 'Abdu'l-Bahá, He had commended them all to His care. The first time the Kitáb-i-'Ahd was read aloud in the presence of a number of friends was on the ninth day after the ascension of Bahá'u'lláh, and soon afterwards its text was released to the believers.

Immediately after the ascension of Bahá'u'lláh the Covenant was violated and opposition to 'Abdu'l-Bahá, the Centre of the Covenant, began.

Those who are unfamiliar with the history and origins of the Cause of Bahá'u'lláh, or who have a superficial understanding of His Faith, may find it strange that while Bahá'u'lláh explained every subject to His followers and clarified their every question, He did not specifically name His successor during His lifetime. It is customary, and indeed essential, for a monarch to nominate his heir to the throne before his death. In this way his subjects will have every opportunity to become familiar with their future head of state and orient themselves towards him. What prevented Bahá'u'lláh from doing this? Could He not have announced to the entire Bahá'í community during His own days the appointment of 'Abdu'l-Bahá as the Centre of His Covenant? Looking at it from a purely human point of view, it appears that had Bahá'u'lláh made such an appointment during His lifetime, all the differences that arose after His ascension could have been avoided. He, as the Manifestation of God, had the wisdom and authority to settle every misunderstanding, to suppress any opposition, to establish the position of 'Abdu'l-Bahá on a firm foundation in the minds and hearts of the believers, and to ensure the loyal support of His successor by all the members of His family.

But Bahá'u'lláh did none of these things. He did not disclose the identity of the person who was to succeed Him but kept it a well-guarded secret, to be divulged only after His passing. 'Abdu'l-Bahá also did the same thing in relation to His successor. He did not reveal the identity of Shoghi Effendi as Guardian of the Cause of God during His own lifetime. That also was a well-guarded secret, disclosed only when His Will and Testament was read. It is true that 'Abdu'l-Bahá intimated the identity of His successor to one or two individuals but the generality of the Bahá'í community remained unaware of it. The person who was privy to this appointment was the Greatest Holy Leaf. Another person was a non-Bahá'í woman, Dr J. Fallscheer, a German physician who lived in Haifa and attended the ladies of 'Abdu'l-Bahá's household. When Shoghi Effendi was a child, 'Abdu'l-Bahá clearly stated to her that Shoghi Effendi would be His successor. But this information was not communicated to anybody else. In answer to a question from three believers as to whether there would be someone to succeed Him, 'Abdu'l-Bahá wrote a short reply:

> . . . Know verily that this is a well-guarded secret. It is even as a gem concealed within its shell. That it will be revealed is predestined. The time will come when its light will appear, when its evidences will be made manifest, and its secrets unravelled.[43]

Another believer enquired about a verse in Isaiah (11:6), 'a little child shall lead them', wanting to know whether this was true and whether the child who would succeed 'Abdu'l-Bahá was then living. In response 'Abdu'l-Bahá revealed the following Tablet:

> O Maidservant of God!
>
> Verily, that child is born and is alive and from him will appear wondrous things that thou wilt hear of in the future. Thou shalt behold him endowed with the most perfect appearance, supreme capacity, absolute perfection, consummate power and unsurpassed might. His face will shine with a radiance that illumines all the horizons of the world; therefore forget this not as long as thou dost live inasmuch as ages and centuries will bear traces of him.
>
> Upon thee be greetings and praise
>
> 'Abdu'l-Bahá 'Abbás[44]

However, in this Tablet 'Abdu'l-Bahá did not reveal the identity of Shoghi Effendi as that child who would succeed Him.

That the successors of the Centre of the Covenant and of Shoghi Effendi were disclosed only after the ascension of Bahá'u'lláh and of 'Abdu'l-Bahá constitutes one of the most important features of the Covenant. Not until one grasps the purpose and significance of such steps, whether in the appointment of 'Abdu'l-Bahá or Shoghi Effendi, will the believer be able to acquire a true comprehension of the Covenant of Bahá'u'lláh.

Although such an understanding must come about primarily through the individual's meditations upon the holy writings, his study of the history, genesis and workings of the Covenant and his prayers that his heart may become the recipient of divine knowledge, the following explanation may throw some light on this important subject.

The main function of the Manifestation of God is to reveal the teachings of God for the age in which He appears. In so doing, He is ready to explain to His followers the meaning and purpose of His Revelation and to answer any difficult questions for them. Both in His association with the believers and in His Tablets, Bahá'u'lláh was always ready to explain the significance of His writings. Many of His Tablets were revealed in response to questions asked by His followers and others on weighty religious and spiritual matters as well as minor problems that affected the lives and activities of the friends. To all these questions Bahá'u'lláh responded. He expounded His teachings; He interpreted the Scriptures of the past, clarifying many of their abstruse passages and statements; He revealed the mysteries surrounding some of His profound utterances; and He delineated the features of His New World Order, giving details of the application of His laws and ordinances, and explaining, in simple terms, the verities of His Faith.

On one subject, however, Bahá'u'lláh remained silent: designating the person who was to succeed Him. There are many wisdoms in this. Let us use the analogy of the teacher, whose duty is to impart knowledge to his pupils and help them in their work. In so doing, he is always ready to explain the various subjects to his pupils and answer their questions but on one occasion he must remain silent and refrain from helping them or answering their questions. On the examination day the students are left on their own and must find the answers by themselves. Those who pass the examination are elevated to a higher class and those who fail are not.

The history of the Faith demonstrates that the Covenant has always provided great tests for the believers. The Báb gave the glad-tidings of the coming of 'Him Whom God shall make manifest' but did not specifically reveal His identity. Bahá'u'lláh kept the appointment of 'Abdu'l-Bahá a secret, and so in the terms of the above analogy the Kitáb-i-'Ahd became the believers' examination paper. The winds of tests began to blow immediately once the contents of that historic document were published, engulfing the community of the Most Great Name in a tempest of unprecedented severity. Many unfaithful and ambitious souls broke the Covenant and arose with all their might to wrest the leadership of the Cause from the hands of 'Abdu'l-Bahá, persisting in their ignoble activities for years until, by their own deeds, they brought about their own extinction. Those who were faithful to the Covenant, however, were elevated to greater heights of faith and devotion.

Tests* associated with so mighty an institution as the Covenant are inevitable and constitute an integral and enduring feature of the Cause of Bahá'u'lláh. Similar tests appeared when the contents of the Will and Testament of 'Abdu'l-Bahá were made public. Some ambitious people, among them most of the members of 'Abdu'l-Bahá's own family who sought leadership and proved to be insincere in their faith, broke the Covenant and rose up against Shoghi Effendi. Here again, the Will and Testament of 'Abdu'l-Bahá became an examination paper for the believers.

After the passing of Shoghi Effendi, too, the winds of tests blew and some misguided and egotistical personalities broke away and were cast out of the community of the Most Great Name. This time the non-existence of a will and testament by Shoghi Effendi became the examination paper.

The Covenant of Bahá'u'lláh will continue to be a testing ground for the followers of Bahá'u'lláh. Those few who may succumb to the dictates of their own selfish desires and arise in opposition to the divinely ordained institutions of the Faith will cut themselves off from the tree of the Cause of God and will wither and perish in time. Indeed, one of the distinguishing features of the Faith of Bahá'u'lláh is that although many of its outstanding followers rebelled against the Covenant and tried with all their might to undermine its foundations, they did not succeed in creating schisms and breaking the unity of the community.

While a small minority failed in the tests provided by the institution of the Covenant, the majority of Bahá'u'lláh's followers who were loyal to the Covenant became inspired by the Kitáb-i-'Ahd and, at a later epoch, by the Will and Testament of 'Abdu'l-Bahá. They enthusiastically rallied around the Centre of the Cause and devotedly endeavoured to carry out provisions embodied in these two great documents. So important to the faith of the believer are the contents of the Will and Testament of 'Abdu'l-Bahá that Shoghi Effendi has made their observance an article of faith for a true believer who, among other things, must adhere to 'every clause of our Beloved's sacred Will'[45] with loyalty and steadfastness.

The degree of a believer's adherence to every clause of the Master's Will and Testament determines the measure of his faith. There are

* For further discussion of tests in this life see Taherzadeh, *Revelation of Bahá'u'lláh*, vol. 3, and Taherzadeh, *The Covenant of Bahá'u'lláh*, pp. 364–5.

those who obey wholeheartedly the provisions of this sacred document and will not deviate a hair's breath from them though there may be a number of aspects which they do not fully understand. Others, while ready to follow some of the directives of 'Abdu'l-Bahá, may have some reservations about certain statements in the Will and Testament that they cannot accept. Such believers experience doubts in their faith but, if sincere, may be able to dispel them through reading the writings, discussion with deepened Bahá'ís and prayer. Others persist in their doubts and hold views contrary to the teachings of the Faith but cannot, for various reasons, resolve their misunderstandings and strengthen their faith. Such people may remain members of the Bahá'í community provided they keep their opinions strictly to themselves and do not propagate their misgivings to others.

Finally, there are those who, while confessing belief in Bahá'u'lláh, do not accept the provisions of His Covenant and rise against 'Abdu'l-Bahá, Shoghi Effendi or the Universal House of Justice. Or they may acknowledge Bahá'u'lláh and 'Abdu'l-Bahá but actively oppose Shoghi Effendi or the Universal House of Justice. Such people are acting against the Covenant and, after adequate counsels and warnings, may be declared Covenant-breakers.

One of the main factors that turns a believer into a Covenant-breaker is ambition to become prominent in the community, to rise to a high station within the Faith. This is the common objective of most Covenant-breakers. Such individuals have not realized that the only station God has destined for man is that of servitude – to God and to his fellow-man. Bahá'u'lláh has abolished the priesthood and has given no one authority to rule over others. There are no individual leaders in the Bahá'í community and the Faith does not harbour egotistical personalities. Of course, there are learned Bahá'ís, outstanding teachers, administrators and pioneers, but none of these people, however eminent, can exert authority over the community. Their greatness is in their humility, servitude and self-effacement. Those who have rebelled against the Covenant have not understood or paid attention to this principle, which is the cornerstone of the Covenant of God with man.

We may understand the reality of Covenant-breaking by looking into one of the laws of nature. In this life, opposites attract each other like the poles of a magnet, while similar poles repulse each other. God and man may be said to be positioned on the two opposite poles. God is the sovereign Lord of all and man a humble servant, hence there is a force of attraction between the two. 'I loved thy creation, hence I created thee',[46] is the voice of God addressing His servants. While God is the possessor of all divine attributes, by reason of His sovereignty, He cannot be humble. The best gift, then, which man can offer to God is the only one He does not already possess, namely, humility and servitude. These are the most befitting attributes for man. The lordship of God and the servitude of man are opposites bound together by the force of love. On the other hand, in the analogy of the magnet, similar poles repel each other. Therefore, should an individual, having recognized a Manifestation of God, aspire to reach His station or attempt to appear equal to Him, such an act will provoke the wrath of God and there will be a force of repulsion between the two parties. This is Covenant-breaking.

In the Tablet of the Holy Mariner,[47] whose main theme is the Covenant, Bahá'u'lláh confirms that should man desire to rise to that level which is beyond him and is solely ordained for God's Chosen Ones, he will be cast out from the realms on high. These are His words:

> They have desired to ascend unto that state which the Lord hath ordained to be above their stations . . .
>
> Whereupon the burning meteor cast them out from them that abide in the Kingdom of His Presence . . .
>
> And they heard the Voice of Grandeur raised from behind the unseen pavilion upon the Height of Glory . . .
>
> 'O guardian angels! Return them to their abode in the world below . . .
>
> 'Inasmuch as they have purposed to rise to that sphere which the wings of the celestial dove have never attained . . .'[48]

Through his actions Mírzá Yaḥyá proved to be the fulfilment of these words, for he longed to take the place of Bahá'u'lláh and, indeed, when formally apprised in Adrianople of Bahá'u'lláh's claim, made his counter-claim and declared himself to be the bearer of a new revelation.

Mírzá Muḥammad-'Alí was the same. He knew the station of 'Abdu'l-Bahá as the Centre of the Covenant, the One to whom all believers must turn. Yet he wanted to be a partner with Him. The fact that Mírzá Muḥammad-'Alí rose up with all his power to oppose 'Abdu'l-Bahá is a clear sign that he considered himself equal to the Master.

A child will never challenge a giant to a fight because he knows that he is no match for the giant. But a man who chooses to fight with another must believe that he possesses at least the same strength as his opponent; the act of opposition by one party indicates that it considers itself to be on a par with the other. By their very act of opposition, all those who become Covenant-breakers seek to bring themselves to the same level as the Centre of the Covenant and to challenge His authority. Consequently, as in the analogy of the poles of the magnet, they are rejected and are cast out from the community of the Most Great Name.

In His Tablets Bahá'u'lláh has stated that since His Revelation is unimaginably glorious and the spiritual forces to which it has given birth are immensely powerful, so will be the severity of the tests it provides for those who follow Him. In a Tablet known as the Lawḥ-i-Fitnih (Tablet of Tests) revealed in honour of Princess Shams-i-Jihán, Bahá'u'lláh states that through His Revelation all creation will be tried. He affirms that every atom, every created being, every accomplished man of learning, the servants of God and His sincere lovers, the angels that enjoy near access to God, the Concourse on high, every righteous man of discernment, every mature embodiment of wisdom, every prophet sent forth by God – all will be tested.

The history of the Faith amply demonstrates this. There were some disciples of Bahá'u'lláh whose faith and devotion had carried them to great heights. They were very close to His person and had become renowned among the believers. Yet because of their pride and ambition, when the winds of tests blew, the flame of faith was extinguished in their hearts. As a result, they fell from grace and died spiritually.

The Covenant of Bahá'u'lláh, through the instrumentality of the Kitáb-i-'Ahd and the Will and Testament of 'Abdu'l-Bahá, provides the means by which every believer is tested. There is a tradition in Islam quoted by Shoghi Effendi in his Persian writings which sets forth the difficulties and perils encountered by man on his journey to God. It describes how all men will perish and die except the believers; all the believers will perish and die except those who are tested, all who are tested will perish and die except those who are sincere, and those who are sincere will be in great danger.

The tests to which the believers are subjected are not all related to Covenant-breaking. Indeed, tests are an integral part of life. Even in the physical world there are tests: for example, where there is movement there is also resistance, and the faster one moves, the greater the resistance. Therefore a fast-moving object meets enormous resistance from the air because of its sheer speed. This is true in the human world too. Depending on the individual and his circumstances, tests present themselves in different forms. Those whose outlook is predominantly materialistic experience tests that disturb their lives, creating pain and suffering. This form of tests is described in the Qur'án in these words:

> Surely We will try you with something of fear and hunger, and diminution of goods and lives and fruits . . . (Qur'án 2:155)

But tests become much more purposeful when the individual recognizes the Manifestation of God and enters under the shadow of His Cause. Again in the Qur'án we read:

> Do men think that when they say 'we believe' they shall be left alone and not be put to proof? (Qur'án 29:2)

In this day, because of the greatness of Bahá'u'lláh's Revelation, when a person embraces the Faith, his tests are far greater than in former Dispensations and he is tested in many ways, often without realizing it. Each time he is successful in passing a test, he will acquire greater spiritual insight and grow stronger in faith. He will then come closer to God and will be elevated to a higher level of service; the next time his tests will be more difficult. We are not always able to pass a test but God in His mercy will provide other opportunities for us to overcome the barriers. However, if through attachment to this world the ego dominates, tests will weaken one's faith, even causing one to lose it altogether.

To cite an example, the meeting of a Spiritual Assembly may be regarded as the greatest testing ground for its members. The standards, which according to 'Abdu'l-Bahá the members must uphold during their consultation, are high indeed. He calls them to 'purity of motive, radiance of spirit, detachment from all else save God . . . humility and lowliness amongst His loved ones, patience and long-suffering in difficulties . . .'[49] He further exhorts them to conduct their discussion in a spirit of love and harmony, of courtesy and dignity, care and moderation. These are some of the prime requisites of Bahá'í consultation.

The application of these spiritual standards makes Bahá'í consultation a testing ground for every member of the Assembly. All the virtues of the individual – his faith, his courage and his steadfastness in the Covenant – undergo a rigorous test as the members sit around the table to consult. Here the spiritual battle within the soul of the individual begins and will continue as long as the ego is the dictator. Indeed, in many cases this battle lasts a lifetime. In this battlefield the forces of light and darkness are arrayed against each other. On the one side stands the spiritual entity, the soul of the believer; on the other, a great enemy, the self or ego. Whenever the soul hearkens to the lofty standards set by 'Abdu'l-Bahá and applies them during consultation, the ego, defeated, recedes into the background. The soul emerges victorious in this battle and becomes radiant with the light of faith and detachment. The application of these spiritual principles, however, must be genuine and not merely superficial. The feelings of love, unity, detachment and harmony must come from the heart. Humility and servitude, radiance, devotion, courtesy and patience, along with all the other virtues, are qualities of the spirit. These cannot be manifested by paying lip service to them. If this is the case, then the ego is the victor.

The best protection for the believer is steadfastness in the Covenant, which, in simple language, means obedience to Bahá'u'lláh, 'Abdu'l-Bahá, Shoghi Effendi and, today, the Universal House of Justice. This is a matter of faith and every Bahá'í who has recognized Bahá'u'lláh as the Supreme Manifestation of God has already accepted this cardinal principle of the Cause.

There are many teachings or principles in the Faith with which a person may agree. The faith of a believer is tested, however, when he comes across a statement that is contrary to his way of thinking. In this instance, the degree of an individual's steadfastness in the Covenant is determined by the ready manner in which he or she sincerely acknowledges that Bahá'u'lláh and those upon whom He has conferred infallibility are divinely guided, that their words, their teachings and their guidance are free from error and that the mind of man is finite and his judgement often erroneous.

4

The Covenant, A Shield for the Protection of the Faith

1–WT All-Praise to Him Who, by the Shield of His Covenant, hath guarded the Temple of His Cause from the darts of doubtfulness, Who by the Hosts of His Testament hath preserved the Sanctuary of His most Beneficent Law and protected His Straight and Luminous Path, staying thereby the onslaught of the company of Covenant-breakers, that have threatened to subvert His Divine Edifice; Who hath watched over His Mighty Stronghold and All-Glorious Faith, through the aid of men whom the slander of the slanderer affect not, whom no earthly calling, glory and power can turn aside from the Covenant of God and His Testament, established firmly by His clear and manifest words, writ and revealed by His All-Glorious Pen and recorded in the Preserved Tablet.

The opening paragraph of the Will and Testament of ‘Abdu'l-Bahá is an anthem of praise and glorification to Bahá'u'lláh, the Founder of the Covenant; it is also a tribute to those believers who defended His Covenant with great courage and heroism.

This passage describes the Covenant as a shield protecting the temple of the Cause of God from the assaults of the Covenant-breakers. The institution of the Covenant tests the faithfulness of the believers, separating the good from the evil. It also provides the means for preserving the unity and ensuring the healthy development of the community. During His ministry Bahá'u'lláh Himself was the protector of His own Cause. The continuation of the Covenant, the most vital instrument for safeguarding and strengthening the foundations of the Cause of Bahá'u'lláh after His ascension, was established through the revelation of the Kitáb-i-‘Ahd. What was only implicit in the Kitáb-i-Aqdas was now made explicit in the Kitáb-i-‘Ahd: the station of ‘Abdu'l-Bahá as the Centre of the Covenant of Bahá'u'lláh was announced to the believers. The passage, 'Turn your faces toward Him Whom God hath purposed, Who hath branched from this Ancient Root', revealed in the former book, was now clearly stated to mean

'Abdu'l-Bahá. Bahá'u'lláh unequivocally affirms 'The object of this sacred verse is none other except the Most Mighty Branch'.[50]

This clear appointment of 'Abdu'l-Bahá as the Centre of the Covenant safeguards the unity of the Bahá'í community and protects it against schism and all manner of division. Similarly, the appointment of Shoghi Effendi and the Universal House of Justice by 'Abdu'l-Bahá in His Will and Testament perpetuates the process of protection until the end of the Bahá'í Dispensation. No other religion, including that of the Báb, has brought into being an instrument designed so to ensure the unity of its community. Through the institution of the Covenant, the mighty stronghold of the Cause of God has remained invincible in spite of the powerful assaults launched against it over a long period by the Covenant-breakers. For example, Mírzá Muḥammad-'Alí and his supporters viciously attacked the Cause of God with such ferocity that the opposition against the faithful in previous Dispensations fades into insignificance compared to it. In spite of this, the Covenant-breakers failed miserably and the Covenant of Bahá'u'lláh triumphed.

It was not so in past religions. If we look at the history of Islam we note that after the Prophet passed away, His followers almost immediately became divided into the two major sects of Sunní and Shí'ah. As previously recounted, Muḥammad, the Prophet of Islam, had made a verbal statement appointing 'Alí-Ibn-i-Abú Ṭálib, known as Imám 'Alí, as His successor. But this appointment was disputed as Muḥammad left behind no document to support it.

There is an episode widely spoken of, especially among the Shí'ahs, concerning the last days of Muḥammad's earthly life. It is claimed that as He lay on His deathbed, four of His outstanding followers were with Him. They were Abú Bakr, 'Umar, 'Uthmán, and 'Alí. Abú Bakr was the father-in-law of the Prophet and 'Alí was His cousin and son-in-law. Muḥammad is reported to have called for writing materials, wishing to leave some guidance for His followers. But the scheming 'Umar, a shrewd tactician, did not allow the wish of the Prophet to be realized. He said that the Prophet, so near the time of His death, was not of sound mind and therefore no writing materials should be given to Him. The Shí'ahs, who follow Imám 'Alí, claim that had the Prophet been allowed to write His will He would have confirmed the verbal statement He had made at Ghadír-i-Khumm concerning the appointment of 'Alí as His successor.

When Muḥammad passed away, 'Umar rallied the majority of the followers around the old and ailing Abú Bakr, who enjoyed a great deal of prestige among the people. He became the first Khalíf (Caliph) of Islam. Two years later when Abú Bakr died, 'Umar became the second Khalíf and under his direction the military conquests of the Muslims soon began. Through the influence exerted by 'Umar the great majority of the followers of Muḥammad, the Sunnís, rejected the claims of Imám 'Alí to successorship.

It is a fundamental belief of the Bahá'ís that Imám 'Alí was the lawful successor of the Prophet of Islam. After him his lineal male descendants, known as the 'holy Imáms', led the Shí'ah community until the year 260 AH. Bahá'u'lláh regarded the Imáms as the legitimate successors of the Prophet, acknowledged the value of their work in the elucidation of the Qur'án, confirmed many of their sayings as recorded in the books of 'Aḥádíth' (traditions), quoted several of these in His writings, interpreted their words, extolled their station (especially that of Ḥusayn, the third Imám) in glowing terms and referred to them as 'those unquenchable lights of divine guidance'[51] and 'those lamps of certitude'.[52]

Through his misguided opposition to 'Alí, 'Umar frustrated Muḥammad's intentions regarding His successorship and the direction of the affairs of Islam. When Imám 'Alí attempted to assert his position as Muḥammad's verbally designated successor and the expounder of the Word of God as revealed in the Qur'án, 'Umar's response was the fateful remark: 'The Book of God is sufficient unto us.' This short statement has echoed through the centuries. 'Abdu'l-Bahá, in His celebrated Tablet the Lawḥ-i-Hizár Baytí (Tablet of One Thousand Verses), describes its woeful consequences, saying that this statement caused the foundation of the religion of God in the Islamic Dispensation to be shattered and the ignoble worshippers of self and passion to rule over the righteous souls. It became a deadly weapon by which the Imám 'Alí himself was martyred, which caused great divisions within the nation of Islam and which changed the loving spirit of that nation to one of armed warriors. In His Tablet 'Abdu'l-Bahá explains that as a result of this statement Imám Ḥusayn, the most illustrious of the Imáms, was decapitated on the plain of Karbilá, the other holy Imáms were inflicted with great suffering, imprisonment and death, and the blood of countless innocent souls was shed for almost twelve hundred years.

'Abdu'l-Bahá further affirms that 'Umar's statement, 'The Book of God is sufficient unto us', was transformed centuries later into the hundreds of bullets that pierced the breast of the Báb in Tabríz; that it became the chains placed around the blessed neck of Bahá'u'lláh and brought about the untold suffering inflicted upon Him in the course of His successive exiles.

'Abdu'l-Bahá attributes all these and many more atrocities committed during the Islamic Dispensation to the influence of the simple statement 'The Book of God is sufficient unto us'. It deprived the greater part of the Islamic nation not only of divine guidance and the wealth of spiritual knowledge imparted by the holy Imáms to their followers through their interpretation and elucidation of the many abstruse passages in the Qur'án, but also of their illuminating prophecies concerning the advent of the Qá'im, the Promised One of Islam.

The course of history itself changed as a result of 'Umar's opposition to Imám 'Alí. The successful breaking of the Covenant of Muḥammad by 'Umar through his refusal to submit to Imám 'Alí as the lawful successor of the Prophet and the interpreter of His words brought about, according to 'Abdu'l-Bahá, dire consequences for many nations and peoples. Who knows in what manner the Faith of Islam would have spread and its community developed had all its followers remained faithful to the wishes of Muḥammad and followed Imám 'Alí as His lawful successor. 'Abdu'l-Bahá implies in the Lawḥ-i-Hizár Baytí that if the nation of Islam had been faithful to 'Alí, many of the atrocities and cruelties committed since the passing of Muḥammad could have been mitigated or avoided.

Such are the dire consequences of man's violation of the Covenant. Unlike past Dispensations when religions divided into many sects and denominations, in the Bahá'í Dispensation the Covenant of Bahá'u-'lláh, endowed with the mysterious power born of the divine Will, has been instrumental in preventing schisms from occurring within the Faith. The institution of the Covenant has conferred authority on the central institutions of the Cause to expel anyone who publicly rises in opposition against the Centre of the Cause – 'Abdu'l-Bahá, Shoghi Effendi or the Universal House of Justice. It acts as a surging sea, casting onto its shores dead bodies and cleansing itself from their unwholesome effects. It does not harbour those ambitious and learned individuals who, in the guise of reformers, might attempt to substitute, with subtlety and craftiness, the teachings of Bahá'u'lláh with their own doctrines or try to undermine the foundations of the Cause by casting doubt on the sacred verities of the Faith enunciated by the pen of Bahá'u'lláh, 'Abdu'l-Bahá or Shoghi Effendi. Indeed, the Covenant of Bahá'u'lláh has been and will continue to be the inviolable guarantor of the invincibility of the Cause and its divinely-ordained institutions and the means of the fulfilment of Bahá'u'lláh's words, that this is 'the Day which shall not be followed by night'.[53]

In the opening paragraph of the Will and Testament reference is made to 'the onslaught of the company of Covenant-breakers'. We shall see in the following pages the accounts of some of their vicious attacks against the Cause of Bahá'u'lláh and the Centre of His Covenant. In the same passage, mention is made of the protection given to the Cause 'through the aid of men whom the slander of the slanderer affect not, whom no earthly calling, glory and power can turn aside from the Covenant of God and His Testament, established firmly by His clear and manifest words, writ and revealed by His All-Glorious Pen and recorded in the Preserved Tablet'.

To appreciate the role of the believers in protecting the Cause, as mentioned in the foregoing passage, we observe that in every age God bestows upon humanity the precious gift of divine Revelation through the advent of the Manifestation of God who formulates the laws and teachings of a religion. The part that man has to play is to propagate, promote and consolidate the religion. This is the function of the believers and not of the Manifestation of God. Bahá'u'lláh by Himself does not directly promote the interests of His Faith among people but He does assist all those who arise to serve His Cause. If the believer does not arise, Shoghi Effendi states, 'The sustaining strength of Bahá'u'lláh Himself, the Founder of the Faith, will be withheld from every and each individual who fails in the long run to arise and play his part.'[54] In the Lawḥ-i-Ṭibb (Tablet of Medicine) and in other Tablets, Bahá'u'lláh states that if the friends had lived in accordance with His commandments, the majority of the peoples of the world would have embraced His Faith in His days.

These statements clearly indicate that the progress and protection of the Cause depend upon the efforts of the believers which in turn attract the confirmations of Bahá'u'lláh. In the passage above, 'Abdu'l-Bahá confirms that Bahá'u'lláh 'watched over His Mighty Stronghold and All-Glorious Faith, through the aid of men whom the slander of the slanderer affect not, whom no earthly calling, glory and power can turn aside from the Covenant of God and His Testament'. This passage extolling the devotion and exalted character of these men is partially quoted by 'Abdu'l-Bahá from a verse of the Qur'án (24:37), to which He has added His own words.

The Bahá'ís of the East and the West were strengthened in their faith through the untiring and persistent efforts of these men spoken of by 'Abdu'l-Bahá. They were some of the most loyal and learned teachers of the Faith who not only deepened the believers in the subject of the Covenant but also rallied around the Master and, like lions, defended the Covenant against the onslaught of the Covenant-breakers. These holy souls, 'the learned ones in Bahá' whom Bahá'u-'lláh describes as 'the billows of the Most Mighty Ocean' and 'the stars of the firmament of Glory',[55] were the four Hands of the Cause of God as well as outstanding teachers such as Ḥájí Abu'l-Ḥasan-i-Amín, Ḥájí Mírzá Ḥaydar-'Alí, Mírzá Abu'l-Faḍl* and several others. Mírzá Abu'l-Faḍl travelled to the United States where he succeeded in deepening new believers in the subject of the Covenant and helped them to

* For the life story of this great Bahá'í scholar see Taherzadeh, *Revelation of Bahá'u-'lláh*, vols. 2 and 3.

counteract the misrepresentations of the Covenant-breaker Khayru-'lláh and a few others. Soon after the ascension of Bahá'u'lláh these teachers of the Cause travelled extensively throughout Persia and met with the entire community. Lacking modern means of transport, these steadfast souls travelled by donkey to every town and village and met with all the believers, either individually or in gatherings. They explained the verities of the Faith in great detail, helped the believers to study many of the Tablets of Bahá'u'lláh and 'Abdu'l-Bahá, discussed the meanings enshrined in the Kitáb-i-Aqdas and the Kitáb-i-'Ahd, and convincingly clarified any questions raised. These devoted promoters of the Cause were so imbued with the love of Bahá'u'lláh and 'Abdu'l-Bahá that wherever they went they imparted that same love to the believers. Wholly detached from earthly things, they were truly 'a river of life eternal'[56] to the loved ones of God and were instrumental in strengthening the faith of the believers and confirming them in the Covenant of Bahá'u'lláh.

Seldom in the history of the Cause do we find an occasion when the power of the Covenant manifested itself with such intensity and effectiveness as it did in Persia after the expulsion from the Faith of those who rebelled against the Centre of the Covenant. The speed with which the pollution of Covenant-breaking was removed from the community of the Most Great Name in the Cradle of the Faith was spectacular. The reaction of the believers in that country to the news of the defection of some of the great teachers of the Faith was to shun them almost immediately. No less significant was the fact that the entire Bahá'í community of Persia, with the exception of a very few individuals, remained loyal to the Centre of the Covenant of Bahá'u-'lláh. The efforts of the Covenant-breakers to mislead the believers were so ineffective that towards the end of 'Abdu'l-Bahá's ministry there were only a few individuals anywhere in that vast community who could be labelled Covenant-breakers. In the West, too, the friends were steadfast in the Covenant and united in their love for and service to the Cause.

The efforts exerted by outstanding teachers of the Cause were not only directed to the rank and file of the Bahá'í community. Indeed, there were occasions when some devoted believers asked 'Abdu'l-Bahá's permission to counsel the arch-breaker of the Covenant himself that he might recognize his transgression against the Cause and repent for violating His father's Covenant. For example, in the early days of the clandestine opposition by Mírzá Muḥammad-'Alí, an interview took place between him and Ḥájí Mírzá Ḥaydar-'Alí,* a renowned teacher of the Faith. Ḥájí Mírzá Ḥaydar-'Alí was about to leave 'Akká and 'Abdu'l-Bahá advised him, as a matter of courtesy, to visit the Mansion of Bahjí to say farewell to the family of Bahá'u-'lláh. 'Abdu'l-Bahá intimated that Mírzá Muḥammad-'Alí might invite him to meet in private. If this happened, the Ḥájí was advised to accept the invitation and, in a spirit of humility and sincerity, to say whatever his heart and conscience dictated. This is how the Ḥájí records the story of the interview:

> It was late at night when Mírzá Muḥammad-'Alí summoned me to his room. He asked his son Shu'á'u'lláh, who was present, to leave, because he wanted to talk to me confidentially. After much conversation, he said: 'I wish to ask you a question in confidence. Don't you think that I could have also inherited what my brother ['Abdu'l-Bahá] has inherited from the Blessed Beauty?'
>
> I said to him: 'In all His references to 'Abdu'l-Bahá, the Blessed Beauty has assigned to Him all the exalted names and praise-worthy attributes. He enjoined on us all to show forth, for the exaltation of His Cause, the utmost love and humility towards His Person. In the Kitáb-i-'Ahd, He has clearly stated: "It is incumbent upon the Aghṣán, the Afnán and My Kindred to turn, one and all, their faces towards the Most Mighty Branch." Therefore to the extent that you show forth humility, self-effacement and utter nothingness to His blessed Person ['Abdu'l-Bahá], you will accordingly acquire the exalted qualities you wish to have. Based on the same principle, you will lose these qualities to the extent that you lessen the measure of your humility and submissiveness towards Him. The reason for this is that all the praise and honour which are bestowed upon you by Bahá'u'lláh are dependent upon certain conditions. Certain verses of the Kitáb-i-Aqdas and their further elucidation in the Kitáb-i-'Ahd are as unequivocal and clear as the sun in mid-sky. God forbid, if for one moment in your heart you might think the passage in the Kitáb-i-'Ahd ought to have directed the Aghṣán, the Afnán and others to turn their faces to Ghuṣn-i-Akbar [the Greater Branch, i.e. Mírzá Muḥammad-'Alí]. It is clear that you do not possess what the Master possesses. God, exalted be He, does not act hypocritically, nor does He create means of division among people. It is impossible for the One True God to entrust the guardianship of His Cause to two individuals at the same time . . . Apart from all this, who is it in this world of being that can claim to rival the Master on any level?'
>
> I was talking on these lines when he arose from his seat saying it was time to go to bed, so I left him.[57]

* For a brief account of his life and achievements see Taherzadeh, *Revelation of Bahá'u'lláh*, vol. 2.

The Covenant of Bahá'u'lláh may be regarded as a protective wall surrounding the great ocean of Bahá'u'lláh's Revelation. There were many unscrupulous attempts to break through that wall and serious attacks by several outstanding followers of the Faith who rebelled against the Centre of the Covenant in order to promote their own selfish desires, to introduce their own ideas into the teachings, to divide the Faith of God and consequently to contaminate the heavenly stream of the Word of God; but they did not succeed in creating a breach in the Bahá'í community. Based on a firm foundation, the Covenant of Bahá'u'lláh was an impregnable wall around the ocean of His Revelation. This great ocean surged within the soul of 'Abdu'l-Bahá for 29 years and He bestowed its life-giving waters upon thousands of men and women throughout the East and the West. He left for posterity the unadulterated Word of God, free of every trace of distortion and defilement.

'Abdu'l-Bahá attributes all these achievements to the overshadowing confirmations of Bahá'u'lláh, which assisted those who championed His Cause and stood unswervingly firm and steadfast in 'the Covenant of God and His Testament, established firmly by His clear and manifest words, writ and revealed by His All-Glorious Pen and recorded in the Preserved Tablet'.

5
The Greatest of All Things

3–WT O ye beloved of the Lord! The greatest of all things is the protection of the True Faith of God, the preservation of His Law, the safeguarding of His Cause and service unto His Word. Ten thousand souls have shed streams of their sacred blood in this path, their precious lives they offered in sacrifice unto Him, hastened wrapt in holy ecstasy unto the glorious field of martyrdom, upraised the Standard of God's Faith and writ with their life-blood upon the Tablet of the world the verses of His Divine Unity.

'Abdu'l-Bahá links the protection of the Cause to the heroism and self-sacrifice of countless souls who offered up their lives for the promotion of the Faith. The history of the Cause indicates that the martyrs of the Faith, when faced with the choice of either recanting their faith or holding on steadfastly to the Cause of God, chose the latter. They proclaimed the divine origin of the Faith, defended the integrity of its teachings, stood firm in the face of unbearable suffering and torture, and in the end sacrificed their lives in the path of their Beloved.

But protection of the Cause is not accomplished only through physical martyrdom. By living his life in a spirit of faithfulness to the teachings of Bahá'u'lláh, a believer brings victory to the Cause. Conversely, great damage is done to the reputation and good name of the Faith when a believer conducts himself in a way contrary to the commandments of God in this day. Bahá'u'lláh has testified to this in many of His Tablets. In one, He states:

> He, Who is the Eternal Truth, beareth Me witness! Nothing whatever can, in this Day, inflict a greater harm upon this Cause than dissension and strife, contention, estrangement and apathy, among the loved ones of God. Flee them, through the power of God and His sovereign aid, and strive ye to knit together the hearts of men, in His Name, the Unifier, the All-Knowing, the All-Wise.[58]

'Abdu'l-Bahá, in one of His Tablets,[59] says that if someone mentioned in the presence of Bahá'u'lláh that there was somewhere a slight disunity among the believers, He would become so overwhelmed with grief that His face would display signs of intense pain and displeasure. While human beings generally experience agony when afflicted by calamities pertaining to the material world and the Manifestations of God also feel the pain of physical afflictions, the greatest suffering they endure is when the Cause they manifest becomes tarnished by the reprehensible conduct of those who embrace it. In one of His Tablets Bahá'u'lláh affirms this fact:

> I sorrow not for the burden of My imprisonment. Neither do I grieve over My abasement, or the tribulation I suffer at the hands of Mine enemies. By My life! They are My glory, a glory wherewith God hath adorned His own Self. Would that ye know it! . . .
>
> My sorrows are for those who have involved themselves in their corrupt passions, and claim to be associated with the Faith of God, the Gracious, the All-Praised . . .
>
> They that have tarnished the fair name of the Cause of God, by following the things of the flesh – these are in palpable error![60]

In another Tablet Bahá'u'lláh states:

> My captivity cannot harm Me. That which can harm Me is the conduct of those who love Me, who claim to be related to Me, and yet perpetrate what causeth My heart and My pen to groan.[61]

> My captivity can bring on Me no shame. Nay, by My life, it conferreth on Me glory. That which can make Me ashamed is the conduct of such of My followers as profess to love Me, yet in fact follow the Evil One.[62]

In another Tablet[63] Bahá'u'lláh mentions that when a believer commits a reprehensible misdeed, the ignorant people will ascribe it to the Founder of the Faith.

Thus each and every believer bears the responsibility of protecting the Cause of God. He can either harm the Cause through unseemly conduct or exalt and protect it through goodly deeds and a saintly character. Innumerable passages in the writings of Bahá'u'lláh and 'Abdu'l-Bahá urge the believers to protect the Cause through righteous deeds. They do not call on the believers to die for the Cause as the early martyrs did but to live and serve the Cause. Bahá'u'lláh exhorts His followers:

> Be pure, O people of God, be pure; be righteous, be righteous . . . Say: O people of God! That which can ensure the victory of Him Who is the Eternal Truth, His hosts and helpers on earth, have been set down in the sacred Books and Scriptures, and are as clear and manifest as the sun. These hosts are such righteous deeds,

such conduct and character, as are acceptable in His sight. Whoso ariseth, in this Day, to aid Our Cause, and summoneth to his assistance the hosts of a praiseworthy character and upright conduct, the influence flowing from such an action will, most certainly, be diffused throughout the whole world.[64]

Again He affirms:

O friends! Help ye the one true God, exalted be His glory, by your goodly deeds, by such conduct and character as shall be acceptable in His sight. He that seeketh to be a helper of God in this Day, let him close his eyes to whatever he may possess, and open them to the things of God. Let him cease to occupy himself with that which profiteth him, and concern himself with that which shall exalt the all-compelling name of the Almighty. He should cleanse his heart from all evil passions and corrupt desires, for the fear of God is the weapon that can render him victorious, the primary instrument whereby he can achieve his purpose. The fear of God is the shield that defendeth His Cause, the buckler that enableth His people to attain to victory. It is a standard that no man can abase, a force that no power can rival.[65]

A believer cannot adequately discharge his responsibility to protect the Cause unless he is firm in the Covenant. It is not sufficient for a Bahá'í only to believe in Bahá'u'lláh and to carry out His teachings while remaining aloof from the Covenant or unresponsive to the guidance proceeding from the Head of the Faith upon whom Bahá'u'lláh and 'Abdu'l-Bahá have placed the mantle of authority. Someone with such an unhealthy attitude will not be able to assist the Cause of God; indeed he will hamper its progress. While firmness in the Covenant is a relative term and differs from person to person, to the extent that a believer turns to the Centre of the Cause and readily observes the obligations binding on him through the institution of the Covenant, to the same extent will he be able to play his part in the protection of the Faith, which 'Abdu'l-Bahá described as 'the greatest of all things'.

One aspect of the protection of the Cause is its defence against the onslaught of internal and external enemies. Today, this function is mainly carried out by the institutions of the Faith,[66] although there is also great scope for the individual believer to play a significant part. For example, refuting accusations or misrepresentations of those who oppose the Faith is an activity which certain learned believers can undertake. Bahá'u'lláh confers upon such people great blessings, as affirmed in the following Tablet:

> Warn, O Salmán, the beloved of the one true God, not to view with too critical an eye the sayings and writings of men. Let them rather approach such sayings and writings in a spirit of open-mindedness and loving sympathy. Those men, however, who, in this Day, have been led to assail, in their inflammatory writings, the tenets of the Cause of God, are to be treated differently. It is incumbent upon all men, each according to his ability, to refute the arguments of those that have attacked the Faith of God. Thus hath it been decreed by Him Who is the All-Powerful, the Almighty. He that wisheth to promote the Cause of the one true God, let him promote it through his pen and tongue, rather than have recourse to sword or violence. We have, on a previous occasion, revealed this injunction, and We now confirm it, if ye be of them that comprehend. By the righteousness of Him Who, in this Day, crieth within the inmost heart of all created things: 'God, there is none other God besides Me!' If any man were to arise to defend, in his writings, the Cause of God against its assailants, such a man, however inconsiderable his share, shall be so honoured in the world to come that the Concourse on high would envy his glory. No pen can depict the loftiness of his station, neither can any tongue describe its splendour. For whosoever standeth firm and steadfast in this holy, this glorious, and exalted Revelation, such power shall be given him as to enable him to face and withstand all that is in heaven and on earth. Of this God is Himself a witness.[67]

Finally, an important feature of the protection of the Faith is to safeguard it from intrusion by Covenant-breakers. This subject will be dealt with in greater detail in chapter 24.

6

The Suffering of the Báb and Bahá'u'lláh

3–WT The sacred breast of His Holiness, the Exalted One (may my life be a sacrifice unto Him), was made a target to many a dart of woe . . .

'His Holiness, the Exalted One' is one of the titles of the Báb. He offered up His life and through His supreme sacrifice, as testified by Bahá'u'lláh and 'Abdu'l-Bahá, enormous spiritual forces were released for the advancement of the Cause of God. In the first year after the Declaration of His Message, the Báb expressed His longing to lay down His life in the path of Bahá'u'lláh, to whom He refers as 'The Remnant of God' in the following celebrated passage from the Qayyúmu'l-Asmá':

> O Thou Remnant of God! I have sacrificed myself wholly for Thee; I have accepted curses for Thy sake, and have yearned for naught but martyrdom in the path of Thy love. Sufficient witness unto me is God, the Exalted, the Protector, the Ancient of Days.[68]

About six years later He achieved His heart's desire when He was publicly executed in Tabríz on 9 July 1850. While the circumstances of His martyrdom are recorded in books of history, a brief account of this supreme sacrifice is bound to enlighten the vision and enrich the heart and mind of any believer who embarks on a deeper study of the Will and Testament of 'Abdu'l-Bahá. Here is a short account of this tragic and earth-shaking episode:

After securing the Báb's death warrant from the leading mujtahids of Tabríz, Mírzá Ḥasan K͟hán, as instructed by his brother, the Grand Vizír, took charge of His execution. As a mark of humiliation, the Báb's green turban and sash, the twin emblems of His noble lineage from the Prophet of Islam, were removed. He was conducted by the farrás͟h-bás͟hí (the chief attendant) to a room in the barracks of the city where a few of His disciples, including His amanuensis, were also imprisoned. Shoghi Effendi describes the circumstances leading to the execution of the Báb in these words:

The farrásh-báshí had abruptly interrupted the last conversation which the Báb was confidentially having in one of the rooms of the barracks with His amanuensis Siyyid Ḥusayn, and was drawing the latter aside, and severely rebuking him, when he was thus addressed by his Prisoner: 'Not until I have said to him all those things that I wish to say can any earthly power silence Me. Though all the world be armed against Me, yet shall it be powerless to deter Me from fulfilling, to the last word, My intention.' To the Christian Sám Khán – the colonel of the Armenian regiment ordered to carry out the execution – who, seized with fear lest his act should provoke the wrath of God, had begged to be released from the duty imposed upon him, the Báb gave the following assurance: 'Follow your instructions, and if your intention be sincere, the Almighty is surely able to relieve you of your perplexity.'

Sám Khán accordingly set out to discharge his duty. A spike was driven into a pillar which separated two rooms of the barracks facing the square. Two ropes were fastened to it from which the Báb and one of his disciples, the youthful and devout Mírzá Muḥammad-'Alí-i-Zunúzí surnamed Anís, who had previously flung himself at the feet of his Master and implored that under no circumstances he be sent away from Him, were separately suspended. The firing squad ranged itself in three files, each of two hundred and fifty men. Each file in turn opened fire until the whole detachment had discharged its bullets. So dense was the smoke from the seven hundred and fifty rifles that the sky was darkened. As soon as the smoke had cleared away the astounded multitude of about ten thousand souls, who had crowded onto the roof of the barracks, as well as the tops of the adjoining houses, beheld a scene which their eyes could scarcely believe.

The Báb had vanished from their sight! Only his companion remained, alive and unscathed, standing beside the wall on which they had been suspended. The ropes by which they had been hung alone were severed. 'The Siyyid-i-Báb has gone from our sight!' cried out the bewildered spectators. A frenzied search immediately ensued. He was found, unhurt and unruffled, in the very room He had occupied the night before, engaged in completing His interrupted conversation with His amanuensis. 'I have finished My conversation with Siyyid Ḥusayn' were the words with which the Prisoner, so providentially preserved, greeted the appearance of the farrásh-báshí, 'Now you may proceed to fulfil your intention.' Recalling the bold assertion his Prisoner had previously made, and shaken by so stunning a revelation, the farrásh-báshí quitted instantly the scene, and resigned his post.

Sám Khán, likewise, remembering, with feelings of awe and wonder, the reassuring words addressed to him by the Báb, ordered his men to leave the barracks immediately, and swore, as he left the courtyard, never again, even at the cost of his life, to repeat that act. Áqá Ján-i-Khamsih, colonel of the body-guard, volunteered to replace him. On the same wall and in the same manner the Báb and His companion were again suspended, while the new regiment formed in line and opened fire upon them. This time, however, their breasts were riddled with bullets, and their bodies completely dissected, with the exception of their faces which were but little marred. 'O wayward generation!' were the last words of the Báb to the gazing multitude, as the regiment prepared to fire its volley, 'Had you believed in Me every one of you would have followed the example of this youth, who stood in rank above most of you, and would have willingly sacrificed himself in My path. The day will come when you will have recognized Me; that day I shall have ceased to be with you.'

Nor was this all. The very moment the shots were fired a gale of exceptional violence arose and swept over the city. From noon till night a whirlwind of dust obscured the light of the sun, and blinded the eyes of the people. In Shíráz an 'earthquake', foreshadowed in no less weighty a Book than the Revelation of St John, occurred in 1268 A.H. which threw the whole city into turmoil and wrought havoc amongst its people, a havoc that was greatly aggravated by the outbreak of cholera, by famine and other afflictions.[69]

Bahá'u'lláh, as well as the Báb, suffered grievously at the hands of His enemies, as 'Abdu'l-Bahá has testified:

3–WT . . . and in Mázindarán, the blessed feet of the Abhá Beauty (may my life be offered up for His loved ones) were so grievously scourged as to bleed and be sore wounded.

The story of Bahá'u'lláh's imprisonment in Ámul is recorded in numerous history books but it is appropriate here to give a brief account of His suffering in His native land, Mázindarán. In the winter of 1848 Bahá'u'lláh, accompanied by a few believers including His half-brother Mírzá Yaḥyá, set out from Núr for the fortress of Shaykh Ṭabarsí. Government forces had besieged the fortress and the defenders inside were in great danger. Bahá'u'lláh's intention was to aid them. To Nabíl-i-A'ẓam, the famous chronicler of *The Dawn-Breakers*, He recounted the following:

. . . We had intended to send 'Abdu'l-Vahháb, one of Our companions, in advance of Us, and to request him to announce Our approach to the besieged. Though encompassed by the forces of the enemy, We had decided to throw in Our lot with those steadfast companions, and to risk the dangers with which they were confronted. This, however, was not to be. The hand of Omnipotence spared Us from their fate and preserved Us for the work We were destined to accomplish. In pursuance of God's inscrutable wisdom, the intention We had formed was, before Our arrival at the fort, communicated by certain inhabitants of Núr to Mírzá Taqí, the

> governor of Ámul, who sent his men to intercept Us. While We were resting and taking Our tea, We found Ourselves suddenly surrounded by a number of horsemen, who seized Our belongings and captured Our steeds. We were given, in exchange for Our own horse, a poorly saddled animal which We found it extremely uncomfortable to ride. The rest of Our companions were conducted, handcuffed, to Ámul. Mírzá Taqí succeeded, in spite of the tumult Our arrival had raised, and in the face of the opposition of the 'ulamás, in releasing Us from their grasp and in conducting Us to his own house. He extended to Us the warmest hospitality. Occasionally he yielded to the pressure which the 'ulamás were continuously bringing to bear upon him, and felt himself powerless to defeat their attempts to harm Us.[70]

The suffering Bahá'u'lláh underwent at the hands of the 'ulamá is truly heartrending. Nabíl describes how the bastinado* was inflicted on Him in public with such ferocity that His feet bled. Here is Nabíl's account of the circumstances leading to this tragic outcome:

> . . . Bahá'u'lláh had signified His wish that they should proceed directly to their destination and allow no pause in their journey. His intention was to reach that spot at night, inasmuch as strict orders had been issued . . . that no help should be extended, under any circumstances, to the occupants of the fort. Guards had been stationed at different places to ensure the isolation of the besieged. His companions, however, pressed Him to interrupt the journey and to seek a few hours of rest. Although He knew that this delay would involve a grave risk of being surprised by the enemy, He yielded to their earnest request. They halted at a lonely house adjoining the road. After supper, his companions all retired to sleep. He alone, despite the hardships He had endured, remained wakeful. He knew well the perils to which He and His friends were exposed, and was fully aware of the possibilities which His early arrival at the fort involved.
>
> As He watched beside them, the secret emissaries of the enemy informed the guards of the neighbourhood of the arrival of the party, and ordered the immediate seizure of whatever they could find in their possession. 'We have received strict orders,' they told Bahá'u'lláh, whom they recognized instantly as the leader of the group, 'to arrest every person we chance to meet in this vicinity, and are commanded to conduct him, without any previous investigation, to Ámul and deliver him into the hands of its governor.' . . .

---

*The victim is made to lie on his back on the ground while his feet are inserted into a loop and held up by two men. The soles are then beaten with a cane or a whip.

At daybreak, as they were approaching the town, a message was sent in advance to the acting governor, informing him of the arrival of a party that had been captured on their way to the fort of Ṭabarsí . . . As soon as the message reached him, he went to the masjid of Ámul and summoned the 'ulamás and leading siyyids of the town to gather and meet the party. He was greatly surprised as soon as his eyes saw and recognized Bahá'u'lláh, and deeply regretted the orders he had given. He feigned to reprimand Him for the action He had taken, in the hope of appeasing the tumult and allaying the excitement of those who had gathered in the masjid. 'We are innocent', Bahá'u'lláh declared, 'of the guilt they impute to us. Our blamelessness will eventually be established in your eyes. I would advise you to act in a manner that will cause you eventually no regret.' The acting governor asked the 'ulamás who were present to put any question they desired. To their enquiries Bahá'u'lláh returned explicit and convincing replies . . .

The circumstances which Bahá'u'lláh proceeded to relate in connection with the reply, no less than the manner of His delivery, convinced the arrogant mujtahid of his stupidity and blunder. Unable to contradict so weighty a statement, he preferred to keep silent. A siyyid angrily interjected: 'This very statement conclusively demonstrates that its author is himself a Bábí and no less than a leading expounder of the tenets of that sect.' He urged in vehement language that its followers be put to death. 'These obscure sectarians are the sworn enemies', he cried, 'both of the State and of the Faith of Islám! We must, at all costs, extirpate that heresy.' He was seconded in his denunciation by the other siyyids who were present, and who, emboldened by the imprecations uttered at that gathering, insisted that the governor comply unhesitatingly with their wishes.

The acting governor was much embarrassed, and realized that any evidence of indulgence on his part would be fraught with grave consequences for the safety of his position. In his desire to hold in check the passions which had been aroused, he ordered his attendants to prepare the rods and promptly inflict a befitting punishment upon the captives. 'We will afterwards', he added, 'keep them in prison pending the return of the governor, who will send them to Ṭihrán, where they will receive, at the hands of the sovereign, the chastisement they deserve.'

The first who was bound to receive the bastinado was Mullá Báqir. 'I am only a groom of Bahá'u'lláh,' he urged. 'I was on my way to Mas͟hhad when they suddenly arrested me and brought me to this place.' Bahá'u'lláh intervened and succeeded in inducing his oppressors to release him. He likewise interceded for Ḥájí Mírzá Jání, who He said was 'a mere tradesman' whom He regarded as His 'guest', so that He was 'responsible for any charges brought against him'. Mírzá Yaḥyá, whom they proceeded to bind, was also set free as soon as Bahá'u'lláh had declared him to be His attendant. 'None of these men', He told the acting governor, 'are guilty of any crime. If you insist on inflicting your punishment, I offer Myself as a willing Victim of your chastisement.' The acting governor was reluctantly compelled to give orders that Bahá'u'lláh alone be chosen to suffer the indignity which he had intended originally for His companions . . .

Bahá'u'lláh and His companions remained for a time imprisoned in one of the rooms that formed part of the masjid. The acting governor, who was still determined to shield his Prisoner from the assaults of an inveterate enemy, secretly instructed his attendants to open, at an unsuspected hour, a passage through the wall of the room in which the captives were confined, and to transfer their Leader immediately to his home. He was himself conducting Bahá'u'lláh to his residence when a siyyid sprang forward and, directing his fiercest invectives against Him, raised the club which he held in his hand to strike Him. The acting governor immediately interposed himself and, appealing to the assailant, 'adjured him by the Prophet of God' to stay his hand. 'What!' burst forth the siyyid. 'How dare you release a man who is the sworn enemy of the Faith of our fathers?' A crowd of ruffians had meanwhile gathered around him, and by their howls of derision and abuse added to the clamour which he had raised. Despite the growing tumult, the attendants of the acting governor were able to conduct Bahá'u'lláh in safety to the residence of their master, and displayed on that occasion a courage and presence of mind that were truly surprising.

Despite the protestations of the mob, the rest of the prisoners were taken to the seat of government, and thus escaped from the perils with which they had been threatened. The acting governor offered profuse apologies to Bahá'u'lláh for the treatment which the people of Ámul had accorded Him. 'But for the interposition of Providence,' he said, 'no force would have achieved your deliverance from the grasp of this malevolent people. But for the efficacy of the vow which I had made to risk my own life for your sake, I, too, would have fallen a victim to their violence, and would have been trampled beneath their feet.' He bitterly complained of the outrageous conduct of the siyyids of Ámul, and denounced the baseness of their character. He expressed himself as being continually tormented by the effects of their malignant designs. He set about serving Bahá'u'lláh with devotion and kindness, and was often heard, in the course of his conversation with Him, to remark: 'I am far from regarding you a prisoner in my home. This house, I believe, was built for the very purpose of affording you a shelter from the designs of your foes.'

I have heard Bahá'u'lláh Himself recount the following: 'No prisoner has ever been accorded the treatment which I received at the hands of the acting governor of Ámul. He treated Me with the utmost consideration and esteem. I was generously entertained by him, and the fullest attention was given to everything that affected My security and comfort.'[71]

A few days later arrangements were made for the safe departure of Bahá'u'lláh and His companions for Ṭihrán. Thus the intention of Bahá'u'lláh to join the defenders of the fortress of Ṭabarsí did not materialize. The protecting Hand of the Almighty preserved Him for His future mission of revealing Himself as the Supreme Manifestation of God for all time.

Referring to the suffering of Bahá'u'lláh, the Master states in His Will and Testament:

> **3–WT His neck also was put into captive chains and His feet made fast in the stocks. In every hour, for a period of fifty years, a new trial and calamity befell Him and fresh afflictions and cares beset Him. One of them: after having suffered intense vicissitudes, He was made homeless and a wanderer and fell a victim to still new vexations and troubles.**

This statement refers to Bahá'u'lláh's imprisonment in the Síyáh-Chál of Ṭihrán. Since this is a well-known story, a brief summary of events will suffice.

In the summer of 1852, obsessed by the tragedy of the martyrdom of the Báb and many of His outstanding disciples, a few irresponsible Bábís made an unsuccessful attempt on the life of Náṣiri'd-Dín Sháh to avenge the blood shed by his orders. Immediately afterwards a fierce onslaught was unleashed against anyone suspected of being a Bábí and a ruthless campaign of killing resulted in the martyrdom of a great many souls. Bahá'u'lláh's position as an outstanding figure in the Bábí community was well-known to the Sháh and his government. His open championship of the Báb, His irresistible eloquence when expounding upon the newly born Faith to groups of learned divines and the public, together with His resourcefulness, His penetrating judgement and His unobtrusive yet effective leadership of the Bábí community during the imprisonment of the Báb and following His martyrdom, were widely known. He was thus suspected as the chief director of this assassination attempt by the Sháh and especially his mother, who openly denounced Bahá'u'lláh as the would-be murderer of her youthful son. But again the Hand of God protected Bahá'u'lláh and His life was miraculously spared. He was arrested and forced to walk before royal horsemen at their pace from Níyávarán to Ṭihrán, a distance of about 15 miles, in the burning heat of a summer day, barefoot and in chains. To further humiliate Him, they removed His hat, which in those days was the symbol of a man's dignity. His destination was the Síyáh-Chál (Black Pit).

The Síyáh-Chál was no ordinary prison but a huge underground pit which had once served as a reservoir for one of the public baths of the city. It had only one entrance. It was situated in the heart of Ṭihrán close to a palace of the Sháh and adjacent to the Sabzih-Maydán, where the Seven Martyrs of Ṭihrán were executed. This dungeon was occupied by many prisoners, some of whom were without clothes or bedding. Its atmosphere was humid and dark, its air fetid and filled with a loathsome smell, its ground damp and littered with filth. These conditions were matched by the brutality of the guards and officials towards the Bábí victims who were chained together in that dismal place. The notorious chains of Qará-Guhar and Salásil, one of which was placed around Bahá'u'lláh's neck at all times, cut through His flesh and left their marks on His blessed body until the end of His life. They were so heavy that a special wooden fork was provided to support their weight.*

Through the kindness of one of the prison officials who was friendly towards Bahá'u'lláh, His eldest son, 'Abdu'l-Bahá, then nine years of age,† was taken one day to visit His father at the Síyáh-Chál. He had come only half-way down the steps when Bahá'u'lláh caught sight of Him and ordered that the child be taken out immediately. 'Abdu'l-Bahá was permitted to wait in the prison yard until noon, when the prisoners were allowed an hour of fresh air. 'Abdu'l-Bahá saw His father in chains and tied to His nephew, Mírzá Maḥmúd. Bahá'u'lláh walked with great difficulty, His beard and hair were unkempt, His neck bruised and swollen from the pressure of a heavy steel collar, and His back was bent with the weight of the chain. On witnessing this sight 'Abdu'l-Bahá fainted and was carried home, unconscious.

While breathing the foul air of the Síyáh-Chál, with His feet in stocks and His head weighed down by the mighty chain, Bahá'u'lláh received, as attested by Him in His Epistle to the Son of the Wolf, the first intimations of His station as the Supreme Manifestation of God – He whose appearance had been foretold by the Prophets of old in such terms as the 'reincarnation of Krishna', the 'fifth Buddha', the 'Sháh Bahrám', the 'Lord of Hosts', the Christ returned 'in the glory of the Father', the 'Spirit of God', and by the Báb as 'Him Whom God shall make manifest'. These are Bahá'u'lláh's words describing this initial experience of the 'Most Great Spirit' stirring within His soul:

> During the days I lay in the prison of Ṭihrán, though the galling weight of the chains and the stench-filled air allowed Me but little sleep, still in those infrequent moments of slumber I felt as if

---

* Qará-Guhar, heavier than Salásil, weighed about 17 'man' (51 kilos).

† According to the lunar calendar. 'Abdu'l-Bahá was born on 23 May 1844 and was at this time in His ninth year.

something flowed from the crown of My head over My breast, even as a mighty torrent that precipitateth itself upon the earth from the summit of a lofty mountain. Every limb of My body would, as a result, be set afire. At such moments My tongue recited what no man could bear to hear.[72]

While Bahá'u'lláh lay in the prison of Ṭihrán, Náṣiri'd-Dín Sẖáh ordered his prime minister, Mírzá Áqá Kẖán, to send troops to the province of Núr and arrest the followers of the Báb in that area. The prime minister – who also came from Núr and was related to Bahá'u-'lláh by the marriage of his niece to Mírzá Muḥammad-Ḥasan, Bahá'u'lláh's half-brother – made efforts to protect Bahá'u'lláh's relatives in Núr but failed.

Bahá'u'lláh's properties were confiscated by the Sẖáh and His house in Núr was razed to the ground. Even the prime minister took advantage of the situation and, without recompense, transferred the deeds of some of Bahá'u'lláh's properties into his own name. The luxurious house of Bahá'u'lláh in Ṭihrán was plundered and its valuable furnishings were removed. Some unique articles, together with many more of great value, fell into the hands of the prime minister. Among them were part of a Tablet, inscribed on leather by the hand of Imám 'Alí, successor to Muḥammad, which was over a thousand years old and known to be priceless, and a rare manuscript of the poems of Ḥáfiẓ written by a celebrated calligrapher.*

Although most of the Bábís were taken from the prison, one by one, and martyred in the adjoining market square of Sabzih-Maydán, Bahá'u'lláh's life was providentially spared. After four months He was released but was ordered to leave Persia within a month.

When Bahá'u'lláh came out of prison, stripped of His possessions, His back bent by the weight of the fetters, His neck swollen and injured and His health impaired, He did not intimate to anyone His experience of divine revelation. Yet those who were close to Him could not fail to witness a transformation of spirit, a power and a radiance never seen in Him before.

The following is an extract from the spoken chronicle of the Greatest Holy Leaf recounting her impressions of Him at the time of His release from the Síyáh-Cẖál:

Jamál-i-Mubárak [lit. the Blessed Beauty, referring to Bahá'u'lláh] had a marvellous divine experience whilst in that prison.

---

* Muḥammad Sẖáh had once been eager to own this manuscript but when he learned that for each of its twelve thousand verses he would have to pay one golden sovereign, he abandoned the idea.

> We saw a new radiance seeming to enfold him like a shining vesture, its significance we were to learn years later. At that time we were only aware of the wonder of it, without understanding, or even being told the details of the sacred event.[73]

Bahá'u'lláh spent the month preceding His exile in the house of His half-brother Mírzá Riḍá-Qulí, a physician. The latter was not a believer, though his wife Maryam, a cousin of Bahá'u'lláh, had been converted by Him in the early days of the Faith and was one of His most sincere and faithful followers within the family. With great care and affection Maryam, together with Ásíyih Khánum, nursed Bahá'u'lláh until His condition improved and, though not fully recovered, He had gathered sufficient strength to enable Him to leave Ṭihrán for Iraq. Those who accompanied Him on this great journey were members of His family, including 'Abdu'l-Bahá, the Greatest Holy Leaf, Navváb and His two brothers Áqáy-i-Kalím and Mírzá Muḥammad-Qulí.

The journey to Baghdád, undertaken in the middle of a severe winter across the snow-bound mountains of western Persia, inflicted much hardship and suffering on the exiles. The following is an extract from one of the prayers revealed by Bahá'u'lláh at that time; it portrays the suffering and hardship which befell Him in the early days of His ministry:

> My God, My Master, My Desire! . . . Thou hast created this atom of dust through the consummate power of Thy might, and nurtured Him with Thine hands which none can chain up . . . Thou hast destined for Him trials and tribulations which no tongue can describe, nor any of Thy Tablets adequately recount. The throat Thou didst accustom to the touch of silk Thou hast, in the end, clasped with strong chains, and the body Thou didst ease with brocades and velvets Thou hast at last subjected to the abasement of a dungeon. Thy decree hath shackled Me with unnumbered fetters, and cast about My neck chains that none can sunder. A number of years have passed during which afflictions have, like showers of mercy, rained upon Me . . . How many the nights during which the weight of chains and fetters allowed Me no rest, and how numerous the days during which peace and tranquillity were denied Me, by reason of that wherewith the hands and tongues of men have afflicted Me! Both bread and water which Thou hast, through Thy all-embracing mercy, allowed unto the beasts of the field, they have, for a time, forbidden unto this servant, and the things they refused to inflict upon such as have seceded from Thy Cause, the same have they suffered to be inflicted upon Me, until, finally, Thy decree was irrevocably fixed, and Thy behest summoned this servant to depart out of Persia,

accompanied by a number of frail-bodied men and children of tender age, at this time when the cold is so intense that one cannot even speak, and ice and snow so abundant that it is impossible to move.[74]

7

Bahá'u'lláh's Retirement to the Mountains of Kurdistan

3–WT In 'Iráq, the Day-Star of the world was so exposed to the wiles of the people of malice as to be eclipsed in splendour.

This passage refers to Bahá'u'lláh's retirement to the mountains of Kurdistan. On 8 April 1853, Bahá'u'lláh and His family arrived in Baghdád, from which centre the light of the new Revelation was progressively diffused throughout the Bábí community. Soon after Bahá'u'lláh's arrival, through the outpouring of His guidance, new courage and new confidence were instilled in the minds and hearts of the Báb's followers in Iraq. The power of divine authority emanating from Bahá'u'lláh was so compelling that the fortunes of a Faith that had seemed ready to sink into oblivion were revived.

In the first year of Bahá'u'lláh's residence in Baghdád, the Bábís, both the locals and those who trickled into Baghdád from Persia, evinced an ever deepening veneration of Him. Their hearts were filled with a new spirit of devotion and adoration for His person. Many inhabitants of the city were also drawn to Bahá'u'lláh during this period, their numbers increasing day by day. Among them were outstanding personalities and government officials, including the city's governor. Thus the circle of His admirers steadily extended and His fame spread throughout the land.

While these highly encouraging developments were taking place, a grim crisis, purely internal and with far-reaching consequences, erupted in the community. Instigated by the notorious Siyyid Muḥammad-i-Iṣfahání,* an embodiment of evil and the Antichrist of Bahá'u'lláh's Revelation, a clandestine opposition to Bahá'u'lláh was set in motion by His half-brother Mírzá Yaḥyá. Yaḥyá was a cowardly yet ambitious person who, at the suggestion of Bahá'u'lláh, had been appointed as the nominal head of the Bábí community. In Baghdád, while hiding himself from the members of the community and wearing the disguise of an Arab, he, prompted by Siyyid Muḥammad,

* For information about him see Taherzadeh, *Revelation of Bahá'u'lláh*, vol. 2.

spread his preposterous claim to be the successor of the Báb and began secretly to misrepresent Bahá'u'lláh's activities, kindling dissension and conflict within the community. Shoghi Effendi describes the shameful behaviour of Mírzá Yaḥyá and Siyyid Muḥammad in these words:

> A clandestine opposition, whose aim was to nullify every effort exerted, and frustrate every design conceived, by Bahá'u'lláh for the rehabilitation of a distracted community, could now be clearly discerned. Insinuations, whose purpose was to sow the seeds of doubt and suspicion and to represent Him as a usurper, as the subverter of the laws instituted by the Báb, and the wrecker of His Cause, were being incessantly circulated. His Epistles, interpretations, invocations and commentaries were being covertly and indirectly criticized, challenged and misrepresented. An attempt to injure His person was even set afoot but failed to materialize.[75]

The cup of Bahá'u'lláh's sorrows was now running over. All His exhortations, all His efforts to remedy a rapidly deteriorating situation, had remained fruitless. The velocity with which His manifold woes grew was hourly and visibly increasing. Upon the sadness that filled His soul and the gravity of the situation confronting Him, His writings, revealed during that sombre period, throw abundant light. In some of His prayers He poignantly confesses that 'tribulation upon tribulation' had gathered about Him, that 'adversaries with one consent' had fallen upon Him, that 'wretchedness' had grievously touched Him and that 'woes at their blackest' had befallen Him.

> 'In these days,' He, describing in the Kitáb-i-Íqán the virulence of the jealousy which, at that time, was beginning to bare its venomous fangs, has written, 'such odours of jealousy are diffused, that ... from the beginning of the foundation of the world ... until the present day, such malice, envy and hate have in no wise appeared, nor will they ever be witnessed in the future.' ...
>
> Mírzá Áqá Ján* himself has testified: 'That Blessed Beauty evinced such sadness that the limbs of my body trembled.' He has, likewise, related, as reported by Nabíl in his narrative, that, shortly before Bahá'u'lláh's retirement, he had on one occasion seen Him, between dawn and sunrise, suddenly come out from His house, His night-cap still on His head, showing such signs of perturbation that he was powerless to gaze into His face, and while walking, angrily remark: 'These creatures are the same creatures who for three thousand years have worshipped idols, and bowed down before the Golden Calf. Now, too, they are fit for nothing better. What rela-

* Bahá'u'lláh's amanuensis. For his life story see Taherzadeh, *Covenant of Bahá'u'lláh*, chapter 15.

tion can there be between this people and Him Who is the Countenance of Glory? What ties can bind them to the One Who is the supreme embodiment of all that is lovable?' 'I stood,' declared Mírzá Áqá Ján, 'rooted to the spot, lifeless, dried up as a dead tree, ready to fall under the impact of the stunning power of His words. Finally, He said: "Bid them recite: 'Is there any Remover of difficulties save God? Say: Praised be God! He is God! All are His servants, and all abide by His bidding!' Tell them to repeat it five hundred times, nay, a thousand times, by day and by night, sleeping and waking, that haply the Countenance of Glory may be unveiled to their eyes, and tiers of light descend upon them." He Himself, I was subsequently informed, recited this same verse, His face betraying the utmost sadness . . . Several times during those days, He was heard to remark: "We have, for a while, tarried amongst this people, and failed to discern the slightest response on their part." Oftentimes He alluded to His disappearance from our midst, yet none of us understood His meaning.'

Finally, discerning, as He Himself testifies in the Kitáb-i-Íqán, 'the signs of impending events', He decided that before they happened He would retire. 'The one object of Our retirement', He, in that same Book affirms, 'was to avoid becoming a subject of discord among the faithful, a source of disturbance unto Our companions, the means of injury to any soul, or the cause of sorrow to any heart.' 'Our withdrawal', He, moreover, in that same passage emphatically asserts, 'contemplated no return, and Our separation hoped for no reunion.'

Suddenly, and without informing any one even among the members of His own family, on the 12th of Rajab 1270 A.H. (April 10, 1854), He departed, accompanied by an attendant, a Muḥammadan named Abu'l-Qásim-i-Hamadání, to whom He gave a sum of money, instructing him to act as a merchant and use it for his own purposes. Shortly after, that servant was attacked by thieves and killed, and Bahá'u'lláh was left entirely alone in His wanderings through the wastes of Kurdistán, a region whose sturdy and warlike people were known for their age-long hostility to the Persians, whom they regarded as seceders from the Faith of Islám, and from whom they differed in their outlook, race and language.

Attired in the garb of a traveller, coarsely clad, taking with Him nothing but his ka<u>sh</u>kúl (alms-bowl) and a change of clothes, and assuming the name of Darví<u>sh</u> Muḥammad, Bahá'u'lláh retired to the wilderness, and lived for a time on a mountain named Sar-Galú, so far removed from human habitations that only twice a year, at seed sowing and harvest time, it was visited by the peasants of that region. Alone and undisturbed, He passed a considerable part of His retirement on the top of that mountain in a rude structure, made of stone, which served those peasants as a shelter against the extremities of the weather.[76]

With Bahá'u'lláh's retirement to the mountains of Kurdistan, a new chapter opened in the history of His Revelation. Here He lived in utter seclusion far away from the world; He left behind His loved ones and admirers, as well as those who had betrayed Him and brought about, through their evil designs, the near extinction of the Cause of the Báb.

After Bahá'u'lláh had spent some time in that area, a certain Shaykh Ismá'íl, the leader of the Khálidíyyih Order, a sect of Sunní Islam, came in contact with Him and was intensely attracted to His person. In the end he succeeded in persuading Bahá'u'lláh to leave His abode for the town of Sulaymáníyyih. There, within a short period of time, His greatness became manifest not only to the leaders of religion and men of learning but also to all the inhabitants of the area.

Their recognition of Him as a man of outstanding qualities and knowledge occurred when His exquisite penmanship was first noticed, as well as His masterly composition and the stylistic beauty of the letters He wrote acknowledging receipt of messages from a few religious leaders. Some of these letters written by Bahá'u'lláh to eminent personalities such as Shaykh 'Abdu'r-Raḥmán, the leader of the Qádiríyyih Order, Mullá Ḥámid, a celebrated divine of Sulaymáníyyih, and a few others, have been left to posterity and testify to His sorrow and anguish in those days. In a letter He wrote to Shaykh 'Abdu'r-Raḥmán He laments the loss of His trusted Muslim servant, Abu'l-Qásim-i-Hamadání, who accompanied Him from Baghdád and was attacked and killed by brigands.

Bahá'u'lláh's fame spread to Sulaymáníyyih and to neighbouring towns. He soon became the focal point for many who thirsted after true knowledge and enlightenment. Without disclosing His identity, He appeared among them day after day, and with simplicity and eloquence answered their questions on various abstruse and perplexing features of their religious teachings. Soon the people of Kurdistan, as 'Abdu'l-Bahá has testified, were magnetized by His love. Some of His admirers even believed that His station was that of a Prophet. Bahá'u'lláh has left in His own handwriting a few Tablets and odes revealed during this period. Notable among them is the Qaṣídiy-i-Varqá'iyyih, the revelation of which had an electric effect on the leaders of the Kurdish community.* The reputation of 'Darvísh Muḥammad', the name Bahá'u'lláh assumed during His two-year absence from Baghdád, now spread beyond Kurdistan. When the reports of His innate greatness and knowledge reached Baghdád, His family and friends realized that this figure could be none other than

* For more information see Taherzadeh, *Revelation of Bahá'u'lláh*, vol. 1.

Bahá'u'lláh Himself. This was confirmed when officials discovered the will of Abu'l-Qásim-i-Hamadání, Bahá'u'lláh's murdered servant, bequeathing all his possessions to a Darvísh Muḥammad in the mountains of Kurdistan. His family immediately dispatched the venerable Shaykh Sulṭán, the father-in-law of Bahá'u'lláh's faithful brother Mírzá Músá, to Kurdistan to seek out Bahá'u'lláh. He and a servant travelled for two months before being led to Him in the neighbourhood of Sulaymáníyyih. After a time, Bahá'u'lláh responded favourably to Shaykh Sulṭán's insistent pleading that He end His two-year retirement. He returned to Baghdád, leaving behind a host of admirers and supporters who bitterly lamented His departure.

The physical hardships that Bahá'u'lláh endured as a result of inadequate food and clothing, and living alone in the wilderness of a desolate and uninhabitable mountain in extreme weather conditions, are unimaginable. These hardships, however, were dwarfed by the intensity of the suffering He felt as He contemplated the harm inflicted by the unfaithful on the Cause of which He was the only divinely chosen Author. Yet, in spite of the great difficulties and privations of a solitary life in such inhospitable surroundings, He communed with the Divine Spirit and chanted aloud many prayers and odes extolling the attributes and glorifying the character of His Revelation. While these outpourings could have revived the souls of men and illuminated the world of humanity, they were instead confined to this remote land and were, alas, forever lost.

Bahá'u'lláh also meditated on such things as the Cause of God which He would manifest, the fierce opposition His enemies would launch, the adversities that had already befallen Him and those that were still to come, and the perversity and unfaithfulness of the leaders of the Bábí community who had stained the good name of the Cause of the Báb and brought shame upon it.

Shoghi Effendi, quoting the words of Bahá'u'lláh Himself, highlights the agony of His soul:

> At times His dwelling-place was a cave to which He refers in His Tablets addressed to the famous Shaykh 'Abdu'r-Raḥmán and to Maryam, a kinswoman of His. 'I roamed the wilderness of resignation' He thus depicts, in the Lawḥ-i-Maryam, the rigours of His austere solitude, 'travelling in such wise that in My exile every eye wept sore over Me, and all created things shed tears of blood because of My anguish. The birds of the air were My companions and the beasts of the field My associates.' 'From My eyes,' He, referring in the Kitáb-i-Íqán to those days, testifies, 'there rained tears of anguish, and in My bleeding heart surged an ocean of agonizing pain. Many a night I had no food for sustenance, and

> many a day My body found no rest . . . Alone I communed with My spirit, oblivious of the world and all that is therein.'[77]

As a result of Bahá'u'lláh's retirement, the Bábí community in general and the lovers of His Beauty in particular were entirely cut off from the effulgence of His light. How fitting are the words of 'Abdu'l-Bahá describing this period as a time when:

> **3–WT . . . the Day-Star of the world was . . . eclipsed in splendour.**

8

Bahá'u'lláh's Exiles

3–WT Later on He was sent an exile to the Great City (Constantinople) and thence to the Land of Mystery (Adrianople), whence grievously wronged, He was eventually transferred to the Most Great Prison ('Akká). He Whom the world hath wronged (may my life be offered up for His loved ones) was four times banished from city to city, till at last, condemned to perpetual confinement, He was incarcerated in this prison, the prison of highway robbers, of brigands and of man-slayers. All this is but one of the trials that have afflicted the Blessed Beauty, the rest being even as grievous as this.

Bahá'u'lláh in Baghdád

With the return of Bahá'u'lláh from Kurdistan to Baghdád in March 1856, a new day opened for the company of exiles in Iraq. During His absence it had become apparent to friend and foe alike that the Bábí community, left for so long to the leadership of unfaithful persons such as Mírzá Yaḥyá and Siyyid Muḥammad-i-Iṣfahání, had degenerated completely. Most of its members were now dispirited; unlike the early heroes and martyrs who only a decade before had demonstrated with their lifeblood the staunchness of their faith, the loftiness of their character, and the depth of their love, the Bábís were now devoid of such virtues and were spiritually dead. They were also divided among themselves. The degradation to which many of the so-called followers of the Báb in Iraq had sunk was evident in the eyes of the public. They were involved in the most shameful crimes. The Kurds and Persians heaped abuse upon them in the streets and denounced their Faith in vile language.

When the fortunes of the Bábí community had reached their lowest ebb, Bahá'u'lláh returned and took the reins of the Cause into His hands. The clouds of uncertainty and misfortune which had hung over the community's members during His absence now began to lift. Through His exhortations and encouragement, both verbal and written, He breathed a new life into the dying community and, in a short time, succeeded in transforming some of its members into the spiritual giants of His Dispensation. Bahá'u'lláh Himself has testified:

> By the aid of God and His divine grace and mercy, We revealed, as a copious rain, Our verses, and sent them to various parts of the world. We exhorted all men, and particularly this people, through Our wise counsels and loving admonitions, and forbade them to engage in sedition, quarrels, disputes or conflict. As a result of this, and by the grace of God, waywardness and folly were changed into piety and understanding, and weapons of war converted into instruments of peace.[78]

The influence that Bahá'u'lláh exerted on the public in Iraq was no less impressive. For eight years the Supreme Manifestation of God lived freely among the inhabitants of Baghdád. He walked among them, sat with them and poured out His affection and bounties upon them. Although He did not disclose His station to them, multitudes of people from all walks of life were attracted to His person and longed to attain His presence, to hear His words, or even to catch a glimpse of Him as He walked in the streets or paced along the bank of the Tigris rapt in meditation. During this period, also, many Bábís from Persia came into contact with Bahá'u'lláh and some became great heroes of His Faith.

The transformation which took place in the lives of the companions of Bahá'u'lláh, the outpouring of His Revelation which revitalized the faith of many dispirited believers in Persia, the range and magnificence of Bahá'u'lláh's rising power and the high esteem in which He was held by many high-ranking government officials alarmed the authorities in Persia. Consequently the government of Náṣiri'd-Dín Sháh asked the Ottoman government to hand Bahá'u'lláh over to the Persian authorities. This request was met with outright refusal because the authorities in Baghdád had been highly impressed with His person. Having failed to carry out its intention, the Persian government brought much pressure to bear upon 'Álí Páshá, the Grand Vizír, to remove Bahá'u'lláh from Baghdád, which was close to its frontiers. Government representatives complained that Bahá'u'lláh's influence in the area was creating a serious problem for Persian pilgrims to the Islamic holy sites. Eventually the Grand Vizír issued orders to Námiq Páshá, the Governor of Baghdád, to invite Bahá'u'lláh to travel to Constantinople as a guest of the government. Námiq Páshá was an ardent admirer of Bahá'u'lláh whom he regarded as one of the lights of the age. So profound was the measure of his esteem that he could not bring himself to convey the government's decision to Him personally. Instead He sent his deputy to apprise Bahá'u'lláh of the invitation extended to Him by the Sulṭán to transfer His residence to the capital of the Ottoman Empire. Shoghi Effendi describes this interview in these words:

> By the following day the Deputy-Governor had delivered to Bahá'u'lláh in a mosque, in the neighbourhood of the governor's house, 'Álí Pá<u>sh</u>á's letter, addressed to Námiq Pá<u>sh</u>á, couched in courteous language, inviting Bahá'u'lláh to proceed, as a guest of the Ottoman government, to Constantinople, placing a sum of money at His disposal, and ordering a mounted escort to accompany Him for His protection. To this request Bahá'u'lláh gave His ready assent, but declined to accept the sum offered Him. On the urgent representations of the Deputy that such a refusal would offend the authorities, He reluctantly consented to receive the generous allowance set aside for His use, and distributed it, that same day, among the poor.
>
> The effect upon the colony of exiles of this sudden intelligence was instantaneous and overwhelming. 'That day,' wrote an eyewitness, describing the reaction of the community to the news of Bahá'u'lláh's approaching departure, 'witnessed a commotion associated with the turmoil of the Day of Resurrection. Methinks, the very gates and walls of the city wept aloud at their imminent separation from the Abhá Beloved. The first night mention was made of His intended departure His loved ones, one and all, renounced both sleep and food . . . Not a soul amongst them could be tranquillized. Many had resolved that in the event of their being deprived of the bounty of accompanying Him, they would, without hesitation, kill themselves . . . Gradually, however, through the words which He addressed them, and through His exhortations and His loving-kindness, they were calmed and resigned themselves to His good-pleasure.'[79]

The expressions of love and devotion for Bahá'u'lláh were not confined to the Bábí community in Iraq. The love and admiration of the people for Bahá'u'lláh was fully demonstrated on the day of His departure from His 'Most Great House' in Ba<u>gh</u>dád. Then His majesty and greatness were evident to both friend and foe. The news of His forthcoming departure for Constantinople had spread rapidly among the inhabitants of Ba<u>gh</u>dád and its neighbouring towns, and large numbers wished to attain His presence and pay their last tributes to Him. But soon it became apparent that His house was too small for the purpose. Arrangements were made for Bahá'u'lláh to proceed to the garden-park of Najíbíyyih. This beautiful garden, designated by His followers as the Garden of Riḍván (Paradise), was situated on the outskirts of Ba<u>gh</u>dád, across the river from His house.

Thirty-one days after Naw-Rúz, on 22 April 1863,* in the afternoon, Bahá'u'lláh moved to this garden, where He remained for twelve days. On the first day He declared His mission to His companions.† These twelve days are celebrated by the Bahá'ís as the Festival of Riḍván.

The departure of Bahá'u'lláh from His house witnessed a commotion the like of which Baghdád had rarely seen. People of all walks of life, men and women, rich and poor, young and old, men of learning and culture, princes, government officials, tradesmen and workers, and above all His companions, thronged the approaches to His house and crowded the streets and roof-tops situated along His route to the river. They were weeping and lamenting the departure of One who, for a decade, had imparted to them the warmth of His love and the radiance of His spirit, who had been a refuge and guide for them all.

When Bahá'u'lláh appeared in the courtyard of His house, His companions, grief-stricken and disconsolate, prostrated themselves at His feet. For some time He stood there, amid the weeping and lamentations of His loved ones, speaking words of comfort and promising to receive each of them later in the garden. In a Tablet Bahá'u'lláh mentions that when He had walked some way towards the gate, amid the crowds, a child‡ of only a few years ran forward and, clinging to His robes, wept aloud, begging Him in his tender young voice not to leave. In such an atmosphere, where emotions had been so deeply stirred, this action on the part of a small child moved the hearts and brought further grief to everyone.

Outside the house, the lamentation and weeping of those who did not confess to be His followers were no less spectacular and heart-rending. Everyone in the crowded street sought to approach Him. Some prostrated themselves at His feet, others waited to hear a few words and yet others were content with a touch of His hands or a glance at His face. A Persian lady of noble birth, who was not herself a believer, pushed her way into the crowd and with a gesture of sacrifice threw her child at the feet of Bahá'u'lláh. These demonstrations continued all the way to the riverbank.

Before crossing the river, Bahá'u'lláh addressed His companions who had gathered around Him, saying:

---

* Thirty-one days after Naw-Rúz usually falls on 21 April. Occasionally, as in the year 1863, when the vernal equinox takes place after sunset, Naw-Rúz is celebrated on 22 March.

† This is stated by 'Abdu'l-Bahá in a talk given at Bahjí on 29 April 1916.

‡ He was Áqá 'Alí, the son of Ḥájí Mírzá Kamálu'd-Din-Naráqí.

> O My companions, I entrust to your keeping this city of Baghdád, in the state ye now behold it, when from the eyes of friends and strangers alike, crowding its housetops, its streets and markets, tears like the rain of spring are flowing down, and I depart. With you it now rests to watch lest your deeds and conduct dim the flame of love that gloweth within the breasts of its inhabitants.[80]

Bahá'u'lláh was then ferried across the river, accompanied by three of His sons: 'Abdu'l-Bahá, Mírzá Mihdí (the Purest Branch) and Muḥammad-'Alí, who were 18, 14 and 10 years of age, respectively. With them also was His amanuensis, Mírzá Áqá Ján. The identity of others who may have accompanied Him, of those in the garden who pitched His tent and made preparations for His arrival, or of those who might have followed Him on that day, is not clearly known.

The call to afternoon prayer was raised from the mosque and the words 'Alláh'u'Akbar' (God is the Greatest), chanted by the muezzin,* reverberated through the garden as the King of Glory entered it. There, Bahá'u'lláh appeared in the utmost joy, walking majestically in its flower-lined avenues and among its trees. The fragrance of the roses and the singing of the nightingales created an atmosphere of beauty and enchantment.

Bahá'u'lláh's companions had, for some time, known the declaration of His station to be imminent. This realization came to them not only as a result of many remarks and allusions made by Him during the last few months of His sojourn in Baghdád but also through a noticeable change in His demeanour. Another sign which unmistakably pointed to this approaching hour was His adoption, on the day of His departure from His house in Baghdád, of a different type of headdress known as *táj* (tall felt hat), which He wore throughout His ministry. 'Abdu'l-Bahá has described how, upon His arrival in the garden, Bahá'u'lláh declared His station to those of His companions who were present and announced with great joy the inauguration of the Festival of Riḍván.[81] Sadness and grief vanished and the believers were filled with delight. Although Bahá'u'lláh was being exiled to far-off lands and knew the sufferings and tribulations which were in store for Him and His followers, yet through this historic declaration He changed all sorrow into blissful joy and spent the most delightful time of His ministry in the Garden of Riḍván. Indeed, in one of His Tablets He referred to the first day of Riḍván as the 'Day of supreme felicity' and called on His followers to 'rejoice with exceeding gladness' in remembrance of that day.[82]

---

* The one who calls to prayer.

Departure for Constantinople

Bahá'u'lláh left the Garden of Riḍván on the first leg of His journey to Constantinople on 3 May 1863. Shoghi Effendi recounts this historic journey in these words:

> The departure of Bahá'u'lláh from the Garden of Riḍván, at noon, on the 14th of Dhi'l-Qa'dih 1279 A.H. (May 3, 1863), witnessed scenes of tumultuous enthusiasm no less spectacular, and even more touching, than those which greeted Him when leaving His Most Great House in Baghdád. 'The great tumult', wrote an eyewitness, 'associated in our minds with the Day of Gathering, the Day of Judgement, we beheld on that occasion. Believers and unbelievers alike sobbed and lamented. The chiefs and notables who had congregated were struck with wonder. Emotions were stirred to such depths as no tongue can describe, nor could any observer escape their contagion.'
>
> Mounted on His steed, a red roan stallion of the finest breed, the best His lovers could purchase for Him, and leaving behind Him a bowing multitude of fervent admirers, He rode forth on the first stage of a journey that was to carry Him to the city of Constantinople. 'Numerous were the heads,' Nabíl himself a witness of that memorable scene, recounts, 'which, on every side, bowed to the dust at the feet of His horse, and kissed its hoofs, and countless were those who pressed forward to embrace His stirrups.' 'How great the number of those embodiments of fidelity,' testifies a fellow-traveller, 'who, casting themselves before that charger, preferred death to separation from their Beloved! Methinks, that blessed steed trod upon the bodies of those pure-hearted souls.' 'He (God) it was,' Bahá'u'lláh Himself declares, 'Who enabled Me to depart out of the city (Baghdád), clothed with such majesty as none, except the denier and the malicious, can fail to acknowledge.'[83]

The journey to Constantinople was arduous and fatiguing, taking 110 days to reach the Port of Sámsún on the Black Sea. The route took the party across uplands, woods, valleys and mountain passes which entailed the careful negotiation of narrow roads above dangerous precipices. Accompanying Bahá'u'lláh were members of His family, including His faithful brothers Áqáy-i-Kalím and Mírzá Muḥammad-Qulí, and 26 men, among them His disciples and Siyyid Muḥammad Iṣfahání, as well as Mírzá Yaḥyá, who joined the party en route.

A mounted guard of ten soldiers accompanied the caravan of 50 mules and seven howdahs.* Most of the time Bahá'u'lláh sat in one pannier with His wife Navváb in the other. Although the howdah was considered a comfortable means of transportation in those days, on long journeys it could be extremely tiring, for one has to sit cross-legged for hours while the panniers continually rise and fall with the movement of the mule's body. 'Abdu'l-Bahá describes how many a night He and Jináb-i-Muníb, a devoted lover of Bahá'u'lláh, walked on either side of the howdah. Every time the party approached a village, or was about to depart from it, Bahá'u'lláh would mount His horse – a practice befitting His station as He appeared in public. On such occasions 'Abdu'l-Bahá would replace Him in His howdah. By virtue of a written order of Námiq Páshá, the Governor of Baghdád, Bahá'u'lláh was enthusiastically welcomed by various high-ranking officials at every village and town as He travelled northward. Shoghi Effendi writes:

> In Karkúk, in Irbíl, in Mosul, where He tarried three days, in Níṣíbín, in Márdín, in Díyár-Bakr, where a halt of a couple of days was made, in Khárpút, in Sívas, as well as in other villages and hamlets, He would be met by a delegation immediately before His arrival, and would be accompanied, for some distance, by a similar delegation upon His departure. The festivities which, at some stations, were held in His honour, the food the villagers prepared and brought for His acceptance, the eagerness which time and again they exhibited in providing the means for His comfort, recalled the reverence which the people of Baghdád had shown Him on so many occasions.[84]

Those who have travelled in the deserts or the valleys and uplands of the Middle East on the backs of mules and horses know how slow and monotonous the pace is. For miles there is no sign of life and those who travel in the party are not always able to talk and communicate easily with each other. Under these circumstances nothing can be more exhilarating than to hear a pleasant voice singing beautiful songs. Jináb-i-Muníb was one of those whose melodious voice, chanting various odes and poems, rang out through the open fields and mountains of Turkey and brought joy and relaxation to those who travelled with Bahá'u'lláh. The odes that he sang were all indicative of his love for Bahá'u'lláh, and the prayers he chanted in the dead of night were a testimony to the yearning of his heart for his Lord.

---

* A litter consisting of a pair of panniers in which two individuals can ride to balance each other's weight. It is carried by a beast of burden, in this case a mule.

On this journey many undesirable problems had to be dealt with, apart from providing food and shelter for a large party of men, women and children, and the daily feeding of mules and horses. The organization of such tasks was undertaken by 'Abdu'l-Bahá, who chose a number of men to assist him in carrying out various duties. Áqá Mírzá Maḥmúd of Ká<u>sh</u>án, together with Áqá Riḍá of <u>Sh</u>íráz, went all the way to the port of Sámsún ahead of the howdah of Bahá'u'lláh. They would arrive at each halting place hours before the party and would take up the task of preparing and cooking the food for everyone. These two souls were so dedicated that, in spite of the fatigue and rigours of the journey, they were constantly engaged until midnight in serving the friends with great devotion. Not only did they cook the meals and wash the dishes but they ensured that every person was comfortable and had sufficient rest. They were the last to retire at night and the first to arise in the morning, rendering this vital service with an exemplary dedication each day of the journey from Bag<u>h</u>dád to Constantinople.

Yet another person who performed a difficult task on this journey was the learned divine Mírzá Ja'far-i-Yazdí. In spite of his great learning he was humble and self-effacing and for some time served in the household of Bahá'u'lláh in Bag<u>h</u>dád. On the way to Constantinople he served the friends in every possible manner. While everyone was resting or sleeping at a stopping-place, Mírzá Ja'far and 'Abdu'l-Bahá would go to surrounding villages to purchase straw and other provisions for the mules and horses. Sometimes this would take hours as there was a famine in the area and it was very difficult to obtain food.

Another soul who was truly enamoured of Bahá'u'lláh was Darví<u>sh</u> Ṣidq-'Alí. He begged Bahá'u'lláh to allow him to join the party travelling to Constantinople and when permission was granted he undertook to serve as groom on the journey. He would walk all day beside the convoy, singing poems which brought joy to the friends, and at night would attend to the horses.

There were others also who carried out various duties with the utmost devotion and self-sacrifice.* Apart from the notorious Siyyid Muḥammad-i-Iṣfahání who travelled with Bahá'u'lláh and Mírzá Yaḥyá, who joined Him on the way, the disciples of Bahá'u'lláh, as always, demonstrated such love, devotion and humility towards Him as no pen can ever describe. The inestimable privilege conferred upon them of accompanying Him to Constantinople completely overwhelmed them. They were so inspired with joy and contentment that

---

* For more information see Taherzadeh, *Revelation of Bahá'u'lláh*, vol. 1.

the hardships of the journey, whether on foot or by mule, had very little effect upon their health.

The marks of respect and veneration shown to Bahá'u'lláh by the people along the way continued until He reached the port of Sámsún. From there He travelled by sea to Constantinople, a journey recounted by Shoghi Effendi in *God Passes By*:

> In Sámsún the Chief Inspector of the entire province, extending from Baghdád to Constantinople, accompanied by several páshás, called on Him, showed Him the utmost respect, and was entertained by Him at luncheon. But seven days after His arrival, He, as foreshadowed in the Tablet of the Holy Mariner, was put on board a Turkish steamer and three days later was disembarked, at noon, together with His fellow-exiles, at the port of Constantinople, on the first of Rabí'u'l-Avval 1280 A.H. (August 16, 1863). In two special carriages, which awaited Him at the landing-stage, He and His family drove to the house of Shamsí Big, the official who had been appointed by the government to entertain its guests, and who lived in the vicinity of the Khirqiy-i-Sharíf mosque. Later they were transferred to the more commodious house of Vísí Páshá, in the neighbourhood of the mosque of Sulṭán Muḥammad.[85]

Bahá'u'lláh in Constantinople

The arrival of Bahá'u'lláh in Constantinople, the capital city of the Ottoman Empire, marks a significant milestone in the unfoldment of His mission. It was during His sojourn in the capital that the conciliatory attitude of the authorities changed to one of hostility as a direct consequence of the intrigues and misrepresentations of Ḥájí Mírzá Ḥusayn Khán, the Mushíru'd-Dawlih, the Persian ambassador. It was also during the same eventful period that the initial phase of the proclamation of the message of Bahá'u'lláh to the kings and rulers of the world was ushered in by the revelation of a Tablet addressed to Sulṭán 'Abdu'l-'Azíz and his ministers, sternly rebuking them for their actions against the new-born Faith of God and its leader.

The house of Vísí Páshá, like most houses in those days, consisted of an inner and an outer apartment. Each consisted of three storeys. Bahá'u'lláh resided in the inner section on the first floor and His family occupied the remainder. In the outer apartment, 'Abdu'l-Bahá lived on the first floor, the believers on the ground floor and the top floor was turned into a store and a kitchen.

Shamsí Big, on behalf of the government, would call every morning and attend to any matter pertaining to the needs and well-being of Bahá'u'lláh and His companions. In the courtyard a tent was pitched for two Christian servants sent by the government to attend to shopping and various other duties.

Several eminent personalities, including state ministers, called on Bahá'u'lláh to pay their respects to Him. Among them was Kamál Páshá, a former Ṣadr-i-A'ẓam (prime minister), who was at that time one of the ministers of the Sulṭán. He knew several languages well and prided himself on this accomplishment.

Now that Bahá'u'lláh was in Constantinople, the Persian ambassador was making a desperate bid to misrepresent Him to the authorities and thereby secure their support for banishing Him further. The day after Bahá'u'lláh's arrival in Constantinople, the ambassador sent Prince Shujá'u'd-Dawlih and Ḥájí Mírzá Ḥasan-i-Ṣafá, the two most prominent men in his circle, to call on Bahá'u'lláh on his behalf. He expected that Bahá'u'lláh would return the call and see him in person but he soon found that this was not going to happen. In those days it was customary for prominent guests of the government, soon after their arrival in the capital, to call on the prime minister and other high-ranking officials. It was on the occasion of these visits that people solicited all kinds of favours, made deals and secured the support of the authorities for themselves. Bahá'u'lláh refused to do this and did not even return the visits of some of the Sulṭán's ministers who had already called on Him to pay their respects.

Kamál Páshá and a few others went so far as to remind Bahá'u'lláh of this custom. Bahá'u'lláh responded by saying that He was aware of the practice but had no demands to make of anyone nor did He require favours from them; therefore there was no reason for Him to call.

This attitude of detachment played into the hands of the Persian ambassador who introduced Bahá'u'lláh to the Sublime Porte as one who was arrogant and proud, considering Himself subject to no law. The ambassador did this mainly through the influence of Ḥájí Mírzá Ḥasan-i-Ṣafá. At last the machinations of the Persian ambassador yielded their fruit. 'Álí Páshá, the prime minister, presented a report to the Sulṭán informing him of the Persian government's request that Bahá'u'lláh be banished either to Boursa or Adrianople. He asked the Sulṭán's approval for banishment to Adrianople and suggested that an allowance of 5,000 qurúsh per month be given to Bahá'u'lláh for subsistence, adding that during His stay in Constantinople He had been a guest of the government. He also enclosed the list of all those who had accompanied Him from Baghdád to Constantinople.

Immediately upon receipt of this report the Sulṭán endorsed these measures and the edict was issued the following day. Shoghi Effendi has summarized the events leading to Bahá'u'lláh's further banishment in these words:

No less a personage than the highly-respected brother-in-law of the Ṣadr-i-A'ẓam was commissioned to apprise the Captive of the edict pronounced against Him – an edict which evinced a virtual coalition of the Turkish and Persian imperial governments against a common adversary, and which in the end brought such tragic consequences upon the Sultanate, the Caliphate and the Qájár dynasty. Refused an audience by Bahá'u'lláh that envoy had to content himself with a presentation of his puerile observations and trivial arguments to 'Abdu'l-Bahá and Áqáy-i-Kalím, who were delegated to see him, and whom he informed that, after three days, he would return to receive the answer to the order he had been bidden to transmit.

That same day a Tablet, severely condemnatory in tone, was revealed by Bahá'u'lláh, was entrusted by Him, in a sealed envelope, on the following morning, to Shamsí Big, who was instructed to deliver it into the hands of 'Alí Páshá, and to say that it was sent down from God. 'I know not what that letter contained,' Shamsí Big subsequently informed Áqáy-i-Kalím, 'for no sooner had the Grand Vizir perused it than he turned the colour of a corpse, and remarked: "It is as if the King of Kings were issuing his behest to his humblest vassal king and regulating his conduct." So grievous was his condition that I backed out of his presence.' 'Whatever action,' Bahá'u'lláh, commenting on the effect that Tablet had produced, is reported to have stated, 'the ministers of the Sulṭán took against Us, after having become acquainted with its contents, cannot be regarded as unjustifiable. The acts they committed before its perusal, however, can have no justification.'

That Tablet, according to Nabíl, was of considerable length, opened with words directed to the sovereign himself, severely censured his ministers, exposed their immaturity and incompetence, and included passages in which the ministers themselves were addressed, in which they were boldly challenged, and sternly admonished not to pride themselves on their worldly possessions, nor foolishly seek the riches of which time would inexorably rob them.

Bahá'u'lláh was on the eve of His departure, which followed almost immediately upon the promulgation of the edict of His banishment, when, in a last and memorable interview with the afore-mentioned Ḥájí Mírzá Ḥasan-i-Ṣafá, He sent the following message to the Persian Ambassador: 'What did it profit thee, and such as are like thee, to slay, year after year, so many of the oppressed, and to inflict upon them manifold afflictions, when they have increased a hundredfold, and ye find yourselves in complete bewilderment, knowing not how to relieve your minds of this oppressive thought . . . His Cause transcends any and every plan ye devise. Know this much: Were all the governments on earth to unite and take My life and the lives of all who bear this Name, this Divine Fire would never be quenched. His Cause will rather encompass all the kings of the earth, nay all that hath been created

> from water and clay . . . Whatever may yet befall Us, great shall be our gain, and manifest the loss wherewith they shall be afflicted.'[86]

In one of the coldest Decembers that Turkey had seen for years, Bahá'u'lláh and His family – including His two faithful brothers Mírzá Músá, entitled Áqáy-i-Kalím, and Mírzá Muḥammad-Qulí, together with Mírzá Yaḥyá* – set out on their journey to the city of Adrianople. The officer commissioned to take charge of the journey was 'Alí Big Yúz-Báshí. According to a statement by Mírzá Áqá Ján, it appears that Bahá'u'lláh was accompanied by 12 of His companions. Among them was the notorious Siyyid Muḥammad-i-Iṣfahání, whose evil spirit was increasingly casting its shadow upon the exiles. Through his satanic influence he brought much pain and anguish to their hearts and created severe tests and trials for them.

In the Súriy-i-Mulúk, addressing Sulṭán 'Abdu'l-'Azíz, Bahá'u'lláh speaks of His arrival in the city of Constantinople in conspicuous glory and His departure 'with an abasement with which no abasement on earth can compare'.[87] He also describes the manner in which He and His loved ones were banished to Adrianople and the sufferings they were made to endure both on their way to that city and on their arrival there. These are some of His words: 'Neither My family, nor those who accompanied Me, had the necessary raiment to protect them from the cold in that freezing weather,' and 'The eyes of Our enemies wept over Us, and beyond them those of every discerning person.'[88]

The circumstances of Bahá'u'lláh's banishment were tragic as well as humiliating. The authorities did not give Him and His party adequate time to prepare themselves for this long and hazardous journey. The weather was unusually cold, many rivers were frozen and the only way to obtain water on the journey was by lighting a fire and melting ice. The members of the party, which included women and children, were inadequately clad, yet some of them were made to ride in wagons normally used for carrying goods, while others had to ride on animals. Of this journey Shoghi Effendi writes:

> Travelling through rain and storm, at times even making night marches, the weary travellers, after brief halts at Kúchik-Chakmachih, Búyúk-Chakmachih, Salvarí, Birkás, and Bábá-Ískí, arrived at their destination, on the first of Rajab 1280 A.H. (December 12, 1863), and were lodged in the Khán-i-'Arab, a two-story caravanserai, near the house of 'Izzat-Áqá. Three days later,

* On leaving Baghdád he had acquired a passport in the name of Mírzá 'Alí, a newly assumed name. During his sojourn in Adrianople and later in Cyprus, the authorities referred to him by this name.

Bahá'u'lláh and His family were consigned to a house suitable only for summer habitation, in the Murádíyyih quarter, near Takyiy-i-Mawlaví, and were moved again, after a week, to another house, in the vicinity of a mosque in that same neighbourhood. About six months later they transferred to more commodious quarters, known as the house of Amru'lláh (House of God's command) situated on the northern side of the mosque of Sulṭán Salím.[89]

Soon after their arrival the companions of Bahá'u'lláh found their own accommodation and, as instructed by Him, engaged in trades and professions in the city.

Bahá'u'lláh in Adrianople

Adrianople's inhabitants soon became aware of Bahá'u'lláh's greatness and were deeply impressed by His genuine love and exalted character. Their leaders, including the governor of the city and other high-ranking officials, as well as men of culture and learning, were drawn to Him and soon discovered that He was the source of all knowledge and the embodiment of virtues. Some of these people earnestly sought His presence, sat at His feet and received spiritual enlightenment from Him. Such were the marks of honour and esteem shown to Bahá'u'lláh that on occasions when He walked in the streets and bazaars the people spontaneously stood and bowed before Him. Their veneration for Him was profound and whole-hearted. Among the people He was referred to as 'Shaykh Effendi', a designation that carried great prestige.

In Adrianople Bahá'u'lláh did not appear in public as much as He had in Baghdád. Instead He allowed 'Abdu'l-Bahá to do this for Him. But He did occasionally visit the mosques of Murádíyyih and Sulṭán Salím where some of the learned and devout came in contact with Him, recognized His greatness and became His admirers. This is one of the remarkable features of the life of Bahá'u'lláh – that although the powerful machinery of a despotic and tyrannical government was directed against Him, bringing about untold personal suffering and persecution, He yet evinced such glory and imparted such love that a great many people were magnetized by Him and were deeply affected by His peerless and exalted character. That a prisoner and an exile could exert such abiding influence upon both high and low is one of the evidences of His divine power and a sign of His authority as the Supreme Manifestation of God.

In spite of the hardships and rigours of yet another exile, the outpourings of the Revelation of Bahá'u'lláh continued unabated in Adrianople. In one of his writings dated 17th Jamádí 1281 A.H. (19

October 1864), Mírzá Áqá Ján has testified that from Bahá'u'lláh's time in Iraq up to that day, Tablets had been sent down successively and unceasingly from the heaven of the Will of God. This process acquired still greater momentum in Adrianople. From the tone of these Tablets it became clear that the Revelation of Bahá'u'lláh had already entered a new phase and that He, who in previous years had only alluded to His station, was now openly summoning the believers to Himself as the Supreme Manifestation of God.

The five years that Bahá'u'lláh spent in Constantinople and Adrianople may be regarded as one of the most eventful and momentous times in His ministry. In this short period the sun of His Revelation mounted to its zenith and, in the plenitude of its splendour, shed its radiance upon all mankind. This was also a most turbulent period in which He bore with much resignation and fortitude the pains, the betrayals and calamities heaped upon Him by His unfaithful brother Mírzá Yaḥyá who broke the Covenant of the Báb and rose up in rebellion against the One whom the world had wronged. Shoghi Effendi describes the outpourings of Bahá'u'lláh's Revelation in these words:

> A period of prodigious activity ensued which, in its repercussions, outshone the vernal years of Bahá'u'lláh's ministry. 'Day and night,' an eye-witness has written, 'the Divine verses were raining down in such number that it was impossible to record them. Mírzá Áqá Ján wrote them as they were dictated, while the Most Great Branch was continually occupied in transcribing them. There was not a moment to spare.' 'A number of secretaries,' Nabíl has testified, 'were busy day and night and yet they were unable to cope with the task. Among them was Mírzá Báqir-i-Shírází . . . He alone transcribed no less than two thousand verses every day. He laboured during six or seven months. Every month the equivalent of several volumes would be transcribed by him and sent to Persia. About twenty volumes, in his fine penmanship, he left behind as a remembrance for Mírzá Áqá Ján.' Bahá'u'lláh, Himself, referring to the verses revealed by Him, has written: 'Such are the outpourings . . . from the clouds of Divine Bounty that within the space of an hour the equivalent of a thousand verses hath been revealed.' 'So great is the grace vouchsafed in this day that in a single day and night, were an amanuensis capable of accomplishing it to be found, the equivalent of the Persian Bayán would be sent down from the heaven of Divine holiness.' 'I swear by God!' He, in another connection has affirmed, 'In those days the equivalent of all that hath been sent down aforetime unto the Prophets hath been revealed.' 'That which hath already been revealed in this land (Adrianople),' He, furthermore, referring to the copiousness of His writings, has declared, 'secretaries are incapable of transcribing. It has, therefore, remained for the most part untranscribed.'[90]

During Bahá'u'lláh's sojourn in Adrianople the proclamation of His message to the kings was made. He addressed the Súriy-i-Mulúk to the kings of the world collectively. He revealed the Lawḥ-i-Sulṭán for Náṣiri'd-Dín Sháh – a Tablet sent to him from 'Akká. He also addressed His first Tablet to Napoleon III. The first Súriy-i-Ra'ís addressed to 'Álí Páshá, the Grand Vizír of the Sulṭán, was revealed on the way to the port of Gallipoli. And finally, the proclamation of His message reached its consummation when in 'Akká He revealed individual Tablets to certain monarchs and ecclesiastical leaders.*

While the foundations of the Cause of God were being strengthened through the outpouring of revelation in Adrianople, a crisis of unprecedented severity – namely the rebellion of Mírzá Yaḥyá – overtook the Faith and shook it to its roots. This act of treachery created a major internal convulsion in the Faith and brought untold suffering to Bahá'u'lláh, which left its mark on His person until the end of His life.

Neither the proclamation of the Cause nor the internal disruption it was undergoing escaped the attention of Bahá'u'lláh's enemies in the capital city. The revelation of so many important Tablets and the proclamation of Bahá'u'lláh's message to the kings and rulers of the world had endowed the Faith with such ascendancy that by the summer of 1868 the authorities in Constantinople had become apprehensive of its rising prestige and power. The exaggerated reports and calumnies of Mírzá Yaḥyá, Siyyid Muḥammad and his accomplice Áqá Ján,† together with further representations by the Persian ambassador to the Sublime Porte, induced the Ottoman government to remove the author of such a dynamic Faith from the mainland and sentence Him to solitary confinement in a far-off prison.

The authorities in Constantinople were alarmed by the news that several outstanding personalities, including Khurshíd Páshá, the Governor of Adrianople, were among the fervent admirers of Bahá'u'lláh, were frequenting His house and were showing Him veneration worthy of a king. They knew that the consuls of foreign governments had also been attracted to Him and often spoke about His greatness. The movement of many pilgrims in and out of Adrianople further aggravated the situation. Fu'ád Páshá, the Turkish foreign minister, passed through Adrianople, made a tour of inspection and submitted exaggerated reports about the status and activities of the community.

* For more information about Bahá'u'lláh's proclamation to the kings and rulers see Taherzadeh, *Revelation of Bahá'u'lláh*, vols. 2, 3 and 4.

† He was known as 'Kaj Kuláh', a retired officer in the Turkish army.

Furthermore, a few among the authorities had come across some of Bahá'u'lláh's writings and had become aware of His stupendous claims. All these were important factors in deciding the fate of Bahá'u-'lláh and His companions.

Those mainly responsible for Bahá'u'lláh's final banishment were the prime minister, 'Áli Pá<u>sh</u>á, the foreign minister, Fu'ád Pá<u>sh</u>á, and the Persian ambassador, Ḥájí Mírzá Ḥusayn <u>Kh</u>án (the Mu<u>sh</u>íru'd-Dawlih). These three worked together closely until they succeeded in their efforts to banish Bahá'u'lláh to 'Akká and to impose on Him life imprisonment there. 'Álí Pá<u>sh</u>á secured from Sulṭán 'Abdu'l-'Azíz an imperial edict dated 5th Rabí'u'l-Á<u>kh</u>ir 1285 A.H. (26 July 1868) ordering Bahá'u'lláh's exile to the fortress of 'Akká and His life imprisonment within the walls of that prison city. In the same edict five others, mentioned by name, were to be exiled with Him. They were the two faithful brothers of Bahá'u'lláh, Áqáy-i-Kalím and Mírzá Muḥammad-Qulí; His faithful servant Darví<u>sh</u> Ṣidq-'Alí; the Antichrist of the Bahá'í Revelation Siyyid Muḥammad-i-Iṣfahání; and his accomplice Áqá Ján Kaj Kuláh. Mírzá Yaḥyá was condemned to life imprisonment in Famagusta along with four of Bahá'u'lláh's followers: Mírzá Ḥusayn entitled Mi<u>sh</u>kín Qalam, 'Alíy-i-Sayyáḥ, Muḥammad-Báqir-i-Qahvih-<u>ch</u>í and 'Abdu'l-<u>Gh</u>affár.

Strict orders were issued in the edict to the authorities in 'Akká directing them to accommodate the prisoners inside a house in the fortress, to guard it most effectively and to ensure that the exiles did not associate with anyone.

When <u>Kh</u>urshíd Pá<u>sh</u>á, the Governor of Adrianople, was informed of the edict and learned of Bahá'u'lláh's immediate banishment he knew that he could not bring himself to notify Bahá'u'lláh of the contents of the Sulṭán's order. He was so embarrassed that he absented himself from his office and left the task to the registrar.

Shoghi Effendi has briefly described Bahá'u'lláh's departure from Adrianople:

> On the twenty-second of the month of Rabí'u'<u>th</u>-<u>Th</u>ání 1285 A.H. (August 12, 1868) Bahá'u'lláh and His family, escorted by a Turkish captain, Ḥasan Effendi by name, and other soldiers appointed by the local government, set out on their four-day journey to Gallipoli, riding in carriages and stopping on their way at Uzún-Kúprú and Ká<u>sh</u>ánih, at which latter place the Súriy-i-Ra'ís was revealed. 'The inhabitants of the quarter in which Bahá'u'lláh had been living, and the neighbours who had gathered to bid Him farewell, came one after the other,' writes an eye-witness, 'with the utmost sadness and regret to kiss His hands and the hem of His robe, expressing meanwhile their sorrow at His departure. That day, too, was a strange day. Methinks the city, its

walls and its gates bemoaned their imminent separation from Him.' 'On that day,' writes another eye-witness, 'there was a wonderful concourse of Muslims and Christians at the door of our Master's house. The hour of departure was a memorable one. Most of those present were weeping and wailing, especially the Christians.' 'Say,' Bahá'u'lláh Himself declares in the Súriy-i-Ra'ís, 'this Youth hath departed out of this country and deposited beneath every tree and every stone a trust, which God will erelong bring forth through the power of truth.'

Several of the companions who had been brought from Constantinople were awaiting them in Gallipoli. On his arrival Bahá'u'lláh made the following pronouncement to Ḥasan Effendi, who, his duty discharged, was taking his leave: 'Tell the king that this territory will pass out of his hands, and his affairs will be thrown into confusion.' 'To this,' Áqá Riḍá, the recorder of that scene has written, 'Bahá'u'lláh furthermore added: "Not I speak these words, but God speaketh them." In those moments He was uttering verses which we, who were downstairs, could overhear. They were spoken with such vehemence and power that, methinks, the foundations of the house itself trembled.'

Even in Gallipoli, where three nights were spent, no one knew what Bahá'u'lláh's destination would be. Some believed that He and His brothers would be banished to one place, and the remainder dispersed, and sent into exile. Others thought that His companions would be sent back to Persia, while still others expected their immediate extermination. The government's original order was to banish Bahá'u'lláh, Áqáy-i-Kalím and Mírzá Muḥammad-Qulí, with a servant to 'Akká, while the rest were to proceed to Constantinople. This order, which provoked scenes of indescribable distress, was, however, at the insistence of Bahá'u'lláh, and by the instrumentality of 'Umar Effendi, a major appointed to accompany the exiles, revoked. It was eventually decided that all the exiles, numbering about seventy, should be banished to 'Akká. Instructions were, moreover, issued that a certain number of the adherents of Mírzá Yaḥyá, among whom were Siyyid Muḥammad and Áqá Ján, should accompany these exiles, whilst four of the companions of Bahá'u'lláh were ordered to depart with the Azalís for Cyprus.

So grievous were the dangers and trials confronting Bahá'u'lláh at the hour of His departure from Gallipoli that He warned His companions that 'this journey will be unlike any of the previous journeys,' and that whoever did not feel himself 'man enough to face the future' had best 'depart to whatever place he pleaseth, and be preserved from tests, for hereafter he will find himself unable to leave' – a warning which His companions unanimously chose to disregard.

On the morning of the 2nd of Jamádíyu'l-Avval 1285 A.H. (August 21, 1868) they all embarked in an Austrian-Lloyd steamer for Alexandria, touching at Madellí, and stopping for two days at

Smyrna, where Jináb-i-Munír, surnamed Ismu'lláhu'l-Muníb, became gravely ill, and had, to his great distress, to be left behind in a hospital where he soon after died. In Alexandria they transhipped into a steamer of the same company, bound for Haifa, where, after brief stops at Port Said and Jaffa, they landed, setting out, a few hours later, in a sailing vessel, for 'Akká, where they disembarked, in the course of the afternoon of the 12th of Jamádíyu'l-Avval 1285 A.H. (August 31, 1868). It was at the moment when Bahá'u'lláh had stepped into the boat which was to carry Him to the landing-stage in Haifa that 'Abdu'l-Ghaffár, one of the four companions condemned to share the exile of Mírzá Yaḥyá, and whose 'detachment, love and trust in God' Bahá'u'lláh had greatly praised, cast himself, in his despair, into the sea, shouting 'Yá Bahá'u'l-Abhá', and was subsequently rescued and resuscitated with the greatest difficulty, only to be forced by adamant officials to continue his voyage, with Mírzá Yaḥyá's party, to the destination originally appointed for him.[91]

Bahá'u'lláh in 'Akká

Bahá'u'lláh's journey from Adrianople to 'Akká was laden with enormous hardship and suffering. It once again highlighted the abasement to which Bahá'u'lláh and His companions were subjected and the indignities heaped upon Him by the actions of His enemies. When He arrived in the prison of 'Akká, these sufferings were intensified to such an extent that He designated that city as the 'Most Great Prison'. Referring to the first nine years of His exile in 'Akká, the Pen of the Most High has recorded these moving words in one of His Tablets:

> Know thou that upon Our arrival at this Spot, We chose to designate it as the 'Most Great Prison'. Though previously subjected in another land (Ṭihrán) to chains and fetters, We yet refused to call it by that name. Say: Ponder thereon, O ye endued with understanding![92]

At Haifa, Bahá'u'lláh and His companions – 70 in all – disembarked from the ship in sailing boats.* All their belongings were also ferried across with them. There, the prisoners were all counted and handed over to government officials. A few hours later they were all taken aboard a sailing vessel which took them to 'Akká in the afternoon of

* According to the shipping records, the Austrian Lloyd steamer was due to leave Alexandria at 11 a.m. on Friday, arriving at Port Said on Saturday at 5 p.m., at Jaffa on Sunday at 6 p.m., at Haifa on Monday at 8 a.m. and in Cyprus at noon two days later.

the same day. As there were no landing facilities at 'Akká, the men had to wade ashore from the boat and the women were to be carried on the backs of men. But at 'Abdu'l-Bahá's insistence the women were carried ashore one by one, seated on a chair which He Himself procured.

When Bahá'u'lláh arrived in 'Akká, the city was a penal colony. Its population in the 1880s was estimated to be about nine thousand. The Turkish government had consigned to it from its vast empire a great number of criminals, murderers, political detainees and every type of troublemaker. The inhabitants, whom Bahá'u'lláh had stigmatized as the 'generation of vipers',[93] had sunk to a very low level. Just prior to the arrival of Bahá'u'lláh and His followers wild rumours and false accusations circulated. The company of exiles, those God-intoxicated heroes who had accompanied their Lord to this most desolate of cities, were considered to be evil men, criminals of the worst type who deserved to be treated most cruelly. Great numbers from among the inhabitants of 'Akká assembled at the landing site to jeer at them and at their leader, to whom they referred as 'the God of the Persians'.

Yet among the crowd there were some endowed with a measure of spiritual perception. These, as they gazed upon the countenance of Bahá'u'lláh, were struck by His majesty and witnessed a glory they had never seen before. Among them was a certain Khalíl Aḥmad 'Abdú, a venerable old man who used to say to the inhabitants of 'Akká that he could see in the face of Bahá'u'lláh signs of greatness and of majesty and truthfulness. He often said that the people of 'Akká should rejoice and be thankful to God for having ennobled their homeland by the footsteps of this great personage. He prophesied that through Him the inhabitants would be blessed and prosper, and this, of course, literally came to pass.

How incomparable is the difference between the vision of those assembled at the sea gate of 'Akká to jeer at the company of exiles and their leader, and the vision of Bahá'u'lláh. A few years before, in the Tablet of Sayyáḥ foreshadowing His arrival in the city of 'Akká, He had disclosed to those endowed with spiritual insight a vastly different spectacle:

> Upon Our arrival We were welcomed with banners of light, whereupon the Voice of the Spirit cried out saying: 'Soon will all that dwell on earth be enlisted under these banners.'[94]

The reaction of these onlookers, blind to the world of the spirit and the all-encompassing vision of Bahá'u'lláh, is characteristic of man's attitude to the Revelation of God in every age. Over one hundred years have passed since Bahá'u'lláh uttered these words. The majority of mankind, its rulers and wise men, have so far failed to recognize their truth, either remaining unaware of the coming of the Lord or turning a deaf ear to His voice. But those who have embraced His Cause believe in the vision of their Lord that 'soon will all that dwell on earth be enlisted under these banners'.

Bahá'u'lláh and His party entered 'Akká through the sea gate and were conducted to the barracks along the city's narrow and twisting streets. The hardships of the long and arduous journey from Adrianople to 'Akká in the burning heat of the midsummer season, with inadequate and primitive facilities on board the crowded ships, had exhausted everyone. Now, added to all this were the appalling conditions of their confinement in the barracks, especially during the first night after their arrival. Bahá'u'lláh was placed in a filthy room that was completely bare. Later He was moved into a room on the upper floor of the barracks; this room, the interior of which is now kept in good condition and visited by Bahá'í pilgrims, was in the days of Bahá'u'lláh unfit for habitation. He Himself has recounted in a Tablet that its floor was covered with earth and what plaster remained on the ceiling was falling.

Bahá'u'lláh's followers were huddled into another room, the floor of which was covered with mud. Ten soldiers were posted at the gate to guard the prisoners. The foul air and the stench in the prison, coupled with the sultry heat of the summer, were so offensive that on arrival Bahíyyih Khánum, the daughter of Bahá'u'lláh entitled the 'Greatest Holy Leaf', was overcome and fainted.

There was no drinking water except that in a small pool which had already been used for washing and was so filthy that the mere thought of drinking it would make one sick. That first night, in those hot surroundings when everyone was so thirsty that some of the women and children were overcome, water was withheld from the prisoners. Mothers with suckling babes were unable to feed them and for hours the children cried for food and water. 'Abdu'l-Bahá made several appeals to the guards to show mercy to the children and even sent a message to the governor of 'Akká but to no avail. At last in the morning some water was given to the prisoners and each received three loaves of bread as a daily ration. The bread was unfit to eat but after some time they were allowed to take it to the market and exchange it for two loaves of a better quality.

Soon after the arrival of the prisoners the governor visited the barracks for inspection. 'Abdu'l-Bahá, accompanied by a few believers, went to see him. But the governor was discourteous and spoke to them in a provocative manner. He threatened to cut the supply of bread if one of the prisoners went missing and then ordered them back to their room. Ḥusayn-i-Áshchí, one of 'Abdu'l-Bahá's attendants, could not bear to remain silent after such insulting treatment. He retorted with rage and hurled back at the governor some offensive remarks.

'Abdu'l-Bahá immediately chastised Ḥusayn by slapping him hard in the face in front of the governor and ordering him to return to his room. This action by 'Abdu'l-Bahá not only defused a dangerous situation but also opened the eyes of the governor to the existence of a real leader among the prisoners, who would act with authority and justice.

Ḥusayn-i-Á<u>sh</u>chí, who has recorded this incident in his memoirs, and who prided himself on being chastised by the Master on that occasion, recalls that because of this action the governor's attitude towards 'Abdu'l-Bahá changed. He realized that, contrary to the wild rumours circulating in 'Akká at the time, 'Abdu'l-Bahá and His family were from a noble background and not criminals as he had been led to believe. The governor therefore began to act in a more humane way towards the prisoners. He eventually agreed to substitute a sum of money for the allotted ration of bread and allowed a small party of the prisoners, escorted by guards, to visit the markets of 'Akká daily to buy their provisions.

Three days after the arrival of Bahá'u'lláh and His companions, the edict of the Sulṭán condemning Him to life imprisonment was read out in the mosque. The prisoners were introduced as criminals who had corrupted the morals of the people. It was stated that they were to be confined to prison and were not allowed to associate with anyone.

In the course of a talk[95] to the friends in Haifa years later, 'Abdu'l-Bahá described His being summoned by the governor of 'Akká to hear the contents of the edict. When it was read out to Him that they were to remain in prison forever,* 'Abdu'l-Bahá responded by saying that the contents of the edict were meaningless and without foundation. Upon hearing this remark, the governor became angry and retorted that the edict was from the Sulṭán and he wanted to know how it could be described as meaningless. 'Abdu'l-Bahá replied that it was impossible for His imprisonment to last forever, for man lives in this world only for a short period and sooner or later the captives would leave this prison, whether dead or alive. The governor and his officers were impressed by the vision of 'Abdu'l-Bahá and felt easier in His presence.

In the meantime, life in the prison of 'Akká in the early days was extremely difficult. The conditions were appallingly unhygienic. The heat was severe during the day and there was no adequate water for

---

* In Arabic the term used for life imprisonment is often 'prisoner forever'.

washing. For three months the authorities did not allow Bahá'u'lláh to go to the public bath, which in those days was the only place where people could take a bath. The guards had been given strict orders not to allow any person to visit Him. Even when a barber came to attend to Bahá'u'lláh's hair, he was accompanied by a guard and was not allowed to talk to Him. 'Abdu'l-Bahá had to live in a room on the ground floor which had been formerly used as a morgue. Its moist air affected His health for the rest of His life. As for the other prisoners, the filthy conditions under which they were living, the lack of proper food and hygiene and the severity of restrictions took their toll. Shortly after their arrival in the barracks all but two fell sick and nine of the ten guards were also struck down by illness. Malaria and dysentery added to their ordeal. The only two unaffected at that stage were 'Abdu'l-Bahá and Áqá Riḍáy-i-Qannád, although both of them were taken ill later. The Master, helped by this believer, attended to the needs of the sick, nursing them day and night. The authorities did not call for a doctor to administer medicine and with the few provisions at His disposal all that 'Abdu'l-Bahá could do was to cook them a simple broth and some rice each day.

In these circumstances three people died. The first victim was a certain Abu'l-Qásim-i-Sulṭán Ábádí. Then two brothers, Ustád Muḥammad-Báqir and Ustád Muḥammad-Ismá'íl, both tailors by profession, died one evening within a few hours of each other, locked in each other's arms as they lay on the floor. Bahá'u'lláh particularly expressed His grief at these tragic deaths and stated that never before had two brothers passed away from this dark world and entered the realms of glory in such unity. As stated in a Tablet, He praised them, showered His bounties upon them and blessed their parents.

The burial of these three posed a difficult problem for the company of exiles. The government refused to allow anyone from among the prisoners to bury them, nor did they provide funds for their burial. The guards demanded payment of necessary expenses before removing the bodies, and as there were very few possessions which could be sold, Bahá'u'lláh gave up the only luxury He had, a small prayer carpet. When the proceeds of the sale were handed to the guards, they pocketed the money and buried the dead in the clothes they wore, without coffins and without the customary Muslim rites of washing and wrapping the bodies in shrouds. As they were not allowed to be buried inside the Muslim cemetery, they were laid to rest outside it. Some years later 'Abdu'l-Bahá arranged for one of the believers to build their graves, which are joined together.

After the death of these three men, Bahá'u'lláh revealed a short healing prayer especially for the believers in the barracks and asked them to chant it repeatedly and with absolute sincerity. This the friends did and soon everyone recovered.

In the meantime, the Persian ambassador to the Sublime Porte did everything in his power to enforce Bahá'u'lláh's imprisonment in 'Akká. The following is a translation of a letter he wrote to his government a little over a year after Bahá'u'lláh's arrival in 'Akká.

> I have issued telegraphic and written instructions, forbidding that He (Bahá'u'lláh) associate with any one except His wives and children, or leave under any circumstances, the house wherein He is imprisoned. 'Abbás-Qulí Khán, the Consul-General in Damascus . . . I have, three days ago, sent back, instructing him to proceed direct to 'Akká . . . confer with its governor regarding all necessary measures for the strict maintenance of their imprisonment . . . and appoint, before his return to Damascus, a representative on the spot to insure that the orders issued by the Sublime Porte will, in no wise, be disobeyed. I have, likewise, instructed him that once every three months he should proceed from Damascus to 'Akká, and personally watch over them, and submit his report to the Legation.[96]

Long before His departure from Adrianople, Bahá'u'lláh had prophesied the impending calamities which were to befall Him in His forthcoming exile to 'Akká. In some of His Tablets revealed in Adrianople He had alluded to that city, in others He had mentioned 'Akká by name as being the next place of His exile. For instance, in the Lawḥ-i-Sulṭán, the Tablet to Náṣiri'd-Dín Sháh of Persia, He had clearly prophesied that the next place of His exile would be 'Akká. Concerning that city He wrote: 'According to what they say, it is the most desolate of the cities of the world, the most unsightly of them in appearance, the most detestable in climate, and the foulest in water.'[97]

In another Tablet, as yet unpublished, revealed soon before His departure from Adrianople, He predicted a new wave of calamities that would soon encompass Him in the fortress of 'Akká. He described the conditions of the city in terms similar to those in the Lawḥ-i-Sulṭán but declared that soon its climate would improve because its builder would enter it and adorn it with the ornament of His Greatest Name.

The foulness of 'Akká's air was summed up in the proverb that a bird flying over the city would drop dead. But the climate changed soon after Bahá'u'lláh's arrival. To this the inhabitants of 'Akká testified and many attributed it to the presence of Bahá'u'lláh. The edict of the Sulṭán condemning Bahá'u'lláh to solitary life imprisonment and forbidding Him to meet anyone, including His companions, was at the beginning carried out strictly. But soon the prison authorities became aware of the striking majesty of Bahá'u'lláh, the loftiness of His standards and the exalted character of His person. They were also deeply impressed by the loving disposition of the Master, His divine qualities and virtues; they increasingly turned to Him for advice and guidance. As a result, the authorities became lenient and relaxed some of the restrictions.

As time went on the companions of Bahá'u'lláh were allotted rooms in different parts of the barracks. Some of them took on essential duties such as cooking, cleaning, water delivery or shopping, and some were able to spend their free time in other useful work. As restrictions became more relaxed the companions were able to communicate with Bahá'u'lláh and even attain His presence.

Although the barracks was a depressing place to live, soon the companions of Bahá'u'lláh, mainly through 'Abdu'l-Bahá's leadership and guidance, organized their daily lives in such a way as to create the best possible conditions for the whole community. Their greatest source of joy was nearness to their Lord and sometimes Bahá'u'lláh visited them in their quarters where they entertained Him with what meagre food or refreshments they could provide.

The sufferings of Bahá'u'lláh in 'Akká were so intense in their severity and so extensive in their range that it would require volumes to recount them. Not confined only to what He endured in the barracks, culminating in the martyrdom of the Purest Branch, these distressing afflictions continued throughout His entire ministry in the Holy Land. These are Bahá'u'lláh's own words:

> Ponder a while on the woes and afflictions which this Prisoner hath sustained. I have, all the days of My life, been at the mercy of Mine enemies, and have suffered each day, in the path of the love of God, a fresh tribulation. I have patiently endured until the fame of the Cause of God was spread abroad on the earth.[98]

And again:

> O My servant that believest in God! By the righteousness of the Almighty! Were I to recount to thee the tale of the things that have befallen Me, the souls and minds of men would be incapable of sustaining its weight. God Himself beareth Me witness.[99]

Bahá'u'lláh's trials and tribulations were not only those inflicted on Him by His enemies. He suffered greatly from the reprehensible conduct of those who were reckoned among His own followers. In His Tablets, Bahá'u'lláh testifies to this truth.

9
Mírzá Yaḥyá

4–WT And still another of His trials was the hostility, the flagrant injustice, the iniquity and rebellion of Mírzá Yaḥyá. Although that Wronged One, that Prisoner, had through His loving-kindness nurtured him in His own bosom ever since his early years, had showered at every moment His tender care upon him, exalted his name, shielded him from every misfortune, endeared him to them of this world and the next, and despite the firm exhortations and counsels of His Holiness, the Exalted One (the Báb) and His clear and conclusive warning; – 'Beware, beware, lest the Nineteen Letters of the Living and that which hath been revealed in the Bayán veil thee!'

Mírzá Yaḥyá, Ṣubḥ-i-Azal, was a paternal half-brother of Bahá'u'lláh. He was about 14 years younger and when their father died he was only a boy of eight. He thus grew up under the care and protection of Bahá'u'lláh, Who paid special attention to his education and upbringing. When the Báb declared His mission in 1844, Mírzá Yaḥyá was 13 years old. When the message of the Báb reached Bahá'u'lláh, He helped Mírzá Yaḥyá to recognize the station of the Báb and to embrace the newly born Faith and encouraged him to read the writings of the Báb and become familiar with their style of composition.

A few months before the Báb was martyred in 1850, Sayyáḥ, one of His distinguished disciples, attained the presence of Bahá'u'lláh in Ṭihrán. On this occasion Bahá'u'lláh sent a communication to the Báb through Sayyáḥ, about which Nabíl-i-A'ẓam writes:

> Ere the departure of Sayyáḥ from Ṭihrán, Bahá'u'lláh entrusted him with an epistle, the text of which He had dictated to Mírzá Yaḥyá, and sent it in his name. Shortly after, a reply, penned in the Báb's own handwriting, in which He commits Mírzá Yaḥyá to the care of Bahá'u'lláh and urges that attention be paid to his education and training, was received.[100]

Thus Mírzá Yaḥyá grew up under the guidance of Bahá'u'lláh and became conversant with the writings of the Báb.

In those days the believers who were educated used to make handwritten copies of the holy word. In order to deepen his half-brother's understanding of the writings of the Báb, Bahá'u'lláh especially assigned Mírzá Yaḥyá the task of transcribing them. Consequently Mírzá Yaḥyá learned not only the style of the composition of the Báb's writings but was also able to write in the same fashion and imitate the Báb's handwriting – an art which served him well some years later when he rebelled against Bahá'u'lláh and, by forging the Báb's handwriting, interpolated his own words into the Báb's writings to produce texts in his own favour.

The appointment by the Báb of Mírzá Yaḥyá as the leader of the Bábí community took place on the advice of Bahá'u'lláh. 'Abdu'l-Bahá states that some time after the death of Muḥammad Sháh it became evident that Bahá'u'lláh's fame had spread far and wide in Persia and it was essential to divert public attention away from His person. To achieve this aim Bahá'u'lláh advised the Báb to appoint Mírzá Yaḥyá as His nominee. This advice was communicated through the medium of a trusted believer, Mullá 'Abdu'l-Karím of Qazvín, otherwise known as Mírzá Aḥmad, who was able to make contact with the Báb. The appointment of Mírzá Yaḥyá, who was then in his late teens, had the obvious advantage of enabling Bahá'u'lláh to direct the affairs of the community behind the scenes through the instrumentality of Mírzá Yaḥyá, who, in reality, was merely the ostensible head until the advent of 'Him Whom God shall make manifest'.

The Bábí community was not informed of the reasons behind this appointment. It must have come as a surprise to many when they realized that the appointee of the Báb was a youth in his teens and those who knew his personality were aware of his shallowness and vanity. Apart from Mullá 'Abdu'l-Karím, the only other person who was privy to this secret arrangement was Bahá'u'lláh's faithful brother Mírzá Músá, entitled Áqáy-i-Kalím. It must be stated here that the Báb in all His writings urged the believers to be ready for the manifestation of 'Him Whom God shall make manifest' and no one else. So imminent was His advent that the Báb never contemplated the appointment of a successor to Himself. Indeed, He confirms this in the Bayán saying that in His Dispensation there was to be no mention of successorship. Yet Mírzá Yaḥyá, as we shall see later, broke the Covenant of the Báb and claimed to be His successor.

Mírzá Yaḥyá was devoid of outstanding qualities. He was easily influenced by people, ambitious and, above all, very timid by nature. At the age of 19 he married his cousin and for some time they lived in the village of Tákur in the province of Núr. The Bábí community of Tákur was one of the most thriving communities in Persia at the time because as soon as the news of the declaration of the Báb had reached Bahá'u'lláh, He had arisen to teach the Faith to the members of His family and others in Núr. Many relatives and friends in that area had embraced the Faith and through the influence of Bahá'u'lláh had become staunch believers.

When the news of the martyrdom of the Báb reached Mírzá Yaḥyá, he was so frightened for his own life that he disguised himself in the garb of a dervish and, leaving his wife and child behind, fled into the mountains of Mázindarán. Two years later, when Bahá'u'lláh was exiled from Persia to Iraq, Mírzá Yaḥyá could no longer avail himself of His protection and guidance. Thus he roamed the countryside in fear and trepidation. This behaviour, especially at a time when Bahá'u'lláh was absent from Persia, had a deadly effect upon the believers in the province of Núr. Through Mírzá Yaḥyá's cowardly behaviour and lack of faith in the religion of the Báb, many believers were disappointed in him as a leader, became disenchanted and left the Faith altogether.

This tragic situation brought great sorrow to Bahá'u'lláh. Some years later in 'Akká, He uttered these words on the subject, as recounted by Nabíl:

> God knows that at no time did We attempt to conceal Ourself or hide the Cause which We have been bidden to proclaim. Though not wearing the garb of the people of learning, We have again and again faced and reasoned with men of great scholarship in both Núr and Mázindarán, and have succeeded in persuading them of the truth of this Revelation. We never flinched in Our determination; We never hesitated to accept the challenge from whatever direction it came. To whomsoever We spoke in those days, We found him receptive to our Call and ready to identify himself with its precepts. But for the shameful behaviour of the people of Bayán, who sullied by their deeds the work We had accomplished, Núr and Mázindarán would have been entirely won to this Cause and would have been accounted by this time among its leading strongholds.[101]

When the attempt was made on the life of Náṣiri'd-Dín Shāh by a few mentally disturbed Bábís in 1852, the Bábí community was engulfed by a wave of persecution. Many of the followers of the Báb were martyred in the most cruel circumstances and Bahá'u'lláh, along with others, was imprisoned in the Síyáh-Chál. The Sháh ordered his prime minister, Mírzá Áqá Khán,* a native of Núr himself, to send troops to Núr and arrest all the followers of the Báb in that area. The

* He was related to Bahá'u'lláh through the marriage of his niece to Mírzá Muḥammad-Ḥasan, an elder half-brother of Bahá'u'lláh.

troops carried out their orders; some believers were killed and some were taken to the Síyáh-Chál, their houses demolished and their properties confiscated. The house of Bahá'u'lláh, which was royally furnished, was turned into ruins. Its roof was destroyed and all its exquisite furnishings confiscated. So terrified was Mírzá Yaḥyá as a result of these persecutions that once again he fled, this time to Gílán in disguise and then to Kirmánsháh in the west of Persia. There he decided to engage himself in a profession so that no one could identify him. He took work as a salesman with a certain 'Abdu'lláh-i-Qazvíní, a maker of shrouds.

Some months later Bahá'u'lláh and His family passed through Kirmánsháh on their way to Baghdád. In Kirmánsháh several people of rank and position came to visit Bahá'u'lláh to pay their respects but Mírzá Yaḥyá was afraid to contact Him. Such was his state of mind that when Áqáy-i-Kalím, Bahá'u'lláh's faithful brother, called on him, Mírzá Yaḥyá was apprehensive lest someone should recognize his true identity. After some persuasion by Áqáy-i-Kalím, he went and visited Bahá'u'lláh, knowing that Bahá'u'lláh would extend to him His protection and guidance. Feeling secure in His presence, he expressed the desire to go to Baghdád and live alone, incognito, in a house close to Bahá'u'lláh's, and engage in a trade there. Bahá'u'lláh gave him a small sum of money and he bought a few bales of cotton, disguised himself as an Arab and, soon after Bahá'u'lláh's arrival in Baghdád, found his way to that city.

Being a master in the art of disguise, he arrived at Bahá'u'lláh's doorstep in Baghdád dressed as a dervish, kashkúl (alms box) in hand. So well was he disguised that Áqáy-i-Kalím, who answered the door, did not recognize him at first. He stayed for a few days in the house of Bahá'u'lláh but asked that neither his identity nor his arrival in the city be divulged to the believers in Iraq. He was helped to secure a residence in the Arab quarter of the city where no Persians resided. There he spent his time in hiding during the day, emerging only at night when he would go to the house of Bahá'u'lláh, meet with Áqáy-i-Kalím and then return home in the late hours. He even had threatened that if anyone insisted on visiting him and revealing his identity, he would excommunicate him from the Bábí community.

The majesty of Bahá'u'lláh was apparent to the members of His family. In the light of this the two faithful brothers, Áqáy-i-Kalím and Mírzá Muḥammad-Qulí, who accompanied Bahá'u'lláh on His exile, showed the utmost humility to Him. Even Mírzá Yaḥyá showed great respect to Bahá'u'lláh until he fell under the spell of Siyyid Muḥammad-i-Iṣfahání, who duped him. Some individuals who were close to Mírzá Yaḥyá have testified that he felt so inadequate to meet with Bahá'u'lláh that whenever he entered into His presence and came face to face with His majestic person, he was unable to put forward his thoughts and became utterly speechless. Mírzá Áqá Ján, Bahá'u'lláh's amanuensis, was at first surprised to find Mírzá Yaḥyá so helpless and mute in the presence of Bahá'u'lláh until later he realized that Mírzá Yaḥyá was like anyone else.

Since the martyrdom of the Báb, it was Bahá'u'lláh who had guided the Bábí community. During the days before Mírzá Yaḥyá's rebellion, at times when he was in a place accessible to Him, Bahá'u'lláh used to call him into His presence and dictate to him His utterances. His message would then be communicated to the Bábí community in Mírzá Yaḥyá's name. Many years after Mírzá Yaḥyá's rebellion, Bahá'u-'lláh, in the following passage in the Kitáb-i-Aqdas, reminds him of earlier days when he used to attain His presence and take down His words:

> Granted that the people were confused about thy station, is it conceivable that thou thyself art similarly confused? Tremble before thy Lord and recall the days when thou didst stand before Our throne, and didst write down the verses that We dictated unto thee – verses sent down by God, the Omnipotent Protector, the Lord of might and power.[102]

The main reason that the Báb, at the suggestion of Bahá'u'lláh, appointed Mírzá Yaḥyá the leader of the Bábí community was to protect Bahá'u'lláh from the assaults of an implacable enemy. Thus the Báb diverted public attention from Bahá'u'lláh and at the same time provided a means for Him to unobtrusively direct the affairs of the Bábí community until such time as His station was revealed. The fact that various communications to the Bábís were issued in the name of Mírzá Yaḥyá caused certain uninformed Bábís to think that he was the author.

Around the time that the followers of Mírzá Yaḥyá were cast out of the community of the Most Great Name, Bahá'u'lláh revealed a beautiful Tablet in Adrianople, known as the Tablet of Zá<u>gh</u> va Bulbul (the Raven and the Nightingale).* Its imagery depicts a delightful drama in which several figures conduct two-way dialogues. Among them are the rose and the nightingale, both symbolic of Bahá'u'lláh. There are also birds disguised as nightingales, symbolizing the unfaithful. The raven represents Mírzá Yaḥyá and the owl one of his

---

* For further information about this Tablet see Taherzadeh, *Revelation of Bahá'u-'lláh*, vol. 2, pp. 241–3. In Persian literature the raven's coarse croak is symbolic of evil while the owl is a symbol of doom and ruin.

followers. Here is a summary of part of the Tablet, paraphrased by the author:

> The owl argues that the song of the crow is much more melodious than that of the nightingale. Challenging this statement, the nightingale demands some evidence and invites the owl to investigate the truth by listening to the melody of each bird, so that the sweet music of the Bird of Heaven can be distinguished from the croaking of the raven. But the owl refuses and says, 'Once from inside a rose-garden the enchanting voice of a bird reached my ears and when I enquired its origin, I was informed that the voice was that of the raven. Simultaneously, a raven flew out of the garden and it became clear to me who the singer was.'
>
> 'But that was my voice,' said the nightingale to the owl, 'and to prove it I can warble similar if not more beautiful melodies now.'
>
> 'I am not interested in hearing thy songs,' the owl replied, 'for I saw the raven and have been assured by others that the melody from inside the garden was his. If the tune of this heavenly music was thine, how is it that thou wert hidden from the eyes of men and thy fame did not reach them?'
>
> 'Because of my beauty,' replied the nightingale, 'I have been despised by my enemies. They were resolved to put an end to my life and for this reason my melodies were noised abroad in the name of the raven. But those with unsullied hearts and sanctified ears have been able to distinguish the voice of the true nightingale from the croaking of the raven.'

It must be remembered that ever since the days of Bahá'u'lláh in Baghdád the great majority of the believers in Persia had turned to Him as the focal point of the Bábí community. To Him they went for help and enlightenment and from Him received their guidance. His spiritual ascendancy and influence were so strikingly manifest that even the enemies of the Cause felt their force. To a great many believers Mírzá Yaḥyá was only a name. There were some, however, who, either because of their ignorance of the facts, or through their devotion to the Báb who had appointed him as His nominee, were eager to meet Mírzá Yaḥyá.

One such person was Siyyid 'Abdu'r-Raḥím-i-Iṣfahání, a well-known believer who had collected certain extracts from the Bayán and other books of the Báb which he used to prove that Bahá'u'lláh was the Promised One of the Bayán and that Azal was only a name without a reality, like a body without a soul. As a result of such pronouncements Áqá Siyyid 'Abdu'r-Raḥím was denounced by some. He used to give the following account:

> After the martyrdom of the Báb when Azal had become famous, I travelled from Iṣfahán to Ṭihrán with the express purpose of meeting him. In the bazaar I met Bahá'u'lláh, the Day-Star of Revelation, the Speaker of Sinai . . . the mention of whose name has adorned the Books and Tablets of the Báb. I attained His presence at a time when His glory was hidden behind a myriad veils of light. He asked me if I had come to meet Azal. I answered in the affirmative. I had actually attained the presence of Bahá'u'lláh before this at Badasht. I had recognized His glory and greatness, His uniqueness and magnanimity by the manner in which Quddús and Ṭáhirih used to bow before Him. I also knew the deeds and actions of Azal; nevertheless since he was known as the nominee of the Báb I considered meeting with him as a means of nearness to God. I went, in the company of Bahá'u'lláh, to His house. He asked for tea to be served. Thereupon Azal brought the samovar and served the tea. He was standing in the presence of Bahá'u'lláh, from Whose tongue were flowing the rivers of wisdom and knowledge. After drinking tea, Bahá'u'lláh rose, and turning to Azal said, 'He has come to see you' and then went into the inner court of the house. Azal sat down, I bowed and expressed my devotion to him, but he had nothing to say to me.[103]

Another person of wide repute who was eager to meet Mírzá Yaḥyá was Shaykh Salmán,* honoured by Bahá'u'lláh as the 'Messenger of the Merciful' and one of the outstanding believers who for almost 40 years carried Tablets and messages from Bahá'u'lláh and 'Abdu'l-Bahá to the believers. This encounter occurred in the early days of Bahá'u'lláh's sojourn in Baghdád. After much pleading by Shaykh Salmán, Mírzá Yaḥyá agreed to meet him outside the city on a hill-top. When the interview took place, Mírzá Yaḥyá had nothing to say except trivialities. He was interested in the telegraph poles (a novelty in those days) and wanted Shaykh Salmán to guess the distance between two poles! The few others who succeeded in meeting Mírzá Yaḥyá in Baghdád also quickly recognized his ignorance and shallow-mindedness.

In His Will and Testament 'Abdu'l-Bahá quotes the exhortations of the Báb:

> **4–WT Beware, beware, lest the Nineteen Letters of the Living and that which hath been revealed in the Bayán veil thee!**

As we survey the ministry of the Báb, which lasted a little over six years, we note that the most significant part of His writings was devoted to establishing a mighty Covenant with His followers concern-

* See Taherzadeh, *Revelation of Bahá'u'lláh*, vol. 1.

ing the Revelation of 'Him Whom God shall make manifest' – Bahá'u-'lláh. Indeed, no Manifestation of God before Him ever devoted so much of His Revelation to the subject of the Covenant. When we carefully study the Bayán, the Mother Book of the Bábí Dispensation, we note that on practically every page of that book there is a mention of 'Him Whom God shall make manifest', stating some aspect of His Revelation but always extolling His station and mentioning His name with a reverence that staggers the imagination. The Báb mentioned 'Him Whom God shall make manifest' in the Persian Bayán more than three hundred times and in the Arabic Bayán more than 70. There are also references to Him without mentioning this designation. In several instances the Báb identifies 'Him Whom God shall make manifest' with the designation Bahá'u'lláh.

The announcement of the Revelation of 'Him Whom God shall make manifest' is not limited to the Bayán. In the great majority of His writings the Báb directed the attention of the Bábís to that great Revelation which was to follow Him, established a firm Covenant with them and directed all the forces of His Revelation towards the spiritual enrichment of the Bábí community in order to rear a new race of men worthy to attain the presence of 'Him Whom God shall make manifest', recognize His station and embrace His Cause.

The laws He promulgated, some very severe, were designed to shake up the lethargic people of Persia and to inflame His own followers with the zeal and fervour of a new and dynamic Faith. In past Dispensations, the energies latent within God's Revelation have taken about a thousand years to be fully released and diffused gradually throughout human society. In the Dispensation of the Báb, however, the energies of a mighty Revelation had to be released within a very short period of time. Therefore, everything associated with His Faith – His laws, His teachings, His own public appearances, His ministry, His personal life and His martyrdom – were all characterized by a dynamism and forcefulness unparalleled in the annals of past religions and which exerted a most potent and electrifying influence upon friend and foe alike.

The laws of the Bayán were promulgated for the sake of 'Him Whom God shall make manifest'. The aim of the Báb in revealing the laws of His Dispensation was to edify the souls of His followers and mould their conduct so they would be worthy to embrace the Cause of Bahá'u'lláh. In the Kitáb-i-Asmá', one of His celebrated writings, He reveals these thought-provoking words:

> But for the sole reason of His being present amongst this people, We would have neither prescribed any law nor laid down any prohibition. It is only for the glorification of His Name and the

> exaltation of His Cause that We have enunciated certain laws at Our behest, or forbidden the acts to which We are averse, so that at the hour of His manifestation ye may attain through Him the good-pleasure of God and abstain from the things that are abhorrent unto Him.[104]

The Covenant that the Báb made with His followers concerning 'Him Whom God shall make manifest' was firm and irrevocable. Because His advent was unquestionable, assured as the midday sun, the Báb did not appoint a successor. Instead, He appointed Mírzá Yaḥyá as the leader of the community until the advent of 'Him Whom God shall make manifest'. So real was His advent that the Báb in the early days of His Revelation in Shíráz despatched Mullá Ḥusayn, the first to believe in the Báb, to Ṭihrán for the sole purpose of searching for and establishing contact with 'Him Whom God shall make manifest', the One who was the source of the Revelation of the Báb, the object of His adoration and the One in whose path He longed to lay down His life.

Innumerable are the passages in the Báb's writings in which He extols the station of 'Him Whom God shall make manifest', portrays His person as majestic, awe-inspiring, incomparable and infinitely glorious, describes the inconceivable greatness of His Revelation, regards Himself as the lowliest servant of His threshold, recognizes Him as the Source of His own Revelation and the object of His adoration and cherishes the desire to lay down His life in His path. Indeed, no Manifestation of God has ever made such a mighty Covenant with His followers regarding the Manifestation who was to follow. The following passages from the writings of the Báb are among those that reveal the greatness of the Revelation of Bahá'u'lláh and the exalted station of its author. He writes:

> Of all the tributes I have paid to Him Who is to come after Me, the greatest is this, My written confession, that no words of Mine can adequately describe Him, nor can any reference to Him in My Book, the Bayán, do justice to His Cause.[105]

The Báb has clearly stated to His followers that His Revelation is entirely dependent upon 'Him Whom God shall make manifest' and that He is only a servant at His threshold. In His Qayyúmu'l-Asmá', the first emanations of His pen, the Báb communes with Bahá'u'lláh in these words:

> Out of utter nothingness, O great and omnipotent Master, Thou hast, through the celestial potency of Thy might, brought me forth

and raised me up to proclaim this Revelation. I have made none other but Thee my trust; I have clung to no will but Thy will . . .[106]

And in the same book He craves for martyrdom in the path of Bahá'u-'lláh, whom He addresses as the 'Remnant of God'.

> . . . O Thou Remnant of God! I have sacrificed myself wholly for Thee; I have accepted curses for Thy sake, and have yearned for naught but martyrdom in the path of Thy love. Sufficient witness unto me is God, the Exalted, the Protector, the Ancient of Days.[107]

In a Tablet addressed to 'Him Whom God shall make manifest', the Báb writes:

> This is an epistle from this lowly servant to the All-Glorious Lord – He Who hath been aforetime and will be hereafter made manifest. Verily He is the Most Manifest, the Almighty.[108]

There are many passages in the writings of the Báb in which He states that He will be the first to acknowledge the Cause of 'Him Whom God shall make manifest' and bow before Him as a lowly servant. A few examples follow:

> Were He to appear this very moment, I would be the first to adore Him, and the first to bow down before Him.[109]

> 'I, verily, am a believer in Him, and in His Faith, and in His Book, and in His Testimonies, and in His Ways, and all that proceedeth from Him concerning them. I glory in My kinship with Him, and pride Myself on My belief in Him.' And likewise, He saith: 'O congregation of the Bayán and all who are therein! Recognize ye the limits imposed upon you, for such a One as the Point of the Bayán Himself hath believed in Him Whom God shall make manifest, before all things were created. Therein, verily, do I glory before all who are in the kingdom of heaven and earth.'[110]

> 'The whole of the Bayán is only a leaf amongst the leaves of His Paradise.' And likewise, He saith: 'I am the first to adore Him, and pride Myself on My kinship with Him.'[111]

The following are utterances of the Báb gleaned from His various writings as He extols the person of 'Him Whom God shall make manifest'. In the Persian Bayán, the Báb states that 'He Whom God shall make manifest', as the Mouthpiece of God, will proclaim:

> Verily, verily, I am God, no God is there but Me; in truth all others except Me are My creatures. Say, O My creatures! Me alone, therefore, should ye fear.[112]

and again:

> He, verily is the One Who, under all conditions, proclaimeth: 'I, in very truth, am God.'[113]

> The glory of Him Whom God shall make manifest is immeasurably above every other glory, and His majesty is far above every other majesty. His beauty excelleth every other embodiment of beauty, and His grandeur immensely exceedeth every other manifestation of grandeur. Every light paleth before the radiance of His light, and every other exponent of mercy falleth short before the tokens of His mercy. Every other perfection is as naught in the face of His consummate perfection, and every other display of might is as nothing before His absolute might. His names are superior to all other names. His good-pleasure taketh precedence over any other expression of good-pleasure. His pre-eminent exaltation is far above the reach of every other symbol of exaltation. The splendour of His appearance far surpasseth that of any other appearance. His divine concealment is far more profound than any other concealment. His loftiness is immeasurably above every other loftiness. His gracious favour is unequalled by any other evidence of favour. His power transcendeth every power. His sovereignty is invincible in the face of every other sovereignty. His celestial dominion is exalted far above every other dominion. His knowledge pervadeth all created things, and His consummate power extendeth over all beings.[114]

> If ye seek God, it behooveth you to seek Him Whom God shall make manifest . . .[115]

Similarly He states:

> From the beginning that hath no beginning all men have bowed in adoration before Him Whom God shall make manifest and will continue to do so until the end that hath no end. How strange then that at the time of His appearance ye should pay homage by day and night unto that which the Point of the Bayán hath enjoined upon you and yet fail to worship Him Whom God shall make manifest.[116]

In the Persian Bayán the Báb states that attaining unto the presence of God as promised in the Holy Books would be none other than attaining the presence of 'Him Whom God shall make manifest', for man has no access to the Essence of God.[117] In another passage[118] He mentions Bahá'u'lláh by name and categorically states that He is the 'Primal Will' of God. In several other instances the Báb refers to Bahá'u'lláh by name. In a celebrated passage in the Persian Bayán He states:

> Well is it with him who fixeth his gaze upon the Order of Bahá'u'lláh, and rendereth thanks unto his Lord. For He will assuredly be made manifest. God hath indeed irrevocably ordained it in the Bayán.[119]

The Báb considered His own Revelation to be a gift to 'Him Whom God shall make manifest'. These are some of His utterances concerning the Bayán, the Mother Book of the Bábí Dispensation:

> Suffer not yourselves to be shut out as by a veil from God after He hath revealed Himself. For all that hath been exalted in the Bayán is but as a ring upon My hand, and I Myself am, verily, but a ring upon the hand of Him Whom God shall make manifest – glorified be His mention! He turneth it as He pleaseth, for whatsoever He pleaseth, and through whatsoever He pleaseth. He, verily, is the Help in Peril, the Most High.[120]

> The whole of the Bayán is only a leaf amongst the leaves of His Paradise.[121]

> The Bayán is from beginning to end the repository of all of His attributes, and the treasury of both His fire and His light.[122]

> I swear by the most holy Essence of God – exalted and glorified be He – that in the Day of the appearance of Him Whom God shall make manifest a thousand perusals of the Bayán cannot equal the perusal of a single verse to be revealed by Him Whom God shall make manifest.[123]

> I swear by the most sacred Essence of God that but one line of the Words uttered by Him is more sublime than the words uttered by all that dwell on earth. Nay, I beg forgiveness for making this comparison. How could the reflections of the sun in the mirror compare with the wondrous rays of the sun in the visible heaven?[124]

> The year-old germ that holdeth within itself the potentialities of the Revelation that is to come is endowed with a potency superior to the combined forces of the whole of the Bayán.[125]

In a Tablet to Mullá Báqir, a Letter of the Living, the Báb testifies, in these words, to the exalted character of 'Him Whom God shall make manifest':

> I have written down in My mention of Him these gem-like words: 'No allusion of Mine can allude unto Him, neither anything mentioned in the Bayán' . . . 'Exalted and glorified is He above the power of any one to reveal Him except Himself, or the description of any of His creatures. I Myself am but the first servant to believe in Him and in His signs, and to partake of the sweet savours of His words from the first-fruits of the Paradise of His knowledge. Yea, by His glory! He is the Truth. There is none other God but Him. All have risen at His bidding.'[126]

The Báb repeatedly gave the year nine as the date of the appearance of 'Him Whom God shall make manifest'. The declaration of the Báb took place in the year 1260 AH (AD 1844). The year nine is 1269 AH, which began about the middle of October 1852 when Bahá'u'lláh had already been imprisoned for about two months in the Síyáh-C͟hál of Ṭihrán, the scene of the birth of His Revelation. The following are a few passages concerning the year nine:

> 'In the year nine ye will attain unto all good.' On another occasion He saith: 'In the year nine ye will attain unto the Presence of God.'[127]

> Ere nine will have elapsed from the inception of this Cause, the realities of the created things will not be made manifest. All that thou hast as yet seen is but the stage from the moist germ until We clothed it with flesh. Be patient, until thou beholdest a new creation. Say: 'Blessed, therefore, be God, the most excellent of Makers!'[128]

The Báb also mentioned the year nineteen with regard to the Revelation of 'Him Whom God shall make manifest'. This is a reference to the public declaration of Bahá'u'lláh in the Garden of Riḍván in Bag͟hdád which occurred 19 years after the inception of the Bahá'í Era in 1844:

> The Lord of the Day of Reckoning will be manifested at the end of Váḥid (19) and the beginning of eighty (1280 AH).[129]

Although the Báb has made several references to the years nine and nineteen, nevertheless He makes it abundantly clear that the time of the advent of 'Him Whom God shall make manifest' is entirely in His own hands. Whenever He appears, all must follow Him.

There are innumerable passages in the Báb's writings exhorting His followers to be watchful, and as soon as the Supreme Manifestation of God reveals Himself, to recognize and follow Him immediately. He counsels them to allow no doubt to enter their minds when informed of the appearance of 'Him Whom God shall make manifest'. He warns them repeatedly to beware lest anything in the world, including the Bayán or any other of the Báb's writings, should become a barrier between them and 'Him Whom God shall make manifest'. The following utterance of the Báb, urging His followers to be faithful to 'Him Whom God shall make manifest', is one quotation gleaned from among many:

> At the time of the manifestation of Him Whom God shall make manifest everyone should be well trained in the teachings of the Bayán, so that none of the followers may outwardly cling to the Bayán and thus forfeit their allegiance unto Him. If anyone does so, the verdict of 'disbeliever in God' shall be passed upon Him.[130]

The Báb enjoined His followers to read once every 19 days chapter VI:8 of the Bayán so that they might prepare themselves for the Revelation of 'Him Whom God shall make manifest':

> Beware, beware lest, in the days of His Revelation, the Váḥid of the Bayán (eighteen Letters of the Living) shut thee not out as by a veil from Him, inasmuch as this Váḥid is but a creature in His sight. And beware, beware that the words sent down in the Bayán shut thee not out as by a veil from Him.[131]

10

The Breaker of the Covenant of the Báb

4–WT . . . notwithstanding this, Mírzá Yaḥyá denied Him, dealt falsely with Him, believed Him not, sowed the seeds of doubt, closed his eyes to His manifest verses and turned aside therefrom.

Shortly after Mírzá Yaḥyá had settled in Baghdád he decided to engage in a profession to hide his identity. At first he changed his headgear, adopting a large turban and assuming the name of Ḥájí 'Alí, the Lás-Furúsh.* He then took a shop in a bazaar in a dilapidated part of the city and started working. In the meantime, a man of great evil, described by Bahá'u'lláh as 'the embodiment of wickedness and impiety', 'the prime mover of mischief' and 'one accursed of God', entered the scene to influence Mírzá Yaḥyá. He was the notorious Siyyid Muḥammad-i-Iṣfahání, known as the 'Antichrist of the Bahá'í Revelation'.[132] In the early days of the Faith this man was a student at a theological school in Iṣfahán but was expelled for reprehensible conduct. He embraced the Faith during the early part of the ministry of the Báb and later went to Karbilá where he joined the ranks of the believers. In the Kitáb-i-Íqán Bahá'u'lláh alludes to him as that 'one-eyed man, who . . . is arising with the utmost malevolence against Us'.[133] Of him Shoghi Effendi writes:

> The black-hearted scoundrel who befooled and manipulated this vain and flaccid man [Mírzá Yaḥyá] with consummate skill and unyielding persistence was a certain Siyyid Muḥammad, a native of Iṣfáhán, notorious for his inordinate ambition, his blind obstinacy and uncontrollable jealousy. To him Bahá'u'lláh had later referred in the Kitáb-i-Aqdas as the one who had 'led astray' Mírzá Yaḥyá, and stigmatized him, in one of His Tablets, as the 'source of envy and the quintessence of mischief', while 'Abdu'l-Bahá had described the relationship existing between these two as that of 'the sucking child' to the 'much-prized breast' of its mother.[134]

* Lás-Furúsh means a dealer in silk. It is interesting that Mírzá Yaḥyá was known inofficial circles as Ḥájí 'Alí until the end of his life.

Siyyid Muḥammad was in Karbilá when Bahá'u'lláh visited that city in 1851. As soon as he met Bahá'u'lláh, whom he considered as merely another Bábí, he was struck by His authority and majesty, and when he saw the honour and reverence shown to Him by the Bábís and the Shaykhís, he was filled with an uncontrollable envy which never left him till the end of his tragic life.

As already stated, when Bahá'u'lláh was exiled to Iraq in 1853, the Bábís were in great disarray. They were frightened and helpless people who since the martyrdom of the Báb had been driven underground. They did not dare associate with each other in public for fear of being persecuted. When Bahá'u'lláh arrived in Iraq, He inspired them to come out into the open and gradually through His wise and loving leadership the Bábí community acquired a new lease of life. The ascendancy of Bahá'u'lláh in public and His rising prestige intensified the fire of jealousy now burning fiercely in Siyyid Muḥammad's heart.

Describing the circumstances in which some of the followers of the Báb in Baghdád recognized the station of Bahá'u'lláh and turned to Him in adoration, Shoghi Effendi recounts the reaction shown by Siyyid Muḥammad:

> To these evidences of an ever deepening veneration for Bahá'u'lláh and of a passionate attachment to His person were now being added further grounds for the outbreak of the pent-up jealousies which His mounting prestige evoked in the breasts of His ill-wishers and enemies. The steady extension of the circle of His acquaintances and admirers; His friendly intercourse with officials including the governor of the city; the unfeigned homage offered Him, on so many occasions and so spontaneously, by men who had once been distinguished companions of Siyyid Káẓim; the disillusionment which the persistent concealment of Mírzá Yaḥyá, and the unflattering reports circulated regarding his character and abilities, had engendered; the signs of increasing independence, of innate sagacity and inherent superiority and capacity for leadership unmistakably exhibited by Bahá'u'lláh Himself – all combined to widen the breach which the infamous and crafty Siyyid Muḥammad had sedulously contrived to create.[135]

Knowing Mírzá Yaḥyá's weaknesses and fully aware of his ambitions, this scheming Siyyid allied himself closely with him. His influence upon Mírzá Yaḥyá was as effective as it was satanic. As a result of this close association, Mírzá Yaḥyá began to sow the seeds of doubt in the minds of those who had become Bahá'u'lláh's ardent admirers and were attracted to His person. By various means, sometimes openly and sometimes subtly, he began to try to discredit Bahá'u'lláh and misrepresent His motives in reviving the declining fortunes of the Bábí community.

While in hiding, Mírzá Yaḥyá employed a Persian merchant named Abu'l-Qásim as an intermediary between himself and the believers. As the nominee of the Báb, Mírzá Yaḥyá began, with the help of Siyyid Muḥammad and through Abu'l-Qásim, to disseminate his misguided directives to all the Bábís in Baghdád. As this campaign of misrepresentation gathered momentum, the fortunes of the Faith began to decline and many Bábís became confused and disenchanted.

It was during these days, too, that Siyyid Muḥammad and Mírzá Yaḥyá found a way to legitimize their own foul conduct in the community. This they did by abusing the proclamation which had been made at Badasht concerning the abrogation of the laws of Islam.* They claimed that the Bábí Dispensation had lifted the bounds (Kasr-i-Ḥudúd) which the laws of God had imposed upon the faithful. This refers to the annulment of the laws of Islam which had indeed been swept away through the Dispensation of the Báb and not to the annulment of the bounds of human decency and morality. Mírzá Yaḥyá misinterpreted this 'lifting of the bounds' to mean the abrogation of moral principles as well. Thus he began to commit many reprehensible acts. For instance, he ordered his servant to assassinate several outstanding individuals among the Bábís, as we shall see.

Bahá'u'lláh is referring to this misleading concept when He admonishes the believers in the Kitáb-i-Aqdas:

> We verily, have commanded you to refuse the dictates of your evil passions and corrupt desires, and not to transgress the bounds which the Pen of the Most High hath fixed . . .[136]

Encouraged by Siyyid Muḥammad, Mírzá Yaḥyá then made the preposterous claim of being the successor of the Báb – a position never contemplated by Him. Indeed, He categorically states in the Persian Bayán that He appointed no successor to Himself. As a result of such harmful propaganda and acts of treachery and deceit, which kindled dissension among the believers, 'the fire of the Cause of God', as testified by Nabíl, 'had been well-nigh quenched in every place'.[137]

Bahá'u'lláh, in some Tablets revealed during that period, foreshadows the appearance of severe tests and trials as a result of the machinations of Mírzá Yaḥyá and Siyyid Muḥammad. In one Tablet He utters these words of warning:

---

* See Shoghi Effendi, *God Passes By*, p. 403 and Nabíl, *Dawn-Breakers*, pp. 193–8.

> The days of tests are now come. Oceans of dissension and tribulation are surging, and the Banners of Doubt are, in every nook and corner, occupied in stirring up mischief and in leading men to perdition.[138]

In the Tablet of Qullu'ṭ-Ṭa'ám,* Bahá'u'lláh alludes to His intention to depart from Baghdád; this He did when tests and tribulations reached a climax.† When Bahá'u'lláh left Baghdád and retired to the mountains of Kurdistan, Mírzá Yaḥyá, disguised as a shopkeeper and sometimes hidden in a house, was emboldened by His absence. Directed by Siyyid Muḥammad, he embarked upon some of his cowardly activities, both within and outside the Bábí community. As we shall see later, the atrocities committed in his name and on his orders constitute some of the most shameful events in the history of the Faith, events which helped to bring about the near extinction of the Bábí religion.

It must be noted that in order to preserve the integrity of the Faith, Bahá'u'lláh for several years neither questioned the validity of Mírzá Yaḥyá's appointment as the leader of the Bábí community nor announced the nullification of his leadership. The separation between Bahá'u'lláh and Mírzá Yaḥyá took place in Adrianople when a complete break occurred between the Bahá'í and Bábí Faiths.

The following account by the Greatest Holy Leaf depicting the hardships and difficulties suffered by the Holy Family during Bahá'u'lláh's absence in the mountains of Kurdistan throws light on their relationship with this unfaithful brother of Bahá'u'lláh and reveals some of his reprehensible conduct:

> At length my father decided to leave Baghdád for a time. During his absence, Ṣubḥ-i-Azal [Mírzá Yaḥyá] could convince himself whether or no the Bábís desired to turn their faces to him as their leader, as he, in the petty conceit of a small mind and undisciplined nature, asserted, would, if given an opportunity, prove to be the case.
>
> Before my father left for his retreat into the wilderness, he commanded the friends to treat Ṣubḥ-i-Azal with consideration. He offered him and his family the shelter and hospitality of our house.

---

* For a more detailed study of this Tablet see Taherzadeh, *Revelation of Bahá'u'lláh*, vol. 1, p. 55.

† See Shoghi Effendi, *God Passes By*, pp. 117–24, quoted in chapter 7 above, for a description of the circumstances leading to Bahá'u'lláh's retirement to the mountains of Kurdistan.

He asked Mírzá Músá, my mother and me, to care for them and to do everything in our power to make them comfortable.

Our grief was intense when my father left us. He told none of us either where he was going or when he would return. He took no luggage, only a little rice, and some coarse bread.

So we, my mother, my brother 'Abbás and I, clung together in our sorrow and anxiety.

Ṣubḥ-i-Azal rejoiced, hoping to gain his ends, now that Jamál-i-Mubárak [Bahá'u'lláh] was no longer present.

Meanwhile, he was a guest in our house. He gave us much trouble, complaining of the food. Though all the best and most dainty things were invariably given to him.

He became at this time more than ever terrified lest he should one day be arrested. He hid himself, keeping the door of our house locked, and stormed at anybody who opened it.

As for me, I led a very lonely life, and would have liked sometimes to make friends with other children. But Ṣubḥ-i-Azal would not permit any little friends to come to the house, neither would he let me go out!

Two little girls about my own age lived in the next house. I used to peep at them; but our guest always came and shouted at me for opening the door, which he promptly locked. He was always in fear of being arrested, and cared for nothing but his own safety.

We led a very difficult life at this time as well as a lonely one. He would not even allow us to go to the Hammám to take our baths. Nobody was permitted to come to the house to help us, and the work therefore was very hard.

For hours every day I had to stand drawing water from a deep well in the house; the ropes were hard and rough, and the bucket was heavy. My dear mother used to help, but she was not very strong, and my arms were rather weak. Our guest never helped.

My father having told us to respect and obey this tyrannical person, we tried to do so, but this respect was not easy, as our lives were made so unhappy by him.

During this time the darling baby brother, born after our arrival in Baghdád, became seriously ill. Our guest would not allow a doctor, or even any neighbour to come to our help.

My mother was heart-broken when the little one died; even then we were not allowed to have anybody to prepare him for burial.

The sweet body of our beautiful baby was given to a man, who took it away, and we never knew even where he was laid. I remember so clearly the sorrow of those days.

A little while after this, we moved into a larger house – fortunately Ṣubḥ-i-Azal was too terrified of being seen, if he came with us – so he preferred to occupy a little house behind ours. We still sent his food to him, also provided for his family, now increased, as he had married another wife, a girl from a neighbouring village.

His presence was thus happily removed from our daily life; we were relieved and much happier.[139]

During Bahá'u'lláh's absence, news reached Baghdád of the martyrdom of a certain believer of Najaf-Ábád, near Iṣfahán. Mírzá Yaḥyá was highly alarmed, fearing that an outbreak of persecution could lead the enemies of the Faith to him, the nominee of the Báb, and cost him his life. With these thoughts in mind, he decided to change his residence. With the help of a certain Mírzá 'Alíy-i-Tabrízí, he bought a consignment of shoes, disguised himself as a Jew and went to Basra where he remained for some time and occupied himself in his newfound profession of shoe merchant. Later, when he realized that there was no need for alarm, he returned to Baghdád.

It was during this period under the leadership of Mírzá Yaḥyá, inspired by his wicked advisor Siyyid Muḥammad, that some of the most heinous atrocities were committed. Mírzá Asadu'lláh of Khúy, who was surnamed Dayyán by the Báb and was one of His outstanding followers, was murdered on Mírzá Yaḥyá's orders.* Another victim was Mírzá 'Alí-Akbar, a paternal cousin of the Báb. These criminal activities of Mírzá Yaḥyá were matched only by certain acts of infamy which he committed, bringing dishonour to the Cause of the Báb. He betrayed the honour of the Báb while Bahá'u'lláh was in Kurdistan by marrying Fáṭimih, the Báb's second wife,† and after a few days giving her in marriage to Siyyid Muḥammad. When Bahá'u'lláh learned of this shameful act, His grief knew no bounds. In several Tablets He severely condemned this outrageous betrayal by one who professed to be the nominee of the Báb. In the Epistle to the Son of the Wolf, He states:

> Reflect a while upon the dishonour inflicted upon the Primal Point. Consider what hath happened. When this Wronged One, after a retirement of two years during which He wandered through the deserts and mountains, returned to Baghdád, as a result of the intervention of a few, who for a long time had sought Him in the wilderness, a certain Mírzá Muḥammad-'Alí of Rasht came to see Him, and related, before a large gathering of people, that which had been done, affecting the honour of the Báb, which hath truly overwhelmed all lands with sorrow. Great God! How could they have countenanced this most grievous betrayal? Briefly, We beseech God to aid the perpetrator of this deed to repent, and return unto Him. He, verily, is the Helper, the All-Wise.[140]

* For more information about Dayyán and other atrocities committed by Mírzá Yaḥyá see Taherzadeh, *Revelation of Bahá'u'lláh*, vols. 1 and 2, and Taherzadeh, *Covenant of Bahá'u'lláh*.

† See Taherzadeh, *Revelation of Bahá'u'lláh*, vol. 2, p. 262.

Those who were in close contact with Mírzá Yaḥyá were fully aware of his immoderate sexual appetites. In the Epistle to the Son of the Wolf, Bahá'u'lláh alludes to this when He addresses Hádíy-i-Dawlat-Ábádí* in these words:

> Regardest thou as one wronged he who in this world was never dealt a single blow, and who was continually surrounded by five of the handmaidens of God? And imputest thou unto the True One, Who, from His earliest years until the present day, hath been in the hands of His enemies, and been tormented with the worst afflictions in the world, such charges as the Jews did not ascribe unto Christ? Hearken unto the voice of this Wronged One, and be not of them that are in utter loss.[141]

'Abdu'l-Bahá mentions that one of Mírzá Yaḥyá's preoccupations was to marry one wife after another. He mentions eleven wives but some historians have counted three more.

When Bahá'u'lláh was in the mountains of Kurdistan, Mírzá Yaḥyá was driven by an insatiable appetite to satisfy his base and carnal desires. In one of His Tablets Bahá'u'lláh describes an episode which brought further shame to his already shameful career. Mírzá Yaḥyá sent a message to a certain believer, Áqá Muḥammad-Karím, asking for the hand of his daughter in marriage. The parents of the girl refused to comply and instead gave their daughter in marriage to Abu'l-Qásim, the Persian merchant who had been in the service of Mírzá Yaḥyá for some years. No sooner had this happened than Mírzá Yaḥyá ordered the elimination of Abu'l-Qásim and he was never seen again.

As a result of such atrocities committed in the name of religion, the Bábí community was utterly degraded in the eyes of the public. When Bahá'u'lláh returned from the mountains of Kurdistan the Bábís were dispirited and spiritually as dead. Once again Bahá'u'lláh took the reins of the Cause in His hands. He breathed new life into the dying community of the Báb, and through His loving advice and exhortations, both verbally and in writing, raised the morale of the believers in Baghdád and the neighbouring towns. As indicated earlier, Bahá'u'lláh Himself testified to the change in these words:

> After Our arrival, We revealed, as a copious rain, by the aid of God and His Divine Grace and mercy, Our verses, and sent them to various parts of the world. We exhorted all men, and particularly

---

* Successor of Mírzá Yaḥyá. For details see Taherzadeh, *Revelation of Bahá'u'lláh*, vol. 4.

> this people, through Our wise counsels and loving admonitions, and forbade them to engage in sedition, quarrels, disputes and conflict. As a result of this, and by the grace of God, waywardness and folly were changed into piety and understanding, and weapons converted into instruments of peace.[142]

'Abdu'l-Bahá also states:

> Bahá'u'lláh after His return (from Sulaymáníyyih) made such strenuous efforts in educating and training this community, in reforming its manners, in regulating its affairs and in rehabilitating its fortunes, that in a short while all these troubles and mischiefs were quenched, and the utmost peace and tranquillity reigned in men's hearts.[143]

This transformation of spirit and the ascendancy of the community in Iraq and Persia, in spite of Mírzá Yaḥyá, continued until the end of Bahá'u'lláh's stay in that country.

The outpouring of Bahá'u'lláh's Revelation in Bag͟hdád began to revive the community of the Báb, not only in Iraq but also in Persia, where thousands of Bábís had been left leaderless. The many Tablets and Epistles which flowed from the Pen of the Most High, especially the Kitáb-i-Íqán and Hidden Words, inspired the believers and breathed a new spirit into their souls. At the same time, the evidences of ascendancy and grandeur which were increasingly manifested by Bahá'u'lláh served to inflame the fire of jealousy smouldering in the heart of Mírzá Yaḥyá. Since he could never find the courage to utter a word of opposition to Bahá'u'lláh when he came into His presence, he sowed the seeds of doubt in the minds of the believers and spread false rumours concerning Bahá'u'lláh throughout the community in Persia.

The person who conceived and carried out these misguided plans aimed at discrediting Bahá'u'lláh was Siyyid Muḥammad. To cite one example: Soon after the Kitáb-i-Íqán was revealed in honour of Ḥájí Siyyid Muḥammad, the uncle of the Báb, several copies were made and circulated among the believers. This book came as a shattering blow to Mírzá Yaḥyá, who could see its overpowering influence on the friends. Siyyid Muḥammad circulated rumours that the Kitáb-i-Íqán was the work of Mírzá Yaḥyá which had been published in Bahá'u'lláh's name.* Such a preposterous claim and similar falsehoods did not influence the rank and file of the believers who, by then, had recognized the corruption and perfidy of Mírzá Yaḥyá as compared

* For more information about this see Taherzadeh, *Revelation of Bahá'u'lláh*, vol. 2, pp. 68–73.

with Bahá'u'lláh's righteousness and divine virtues. In spite of Mírzá Yaḥyá's iniquitous deeds, whether carried out clandestinely or in the open, Bahá'u'lláh always counselled him to uprightness and purity. This state of affairs continued until Bahá'u'lláh was invited to move to Constantinople.

The news of Bahá'u'lláh's imminent departure from Baghdád to Istanbul disturbed and frightened Mírzá Yaḥyá. He who had hidden himself from the public eye in Baghdád over the years and who, in spite of his iniquitous deeds, relied heavily on Bahá'u'lláh's protection and loving-kindness, found himself suddenly plunged into a grievous situation. The thought of remaining alone in Baghdád was deeply distressing to him. Bahá'u'lláh advised him that since he was free to travel, he should proceed to Persia and there disseminate the writings of the Báb among the believers.* But Mírzá Yaḥyá had no interest in teaching the Cause of the Báb or in disseminating its holy scriptures. He refused to comply with Bahá'u'lláh's advice on the grounds that the authorities in Persia were ruthlessly persecuting the Bábís and therefore his life would be in great danger if he went there.

At one point Mírzá Yaḥyá decided to flee to India or Abyssinia (Ethiopia), where he thought he would be free from persecution. But soon he changed his mind and resigned himself to remaining in Iraq, asking Bahá'u'lláh to arrange the building of a secure hiding place for him. He wanted a cottage in Huvaydar, near Baghdád, in a garden owned by Shaykh Sulṭán. Bahá'u'lláh acceded to his request and asked Shaykh Sulṭán, who was one of His devoted Arab followers, to build the cottage for him. But as the building work proceeded Mírzá Yaḥyá felt increasingly insecure and eventually cancelled his plans in favour of going to Istanbul incognito. However, he made it clear that he did not intend to travel with Bahá'u'lláh, for he was very suspicious of the authorities' intention in inviting Bahá'u'lláh to Istanbul. He feared that Bahá'u'lláh and his companions might either be handed over to Persian officials or killed on the way.

To go on this long journey Mírzá Yaḥyá needed a passport. Not wishing to identify himself to the authorities, he sent a certain Ḥájí Muḥammad-Káẓim, who resembled him, to the government house to procure a passport for him in his newly assumed name of Mírzá 'Alíy-i-Kirmánsh- áhi. He then proceeded to Mosul in disguise, accompanied by an Arab servant, and reached there before Bahá'u'lláh's caravan arrived.

Bahá'u'lláh allowed Siyyid Muḥammad-i-Iṣfahání to be included in the party that accompanied Him to Istanbul. Whenever possible,

* At Bahá'u'lláh's direction these writings had been transcribed by Mírzá Yaḥyá some years before and were ready to be taken to Persia.

Bahá'u'lláh ensured that the trouble-makers and those who were not inwardly faithful to Him were not left at large among the believers, often keeping such people close to His own person so as to be able to check their mischief. Although Siyyid Muḥammad was a treacherous individual who caused untold difficulties for Bahá'u'lláh and His devoted companions, he was never barred, while in Baghdád, from attaining His presence or taking part in the gatherings of the believers. By allowing Siyyid Muḥammad to accompany Him in His exile, Bahá'u'lláh protected the believers in Iraq and elsewhere from the man's satanic influence. Of course, the faithful companions of Bahá'u'lláh, both those who travelled with Him and those who remained behind, were fully aware of the iniquitous deeds of that evil and hypocritical individual who used to pretend, whenever he came into their gatherings, to be a loyal believer himself.

Mírzá Yahyá waited in Mosul until Bahá'u'lláh's caravan arrived. Then he sent his servant to inform Áqáy-i-Kalím (Bahá'u'lláh's most faithful brother, known also as Mírzá Músá) of his whereabouts in the city. In one of His Tablets 'Abdu'l-Bahá tells the story in these words:

> When we reached Mosul, and a camp was set up on the bank of the Tigris, where the notables of the town flocked group after group to come into His blessed presence [Bahá'u'lláh's], on a midnight that aforementioned Arab, Ẓáhir, came to say that his Honour [Mírzá Yaḥyá] was staying at an inn outside the city, and wished to meet someone. My uncle, Mírzá Músá, went there at midnight and met him. Mírzá Yaḥyá asked about his family, and was told that they were there and had their own tent and he could visit them. He said that he did not at all consider it advisable to do so, but he would accompany the caravan with which his family too would be travelling. Thus he continued to Diyárbakr, a black cord round his head, and a begging-bowl in his hand, consorting only with the Arabs and the Turks in the caravan. At Diyárbakr, he sent word that he would visit his family at night and join the main body of the caravan in the morning. That was done. Since Ḥájí Siyyid Muḥammad knew him, he gave out that he was a Persian dervish, an acquaintance of his, and visited him, but other friends because they had never seen him [Mírzá Yaḥyá], did not recognize him.[144]

Mírzá Yaḥyá, who was now introducing himself as Ḥájí 'Alí, pretended that he did not know anybody in the party, including Bahá'u'lláh, and claimed to be returning from Mecca. He was not recognized by most of the companions because he had been living in disguise and hiding himself from the believers while in Iraq. The crafty Siyyid Muḥammad had the nerve to introduce Mírzá Yaḥyá as a dervish friend of his to Bahá'u'lláh's companions but they discovered his real identity as they approached their destination. In this fashion Mírzá Yaḥyá, whose wives were among the female group travelling with Bahá'u'lláh, accompanied them until they reached the shores of Istanbul. There his identity was disclosed and everyone knew who he was. But during his stay in Istanbul, Mírzá Yaḥyá did not dare to reveal his true identity to the authorities. To Shamsí Big, who was appointed by the government to act as host to Bahá'u'lláh, he introduced himself as a servant in Bahá'u'lláh's household and he would sometimes sleep in the servants' quarters to prove his case.

When Bahá'u'lláh was exiled to Adrianople, Mírzá Yaḥyá and Siyyid Muḥammad went with him. Bahá'u'lláh, in the Epistle to the Son of the Wolf, mentions that Mírzá Yaḥyá followed Him from place to place:

> Wherever this Wronged One went Mírzá Yaḥyá followed Him . . . The Siyyid of Iṣfáhán, however, surreptitiously duped him. They committed that which caused the greatest consternation.[145]

11

Open Rebellion of Mírzá Yaḥyá

4–WT Would that he had been content therewith! Nay, he even attempted to shed the sacred blood (of Bahá'u'lláh) and then raised a great clamour and tumult around him, attributing unto Bahá'u'lláh malevolence and cruelty towards himself. What sedition he stirred up and what a storm of mischief he raised whilst in the Land of Mystery (Adrianople)! At last, he wrought that which caused the Day-Star of the world to be sent an exile to this, the Most Great Prison, and sorely wronged, and in the West of this Great Prison He did set.

Shedding of the sacred blood is a reference to Mírzá Yaḥyá's attempt on the life of Bahá'u'lláh.

Soon after his arrival in Adrianople, Mírzá Yaḥyá realized that there was no longer any danger to his life because within a short period Bahá'u'lláh had won the respect and admiration of the dignitaries, including the governor of Adrianople. The inhabitants of the city showed such a spirit of friendliness and cooperation towards the exiled community that Bahá'u'lláh instructed the believers to engage in some work or profession and integrate themselves into the community. Since there was no apparent reason for persecution of the Bahá'ís, Mírzá Yaḥyá, emboldened by Siyyid Muḥammad, decided to emerge from his self-imposed seclusion.

Through his constant association with Siyyid Muḥammad and a certain Ḥájí Mírzá Aḥmad-i-Ká<u>sh</u>ání, an infamous mischief-maker notorious for his vulgar conduct and foul language, Mírzá Yaḥyá began openly to sound his rebellion against Bahá'u'lláh. He who always felt so insignificant when he came face to face with Bahá'u'lláh and fell speechless in His presence, was now, prompted by his wicked lieutenant, to rise up against Him and attempt to wrest the leadership of the community from His hands.

To achieve this long-cherished ambition, Mírzá Yaḥyá embarked upon a plan which involved him in further acts of crime. He decided that the only way to accomplish his goal was to take Bahá'u'lláh's life, for he knew that he had neither the courage nor the personality to confront Him. Indeed, it was not unthinkable for a man who had already masterminded the assassination of several believers in

Baghdád, including the Báb's own cousin, to contemplate ways and means of taking Bahá'u'lláh's life.

The first attempt was carried out by Mírzá Yaḥyá's own hands when he poisoned Bahá'u'lláh with a deadly substance. Shoghi Effendi describes this shameful episode:

> Desperate designs to poison Bahá'u'lláh and His companions, and thereby reanimate his own defunct leadership, began, approximately a year after their arrival in Adrianople, to agitate his mind. Well aware of the erudition of his half-brother, Áqáy-i-Kalím, in matters pertaining to medicine, he, under various pretexts, sought enlightenment from him regarding the effects of certain herbs and poisons, and then began, contrary to his wont, to invite Bahá'u'lláh to his home, where, one day, having smeared His tea-cup with a substance he had concocted, he succeeded in poisoning Him sufficiently to produce a serious illness which lasted no less than a month, and which was accompanied by severe pains and high fever, the aftermath of which left Bahá'u'lláh with a shaking hand till the end of His life. So grave was His condition that a foreign doctor, named Shíshmán, was called in to attend Him. The doctor was so appalled by His livid hue that he deemed His case hopeless, and, after having fallen at His feet, retired from His presence without prescribing a remedy. A few days later that doctor fell ill and died. Prior to his death Bahá'u'lláh had intimated that doctor Shíshmán had sacrificed his life for Him. To Mírzá Áqá Ján, sent by Bahá'u'lláh to visit him, the doctor had stated that God had answered his prayers, and that after his death a certain Dr Chúpán, whom he knew to be reliable, should, whenever necessary, be called in his stead.[146]

Despite this heinous crime, Bahá'u'lláh advised His followers not to spread the news of the poisoning. But Mírzá Yaḥyá lost his nerve and shamefully accused Bahá'u'lláh of trying to poison *him*, and as a result, the story had to be told. The believers and those who were in close contact with them then became aware that the poison administered by Mírzá Yaḥyá had been the cause of Bahá'u'lláh's serious illness. The contrast between light and darkness, between truth and falsehood, Bahá'u'lláh's sin-covering eye and Mírzá Yaḥyá's corruption and wickedness, was evident to all.

This episode created deep turmoil and agitation within the community. Some time passed and the situation was beginning to simmer down when another serious attempt by Mírzá Yaḥyá to assassinate Bahá'u'lláh brought about an unprecedented commotion within the community, resulting in the final parting of the ways between Bahá'u'lláh and His unfaithful half-brother.

This time Mírzá Yaḥyá made plans to carry out his sinister designs in the public bath* frequented by Bahá'u'lláh. For some time he began to show favours to Ustád Muḥammad-'Alíy-i-Salmání,† a barber who served in the household of Bahá'u'lláh and was His bath attendant. Eventually Mírzá Yaḥyá intimated to Salmání in a subtle way that he could render a great service to the Cause if he were to assassinate Bahá'u'lláh while attending Him in the bath.

The following is a summary translation of Salmání's memoirs describing this shameful incident:

> One day I went to the bath and awaited the arrival of the Blessed Beauty. Azal [Mírzá Yaḥyá] arrived first. I attended to him and applied henna. He began to talk to me. For some time he had been trying hard to make me his follower but he was doing this in a secret way. He said to me: 'Last night I dreamt that someone had a sweeping brush in his hand and was sweeping the area around me.'‡ He gave me to understand that this person was the Blessed Beauty. From the tone of his conversation, I knew that he wanted me to do something for him but he did not tell me anything and soon left the bath . . .
>
> I was deep in my thoughts concerning the words of Azal. I did not understand his purpose in implying that the Blessed Beauty was sweeping the floor around him. However, it was quite clear that he wanted me to carry out a special task for him. At the same time I noted that Ḥájí Mírzá Aḥmad was trying to convert me to follow Azal. During the course of several days he persisted in trying to win me over.
>
> He said, 'A certain Mírzá Na'ím, the former Governor of Nayríz, killed many believers and perpetrated many crimes against the Cause.' He then praised courage and bravery in glowing terms. He said that some were brave by nature and at the right time they would manifest that quality in their actions. He then continued the

* Public baths, known in the West as Turkish baths, were the only type available to people in those days because houses had no baths built in them. These baths, with their warm and steamy atmosphere, were used by people as a place to wash and relax for hours. This meant that a public bath was a place for social occasions where people gathered, exchanged news and discussed many topics. In these baths people were not fully naked and wore loin-cloths. Often, friends used to go to the bath on the same day in order to spend time together. The baths provided customers with attendants who washed them and performed other services such as the applying of henna, shaving and massaging. Important people usually had their own bath attendants.

† For a story of his life and services, see Taherzadeh, *Revelation of Bahá'u'lláh*, vol. 2, p. 155. Salmání should not be confused with Shaykh Salmán.

‡ The connotation of these words in Persian is that Bahá'u'lláh was a humble servant of Mírzá Yaḥyá.

story of Mírzá Na'ím. 'From the persecuted family of the believers there remained a young boy aged ten or eleven. One day, when Mírzá Na'ím went into the bath, this boy went in with a knife. As he was coming out of the water, the boy stabbed him and ripped his belly open. Mírzá Na'ím screamed and his servants who were in the ante-room rushed in. They went for the boy, attacked and beat him. Then they went to see how their master was. The boy, although wounded, rose up and stabbed him again.' Azal praised courage again and said, 'How wonderful it is for a man to be brave. Now, see what they are doing to the Cause of God. Everybody harms it, everyone has arisen against me, even my brother. I have no comfort whatsoever and am in a wretched state.' His tone implied that he, the nominee of the Báb, was the wronged one, and his Brother (I take refuge in God!) was the usurper and aggressor. Then he once more praised courage and said that the Cause of God needed help. In all this talk, the tone of his remarks, the story of Mírzá Na'ím, the praise of courage and his encouragement to me, he was in fact telling me to kill Bahá'u'lláh.

The effect of all this upon me was so disturbing that in all my life I had never felt so shattered. It was as if the whole building was falling upon my head. I was frightened; without uttering a word I went out to the ante-room. My mind was in a state of the utmost agitation. I thought to myself that I would go inside and cut Azal's head off regardless of consequences. Then I thought, to kill him is easy but perhaps I would offend the Blessed Beauty. One thing which prevented me from carrying out my intention was the thought that if I killed him and then went into the presence of the Blessed Beauty, and He asked me why I had killed him, what answer could I give?

I returned to the bath and being extremely angry, I shouted at him, 'Go and get lost, clear off!' He whimpered and trembled and asked me to pour water over him. I complied. Washed or unwashed he went out in a state of great trepidation and I have never seen him since.

My state of mind, however, was such that nothing could calm me. As it happened, that day the Blessed Beauty did not come to the bath, but Áqá Mírzá Músáy-i-Kalím [Bahá'u'lláh's faithful brother] came. I told him that Azal had set me on fire with his sinister suggestion. Áqá Mírzá Músá said: 'He has been thinking of this for years, this man has always been thinking in this way. Do not pay any attention to him.' He counselled me to disregard the whole thing and went inside the bath.

However, when my work was finished in the bath, I went to the Master ['Abdu'l-Bahá] and reported to Him what Mírzá Yaḥyá had told me, and how I was filled with rage and wanted to kill him . . . the Master said, 'This is something that you alone know. Do not mention it to anyone, it is better that it remain hidden.' I then went to Mírzá Áqá Ján, reported the details of the incident, and asked

> him to tell Bahá'u'lláh. He returned and said, 'Bahá'u'lláh says to tell Ustád Muḥammad-'Alí not to mention this to anyone.'
>
> That night I collected all the writings of Azal and went to the tea-room* of Bahá'u'lláh's house and burnt them all in the brazier. Before doing so, I showed them to seven or eight of the believers who were present. They all saw that they were the writings of Azal. They all protested to me and asked me the reason for doing this. I said, 'Until today I esteemed Azal highly, but now he is less than a dog in my sight.'†

Because of Bahá'u'lláh's sin-covering eye and His loving kindness towards Mírzá Yaḥyá and because Yaḥyá was Bahá'u'lláh's half-brother, the faithful believers treated him with respect and consideration. But after these vicious attacks on Bahá'u'lláh, it was natural for them to turn their backs on him. After Salmání failed to keep the details of the incident to himself, the news spread and created a great upheaval in the community.

At this point Bahá'u'lláh decided to formally declare to Mírzá Yaḥyá, as the nominee of the Báb, His claim to be the Author of a new Revelation, 'Him Whom God shall make manifest', as foretold by the Báb. Of course, Mírzá Yaḥyá was well aware of Bahá'u'lláh's declaration in the Garden of Riḍván and the Tablets subsequently revealed by Him. But now the time had come for the Supreme Manifestation of God to formally announce His station to the one who was nominated by the Báb to be the leader of His followers until the advent of 'Him Whom God shall make manifest'.

In order to communicate this message to Mírzá Yaḥyá, Bahá'u'lláh revealed the Súriy-i-Amr (Súrih of Command) in His own handwriting and instructed His amanuensis Mírzá Áqá Ján to take the Tablet to Mírzá Yaḥyá, read it aloud and demand a conclusive reply from him. On being apprised of the contents of the Tablet and the claims of Bahá'u'lláh, Mírzá Yaḥyá indicated that he needed some time during which to meditate on the subject. The following day he sent a message to Bahá'u'lláh that he himself had become the recipient of divine Revelation and it was incumbent upon all to obey and follow him.

Such a claim maintained by so perfidious a person evoked the wrath of God and brought about the eventual split between Bahá'u'lláh and Mírzá Yaḥyá. It must be remembered that the majority of the believers in Adrianople were faithful to Bahá'u'lláh and until then

---

* Reception room of Bahá'u'lláh where the believers usually gathered.

† In Persian, this designation is much more insulting than it sounds in English.

had associated freely with Mírzá Yaḥyá and a small number of his henchmen; now the situation changed.

Mírzá Yaḥyá's response to the Súriy-i-Amr was a clear signal for separation. Bahá'u'lláh, who was then residing in the house of Amru-'lláh, changed His residence to the house of Riḍá Big. This was on 10 March 1866. Only the members of His own family and one servant moved to this house and He allowed no one else to attain His presence. As a result, the community of exiles was cut off from His blessed person and left entirely on its own. This withdrawal, similar to His withdrawal to the mountains of Kurdistan a few years earlier, plunged the community into a grievous state and created severe tests and trials for the believers. On the other hand, it afforded each one of the exiles the opportunity to choose between Bahá'u'lláh and His unfaithful brother.

Bahá'u'lláh's faithful followers, those lovers of His beauty, became dispirited. The light had departed from their midst and they were enveloped in a darkness that obscured their vision and left them helpless and disconsolate. Áqáy-i-Kalím, Bahá'u'lláh's faithful brother who carried the weight of responsibility during Bahá'u'lláh's retirement in the house of Riḍá Big, recounted to Nabíl these words:

> That day witnessed a most great commotion. All the companions lamented in their separation from the Blessed Beauty.[147]

Another witness to those grievous days has recorded:

> Those days were marked by tumult and confusion. We were sore-perplexed and greatly feared lest we be permanently deprived of the bounty of His presence.[148]

Even those who were unfaithful to Bahá'u'lláh were disturbed by His withdrawal, as they knew only too well that it was through His guiding influence that they were living in relative safety and security. These men were now left to their own devices and were soon engulfed in a most troublesome situation created by their own hands.

The retirement of Bahá'u'lláh to the house of Riḍá Big and His refusal to meet with any of the exiles created a situation in which everyone was left by himself to decide his own spiritual destiny. Those few who were inclined towards Mírzá Yaḥyá congregated together and began to launch their attacks on the faithful ones, while the rest occupied their time mostly in prayer and devotions, supplicating God to relieve them of this grievous separation from their Lord.

Before taking up residence in the house of Riḍá Big, Bahá'u'lláh ordered His brother Áqáy-i-Kalím to send half of the furniture, bedding and utensils to the house of Mírzá Yaḥyá. He also sent him certain historic relics such as the rings of the Báb, His seals and manuscripts. These were the items which the Báb had sent to Bahá'u'lláh prior to His martyrdom and which were coveted by Mírzá Yaḥyá. Bahá'u'lláh also asked Darvís͟h Ṣidq-'Alí, one of His faithful followers, to act as a servant in the household of Mírzá Yaḥyá. Although loath to serve the one who was in his sight the embodiment of deceit and falsehood, this devoted soul wholeheartedly obeyed Bahá'u'lláh and engaged himself in Mírzá Yaḥyá's service. Soon other circumstances relieved him of this most unpleasant task. As already mentioned, those few individuals who were weak and vacillating in their faith joined Mírzá Yaḥyá and, emboldened by the absence of Bahá'u'lláh, began their contemptible activities against the Faith of God.

Mírzá Yaḥyá and Siyyid Muḥammad started a vigorous letter-writing campaign to discredit Bahá'u'lláh in the eyes of the believers and the authorities. They loaded their letters with lies and disgraceful calumnies, accusing Bahá'u'lláh of the very crimes they themselves had committed, and disseminated them far and wide among the believers in Persia and Iraq. These slanderous letters disturbed the Bábí community and confused many. Some weaker believers lost their faith altogether; a small number were inclined towards Mírzá Yaḥyá. A few wrote to Bahá'u'lláh for clarification. As a result several Tablets were revealed in this period describing the true state of affairs. However, the majority of the believers remained faithful to the Cause of Bahá'u'lláh. These souls arose with determination and dedication to vindicate the truth of the Cause of God. Many of them, such as Nabíl-i-A'ẓam, Muníb and Aḥmad-i-Yazdí,* who travelled throughout Persia, championed the Cause of Bahá'u'lláh and defended it valiantly against the onslaught of the unfaithful.

It was through Mírzá Yaḥyá's own actions that the news of his infidelity to the Cause of God was effectively communicated to the community in Persia and signalled the permanent rupture between him and his illustrious brother. While Bahá'u'lláh had withdrawn Himself from the community in Adrianople, Siyyid Muḥammad and Mírzá Yaḥyá were actively engaged in damaging His reputation in government circles. The latter sent a petition to the governor, K͟hurs͟híd Pás͟há, and his assistant, 'Azíz Pás͟há. It was couched in obsequious language, contained false statements about Bahá'u'lláh, and was aimed at discrediting Him in the eyes of the governor who was one of His ardent admirers.

* See Taherzadeh, *Revelation of Bahá'u'lláh*, vol. 2 for accounts of these two.

Later, the governor shared this letter with Bahá'u'lláh and its contents became known to the believers. Ḥájí Mírzá Ḥaydar-'Alí,* who arrived in Adrianople a few months after this shameful episode, writes of Mírzá Yaḥyá's petition to the authorities in these words:

> When Azal arose in hostility with his satanic spirit to oppose and challenge the Blessed Beauty, through calumnies and false accusations, he wrote a letter to the Governor of Adrianople. We all saw this letter. It opened with these words: 'May my soul and body be a sacrifice to thee.' It went on to say: 'O thou 'Azíz ['Azíz Páshá], we come to you in destitution, grant us some corn.' He continues falsely to accuse the Ancient Beauty of having cut off his livelihood.
>
> The opening sentence of his letter, the statement of his needs and the complaints all demonstrate that God cannot be confused with man, and that there is no likeness between the two. We see the contrast, for instance, in these words of the Ancient Beauty as He addressed the late Sulṭán 'Abdu'l-'Azíz:† 'O thou Ra'ís [Chief], hearken to the voice of God, the Supreme Ruler, the Help in Peril, the Self-Subsisting. He verily calleth between earth and heaven and summoneth mankind to the scene of effulgent glory.'
>
> In this blessed Tablet, Bahá'u'lláh prophesies that the Sulṭán will lose his throne and the country will pass out of his hands . . . To return to our subject: Bahá'u'lláh had, through an intermediary, proved to the Governor that these allegations [by Mírzá Yaḥyá] were false and, in a message, explained to him that these calumnies were designed to hurt and humiliate Him.[149]

Concerning these distasteful events, Shoghi Effendi writes:

> He [Bahá'u'lláh] was soon after informed that this same brother [Mírzá Yaḥyá] had despatched one of his wives to the government house to complain that her husband had been cheated of his rights, and that her children were on the verge of starvation – an accusation that spread far and wide and, reaching Constantinople, became, to Bahá'u'lláh's profound distress, the subject of excited discussion and injurious comment in circles that had previously been greatly impressed by the high standard which His noble and dignified behaviour had set in that city.[150]

Some time later in a Tablet‡ to Shaykh Salmán, Bahá'u'lláh reveals the agony of His heart during this period and recounts the calumnies

---

* For his story see Taherzadeh, *Revelation of Bahá'u'lláh*, vol. 2.

† This Tablet is actually addressed to 'Alí Páshá, the Grand Vizír of the Sulṭán.

‡ See Taherzadeh, *Revelation of Bahá'u'lláh*, vol. 2, ch. 13, and vol. 1, pp. 109–13.

of Mírzá Yaḥyá concerning his share of the government allowance, which was always divided equitably between the exiles. In this Tablet Bahá'u'lláh explains that had it not been for the sake of His companions in exile, He would have never accepted any allowance from the authorities. Indeed, soon after these heart-rending events, Bahá'u'lláh refused to draw this allowance and sometimes had to sell some of His belongings in order to provide for His daily needs.

As a result of the many calumnies which were circulating in Adrianople and were extremely hurtful to Him and His loved ones, Bahá'u'lláh ended His retirement which had lasted about two months and came forward to check the misdeeds of His wicked opponents. It was at this time that Siyyid Muḥammad-i-Iṣfahání was finally and effectively expelled from the community and the parting of Bahá'u'lláh and Mírzá Yaḥyá – referred to as 'the Most Great Separation' – became official. The two-month withdrawal of Bahá'u'lláh was an act of providence in that it identified the unfaithful. When Bahá'u'lláh emerged every one of the exiles knew to which side he belonged. The few gathered around Mírzá Yaḥyá intensified their evil activities and spread their shameful calumnies further to the heart of the Ottoman Empire, poisoning the minds of the Grand Vizír and the Sulṭán against Bahá'u'lláh.

The announcement by Bahá'u'lláh of 'the Most Great Separation' had an electrifying effect on the community of believers in Persia. The great majority of the followers of the Báb, estimated by Ḥájí Mírzá Ḥaydar-'Alí in his immortal *Bihjatu'ṣ-Ṣudúr* to be about 99 percent, embraced the Cause of Bahá'u'lláh. From that time onward those who followed Mírzá Yaḥyá were identified as the breakers of the Covenant of the Báb and became known as Azalís, after Mírzá Yaḥyá's title Ṣubḥ-i-Azal. At the same time the followers of Bahá'u'lláh were designated as the people of Bahá, the Bahá'ís.

The separation between Bahá'u'lláh and Mírzá Yaḥyá was a clear signal for the followers of Bahá'u'lláh to dissociate themselves from Mírzá Yaḥyá and those who had gathered around him. Mírzá Yaḥyá was now living with his family in a separate house and Siyyid Muḥammad was among the Muslims. For about 18 months these two continued to devise ways and means of discrediting Bahá'u'lláh and His faithful companions. They spread calumnies and falsehoods among the citizens of Adrianople and the authorities in Istanbul, all aimed at undermining the foundations of the Cause of God and tarnishing the good reputation and honour of its Author. In Persia, too, Mírzá Yaḥyá distributed among the believers his letters loaded with untrue stories. The confusion created by his venomous statements gave rise to much conflict and disturbance in that community.

About one-and-a-half years passed and Mírzá Yaḥyá's intrigues and machinations had reached their climax when suddenly the hand of God struck him down, brought about his doom and degraded him in the eyes of his supporters and the authorities in Adrianople. The incident that precipitated this downfall was entirely of his own making.

Siyyid Muḥammad was heavily engaged in his activities aimed at publicly discrediting Bahá'u'lláh. In the course of his plottings he came up with the idea of arranging a public confrontation between Bahá'u'lláh and Mírzá Yaḥyá. In advocating this confrontation, Siyyid Muḥammad was confident that Bahá'u'lláh would never accept such a challenge because he had observed over the years that Bahá'u'lláh usually did not seek to appear in public. He also knew of His forbearance and sin-covering attitude whenever He was confronted with those who opposed Him. For these reasons he apprised his Muslim associates of his plans.

This type of event, known in Islam as 'mubáhilih', goes back to the days of Muḥammad when a deputation of the unbelievers of Najrán in Medina challenged the Prophet to a confrontation. It is a challenge between truth and falsehood. The two parties come together face to face and it is believed that in such a confrontation the power of truth will destroy the ungodly. Siyyid Muḥammad confidently asserted to the Muslim community that whereas Mírzá Yaḥyá was ready and willing to take part in a public confrontation, Bahá'u'lláh was not.

While these wild statements were circulating in Adrianople, the believers in Persia were in a state of agitation because of Mírzá Yaḥyá's false propaganda. One of the believers from Shíráz, a certain Mír Muḥammad-i-Mukárí (driver of beasts of burden) came to Adrianople. This believer had accompanied the Báb as a caravan-driver from Baghdád to Mecca and, later, accompanied Bahá'u'lláh from Baghdád to Istanbul.

Mír Muḥammad was of the opinion that a public confrontation would help to clarify the situation. He urged Siyyid Muḥammad to induce Mírzá Yaḥyá to meet Bahá'u'lláh in a public place for all to see and he himself promised to invite Bahá'u'lláh to accept the challenge. This he did and Bahá'u'lláh responded positively to his request. Shoghi Effendi describes this episode:

> Foolishly assuming that his illustrious Brother would never countenance such a proposition, Mírzá Yaḥyá appointed the mosque of Sulṭán Salím as the place for their encounter. No sooner had Bahá'u'lláh been informed of this arrangement than He set forth, on foot, in the heat of midday, and accompanied by this same Mír Muḥammad, for the afore-mentioned mosque, which was situated

in a distant part of the city, reciting, as He walked, through the streets and markets, verses, in a voice and in a manner that greatly astonished those who saw and heard Him.

'O Muḥammad!', are some of the words He uttered on that memorable occasion, as testified by Himself in a Tablet, 'He Who is the Spirit hath, verily, issued from His habitation, and with Him have come forth the souls of God's chosen ones and the realities of His Messengers. Behold, then, the dwellers of the realms on high above Mine head, and all the testimonies of the Prophets in My grasp. Say: Were all the divines, all the wise men, all the kings and rulers on earth to gather together, I, in very truth, would confront them, and would proclaim the verses of God, the Sovereign, the Almighty, the All-Wise. I am He Who feareth no one, though all who are in heaven and all who are on earth rise up against Me . . . This is Mine hand which God hath turned white for all the worlds to behold. This is My staff; were We to cast it down, it would, of a truth, swallow up all created things.' Mír Muḥammad, who had been sent ahead to announce Bahá'u'lláh's arrival, soon returned, and informed Him that he who had challenged His authority wished, owing to unforeseen circumstances, to postpone for a day or two the interview. Upon His return to His house Bahá'u'lláh revealed a Tablet, wherein He recounted what had happened, fixed the time for the postponed interview, sealed the Tablet with His seal, entrusted it to Nabíl, and instructed him to deliver it to one of the new believers, Mullá Muḥammad-i-Tabrízí, for the information of Siyyid Muḥammad, who was in the habit of frequenting that believer's shop. It was arranged to demand from Siyyid Muḥammad, ere the delivery of that Tablet, a sealed note pledging Mírzá Yaḥyá, in the event of failing to appear at the trysting-place, to affirm in writing that his claims were false. Siyyid Muḥammad promised that he would produce the next day the document required, and though Nabíl, for three successive days, waited in that shop for the reply, neither did the Siyyid appear, nor was such a note sent by him. That undelivered Tablet, Nabíl, recording twenty-three years later this historic episode in his chronicle, affirms was still in his possession, 'as fresh as the day on which the Most Great Branch had penned it, and the seal of the Ancient Beauty had sealed and adorned it', a tangible and irrefutable testimony to Bahá'u'lláh's established ascendancy over a routed opponent.[151]

Ḥájí Mírzá Ḥaydar-'Alí, the celebrated Bahá'í teacher, was in Adrianople at the time and recounts the events as he witnessed them on that memorable day. The following is a summary translation of his memoirs:

> The meeting was to be on Friday at the mosque of Sulṭán Salím at the time of the congregational prayer when the Muslims gather

inside in great numbers . . . Mír Muḥammad-i-Mukárí from Shíráz who was a Bábí . . . could not imagine that Azal had broken the Covenant. So he begged the Blessed Beauty to enlighten him. Bahá'u'lláh said to him that if ever Azal came face to face with Him at a meeting-place, then he could consider Azal's claims to be true. Mír Muḥammad accepted this statement as a criterion for distinguishing between truth and falsehood and he endeavoured to bring this meeting about.

The news and date of the confrontation became known among the peoples of the Muslim, Christian and Jewish religions in the city. All of them had heard of the miracles of Moses and the story of His confrontation with Pharaoh. And now they were expecting the meeting face to face in the mosque between His Holiness the Shaykh Effendi [a designation by which the people called Bahá'u'lláh to express their reverence for Him] and Mírzá 'Alí [for fear of being recognized, Azal called himself by this name], who had denied Him. Therefore, from the morning of Friday until noon, a large multitude drawn from the followers of these three religions had thronged the area between the house of Amru'lláh . . . and the entrance to the mosque. The crowd was so large that it was difficult to move about. Bahá'u'lláh, the Day-Star of Glory, emerged from His home . . . and as He passed through the crowd, people showed such reverence as is difficult to describe. They greeted Him with salutations, bowed and opened the way for Him to pass. Many of them prostrated themselves at His feet and kissed them. Bahá'u'lláh, the countenance of majesty and omnipotence, in acknowledgement greeted the crowd by raising His hands (as was customary among the Ottomans), and expressed His good wishes. This continued all the way to the mosque. As soon as He entered the mosque, the preacher, who was delivering his discourse, became speechless or perhaps he forgot his words. Bahá'u'lláh went forward, seated Himself and then gave permission for the preacher to continue. Eventually the preaching and prayers came to an end. But Azal did not turn up. We heard that he had feigned illness and asked to be excused.

. . . When Bahá'u'lláh was about to leave the mosque He said: 'We owe a visit to the Mawlavís. We had better go to their takyih.' As He rose to go, the Governor of Adrianople and other dignitaries, together with the divines, availed themselves of the opportunity to be in His presence and so they accompanied Him. As a token of their humility and courtesy, the Governor, the Shaykhu'l-Islám, the 'ulamá [divines and men of learning] and other dignitaries walked four or five steps behind Bahá'u'lláh while the stream of His utterance was flowing. Sometimes, through His grace and loving-kindness, Bahá'u'lláh would stop and beckon the Governor

> and the others to walk in front.* But they would refuse to do so. In this way, with majesty and glory born of God, Bahá'u'lláh arrived in the takyih.[152]

Mírzá Yaḥyá was now discredited in the eyes of many in Adrianople. In Persia the news of this episode spread among the believers. A Tablet known as Lawḥ-i-Mubáhilih, addressed to Mullá Ṣádiq-i-Khurásání and describing this event, reached the Bahá'í community in that land and caused some wavering souls among the friends to recognize the power and majesty of Bahá'u'lláh in breaking up, once and for all, this great 'idol' of the Bábí community.

This dramatic downfall of Mírzá Yaḥyá was, as testified by Shoghi Effendi, clearly foretold by St Paul in the following passage:

> Let no man deceive you by any means; for [that day shall not come], except there come a falling away first, and that man of sin be revealed, the son of perdition; who opposeth and exalteth himself above all that is called God, or that is worshipped; so that he as God sitteth in the temple of God, showing himself that he is God . . .
>
> And then shall that Wicked be revealed, whom the Lord shall consume with the spirit of His mouth, and shall destroy with the brightness of His coming . . .[153]

The downfall of this perfidious figure who betrayed his Lord and rose up against Him coincided with an unprecedented outpouring from the Supreme Pen. The verses of God were sent down in great profusion and resulted, soon afterwards, in the proclamation of His Message to the kings and rulers of the world.

The casting out of Mírzá Yaḥyá and his followers from the community of the Most Great Name brought about his gradual downfall and ultimate extinction in later years. In the summer of 1868 the edict of Sulṭán 'Abdu'l-'Azíz, which condemned Bahá'u'lláh to life-long imprisonment in the fortress-city of 'Akká in the Holy Land, sent Mírzá Yaḥyá to the island of Cyprus. There he was confined in the city of Famagusta until 1878 when the island passed from Turkish to British rule. He then decided to remain in Cyprus and receive a pension from the British government, living freely on that island until his death in 1912. During this time he achieved nothing significant.

---

* When an important person walked, it was considered discourteous if his subordinates walked in front of, or abreast of, him except at night, when someone would carry a lantern before him. In order to show their humility, subordinates always walked a few steps behind. For example, this is how the oriental believers conducted themselves when they were walking with Bahá'u'lláh, 'Abdu'l-Bahá or Shoghi Effendi.

'Abdu'l-Bahá, in one of His talks, describes how in all these years Mírzá Yaḥyá did not succeed in converting a single soul on that island to his cause. Instead he spent his life in the company of his many wives and was father to several ill-bred children of low intelligence and capacity.

4–WT At last, he wrought that which caused the Day-Star of the world to be sent an exile to this, the Most Great Prison, and sorely wronged, and in the West of this Great Prison He did set.

The circumstances that brought about the exile of Bahá'u'lláh to the Most Great Prison in 'Akká are briefly described in chapter 8.

One of the main contributory factors prompting 'Álí-Pás͟há, the Grand Vizír, to submit to the Sulṭán his recommendation for Bahá'u-'lláh's exile, was the exaggerated reports and falsehoods he received from Mírzá Yaḥyá and Siyyid Muḥammad. Their campaign of misrepresentation, lasting almost 18 months, included letters from Mírzá Yaḥyá to government officials. These were filled with calumnies confirmed by a constant flow of anonymous letters written by Siyyid Muḥammad and his accomplice, Áqá Ján Big, known as Kaj Kuláh, and were all aimed at discrediting Bahá'u'lláh. They perverted the writings of Bahá'u'lláh and accused Him, among other things, of having conspired, with the aid of His Persian followers, with the Bulgarian leaders and high-ranking officials of certain European powers, to conquer Constantinople and overthrow the government. Such preposterous claims alarmed the authorities and hastened their resolve to banish Bahá'u'lláh to the prison city of 'Akká where they thought His Cause would die away and be consigned to oblivion forever!

12

The Arch-Breaker of the Covenant of Bahá'u'lláh

5–WT O ye that stand fast and firm in the Covenant! The Centre of Sedition, the Prime Mover of mischief, Mírzá Muḥammad 'Alí, hath passed out from under the shadow of the Cause, hath broken the Covenant . . .

In many of His Tablets, as in His Will and Testament, 'Abdu'l-Bahá has referred to His half-brother Mírzá Muḥammad-'Alí as the Centre of Sedition, the Prime Mover of Mischief and the Arch-breaker of the Covenant of Bahá'u'lláh. These designations indicate that it was he who, immediately after the passing of Bahá'u'lláh, initiated the act of Covenant-breaking, was the motivating force misleading many believers and was the one who, for over half a century, led the Covenant-breakers against 'Abdu'l-Bahá and Shoghi Effendi.

Ambition for leadership of the Bahá'í community is the most common feature of those who have violated the Covenant. In the case of Mírzá Muḥammad-'Alí, an excessive lust for leadership so possessed him that he was driven to commit acts of infamy and crime in his struggle to wrest the reins of the Cause of God from 'Abdu'l-Bahá. Another factor contributing greatly to his downfall was the uncontrollable jealousy he entertained in his heart for 'Abdu'l-Bahá. A feeling of inferiority in relation to Him had been engendered in his mind from childhood, mainly through the resentful attitude which his mother, Mahd-i-'Ulyá, showed towards 'Abdu'l-Bahá. The fire of jealousy burning in his heart intensified as a result of the outpouring of Bahá'u'lláh's abundant favours upon the one He designated as the Master when 'Abdu'l-Bahá was in His early teens in Baghdád. The many expressions of praise and glorification flowing from the Pen of Bahá'u'lláh as He extolled the virtues and superhuman qualities of 'Abdu'l-Bahá, whom He appointed as the Centre of His Covenant and the Interpreter of His words, aggravated the feeling of enmity towards 'Abdu'l-Bahá which Mírzá Muḥammad-'Alí had concealed in his heart.

Indeed, one of the reasons that 'Abdu'l-Bahá did not join Bahá'u'lláh when He moved His residence from 'Akká to the Mansion of

Mazra'ih and then to Bahjí was to ensure that by staying away from Bahá'u'lláh the fire of jealousy in Mírzá Muḥammad-'Alí's heart would be somewhat dampened. Bahá'u'lláh always cherished being close to 'Abdu'l-Bahá and whenever the Master came to visit Him, Bahá'u'lláh would show great excitement and, in glowing terms, would extol His station. On these occasions the radiance of His countenance betrayed such adoration and love towards the Master that the sincere believers became joyful and the few unfaithful became envious and dispirited.

During the lifetime of Bahá'u'lláh, Mírzá Muḥammad-'Alí and his mother, brothers and sisters were all subdued by His authority and kept under control through His loving exhortations. In those days, Mírzá Muḥammad-'Alí, as a son of Bahá'u'lláh, was highly respected by the believers and basked in the sunshine of his father's majesty and greatness. His insincerity and lack of spirituality were apparent, however, to some of the believers who were endowed with insight and pure hearts. One such example is drawn from *Khaṭirát-i-Málmírí*, the memoirs of Ḥájí Muḥammad-Ṭáhir-i-Málmírí,* when he describes his arrival in 'Akká around 1878 and his first meeting with Mírzá Muḥammad-'Alí:

> When we† arrived in Haifa . . . we were taken to the home of Áqá Muḥammad-Ibráhím-i-Káshání. He was directed by Bahá'u'lláh to make his residence in Haifa, to handle the distribution of letters and to give assistance and hospitality to Bahá'í pilgrims. When Bahá'u'lláh was informed that the three of us had arrived, He advised, through Mírzá Áqá Ján . . . that in 'Akká I should stay with my brother Ḥájí 'Alí.‡ We were driven from Haifa to 'Akká in 'Abdu'l-Bahá's carriage. I was taken to Ḥájí 'Alí's residence, which was situated in the Khán-i-Súq-i-Abiyaḍ (White Market), in close proximity to the residence of Mírzá Músá, Bahá'u'lláh's brother, and several other Bahá'ís such as Nabíl-i-A'ẓam . . . That day I was most happy. Joy and ecstasy filled my soul. The next day, Mírzá Muḥammad-'Alí, accompanied by his two brothers, Mírzá Ḍíyá'u-'lláh and Mírzá Badí'u'lláh, came to Nabíl-i-A'ẓam's quarters to meet me. Very eagerly my brother and I went there to meet them. But no sooner had I met Mírzá Muḥammad-'Alí and Badí'u'lláh than I became depressed and all the joy in my heart was transformed into sadness and grief. I was distressed . . . and bitterly disappointed with myself. I was wondering what had happened so suddenly that, in spite of all the eagerness and excitement which had filled my

* The father of the author. For a brief account of his life see Taherzadeh, *Revelation of Bahá'u'lláh*, vol. 1.

† Ḥájí Muḥammad-Ṭáhir and two of his fellow pilgrims.

‡ See *Bahá'í World*, vol. 9, pp. 624–5.

being on arrival in 'Akká, I had become so utterly gloomy and dispirited. I was convinced at that time that I had been rejected by God . . .

I was plunged into such a state of distress and anguish that I wanted to leave that gathering forthwith but did not dare to do so. In my heart I was communing with God . . . anxiously waiting for the visitors to leave so that I could go out and try to find a solution for my sad condition. I noticed that whereas my brother and Nabíl-i-A'ẓam were enjoying themselves talking most happily with these sons of Bahá'u'lláh, I was in a state of mental turmoil and agony throughout the meeting . . . After about an hour, when the visitors were leaving, my brother thanked them most warmly and joyfully.

In the evening he informed me that we were to go and attain the presence of the Master in His reception room. Although depressed and grief-stricken as a result of meeting Mírzá Muḥammad-'Alí, I went with him. As soon as I came into the presence of the Most Great Branch, a new life was breathed into me. My whole being was filled with such joy and felicity that all the agonies and disturbances of the past vanished in an instant.

A few days later my brother invited me to go with him to meet Mírzá Muḥammad-'Alí again, but in spite of much persuasion on his part I refused to go . . . During the period that I stayed in 'Akká, Mírzá Muḥammad-'Alí came several times to the residence of Nabíl-i-A'ẓam but I always found some excuse not to go there.

The breaking of the Covenant by Mírzá Muḥammad-'Alí began immediately after the passing of Bahá'u'lláh. Indeed, 28 May 1892 marks the beginning of the most turbulent period within the Bahá'í community, which witnessed the onslaught of the unfaithful against the Cause on a far greater scale than any so far encountered in the course of its eventful history, including the rebellion of Mírzá Yaḥyá. The blessed remains of Bahá'u'lláh were not yet laid to rest when Mírzá Muḥammad-'Alí revealed his true self. Until then he had given the appearance of being loyal to his father and to 'Abdu'l-Bahá but now he launched his ignoble plans to undermine the foundation of the Covenant and overthrow 'Abdu'l-Bahá, its Centre.

In a celebrated Tablet, the Lawḥ-i-Hizár Baytí (Tablet of One Thousand Verses) 'Abdu'l-Bahá describes the grievous events which occurred immediately before and just after the ascension of Bahá'u'lláh. He states that during the days of Bahá'u'lláh's illness, He, 'Abdu'l-Bahá, was in attendance on His blessed person by day and by night, most of the time in a state of deep sorrow and depression. One day as He lay in His sick-bed, Bahá'u'lláh ordered 'Abdu'l-Bahá to gather all of His papers that were in the room and place them in two special cases. It was Bahá'u'lláh's practice that whenever He left the Mansion for 'Akká or elsewhere, He would put all His papers in these large cases. Aware of the implications of this command, 'Abdu'l-Bahá was shaken to the very depths of His being. As He hesitated to comply, Bahá'u'lláh reiterated His orders. With trembling hands and tearful eyes, 'Abdu'l-Bahá was beginning to gather the papers when Majdu'd-Dín entered the room.

Majdu'd-Dín was a son of Bahá'u'lláh's faithful brother Áqáy-i-Kalím but he was utterly different from his father. The most treacherous among the family, he was 'Abdu'l-Bahá's most formidable enemy. Indeed, as we shall see later, he was the backbone, if not the principal instigator, of Mírzá Muḥammad-'Alí, the Arch-breaker of the Covenant of Bahá'u'lláh.

In the Lawḥ-i-Hizár Baytí, 'Abdu'l-Bahá describes the agony of His heart as He forced Himself to gather Bahá'u'lláh's papers. Seeing Majdu'd-Dín, He asked for his assistance so that this task, so extremely painful to Him, might soon be finished. When all the papers, the seals and other items had been locked into the cases, Bahá'u'lláh said to 'Abdu'l-Bahá, 'These two now belong to you.' These words, implying the approach of the final hours of Bahá'u'lláh's earthly life, pierced 'Abdu'l- Bahá's heart like an arrow.

When the ascension took place, 'Abdu'l-Bahá's grief knew no bounds. The shock He sustained as a result of this calamitous event was so intense that He found it difficult to describe. He says that in the morning, along with His brother, He began the task of preparing the remains for burial. When they were about to wash Bahá'u'lláh's blessed body, Mírzá Muḥammad-'Alí suggested to 'Abdu'l-Bahá that since the floor would become wet, it would be better to move the two cases into Badí'u'lláh's room. 'Abdu'l-Bahá was at that point in such a state of shock and grief that He was almost unconscious of His surroundings. He never thought that behind this suggestion could be a treacherous plot designed to rob Him of that precious trust.

He agreed, and the two cases were taken out and that was the last He saw of them.

The sacred remains were laid to rest that same day. 'Abdu'l-Bahá was disconsolate and heartbroken. He says that for three consecutive days and nights He could not rest a single moment. He wept for hours and was in a state of unbearable grief. The Light of the World had disappeared from His sight and all around Him had been plunged into darkness. On the fourth night after the ascension, He arose from His bed around midnight and walked a few steps, hoping that it might help to bring a measure of tranquillity to His agonized heart. As He began to pace the room, He saw through the window a scene His eyes could scarcely believe. His unfaithful brothers had opened the cases and were looking through Bahá'u'lláh's papers – those papers that had been entrusted to Him!

'Abdu'l-Bahá was deeply disturbed by the treachery of His brothers so soon after the ascension of their father. This act of unfaithfulness, committed so dishonourably against the most sacred trust of God, inflicted further pain and suffering upon His sorrow-laden heart. He returned to His bed immediately after this incident, for He did not wish His brothers to know He had seen them interfering with the contents of the cases. At this point 'Abdu'l-Bahá thought that since His brothers had not seen the Will and Testament of Bahá'u'lláh, which was in 'Abdu'l-Bahá's possession, they were trying to find some document among His writings with which to justify their intended action of undermining the foundation of the Cause of God and creating a division within the ranks of its avowed supporters. However, 'Abdu'l-Bahá hoped that when they saw the Will and Testament, their efforts would be frustrated and they would then return His trust to Him.

But alas, this did not happen! The Kitáb-i-'Aḥd was read by Áqá Riḍáy-i-Qannád* on the ninth day after the ascension of Bahá'u'lláh in the presence of nine witnesses chosen from among Bahá'u'lláh's companions and members of His family, including Mírzá Muḥammad-'Alí. On the afternoon of the same day it was read by Majdu'd-Dín in the Shrine of Bahá'u'lláh before a large company of the friends, consisting of the Aghṣán, the Afnán, the pilgrims and resident believers. 'Abdu'l-Bahá says that after the Kitáb-i-'Ahd was read and its contents noted, some rejoiced with exceeding gladness and some grieved with great sorrow. The faces of the faithful were illumined with the light of joy and those of the falsehearted were covered in the dust of despondency and gloom. On that day, 'Abdu'l-Bahá states, the foundations of Covenant-breaking were laid, the ocean of vain imagining began to surge, and the fire of dissension and strife was lit, its flame burning more fiercely with the passage of time and consuming the hearts and souls of the faithful in its tormenting heat.

Soon after the reading of the Kitáb-i-'Ahd, one of the Afnán asked 'Abdu'l-Bahá to use one of Bahá'u'lláh's seals on a Tablet which had been revealed by Bahá'u'lláh in his honour. When 'Abdu'l-Bahá asked His brothers to give Him the seals which had been placed in the two cases, they pleaded ignorance, saying they did not know anything about the cases! Bewildered and perplexed by such a remark, 'Abdu'l-Bahá was plunged further into sorrow and grief. He describes how His whole being began to tremble when He heard such a response from His brothers and He knew that great tests and trials lay ahead.

---

* For a brief account of his life see Taherzadeh, *Revelation of Bahá'u'lláh*, vol. 2.

Indeed the Kitáb-i-'Ahd had the same effect on the believers as an examination paper does on pupils: they were divided into two categories, those who pass and those who fail. Those who remained faithful to its sacred provisions rose to exalted realms of certitude and entered the ark of salvation. Those who violated the provisions were spiritually cast out of the community and returned to the deadly abodes of their own selves and passions.

Although the violation of the Covenant of Bahá'u'lláh began in earnest immediately after His ascension, 'Abdu'l-Bahá tried very hard to stop the foul odour of Covenant-breaking from spreading among the believers of the East and the West. He succeeded, through painstaking effort; the news of the Covenant-breakers' defection was not made public for about four years.

This four-year lapse was made possible because the rebellion was at first covert and only those who were close to the Holy Family were aware of it. As the years went by Mírzá Muḥammad-'Alí became more vociferous in his opposition and the news of his dissension gradually leaked out. During these four years 'Abdu'l-Bahá instructed that all letters written by the believers in the Holy Land addressed to the friends in Persia were to be submitted to Him for approval. He usually placed His seal on the letters if the contents met with His approval. Even most of the dissidents used to comply. In this way 'Abdu'l-Bahá tried to contain the deadly disease of Covenant-breaking within the Holy Land. During this period He also made every effort to guide these misguided souls to the straight path of truth. He even intimated to Mírzá Muḥammad-'Alí that since Bahá'u'lláh had appointed him to succeed 'Abdu'l-Bahá he could achieve his heart's desire at a later time.* But Mirza Muḥammad-'Alí is reported have responded: 'How can I be sure that I shall survive you?'

Unfortunately, the more 'Abdu'l-Bahá showered loving counsel upon the Covenant-breakers, the more haughty and rebellious they became. At last it was they themselves who announced their rebellion by distributing their messages of calumny and falsehood to the believers in the East. They made subtle remarks in their letters to Persia designed to undermine the faith of the believers in the person of 'Abdu'l-Bahá. The following is a summary translation of an account given by Ḥájí Mírzá Ḥaydar-'Alí, that renowned teacher of the Faith of Bahá'u'lláh, of a letter he received in Persia from Muḥammad-

* For the significance and far-reaching consequences of this appointment by Bahá'u'lláh see chapter 26.

Javád-i-Qazvíní,* one of the Covenant-breakers resident in the Holy Land.

> Since the days of Bahá'u'lláh in Adrianople I had a close relationship with Muḥammad-Javád-i-Qazvíní. He was my correspondent through whom I used to dispatch my letters to His Holy Presence. I received a confidential letter from Javád [during the early years of 'Abdu'l-Bahá's ministry] in which he advised me that in my letters to the friends, I should not write the usual words 'May my life be a sacrifice for you' nor begin my letters [to 'Abdu'l-Bahá] with words of praise or supplication to Him. Neither should I address them to any single Ghuṣn [Branch], instead they should be addressed to the Aghṣán [Branches]. This letter indicated to me that some form of secret opposition to the Centre of the Covenant was taking place and that Muḥammad-Javád himself was one of the dissidents. . .
>
> In reply I wrote him a letter in which I rejected his proposals and stated that unless 'Abdu'l-Bahá made such a demand, I would not pay any attention to such advice. I also told him not to write to me again. Since Muḥammad-Javád did not respond to my letter I was assured that the birds of darkness were on the move and the clamour of the foreboders of evil would be heard soon. I felt certain that Javád and Jamál-i-Burújirdí† were both secretly involved, so with all my heart and soul I used to pray on their behalf so that they might return to the path of truth. I kept this matter confidential, but it never occurred to me that the source of sedition was Mírzá Muḥammad-'Alí along with other members of Bahá'u'lláh's family because I did not think they were so foolish and egotistical.[154]

Soon after these developments, Ḥájí Mírzá Ḥaydar-'Alí, with 'Abdu'l-Bahá's permission, proceeded to the Holy Land. En route he visited the believers in many towns and villages including Ishqábád, Bákú, Nakhjaván, Ganjih and Tiflís (Tbilisi). Everywhere he found the believers steadfast in the Covenant, enchanted by the utterances of 'Abdu'l-Bahá in His Tablets and serving the Faith with enthusiasm and devotion. Being assured in his heart that severe tests and trials were about to engulf the community, Ḥájí encouraged the believers to turn with heart and soul to no one but the Master, to regard His words and utterances to be as valid as the words of Bahá'u'lláh Himself and to refrain from any action which ran counter to His good-pleasure. The loving counsels of Ḥájí were warmly welcomed everywhere and the

---

* See chapter 13.

† A teacher of the Cause who rebelled against the Covenant. See Taherzadeh, *Covenant of Bahá'u'lláh*, pp. 308–25.

believers vowed to remain steadfast in the Covenant, come what might.

When Ḥájí arrived in Beirut he stayed with a devoted believer, Áqá Muḥammad-Muṣṭafáy-i-Baghdádí, who intimated to him the opposition and rebellion of Mírzá Muḥammad-'Alí and a few others, contained so far by 'Abdu'l-Bahá within the family and a small circle of friends. Immediately upon his arrival at the pilgrim house in 'Akká, Ḥájí wrote a letter to the Master. In his memoirs he talks about his letter, tells the story of attaining the presence of 'Abdu'l-Bahá and of other events associated with his pilgrimage during those turbulent months. This is a summary translation of his reminiscences:

> In this letter I stated that I do not turn to anybody except the Master and I do not wish to meet with any believer except those whom the Beloved wishes me to meet. Even praying at the Holy Shrine of Bahá'u'lláh and circumambulating that exalted spot around which circle in adoration the Concourse on high, are dependent on the will of the Master. Praise and thanksgiving be to God that on the day of my arrival I was given the privilege of praying at and circumambulating the Shrine in the presence of 'Abdu'l-Bahá who chanted the Tablet of Visitation Himself. In what a radiant condition I found myself and to what heights of spirituality I was carried as a result of this experience are impossible for me to describe. With my inner eyes I saw the Heavenly Kingdom, witnessed the Blessed Beauty, exalted be His glory, seated upon the Throne of His majesty and authority, and was assured of the penetration of His Holy Word in the hearts of men . . .
>
> Through the flattery and empty compliments of some hypocrites, Mírzá Muḥammad-'Alí, in the prime of his youth, entertained the thought of rebellion, cherished the inordinate ambition of becoming great, and lusted for leadership . . . and a few others were watering the tree of his rebelliousness. They were secretly engaged in intrigues and satanic ambitions. Some believers were aware of their condition but for the sake of God they did not reveal it. This situation continued until the last years of the ministry of the Day-Star of the World [Bahá'u'lláh], when Muḥammad-Javád-i-Qazvíní and Jamál-i-Burújirdí secretly united with Mírzá Muḥammad-'Alí in their plots to create discord and dissension within the community. They succeeded in enlisting a few others within their fold. These two men convinced Mírzá Muḥammad-'Alí that since the bulk of the believers in Persia were looking up to them, he would become the one to whom all would turn and he could present himself as the Centre of the Cause. Their deceitfulness and hypocrisy were fully disclosed through their misdeeds after the setting of the Sun of Truth . . .
>
> These insinuations continued until the believers noticed that 'Abdu'l-Bahá treated Mírzá Muḥammad-'Alí with much greater respect than at the time of Bahá'u'lláh. On the other hand, the

Arch-breaker of the Covenant and his entourage had considerably lessened the measure of honour and respect that they humbly used to show the Master in the days of the Blessed Beauty. Added to this treatment, the Covenant-breakers through their words and deeds and by subtle hints were attempting to belittle the Master and to dishonour Him. When the believers realized this, they kept away from the unfaithful and as far as possible did not seek to associate with them in private.

Two devoted believers, Áqá Muḥammad-Riḍáy-i-Shírází and Mírzá Maḥmúd-i-Kashání, went together to meet Mírzá Muḥammad-'Alí. They showed the utmost respect to him, and in a spirit of humility and loving kindness counselled him with genuine concern. By giving some hints or relating certain stories, they conveyed to him the dire consequences of his rebellion. But instead of taking to heart their admonitions and heeding their loving advice to change his ways, he was hurt that they counselled him in this manner.

The Master continued to overlook Mírzá Muḥammad-'Alí's wrongdoings and treated him with the utmost love and kindness in spite of his rebellion. Whereas in the days of the Blessed Beauty Mírzá Muḥammad-'Alí showed so much respect to 'Abdu'l-Bahá that he would not take a seat in His presence without His permission, now it was different; it was the Master who as a sign of loving respect would arise from His seat when he or his associates arrived in a gathering. At first 'Abdu'l-Bahá's counsels were given to them in private, through hints and suggestions which pointed the way to their everlasting salvation and glory. But since through their rebellion they gradually tore apart the veil which had until then concealed their wrongdoings, the Master began to counsel them publicly in words such as these: 'Do not by your actions quench the fire and extinguish the light of God. Take not a step that would lead to the degradation of the Word of God. Do not behave in such a way as to cause the enemies to rejoice and the loved ones to lament.'* 'Abdu'l-Bahá warned them lovingly and repeatedly about the dire consequences of their evil doings but all these counsels fell on deaf ears and they followed the path of pride, hate and rebellion.

About three months after my arrival in the Holy Land, the Master sent me to Egypt. Since 'Abdu'l-Bahá had warned the friends not to discuss the rebellion of Mírzá Muḥammad-'Alí, I addressed a letter to him when I was in Egypt, the gist of which was as follows: 'The people of Bahá expected that after the setting of the Sun of Truth, you would show the same measure of humility, submissiveness and obedience to the Centre of the Covenant that you demonstrated in the Holy Presence of Bahá'u'lláh. We have all observed that in the days of the Blessed Beauty, you would not have

* These are not the exact words of 'Abdu'l-Bahá but they convey the gist of what He said on that occasion.

taken your seat in the presence of the Master without His permission. Each time that He came to Bahjí to attain the presence of His beloved Father, you along with others, as commanded by Bahá'u-'lláh, went as a welcoming party as far as the Garden of Jammál* to greet Him. Now we see that when any one of you arrives in the room, it is the Master who as a token of respect for you arises from His seat and will not sit down until the person takes his seat. We have also noticed that when His Blessed Person arrives at Bahjí after having walked all the way from 'Akká as a token of His utter humility to the sacred Threshold,† not only do you refuse to go out to welcome Him but after He enters the Sacred Shrine, those who are in your company come down the steps of the Mansion slowly one by one and go towards the Shrine, and you yourself are the last one to appear. Again, when He has come out of the Shrine and is about to depart for 'Akká, you walk away towards the Mansion before being dismissed from His presence.‡ Indeed, you are back inside the Mansion before He leaves. Now that you do not go to welcome Him at the entrance of the Garden of Jammál, you could at least ask permission to leave His presence or wait outside the Shrine until He departs.

'In the past you always addressed Him as "the Master" but now refer to Him as "my brother". We are surprised and do not know the reason for all this humiliating treatment to which you have subjected His blessed Person. Is your contemptuousness because of all the services that He has rendered to the Cause and to the Person of the Blessed Beauty? Or is it because He was the One who brought about your exaltation and honour among the people and enabled you to live in the utmost comfort and luxury? While you enjoyed a life of pleasure and engaged in pastimes such as hunting and other recreations, His blessed Person did not have a moment to rest. Do you behave towards Him in a disdainful manner because it was He who, from the early days of the rising of the Day-Star of the World [Bahá'u'lláh] from the horizon of Ṭihrán and Iraq was the Master and the leader of all the people of Bahá? Or is your behaviour towards Him due to all the sufferings and hardships that were, and are, being inflicted upon His blessed Person from every quarter? He has stood up with the utmost firmness and strength in resisting the onslaught of the enemy and has, singly and alone, exerted every effort in the promotion of the

---

* Properties lying at the south entrance to the Mansion.

† It is an expression of humility and self-effacement for a servant to walk to his master rather than to ride.

‡ It was considered highly discourteous for a man to take his seat in the presence of an eminent person without his permission. Similarly, it was discourteous to leave his presence before being dismissed. The believers always observed the utmost courtesy when they came into the presence of Bahá'u'lláh, 'Abdu'l-Bahá and Shoghi Effendi.

word of God and the diffusion of its fragrances, while you are conducting a life of luxury and spending your time in riding and sightseeing. Does the particular text of the Kitáb-i-Aqdas which was later confirmed in the Kitáb-i-'Ahd, that all the Aghṣán must turn to Him, and gird up their loins in His obedience, provide justification for you to belittle His exalted station?

'Besides all this, when this servant and other believers notice the extraordinary loving kindness and humility the Centre of the Covenant shows to you, while you appear proud and haughty before His peerless and incomparable Person, what conclusion do we reach? In the light of all this, whom should we regard as a true believer in the Blessed Beauty and whom should we consider steadfast in His Covenant?

'The believers have endured all manner of oppression. They have suffered imprisonment and exile and been inflicted with hardship and persecution. These souls will not deviate from the straight path. They will cling fast to the Covenant of Bahá'u'lláh and its Centre, He "who hath branched from this Ancient Root". They will not loosen their hold on that "excellent and priceless heritage" which Bahá'u'lláh has bequeathed to His heirs . . .'[155]

As the years passed, the clandestine opposition to 'Abdu'l-Bahá gathered further momentum. Soon after his violation of the Covenant, Muḥammad-'Alí established secret links with Jamál-i-Burújirdí and a few others in Persia. Together they designed a strategy which was kept secret until, at a propitious time, they would make their rebellion public and divide the community. While the rank and file of the believers in Persia were not fully informed of what was happening in the Holy Land during this four-year period, a number of prominent Bahá'ís felt that there was a serious problem at the World Centre of the Faith. Some decided not to make any statements concerning the situation, except that they remained steadfast in the Covenant and adhered to the provision of the Kitáb-i-'Ahd, the Will and Testament of Bahá'u'lláh. Notable among them was the renowned scholar of the Faith Mírzá Abu'l-Faḍl. For a few years, he, who used to write profusely to defend the Faith or to expound its teachings for the believers and others, refused to make a statement about the affairs of the Cause. Later he explained the reason for his silence on the matter, saying that he was waiting for 'Abdu'l-Bahá, the Centre of the Covenant, to make a statement, fearing that one word uttered by him could be the wrong one and might harm the Faith.

In His Will and Testament, 'Abdu'l-Bahá states:

49–WT When, in all parts of the earth, the enemies of God profiting by the passing away of the Sun of Truth, suddenly and with all their might launched their attack; at such a time and in

the midst of so great a calamity, the Covenant-breakers arose with the utmost cruelty, intent upon harm and the stirring up of the spirit of enmity. At every moment a misdeed they did commit and bestirred themselves to sow the seeds of grievous sedition, and to ruin the edifice of the Covenant. But this wronged one, this prisoner, did his utmost to hide and veil their doings, that haply they might regret and repent. His long-suffering and forbearance of these evil deeds, however, made the rebellious ones still more arrogant and daring; until, through leaflets written with their own hands, they sowed the seeds of doubt, printing these leaflets and scattering them broadcast throughout the world, believing that such foolish doings would bring to naught the Covenant and the Testament.

32–WT Adversities have waxed still more severe as they rose with unbearable cruelty to overpower and crush me, as they scattered far and wide their scrolls of doubt and in utter falsehood hurled their calumnies upon me.

As previously stated, for four years 'Abdu'l-Bahá did everything in His power to guide these people to the straight path and He did not reveal their breaking of the Covenant to the Bahá'ís outside the Holy Land. However, after four years of strengthening their position, Mírzá Muḥammad-'Alí and his party felt that it was time to unmask themselves. They did this by printing letters loaded with falsehoods, misleading statements and calumnies against the Centre of the Covenant, casting themselves as the voice of truth trying to purify the Cause which they shamelessly claimed to have been polluted by those who were faithful to 'Abdu'l-Bahá. In his propaganda, Mírzá Muḥammad-'Alí did not contest the authenticity of the Kitáb-i-'Ahd, rather he expressed his grievance that he had been barred from partnership with 'Abdu'l-Bahá in directing the affairs of the Cause. He wanted to share with Him the station of the Centre of the Covenant.

As a result of these letters by Mírzá Muḥammad-'Alí, 'Abdu'l-Bahá in His Tablets began openly to refer to the breaking of the Covenant by His unfaithful brother; from then on, right up to the end of His life, He explained in innumerable Tablets the significance of the Covenant, expelled the Covenant-breakers from the community of the Most Great Name and urged the friends to remain steadfast in the Cause of God.

Concerning the dispatch for the first time of Mírzá Muḥammad-'Alí's letters to Persia, Dr Yúnis Khán-i-Afrúkhtih, one of the faithful secretaries of the Master, relates the following story.

'Abdu'l-Bahá often used to say: 'One day Mírzá Ḍíyá'u'lláh came to see Me. I noticed he was looking at his fingers which were

> stained with ink and was expecting Me to comment on them. I did not say anything, so he himself volunteered the information, saying, "Last night until the early hours of the morning we were engaged in writing letters and gelatine printing, consequently my fingers have been stained. My brother [Mírzá Muḥammad-'Alí] had written a letter of which we printed several copies and sent them away this morning." I asked him: Did you really write and dispatch them? And when he answered in the affirmative, I said: I swear by the Righteousness of God, a day shall come when Mírzá Muḥammad-'Alí would wish that his fingers had been cut off so that he could not have taken the pen to announce his breaking of the Covenant. For four years I have concealed this matter so that the beloved of God might not learn of your unfaithfulness to the Covenant. It is now beyond my power to conceal it any longer. You have announced yourselves to the believers.'[156]

The timing of the public announcement of the Covenant-breakers' rebellion was no doubt influenced by their apparent success in converting a considerable number to their side, as well as the encouragement they received from Jamál-i-Burújirdí and others in Persia who were anxiously waiting and hoping to become the leaders of the community there – hopes which, through the power of the Covenant, were dashed forever.

However, for some time, Mírzá Muḥammad-'Alí used to dispatch his letters of propaganda which were stigmatized by the believers as Awráq-i-Náríyyih (the Infernal Letters). Soon after receiving the initial dispatches, the believers, as advised by the Hands of the Cause, did not open the envelopes and used to send them back to Mírzá Muḥammad-'Alí – an intelligent way to deter him from sending further letters.

13

Attacks on the Centre of the Covenant

5–WT [Mírzá Muḥammad-'Alí] hath falsified the Holy Text . . .*

5–WT . . . [Mírzá Muḥammad-'Alí] hath inflicted a grievous loss upon the true Faith of God, hath scattered His people, hath with bitter rancour endeavoured to hurt 'Abdu'l-Bahá and hath assailed with the utmost enmity this servant of the Sacred Threshold. Every dart he seized and hurled to pierce the breast of this wronged servant, no wound did he neglect to grievously inflict upon me, no venom did he spare but he poisoned therewith the life of this hapless one. I swear by the most holy Abhá Beauty and by the Light shining from His Holiness, the Exalted One (may my soul be a sacrifice for Their lowly servants), that because of this iniquity the dwellers in the Pavilion of the Abhá Kingdom have bewailed, the Celestial Concourse is lamenting, the Immortal Maids of Heaven in the All-Highest Paradise have raised their plaintive cries and the angelic company sighed and uttered their moanings.

The cruelties heaped upon 'Abdu'l-Bahá by Mírzá Muḥammad-'Alí, supported by most members of Bahá'u'lláh's family, were ruthless and unrelenting. That 'Abdu'l-Bahá describes the agony and lamentations of the Concourse on high is indicative of the grievous nature of the attacks carried out by a faithless band of Covenant-breakers. 'Abdu'l-Bahá's account of the sufferings He endured at their hands, as mentioned in the section of the Will and Testament cited above, will become clear to readers with the perusal of the forthcoming pages of this book.

Further, in the Will and Testament 'Abdu'l-Bahá makes the following statement:

5–WT So grievous the deeds of this iniquitous person became that he struck with his axe at the root of the Blessed Tree, dealt a heavy blow at the Temple of the Cause of God, deluged with tears of blood the eyes of the loved ones of the Blessed Beauty, cheered and encouraged the enemies of the One True God, by

---

* For a full discussion of this subject see chapter 16.

his repudiation of the Covenant turned many a seeker after Truth aside from the Cause of God, revived the blighted hopes of Yaḥyá's following, made himself detested, caused the enemies of the Greatest Name to become audacious and arrogant, put aside the firm and conclusive verses and sowed the seeds of doubt.

As mentioned in the preceding chapter, for four years Mírzá Muḥammad-'Alí's rebellion was kept a well-guarded secret by 'Abdu'l-Bahá. During this period and afterwards, almost the entire family of Bahá'u-'lláh, including three of His sons and two daughters, together with their families, as well as the two surviving wives of Bahá'u'lláh and their relatives, rose up against 'Abdu'l-Bahá. They fought Him fiercely on every issue which related to His being the Head of the Faith and the Centre of the Covenant of Bahá'u'lláh. Indeed, members of Bahá'u'lláh's family were foremost among those who violated the Covenant.

After Bahá'u'lláh's passing the only members of His family who remained firm in the Covenant, in the face of great opposition, were Mírzá Muḥammad-Qulí and his family, 'Abdu'l-Bahá and His family and the Greatest Holy Leaf. Mírzá Muḥammad-Qulí, the youngest half-brother of Bahá'u'lláh, was about seven years older than 'Abdu'l-Bahá. He was very young when his father died and was brought up by Bahá'u'lláh. He travelled with Him on His exiles and shared, in a spirit of resignation and fortitude, the sufferings inflicted on him in the course of four successive banishments. He had a quiet and loving disposition and took great pride in serving Bahá'u'lláh in domestic affairs.

In order to survey, however briefly, the nefarious activities of the Covenant-breakers during 'Abdu'l-Bahá's ministry, it is necessary to mention a few individuals who were the props and mainstays of Mírzá Muḥammad-'Alí in his activities. Foremost among them in the Holy Land was Majdu'd-Dín, the son of Áqáy-i-Kalím, the noble brother of Bahá'u'lláh. Majdu'd-Dín was the backbone, the motivating force behind Mírzá Muḥammad-'Alí. He had married Ṣamadíyyih, Mírzá Muḥammad-'Alí's sister, and was a bitter enemy of 'Abdu'l-Bahá. 'Abdu'l-Bahá prophesied that Majdu'd-Dín would live a long life to see the triumph of the Cause and the frustration of his evil plots. This prophecy was fulfilled: he lived to be over a hundred years old and saw the birth of the Administrative Order, the child of the Covenant, and the strengthening of its foundations by Shoghi Effendi. Majdu'd-Dín died in 1955, two years after the Ten Year Crusade was launched by the Guardian, having witnessed the indisputable ascendancy of the Covenant and the extinction of his hopes and evil designs.

Another ally and close companion of Mírzá Muḥammad-'Alí was his youngest brother Mírzá Badí'u'lláh. His shameful activities against the Centre of the Covenant and his opposition at a later date to Shoghi Effendi will be referred to in the following pages. Mírzá Badí'u'lláh also lived a long life and died at an advanced age.

Bahá'u'lláh's other son, Mírzá Ḍíyá'u'lláh, was a vacillating person who wavered in his allegiance to the Centre of the Covenant; he was easily manipulated and became a willing tool in the hands of Mírzá Muḥammad-'Alí. He lived in the Mansion of Bahjí along with the rest of the family, all of whom were affected by the spirit of Covenant-breaking. Mírzá Ḍíyá'u'lláh died in 1898, only six years after the passing of Bahá'u'lláh. He did not live to take an effective part in all the hostile activities which his brother conducted against 'Abdu'l-Bahá.

Another veteran Covenant-breaker was Ḥájí Siyyid 'Alí Afnán, a son of the venerable Ḥájí Mírzá Siyyid Ḥasan, entitled Afnán-i-Kabír (Great Afnán),* brother of the wife of the Báb. Siyyid 'Alí joined hands with the Arch-breaker of the Covenant and became one of 'Abdu'l-Bahá's great enemies. He had risen to eminence through the efforts of the wife of the Báb, who sent a special message to Bahá'u'lláh through Munírih Khánum, the wife of 'Abdu'l-Bahá, when she visited her in Shíráz. Munírih Khánum has written the following account:

> The wife of the Báb said: 'Please supplicate the Blessed Perfection to grant two wishes of mine. One, that one of the exalted Leaves† of the blessed Family may be permitted to join in wedlock with a member of the family of the Báb, so that the two holy Trees may be outwardly knit together. The other, to grant me permission to attend His presence.' I conveyed this message when I attained the presence of Bahá'u'lláh; He readily assented to both her requests.[157]

The person the wife of the Báb had in mind was Ḥájí Siyyid 'Alí. Bahá'u'lláh granted her wish and he was joined in wedlock with Furúghíyyih, a daughter of Bahá'u'lláh. As a token of his appreciation, Siyyid 'Alí promised his aunt, the wife of the Báb, that he would accompany her to the Holy Land if Bahá'u'lláh accepted the proposal for his marriage. However, when the time arrived he left for 'Akká alone. Thus he broke his promise and with it the heart of that noble lady. Being unable to travel on her own, she was sorrowful and

---

* For an account of his life see Taherzadeh, *Revelation of Bahá'u'lláh*, vol. 4.

† Bahá'u'lláh referred to His male descendants as Aghṣán (Branches) and His female descendants of Varaqát (Leaves).

disconsolate as a result of this cruel treatment. Soon her health was impaired and a few months later she passed away.

After the ascension of Bahá'u'lláh, Siyyid 'Alí and his wife Furúghíyyih sided with Mírzá Muḥammad-'Alí and rose up in opposition to 'Abdu'l-Bahá. After inflicting much pain upon the Centre of the Covenant for several years, Siyyid 'Alí repented of his iniquitous deeds and the Master forgave him. But his repentance was short-lived; he returned to his den again and resumed his odious activities against 'Abdu'l-Bahá. It was the members of his family who were chiefly responsible for delivering the most painful blows upon the person of Shoghi Effendi during his ministry. They caused havoc in the family of the Master and tore it apart altogether.

Apart from these members of Bahá'u'lláh's family who rose up against 'Abdu'l-Bahá, there were others in the Holy Land who joined hands with them. Notorious among them was Mírzá Áqá Ján, Bahá'u-'lláh's amanuensis, who had fallen from grace during the last months of Bahá'u'lláh's ministry.* His rebellion against the Centre of the Covenant erased his 40–year record of service to Bahá'u'lláh and stained the annals of the Faith.

Another opponent of the Covenant was Muḥammad-Javád-i-Qazvíní. He first attained the presence of Bahá'u'lláh in Baghdád; some years later he went to Adrianople and remained in the service of Bahá'u'lláh there. He was among those who accompanied Him to 'Akká, was the recipient of His boundless favours, transcribed His writings and was entitled 'Ismu'lláhu'l-Javád' (the Name of God Javád) by Him. Muḥammad-Javád was an arrogant man who after the ascension of Bahá'u'lláh betrayed his Lord and became one of the adversaries of 'Abdu'l-Bahá in spite of His efforts to protect him from Mírzá Muḥammad-'Alí's wicked designs. But the Master did not succeed in His efforts to save Javád, for Javád had been irremediably corrupted by Mírzá Muḥammad-'Alí, especially as he had established a family link by marrying a sister of one of the wives of Mírzá Muḥammad-'Alí. Although he was devoid of knowledge and learning, he attacked the Centre of the Covenant in his venomous writings, which contain many inaccuracies, falsehoods and calumnies. Professor Edward Browne of Cambridge was misled by him when he translated some of Javád's writings and published them in one of his works.

At the same time as the believers in the Holy Land were being tested by the disease of Covenant-breaking, a number of outstanding teachers of the Faith in Persia who were ambitious for the leadership of that community also defected and rose up in opposition to the

* See Taherzadeh, *Covenant of Bahá'u'lláh*, chapter 15.

Centre of the Covenant. The main source of rebellion was the proud and egotistical Jamál-i-Burújirdí.* For many years during Bahá'u'lláh's ministry this ambitious and deceitful man was foremost among the teachers of the Faith and his fame had spread throughout the community. Bahá'u'lláh concealed his faults, revealed many Tablets in his name, entitled him 'Ismu'lláhu'l-Jamál' (the Name of God Jamál), exhorted him to faithfulness and purity of motive, at times admonished him for those of his actions which were harmful to the Faith and overlooked his shortcomings with forbearance and magnanimity. However, his hypocrisy was known to those who were close to him. Before embracing the Faith of Bahá'u'lláh, Jamál had been a learned mujtahid from the town of Burújird. Many Bahá'ís in Persia who could not see his deceitful and egotistical nature looked upon him as a man of God and treated him with great respect. It was after the passing of Bahá'u'lláh that Jamál showed his true colours, rejected the Covenant and rebelled against its Centre.

There were other teachers of the Faith in Persia who were also proud and ambitious. Notorious among them was Siyyid Mihdíy-i-Dahají entitled by Bahá'u'lláh 'Ismu'lláhu'l-Mihdí' (the Name of God Mihdí).† He too was treated with loving kindness and forbearance by Bahá'u'lláh, was an eloquent teacher of the Cause and was highly esteemed by the believers. Jalíl-i-Khú'í‡ was another well-known believer, for whom Bahá'u'lláh revealed the Tablet of Ishráqát. These men and several others who were engaged in the service of the Cause during Bahá'u'lláh's ministry lusted in their hearts for glory and leadership of the community and were tested through the institution of the Covenant. When they failed to comply with the provisions of the Kitáb-i-'Ahd and broke the Covenant, they were expelled from the community.

Mírzá Muḥammad-'Alí's campaign of opposition against 'Abdu'l-Bahá acquired greater momentum as the years went by. Soon after the passing of Bahá'u'lláh, Mírzá Muḥammad-'Alí, who had already won the support of most members of Bahá'u'lláh's family, began secretly to undermine the faith of the believers in 'Akká, to weaken their love and loyalty towards the Master and eventually win them over to his own camp.

The first thing he did was to launch among the believers a clandestine campaign of calumny against 'Abdu'l-Bahá. At a time when He

---

* For a detailed story of his nefarious activities see Taherzadeh, *Covenant of Bahá'u-'lláh*.

† For more information see Taherzadeh, *Revelation of Bahá'u'lláh*, vol. 2.

‡ For more information see Taherzadeh, *Revelation of Bahá'u'lláh*, vol. 4.

had, as a sign of humility among the believers, adopted the title of '‘Abdu'l-Bahá' (Servant of Bahá'u'lláh) and requested the friends to call Him by this new name rather than by such exalted titles as the 'Master', 'the Most Great Branch' and others conferred upon Him by Bahá'u'lláh, Mírzá Muḥammad-‘Alí spread rumours that ‘Abdu'l-Bahá had claimed to be an independent Manifestation of God. He shamelessly accused ‘Abdu'l-Bahá of aiming to destroy Bahá'u'lláh's Faith, to abrogate its laws and to completely wipe out every trace of His Revelation. He went so far as to impute to ‘Abdu'l-Bahá the claim of divinity for Himself. To strengthen these false accusations, the Covenant-breakers began to preach to everyone the principle of the oneness of God and that no one can claim partnership with Him. In order to draw attention to this point, they called themselves Muvaḥḥidín (Believers in the Unity of God). It is this appellation to which ‘Abdu'l-Bahá refers in the following passage of His Will and Testament:

> **17–WT . . . the Centre of Sedition waxed haughty and rebellious and with Divine Unity for his excuse deprived himself and perturbed and poisoned others.**

So widespread was this propaganda that even in the early days when the believers in Persia heard of this they were puzzled by the emphasis placed on the oneness of God. Ḥájí Mírzá Ḥaydar-‘Alí wrote about this. The following is a summary translation of his words:

> As the Day-Star of the Incomparable Beauty hid itself from the eyes of men and began to shed its light from the Realm of Glory upon the peoples of the world, and His confirmations and assistance were showered upon the Centre of His Covenant, these unfaithful ones began to promote their designs. When they came in contact with the believers, whether residents or pilgrims, they opened the subject of the oneness of God saying that God is one, there is no partner with Him, and the Most Great Infallibility belongs to Him, exalted be His Glory. The believers were surprised and bewildered at such statements. They could not understand to whom they were imputing their strange suggestions, for no one had claimed to be a partner with God or be a possessor of the Most Great Infallibility.[158]

Mírzá Muḥammad-‘Alí and his associates tried by various methods to undermine the faith of some believers and convert them to their side. For example, they knew those who were steadfast in the Covenant and those who were weak, simple-hearted or proud and ambitious. They bypassed the former and concentrated on sowing the seeds of doubt in the hearts of the latter, adopting different methods to achieve their purpose. In all these they hid themselves under the cloak of hypocrisy and did their best to pose as the most devoted, the most pious and the most humble Bahá'ís in the land. For example, one way of misleading a simple-hearted believer was for a few agents of Mírzá Muḥammad-'Alí to get close to him personally and establish bonds of friendship with him. The Covenant-breakers posed as the most humble followers of 'Abdu'l-Bahá and in the course of conversation praised the Master with unusual exaggeration, saying that He was a Manifestation of God, that His station was equal to Bahá'u'lláh's, that He was the embodiment of divinity Himself and that in their prayers they turned to Him instead of God. One after the other would convey to the individual such preposterous thoughts and assure him falsely that 'Abdu'l-Bahá had claimed such a station for Himself. When they were sure that the loyal Bahá'í was beginning to have doubts about 'Abdu'l-Bahá's station, they would then despatch other persons to him who would disprove and strongly criticize fabricated claims which they had slanderously attributed to 'Abdu'l-Bahá. In this way, through deceit and falsehood, they would weaken the faith of the believer to a point where he would be invited to join the group of dissidents.

Another trick played by Mírzá Muḥammad-'Alí was to shower praise upon an outstanding teacher of the Faith who was steadfast in the Covenant. Consequently, some believers would conclude that the famous Bahá'í teacher must have joined the ranks of the Covenant-breakers. This could result in the defection of some weak and uninformed believers. Once, Mírzá Muḥammad-'Alí's associates published a paper in which they paid great tribute to the famous Bahá'í scholar Mírzá Abu'l-Faḍl and extolled him in superlative terms. No sooner was Mírzá Abu'l-Faḍl informed of this than he wrote an open letter saying that they had no right to praise him and that this action alone had exposed their hypocrisy, for he was abhorred in their sight. If any praise was due to him, it ought to come from the friends of 'Abdu'l-Bahá. He handed this letter to the Master who directed that it be read aloud at a meeting of the friends.

For some years the Covenant-breakers used to mix freely with the believers, especially a few who cast themselves as the most steadfast in the Covenant but who, in reality, were acting as spies. In the gatherings of the friends, these men would speak with eloquence and feigned sincerity about the importance of firmness in the Covenant. At every meeting they would urge the believers to remain loyal to 'Abdu'l-Bahá. Having established their credibility in the community, they would then intimate to the friends that a certain steadfast believer whom they knew to be rather naive and simple-hearted had secretly joined the Covenant-breakers. Such an accusation, which was entirely false, would disturb the steadfast believers but these unscrupulous men would bring forth all kinds of reasons in support of their claim. For instance, one would say, I saw this person in the street bowing to Mírzá Muḥammad-ʻAlí. Another would say, I saw many pages of the writings of Mírzá Muḥammad-ʻAlí in his possession. One would say, I saw him in the street turning his back to ʻAbdu'l-Bahá.

Naturally, having heard and believed such accusations against this poor individual, the faithful believers would avoid his company. Having isolated this person from the community, then Mírzá Muḥammad-ʻAlí would send his men to win him over to his side through artful manipulations and stories about ʻAbdu'l-Bahá and the steadfast believers. There were also other deceitful practices through which the Covenant-breakers succeeded in gathering a number of people around themselves.

By such means a temporary breach was made in the ranks of the believers but the Covenant-breakers did not limit their activities to the Bahá'í community. Soon after the ascension of Bahá'u'lláh they began a campaign of defamation against ʻAbdu'l Bahá among prominent people in ʻAkká and other cities of Syria.* The breaking of the Covenant and rising against its Centre brought great sorrow to the hearts of the believers. Dr Yúnis K͟hán, a trusted secretary of ʻAbdu'l- Bahá and a well-known defender of the Covenant, wrote an account of the condition of the believers and Covenant-breakers in ʻAkká. The following is a summary translation of his observations during a period when the Covenant-breakers were openly attacking the Cause:

> Each one of the Ag͟hṣán played a special role. The Arch-breaker of the Covenant, similar to Mírzá Yaḥyá, kept out of sight and retired to the sanctuary of the Mansion of Bahjí. Instead, he dispatched Mírzá Badí'u'lláh into the field of action. The vacillating Mírzá Ḍíyá'u'lláh, a person who was undecided and shifted his position from one side to the other, often acted as a link between the believers and the Covenant-breakers.
>
> Mírzá Badí'u'lláh was actively engaged, from morning till night, in stirring up sedition in the land. He was an artful player as he moved in different circles. He was a two-faced hypocrite who adapted himself to every situation and changed his style and disposition to conform to the often conflicting customs of various groups of people. He even attended private merrymaking parties held for the enjoyment of sensual pleasures. The late Ḍíyá'u'lláh, that poor wavering person, did not have a steady outlook. At times he was friendly towards the believers, at other times unfriendly;

* See chapter 17 for a detailed account of their efforts to discredit ʻAbdu'l-Bahá.

> for a while he would be steadfast in the Covenant, then he would change his allegiance and join the Covenant-breakers. He was always vacillating and often would bring messages from the Covenant-breakers to the Master.[159]

Dr Yúnis Khán also observed that the Covenant-breakers could be divided into three categories:

> The first were those who had completely cut themselves off from the community; they showed their animosity quite openly and had the audacity to speak disrespectfully to 'Abdu'l-Bahá whenever they met Him.
>
> The second group were those who were cut off from the community and were at a loose end, wandering in the streets of Haifa and 'Akká.
>
> The third were the hesitating and wavering types who used to associate freely with the believers and usually were the cause of mischief. They acted as spies and informers, would pass on the news of the believers to the Covenant-breakers who, acting upon the information, would then formulate their stratagem accordingly.

Dr Yúnis Khán described the state of the believers in those days. Here is a summary translation of his words:

> In those difficult times, the believers had special feelings and concerns which are impossible to appreciate in these days, unless one has lived through the events of that period. For instance, those steadfast believers, especially the older ones, had witnessed from the early days of Bahá'u'lláh's successive banishments until the final transfer of His residence to the Mansion of Bahjí, the manner in which the Centre of the Covenant was cherished in the presence of Bahá'u'lláh. They remembered how He was treated with extreme reverence, honour and deepest affection. They recalled the attitude of the Aghṣán and the Afnán as they showed the utmost submissiveness, humility and obedience to Him. All these had changed and the believers were now utterly heartbroken and filled with grief as they observed Him woefully wronged and treated with malice.
>
> Each day the Covenant-breakers created a new mischief. They spread so much calumny against the Master throughout the land that the public in the whole of Syria were perplexed and led astray. Even those people whose daily sustenance had been provided through the generosity of the Master arose against Him. Many prominent people of Haifa and 'Akká who used to attribute miracles to Him in the past now shunned Him and secretly joined hands with Covenant-breakers against Him . . . Each day the number of His admirers reduced while the number of stirrers of sedition increased.

> It is because of these developments that the believers who were steadfast in the Covenant were sorrowful and grieved. The extent of their distress and anguish was beyond description. But when they attained the presence of the Master and heard His inspiring words and came into contact with His heavenly spirit, a new life was breathed into their souls and the light of hope shone forth in their sorrowful hearts.
>
> In those days the Cause of God had been promoted in the West. Each week a bundle of letters of declaration of faith or questions about spiritual matters was received. These were translated and read to the friends in the birúní (outer quarters) of the Master's house. The believers were highly exhilarated by hearing the news of the spread of the Cause in the West . . . Such exciting news was instantly carried to the Mansion of Bahjí by a few individuals who acted as spies in the midst of the friends. This would activate the Covenant-breakers to intensify their campaign of opposition by fabricating new calumnies against the Master and publishing them in their inflammatory letters.[160]

The Covenant-breakers tried very hard, with the help of the notorious Jamál-i-Burújirdí and a few others, to undermine the faith of the believers in Persia but they failed miserably. Only a very small handful of ambitious men carried on a campaign of opposition against the Covenant but they were effectively silenced by a devoted and steadfast community whose members were deepened in the Covenant and were brought up with an intense love for the Master.

Jamál, who was foremost amongst the teachers of the Cause in Persia, became very tense and agitated after the ascension of Bahá'u-'lláh. When he saw the first message sent by 'Abdu'l-Bahá to the Bahá'ís of the East, he dismissed it, saying, 'The Ag͟hṣán are young and immature.' This remark was a reference to 'Abdu'l-Bahá. Jamál was the first among the Bahá'ís of Persia to travel to the Holy Land, very soon after the ascension. He went there without seeking permission from 'Abdu'l-Bahá, met with Mírzá Muhammad-'Alí, stayed there for a few months and returned to Persia. From that time onwards, his attitude and feelings disturbed the hearts of those who came into close contact with him. The words and counsels of 'Abdu'l-Bahá exhorting him to servitude and detachment went unheeded. The poison of Covenant-breaking had been effectively injected into his whole being by Mírzá Muḥammad-'Alí, and although outwardly he professed loyalty to 'Abdu'l-Bahá, inwardly he was preparing himself for the day when he would become the head of the Faith in Persia. To this end, he influenced certain individuals in each province to act as his representatives. This was not difficult for him to achieve, since several teachers of the Faith in different parts of the country were his supporters. Because the rebellion of Mírzá Muḥammad-'Alí was kept a secret for a few years, Jamál had no choice but to continue his activities within the Bahá'í community.

Over the course of several decades Jamál had acquired many admirers. For example, many believers in the city of Qazvín were his staunch supporters and he considered that city to be his stronghold and refuge. He was also very popular among the believers in the province of Mázindarán.

During this time, 'Abdu'l-Bahá continually exhorted Jamál to steadfastness in the Covenant and to purity of motive, in Tablets indicative of His loving concern for Jamál's spiritual survival. But, alas, in the end Jamál lost this battle. When the rebellion of Mírzá Muḥammad-'Alí became public knowledge and his circular letters misrepresenting the station of 'Abdu'l-Bahá reached the Bahá'ís of Persia, Jamál threw in his lot with the Arch-breaker of the Covenant. By transferring his loyalty to Mírzá Muḥammad-'Alí, Jamál expected to become the indisputable head of the Faith in Persia, a position promised him by Mírzá Muḥammad-'Alí himself, but after Jamál became involved in activities against the Covenant, he was expelled from the Faith by 'Abdu'l-Bahá. No sooner did the believers become informed of this than the entire Bahá'í community in Persia, with the exception of a handful of people, shunned his company. Those very few individuals who joined him in his odious activities were likewise cast out of the community and isolated.

The manner in which the believers swiftly cut their association with Jamál came as a surprise to many observers. For example, he was rejected by almost the entire community in Qazvín, where he had his most ardent admirers. The same thing happened in Mázindarán. While the believers had previously given him respect and veneration, after his defection he was shunned so effectively that he could not find even one family to offer him hospitality in that province. In some places, for example in Ádhirbáyján, he found a few individuals who harboured him but he and his dwindling associates swiftly sank into oblivion.

At the height of Jamál's popularity and success, 'Abdu'l-Bahá wrote him a Tablet[161] in which He emphasized the importance of steadfastness in the Covenant, stating that in this day the confirmations of Bahá'u'lláh will reach only those who are firm in the Covenant. He affirmed that even should the one who was an embodiment of the Holy Spirit fail to turn to the Centre of the Covenant, he would become a dead body, whereas a child who remained steadfast in the Covenant would be assisted by the hosts of the Supreme Concourse. Ironically, this Tablet of 'Abdu'l-Bahá found its fulfilment in Jamál and his few assistants, who withered away spiritually.

There were a few other teachers in Persia who also rebelled against the Covenant. Siyyid Mihdíy-i-Dahají was one. Like Jamál he was a learned man and a very capable teacher of the Faith. As mentioned above, Bahá'u'lláh had conferred upon him the title of 'Ismu'lláhu'l-Mihdí' (the Name of God Mihdí) and had revealed many Tablets in his honour. Siyyid Mihdí was a native of Dahaj in the province of Yazd. He attained the presence of Bahá'u'lláh in Baghdád, Adrianople and 'Akká and received His unfailing bounties. Like Jamál, he travelled widely throughout Persia and was much honoured by the believers. Yet people who were endowed with discernment found him to be insincere, egotistical and deeply attached to the things of this world. Notable among those who have written their impressions of him is Ḥájí Mírzá Ḥaydar-'Alí, who also wrote about Jamál-i-Burújirdí. A perusal of his narratives makes it clear that these two men had at least one thing in common, namely their insatiable lust for leadership. For example, Siyyid Mihdí always entered Bahá'í gatherings with an air of superiority. He loved to have a retinue of the faithful walk behind him and at night, in the absence of public lighting, he was preceded by a number of believers who carried lanterns for him. This made a spectacular scene in those days, for normally only one servant or a friend with a lantern accompanied a prominent person at night. In Siyyid Mihdí's case some believers even vied with each other to perform this service and Ḥájí Mírzá Ḥaydar-'Alí recalls an evening when no less than 14 men, with lanterns in hand, escorted him to a meeting!

Men such as these always fall. The Faith of Bahá'u'lláh does not harbour people who are egotistical and seek to glorify themselves. Its hallmark is servitude and the standard it demands is sincerity and purity of motive. It is not therefore surprising that, like Jamál, Siyyid Mihdí was toppled to the ground when the winds of tests began to blow. He ultimately broke the Covenant of Bahá'u'lláh and, in the hope of becoming one of the undisputed leaders of the Faith in Persia, joined hands with Mírzá Muḥammad-'Alí and rebelled against the appointed Centre of the Cause of God. When this became known, the believers left him to his own devices and soon his glory was turned into abasement and the power of the Covenant swept him into the abyss of ignominy and perdition.

The swift downfall of the Covenant-breakers in Persia and the complete frustration of their evil plans resulted in a great upsurge of activity in the Bahá'í community, which had cleansed itself from this pollution. Notwithstanding such an achievement, the believers were deeply distressed by the acts of treachery and deceit perpetrated by Mírzá Muḥammad-'Alí and his associates. Their grief knew no bounds as they contemplated the wrongs inflicted upon the Centre of the Covenant.

The news of the uprising of Bahá'u'lláh's family members against 'Abdu'l-Bahá, known by the public as the Head of the Faith, was greeted enthusiastically by the enemies of the Cause in Persia who, as the years went by, increased their attacks against the community. These reached their climax in the summer of 1903 with the massacre of great numbers of Bahá'ís in the city of Yazd and neighbouring villages – the greatest upheaval since the blood-bath of 1852 in Ṭihrán. Another consequence of the calumnies which the Covenant-breakers published widely against 'Abdu'l-Bahá was the disillusionment of many prominent people who were His admirers. The dwindling followers of Mírzá Yaḥyá who were influential in political circles in Persia also took advantage of propaganda against 'Abdu'l-Bahá and, highlighting the leadership crisis in the Bahá'í community, hoped to revive the fortunes of their tottering movement.

14

Confirmations of Bahá'u'lláh Bestow Victory

5–WT Had not the promised aid of the Ancient Beauty been graciously vouchsafed at every moment to this one, unworthy though he be, he [Mírzá Muḥammad-'Alí] surely would have destroyed, nay exterminated the Cause of God and utterly subverted the Divine Edifice. But, praised be the Lord, the triumphant assistance of the Abhá Kingdom was received, the hosts of the Realm above hastened to bestow victory. The Cause of God was promoted far and wide, the call of the True One was noised abroad, ears in all regions were inclined to the Word of God, His standard was unfurled, the ensigns of Holiness gloriously waved aloft and the verses celebrating His Divine Unity were chanted.

'This one, unworthy though he be' is how 'Abdu'l-Bahá refers to Himself. Throughout His life, 'Abdu'l-Bahá attributed all His achievements to the confirmations of Bahá'u'lláh. Here He affirms that He was the recipient of 'the promised aid of the Ancient Beauty'. One may come to the obvious conclusion that Bahá'u'lláh would assist 'Abdu'l-Bahá, whom He had appointed as the Centre of His Covenant, unconditionally and at all times but Bahá'u'lláh has promised the believers that they, too, will receive His confirmations upon the fulfilment of certain conditions.

The study of the holy writings makes it clear that the growth and progress of the Faith and the development of its institutions depend upon the interaction of two forces. One is released from the realms on high while the other is generated through the efforts of the believers who serve the Cause with devotion and sincerity. When these two forces combine, the Faith of God is promoted. In His bounty, God has ordained that the believers will receive divine confirmations only when they make the effort to serve Him.

The progress of the Cause of Bahá'u'lláh is dependent upon the actions of the believers. Every pure deed attracts the confirmations of Bahá'u'lláh, which in turn bring victory to the Cause. But the first step must be taken by the individual; without it, God's assistance cannot reach the Bahá'í community. This is one of the irrevocable laws of the Covenant of God, which has two sides: God's and man's. God's part of the Covenant cannot be confused with man's. God pours out His bounties and grace upon man but man must take the necessary action to receive them. Unless he opens his heart and submits himself, God's gifts cannot reach him. In the Hidden Words Bahá'u'lláh has laid down the law of this Covenant in these words:

> Love Me, that I may love thee. If thou lovest Me not, My love can in no wise reach thee. Know this, O servant.[162]

Indeed, the greatest source of strength for a Bahá'í is to draw from the power of Bahá'u'lláh. It is the only way through which the believer can effectively promote His Cause. The essential prerequisite for gaining access to this limitless source of spiritual energy is to have faith in Bahá'u'lláh and to believe wholeheartedly that this power exists. Without a sincere belief that Bahá'u'lláh is the Manifestation of God for this age and that He, and He alone, is the source of all creative energies destined to vivify the souls of all men, a Bahá'í cannot succeed in tapping this mighty reservoir of celestial strength. It is the same in nature. How can a person use a form of energy without knowing its source? To have certitude in the Faith is the first condition for success in drawing on the power of Bahá'u'lláh.

The second condition is to become humble and consider oneself as utter nothingness in relation to God and His Manifestation. To appreciate this, let us turn to the laws of nature, which are similar to those of the spiritual world. This is because God's creation, both physical and spiritual, is one. The laws of the lower kingdom exist in the higher one but are applied on a higher level.

In the physical world, energy can be generated between two points where there is a difference of levels. Water can flow from a higher plane onto a lower one. Electrical energy may be generated when there is a difference of potential between two points in the circuit. Similarly, to draw on the power of Bahá'u'lláh, the believer must assume a lowly position in relation to Bahá'u'lláh's lofty station. Bahá'u'lláh may be likened to the summit of a mountain and the believers to the valley below. In the same way that water pours from the mountaintop into the valley, the energies of the Revelation of Bahá'u'lláh and the token of His power and might can reach a Bahá'í who turns to Him in a spirit of true humility and servitude. The writings of the Central Figures of the Faith bear abundant testimony to this basic principle which governs the relationship of man to his Creator. In the Hidden Words Bahá'u'lláh prescribes: 'Humble thyself before Me, that I may graciously visit thee.'[163] When the believer assumes the position of humility and utter nothingness towards God, he will long to commune with Him in a spirit of prayer that is without desire and 'transcends the murmur of syllables and sounds'[164] – a prayer of praise and glorification of God.

To have faith, to become humble and to raise one's voice in prayer and glorification of God are not sufficient prerequisites for drawing on the power of Bahá'u'lláh. There is yet another vital condition which the individual must fulfil, namely, to arise to serve the Cause. If he does not act, the channels of grace will remain closed and no amount of devotion to Bahá'u'lláh or humility before Him can release the powers from on high. The very act of arising is, in itself, bound to attract the confirmations of Bahá'u'lláh. In many of His Tablets Bahá'u'lláh has assured His followers that if they arise with faith and devotion to promote His Cause, the unseen hosts of His confirmations will descend upon them and make them victorious. The following passage gleaned from the Kitáb-i-Aqdas is one such statement among many:

> Verily, we behold you from Our realm of glory, and shall aid whosoever will arise for the triumph of Our Cause with the hosts of the Concourse on high and a company of Our favoured angels.[165]

The belief that the power of Bahá'u'lláh can, by itself, accomplish the promotion and establishment of the Faith throughout the world without the believers fulfilling their obligations to teach and build up the institutions of the Cause, is unfounded and completely against the laws of the Covenant of God. Indeed, the hands of Bahá'u'lláh are tied if the individual does not arise to serve His Cause. In some of His writings going as far back as the days of 'Akká, Bahá'u'lláh has stated[166] that if all the believers had fully carried out His teachings in their daily lives, the great majority of the peoples of the world would have recognized Him and embraced His Cause in His days.

From the beginning of this Dispensation up to the present time, every victory that the Faith of Bahá'u'lláh has achieved is due to divine confirmations and assistance; and it shall be so in the future. The power released from on high has been responsible for the progress of the Cause and the building of its embryonic institutions. With insignificant resources, handicapped by the lack of facilities and manpower, and often devoid of much knowledge and learning, thousands of men and women have scattered throughout the world and pioneered to the most inhospitable areas of the globe. And yet, in spite of their powerlessness and inadequacy, these souls have won astounding victories for the Cause of Bahá'u'lláh. All who have arisen with devotion have experienced the unfailing confirmations of Bahá'u-'lláh reaching them in miraculous ways, enabling them to teach the

Faith and build its institutions in spite of great and at times seemingly insurmountable obstacles.

The outpouring of confirmations pledged in the Kitáb-i-Aqdas is clearly conditional upon the activity of the individual believer. It depends upon one action which may be summed up by the single word 'arise'. It is to the believer's inner urge to teach the Faith and his act of 'arising' that God responds, releasing His powers from on high to sustain and strengthen him in his efforts to promote the word of God. Through the mere act of stepping forward to serve the Cause, great bounties will flood the soul, transforming its weakness into strength and its ignorance into wisdom and understanding.

In many of His Tablets Bahá'u'lláh makes similar promises. For example, He utters these assuring words:

> By the righteousness of God! Whoso openeth his lips in this Day and maketh mention of the name of his Lord, the hosts of Divine inspiration shall descend upon him from the heaven of My name, the All-Knowing, the All-Wise. On him shall also descend the Concourse on high, each bearing aloft a chalice of pure light. Thus hath it been foreordained in the realm of God's Revelation, by the behest of Him Who is the All-Glorious, the Most Powerful.[167]

From 'Abdu'l-Bahá, in many Tablets, have come similar assurances, such as this one:

> By the Lord of the Kingdom! If one arise to promote the Word of God with a pure heart, overflowing with the love of God and severed from the world, the Lord of Hosts will assist him with such a power as will penetrate the core of the existent beings.[168]

And Shoghi Effendi, too, reaffirms these overwhelming promises, writing through his secretary:

> Today, as never before, the magnet which attracts the blessings from on high is teaching the Faith of God. The Hosts of Heaven are poised between heaven and earth, just waiting, and patiently, for the Bahá'í to step forth, with pure devotion and consecration, to teach the Cause of God, so they may rush to his aid and assistance . . . Let those who wish to achieve immortality step forth and raise the Divine Call. They will be astonished at the spiritual victories they will gain.[169]

In the passage of the Will and Testament cited above, 'Abdu'l-Bahá attributes the progress of the Cause to the confirmations of Bahá'u'lláh. When He wrote the Will and Testament the Covenant-breakers were at the height of their activities against the Master but those who were steadfast in the Covenant rallied around 'Abdu'l-Bahá and arose with vigour and devotion to defend the Covenant and thus attracted the bountiful confirmations of Bahá'u'lláh to themselves. These souls were enabled to turn the machinations of the Covenant-breakers into victory for the Cause.

This is why 'Abdu'l-Bahá states that 'the Cause of God was promoted far and wide . . .' A study of the history of the Faith during this period demonstrates that in spite of great opposition from Mírzá Muḥammad-'Alí and his followers, who created much confusion among the Bahá'ís, the believers succeeded in promoting the Faith and increasing the number of its steadfast and avowed supporters in the East and the West.

In Persia the expansion of the Faith continued over the years and the martyrdom of many released a new power and strength within the Bahá'í community. As already mentioned, the efforts of Covenant-breakers in Persia soon ended in failure, which in turn created much enthusiasm and devotion in the hearts of the believers. Steadfastness in the Covenant was the main challenge of the day and every Bahá'í turned his heart and soul to the Master. Many Bahá'í families chose new surnames, consisting of derivatives of the words 'Covenant', 'steadfast', 'firm', etc. The more Mírzá Muḥammad-'Alí spread falsehoods about 'Abdu'l-Bahá, the greater became the zeal and fervour with which the friends extolled His station.

The Message of Bahá'u'lláh was introduced to the West in the early days of 'Abdu'l-Bahá's ministry. The first person who began to teach the Faith in Chicago in 1894 was a Syrian doctor by the name of Ibráhím Khayru'lláh. In the following passages, Shoghi Effendi describes the conversion of the early believers in North America:

> [Dr Khayru'lláh] established his residence in Chicago, and began to teach actively and systematically the Cause he had espoused. Within the space of two years he had communicated his impressions to 'Abdu'l-Bahá, and reported on the remarkable success that had attended his efforts. In 1895 an opening was vouchsafed to him in Kenosha, which he continued to visit once a week, in the course of his teaching activities. By the following year the believers in these two cities, it was reported, were counted by hundreds. In 1897 he published his book, entitled the Bábu'd-Dín, and visited Kansas City, New York City, Ithaca and Philadelphia, where he was able to win for the Faith a considerable number of supporters. The stout-hearted Thornton Chase, surnamed Thábit (Steadfast) by 'Abdu'l-Bahá and designated by Him 'the first American believer', who became a convert to the Faith in 1894, the immortal Louisa A. Moore, the mother teacher of the West, surnamed Livá (Banner) by 'Abdu'l-Bahá, Dr Edward Getsinger, to whom she was later

married, Howard McNutt [sic], Arthur P. Dodge, Isabella D. Brittingham, Lillian F. Kappes, Paul K. Dealy, Chester I. Thacher and Helen S. Goodall, whose names will ever remain associated with the first stirrings of the Faith of Bahá'u'lláh in the North American continent, stand out as the most prominent among those who, in those early years, awakened to the call of the New Day, and consecrated their lives to the service of the newly proclaimed Covenant.

By 1898 Mrs Phoebe Hearst, the well-known philanthropist (wife of Senator George F. Hearst), whom Mrs Getsinger had, while on a visit to California, attracted to the Faith, had expressed her intention of visiting 'Abdu'l-Bahá in the Holy Land, had invited several believers, among them Dr and Mrs Getsinger, Dr Khayru'lláh and his wife, to join her, and had completed the necessary arrangements for their historic pilgrimage to 'Akká. In Paris several resident Americans, among whom were May Ellis Bolles, whom Mrs Getsinger had won over to the Faith, Miss Pearson, and Ann Apperson, both nieces of Mrs Hearst, with Mrs Thornburgh and her daughter, were added to the party, the number of which was later swelled in Egypt by the addition of Dr Khayru'lláh's daughters and their grand-mother whom he had recently converted.

The arrival of fifteen pilgrims, in three successive parties, the first of which, including Dr and Mrs Getsinger, reached the prison-city of 'Akká on December 10, 1898; the intimate personal contact established between the Centre of Bahá'u'lláh's Covenant and the newly arisen heralds of His Revelation in the West; the moving circumstances attending their visit to His Tomb and the great honour bestowed upon them of being conducted by 'Abdu'l-Bahá Himself into its innermost chamber; the spirit which, through precept and example, despite the briefness of their stay, a loving and bountiful Host so powerfully infused into them; and the passionate zeal and unyielding resolve which His inspiring exhortations, His illuminating instructions and the multiple evidences of His divine love kindled in their hearts – all these marked the opening of a new epoch in the development of the Faith in the West, an epoch whose significance the acts subsequently performed by some of these same pilgrims and their fellow-disciples have amply demonstrated.[170]

The pilgrims returned home exhilarated and filled with a new spirit of love and devotion to the Faith. Some went to France and others to the United States. But soon the believers in the West were confronted with a devastating crisis. Khayru'lláh,* who had taught the Faith to many of them, joined hands with Mírzá Muḥammad-'Alí and arose

* For more information about him see, see chapter 18.

in opposition to 'Abdu'l-Bahá, creating great turmoil. To support his activities, Mírzá Muḥammad-'Alí dispatched his son S͟hu'á'u'lláh, accompanied by G͟hulámu'lláh, a son of Javád-i-Qazvíní,* to the United States. Along with K͟hayru'lláh, these two tried to undermine the faith of the believers. But the power of the Covenant overwhelmed them and they failed utterly to carry out their designs. A number of devoted souls, some of whom had attained the presence of the Master, arose with heroic spirit and defended the Covenant. The friends turned away from K͟hayru'lláh and ignored his misguided claims. He was soon cast out of the community as a Covenant-breaker; his influence ebbed and eventually declined into the abyss of ignominy and perdition.

Cleansed from the pollution of Covenant-breaking, the North American Bahá'í community became stronger. Teaching work acquired a new vitality and more souls embraced the Faith. Consequently centres were opened in Washington, San Francisco, Los Angeles, Boston, Baltimore, Cleveland, Minneapolis, Buffalo, Pittsburg, Seattle, St Paul and other places.

In Europe, the first centre was established in Paris when May Bolles, after having attained the presence of 'Abdu'l-Bahá, returned to that city. There she taught the Faith to Thomas Breakwell and Hippolyte Dreyfus, the first English and French believers respectively. In England the nucleus of the Bahá'í community was created through the efforts of Mrs Thornburgh-Cropper and Miss Ethel Rosenberg, both of whom had visited the Master in 'Akká.

Another significant development was the publication of Bahá'í literature in the United States. Shoghi Effendi states:

> In 1902 a Bahá'í Publishing Society, designed to propagate the literature of a gradually expanding community, was formed in Chicago. A Bahá'í Bulletin, for the purpose of disseminating the teachings of the Faith was inaugurated in New York. The 'Bahá'í News', another periodical, subsequently appeared in Chicago, and soon developed into a magazine entitled 'Star of the West'. The translation of some of the most important writings of Bahá'u-'lláh, such as the 'Hidden Words', the 'Kitáb-i-Íqán', the 'Tablets to the Kings', and the 'Seven Valleys', together with the Tablets of 'Abdu'l-Bahá, as well as several treatises and pamphlets written by Mírzá Abu'l-Faḍl and others, was energetically undertaken. A considerable correspondence with various centres throughout the Orient was initiated, and grew steadily in scope and importance. Brief histories of the Faith, books and pamphlets written in its defence, articles for the press, accounts of travels and pilgrim-

---

* See chapter 13.

> ages, eulogies and poems, were likewise published and widely disseminated.[171]

Many other developments took place in the West, all indicative of the onward march of the Faith. Although the Bahá'í community in Persia was also progressing rapidly, news of the advancement of the Cause in the United States was greeted with much more excitement in the Holy Land. This was because the Persian believers had, from the early days of the Faith, longed to witness a day when the people of the West would enter the Cause of God and lend their assistance in its promotion.

That the Bahá'í community was steadily growing in both East and West at a time when the Covenant-breakers seemed to be successful in their attacks against the Faith was mainly due to the outpouring of love and encouragement by the Master upon the believers. During a period when He was being attacked on every side by the Covenant-breakers and the believers were dispirited and disconsolate, He cheered the friends, strengthened their faith, assured them of the invincibility of the Covenant and widened their vision to see the greatness of the Cause and its ultimate victory.

'Abdu'l-Bahá's trusted secretary and confidant Dr Yúnis Khán has left to posterity his reminiscences of the Master during this most turbulent period of His ministry. The following is a summary translation of his celebrated memoirs:

> In those days when the showers of sedition and conspiracy were raining down and the storms of tests and trials were blowing with fury, a fierce hurricane was raging around the Ark of the Cause of God. But it was the Centre of the Covenant who was at the helm. Through the potency of His words and the authority of His directives, He was navigating the Sacred Ark towards the shores of salvation. The sway of His pen and the influence of His utterances were both means whereby He was guiding the people to the highway of blissfulness and prosperity. In the same way that the traces of His pen are imprinted for all time upon the pages of His Tablets, His blessed words were engraved upon the hearts of those who were privileged to hear Him and their recollections were transmitted from heart to heart. His utterances in those days were as varied as His writings.
>
> In His talks He often used to share with us many glad-tidings of the future progress of the Cause of God. He likened our days of anguish and sadness to the early days of Christianity and Islam which had also been very turbulent; but these religions were later exalted in the land. Similarly, He assured us in clear terms of the ascendancy and victory of the Cause of Bahá'u'lláh . . . His utterances on the future of the Cause were delivered with eloquence and

> effectiveness and were imbued with a power and authority born of the heavenly realms such that they penetrated the depths of our hearts. Our souls were so assured and uplifted that we, His hearers, did not have to imagine forthcoming events. Rather, we found ourselves experiencing all the bountiful happenings of the future. The eternal glory and ultimate successes of the Cause of God were so vividly portrayed by Him that the passage of time was irrelevant, for we saw the past, present and the future at the same time. All of this was because the promises of the Master concerning the ascendancy of the Cause were absolutely clear, explicit and irrevocable . . . Now [after a few decades] many of the prophecies of 'Abdu'l-Bahá have already been fulfilled. For instance who could ever have imagined that the small village of Haifa would become, within so short a period, as foreshadowed by 'Abdu'l-Bahá, a great city and an important port . . .[172]

Thus through the spiritual powers conferred upon Him by Bahá'u-'lláh, 'Abdu'l-Bahá strengthened the faith of those loved ones who attained His presence and enabled them to withstand the onslaught of the Covenant-breakers. This privilege was the experience of those believers who were resident in the Holy Land and the pilgrims who arrived from time to time. But the great majority of the friends who were living in other parts of the world received their spiritual sustenance from the Master through the innumerable Tablets which flowed from His pen.

Again we turn to Dr Yúnis Khán's memoirs for a glimpse of the manner in which 'Abdu'l-Bahá wrote Tablets or dictated them in the presence of the believers:

> There are various accounts by Bahá'í pilgrims and visitors concerning the revelation of Tablets by 'Abdu'l-Bahá. Some have said that at the time of revelation their souls were transported into realms of the spirit while their whole beings were shaking with excitement. Others have testified that they saw with their own eyes that while the Master was entertaining believers and non-believers and speaking to them in Turkish he was, at the same time, dictating His Tablets in Arabic and the secretary was taking down His words. Some have said that they saw the Master Himself writing Tablets in Arabic while speaking in Turkish to the friends. Others have seen Him writing a Tablet in His own hand in Persian, while at the same time dictating one to His secretary in Arabic. Some speak of the unusual speed of His writing as well as the majesty of His utterances. There are no exaggerations in the above statements. Each person has described his observations in accordance with his own understanding . . .
>
> The revelation of Tablets had a greater effect on the believers than other experiences in the presence of 'Abdu'l-Bahá. His

Tablets were written in the following manner. Whenever 'Abdu'l-Bahá was freed from His various daily engagements, He summoned Mírzá Núru'd-Dín, His secretary, and began dictating to him. At times He would simultaneously review the Tablets previously revealed, inscribed and ready for His signature. It was on such occasions that He wrote and dictated at the same time. He was truly the embodiment of the verse: 'Nothing whatsoever keepeth Him from being occupied with any other thing.' There was no thought or action which could distract Him.

As the revelation of Tablets continued, the believers, who were usually gathered in the room below or in the Pilgrim House or were walking in the streets of 'Akká, were all eager to attain the presence of the Master and hear His words as He dictated to His secretary in answer to letters He had received. When summoned, they would arrive and be seated. After greeting them lovingly, the revelation of Tablets would begin. Sometimes He would dictate in a loud, clear voice; sometimes He would chant His dictation in the same melodious voice He used to chant the Tablet of Visitation at the Shrine of Bahá'u'lláh. As a result of this marvellous experience, those present were immersed in the sea of astonishment. Some would find that their questions were answered and some learned a lesson from this heavenly experience. As the revelation of the Tablets continued, all became exhilarated and turned their hearts and souls to the Kingdom on high.

But alas, such meetings of fellowship and love would often be interrupted by visiting strangers. The house of the Master was open to all. There being no guards posted at the gate, people would come in. If the new arrivals were not antagonistic towards the Faith and were worthy to listen to the exalted words of the Master, then after welcoming them and showing His loving kindness to each one, He would resume dictating His words to His secretary. But if they were not worthy, or if they overcrowded the room, the Master dismissed the believers and dealt with the situation as He deemed proper. This was how 'Abdu'l-Bahá dictated to His secretary.

But most of the time He wrote the Tablets with His own hand in the circumstances described above. Whenever He was free, He would take the pen and begin to write. But as He did not wish the believers who were assembled in the room to become tired or bored, He would talk to them while He was writing . . . As others arrived, He would welcome each and shower upon all His loving kindness, and yet His pen was moving. Occasionally He would read aloud what He was writing. There were also periods of silence. The Master, as He continued to write, often broke the silence saying: 'Talk among yourselves. I will be able to hear you.' However, the believers were so carried away by His peerless Beauty that they would remain silent.

Only the new arrivals, those who had not been invited, such as an Arab Shaykh or an Ottoman dignitary, would break the silence.

After the usual greetings and words of welcome which befitted the guests, the pen of 'Abdu'l-Bahá would begin to move while He conversed with them. Whenever there was silence, He would ask the newly-arrived guests to broach a subject and discuss it together. Then He Himself entered the conversation . . . Sometimes the guests conducted heated arguments and yet throughout the noise and clamour they created, the Master's pen kept on moving on His Tablets . . .

My purpose in describing the revelation of the Tablets in detail is to enable the people to appreciate the manner in which these Tablets, which uplift the souls and exhilarate the hearts, were written under such difficult and trying circumstances. Another amazing aspect of these Tablets is that it was not only the believers who heard the Master reciting them who were inspired but also the deniers and mischief-makers, who were deeply moved and humbled by this experience.[173]

During those turbulent years when the Covenant-breakers were engaged in making mischief in the Holy Land, the believers' only refuge was the shelter of 'Abdu'l-Bahá's presence. He could be likened to a vast ocean at whose shores His loved ones gathered in order to receive a portion of its life-giving waters. Each believer received his share in accordance with his capacity. Some who had come empty-handed merely enjoyed seeing that vast and fathomless ocean. Others who had more capacity had come with a vessel in hand and each one received a draught of the water of life. Still others, yet unsatisfied, immersed themselves in that ocean and found some of the inestimable pearls of wisdom and knowledge which lay concealed in its depths.

That ocean – the person of 'Abdu'l-Bahá – appeared in various forms on different occasions. At times it was calm, at others surging with mighty waves. When it was calm, every beholder would find himself in a state of joy and tranquillity. When its billowing waves surged, it cast gems of inestimable value upon the shores. At such times, the utterances of 'Abdu'l-Bahá captivated the hearts of His loved ones, who were carried away into spiritual realms utterly oblivious of their own selves and wholly devoted to Him. The effect of the presence of 'Abdu'l-Bahá upon the believers cannot be adequately explained by the above analogy. Suffice it to say that the pure in heart who attained His presence were transformed into a new creation; they became spiritual giants who championed the Cause of the Covenant and defended it with heroism and sacrifice.

In his memoirs Dr Yúnis Khán asserts that the mere glance of 'Abdu'l-Bahá upon a believer released mysterious forces which at times were capable of transforming his life. This is a summary of his observations as he describes the various effects of the Master's glances:

One glance, which thankfully did not appear except on rare occasions, was that of wrath and anger. It reflected the wrath of God from which one had to flee for refuge to Him . . .

There was a glance of love and compassion which was evident at all times. It conferred life and brought joy to everyone . . .

Another glance was that which enchanted the hearts and attracted the souls. I observed many a time in the narrow and dark streets of 'Akká that with one look, the strangers were so attracted to 'Abdu'l-Bahá as to follow Him until He dismissed them. This particular glance has many aspects which I am not in a position to describe . . .

There was a glance by which He expressed His satisfaction and pleasure to a person, as if to say, 'I am pleased with you.' This glance was shown to both the obedient and the rebellious.

Another glance was one which released great spiritual potency. If ever He cast such a glance upon a person, that person's greatest wish would have been granted, if he so desired. But who is it that in such an atmosphere could have any desire other than to seek the good-pleasure of His Lord? I myself have seen this type of a glance many a time. In this mood, one longs for sufferings in the path of God. And some, like Varqá,* have, under the influence of this glance, gone to the field of martyrdom.

There was a glance through which a person realized that all that was hidden in his heart, whether of the past or of the future, was known to the Master.

Above all, there was a glance which, if ever it was directed to an individual, caused that individual to become the recipient of knowledge and understanding. At one time we all saw two believers who were enchanted by this glance and became the possessors of divine knowledge. One was Fáḍil-i-Shírází,† the other Shaykh 'Alí-Akbar-i-Qúchání‡ . . .[174]

* For a story of his life see Taherzadeh, *Revelation of Bahá'u'lláh*, vol. 4.

† An outstanding teacher of the Faith.

‡ He was martyred during the ministry of 'Abdu'l-Bahá.

15

Mírzá Muḥammad-'Alí Claims Partnership with Bahá'u'lláh

5–WT Now, that the true Faith of God may be shielded and protected, His Law guarded and preserved and His Cause remain safe and secure, it is incumbent upon everyone to hold fast unto the Text of the clear and firmly established blessed verse, revealed about him. None other transgression greater than his can be ever imagined. He (Bahá'u'lláh) sayeth, glorious and holy is His Word: – 'My foolish loved ones have regarded him even as my partner, have kindled sedition in the land and they verily are of the mischief-makers.' Consider, how foolish are the people! They that have been in His (Bahá'u'lláh's) Presence and beheld His Countenance, have nevertheless noised abroad such idle talk, until, exalted be His explicit words, He said: – 'Should he for a moment pass out from under the shadow of the Cause, he surely shall be brought to naught.' Reflect! What stress He layeth upon one moment's deviation: that is, were he to incline a hair's breadth to the right or to the left, his deviation would be clearly established and his utter nothingness made manifest.

The basis for Mírzá Muḥammad-'Alí's expulsion from the Faith and his disqualification to succeed 'Abdu'l-Bahá as anticipated in the Kitáb-i-'Ahd is found in the above passage in the Will and Testament of 'Abdu'l-Bahá. Central to this subject is the word 'deviation'. In the next five paragraphs of the Will and Testament, 'Abdu'l-Bahá further elaborates on the same topic and establishes, beyond the shadow of doubt, Mírzá Muḥammad-'Alí's ineligibility to succeed Him. To appreciate 'Abdu'l-Bahá's exhortation in the above passage, it is necessary to study a shameful episode in Mírzá Muḥammad-'Alí's life when he was a young teenager in Adrianople.

Mírzá Muḥammad-'Alí was about ten years old when he accompanied Bahá'u'lláh to Adrianople. He left that city at the age of 15. Bahá'u'lláh granted him a special ability in his childhood – the power of utterance – and this became obvious to everybody who came into contact with him. But instead of using this gift to promote the Cause of God, he embarked on a career which hastened his downfall. When he was in his early teens in Adrianople, he composed a series of passages in Arabic and, without Bahá'u'lláh's permission, disseminated them among some of the Persian Bahá'ís, introducing them as verses of God which, he claimed, were revealed to him. He intimated to the believers that he was a partner with Bahá'u'lláh in divine revelation. In Qazvín several believers were influenced by him and drawn to him, creating a great controversy and resulting in disunity among some of the believers there. The city was already notorious for its different factions among the Bábís and there were some followers of Mírzá Yaḥyá actively disseminating false propaganda against the followers of Bahá'u'lláh.

Now, in the midst of these conflicting groups, Mírzá Muḥammad-'Alí's claim to be the revealer of the verses of God brought about an added confusion among Bahá'u'lláh's followers. In his writings, which are of considerable length, the teenaged Muḥammad-'Alí refers to himself as, among other things, 'the King of the spirit'; he calls on the believers to 'hear the voice of him who has been manifested to man', admonishes those who deny his verses revealed in his childhood, declares his revelation to be 'the greatest of God's revelations', asserts that 'all have been created through a word from him', considers himself to be 'the greatest divine luminary before whose radiance all other suns pale into insignificance', and proclaims himself to be 'the sovereign ruler of all who are in heaven and on earth'.[175]

Such preposterous claims and such a display of personal ambition evoked the wrath of Bahá'u'lláh, who rebuked him vehemently and chastised him with His own hands. Meanwhile, the controversy in Qazvín continued for some time. Three believers in particular fell under the spell of Muḥammad-'Alí: Mírzá 'Abdu'lláh, Ḥájí Ḥasan and his brother, Áqá 'Alí. They and a few others, who considered their youthful candidate to be a partner with Bahá'u'lláh and of equal station to Him, entered into argument with several believers who refuted their claims. Shaykh Káẓim-i-Samandar,* a tower of strength for the Bahá'ís of Qazvín, emphatically rejected the claims of Muḥammad-'Alí and declared that his writings amounted to no more than a string of Arabic sentences which in no way could be the Word of God.

This controversy prompted Ḥájí Muḥammad-Ibráhím, entitled Khalíl, to write a letter to Bahá'u'lláh begging Him to clarify His own station and the station of His sons. Ḥájí Khalíl was already confused about the claims of Mírzá Yaḥyá and wished to be enlightened and

* See Taherzadeh, *Revelation of Bahá'u'lláh*, vol. 3, pp. 88–91.

find the truth. In his petition he also asked other questions. Bahá'u-'lláh responded by revealing a Tablet in his honour, known as the Lawḥ-i-Khalíl (Tablet of Khalíl).*

In this Tablet He declares His own station and states that as long as His sons observe the commandments of God, persevere in edifying their souls, testify to what has been revealed by God, believe in 'Him Whom God shall make manifest', do not create divisions in His Cause and do not deviate from His revealed laws, they can be considered as the leaves and branches of His tree of holiness and members of His family. Through them will the light of God be diffused and the signs of His bounty be made manifest.

Mírzá Muḥammad-'Alí did not live up to these standards. Apart from his shameful claim of equality with Bahá'u'lláh, he became a source of sedition in the community, inflicted severe injuries upon the Cause of God and, after Bahá'u'lláh's ascension, broke His Covenant and rose up to extinguish the light of His Faith.

In the Tablet of Khalíl Bahá'u'lláh alludes to 'Abdu'l-Bahá in terms which immensely exalt Him above His other sons. He refers to Him as One 'from Whose tongue God will cause the signs of His power to stream forth' and as the One Whom 'God hath specially chosen for His Cause'.[176]

In another Tablet[177] revealed at this time when a few believers had been influenced by Mírzá Muḥammad-'Alí's claim, Bahá'u'lláh asserts that when Muḥammad-'Alí was a child of tender years He conferred upon him the power of utterance, so that people might witness His might and glory. He grieves in this Tablet at the state of some of His foolish followers who have thought to recognize a partner with Him in revelation and who have made great mischief in the land. He expresses astonishment at the behaviour of some who have attained His presence and witnessed the outpouring of His Revelation and yet have spread such shameful rumours among the believers. Referring to Muḥammad-'Alí in this Tablet, He further states:

> He verily, is but one of My servants. . . Should he for a moment pass out from under the shadow of the Cause, he surely shall be brought to naught.[178]

In this Tablet Bahá'u'lláh further confirms that all beings are created through a word from Him and that no one can claim equality, likeness or partnership with Him. He and He alone is the possessor of the

---

* Parts of this Tablet are translated by Shoghi Effendi in *Gleanings from the Writings of Bahá'u'lláh*, nos. XXXIII, XXXVIII, LXXVII and CXXVII.

Most Great Infallibility which is the prerogative of every Manifestation of God.

Concerning the three believers in Qazvín who were misled by Muḥammad-'Alí's claim, Bahá'u'lláh invited Ḥájí Ḥasan and his brother to come to Adrianople. Here they attained His presence and fully recognized their folly.

In distinct contrast to Mírzá Muḥammad-'Alí's claim was 'Abdu'l-Bahá's utter self-effacement. Many believers during Bahá'u'lláh's ministry used to write letters to 'Abdu'l-Bahá but He would not respond to them. For instance, Mírzá 'Alí-Muḥammad-i-Varqá,* who was later martyred, wrote a great many letters to 'Abdu'l-Bahá. To none of these did 'Abdu'l-Bahá send a reply. In the end, Varqá wrote to Mírzá Áqá Ján, Bahá'u'lláh's amanuensis, and complained. When Bahá'u'lláh was informed about this He summoned 'Abdu'l-Bahá to His presence and directed Him to send a reply to Varqá. 'Abdu'l-Bahá wrote a brief letter to him saying that when the Pen of the Most High is moving upon His Tablets, how could 'Abdu'l-Bahá be expected to write? Indeed, whatever 'Abdu'l-Bahá wrote during the lifetime of Bahá'u'lláh was directed by Him and received His sanction. This episode alone demonstrates the vast different between the two: 'Abdu'l-Bahá, a true servant, humble and lowly before His Lord; Mírzá Muḥammad-'Alí, ambitious, vain and faithless.

Mírzá Muḥammad-'Alí's claim was not the only sign pointing to his ambitious nature and his craving for leadership from this early age. His daily behaviour, even during Bahá'u'lláh's lifetime, gave clear indications of his lack of spirituality and purity of motive, and his jealousy of 'Abdu'l-Bahá was apparent to those who were close to him. As Mírzá Muḥammad-'Alí grew older, he acquired great prestige among the believers. He thrived on the special consideration shown him by Bahá'u'lláh's followers in order to honour his father. But many of Bahá'u'lláh's disciples who had spiritual eyes soon discovered his real nature and found him devoid of those divine virtues and spiritual qualities that characterize a true believer. Long before he broke the Covenant they were able to detect in him an air of superiority and self-glorification and a craving for leadership and power.[179]

---

* See Taherzadeh, *Revelation of Bahá'u'lláh*, vol. 4.

16

Deviations of Mírzá Muḥammad-'Alí (1)

6–WT What deviation can be greater than breaking the Covenant of God! What deviation can be greater than interpolating and falsifying the words and verses of the Sacred Text, even as testified and declared by Mírzá Badí'u'lláh!

32–WT Not content with this, their chief, O my God, hath dared to interpolate Thy Book, to fraudulently alter Thy decisive Holy Text and falsify that which hath been revealed by Thy All-Glorious Pen. He did also maliciously insert that which Thou didst reveal for the one that hath wrought the most glaring cruelty upon Thee, disbelieved in Thee and denied Thy wondrous Signs, into what Thou didst reveal for this servant of Thine that hath been wronged in this world. All this he did that he might beguile the souls of men and breathe his evil whisperings into the hearts of Thy devoted ones. Thereunto did their second chief testify, confessing it in his own handwriting, setting thereupon his seal and spreading it throughout all regions. O my God! Could there be a more grievous injustice than this?

38–WT Ye know well what the hands of the Centre of Sedition, Mírzá Muḥammad 'Alí, and his associates have wrought. Among his doings, one of them is the corruption of the Sacred Text whereof ye are all aware, the Lord be praised, and know that it is evident, proven and confirmed by the testimony of his brother, Mírzá Badí'u'lláh, whose confession is written in his own handwriting, beareth his seal, is printed and spread abroad. This is but one of his misdeeds. Can a transgression be imagined more glaring than this, the interpolation of the Holy Text? Nay, by the righteousness of the Lord! His transgressions are writ and recorded in a leaflet by itself. Please God, ye will peruse it.

These passages refer to one of the most ignoble acts perpetrated by Mírzá Muḥammad-'Alí, namely interpolation of the sacred writings of Bahá'u'lláh, which took place after His ascension. This was not the first time that the Arch-breaker of the Covenant had committed this offence. During the last years of Bahá'u'lláh's ministry he succeeded in altering certain passages of the revealed word. We shall refer to this episode further in this chapter. However, the interpolation of the writings described in the Will and Testament relates to the period after the ascension.

Having observed the ascendancy of ‘Abdu’l-Bahá and the loyalty of the rank and file of the believers to the Covenant, Mírzá Muḥammad-‘Alí in the early days of his rebellion embarked upon various dishonourable schemes to undermine ‘Abdu’l-Bahá’s influence in the community. An account of his stealing two cases containing various Tablets by Bahá’u’lláh which had been entrusted to ‘Abdu’l-Bahá has been given in chapter 12. He went through these original Tablets and found certain ones, condemnatory in tone, which referred to Mírzá Yaḥyá. He easily removed Mírzá Yaḥyá’s name and substituted that of ‘Abdu’l-Bahá. As the ink used in those days was soluble in water or saliva, it was a usual practice by all scribes to remove part of a written page by licking it and, once it had dried, to write on it again. Being a writer himself, Mírzá Muḥammad-‘Alí was accustomed to this practice.

One of the people who informed the Master about Mírzá Muḥammad-‘Alí’s interpolation of the writings was Mírzá Badí‘u’lláh, who conveyed the information to ‘Abdu’l-Bahá by releasing a document known as the ‘Epistle of Repentance’. We have, in chapter 13, referred to Mírzá Badí‘u’lláh’s iniquitous activities against the Covenant, when he acted in concert with his older brother, the Centre of Sedition. For some years he continued in this way until early in 1903 when rumours began to circulate that he intended to repent and return to the fold. While the friends who were steadfast in the Covenant were apprehensive that if the rumours were true there might be a fresh plan by the Covenant-breakers to deceive the believers, the news was soon confirmed and Mírzá Badí‘u’lláh announced his repentance for all his activities against the Covenant.

This move proved to be of great material benefit to him because he had lived extravagantly and had spent all his possessions in promoting the cause of Covenant-breaking. When he found himself in financial need and realized that Mírzá Muḥammad-‘Alí’s assistance was not forthcoming owing to a rift between the two brothers, Mírzá Badí‘u’lláh took revenge by announcing his decision to leave the band of Covenant-breakers. He repented for his past actions, turned to ‘Abdu’l-Bahá and begged for forgiveness. Of course the Master knew that he was not sincere and that his repentance was an expedient measure to satisfy his needs. But with the Master’s characteristic loving kindness, he was forgiven.

Arrangements were made for him to make a public statement about this matter. On the appointed day, Mírzá Badí‘u’lláh arrived in the Master’s house where all the friends had gathered. He showed the utmost respect to everyone, prostrated himself at the feet of the

Master, begged forgiveness and read his 'Epistle of Repentance'. Dr Yúnis Khán in his memoirs describes that day as an historic occasion and states that some of the friends endowed with spiritual insight readily recognized Mírzá Badí'u'lláh's insincerity in that meeting. They knew that his association with the friends would create great problems for the community which certain unfaithful individuals had already infiltrated. Soon their fears were realized.

For some time after this event Mírzá Badí'u'lláh attended the gatherings of the friends who showed him every courtesy. The Master provided him and his family with a suitable residence in 'Akká and supplied his needs. He would often go to the Master's house and attain His presence. During this period Mrs Lua Getsinger, an outstanding believer of the West, referred to by Shoghi Effendi as a Disciple of 'Abdu'l-Bahá, was in the Holy Land. Mírzá Badí'u'lláh asked her to teach him English. Lua very happily agreed, thinking that by coming in contact with him, she would become the recipient of knowledge, spirituality and divine virtues. But very soon, after the first two lessons, she realized her great mistake in this undertaking. She found him devoid of spiritual qualities and knowledge of the Faith and felt the influence of his dishonesty and treacherous nature. Knowing that if he learned English he could poison the minds of the Western believers, she refused to continue teaching him and told him, in no uncertain terms, to abandon the plan altogether.

The 'Epistle of Repentance', which was addressed to the people of Bahá, was translated from Persian into English and printed and published in both languages. The original manuscript bears Mírzá Badí'u'lláh's signature and seal. In this document he reveals, among other things, some of Mírzá Muḥammad-'Alí's ignoble works, including the interpolation of the writings carried out immediately after the ascension of Bahá'u'lláh. The following is a summary translation of his account of this episode:

> During His last illness, Bahá'u'lláh directed 'Abdu'l-Bahá to place His papers and Tablets in two special large cases . . . These were entrusted by Him to 'Abdu'l-Bahá . . . When the time came to wash the sacred body of Bahá'u'lláh, they brought water into the room. Mírzá Muḥammad-'Alí said to 'Abdu'l-Bahá that since water would be poured around the room, it would be better to remove the two cases to another room so that they would not get wet. 'Abdu'l-Bahá assented and Mírzá Muḥammad-'Alí asked Majdu'd-Dín to move them to my room. This was done and the cases were placed in a special cabinet and locked.
>
> Three days after the ascension of Bahá'u'lláh, Mírzá Muḥammad-'Alí asked me to give him the keys so that he might open the cases. He said: 'Bahá'u'lláh has placed a certain document in these

cases which needs to be studied.' He took the keys from me. The next thing I noticed was that with the help of Majdu'd-Dín, 'Alí Riḍá,* his sister, and the mother of Shu'á'u'lláh the cases were taken out of the window onto the balcony of the mansion and from there into the room of Mírzá Muḥammad-'Alí. He took out all the Tablets of Bahá'u'lláh which were addressed to individual believers. When I protested at his action, he explained, among other things, that the responsibility of the protection of the holy writings had been given to him by Bahá'u'lláh and that he had a Tablet to this effect. However, he did not show me any such Tablet . . . He also indicated to me in a subtle way that the Most Great Branch was against the Cause of Bahá'u'lláh and if these holy writings were to fall into His hands, He would destroy them and would obliterate the name and every trace of the Blessed Beauty from this world!

Another violation by Mírzá Muḥammad-'Alí was the interpolation of the holy writings. For a long time . . . he used to say that he possessed a Tablet from the Supreme Pen concerning the person of 'Abdu'l-Bahá and that if he were to publish it, the credibility of 'Abdu'l-Bahá would be finished and His name effaced forever. He spoke of this on numerous occasions to members of the family. Some time elapsed, during which a few individuals questioned me concerning the Tablet in question. I, therefore, asked Mírzá Muḥammad-'Alí to show it to us but every time I mentioned it to him, he offered me an excuse and sought a pretext to avoid it. Then one day he took out of the case a blessed Tablet which was revealed before Bahá'u'lláh's imprisonment in the Most Great Prison and gave it to me to read. In it Bahá'u'lláh condemns the iniquities and wicked deeds perpetrated by His brother Mírzá Yaḥyá, whom He addresses as 'My brother'. I said to Mírzá Muḥammad-'Alí that this Tablet had no relevance to the present situation. He said: 'I have permission from Bahá'u'lláh to use my pen and interpolate His writings for the protection of the Cause. Now since some individuals have exaggerated the station of 'Abdu'l-Bahá and the Master claims to be the embodiment of divinity, I will erase the words "My brother" and insert in its place "My Greatest Branch". This I will show to some people in order to check His influence.'

. . . After a few minutes, he carried out this interpolation in front of my eyes. Successfully, he changed the words 'My brother' to 'My Greatest Branch'. I pointed out to him that this action amounted to the betrayal of God's trust and constituted a sin. I warned him that if he showed the Tablet in this form to anyone, I would divulge the whole event and report the act of interpolation . . . On hearing these words he became disturbed and promised that he would not show the Tablet to anyone. He also requested me not to reveal the matter.

* A son of Áqáy-i-Kalím, i.e. Majdu'd-Dín's brother.

In his 'Epistle of Repentance' Mírzá Badí'u'lláh discloses further interpolations of the holy Tablets. He states that Mírzá Muḥammad-'Alí interpolated all other Tablets which were addressed to the Bábís who had rebelled against Bahá'u'lláh, replacing Mírzá Yaḥyá's name with that of the Most Great Branch.

Mírzá Badí'u'lláh's repentance was short-lived. It did not take him long to realize that there was no room for leadership in the Bahá'í community for him, especially as in those days 'Abdu'l-Bahá chose to talk at great length about the glorious future of the Faith under the leadership of the Universal House of Justice. Mírzá Badí'u'lláh did not attend the friends' meetings for some time, established secret links with Mírzá Muḥammad-'Alí and eventually rejoined him and resumed his nefarious activities against the Centre of the Covenant. During the time that he was with the steadfast believers he created great tension within the community and it brought the friends a sense of relief when he left them and rejoined the ignoble band of Covenant-breakers. This matter is referred to by 'Abdu'l-Bahá in the following passage of the Will and Testament:

> **40–WT Gracious God! After Mírzá Badí'u'lláh had declared in his own handwriting that this man (Muḥammad 'Alí) had broken the Covenant and had proclaimed his falsification of the Holy Text, he realized that to return to the True Faith and pay allegiance to the Covenant and Testament would in no wise promote his selfish desires. He thus repented and regretted the thing he had done and attempted privily to gather in his printed confessions, plotted darkly with the Centre of Sedition against me and informed him daily of all the happenings within my household. He has even taken a leading part in the mischievous deeds that have of late been committed. Praise be to God affairs recovered their former stability and the loved ones obtained partial peace. But ever since the day he entered again into our midst, he began afresh to sow the seeds of sore sedition. Some of his machinations and intrigues will be recorded in a separate leaflet.**

It is interesting to note that Bahá'u'lláh had revealed a special Tablet addressed to His son Badí'u'lláh. Had he followed the exhortations of His father in that celebrated Tablet, he could have become a brilliant light in the firmament of the Cause but his close association with the Arch-breaker of the Covenant extinguished the light of faith in his heart. The following is the text of the Tablet by Bahá'u'lláh:

> Be generous in prosperity, and thankful in adversity. Be worthy of the trust of thy neighbour, and look upon him with a bright and friendly face. Be a treasure to the poor, an admonisher to the rich, an answerer of the cry of the needy, a preserver of the sanctity of

> thy pledge. Be fair in thy judgement, and guarded in thy speech. Be unjust to no man, and show all meekness to all men. Be as a lamp unto them that walk in darkness, a joy to the sorrowful, a sea for the thirsty, a haven for the distressed, an upholder and defender of the victim of oppression. Let integrity and uprightness distinguish all thine acts. Be a home for the stranger, a balm to the suffering, a tower of strength for the fugitive. Be eyes to the blind, and a guiding light unto the feet of the erring. Be an ornament to the countenance of truth, a crown to the brow of fidelity, a pillar of the temple of righteousness, a breath of life to the body of mankind, an ensign of the hosts of justice, a luminary above the horizon of virtue, a dew to the soil of the human heart, an ark on the ocean of knowledge, a sun in the heaven of bounty, a gem on the diadem of wisdom, a shining light in the firmament of thy generation, a fruit upon the tree of humility.[180]

This Tablet begins with ‘O Badí‘’ and ends with a passage (not yet translated into English) in which Bahá’u’lláh prays that God may protect Mírzá Badí‘u’lláh from the all-consuming fire of envy and jealousy. However, through his violation of the Covenant, Bahá’u-’lláh’s prayer for him remained unfulfilled.

Returning to the activities of Mírzá Muḥammad-‘Alí, it is a well-known fact that he had also interpolated the writings of Bahá’u’lláh during His ministry. This may be regarded as his most successful act of interfering with the holy writings because the passage he altered was printed and published in a book whereas the other interpolations were made to Tablets that remain unpublished. The story behind this disloyal act is as follows. Since Mírzá Muḥammad-‘Alí was highly skilled in the art of calligraphy, Bahá’u’lláh sent him from ‘Akká on a mission to India to help print a few books including the Kitáb-i-Aqdas and a selected compilation of His writings. This compilation, known as the Kitáb-i-Mubín, contains some of His most important Tablets, including the Súriy-i-Haykal.* The book was printed in the handwriting of Mírzá Muḥammad-‘Alí by the printing firm of Násirí, which was part of a business organization established in Bombay by a few members of the Afnán family. Mírzá Muhammad-‘Alí took advantage of this opportunity and betrayed Bahá’u’lláh by changing an important passage in this book. The passage refers to the one who will come after Bahá’u’lláh. Mírzá Muḥammad-‘Alí considered this passage to allude to ‘Abdu’l-Bahá and therefore he deleted all reference to Him and substituted it with a few words of his own. Of course this treacherous act of interpolation was soon exposed by comparing the passage with the authentic writings of Bahá’u’lláh.

---

* See Taherzadeh, *Revelation of Bahá’u’lláh*, vol. 3.

17

Deviations of Mírzá Muḥammad-'Alí (2)

6–WT What deviation can be greater than calumniating the Centre of the Covenant himself!

In studying this subject it is helpful to look into the living conditions of the family of Bahá'u'lláh and their attitude towards the Master. As stated in previous chapters, 'Abdu'l-Bahá and His family lived in 'Akká but the rest of Bahá'u'lláh's family resided in the Mansion of Bahjí. Only a few rooms on the ground floor were reserved for 'Abdu'l-Bahá's use when He visited and even these were taken over by the Covenant-breakers once their opposition to Him intensified and became public. At that time 'Abdu'l-Bahá took over the rooms, known as the pilgrim house, in the vicinity of the Shrine of Bahá'u'lláh, for His own use. Here He rested after the fatigue of the journey from 'Akká and received the believers.

The members of Bahá'u'lláh's family who became Covenant-breakers led a very comfortable life in the Mansion of Bahjí. During Bahá'u'lláh's lifetime His three sons and His amanuensis Mírzá Áqá Ján had hoarded a great many valuable gifts which the believers had presented to Bahá'u'lláh and which He had declined to accept for Himself. He was detached from all earthly possessions, as were 'Abdu'l-Bahá, His mother and His sister, the Greatest Holy Leaf. In contrast, Mírzá Áqá Ján and Mírzá Muḥammad-'Alí coveted these gifts. Consequently they had amassed considerable wealth. Indeed, Mírzá Muḥammad-'Alí and his brothers at one time plotted to kill Mírzá Áqá Ján in order to seize his possessions.*

After the passing of Bahá'u'lláh, the family lived prosperously. 'Abdu'l-Bahá continued for many years to send funds and large supplies of food to the inhabitants of the Mansion – everything needed to make them comfortable. The three brothers, their families and close relatives all enjoyed a life of luxury and leisure. The following is a summary translation of Ḥájí Mírzá Ḥaydar-'Alí's remarks on this subject:

---

* For details, see Taherzadeh, *Covenant of Bahá'u'lláh*, chapter 15.

All the gifts that the Master received, as well as the funds relating to the Ḥuqúqu'lláh, He used to send to the Mansion for the upkeep of the family. Also He had bought for them a number of horses of the best breed which were kept in the stables at the Mansion. The Covenant-breakers often spent their time riding and hunting. When they went to 'Akká, they rode horses* flanked on each side by ten or twelve armed horsemen as guards. In this way they impressed everyone. They entered the city with a pomp and grandeur usually reserved for the governor and the chiefs. In contrast to this, the Master often used to walk and occasionally rode a donkey as He went alone to the Shrine of Bahá'u'lláh. Thus they considered themselves victorious when they reflected on their outward pomp and glory, while they regarded 'Abdu'l-Bahá's lowliness and simplicity as a sign of His weakness and defeat . . .

The Master had instructed Áqá Faraju'lláh, who was His caterer, to send to the Mansion any amount of food and other supplies which the Covenant-breakers requested. But they used to demand five or six times more than their needs. They were determined to take excessive funds from the Master so as to make Him helpless and force upon Him the humiliation of borrowing money from the people. In spite of all this, 'Abdu'l-Bahá ensured that they received large supplies of food, clothing and other necessities of life. Moreover, every gift which was sent to Him 'Abdu'l-Bahá would dispatch to the Mansion and many of the funds which He received as Ḥuqúqu'lláh were given to them. These manifestations of generosity and compassion which 'Abdu'l-Bahá showered upon them in spite of their malevolence were interpreted by them as fear and helplessness. Consequently the more they received His gracious gifts and favours, the more haughty they became and progressively intensified their opposition to His blessed Person.[181]

During the early years of their rebellion, the Covenant-breakers, noticing on the one hand their own prosperity and apparent success in converting a considerable number to their side and on the other 'Abdu'l-Bahá's humility and loving generosity, were convinced that theirs would be a victorious outcome. Dr Yúnis Khán recounts:

I heard several times from the Master saying: 'Once I was counselling Majdu'd-Dín and trying to guide him in a spirit of love and compassion. I admonished him to abandon the path of error and warned him of the remorseful consequences of his deeds. But I spoke to him with such fervour that tears came to My eyes. Then I noticed that upon seeing my emotions, Majdu'd-Dín was scornfully smiling at Me, thinking in his heart how well I had been

* In those days important people rode horses as a sign of their eminence in the community. Ordinary people either walked or rode donkeys.

> defeated! Thereupon I raised my voice at him saying: "O wretched one! My tears were shed when, out of pity, I reflected upon your miserable state and not for myself. Did you think I had become helpless and impotent because of my pleading to you?"'[182]

'Abdu'l-Bahá's patience and loving-kindness, as demonstrated in this story, were thus interpreted by the Covenant-breakers as weakness. This misconception, coupled with the notion that theirs was a life of prosperity and honour, while 'Abdu'l-Bahá and His family were living an austere life burdened by having to supply the exorbitant expenses they demanded, emboldened the Covenant-breakers to step up their campaign of misrepresentation against 'Abdu'l-Bahá. In this they received encouragement from the enemies of the Faith, as well as from the aides and deputies of Mírzá Muḥammad-'Alí in Persia.

As Mírzá Muḥammad-'Alí's campaign to discredit 'Abdu'l-Bahá in the eyes of the Bahá'ís gathered momentum, he began to direct his attention to the non-Bahá'í public, fertile ground for spreading false accusations against Him. It was much easier to poison the minds of those who, although they knew the Master, were not spiritually close to Him. The Covenant-breakers invented several stories of different kinds and began to propagate calumnies against 'Abdu'l-Bahá among influential people who held important positions in 'Akká and neighbouring towns. Thus they completely disregarded the interests of the Faith they claimed to believe in and acted in a manner that clearly demonstrated their disbelief in Bahá'u'lláh and their denunciation of His Cause.

One of the most shameful pieces of propaganda was their accusation that 'Abdu'l-Bahá had cut off their livelihood by withholding funds and provisions to which they were entitled. As Dr Yúnis Khán noted, nothing could have been further from the truth. 'Abdu'l-Bahá used to send to Mírzá Muḥammad-'Alí a great part of the funds which He received from the believers in Persia. He had also made ample arrangements for all members of Bahá'u'lláh's family to receive food and other provisions, amounting to many times more than their needs. Whereas the Master and His family lived a life of austerity, His unfaithful brothers and the rest of Bahá'u'lláh's family lived luxuriously in the Mansion of Bahjí. Despite 'Abdu'l-Bahá's solicitude for them, Mírzá Muḥammad-'Alí and his younger brothers used to complain to people that they were destitute and their families on the verge of starvation.

It must be remembered that in all the years that 'Abdu'l-Bahá lived in 'Akká no one except a few enemies had ever doubted His exalted character, His magnanimity, His loving-kindness and generosity towards the inhabitants of the Holy Land in general and 'Akká in particular. He was a compassionate father to all, a refuge to the poor, a true guide to the rich and a wise counsellor to the rulers of the land. But now owing to the falsehoods invented by the Covenant-breakers, people who had hitherto been great admirers of 'Abdu'l-Bahá became confused and, in the course of time when similar accusations were repeated, disillusioned and lost their faith and confidence in Him altogether.

In order to deceive people into believing that he had become destitute, Mírzá Muḥammad-'Alí used to send his sons, dressed in rags, to the homes of important people where they begged for money. They pretended that they did not have even a loaf of bread in their home and that the whole family was on the verge of starvation. In spite of the fact that they were living a life of luxury owing to the care and protection of 'Abdu'l-Bahá, they accused Him of withholding their source of livelihood. Dr Yúnis Khán tells an interesting story, summarized below:

> One of the deceitful schemes contrived by Covenant-breakers after the ascension of Bahá'u'lláh was that, on the one hand, they placed a great financial burden on 'Abdu'l-Bahá, receiving exorbitant sums of money from Him, and on the other, claimed poverty, destitution and hunger. At the same time they spread false rumours among the believers (in Persia) that some of 'Abdu'l-Bahá's companions had stolen His seals, with which they were issuing receipts for Ḥuqúqu'lláh* and pocketing the proceeds. The Master often told us that the Covenant-breakers had done this so that the believers might stop sending funds and cause financial hardship for Him.
>
> Their claims of poverty however, became so serious . . . that eventually they began to beg. They continued to carry out this shameful practice of begging from people both high and low, and consequently they brought about great degradation for the Cause of God . . . Whenever they received a gift of money from the Master they would intensify their begging operation. When the news of such activities reached 'Abdu'l-Bahá, He would usually be overcome with grief and sorrow. To cite an example:
>
> One afternoon, when a number of visitors and resident believers had assembled in the Bírúní [outer apartment] of the house of 'Abdu'l-Bahá, a certain respectable Shaykh (his name I do not recall) arrived. He was well known to the Master and trusted by Him. He was held in high esteem by the people of Syria and Palestine and was a successful merchant in these regions. Since he was a pious man, he had been appointed by the Ottoman government as the Mufti of 'Akká and was a centre of attention to all the

---

* For information about Ḥuqúqu'lláh, see Taherzadeh, *Revelation of Bahá'u'lláh*, vol. 4.

people. He sat next to the Master and after a brief exchange of greetings he began to convey some information to 'Abdu'l-Bahá by whispering into His ear.

At this time everyone was silently gazing upon the face of the Master. His countenance displayed various modes of expression – anger, astonishment and a mild smile. When the whispering came to an end, 'Abdu'l-Bahá . . . asked the Shaykh to recount his story to the assembled friends . . . which he did in these words: 'A certain honoured person [one of the dignitaries known to the Master] came to see me in my office this morning . . . I noticed he was very sad and depressed . . . After much persuasion on my part he said: "A person ['Abdu'l-Bahá] whom up to now I considered to be equal to a Prophet of God is, today, in my sight . . ." He did not finish the sentence.

'After much insistence on my part, promising that I should keep his story confidential, he continued: "Today I met Mírzá Muḥammad-'Alí. He complained bitterly about his brother, 'Abbás Effendi.* He told me many stories which deeply surprised and saddened me . . . This poor man is now destitute . . . He is in need of daily bread. Mírzá Muḥammad-'Alí told me that his children were today crying for a piece of bread and he could not provide for them . . . I was so shaken and upset hearing Mírzá Muḥammad-'Alí's story that I was about to give him some money, but decided instead to send him some wheat . . ."

'When his story was finished, not wishing to disclose to my friend that Mírzá Muḥammad-'Alí had a credit account with me, and that I keep his money for him in my bank, I said to him, "There is no need for you to send wheat or other provisions. Please go and tell Mírzá Muḥammad-'Alí that he can come to me for funds up to a thousand liras." My friend, who did not understand me, said, "Mírzá Muḥammad-'Alí is a respectable person, he will never beg for money."

'Realizing that my friend could not see that Mírzá Muḥammad-'Alí had been lying to him, I decided to disclose to him the true situation. I said to him, "Please go to Mírzá Muḥammad-'Alí and tell him that the Shaykh says that he should take a fraction of the 60 liras he received the other day from his office and purchase some bread for his children." My friend still could not understand. He said, "If Mírzá Muḥammad-'Alí had even a piece of bread to eat, he would not have come to me in such a state of degradation and humility." At this point I opened my safe and showed him a cheque which bore Mírzá Muḥammad-'Alí's signature and which I had cashed for him only the day before. I said, "Now that you have seen the cheque with his signature, go and tell Mírzá Muḥammad-'Alí that he should be ashamed of himself feigning poverty and resorting to beggary. Tell him that no one will be deceived by his imposture."

* 'Abdu'l-Bahá

'Upon seeing the cheque, my friend was stunned. He was overcome by an inner agitation which showed itself outwardly in his face. He was so highly disturbed that for a few minutes he remained speechless. Then, with tears flowing down his face, he said, "What a fool I have been. I was deceived by this Satan and uttered some disparaging remarks about my Lord. Now how can I atone for this transgression?" He then asked me to come here and beg forgiveness for him, saying "I will go myself later to the presence of 'Abdu'l-Bahá and will kiss the hem of His garment."'*

Before leaving us, the Shaykh said to 'Abdu'l-Bahá: 'My Lord, in this world you have no enemy except Your own brother.'

When the Shaykh departed, the Master spoke about the Covenant-breakers and said that they had girded up their loins for the extinction of the Cause of God. He spoke in this vein for a short time and when He saw that the friends were all becoming sad, He changed the subject and with His soul-stirring utterances, He gave us the glad-tidings of the ascendancy of the Cause of God in the future. He categorically stated that ere long these dark clouds would be dispersed and that the domain of the Covenant-breakers would be rolled up and assured us that the Cause of God would not become the plaything of children. He told us to ponder upon the activities of the Covenant-breakers. Because of their enmity towards Him, they go through so much degradation and abasement, appear in the guise of beggars and solicit alms for themselves. Yet they have achieved nothing except to bring upon themselves further humiliation and dishonour.[183]

There are many accounts left by 'Abdu'l-Bahá's friends describing similar activities by the Covenant-breakers. Ḥájí 'Alí Yazdí,† who was one of the resident Bahá'ís in 'Akká during the days of Bahá'u'lláh and 'Abdu'l-Bahá and who lived to serve the Cause of God during Shoghi Effendi's ministry, recounts a similar story. He writes:

One day the Master received from 'Adasíyyih a large quantity of wheat, the annual income from a certain property [owned by the Faith]. He sent it all to the Mansion of Bahjí but Mírzá Muḥammad-'Alí returned it to Him. At the same time, he sent a petition to the local government complaining that 'Abdu'l-Bahá owed him his share of the annual income of that same property which he had earlier refused to accept and pleaded with the authorities to intervene so that he could remedy a serious shortage of food in his household.

This ignoble action was so manifestly provocative that even some of his supporters warned him that government intervention would harm the Cause. He is reported to have said, 'Which harm

* This action signifies the expression of the utmost humility towards a person.

† The paternal uncle of the author. For his life story see *Bahá'í World*, vol. 9, p. 625.

is greater, this one or 'Abdu'l-Bahá's claim that He is a Manifestation of God, that Bahá'u'lláh and the Báb are His forerunners and that He is determined to eliminate the Cause of Bahá'u'lláh and establish instead His own Cause and new teachings?'

This petition was sent purely to humiliate the Master. The officer in charge sent for 'Abdu'l-Bahá and acquainted Him with His brother's claim. Whereupon 'Abdu'l-Bahá summoned Áqá Riḍá Qannád, who was in charge of His domestic affairs and who in the presence of the officer produced the books and determined the full annual income, which amounted to 520 liras. It was further determined that Mírzá Muḥammad-'Alí's share was only 80 liras. But 'Abdu'l-Bahá informed the officer that upon getting a receipt from Mírzá Muḥammad-'Alí, He would be glad to pay him the full amount of 520 liras to be transferred to him through the government officer. A messenger was sent by the officer to inform Mírzá Muḥammad-'Alí of the offer and to ask him to sign the document.

A day later, 'Abdu'l-Bahá was again invited to the government office and handed a receipt, which, although it was issued by Mírzá Muḥammad-'Alí, bore a signature which had no resemblance to his. 'Abdu'l-Bahá refused to accept it and the officer in charge rebuked the messenger and ordered him to return to Mírzá Muḥammad-'Alí and get a genuine signature this time. When the document arrived a second time 'Abdu'l-Bahá was again invited to the office. Again it was the same story. The signature was not genuine. This time the officer became very angry because of Mírzá Muḥammad-'Alí's deceitful action. He apologized to 'Abdu'l-Bahá and offered to sign the receipt himself and send the money to its recipient – an offer which was accepted by Him.[184]

All these things were done to inflict humiliation upon the Master and to hurt Him as much as possible. For many years the Covenant-breakers carried out this type of campaign to discredit 'Abdu'l-Bahá, not knowing that falsehood can never survive and that the power of truth will prevail in the end. Of course, the Cause of God was ultimately victorious through the potency of the Covenant, and through their actions the Covenant-breakers extinguished their own spiritual life. But in the meantime, until they finally became impotent, they created a great disturbance within the community.

The accusations against 'Abdu'l-Bahá were numerous and are beyond the scope of this book. Mírzá Muḥammad-'Alí devised several plots calumniating the Master on various issues. These calumnies turned out to be much more serious with the passage of time; these will be recounted in chapter 22.

18

Deviations of Mírzá Muḥammad-'Alí (3)

6–WT What deviation can be more glaring than spreading broadcast false and foolish reports touching the Temple of God's Testament!

Although Mírzá Muḥammad-'Alí often remained secluded in the Mansion of Bahjí, he used to employ the services of his aides quite effectively in creating mischief for 'Abdu'l-Bahá. Whenever he met the Bahá'ís, he would behave like a most loyal believer in Bahá'u'lláh, feigning meekness and pretending that he had been wronged after the ascension of Bahá'u'lláh. At the same time, he was engaged in a campaign of undermining the foundation of the Cause. We recall the words of 'Abdu'l-Bahá in the opening paragraph of His Will and Testament referring to 'the onslaught of the company of Covenant-breakers, that have threatened to subvert His Divine Edifice'.

In the 'Infernal Letters" that Mírzá Muḥammad-'Alí published among the friends, he appeared to be defending the Cause of Bahá'u-'lláh. But when addressing the public who were unaware of the real situation, he did not shrink from attacking the Centre of the Covenant and misrepresenting every truth enshrined in the teachings of Bahá'u-'lláh. He even went so far as to say that his father was merely a retiring holy man who believed in Sunní Islam! The following is but one out of many examples of his public attacks on the Faith:

After the defection of Mírzá Áqá Ján, Bahá'u'lláh's amanuensis,* Mírzá Muḥammad-'Alí drew up an official indictment against 'Abdu'l-Bahá replete with preposterous accusations. He did this with the help of Tábúr Áqásí, the chief of police, whom he had bribed heavily. The case was taken to a court in 'Akká; there were five main complaints lodged by the sons of Bahá'u'lláh against 'Abdu'l-Bahá. They claimed that:

- Bahá'u'lláh was only a holy man who did not claim to be a prophet. He had spent His time in seclusion, prayer and meditation, whereas 'Abdu'l-Bahá for political ends exalted the

* For more information, see Taherzadeh, *Covenant of Bahá'u'lláh*, chapter 15.

station of His father to that of a Supreme Manifestation of God and of the Essence of Divinity.

- 'Abdu'l-Bahá did not deal with them in accordance with the provisions of Bahá'u'lláh's Will and Testament.

- They had been deprived of their right to inherit a vast estate left behind by their father, Bahá'u'lláh.

- None of the gifts or funds sent in the name of Bahá'u'lláh were given to them.

- 'Abdu'l-Bahá had caused thousands of their friends in Persia and India to turn against them and shun their company.

Such reckless action by members of Bahá'u'lláh's family against the Cause which they privately claimed to uphold, whose Author they knew was not just a 'holy man' but One who had proclaimed His mission to the kings and rulers of the world as the Promised One of all ages, exposes the hypocrisy of the Covenant-breakers, their treachery and their utter faithlessness. These characteristics are true of the Covenant-breakers of the past, present and future. Cut off from the tree of the Cause, they are devoid of faith and spiritual life. They never shirk from employing any means, however degrading and nefarious, to undermine the foundations of the Cause and rob the believers of their faith.

In taking his case to court, Mírzá Muḥammad-'Alí never imagined that in the defence of the Cause 'Abdu'l-Bahá would go so far as to read aloud the contents of the Kitáb-i-'Ahd, Bahá'u'lláh's Will and Testament, in the courtroom. By reading parts of this momentous document, 'Abdu'l-Bahá made it clear that the station of Bahá'u'lláh was not merely that of a 'holy man' who spent His time in prayer and meditation. Rather, He was the Lord of all men calling the peoples of the world to carry out His teachings and exhorting them to unity and fellowship.

It is reported that in the presence of the officials, 'Abdu'l-Bahá openly declared His own position as the Centre of the Covenant of Bahá'u'lláh, the Promoter of His Cause and the Interpreter of His teachings, the One to whom the Aghṣán, the Afnán, the kindred of Bahá'u'lláh and all the believers must turn. He explained that since the Covenant-breakers had arisen against Him they had violated the provisions of Bahá'u'lláh's Will, and consequently the believers had cut off their relationship with them. He is reported to have told the officials that for four years He had not disclosed their rebellion to the believers but that the Covenant-breakers themselves had announced to the Bahá'í world their opposition to Him and had thereby cut themselves off from the Bahá'í community.

'Abdu'l-Bahá refuted the other claims of His brothers just as forcefully. Quoting the Kitáb i 'Ahd, He demonstrated that they were not entitled to receive any of the funds of the Faith which were donated by the believers, for Bahá'u'lláh in that document states 'God hath not granted them any right to the property of others'.[185] On the question of inheritance, 'Abdu'l-Bahá stated that Bahá'u'lláh had lived a life of austerity and had left no estate for anyone to inherit. He is reported to have quoted the celebrated passage from the Kitáb-i-'Ahd, 'Earthly treasures We have not bequeathed, nor have We added such cares as they entail. By God! in earthly riches fear is hidden and peril is concealed.'[186]

However, 'Abdu'l-Bahá confirmed that there were two priceless items in Bahá'u'lláh's possession – one a rare copy of the Qur'án and the other a set of prayer beads – and that both these items of inestimable value had been seen by a few dignitaries of 'Akká. These unique possessions of Bahá'u'lláh had been taken by Mírzá Muḥammad-'Alí and were kept by him. These and other personal effects of Bahá'u'lláh, such as His garments, had been distributed by him to various officials to serve as chattels of bribery and to provide a means of humiliating 'Abdu'l-Bahá. For Mírzá Muḥammad-'Alí knew that the Master considered Bahá'u'lláh's personal belongings to be sacred and that they should be preserved with reverence. Therefore, in order to hurt 'Abdu'l-Bahá he gave Bahá'u'lláh's prayer beads to one of the enemies of the Faith and persuaded him to try to show them to 'Abdu'l-Bahá. It is reported that one day this man showed the beads to 'Abdu'l-Bahá and asked Him if He could put a price on them, to which 'Abdu'l-Bahá responded that their value depended on who was using them.

The episode of the court case was widely publicized. Once again the Covenant-breakers were frustrated in their actions as they failed to humiliate the Master. On another occasion Mírzá Muḥammad-'Alí gave Bahá'u'lláh's cloak and a pair of His spectacles to the deputy governor of Haifa as a bribe and urged him to wear them when he visited the Master. This he did, appearing before 'Abdu'l-Bahá brazenly spectacled and wearing Bahá'u'lláh's cloak. Soon afterwards, however, this man was dismissed from his post and met with misfortune. He then went to 'Abdu'l-Bahá, begged forgiveness for his shameful behaviour and confessed that he had been urged by Mírzá Muḥammad-'Alí to act as he had. 'Abdu'l-Bahá showered him with kindness and generosity and helped him to resolve his difficulties. This was always 'Abdu'l-Bahá's way – to extend a helping hand with all His love to those enemies who had wronged Him and inflicted sufferings upon Him. In His Will and Testament, 'Abdu'l-Bahá further states:

> **6–WT What deviation can be more odious than his iniquity and rebellion! What deviation can be more shameful than dispersing the gathering of the people of salvation!**

This is a reference to a temporary breach in the ranks of the believers caused by Mírzá Muḥammad-'Alí. We have discussed in chapter 13 the manner in which Mírzá Muḥammad-'Alí tried to establish a following for himself among the believers in the East. Through his main agents, such as Jamál-i-Burújirdí, Siyyid Mihdí Dahají and Jalíl-i-Khú'í, he made every endeavour to split the community of the Most Great Name. Although for a short while he created some controversy among certain believers, as already stated, he failed miserably in his efforts. Cleansed from the pollution of Covenant-breaking, the community emerged much stronger than before.

Mírzá Muḥammad-'Alí also spread his wings over North America, in the following manner: Around the turn of the century the Covenant-breakers became frustrated, for they found themselves impotent to arrest the progress of the Cause of God. The news of the expansion of the Faith, especially the conversion of a number of souls in the West, caused the fire of jealousy to burn more fiercely within their breasts. In December 1898 the first party of Western pilgrims arrived in the Holy Land and attained the presence of 'Abdu'l-Bahá. For the first time these newly enrolled believers came into contact with the magnetic personality of the Master. They felt the warmth of His genuine love and compassion and saw the light of divine spirit shining from His countenance.

During their short visit these pilgrims became galvanized by the soul-stirring words of the Master. They were utterly devoted to Him and longed to serve Him and the Cause He represented with unflinching faithfulness. These souls showed such radiance and heavenly joy as a result of meeting 'Abdu'l-Bahá that the Covenant-breakers became inflamed with rage and envy; their gloom and disappointment knew no bounds. It became imperative for them to counteract these developments and to devise a plan to impede the progress of the Cause in the West. At last Mírzá Muḥammad-'Alí discovered a means whereby he could attempt to disrupt the unity of the believers in America.

Among the party from the West that came to visit the Master was Ibráhím Khayru'lláh, a Lebanese Christian who had embraced the Cause in Egypt during Bahá'u'lláh's lifetime and had moved to the United States in 1892. Two years later he had succeeded in converting

Thornton Chase, the first Western Christian to embrace the Faith of
Bahá'u'lláh. The Master referred to K͟hayru'lláh as 'Bahá's Peter'.
Over the next few years K͟hayru'lláh taught the Faith in various parts
of the United States and was the only teacher to whom the believers
could turn for enlightenment in that vast country.

During the time that K͟hayru'lláh was loyal to 'Abdu'l-Bahá he
succeeded in converting a number of people to the Faith. In one of
his letters to the Master he expressed profound loyalty to Him and
gave the news of these conversions. The following is a translation of
this letter, which he wrote in 1897:

> To the sacred court of my Master and the Master of the entire
> world . . . may my soul be a sacrifice unto the dust of His pathway:
> After offering obedience and servitude unto the sacred threshold
> of my Master, I beg to state that the believers in these regions and
> I greet the morn immersed in the sea of your bounties, and meet
> the night with the grace of your mercy which encompasses the East
> and the West of the earth, because you have turned unto them and
> unto me the glances of your favour. You have revealed of divine
> verses three Tablets: one for the believers in America, one for
> Anṭún Effendi Ḥaddád, and the last one for your servant, who
> forever and ever, lowly and poor, awaits the generous dispensa-
> tions of his bountiful Lord . . . Enclosed with this petition are
> seventy-four petitions from those who have recently come into the
> Faith of God, and shall soon send other petitions. Seekers who wish
> to hear the Word of God and come into the knowledge of truth
> arrive in large numbers . . .[187]

But here is an example of how pride and ambition can extinguish the
fire of faith which burns in the heart of a believer. There is nothing
more vital for a follower of Bahá'u'lláh who becomes successful in
teaching the Cause than genuine humility, utter self-effacement and
complete servitude towards the loved ones of God. But alas,
K͟hayru'lláh was vain and egotistical. As the years went by and he saw
the fruit of his teaching work multiply, he became proud and entertained the thought of dividing the Bahá'í world into two parts, he
becoming the leader of the Bahá'ís of the West and 'Abdu'l-Bahá of
the East!

While nurturing these selfish ambitions in his heart, he arrived in
'Akká and met the Master for the first time. He felt His majesty and
authority as well as His love and compassion. For a short while
K͟hayru'lláh showed his subordination to 'Abdu'l-Bahá, who one day
took him to Mount Carmel and there laid the foundation stone of the
mausoleum of the Báb on the site purchased by Him and chosen by
Bahá'u'lláh Himself.

In the meantime, Mírzá Muḥammad-'Alí had discovered in Khayru'lláh signs of ambition and egotism which he exploited to the full. Soon a clandestine relationship was established between the two and Khayru'lláh became a tool in Mírzá Muḥammad-'Alí's hands. He joined the infamous band of Covenant-breakers, rose up in opposition to 'Abdu'l-Bahá, disseminated his misgivings among the friends and published far and wide some of his own ideas. His defection brought great tests for the believers in the West but the vast majority of the American Bahá'ís remained faithful to the Cause. In order to further his aim of creating division within the community, Mírzá Muḥammad-'Alí sent Shu'á'u'lláh, his son, to the United States to strengthen the hand of Khayru'lláh.

The news of Khayru'lláh's defection brought sorrow to the heart of 'Abdu'l-Bahá, who tried to save him as he was heading towards his spiritual downfall. In 1901 the Master asked 'Abdu'l-Karím-i-Ṭihrání, a merchant from Cairo who had taught the Faith to Khayru'lláh, to go to the United States especially to make this faltering soul realize the error of his ways. When his mission failed, that same year 'Abdu'l-Bahá sent Ḥájí Mírzá Ḥasan-i-Khurásání for the same purpose. He also could not help. When Ḥájí Mírzá Ḥasan returned, Mírzá Asadu'lláh-i-Iṣfahání was dispatched to the United States. He had previously been commissioned by 'Abdu'l-Bahá to transport the remains of the Báb to the Holy Land, a task which he had carried out with great success. He had a link with the Holy Family since he had married a sister of Munírih Khánum, the wife of 'Abdu'l-Bahá. Although he tried to help Khayru'lláh remain faithful to the Covenant, sadly, a few years later, he himself and his son Dr Faríd (Fareed) likewise became Covenant-breakers.

In spite of all Khayru'lláh's attempts to mislead those he had earlier helped to embrace the Faith, he did not succeed in doing so. Only a small number of people gathered around him. He thus created a temporary division but the situation quickly changed. As in Persia, the believers remained loyal to the Covenant of Bahá'u'lláh and thereafter refused to associate with their teacher. This can be credited to a great extent to the arrival in the United States of the celebrated Bahá'í scholar Mírzá Abu'l-Faḍl in 1901. The visit of this eminent teacher, undertaken at the behest of 'Abdu'l-Bahá, lasted for about two years. During this period, Mírzá Abu'l-Faḍl dedicated himself fully to the task of deepening the believers in the verities of the Faith of Bahá'u'lláh. He spent many hours, day and night, discussing various aspects of the Revelation of Bahá'u'lláh, its history, its teachings, its laws and its Covenant, which he pointed out was the guarantor of the unity of the community. In the course of these discussions he was able to clarify those subjects which had hitherto been obscure to the

American Bahá'ís. In this he was assisted by Ali Kuli Khan, who acted as his interpreter. Thus, as a result of Mírzá Abu'l-Faḍl's teaching work, the believers in America became filled with the spirit of faith and vitality and many among them were transformed into spiritual giants of this Dispensation.

Khayru'lláh, who craved power and continued to struggle to become the leader of the Bahá'í community in the West, was continually urged by the Arch-breaker of the Covenant to foment discord and contention among the believers, and the efforts of prominent Bahá'í teachers to purify his heart and mind from the poison of Covenant-breaking failed. 'Abdu'l-Bahá expelled him from the community and commented that as a result of his violation of the Covenant he would be reckoned as dead and that soon the repugnant odour of his deeds would repel people everywhere. In 1917 Khayru'lláh wrote a letter to Professor Edward Browne of Cambridge University which is indicative of his despair:

> The Bahá'í movement in America became slow and dull since the sad dissension reached the West nineteen years ago. I thought then that to call the people to this Great Truth was equivalent to inviting them into a quarrel. But the visit of 'Abbás Efendi 'Abdu'l-Bahá to this country, his false teachings, his misrepresentation of Bahá'ísm, his dissimulation, and the knowledge that his end is nigh, aroused me to rise up for helping the work of God, declaring the Truth, and refuting the false attacks of theologians and missionaries. Now I am struggling hard to vivify the Cause of God, after its having received by the visit of 'Abbas Efendi a death-blow.[188]

Reference has been made in previous chapters to Mírzá Muḥammad-'Alí's iniquity and rebellion – a rebellion unprecedented in the annals of religion because the greatness of the Cause has brought similarly great opposition. Dr Yúnis Khán states in his memoirs that on one occasion, towards the end of 1904, when a few pilgrims were seated in His presence, 'Abdu'l-Bahá described His suffering at the hands of the Covenant-breakers. The stories He recounted were so heart-rending that all who heard Him were deeply distressed. At this point Dr Khán asked the Master to tell him how long these Covenant-breakers would continue to oppose Him. 'Abdu'l-Bahá is reported to have said that in four years' time they would become impotent to act against Him. This prophecy was fulfilled in 1909 when, as a result of the 'Young Turk' Revolution, 'Abdu'l-Bahá was freed from 40 years of imprisonment, the Cause of God made remarkable progress in the East and the West and the Covenant-breakers crept back into their abodes of ignominy and defeat. In that same gathering in 1904

'Abdu'l-Bahá stated that whereas in the future some vestige would remain of Mírzá Yaḥyá's followers in the world, no trace would be left of these Covenant-breakers in the Holy Land, and this is the case today.

In one of His talks the Master is reported to have said that God always assisted the Covenant-breakers during His ministry and enabled them to make every possible breach in the stronghold of the Cause so that the Master might stop them all and ensure that others in the future would not succeed.

As the years went by, the Message of Bahá'u'lláh spread throughout the United States and Canada. It reached the continent of Europe, where a nucleus of Bahá'í communities was established in several countries including Britain, France and Germany. When 'Abdu'l-Bahá was freed from His 40–year confinement He travelled to the West and openly proclaimed the Message of Bahá'u'lláh to the people of Europe and America. So powerful was the influence He exerted on the hearts of the people that great numbers flocked to churches and public halls to see Him and to hear Him speak. The believers in the West who came into contact with 'Abdu'l-Bahá were transformed spiritually and magnetized by His all-encompassing love. He laid such a solid foundation, especially in North America, that a few years later He conferred upon that community a measure of primacy in the execution of His Tablets of the Divine Plan, a series of 14 Tablets addressed to the North American believers, which constitute a charter for the teaching work throughout the world.

19

Deviations of Mírzá Muḥammad-'Alí (4)

6–WT What deviation can be more infamous than the vain and feeble interpretations of the people of doubt!

'The people of doubt' may be understood to be a reference to the Covenant-breakers in the Holy Land and those who were misled by them. Engaged for years in opposing the Covenant, Mírzá Muḥammad-'Alí, assisted by his evil-minded companions, continuously fabricated false stories to promote his plans to foment dissension within the Bahá'í community and create confusion and mistrust among the well-wishers of the Master. One may marvel at the Covenant-breakers' creativity, for every day they concocted and disseminated new falsehoods. While a detailed description of their propaganda lies beyond the scope of this book, a few misleading statements will be mentioned.

In the 'Infernal Letters' that he disseminated among the believers, Mírzá Muḥammad-'Alí maintained that contrary to the provisions of the Kitáb-i-'Ahd, 'Abdu'l-Bahá should not be the sole Centre of authority in the community. He contended that the Ag̲h̲ṣán, meaning the three half-brothers of 'Abdu'l-Bahá, should be involved in the decision-making process in all affairs of the Cause. The reason given was that 'Abdu'l-Bahá could not be trusted since He had allegedly claimed the station of the Divine Being for Himself – a preposterous allegation. At other times 'Abdu'l-Bahá was accused of claiming the station of a Manifestation of God. The Covenant-breakers levelled all these accusations, and many more, against the Master and publicized them far and wide.

In 1903 a bloody upheaval took place in the city of Yazd and its surrounding villages. Within a few days, a great number of believers were martyred, demonstrating to the public the intensity of their faith and proclaiming with their life-blood the truth of the Cause of Bahá'u-'lláh. The scenes of their heroism and self-sacrifice are all recorded in detail in the annals of the Faith. The news of the martyrdom of so many devoted believers brought great sorrow to the heart of 'Abdu'l-Bahá. Mírzá Muḥammad-'Alí and his associates, knowing too well that these souls had laid down their lives in the path of Bahá'u'lláh, spread the news among the inhabitants of the Holy Land in general, and to prominent citizens in particular, that the followers of 'Abdu'l-Bahá in Yazd were all criminals and had therefore been put to death.

Dr Yúnis Khán recounts an interesting story which demonstrates the genius of Mírzá Muḥammad-'Alí in the art of perverting the truth. The following is a summary translation of his words:

> As the news of the sufferings of the Master reached the believers in the West, it stirred them up and aroused the spirit of loving devotion for Him in their hearts. Some believers decided to try to relieve Him from His sufferings. They wrote letters to 'Abdu'l-Bahá and expressed their readiness to do anything in their power to bring about His freedom. They sent letters to this effect signed by a great many souls. Among those who wanted to take action were Mme. Jackson and Hippolyte Dreyfus and two others who collected a large sum of money with a view to journeying to Istanbul and trying to secure 'Abdu'l-Bahá's release from incarceration* in the Most Great Prison. In so doing they intended to give a considerable sum as an award to Káẓim Páshá, the Governor of Beirut, for his assistance in this matter.
>
> As soon as this news reached the Master, He immediately put a stop to it by sending a telegram and forbidding them to take such action . . . One day 'Abdu'l-Bahá told me that His freedom from incarceration was in the hands of God and that it was not permitted for anyone to take action in this regard. As soon as He heard of the plan to try to bring about His freedom, He sent a telegram to Paris and stopped the intended plan. He then told me how the Covenant-breakers exploited this action by the Master. They wrote a letter to Káẓim Páshá and told the whole story to him. They made a false statement accusing 'Abdu'l-Bahá of harbouring animosity towards the Páshá and maintained that because of this animosity, 'Abdu'l-Bahá had stopped His followers from sending him a large sum of money (about thirty thousand liras) which he otherwise would have received. It was because of this devilish misinformation that the Páshá rose up in enmity against 'Abdu'l-Bahá.[189]

Dr Khán further describes the machinations of the Covenant-breakers in casting doubts in the hearts of the people about the activities of the friends, as seen in the following summary translation:

> When Mírzá Badí'u'lláh broke his repentance,† rejoined his brother, and reunited with the rebellious and the deniers, all the Covenant-breakers joined forces in order to arrest the onward progress of the Faith. Mírzá Shu'á'u'lláh went to the United States to assist Khayru'lláh and to confront Mírzá Abu'l-Faḍl. Thus preparations

---

* For further details of 'Abdu'l-Bahá's incarceration see chapter 20.

† See chapter 16.

> were made to embark upon a campaign of misrepresentation of the Cause – a campaign in which all Covenant-breakers were to take part including those in the Holy Land and abroad. Soon they began to deny the indisputable facts connected with the progress of the Faith. In those days, the believers in the East and the West were highly excited about the unprecedented advance of the Faith. The Covenant-breakers in their publications in the West stated that there was no grain of truth concerning the progress of the Cause in the East. Similarly, to the Bahá'ís of the East they emphatically declared the statements about entry into the Faith by the Western people to be untrue. They even publicly announced that there was no truth in the news of the building of the Mas͟hriqu'l-Ad͟hkár in 'Is͟hqábád and that it was merely a propaganda campaign of the Bahá'ís . . .
>
> They continued fabricating false statements for some time. Eventually, there came a time when they saw the futility of their efforts and these activities came to a halt . . . In the meantime some of the Covenant-breakers in 'Akká repented and returned to the community, others were disillusioned and became helpless and began to wander around. In the year 1904 the Arch-breaker of the Covenant, along with two or three of his close allies, crept into the den of oblivion, and like unto a spider, made a web of vain imaginings and feeble interpretations around himself, waiting for some poor soul to be caught in his net, to be indoctrinated and led astray . . . For about two years they remained inactive until the year 1906, when they crept out of their abodes of heedlessness and became active again with the arrival of the Commission of Inquiry.[190]

As we shall see in the following pages, they soon became impotent and lost their cause altogether.

6–WT What deviation can be more wicked than joining hands with strangers and with the enemies of God!

As we have already noted, in their struggle to achieve ascendancy over the Master, the Covenant-breakers did everything in their power to undermine the foundation of the Covenant of Bahá'u'lláh. The basis on which they always acted was falsehood, a universal tool with which they manipulated every situation. They found sympathy among the enemies of the Cause who were longing to harm the Faith. Not satisfied with sowing the seeds of disunity among the Bahá'ís, not content with spreading falsehood among the inhabitants of 'Akká and the neighbouring lands, they took their tales of woe to foreign nationals who were antagonistic towards the Faith. Disguised as paupers, they claimed to have been treated cruelly by 'Abdu'l-Bahá.

One such person in whom the Covenant-breakers confided was Rosamond Dale Owen, the wife of Laurence Oliphant, the Victorian traveller and writer who lived for several years in the Holy Land. Mrs Oliphant, a staunch Christian committed to the defence of her religion, became alarmed at the progress of the Faith, as can be seen from her book *My Perilous Life in Palestine*. Mírzá Badí'u'lláh deceitfully complained to her that 'Abdu'l-Bahá had usurped his rights and those of his brothers and that consequently he was in dire financial need. He and Mírzá Muḥammad-'Alí made other preposterous claims, all designed to discredit 'Abdu'l-Bahá. These brothers knew only too well that Mrs Oliphant was very unhappy about the growth of the Faith and its spread among Christians in the West; they hoped that their slanderous remarks about 'Abdu'l-Bahá might serve as ammunition in her opposition to the Faith and to the Master as its head. And this is exactly what happened.

The following few passages gleaned from Mrs Oliphant's book show the extent to which the calumnies and falsehoods that Mírzá Badí'u'lláh had uttered played into the hands of its author, who used them to discredit the Cause of Bahá'u'lláh:

> He [Mírzá Badí'u'lláh] was a political prisoner in St Jean d'Acre for a number of years, and I found that he and his family of seven persons were about to starve . . .
>
> Abbas Effendi and his family live comfortably, whereas Bedi-Allah [sic] and his family would almost have starved had I not come to the rescue . . .
>
> I understand that Mohammed Ali [sic] the second son, is as great a sufferer, having been saved from extreme poverty only by the exertions of some relatives in America . . .
>
> If the numerous Christian followers of Abbas Effendi, in England and America, consider this a noble course of action, their ideas of brotherly love, must be, so it seems to me, somewhat peculiar . . .
>
> I understand that there are at least three million Christians who are followers and admirers of Abbas Effendi. This scarcely seems possible, but if it be true, then it is for these people to determine whether a man of the character of Abbas Effendi, letting his brother almost starve while he lived comfortably, is fitted to teach Christians a more Christ-like mode of life.[191]

Much has happened since these uncomplimentary remarks were written about the Master. It is evident today that the darkness of falsehood has been vanquished by the light of truth. The Christ-like person of 'Abdu'l-Bahá, the perfect Exemplar of the teachings of Bahá'u'lláh and a stainless mirror reflecting His light, provided a noble example for men to follow in this Dispensation. These disparaging remarks about the Master, whose virtuous life of service to humanity has been acclaimed by friend and foe alike, would have brought great satisfaction to the Covenant-breakers, had it not been for the fact that by the time Mrs Oliphant's book was published they had become powerless and were on the verge of extinction.

20

Deviations of Mírzá Muḥammad-'Alí (5)

6–WT What deviation can be more complete than falsely accusing the loved ones of God! What deviation can be more evil than causing their imprisonment and incarceration! What deviation can be more severe than delivering into the hands of the government the Holy Writings and Epistles, that haply they (the government) might arise intent upon the death of this wronged one! What deviation can be more violent than threatening the ruin of the Cause of God, forging and slanderously falsifying letters and documents so that this might perturb and alarm the government and lead to the shedding of the blood of this wronged one, – such letters and documents being now in the possession of the government!

Much has been said in foregoing pages about the machinations of Mírzá Muḥammad-'Alí and his shameful accusations against the Master and His loved ones. In his endeavour to discredit 'Abdu'l-Bahá he devised every kind of malicious plot, which brought much sorrow to the hearts of the believers. He spread untrue stories in the Bahá'í community and misrepresented the Faith to the local people in the Holy Land. These activities continued unabated until the year 1900, when 'Abdu'l-Bahá began to build the Shrine of the Báb on Mount Carmel. This undertaking played into the hands of Mírzá Muḥammad-'Alí, who exploited it to the utmost and brought about 'Abdu'l-Bahá's greatest sufferings. The difficulties which 'Abdu'l-Bahá had endured since the passing of Bahá'u'lláh until the building work started pale into insignificance when compared with the pain inflicted on the Master by the Covenant-breakers after the start of the construction of the Shrine.

To appreciate the extent of Mírzá Muḥammad-'Alí's machinations, a brief account of the circumstances surrounding the building of the Shrine of the Báb is helpful. In the early part of 1900 Haifa became the focal point of 'Abdu'l-Bahá's attention. He rented three houses there: one for Himself and for occasional visits by members of His family; another, a four-roomed house, for Eastern pilgrims, in which one room was set aside for the Master Himself, another for the office of Ḥájí Siyyid Taqíy-i-Manshádí,* and the other two for pilgrims; and a third house with four rooms, suitably furnished for the increasing number of Western pilgrims who had begun to visit 'Abdu'l-Bahá since late 1898. Before 1900 several pilgrims stayed in these houses but once 'Abdu'l-Bahá began to build the Shrine on Mount Carmel, He discouraged Bahá'ís from coming on pilgrimage and so the houses remained for the most part untenanted.

Dr Yúnis Khán describes the state of affairs in Haifa just after the turn of the century. The following is a summary translation from his fascinating memoirs:

> The work of building the foundation of the Shrine of the Báb was proceeding well. The Blessed Master used to come to Haifa frequently to supervise the construction work. He would stay a few days during which the Bahá'ís and non-Bahá'ís attained His presence . . .
>
> Certain changes had taken place during the three or four years preceding the year 1900.
>
> Mírzá Áqá Ján . . . had passed away.
>
> Mírzá Ḍíyá'u'lláh, the vacillating son of Bahá'u'lláh . . . had also passed away.
>
> The room on the ground floor of the Mansion of Bahjí which was used by the believers had been taken over by the Covenant-breakers . . .
>
> The Covenant-breakers had given up their earlier practice of demanding payment of their expenses from the Master; consequently, the hardships in His own household resulting from the shortage of funds in previous years had somewhat eased. However, from time to time, He would find some reason to send funds to His unfaithful brothers.
>
> The activities of the chief of police of 'Akká, Yaḥyá Ṭábúr Áqásí, against the Cause of God, had produced the opposite effect. He himself was dismissed from his post and later, when he became destitute, he went to the Master and received help from Him.
>
> During these past three years, groups of pilgrims from both the East and the West visited regularly. The town of Haifa had become

---

* This believer served Bahá'u'lláh and the Master in the Holy Land for many years. See 'Abdu'l-Bahá, *Memorials of the Faithful*, p. 54.

> a centre for the believers where meetings and festive gatherings were often held, but in obedience to the advice of the Master, these gatherings had become less frequent.
>
> The Covenant-breakers began to create fresh trouble by causing alarm among the mischievous elements of the population. They misrepresented 'Abdu'l-Bahá's plans for the construction of the mausoleum of the Báb.[192]

The construction of the Shrine of the Báb was the greatest undertaking in the Bahá'í Faith during the opening years of the 20th century. This was a sacred task which, during the last years of His life, Bahá'u-'lláh had specifically asked 'Abdu'l-Bahá to accomplish. The purchase of the site for the Shrine took a long time, for under the influence of the Covenant-breakers the owner at first refused to sell. After many difficulties, when negotiations for the sale of the property were completed and ownership passed to 'Abdu'l-Bahá, it became necessary to purchase another piece of land situated on the south side to provide access to the building site. At the instigation of the Covenant-breakers, the owner demanded an exorbitant price for this land and even when 'Abdu'l-Bahá offered to pay a very large sum for it the owner was determined not to sell. 'Abdu'l-Bahá was heard to make the following remarks concerning this episode:

> Every stone of that building, every stone of the road leading to it, I have with infinite tears and at tremendous cost, raised and placed in position.
>
> One night I was so hemmed in by My anxieties that I had no other recourse than to recite and repeat over and over again a prayer of the Báb which I had in My possession, the recital of which greatly calmed Me. The next morning the owner of the plot himself came to Me, apologized and begged Me to purchase the property.[193]

As the building work on Mount Carmel proceeded the believers were overjoyed at the prospect of the interment of the remains of the Báb in that holy spot. But the Covenant-breakers, who were continually frustrated in their devious activities and forced to witness the ascendancy of the Covenant, particularly in the arrival of pilgrims from the West, were aroused to inflict yet another blow upon the Master.

In 1901 'Abdu'l-Bahá, in the course of His talks with the believers, foretold the approach of some impending tribulation that would be caused by the Covenant-breakers. He is reported to have intimated to the friends that the Covenant-breakers would create great trouble for Him but that they themselves would be the first to be trapped in the mesh of their own devices and that only later would He Himself become a target of their schemes. ʻAbdu'l-Bahá often spoke in this vein to His companions during those days. He intimated to them that whereas He welcomed afflictions in the path of God, His brothers would be the ones who would suffer. The believers were concerned about such predictions and did not know what kind of problems would be created for the Master. Their only prayer was that God might intervene and avert any ordeal which might be in store for Him.

By August 1901 the building work on Mount Carmel had reached an advanced stage and ʻAbdu'l-Bahá was visiting Haifa frequently when suddenly a great upheaval occurred in ʻAkká. On 20 August the believers celebrated the anniversary of the Declaration of the Báb (according to the lunar calendar) at the Shrine of Bahá'u'lláh at Bahjí. On His return to ʻAkká, ʻAbdu'l-Bahá was informed that His brothers had been escorted by soldiers from Bahjí and brought to ʻAkká in great humiliation. Majdu'd-Dín* had also been brought from Tiberias. The Master immediately went to the authorities to enquire about the reason for their arrest. It was then that the governor informed ʻAbdu'l-Bahá of an order from the Sulṭán that He and His brothers were to be confined within the walls of the city of ʻAkká and that the same restrictions previously imposed upon Bahá'u'lláh and His companions in the Most Great Prison were to be re-introduced. Furthermore, none of the believers were to be allowed to leave the city and all their activities were to be monitored by the authorities.

Although in the early days of Bahá'u'lláh's arrival in ʻAkká such restrictions were enforceable, now, after so many years, when the Master was loved and adored by the people, it was impossible to enforce this edict fully. Indeed, the governor himself, who was a great admirer of ʻAbdu'l-Bahá, was so embarrassed by the order that he delayed its implementation for some time.

This re-incarceration was the direct result of Mírzá Muḥammad-ʻAlí's misrepresentations to Náẓim Pá<u>sh</u>á, the governor of the province of Syria. The circumstances of this episode are described by Mírzá Badíʻu'lláh in his 'Epistle of Repentance',† written a few years after this incident. He states that Mírzá Muḥammad-ʻAlí sent Mírzá Majdu'd-Dín to Damascus to present a petition to the governor complaining about the activities of ʻAbdu'l-Bahá. The main purpose of this treacherous act was to alarm the authorities by misrepresenting the purpose of the building on Mount Carmel as a fortress designed

---

* See chapter 13.

† See chapter 16.

to raise rebellion and by informing them of large gatherings in 'Akká and the comings and goings of Americans, whom he described as military advisers!

It is known that Majdu'd-Dín took expensive gifts to the governor as a bribe and asked his help in bringing about 'Abdu'l-Bahá's deportation. Indeed, at other times and in the course of their several appeals to the government authorities in Syria, the Covenant-breakers had to raise large sums of money to bribe various officials. Having used up the entire estate of Mírzá Áqá Ján for this purpose, they sold a one-third share of the Mansion of Bahjí for 1200 liras to Yaḥyá Ṭábúr Áqásí, the chief of police in 'Akká and an inveterate enemy of the Faith, and spent the whole sum in bribes to officials.

Majdu'd-Dín arrived back from his mission to Damascus in a jubilant mood, having secured the governor's promise of aid. But events now took a different turn. Upon receiving the governor's report, Sulṭán 'Abdu'l-Ḥamíd became alarmed and ordered that 'Abdu'l-Bahá, His brothers and His followers be re-incarcerated. Consequently, to the surprise of Majdu'd-Dín, his plans misfired and he himself, as well as his chief, Mírzá Muḥammad-'Alí, together with Mírzá Badí'u'lláh, were incarcerated in the city of 'Akká by the order of the Sulṭán. The prophecy of 'Abdu'l-Bahá was fulfilled: His brothers were the first to fall into their own trap.

The Master, as always, submitted Himself to the cruelties inflicted upon Him by His enemies. He accepted the new restrictions in a spirit of radiant acquiescence. The greatest deprivation for Him was His separation from the Shrine of Bahá'u'lláh, which He could not visit during this time. He was also cut off from the building work on Mount Carmel, although He made arrangements for it to continue. For about seven years while this incarceration was in force 'Abdu'l-Bahá continued to direct the affairs of the Bahá'í world in both the East and the West through the outpouring of His voluminous writings. As the years went by, more pilgrims and visitors were received in His rented house adjacent to the barracks, known as the house of 'Abdu'lláh Pá<u>sh</u>á. On the upper storey of this house He built a small wooden cabin in which He could pray, turning in the direction of the Shrine of Bahá'u'lláh.

As for His brothers, upon being brought to 'Akká where they were ordered to live, Mírzá Muḥammad-'Alí wrote two letters, one after the other, to the governor of Damascus (whom he had already bribed) desperately seeking assistance for his own release. But his letters were left unanswered. However, 'Abdu'l-Bahá met the civil and military authorities and interceded for the release of His brothers, saying that they were not able to endure such restrictions, and they were released. He also secured freedom for the other believers, who were allowed to resume the occupations in which they had been previously engaged, but He assured the authorities that He Himself would remain within the walls of the city.

The cause of the restrictions, Mírzá Muḥammad-'Alí, at first flatly denied having had any communication with the governor of Damascus, as did Majdu'd-Dín. They both alleged that the edict of the Sulṭán for re-incarceration had been issued as a result of the publication of a book by Mírzá Abu'l-Faḍl, the great Bahá'í scholar, but the truth soon surfaced. In his memoirs Ḥájí 'Alí Yazdí has described the circumstances which exposed the treachery of Majdu'd-Dín and Mírzá Muḥammad-'Alí. According to Ḥájí 'Alí, Majdu'd-Dín had delivered two petitions personally, one to Náẓim Pá<u>sh</u>á and the other to Faríq Pá<u>sh</u>á, a high-ranking military officer friendly to 'Abdu'l-Bahá. The second petition was presented in response to a question raised by Faríq Pá<u>sh</u>á, who wanted to know the nature of the disagreements between 'Abdu'l-Bahá and His brothers.

Faríq Pá<u>sh</u>á considered 'Abdu'l-Bahá to be possessed of superhuman powers exclusive to the Prophet of God, as illustrated by the following summarized translation of the story by Dr Yúnis <u>Kh</u>án:

> Sometime before the year 1900, there was a war between the Ottomans and the Greeks. Faríq Pá<u>sh</u>á, a general in the army, was ordered to take part in the battle. Because of his heartfelt belief in the powers of 'Abdu'l-Bahá, he asked Him to write a prayer for him to take with him for his protection. The Master wrote a few lines, sealed it and gave it to him to wear on his arm but told him not to open it. He left the Master and went quite happily to the battlefield. At the end of the war he returned victorious, and in a spirit of humility and servitude, went straight to the presence of 'Abdu'l-Bahá, where he expressed his gratitude to Him. 'Abdu'l-Bahá asked him if he had ever opened the prayer, and when he answered in the negative, He asked him to open and read it. Upon reading it, Faríq Pá<u>sh</u>á's belief in 'Abdu'l-Bahá's superhuman powers was further strengthened when he discovered that 'Abdu'l-Bahá had briefly foretold the events of the war and the highlights of his personal circumstances.[194]

Returning to the story of Mírzá Muḥammad-'Alí's petition to the governor of Syria, Ḥájí 'Alí Yazdí further describes that in order to confuse the issue for Faríq Pá<u>sh</u>á, who was a Sunní Muslim, Mírzá Muḥammad-'Alí and Majdu'd-Dín forged a document, which they attributed to Bahá'u'lláh, and sent it along with their petition. In this document they composed, in the name of Bahá'u'lláh, certain complimentary passages in praise of 'Umar, the second Caliph of Sunní Islam. In so doing, they made it seem that Bahá'u'lláh was a follower of Sunní Islam. The other document which they sent to the Pá<u>sh</u>á contained parts of the Lawḥ-i-Hizár Baytí (Tablet of One Thousand Verses)* in which 'Abdu'l-Bahá condemned 'Umar in strong terms. In their petition they then alleged that 'Abdu'l-Bahá was inciting His followers to arise in enmity against the Sunnís, whereas the rest of Bahá'u'lláh's family were admirers of 'Umar and the Sunní community!

Mírzá Muḥammad-'Alí and Majdu'd-Dín continued to deny having sent any petition to Damascus until Faríq Pá<u>sh</u>á at last sent it to 'Abdu'l-Bahá, who, upon receiving it, sent it to the mother of Mírzá Muḥammad-'Alí so that she could see the treachery of her offspring and son-in-law.

These preposterous activities opened the eyes of some of the Covenant-breakers, who had previously been duped into believing that Mírzá Muḥammad-'Alí was a true follower of the Faith of Bahá'u'lláh. These simple-hearted men, who had been for so long deceived by the Arch-breaker of the Covenant, went to 'Abdu'l-Bahá, expressed remorse for their folly and were bountifully forgiven by Him.

As we look back upon these events, we can only be amazed at the craftiness of such a two-faced hypocrite who, on the one hand, professed to his misguided followers the divine origin of the Revelation of his Father, thereby posing as a holy and truthful person worthy to be emulated by all, and on the other, shamelessly announced that both he and Bahá'u'lláh were followers of Sunní Islam. Mírzá Muḥammad-'Alí knew only too well that Bahá'u'lláh had clearly taught His followers that 'Umar, the second Caliph of Sunní Islam, had broken the unwritten Covenant of Muḥammad and unlawfully usurped the successorship of the Prophet from Imám 'Alí. He also knew that the holy Imáms of the <u>Sh</u>í'ah sect of Islam, whose stations Bahá'u'lláh has extolled in His writings, were the true successors of the Prophet. Despite this, there were no limits to which Mírzá Muḥammad-'Alí would not go in order to destroy 'Abdu'l-Bahá. He was a master in the art of falsification and continued in this vein for years, spreading falsehood and calumnies against the Centre of the Covenant.

When it became public knowledge that the cause of the imposition of this new incarceration of 'Abdu'l-Bahá was Majdu'd-Dín's petition, the Covenant-breakers became subdued and chastened for some time. However, once released from incarceration within the prison city, Mírzá Muḥammad-'Alí and his associates became content with their own freedom and jubilant that the Master, whom they hated so bitterly, was confined within the walls of 'Akká. They considered this a victory and foolishly thought that the end of 'Abdu'l-Bahá and His

* See chapter 4.

leadership was in sight. Little did they know that light cannot be put out by darkness and that the power of God cannot be made ineffective through the opposition of ignoble men.

During the years of His confinement in the city of 'Akká, 'Abdu'l-Bahá was engaged in writing numerous Tablets either in His own handwriting or by dictation to His secretaries. Through these He continued to guide the followers of Bahá'u'lláh in their service to the Cause, urging them to remain steadfast in the Covenant and to diffuse the divine fragrances with wisdom and perseverance. Though restricted in His movements, the Master was now living in relative peace, directing the construction of the Shrine of the Báb on Mount Carmel, while the emanations of His pen continued to enrapture the souls of the faithful, thus enabling them to scale loftier heights of service in His Cause.

Many significant achievements in the history of the Faith occurred during this time. In 1902, through 'Abdu'l-Bahá's instruction and guidance, the foundation stone was laid of the Mas͟hriqu'l-Ad͟hkár* in 'Is͟hqábád, the first Bahá'í House of Worship in the world.

Another significant development during this period was the rise of a new spirit of dedication and steadfastness in the Bahá'í communities of both the East and the West. This spirit was intensified as a result of the upheaval in the summer of 1903 in Yazd and neighbouring villages, when a great many souls were martyred in the most moving circumstances, shedding through their amazing steadfastness and exemplary heroism an imperishable lustre upon the annals of the Faith.

In the Holy Land, while the Covenant-breakers were rejoicing that 'Abdu'l-Bahá had been made a prisoner, many members of the public were moved to sympathize with the Cause. The friendly governor of 'Akká made several attempts to persuade 'Abdu'l-Bahá not to confine Himself within the city walls but to go and visit other places outside 'Akká; however, the Master declined the suggestion. Eventually the governor asked 'Abdu'l-Bahá to accompany him on a visit to the Shrine of Bahá'u'lláh. The Master granted his wish and together they left the city and went to Bahjí. In order to further circumvent the strict edict of the Sulṭán, the governor arranged another visit and this time he invited other high-ranking officials to accompany him, including Faríq Pás͟há.

When the party arrived at Bahjí, the Covenant-breakers witnessed the majestic figure of 'Abdu'l-Bahá walking at the front of the procession and the dignitaries walking behind Him as a mark of respect.

* Literally, 'Dawning Place of the Mention of God'; a Bahá'í House of Worship.

When Mírzá Muḥammad-'Alí saw the honour and reverence which the governor and other officials paid to the Master, he became very disheartened and his hopes that incarceration might diminish 'Abdu'l-Bahá's ascendancy were dashed.

As the year 1902 passed, 'Abdu'l-Bahá again permitted pilgrims from the East and West to come. All who attained the presence of the Master became magnetized by the spiritual forces He released and when they returned home they warmed the hearts of the friends through the fire of the divine love that the Master ignited in their hearts. Far from impeding the progress of the Faith during those perilous years, 'Abdu'l-Bahá's incarceration in the city of 'Akká, with all the hardships it entailed, coincided with an upsurge in activity among the friends and the expansion of the community throughout the world.

Eye-witnesses have testified that during this agitated period in His life the Master, in His own hand, used to pen no less than 90 Tablets a day. The outpouring of these Tablets in such profusion was chiefly responsible for the expansion of the Faith and the exhilaration and upliftment of the believers everywhere.

21

Decreeing the Death of 'Abdu'l-Bahá

6–WT What deviation can be more grievous than decreeing the death of the Centre of the Covenant, supported by the holy verse: – 'He that layeth a claim ere the passing of a thousand years . . . ,' whilst he (Muḥammad 'Alí) without shame in the days of the Blessed Beauty had advanced such a claim as this and been confuted by Him in the aforementioned manner, the text of his claim being still extant in his own handwriting and bearing his own seal.

This passage in the Will and Testament concerns the secret plans of the Covenant-breakers to take 'Abdu'l-Bahá's life. For several years they had tried everything to discredit the Master but the more they intensified their campaign of opposition against Him, the greater was the progress of the Cause and the more desperate they became. Like Mírzá Yaḥyá, who found himself unable to withstand the power of Bahá'u'lláh and resorted to poisoning Him, Mírzá Muḥammad-'Alí tried different means by which to bring about 'Abdu'l-Bahá's death. One of his men, on two different occasions, placed poison in a jug of His drinking water. This was discovered in time. On another occasion one of the Covenant-breakers carried a dagger hidden under his clothes with the intention of taking 'Abdu'l-Bahá's life but he did not succeed in his attempt. Later both men regretted their actions. 'Abdu'l-Bahá forgave one and turned a blind eye to the other. These two later left the Holy Land and went to Ṭihrán.

Before incarceration was imposed on Him, 'Abdu'l-Bahá used to frequent the city of Haifa to supervise the building work on the Shrine of the Báb. He used to meet the believers in the evenings and often late in the night He would proceed to His residence. Always, against His wishes, some believer concerned for His protection would walk a few yards behind Him. Late one night a gunman hired by Mírzá Muḥammad-'Alí fired three shots at the Master, all of which failed to hit Him. The believer who was walking behind rushed forward and the gunman ran away. 'Abdu'l-Bahá did not show the slightest sign of perturbation at this incident and kept on walking, as always, with great dignity and majesty. In this connection the following words of

'Abdu'l-Bahá concerning the sufferings which Mírzá Muḥammad-'Alí inflicted upon Him take on added meaning:

> **5–WT [Mírzá Muḥammad-'Alí] hath with bitter rancour endeavoured to hurt 'Abdu'l-Bahá and hath assailed with the utmost enmity this servant of the Sacred Threshold. Every dart he seized and hurled to pierce the breast of this wronged servant, no wound did he neglect to grievously inflict upon me, no venom did he spare but he poisoned therewith the life of this hapless one. I swear by the most holy Abhá Beauty and by the Light shining from His Holiness, the Exalted One (may my soul be a sacrifice for Their lowly servants), that because of this iniquity the dwellers in the Pavilion of the Abhá Kingdom have bewailed, the Celestial Concourse is lamenting, the Immortal Maids of Heaven in the All-Highest Paradise have raised their plaintive cries and the angelic company sighed and uttered their moanings.**

In another passage of the Will and Testament 'Abdu'l-Bahá says:

> **48–WT O ye the true, the sincere, the faithful friends of this wronged one! Everyone knoweth and believeth what calamities and afflictions have befallen this wronged one, this prisoner, at the hands of those who have broken the Covenant at the time when, after the setting of the Day-Star of the world, his heart was consumed with the flame of His bereavement.**

In order to legitimize their plans for taking 'Abdu'l-Bahá's life, the Covenant-breakers needed to fabricate a reason that would warrant His death and Mírzá Muḥammad-'Alí was well qualified in this regard. As previously outlined, false accusations had been made against the Master to the effect that He claimed to be a Manifestation of God and that He regarded the Báb and Bahá'u'lláh to be His forerunners. All these calumnies were widely spread among the Covenant-breakers who justified the death of 'Abdu'l-Bahá based on the following passage of the Kitáb-i-Aqdas, in which Bahá'u'lláh regards anyone who claims a revelation from God as an imposter:

> Whoso layeth claim to a Revelation direct from God, ere the expiration of a full thousand years, such a man is assuredly a lying imposter. We pray God that He may graciously assist him to retract and repudiate such claim. Should he repent, God will, no doubt, forgive him. If, however, he persisteth in his error, God will, assuredly, send down one who will deal mercilessly with him. Terrible, indeed, is God in punishing![195]

The phrase to 'deal mercilessly with him' was interpreted by Mírzá Muḥammad-'Alí as a decree for taking the life of the imposter. How wicked to calumniate 'Abdu'l-Bahá, the embodiment of servitude, by saying that He claimed the station of the Manifestation of God for Himself! It was common knowledge that in Adrianople Mírzá Muḥammad-'Alí had declared himself to be a partner with Bahá'u'lláh in divine revelation, provoking Bahá'u'lláh's wrathful reaction* to passages in Mírzá Muḥammad-'Alí's writings in which he announced himself to be the source of divine revelation. It is to this that 'Abdu'l-Bahá refers in His Will and Testament:

> . . . whilst he (Muḥammad 'Alí) without shame in the days of the Blessed Beauty had advanced such a claim as this and been confuted by Him in the aforementioned manner, the text of his claim being still extant in his own handwriting and bearing his own seal.

Attempts on the life of 'Abdu'l-Bahá continued for some time. Towards the end of 1905 Shu'a'u'lláh, the eldest son of Mírzá Muḥammad-'Alí, disclosed a clandestine plot by the Covenant-breakers to achieve their aim, to which 'Abdu'l-Bahá refers in this passage of the Will and Testament:

> **9–WT In like manner, the focal Centre of Hate, hath purposed to put 'Abdu'l-Bahá to death and this is supported by the testimony written by Mírzá Shu'á'u'lláh himself and is here enclosed. It is evident and indisputable that they are privily and with the utmost subtlety engaged in conspiring against me. The following are his very words written by him in this letter: – 'I curse at every moment him that hath kindled this discord, imprecate in these words "Lord! have no mercy upon him" and I hope ere long God will make manifest the one that shall have no pity on him, who now weareth another garb and about whom I cannot any more explain.' Reference he doth make by these words to the sacred verse that beginneth as follows: – 'He that layeth a claim ere the passing of a thousand years . . .' Reflect! How intent they are upon the death of 'Abdu'l-Bahá! Ponder in your hearts upon the phrase 'I cannot any more explain' and realize what schemes they are devising for this purpose. They fear lest, too fully explained, the letter might fall into alien hands and their schemes be foiled and frustrated. The phrase is only foretelling good tidings to come, namely that regarding this all requisite arrangements have been made.**

---

* See chapter 15.

As already stated, Shu'a'u'lláh was sent to the United States to assist the notorious Covenant-breaker Khayru'lláh and to counter the activities of the Bahá'í community. Soon after his arrival in that country, however, he found himself unable to carry out effectively the mission entrusted to him by his father. He travelled to various parts of the United States and tried in vain to create dissension among the believers. One of the activities he was involved in while there was a secret plot to take the life of 'Abdu'l-Bahá, to which he clearly refers in a letter, dated 27 November 1905, to Majdu'd-Dín. Somehow this letter fell into the hands of 'Abdu'l-Bahá, who attached such importance to it that He quoted these words of Shu'a'u'lláh in His Will and Testament:

> 'I curse at every moment him ['Abdu'l-Bahá] that hath kindled this discord, imprecate in these words "Lord! have no mercy upon him" and I hope ere long God will make manifest the one that shall have no pity on him, who now weareth another garb and about whom I cannot any more explain.'

The phrase 'Lord! have no mercy upon him' is a reference to the passage in the Kitáb-i-Aqdas quoted above: 'Whoso layeth claim to a Revelation . . . God will, assuredly, send down one who will deal mercilessly with him.'

Apart from this reference to 'Abdu'l-Bahá and the plot against His life, the rest of the letter mostly concerns material things. Shu'a'u'lláh refers to his shortage of funds and describes the ways he has been living in different quarters of the United States since his arrival in the summer of 1904. He also mentions that when he meets the believers, he finds himself inadequate to deal with them in discussions. Shu'a'u'lláh (Light of God), to whom the Master referred as the darkened soul, remained in the United States for several years. There he used to meet with some of the new believers and introduce himself as the grandson of Bahá'u'lláh but when the friends became aware of his violation of the Covenant, they left him to his own devices and shunned his company.

Shu'a'u'lláh was in the United States when the Master visited that country. He tried to undermine the influence which 'Abdu'l-Bahá exerted on the hearts of people. On one occasion, introducing himself as a blood relation of Bahá'u'lláh, he succeeded in misleading a newspaper editor who wrote about him as deserving to inherit the station of the chosen ones of God. 'Abdu'l-Bahá did not pay any attention to this but when asked by a journalist to comment on His nephew's statement, He is reported to have told the story of Christ when He learned His brothers were coming to see Him. Christ has said, 'They are not my brethren but you are my brethren and kindred.' As Christ had not paid attention to His brothers, 'Abdu'l-Bahá continued, the same was true in this case. He then said, 'Notwithstanding, my house is open to all. People are free to come in or go out.' The words of the Master as recorded by the journalist were published in the newspaper.

At one point during the Master's visit to the United States, Shu'a'u'lláh, encouraged by his father, wrote a letter to 'Abdu'l-Bahá and published its contents in a newspaper. In this letter, written in Arabic, he invited 'Abdu'l-Bahá to meet with him and Khayru'lláh in Chicago or elsewhere to resolve the differences that had arisen in the Faith. He had the temerity to accuse 'Abdu'l-Bahá of having divided the Faith and suggested ten points to be discussed in the meeting – all based on the preposterous accusation that 'Abdu'l-Bahá claimed to be and was acting as a Manifestation of God. The Master did not deign to respond.

Soon after the passing of 'Abdu'l-Bahá, Shu'a'u'lláh wrote another letter, on behalf of His father, addressed to the believers in the United States. In it, quoting the verses of the Kitáb-i-'Ahd concerning the station of Mírzá Muḥammad-'Alí, he announced him to be the successor to 'Abdu'l-Bahá. None of the friends was influenced by his appeal to turn to the one who was the Arch-breaker of the Covenant of Bahá'u'lláh.

22

Covenant-Breakers Petition Government against 'Abdu'l-Bahá

7–WT A few months ago, in concert with others, he that hath broken the Covenant, hath prepared a document teeming with calumny and slander wherein, the Lord forbid, among many similar slanderous charges, 'Abdu'l-Bahá is deemed a deadly enemy, the ill-wisher of the Crown. They so perturbed the minds of the members of the Imperial Government that at last a Committee of Investigation was sent from the seat of His Majesty's Government which, violating every rule of justice and equity that befit His Imperial Majesty, nay, with the most glaring injustice, proceeded with its investigations. The ill-wishers of the One True God surrounded them on every side and explained and excessively enlarged upon the text of the document whilst they (the members of the Committee) in their turn blindly acquiesced. One of their many calumnies was that this servant had raised aloft a banner in this city, had summoned the people together under it, had established a new sovereignty for himself, had erected upon Mount Carmel a mighty stronghold, had rallied around him all the peoples of the land and made them obedient to him, had caused disruption in the Faith of Islám, had Covenanted with the following of Christ and, God forbid, had purposed to cause the gravest breach in the mighty power of the Crown. May the Lord protect us from such atrocious falsehoods!

In part two of the Will and Testament, 'Abdu'l-Bahá, referring to the Covenant-breakers, says:

32–WT And still they rested not, but further strove with stubbornness, falsehood and slander, with scorn and calumny to stir up sedition in the midst of the government of this land and elsewhere, causing them to deem me a sower of sedition and filling the minds with the things that the ear abhorreth to hear. The government was thus alarmed, fear fell upon the sovereign, and the suspicion of the nobility was aroused. Minds were troubled, affairs were upset, souls were perturbed, the fire of anguish and sorrow was kindled within the breasts, the Holy Leaves (of the Household) were convulsed and shaken, their eyes rained with

tears, their signs and lamentations were raised and their hearts burned within them as they bewailed this wronged servant of Thine, fallen a victim into the hands of these, his kindred, nay, his very enemies!

These two passages tell the story of the most menacing and the most dangerous episode in the life of the Master, during which the Covenant-breakers came very close to fulfilling their aim of eliminating Him. They failed, through an act of Providence which brought in its wake freedom for the Master and an ignominious decline for Mírzá Muḥammad-'Alí and his henchmen.

As we have already stated, by 1902 pilgrims from the East and the West were attaining the presence of the Master in the Holy Land. As a result of their contact with Him, they were filled with a new divine spirit and returned home illumined, teaching the Cause, inspiring the friends and consolidating the foundations of the Faith. In Persia, a number of the erudite teachers of the Faith defended the Covenant by writing epistles refuting, in compelling terms, the misrepresentations of the Covenant-breakers. Copies of these letters were usually read aloud in the gatherings of the friends in the Holy Land. These activities as well as the onward progress of the Cause aroused the jealousy of the Covenant-breakers who began to take drastic actions against 'Abdu'l-Bahá. The following passage in the Will and Testament describes the extent of their malice and infamous deeds:

50–WT Thereupon the loved ones of the Lord arose, inspired with the greatest confidence and constancy and aided by the power of the Kingdom, by Divine Strength, by heavenly Grace, by the unfailing help and Celestial Bounty, they withstood the enemies of the Covenant in well-nigh three score and ten treatises and supported by conclusive proofs, unmistakable evidences and clear texts from the Holy Writ, they refuted their scrolls of doubt and mischief-kindling leaflets. The Centre of Sedition was thus confounded in his craftiness, afflicted by the wrath of God, sunk into a degradation and infamy that shall be lasting until the Day of Doom. Base and wretched is the plight of the people of evil deeds, they that are in grievous loss!

51–WT And as they lost their cause, grew hopeless in their efforts against the loved ones of God, saw the Standard of His Testament waving throughout all regions and witnessed the power of the Covenant of the Merciful One, the flame of envy so blazed within them as to be beyond recounting. With the utmost vigour, exertion, rancour and enmity, they followed another path, walked in another way, devised another plan: that of kindling the flame of sedition in the heart of the very government

> **itself, and thus cause this wronged one, this prisoner to appear as a mover of strife, inimical to the government and a hater and opponent of the Crown. Perchance 'Abdu'l-Bahá may be put to death and his name be made to perish whereby an arena may be opened unto the enemies of the Covenant wherein they may advance and spur on their charger, inflict a grievous loss upon everyone and subvert the very foundations of the edifice of the Cause of God. For so grievous is the conduct and behaviour of this false people that they are become even as an axe striking at the very root of the Blessed Tree. Should they be suffered to continue they would, in but a few days' time, exterminate the Cause of God, His Word, and themselves.**

These passages refer to the treachery of the Covenant-breakers and their approach to government authorities, misrepresenting the activities of 'Abdu'l-Bahá.

The Covenant-breakers continued to spread their malicious propaganda against the Master until the year 1904 when fresh adversities appeared on the horizon. The Covenant-breakers had assiduously plotted until the friendly governor of 'Akká was replaced by one who was hostile to 'Abdu'l-Bahá. Mírzá Muḥammad-'Alí took full advantage of this and stirred up mischief among certain elements of the population who had shown their opposition to the Master. As a result, newspapers in Syria and Egypt wrote disturbing reports about Him and the partisans of Mírzá Muḥammad-'Alí fanned into flame all the unfounded allegations these articles contained.

The culmination of these activities was reached when the Arch-breaker of the Covenant finally drew up an official indictment against the Master. In it he brought false and outrageous accusations against Him and through bribery gathered a number of signatures from certain inhabitants of 'Akká to support his case. This document was sent to the authorities in Istanbul, the seat of Sulṭán 'Abdu'l-Ḥamíd, in the hope that the Sulṭán, who was a despot, might take measures to destroy 'Abdu'l-Bahá.

Soon a Commission of Inquiry arrived in 'Akká. The news spread immediately and agitation seized the inhabitants of the city. Spies were planted in the neighbourhood and the approaches to the house of the Master were watched day and night. For the protection of the Faith and the community, 'Abdu'l-Bahá advised most of the believers to leave 'Akká and seek residence elsewhere. Pilgrimages of the believers were also temporarily halted.

'Abdu'l-Bahá was summoned by the Commission to face charges brought against Him by the violators of the Covenant. He visited the members of the Commission several times and ably refuted the false accusations, disproving each in such a masterly way as to leave no doubt about their spurious nature. His explanations, delivered with majesty and eloquence, were so convincing that the members of the Commission had no choice but to dismiss the case and return home. Once again Mírzá Muḥammad-'Alí and his fellow conspirators were frustrated. Their shameful public encounter with the Master brought no benefit to them; instead it cost them large sums of money in bribes.

As 1904 drew to a close, the Master's situation gradually returned to normal and the believers returned to their homes in 'Akká. The years 1905 and 1906 passed without major incident, although 'Abdu'l-Bahá was continually harassed by these enemies of the Faith and had to take appropriate measures to protect the Cause from their various manoeuvres. In the meantime the political situation in the heart of the Ottoman Empire was becoming increasingly unstable and the Sulṭán correspondingly alarmed. He was known to be nervous of any popular movement in the country and showed himself ruthless in dealing with dissidents.

The Covenant-breakers, who had lost hope of carrying out their evil plots, were heartened by the political situation in Istanbul. They now decided to take advantage of the Sulṭán's weakness and play on his fears and suspicions. All they had to do was to re-open their case against 'Abdu'l-Bahá and send their complaints to the court of the Sulṭán. This, their last major onslaught against the Master, proved to be a complete failure.

In their petition, Mírzá Muḥammad-'Alí and his associates reaffirmed their false claim that whereas Bahá'u'lláh was merely a holy man and an admirer of Sunní Islam, 'Abdu'l-Bahá had condemned the Sunní Faith and claimed the station of prophethood for Himself. They also charged that 'Abdu'l-Bahá had not only acquired vast tracts of land in 'Akká and neighbouring villages and had gathered a large following in the Holy Land but that He had also built a mighty fortress on Mount Carmel,* had made a banner of 'Yá Bahá'u'l-Abhá' and raised it among the inhabitants, had received American and other Western military advisers† at His home and was about to overthrow the government.

Such inflammatory claims, made at a time when the government was apprehensive of revolt by some of the Turkish factions, disturbed the mind of the Sulṭán, who immediately ordered a new Commission of Inquiry to be despatched to 'Akká. This Commission, consisting of four officials, arrived in the winter of 1907. They had in their possession all the papers relating to the previous Commission of

* This refers to the building of the Shrine of the Báb.

† This refers to Western pilgrims.

Inquiry, which had, ironically enough, found all the allegations against 'Abdu'l-Bahá to be baseless.

The Commission assumed full authority in the administration of the city, dismissed the governor of 'Akká who was friendly towards 'Abdu'l-Bahá, and even disregarded the orders from the governor of the province of Syria who wielded supreme authority over the region. The members of the Commission then established direct contact with Mírzá Muḥammad-'Alí and his associates and planned their course of action in concert with them. They took as their residence the house of 'Abdu'l-Ghaní Bayḍún, a wealthy and influential man who was living in close proximity to the Mansion of Bahjí and was friendly towards the violators of the Covenant.

Their first act was again to plant a number of spies around the house of 'Abdu'l-Bahá. They then began to obtain testimonies from those enemies who had signed Mírzá Muḥammad-'Alí's original petition to the authorities. With the assistance of the Covenant-breakers, the members of the Commission even sought to bring pressure upon people to testify against the Master. Through intimidation people were forced to give false testimony, while a local grocer who refused to comply was put in gaol. The inhabitants of the city became afraid to approach the house of the Master, in case they were incriminated by the authorities. Even the poor of 'Akká, whom 'Abdu'l-Bahá had always succoured, did not dare to come in contact with Him.

At one point the members of the Commission paid a visit to Mount Carmel, examined the six-room building of the Shrine, noted its massive walls and commented on its extraordinary strength. Later in their report, they confirmed the Covenant-breakers' allegation that 'Abdu'l-Bahá had indeed built a fortress on a strategic location on the mountain! They also endorsed the other charges brought against Him. Soon rumours began to circulate far and wide that the Commission was about to exile the Master to Fizán in Tripolitania, situated in the middle of the desert in North Africa.

During this period the Master remained unperturbed and confident. He continued to write His Tablets to the Bahá'ís of the East and the West, spent time planting a few trees in His small garden and, to the astonishment of some notables of 'Akká who considered His banishment to be imminent, was seen to be attending to repairs of His rented house. Their surprise was further intensified when they learned that He had bought and stored fuel for the winter.

The members of the Commission, who were actively engaged in preparing their report in collaboration with the Covenant-breakers, sent one of their agents to 'Abdu'l-Bahá inviting Him to meet with them but He declined the invitation, saying that the Commission was biased against Him and there was no point in meeting with its members. At the same time He made it clear, as on previous occasions, that He was ready to submit Himself to whatever decision they made and reminded them that His greatest ambition was to follow in the footsteps of His Lord the Báb and die a martyr's death.

'Abdu'l-Bahá Himself mentioned this episode in a talk to the friends, recounted as follows:

> Upon their arrival, the Commission of Inquiry invited me to meet with them but I declined. They sent a certain official by the name of Ḥikmat Big to persuade me to call on them. This agent begged me, and even hypocritically brought tears to his eyes, pleading with me to meet with members of the Commission even for a short time. I told him that since they had come to investigate accusations against me, it would be better that I did not meet them. I told him that they had already sent a report to the capital and I had sent a letter to Sulṭán 'Abdu'l-Ḥamíd through Shaykh Badru'd-Dín, the gist of which was as follows:
>
> 'The members of the Commission have come to 'Akká, but I have not met with them. I understand that they have made a report in which they have levelled several accusations against me and for this I am grateful. Their main complaints are as follows:
>
> 1. That I have rebelled against the government and established my own.
>
> 2. That I have built fortifications on Mount Carmel.
>
> 3. That with the help of Mírzá Dhikru'lláh* I have hoisted a banner with the inscription of 'Yá Bahá'u'l-Abhá' [O Glory of the Most Glorious] among the inhabitants including the Bedouins.
>
> 4. That two-thirds of the land in 'Akká is owned by me.
>
> The reason that I am grateful to the members of the Commission for the above accusations is that by their first complaint, they have, in reality, praised me and attributed great powers to me. How can a prisoner and an exile establish a new government? Anyone who could do that deserves to be congratulated.
>
> Similarly, by their second complaint they have also commended me by ascribing to me extraordinary capabilities. It would be a miracle for one who is a captive in the hands of the authorities to build fortifications strong enough to be capable of withstanding bombardment by powerful naval ships.
>
> But one is surprised by their third complaint, for how is it that the many government agents posted all over the country have

* The son of Mírzá Muḥammad-Qulí, the faithful half-brother of Bahá'u'lláh who remained steadfast in the Covenant after the ascension of Bahá'u'lláh.

failed to see the banner which has allegedly been hoisted among the inhabitants of these lands? Perhaps during the last two years these officials have been asleep or some angels have blinded their eyes.

Concerning the fourth complaint, that I own most of the land in 'Akká and neighbouring villages, I am willing to sell them all for the small sum of one thousand liras.'[196]

The ironic language of this letter is indicative of the depravity of those 'Abdu'l-Bahá was addressing. In the meantime, events were moving to a climax in which it was almost certain that 'Abdu'l-Bahá would be exiled or put to death. The atmosphere was becoming more tense with every passing day.

There is an interesting account of an Italian who was Acting Consul for Spain at this time. He was an admirer of the Master and his wife was friendly with the family of 'Abdu'l-Bahá. This man and his relatives were the chief agents of an Italian shipping company. When he was informed that 'Abdu'l-Bahá's life was in danger, he came to the Master in the dead of night and offered to transport Him out of the Holy Land to a safe spot. He even delayed a particular ship's departure for a few days in the hope of rescuing Him. 'Abdu'l-Bahá took the unusual step of inviting some of the elders of the Bahá'í community in 'Akká, including the celebrated Ḥájí Mírzá Ḥaydar-'Alí, to consult together and give their opinion on this offer. It is amusing to see how 'Abdu'l-Bahá wanted to test these people and teach them a lesson. The group unanimously decided to advise the Master to accept the offer of the Italian friend and leave the Holy Land for a place of safety. 'Abdu'l-Bahá looked at them disapprovingly and reminded them that running away had never been the practice of the Chosen Ones of God. His Lord the Báb had offered up His life, so how could 'Abdu'l-Bahá do otherwise? As a result of this episode, each one of the group recognized his own shortsightedness and lack of understanding of the spirit of the Faith.

The following passage from the Will and Testament casts further light on 'Abdu'l-Bahá's resignation to the Will of God and His longing to lay down His life in the path of Bahá'u'lláh:

8–WT According to the direct and sacred command of God we are forbidden to utter slander, are commanded to show forth peace and amity, are exhorted to rectitude of conduct, straightforwardness and harmony with all the kindreds and peoples of the world. We must obey and be the well-wishers of the governments of the land, regard disloyalty unto a just king as disloyalty to God Himself and wishing evil to the government a transgression of the Cause of God. With these final and decisive words, how can it

be that these imprisoned ones should indulge in such vain fancies; incarcerated, how could they show forth such disloyalty! But alas! The Committee of Investigation hath approved and confirmed these calumnies of my brother and ill-wishers and submitted them to the presence of His Majesty the Sovereign. Now at this moment a fierce storm is raging around this prisoner who awaiteth, be it favourable or unfavourable, the gracious will of His Majesty, may the Lord aid him by His grace to be just. In whatsoever condition he may be, with absolute calm and quietness, 'Abdu'l-Bahá is ready for self-sacrifice and is wholly resigned and submitted to His Will.

One wonders what thoughts must have crowded the mind of 'Abdu'l-Bahá, during the days that He waited for the Sulṭán's decree, as He reflected on the adversities which had surmounted Him. How much He must have grieved when He meditated on the unfaithfulness of His brothers and other members of the family who had arisen with all their power to destroy Him and the Cause He represented. The following passage from the Will and Testament describes the tenderness of His heart during those fate-laden days:

33–WT Lord! Thou seest all things weeping me and my kindred rejoicing in my woes. By Thy Glory, O my God! Even amongst mine enemies, some have lamented my troubles and my distress, and of the envious ones a number have shed tears because of my cares, my exile and my afflictions. They did this because they found naught in me but affection and care and witnessed naught but kindliness and mercy. As they saw me swept into the flood of tribulation and adversity and exposed even as a target to the arrows of fate, their hearts were moved with compassion, tears came to their eyes and they testified declaring: – 'The Lord is our witness; naught have we seen from him but faithfulness, generosity and extreme compassion.' The Covenant-breakers, foreboders of evil, however, waxed fiercer in their rancour, rejoiced as I fell a victim to the most grievous ordeal, bestirred themselves against me and made merry over the heartrending happenings around me.

When 'Abdu'l-Bahá wrote parts two and three of the Will and Testament, great dangers surrounded Him. It appears that as He was writing He was waiting patiently for God's will to be realized. He communed with God and in the prayers He wrote in this period, He revealed the agony of His heart and portrayed the evil machinations of the Covenant-breakers. In these prayers, He expressed His longing to lay down His life as a martyr in the path of Bahá'u'lláh. Those who attained the presence of the Master have left behind many stories of His craving for martyrdom. Whenever He spoke about the subject, His whole being would be exhilarated, His face radiant and His heart in great excitement.

Dr Yúnis Khán describes how 'Abdu'l-Bahá, in the midst of intense suffering at the hands of the Covenant-breakers, earnestly prayed that yet more suffering and hardship might descend upon Him. As tribulations increased, His desire to bear them increased correspondingly. He often used to speak about illustrious martyrs such as Varqá and then, in a joyous and excited tone, He would express His heartfelt desire to lay down His life in the path of Bahá'u'lláh. So moving were His words that all His loved ones who heard Him were overcome with emotion, their souls uplifted and their hearts filled with a new spirit of sacrifice in their readiness to follow in the footsteps of their Beloved.

At the time of greatest danger to His life He revealed a number of moving prayers, such as the following:

> **30–WT O my Lord, my heart's Desire, Thou Whom I ever invoke, Thou Who art my Aider and my Shelter, my Helper and my Refuge! Thou seest me submerged in an ocean of calamities that overwhelm the soul, of afflictions that oppress the heart, of woes that disperse Thy gathering, of ills and pains that scatter Thy flock. Sore trials have compassed me round and perils have from all sides beset me. Thou seest me immersed in a sea of unsurpassed tribulation, sunk into a fathomless abyss, afflicted by mine enemies and consumed with the flame of their hate, enkindled by my kinsmen with whom Thou didst make Thy strong Covenant and Thy firm Testament, wherein Thou biddest them turn their hearts to this wronged one, to keep away from me the foolish, the unjust, and refer unto this lonely one all that about which they differ in Thy Holy Book, so that the Truth may be revealed unto them, their doubts may be dispelled and Thy manifest Signs be spread abroad.**

In the following prayer 'Abdu'l-Bahá dwells on the afflictions He has endured and begs God to relieve Him from His ordeals, beseeching Him to fulfil His heart's desire of laying down His life as a martyr:

> **44–7–WT O my God! my Beloved, my heart's Desire! Thou knowest, Thou seest that which hath befallen this servant of Thine, that hath humbled himself at Thy Door, and Thou knowest the sins committed against him by the people of malice, they that have broken Thy Covenant and turned their backs on Thy Testament. In the day-time they afflicted me with the arrows of hate and in the night-season they privily conspired to hurt me. At dawn they committed that which the Celestial Concourse did lament and at eventide they unsheathed against me the sword of tyranny and hurled in the presence of the ungodly their darts**

> **of calumny upon me. Notwithstanding their misdeeds, this lowly servant of Thine was patient and did endure every affliction and trial at their hands, though by Thy power and might he could have destroyed their words, quenched their fire and stayed the flame of their rebelliousness.**
>
> **Thou seest, O my God! how my long-suffering, my forbearance and silence have increased their cruelty, their arrogance and their pride. By Thy Glory, O Beloved One! They have misbelieved in Thee and rebelled against Thee in such wise that they left me not a moment of rest and quiet, that I might arise as it is meet and seemly, to exalt Thy Word amidst mankind, and might serve at Thy Threshold of Holiness with a heart that overfloweth with the joy of the dwellers of the Abhá Kingdom.**
>
> **Lord! My cup of woe runneth over, and from all sides blows are fiercely raging upon me. The darts of affliction have compassed me round and the arrows of distress have rained upon me. Thus tribulation overwhelmed me and my strength, because of the onslaught of the foemen, became weakness within me, while I stood alone and forsaken in the midst of my woes. Lord! Have mercy upon me, lift me up unto Thyself and make me to drink from the Chalice of Martyrdom, for the wide world with all its vastness can no longer contain me.**
>
> **Thou art, verily, the Merciful, the Compassionate, the Gracious, the All-Bountiful!**

And again:

> **10–WT O God, my God! Thou seest this wronged servant of Thine, held fast in the talons of ferocious lions, of ravening wolves, of blood-thirsty beasts. Graciously assist me, through my love for Thee, that I may drink deep of the chalice that brimmeth over with faithfulness to Thee and is filled with Thy bountiful Grace; so that, fallen upon the dust, I may sink prostrate and senseless whilst my vesture is dyed crimson with my blood. This is my wish, my heart's desire, my hope, my pride, my glory. Grant, O Lord my God, and my Refuge, that in my last hour, my end may even as musk shed its fragrance of glory! Is there a bounty greater than this? Nay, by Thy Glory! I call Thee to witness that no day passeth but that I quaff my fill from this cup, so grievous are the misdeeds wrought by them that have broken the Covenant, kindled discord, showed their malice, stirred sedition in the land and dishonored Thee amidst Thy servants.**

Returning to the subject of the Commission of Inquiry, events were moving to their climax, and one day, late in the afternoon, the members of the Commission boarded their ship in Haifa and headed towards 'Akká. The sun was setting as the ship sailed closer to the prison city. Everyone in Haifa and 'Akká was certain that the ship was on its way to take 'Abdu'l-Bahá on board as a prisoner. In the meantime, 'Abdu'l-Bahá was calmly pacing the yard at His house, and the believers, extremely perturbed, were nervously watching the approaching ship. Suddenly, to their great relief, the ship changed course, headed out to sea and sailed towards Istanbul.

In one of His Tablets 'Abdu'l-Bahá states that at that moment the guns of God went into action, removed the chains from the neck of 'Abdu'l-Bahá and placed them on the neck of 'Abdu'l-Ḥamíd, the Sulṭán of Turkey. This was a reference to the ultimate fate of the Sulṭán, who narrowly escaped death when returning from the mosque on a fateful Friday that same year. A bomb which was meant for him exploded, killing and injuring others, and it was this event which prompted the authorities to recall the members of the Commission. Some months later, the 'Young Turk' revolutionaries demanded from the Sulṭán the release of all political prisoners. This was done, and in the summer of 1908 'Abdu'l-Bahá was freed. Within months the tyrannical Sulṭán 'Abdu'l-Ḥamíd was deposed. 'Abdu'l-Bahá's freedom after 40 years of imprisonment enabled Him to fulfil one of the most important undertakings of His ministry, the interment of the remains of the Báb, the Martyr-Prophet of the Faith, in the Shrine built by the Master on Mount Carmel.*

'Abdu'l-Bahá's dramatic release from confinement was the greatest blow that the Covenant-breakers had ever sustained in their entire period of opposition to Him. It signalized the approaching end of their satanic endeavours to uproot the very foundations of the Cause of God. 'Abdu'l-Bahá's prophecy, uttered in 1904 (see chapter 18), that in four years' time they would become impotent, was fulfilled. 'Abdu'l-Bahá foresaw the downfall of Mírzá Muḥammad-'Alí when He wrote these words in His Will and Testament:

> **5–WT And now ye are witnessing how the wrath of God hath from all sides afflicted him and how day by day he is speeding towards destruction. Ere long will ye behold him and his associates, outwardly and inwardly, condemned to utter ruin.**

---

* For more detailed information on this see Taherzadeh, *Revelation of Bahá'u'lláh*, vol. 3, appendix 1; also ibid. vol. 1, p. 268.

23

'Abdu'l-Bahá's Greatness Transcends His Suffering

Around the time that 'Abdu'l-Bahá wrote the passages concerning the Commission of Inquiry, He wrote a long Tablet to the believers in Persia to familiarize them with the distressing situation that endangered His life as He awaited the decision of the Sulṭán on the Commission's report. Here is a translation of part of this Tablet:

> O ye the cherished loved ones of 'Abdu'l-Bahá! It is a long time now since my inward ear hath heard any sweet melodies out of certain regions, or my heart been gladdened; and this despite the fact that ye are ever present in my thoughts and standing clearly visible before my sight. Filled to overflowing is the goblet of my heart with the wine of the love I bear you, and my yearning to set eyes upon you streameth like the spirit through my arteries and veins. From this it is clear how great is my affliction. At this time and throughout this tempest of calamities now tossing its waves to high heaven, cruel and incessant darts are being hurled against me from every point of the compass, and at every moment, here in the Holy Land, terrifying news is received, and every day bringeth its quota of horror. The Centre of Sedition had imagined that it needed but his arrogant rebellion to bring down the Covenant and Testament in ruins; it needed but this, so he thought, to turn the righteous away from the Holy Will. Wherefore he sent out far and wide his leaflets of doubt, devising many a secret scheme. Now he would cry out that God's edifice had been subverted and His divine commands annulled, and that accordingly, the Covenant and Testament was abolished. Again he would set himself to sighing and groaning that he was being held a prisoner and was kept hungry and thirsty day and night. Another day he would raise an uproar, saying that the oneness of God had been denied, since another Manifestation had been proclaimed, prior to the expiration of a thousand years.
>
> When he saw that his calumnies had no effect, he gradually formed a plan to incite a disturbance. He began stirring up mischief, and went knocking at every door. He started making false accusations to the officials of the Government. He approached some of the foreigners, made himself their intimate, and together with them

prepared a document and presented it to the seat of the Sultanate, bringing consternation to the authorities. Among the many slanderous charges was this, that this hapless one had raised up a standard of revolt, a flag bearing the words *Yá Bahá'u'l-Abhá*; that I had paraded this throughout the countryside, to every city, town and village, and even among the desert tribes, and had summoned all the inhabitants to unite under this flag.

O my Lord, verily I seek refuge with Thee from the very thought of such an act, which is contrary to all the commandments of Bahá'u'lláh, and which would indeed be a mighty wrong that none but a grievous sinner would ever perpetrate. For Thou has made it incumbent upon us to obey the rulers and kings.

Another of his slanders was that the Shrine on Mount Carmel was a fortress that I had built strong and impregnable – this when the building under construction compriseth six rooms – and that I had named it Medina the Resplendent, while I had named the Holy Tomb* Mecca the Glorified. Yet another of his calumnies was that I had established an independent sovereignty, and that – God forbid! God forbid! God forbid! – I had summoned all the believers to join me in this massive wrongdoing. How dire, O my Lord, is his slander!

Yet again, he claimeth that since the Holy Shrine hath become a point visited by pilgrims from all over the world, great damage will accrue to this Government and people. He, the Centre of Sedition, averreth that he himself hath had no hand in all these matters, that he is a Sunní of the Sunnites and a devoted follower of Abú-Bakr and 'Umar, and regardeth Bahá'u'lláh as only a pious man and a mystic; all these things, he saith, were set afoot by this wronged one.

To be brief, a Commission of Investigation was appointed by the Sulṭán, may the glory of his reign endure. The Commission journeyed hither and immediately upon arrival betook themselves to the house of one of the accusers. They then summoned the group who, working with my brother, had prepared the accusatory document and asked them whether it was true. The group explained the contents of the document, stated that everything they had reported therein was nothing but the truth, and added further accusations. Thus they functioned at one and the same time as plaintiffs, witnesses, and judge.

The Commission hath now returned to the seat of the Caliphate, and reports of a most frightful nature are coming in daily from that city. However, praised be God, 'Abdu'l-Bahá remaineth composed and unperturbed. To none do I bear ill will because of this defamation. I have made all my affairs conditioned upon His irresistible Will and I am waiting, indeed in perfect happiness, to offer my life and prepared for whatever dire affliction may be in store. Praise be to God, the loving believers also accept and remain

---

* At Bahjí

submissive to God's Will, content with it, radiantly acquiescent, offering thanks.

The Centre of Sedition hath imagined that once the blood of this wronged one is spilled out, once I have been cast away on the wide desert sands or drowned in the Mediterranean Sea – nameless, gone without trace, with none to tell of me – then would he at last have a field where he could urge his steed ahead, and with his mallet of lies and doubts, hit hard at the polo ball of his ambitions, and carry off the prize.

Far from it! For even if the sweet musk-scent of faithfulness should pass, and leave no trace behind, who would be drawn by the stench of perfidy? And even if some gazelle of heaven were to be ripped apart by dogs and wolves, who would go running to seek out a ravening wolf? Even should the day of the Mystic Nightingale draw to its close, who would ever lend his ear to the raven's croak, or the cawing of the crow? What an empty supposition is his! What a foolish presumption! 'Their works are like the vapour in a desert which the thirsty dreameth to be water, until when he cometh unto it, he findeth nothing.'*

O ye loved ones of God! Be ye firm of foot, and fixed of heart, and through the power of the Blessed Beauty's help, stand ye committed to your purpose. Serve ye the Cause of God. Face ye all nations of the world with the constancy and the endurance of the people of Bahá, that all men may be astounded and ask how this could be, that your hearts are as well-springs of confidence and faith, and as mines so rich in the love of God. Be ye so, that ye shall neither fail nor falter on account of these tragedies in the Holy Land; let not these dread events make you despondent. And if all the believers be put to the sword, and only one be left, let that one cry out in the name of the Lord and tell the joyous tidings; let that one rise up and confront all the peoples of the earth.

Gaze ye not upon the dire happenings at this Illumined Spot. The Holy Land is in danger at all times, and here, the tide of calamities is ever at the flood; for this upraised call hath now been heard around the world, and the fame of it hath gone forth to the ends of the earth. It is because of this that foes, both from within and from without, have turned themselves with subtlety and craft to spreading slander. It is clear that such a place as this would be exposed to danger, for there is no defender here, none to arise and take our side in the face of calumny: here are only a few souls that are homeless, hapless, held captive in this stronghold. No champion have they; there is none to succour them, none to ward off the arrows of lies, the darts of defamation that are hurled against them: none except God . . .

O ye loving friends! Strive ye with heart and soul to make this world the mirror-image of the Kingdom, that this nether world may teem with the blessings of the world of God, that the voices

* Qur'án 24:39

of the Company on high may be raised in acclamation, and signs and tokens of the bounties and bestowals of Bahá'u'lláh may encompass all the earth.

Jináb-i-Amín hath expressed the greatest admiration for you honoured men and enlightened women, naming and commending you each by each, telling at length of the firmness and constancy ye all have shown, saying that, God be praised, in all Persia the men and women are standing together, straight, strong, unmovable – a mighty edifice solidly raised up; and that ye are engaged with love and joy in spreading abroad the sweet savours of the Lord.

These were tidings of great joy, especially as they have reached me in these days of extreme peril. For the dearest wish of this wronged one is that the friends be spiritual of heart and illumined of mind, and once this grace is granted me, calamity, however afflictive, is but bounty pouring down upon me, like copious rain.

O God, my God! Thou seest me plunged in an ocean of anguish, held fast to the fires of tyranny, and weeping in the darkness of the night. Sleepless I toss and turn upon my bed, mine eyes straining to behold the morning light of faithfulness and trust. I agonize even as a fish, its inward parts afire as it leapeth about in terror upon the sand, yet I ever look for Thy bestowals to appear from every side.[197]

'Abdu'l-Bahá felt the sufferings inflicted on Him by the Covenant-breakers much more intensely than any human being would have felt them. This is true of Bahá'u'lláh also. He mentions in many Tablets that no one on earth has been, or will be, subjected to such suffering. It may be difficult for those who are not fully familiar with the Faith of Bahá'u'lláh to accept such a statement. They may argue that there have been many people who were afflicted with unbearable tortures and life-long sufferings. In order to appreciate the words of Bahá'u-'lláh let us imagine a community somewhere in the world whose people are savage, barbarous and brutally cruel. Those born and brought up within such a community, who have lived there all their lives and have never been in touch with civilization, would find this life to be normal. Although to the outsider the standard would seem to be very cruel, yet for the members of that community every event that took place in their midst would be a natural happening and accepted as such. As in every other community, there would be moments of joy and comfort as well as sadness and suffering for the people who belonged to this society. However, were a noble person who had lived in a highly civilized society forced to join this uncivilized community, he would suffer much more than the rest. Because he was used to a far superior standard in his life, it could be said of him that he had undergone cruelties and hardships, both mental and physical, that no one else in that community had experienced.

It is the same with the Manifestation of God and His Chosen Ones, sent to live among men. There is a vast contrast between the world of man and the world of the Chosen Ones of God. The former is limited and full of imperfections while the latter is a realm of perfections far exalted above the comprehension of human beings. Coming from such a realm, possessing all the divine virtues and embodying God's attributes, these exalted Beings descend into this world and become prisoners among human beings. Man's ignorance, his cruelty, his ungodliness, his selfishness, his insincerity and all his sins and shortcomings are tools of torture inflicting painful wounds upon the souls of the Chosen Ones of God, who have no alternative but to bear them in silence with resignation and submissiveness, as in the case of 'Abdu'l-Bahá. One act of unfaithfulness – even a glance betraying the insincerity of the individual or an unworthy thought emanating from his mind – is painful torture to them. But they seldom reveal the shortcomings of men or dwell on their own pain and suffering. Like teachers who have to descend to the level of a child and act as if they do not know, the Manifestations of God come as men appearing to be the same as others. They have the sin-covering eye to such an extent that some may think that they do not know.

The perusal of the Will and Testament may leave the reader with the erroneous impression that 'Abdu'l-Bahá was being crushed under the pressure of sufferings inflicted on Him by the Covenant-breakers, and that He could not bear their onslaught any longer. For example, we come across the following statements which, if considered on a human level, may lead one to conclude that a person facing such fierce opposition would collapse and be heard of no more:

> **31–WT Yet now Thou seest them, O Lord, my God! with Thine eye that sleepeth not, how that they have broken Thy Covenant and turned their backs thereon, how with hate and rebelliousness they have erred from Thy Testament and have arisen intent upon malice.**

> **32–WT Adversities have waxed still more severe as they rose with unbearable cruelty to overpower and crush me, as they scattered far and wide their scrolls of doubt and in utter falsehood hurled their calumnies upon me.**

> **36–WT O dearly beloved friends! I am now in very great danger and the hope of even an hour's life is lost to me.**

The study of the life of the Manifestations of God and their Chosen Ones reveals that although they physically endure the pain and agony of persecutions, in the realm of the spirit they are not affected. For instance, while 'Abdu'l-Bahá faced fierce opposition from the Covenant-breakers, He dispelled, through His exemplary life, the gloom that had been surrounding the community of the Most Great Name. During this time, when He Himself was the target of dire afflictions and sufferings, He cast upon everyone around Him the light of truth, of divine virtues and spiritual teachings.

Although we can never understand the reality of Bahá'u'lláh, the Manifestation of God, or of 'Abdu'l-Bahá, the Most Great Mystery of God and the Centre of His Covenant, we can observe some of their superhuman characteristics. Unlike a human being whose mind can only deal with one subject at a time, 'Abdu'l-Bahá, who had all the powers of Bahá'u'lláh conferred upon Him, was free from this limitation. Usually a person becomes overwhelmed when afflicted by sufferings or faced with insurmountable obstacles. Under such circumstances even people of outstanding ability show their weakness and reveal their human frailty. They try to cope with one problem at a time and often seek the assistance of experts and advisors to help them make a decision.

Not so with 'Abdu'l-Bahá. He acted independently, for no individual was qualified to advise or assist Him in His manifold activities. His soul was not bound by the limitations of the world of humanity and His mind was not overwhelmed when faced with a host of problems simultaneously. In the midst of calamities, when the ablest of men would have succumbed to pressure, He remained detached, while directing His attention to whatever He desired. This is one of the distinguishing characteristics of the Manifestation of God and His Chosen Ones. Bahá'u'lláh has explained this in the Kitáb-i-Íqán, quoting the celebrated Islamic passage: 'Nothing whatsoever keepeth Him from being occupied with any other thing.'[198]

Although the Manifestations of God and these specially Chosen Ones such as 'Abdu'l-Bahá feel the agony of sufferings inflicted on them by their enemies, and their human nature experiences both mental and physical pain, their souls are not affected by any man-made affliction. They abide in a realm far beyond the ken of mortal men and wield the spiritual sceptre of authority and power with which they rule over humanity. These powers are at first hidden from the eyes of most people but with the passage of time humanity observes the influence of their word and the spread of their Faith.

To appreciate, even to a limited degree, the superhuman powers and divine perfections with which 'Abdu'l-Bahá was invested, we can do no better than to turn to the writings of Shoghi Effendi. Referring to the station of 'Abdu'l-Bahá and the position He occupies in this Dispensation, the Guardian writes:

It would be indeed difficult for us, who stand so close to such a tremendous figure and are drawn by the mysterious power of so magnetic a personality, to obtain a clear and exact understanding of the rôle and character of One Who, not only in the Dispensation of Bahá'u'lláh but in the entire field of religious history, fulfils a unique function. Though moving in a sphere of His own and holding a rank radically different from that of the Author and the Forerunner of the Bahá'í Revelation, He, by virtue of the station ordained for Him through the Covenant of Bahá'u'lláh, forms together with them what may be termed the Three Central Figures of a Faith that stands unapproached in the world's spiritual history. He towers, in conjunction with them, above the destinies of this infant Faith of God from a level to which no individual or body ministering to its needs after Him, and for no less a period than a full thousand years, can ever hope to rise . . .

. . . we should not by any means infer that 'Abdu'l-Bahá is merely one of the servants of the Blessed Beauty, or at best one whose function is to be confined to that of an authorized interpreter of His Father's teachings. Far be it from me to entertain such a notion or to wish to instil such sentiments. To regard Him in such a light is a manifest betrayal of the priceless heritage bequeathed by Bahá'u'lláh to mankind. Immeasurably exalted is the station conferred upon Him by the Supreme Pen above and beyond the implications of these, His own written statements. Whether in the Kitáb-i-Aqdas, the most weighty and sacred of all the works of Bahá'u'lláh, or in the Kitáb-i-'Ahd, the Book of His Covenant, or in the Súriy-i-Ghuṣn (Tablet of the Branch), such references as have been recorded by the pen of Bahá'u'lláh – references which the Tablets of His Father addressed to Him mightily reinforce – invest 'Abdu'l-Bahá with a power, and surround Him with a halo, which the present generation can never adequately appreciate.

He is, and should for all time be regarded, first and foremost, as the Centre and Pivot of Bahá'u'lláh's peerless and all-enfolding Covenant, His most exalted handiwork, the stainless Mirror of His light, the perfect Exemplar of His teachings, the unerring Interpreter of His Word, the embodiment of every Bahá'í ideal, the incarnation of every Bahá'í virtue, the Most Mighty Branch sprung from the Ancient Root, the Limb of the Law of God, the Being 'round Whom all names revolve', the Mainspring of the Oneness of Humanity, the Ensign of the Most Great Peace, the Moon of the Central Orb of this most holy Dispensation – styles and titles that are implicit and find their truest, their highest and fairest expression in the magic name 'Abdu'l-Bahá. He is, above and beyond these appellations, the 'Mystery of God' – an expression by which Bahá'u'lláh Himself has chosen to designate Him, and which, while it does not by any means justify us to assign to Him the station of Prophethood, indicates how in the person of 'Abdu'l-Bahá the incompatible characteristics of a human nature and superhuman knowledge and perfection have been blended and are completely harmonized.[199]

The tributes which Bahá'u'lláh has paid to 'Abdu'l-Bahá are numerous, as recorded in His Tablets to which Shoghi Effendi refers above. The following passages are gleaned from a wide range of Bahá'u'lláh's writings, some of which are written in His own hand.

In the Súriy-i-Ghuṣn (Súrih of the Branch),* He exalts the station of 'Abdu'l-Bahá in these words:

> There hath branched from the Sadratu'l-Muntahá this sacred and glorious Being, this Branch of Holiness; well is it with him that hath sought His shelter and abideth beneath His shadow. Verily the Limb of the Law of God hath sprung forth from this Root which God hath firmly implanted in the Ground of His Will, and whose Branch hath been so uplifted as to encompass the whole of creation. Magnified be He, therefore, for this sublime, this blessed, this mighty, this exalted Handiwork! . . . Render thanks unto God, O people, for His appearance; for verily He is the most great Favour unto you, the most perfect bounty upon you; and through Him every mouldering bone is quickened. Whoso turneth towards Him hath turned towards God, and whoso turneth away from Him hath turned away from My Beauty, hath repudiated My Proof, and transgressed against Me. He is the Trust of God amongst you, His charge within you, His Manifestation unto you and His appearance among His favoured servants . . .[200]

In another Tablet in His own handwriting, Bahá'u'lláh thus addresses 'Abdu'l-Bahá:

> O Thou Who art the apple of Mine eye! My glory, the ocean of My loving-kindness, the sun of My bounty, the heaven of My mercy rest upon Thee. We pray God to illumine the world through Thy knowledge and wisdom, to ordain for Thee that which will gladden Thine heart and impart consolation to Thine eyes.[201]

In yet another Tablet, these verses have been revealed by Him:

> The glory of God rest upon Thee, and upon whosoever serveth Thee and circleth around Thee. Woe, great woe, betide him that opposeth and injureth Thee. Well is it with him that sweareth fealty to Thee; the fire of hell torment him who is Thine enemy.[202]

And again:

> We have made Thee a shelter for all mankind, a shield unto all who are in heaven and on earth, a stronghold for whosoever hath believed in God, the Incomparable, the All-Knowing. God grant

* See Taherzadeh, *Revelation of Bahá'u'lláh*, vol. 2.

that through Thee He may protect them, may enrich and sustain them, that He may inspire Thee with that which shall be a well-spring of wealth unto all created things, an ocean of bounty unto all men, and the dayspring of mercy unto all peoples.[203]

When 'Abdu'l-Bahá was on a visit to Beirut, Bahá'u'lláh expressed in these words His sorrow at their separation:

> Praise be to Him Who hath honoured the Land of Bá [Beirut] through the presence of Him round Whom all names revolve. All the atoms of the earth have announced unto all created things that from behind the gate of the Prison-city there hath appeared and above its horizon there hath shone forth the Orb of the beauty of the great, the Most Mighty Branch of God – His ancient and immutable Mystery – proceeding on its way to another land. Sorrow, thereby, hath enveloped this Prison-city, whilst another land rejoiceth . . .
>
> Blessed, doubly blessed, is the ground which His footsteps have trodden, the eye that hath been cheered by the beauty of His countenance, the ear that hath been honoured by hearkening to His call, the heart that hath tasted the sweetness of His love, the breast that hath dilated through His remembrance, the pen that hath voiced His praise, the scroll that hath borne the testimony of His writings.[204]

The bounties that Bahá'u'lláh showered upon 'Abdu'l-Bahá were not confined to these and the other Tablets that streamed from His Pen. On innumerable public and private occasions He praised 'Abdu'l-Bahá, described His divine attributes in glowing terms and paid tribute to His noble deeds. Ḥájí Mírzá Ḥaydar-'Alí, that spiritual giant immortalized by the title 'the Angel of Carmel', has left the following record of one of his memorable audiences, when Bahá'u'lláh spoke about 'Abdu'l-Bahá's important role in shielding Him from the pressures of the outside world:*

> During the days of Baghdád We ourself used to visit the coffee house† and meet with everyone. We associated with people whether they were in the community or outside, whether acquaintances or strangers, whether they came from far or near.
>
> We considered those who were distant from us to be near, and the strangers as acquaintances. We served the Cause of God, supported His Word, and exalted His Name. The Most Great Branch ['Abdu'l-Bahá] carried out all these services, withstood all

* These are not to be taken as the exact words of Bahá'u'lláh; they are only recollections of His utterances by Ḥájí Mírzá Ḥaydar-'Alí.

† See Taherzadeh, *Revelation of Bahá'u'lláh*, vol. 3, pp. 250–1.

the difficulties and endured the sufferings and calamities to a great extent in Adrianople and now to a far greater extent in 'Akká. Because while in Baghdád, to all appearances We were not a prisoner and the Cause of God had hardly enjoyed a fame it does today. Those who opposed it and the enemies who fought against it were comparatively few and far between.

In Adrianople We used to meet with some of the people and gave permission to some to attain Our presence. But while in the Most Great Prison We did not meet with anyone* and have completely closed the door of association with the people. Now the Master has taken upon Himself this arduous task for Our comfort. He is a mighty shield facing the world and its peoples and so He has relieved Us [from every care]. At first He secured the Mansion of Mazra'ih for Us and We stayed there, then the Mansion of Bahjí. He is so occupied in the service of the Cause that for weeks He does not find the opportunity to come to Bahjí. We are engaged in meeting with the believers and revealing the verses of God, while He labours hard and faces every ordeal and suffering. Because to deal and associate with these people is the most arduous task of all.[205]

Mírzá Maḥmúd-i-Káshání,† a trusted follower of Bahá'u'lláh who was in His service from the days of Baghdád and accompanied Him to Adrianople and 'Akká, has recounted in his memoirs his recollection of the words of Bahá'u'lláh as He spoke to a number of believers about the exalted station of 'Abdu'l-Bahá. Here is a summary translation of his notes:

> . . . The word Áqá (the Master) was a designation given to 'Abdu'l-Bahá. I recall that one day when Bahá'u'lláh was in the Garden of Vashshásh which was a delightful place situated outside Baghdád, which He occasionally used to visit, someone referred to certain individuals as the Áqá.‡ On hearing this Bahá'u'lláh was heard to say with a commanding voice: 'Who is the Áqá? There is only one Áqá, and He is the Most Great Branch.'
>
> Bahá'u'lláh said the same thing again in the Garden of Riḍván in 'Akká. On that occasion, someone addressed Mírzá Muḥammad-'Alí as Áqá, whereupon Bahá'u'lláh admonished him saying: 'There is one and only one Áqá and He is the Most Great Branch, others should be addressed by their names.' . . .

---

* That is, with non-Bahá'ís.

† See Taherzadeh, *Revelation of Bahá'u'lláh*, vol. 1, p. 288.

‡ As a common noun, the word 'Áqá' in the Persian language is used as a title before a name. It is similar to 'Mr' in English. However, if it is used on its own as a proper noun, it signifies the exalted station of a person.

Many a time I was in the presence of Bahá'u'lláh when the Master was also present. Because of His presence Bahá'u'lláh would be filled with the utmost joy and gladness. One could see His blessed countenance beaming with delight and exultation so lovingly that no words can adequately describe it. Repeatedly He would laud and glorify the Master and the mere mention of His name would suffice to evoke an indescribable feeling of ecstasy in the person of the Blessed Beauty. No pen is capable of fully describing this. In many of His Tablets Bahá'u'lláh has extolled the station of 'Abdu'l-Bahá . . .

Ḥájí Mírzá Ḥabíbu'lláh-i-Afnán, a younger son of Áqá Mírzá Áqá entitled Núru'd-Dín,* one of the distinguished members of the Afnán family, has written in his memoirs some interesting stories of his pilgrimage in 1891. The following is an extract from his notes, summarized and translated:

One evening we were informed that the Beloved of the World [Bahá'u'lláh] intended to visit the Garden of Junaynih† and had directed that all the pilgrims and resident Bahá'ís accompany Him in the morning. That night we could not sleep because we were so excited . . . that we should have the bounty of being in His holy presence for several hours the next day. At the hour of dawn we faced His blessed room and engaged in prayers and devotions. Before sunrise we all assembled outside the gate of the Mansion. It took about one hour until His Blessed Person came downstairs and mounted a white donkey . . . All the believers followed Him on foot to the garden. One of the local believers, Ḥájí Kh̲ávar, was a tall man. He walked alongside Bahá'u'lláh and held an umbrella over His head as a protection against the heat of the sun. The air was refreshing as we arrived in the garden . . . His Blessed Person was extremely happy that day and each one of the friends received his share of the bounties from His presence. We had lunch in the garden, then we assembled together and attained His presence.

It was at that time that 'Abdu'l-Bahá arrived from 'Akká. The Blessed Beauty said, 'The Master is coming, hasten to attend Him' . . . On those days Bahá'u'lláh used to sow the seeds of loyalty and servitude towards 'Him Whom God hath purposed' ['Abdu'l-Bahá] in the hearts of the believers and explained the lofty station and hidden reality of the Master to all.

Attended by everyone, 'Abdu'l-Bahá came with great humility into the presence of the Blessed Beauty. Then the Tongue of Grandeur uttered words to this effect, 'From morning until now this garden was not pleasant but now with the presence of the

---

* For a detailed account of his life and services see Taherzadeh, *Revelation of Bahá'u'lláh*, vol. 4.

† A garden situated in the north of 'Akká, near the Mansion of Mazra'ih.

> Master it has become truly most delightful.' Then, turning to the Master, He remarked, 'You should have come in the morning.' 'Abdu'l-Bahá responded, 'The Governor of 'Akká and some residents had requested to meet with Me. Therefore I had to receive and entertain them.' Bahá'u'lláh, with a smiling face, said, 'The Master is our shield. Everybody here lives in the utmost comfort and peace. Association with the outside people such as these is very, very difficult. It is the Master who stands up to everything and prepares the means of comfort for all the friends. May God protect Him from the evil of the envious and the hostile.'*

In His Will and Testament, having dwelt on the machinations of the Covenant-breakers, the Centre of the Covenant of Bahá'u'lláh and the Supreme Exemplar of His teachings unveils to His loved ones a different picture of His warm and affectionate nature. He gives them a glimmer of that heavenly spirit bestowed upon Him by Bahá'u-'lláh and provides them with a glimpse of His limitless love and compassion, His humility and self-effacement through the following soul-stirring prayer of forgiveness for His enemies:

> **34–5–WT I call upon Thee, O Lord my God! with my tongue and with all my heart, not to requite them for their cruelty and their wrong-doings, their craft and their mischief, for they are foolish and ignoble and know not what they do. They discern not good from evil, neither do they distinguish right from wrong, nor justice from injustice. They follow their own desires and walk in the footsteps of the most imperfect and foolish amongst them. O my Lord! Have mercy upon them, shield them from all afflictions in these troubled times and grant that all trials and hardships may be the lot of this Thy servant that hath fallen into this darksome pit. Single me out for every woe and make me a sacrifice for all Thy loved ones. O Lord, Most High! May my soul, my life, my being, my spirit, my all be offered up for them. O God, My God! Lowly, suppliant and fallen upon my face, I beseech Thee with all the ardour of my invocation to pardon whosoever hath hurt me, forgive him that hath conspired against me and offended me, and wash away the misdeeds of them that have wrought injustice upon me. Vouchsafe unto them Thy goodly gifts, give them joy, relieve them from sorrow, grant them peace and prosperity, give them Thy bliss and pour upon them Thy bounty.**
>
> **Thou art the Powerful, the Gracious the Help in Peril, the Self-Subsisting!**

* These are not to be taken as the exact words of Bahá'u'lláh or 'Abdu'l-Bahá.

24

Dissociation with Covenant-Breakers

The history of the Faith of Bahá'u'lláh is replete with glorious episodes of steadfastness to Bahá'u'lláh and loyalty to His Covenant, of heroism and sacrifice. There are also dark pages of violation and treachery. These contrasting features of light and darkness, of truth and falsehood are interwoven.

The preceding chapters of this book mainly recount stories of the Covenant-breakers' unfaithfulness and betrayal, which caused much agony and hardship for the Master. In His Will and Testament, 'Abdu'l-Bahá describes their attacks on the Cause and the sufferings they inflicted on His person over a period of almost 15 years. He refers to Mírzá Muḥammad-'Alí's hatred, describes his unrelenting attacks on the Cause, enumerates his manifold violations of the Covenant, and foreshadows, in emphatic terms, the frustration of his schemes and his eventual extinction, a prophecy soon fulfilled. Referring to him in His Will and Testament, 'Abdu'l-Bahá states:

> **5–WT And now ye are witnessing how the wrath of God hath from all sides afflicted him and how day by day he is speeding towards destruction. Ere long will ye behold him and his associates, outwardly and inwardly, condemned to utter ruin.**

These passages of the Will and Testament constitute dark and gloomy pages in the history of the Faith. Then, having dwelt at length on these tragic events, 'Abdu'l-Bahá turns His attention to the glorious features of the Cause of Bahá'u'lláh. He directs the believers to observe at all times the ordinances of God, to uphold the standard of faithfulness and to arise in the promotion of the teachings in a spirit of selflessness and detachment from all worldly things, as seen in the following exhortations:

> **23–4–WT O ye beloved of the Lord! In this sacred Dispensation, conflict and contention are in no wise permitted. Every aggressor deprives himself of God's grace. It is incumbent upon everyone to show the utmost love, rectitude of conduct, straightforwardness and sincere kindliness unto all the peoples and kindreds of the world, be they friends or strangers. So intense**

must be the spirit of love and loving kindness, that the stranger may find himself a friend, the enemy a true brother, no difference whatsoever existing between them. For universality is of God and all limitations earthly. Thus man must strive that his reality may manifest virtues and perfections, the light whereof may shine upon everyone. The light of the sun shineth upon all the world and the merciful showers of Divine Providence fall upon all peoples. The vivifying breeze reviveth every living creature and all beings endued with life obtain their share and portion at His heavenly board. In like manner, the affections and loving kindness of the servants of the One True God must be bountifully and universally extended to all mankind. Regarding this, restrictions and limitations are in no wise permitted.

Wherefore, O my loving friends! Consort with all the peoples, kindred and religions of the world with the utmost truthfulness, uprightness, faithfulness, kindliness, good-will and friendliness, that all the world of being may be filled with the holy ecstasy of the grace of Bahá, that ignorance, enmity, hate and rancour may vanish from the world and the darkness of estrangement amidst the peoples and kindreds of the world may give way to the Light of Unity. Should other peoples and nations be unfaithful to you show your fidelity unto them, should they be unjust toward you show justice towards them, should they keep aloof from you attract them to yourselves, should they show their enmity be friendly towards them, should they poison your lives, sweeten their souls, should they inflict a wound upon you, be a salve to their sores. Such are the attributes of the sincere! Such are the attributes of the truthful.

The exhortation to consort with the peoples and religions of the world with the utmost love and fellowship should not be confused with the commandment to shun entirely the Covenant-breakers. Covenant-breaking is a deadly spiritual disease and never before in the history of religion have its pernicious effects been brought to light. In this Dispensation, however, the position of the Covenant-breakers and their spiritual condition have been exposed and fully examined. As we have described in chapter 3, Covenant-breaking provokes the wrath of God. Therefore, when a believer breaks the Covenant, his spiritual lifeline is cut off. Although he may have great knowledge of the teachings and the history of the Faith and may have had a brilliant record of service to the Cause, he becomes a lifeless being. Spiritually he turns blind and deaf; his heart becomes cold and bereft of faith. In reality he is not the same person any more. This is the reason why the violators of the Covenant of Bahá'u'lláh acted in the way they did.

As previously noted, in nature water can only flow from a high level to a lower one. It cannot flow to a point on the same level or to a higher one. Similarly, in order for a believer to receive the bounties of God from on high, he must be positioned at the opposite end of the scale: lowly, humble and self-effacing. The Covenant-breakers were not. They aspired to be equal to the Centre of the Covenant and thus the spiritual energies released by God could not reach them and they became deprived of the outpouring of the spirit of faith. Their lives, once guided by the Light of Truth, were now based on falsehood. Deception, intrigue, dishonesty and violence became their way of life. Throughout the ages these vices have proved to be the weapons which the ungodly use against the righteous. But in the end they are obliterated by the power of truth.

These unholy characteristics are not exclusive to the violators at the time of 'Abdu'l-Bahá. The Covenant-breakers who opposed Shoghi Effendi and those who appeared after his passing conducted their shameful careers in the same manner.

It is necessary here to distinguish between enemies of the Faith and Covenant-breakers. The former attack the Cause of God mainly through ignorance, and perhaps they will be forgiven by God. The latter, however, know where the Source of Truth is but are unable to turn to it; instead, for their own selfish reasons, they knowingly rise up against it. To inflict harm upon a human being is reprehensible in the sight of God and perhaps can be forgiven by Him. But to wilfully oppose the Cause of the Almighty and to strike at its roots, as the violators of the Covenant do, are grave transgressions which without repentance are unforgivable.

The subject of Covenant-breaking was frequently broached by the Master, according to Dr Yúnis Khán's testimony. In order to protect the community from the Covenant-breakers' poisonous influence, 'Abdu'l-Bahá used to speak about their schemes and intrigues, their plots and conspiracies. He often likened Covenant-breaking to a contagious disease: the only way to prevent it from spreading is to confine the patient and place him in quarantine. Infectious disease spreads rapidly and can affect a multitude. For that reason, He said, protecting the believers from this deadly disease was imperative and could be achieved only by cutting off association with the Covenant-breakers.

In one of His last messages to the American believers 'Abdu'l-Bahá warned of the consequences of association with the Covenant-breakers. He cabled them:

> He who sits with leper catches leprosy. He who is with Christ shuns Pharisees and abhors Judas Iscariots. Certainly shun violators . . .[206]

In many of their Tablets Bahá'u'lláh and 'Abdu'l-Bahá have emphatically warned the believers to avoid associating with the Covenant-breakers.

In His Will and Testament, 'Abdu'l-Bahá admonishes them in these words:

> **38–WT And now, one of the greatest and most fundamental principles of the Cause of God is to shun and avoid entirely the Covenant-breakers, for they will utterly destroy the Cause of God, exterminate His Law and render of no account all efforts exerted in the past. O friends! It behoveth you to call to mind with tenderness the trials of His Holiness, the Exalted One, and show your fidelity to the Ever-Blest Beauty. The utmost endeavour must be exerted lest all these woes, trials and afflictions, all this pure and sacred blood that hath been shed so profusely in the Path of God, may prove to be in vain.**

Again 'Abdu'l-Bahá writes in the third part of the Will and Testament:

> **52–WT Hence, the beloved of the Lord must entirely shun them, avoid them, foil their machinations and evil whisperings, guard the Law of God and His religion, engage one and all in diffusing widely the sweet savours of God and to the best of their endeavour proclaim His Teachings.**

In answer to a question about 'shunning', 'Abdu'l-Bahá wrote:

> Thou hadst asked some questions; that why the blessed and spiritual souls, who are firm and steadfast, shun the company of degenerate persons. This is because, that just as bodily diseases . . . are contagious, likewise the spiritual diseases are also infectious. If a consumptive should associate with a thousand safe and healthy persons, the safety and health of these thousand persons would not affect the consumptive and would not cure him of his consumption. But when this consumptive associates with those thousand souls, in a short time the disease of consumption will infect a number of those healthy persons. This is a clear and self-evident question.[207]

To check the spread of this spiritual disease, it is necessary not only to shun the Covenant-breakers but also to expel them from the community in the same way that a cancerous growth is cut out of the body. As has already been stated in the Introduction, the Prophets of old did not establish a firm and explicit Covenant with their followers and so the adherents of past religions did not enjoy this protection. A look at the history of religions, which clearly reveals the many schisms that have taken place, will amply demonstrate the danger. If, in this Dispensation, the Covenant-breakers had not been expelled and had been allowed to associate freely with the believers, after a short time the Bahá'í community, like other religions, would have been divided into sects. Its unity, which is its distinguishing feature, would have been destroyed forever and its goal of establishing the oneness of mankind on this planet brought to naught.

To illustrate this point, let us examine some of the laws of nature as applied to the human body. The Cause of God may be likened to the body of man which, when healthy, can withstand manifold external pressures. It can endure extremes of temperature, overcome thirst and hunger, defend itself when confronted with hardship and preserve its wholesomeness against the effects of disease. Similarly the Cause of Bahá'u'lláh can withstand the onslaught of its external enemies and can resist every opposition from its adversaries. All the persecutions whereby thousands of its followers were martyred have failed to extinguish its light, destroy its unity or undermine its rising institutions.

On the other hand, a healthy person can be fatally afflicted if poison is allowed to enter and circulate in his blood stream. Nature, however, has provided the body with an immune system which removes the unwanted poisonous substances from the blood stream and discharges them at intervals, thus cleansing the body from their deadly effects and ensuring its health and well-being.

It is the same with the Cause of God. Bahá'u'lláh has provided an instrument for casting out any individual who, while claiming to be a believer, opposes the Centre of the Cause and tries to remain in the community to disrupt its foundations. When the unwholesome elements, those egotistical personalities who lust for power and are ready to sacrifice the religion of God to their own selfish desires, are expelled from the Faith, the community, cleansed from the poison of Covenant-breaking, acquires a fresh vitality and vigour. It is enabled to maintain its health and continue its forward march towards ultimate victory.

During the days of Bahá'u'lláh the authority to expel Covenant-breakers was vested only in Him. Later it devolved upon 'Abdu'l-Bahá, as the Centre of the Covenant, and then upon Shoghi Effendi, as the Guardian of the Cause. Today this expulsion takes place by decision of the Hands of the Cause of God* residing in the Holy Land, subject to the approval of the Universal House of Justice.

* The functions of the Hands of the Cause, as defined in the Will and Testament of 'Abdu'l-Bahá, are mainly the protection and propagation of the Faith. Those Hands of the Cause now living were appointed by the Guardian, Shoghi Effendi.

No one is lightly or hurriedly declared a Covenant-breaker by the Centre of the Cause. Great efforts are made to enlighten the individual and guide him to the path of truth. Only when every possible effort to save him from his spiritual downfall has failed will he be expelled from the community. For example, 'Abdu'l-Bahá made every endeavour during the first few years of His ministry to change the attitude of His unfaithful brothers; only after they failed to heed His counsels and intensified their rebellion did He declare them to be Covenant-breakers and cast them out of the community.

Never before has a Manifestation of God created the instrument whereby the breakers of His Covenant, those who oppose the Centre of the Cause from within the community, are cast out. This is one of the unique features of the Revelation of Bahá'u'lláh, providing a means by which the Cause of God is purged from impurities.

It is important to note that should a Covenant-breaker recognize his mistakes, become conscious of his transgressions against the Cause of God and find the urge to repent, the Centre of the Cause, when satisfied he is sincerely repentant, will forgive his past deeds and restore his credibility and status as a Bahá'í in good standing in the community.

The protection of the Cause from the intrusion of the Covenant-breakers is the most vital duty of the institutions of the Faith, both at present and in the future. Around the time when the perils threatening the life of 'Abdu'l-Bahá were greatest and He wrote in His Will and Testament, 'I am now in very great danger and the hope of even an hour's life is lost to me',[208] He took a special measure for the protection of the Cause of God. Since Shoghi Effendi, whom He had designated as the Guardian of the Cause, was at that time a child of about ten years of age, 'Abdu'l-Bahá wrote a Tablet of great significance to Ḥájí Mírzá Muḥammad-Taqí, the Vakílu'd-Dawlih, a cousin of the Báb.* In it He intimated that great dangers surrounded His person, and urged him to make arrangements, if necessary, for the election of the Universal House of Justice. To bring this about, He directed him to gather the Afnán† and the Hands of the Cause in one place and establish this institution in accordance with the provisions of His Will and Testament.

---

* The Vakílu'd-Dawlih was a distinguished believer who was designated by 'Abdu'l-Bahá as one of the 'four and twenty elders which sat before God on their seats' mentioned in chapter 11 of the Revelation of St John the Divine. Of the other 23 'elders', only 19 have been named by 'Abdu'l-Bahá, i.e. the Báb and the 18 'Letters of the Living'.

† The kinsmen of the Báb and those of His wife.

'Abdu'l-Bahá attached great importance to the protection of the Cause. He refers to it several times in His Will and Testament:

> **10–WT Lord! Shield Thou from these Covenant-breakers the mighty Stronghold of Thy Faith and protect Thy secret Sanctuary from the onslaught of the ungodly. Thou art in truth the Mighty, the Powerful, the Gracious, the Strong.**
>
> **36–WT O dearly beloved friends! I am now in very great danger and the hope of even an hour's life is lost to me. I am thus constrained to write these lines for the protection of the Cause of God, the preservation of His Law, the safeguarding of His Word and the safety of His Teachings. By the Ancient Beauty! This wronged one hath in no wise borne nor doth he bear a grudge against any one; towards none doth he entertain any ill-feeling and uttereth no word save for the good of the world. My supreme obligation, however, of necessity, prompteth me to guard and preserve the Cause of God. Thus, with the greatest regret, I counsel you saying: – Guard ye the Cause of God, protect His law and have the utmost fear of discord.**
>
> **42–WT O ye beloved of the Lord! Strive with all your heart to shield the Cause of God from the onslaught of the insincere, for souls such as these cause the straight to become crooked and all benevolent efforts to produce contrary results.**
>
> **43–WT O God, my God! I call Thee, Thy Prophets and Thy Messengers, Thy Saints and Thy Holy Ones, to witness that I have declared conclusively Thy Proofs unto Thy loved ones and set forth clearly all things unto them, that they may watch over Thy Faith, guard Thy Straight Path and protect Thy Resplendent Law. Thou art, verily, the All-Knowing, the All-Wise!**

In one of His Tablets 'Abdu'l-Bahá describes the Covenant-breakers as dead bodies which the ocean casts out upon its shores:

> The tests of every dispensation are in direct proportion to the greatness of the Cause, and as heretofore such a manifest Covenant, written by the Supreme Pen, hath not been entered upon, the tests are proportionately more severe. These trials cause the feeble souls to waver while those who are firm are not affected. These agitations of the violators are no more than the foam of the ocean, which is one of its inseparable features; but the ocean of the Covenant shall surge and shall cast ashore the bodies of the dead, for it cannot retain them. Thus it is seen that the ocean of the Covenant hath surged and surged until it hath thrown out the dead bodies – souls that are deprived of the Spirit of God and are lost in passion and self and are seeking leadership. This foam of

> the ocean shall not endure and shall soon disperse and vanish, while the ocean of the Covenant shall eternally surge and roar . . .
>
> From the early days of creation down to the present time, throughout all the divine dispensations, such a firm and explicit Covenant hath not been entered upon. In view of this fact is it possible for this foam to remain on the surface of the ocean of the Covenant? No, by God! The violators are trampling upon their own dignity, are uprooting their own foundations and are proud at being upheld by flatterers who exert a great effort to shake the faith of feeble souls. But this action of theirs is of no consequence; it is a mirage and not water, foam and not the sea, mist and not a cloud, illusion and not reality. All this ye shall soon see.[209]

Those who are expelled from the Faith as Covenant-breakers are left to their own devices. The believers will never oppose them in their activities and they are left free to continue their actions against the Cause of God. But the history of the Faith demonstrates that by their very opposition to the Centre of the Faith they sow the seeds of their own extinction and after a while fade away ignominiously. Their position is like that of a branch cut off from the tree. At first it is green and appears to have some life, but as it has no root, it will inevitably wither and die.

Severing relationships with Covenant-breakers must not be confused with acts of opposition or hatred towards them. Dr Yúnis Khán recounts a story of 'Abdu'l-Bahá which throws light on this subject. The following is a summary translation of a passage from his memoirs:

> Sometimes in the course of His talks, 'Abdu'l-Bahá used to explain that Covenant-breaking exerts an evil influence upon the conduct and morals of the public. The seed of sedition which the Covenant-breakers have sown among the people is capable of inclining the world of humanity towards ungodliness and iniquity. Therefore the believers must manifest righteousness and divine virtues in their lives, so as to remove the foul odour of this rebellion from the world. At the same time they will have to be vigilant and resourceful lest the Covenant-breakers influence public opinion because whenever their foul breath reaches a certain area, it impairs the spiritual nostrils of the people and obscures their vision. Consequently these people are unable to inhale the sweet savours of holiness or to behold the effulgence of the divine light . . .
>
> One of the important duties enjoined upon the loved ones of God is to make every endeavour to prevent the Covenant-breakers from infiltrating the Bahá'í community.
>
> 'Abdu'l-Bahá quoted Bahá'u'lláh as saying that should one who is a follower of Mírzá Yaḥyá be living in a town, the foul odour of his presence will linger for a long time in that town and the prog-

ress of the Cause of God will be impeded there. The Master gave the example of the city of Kirmán and said that the breath of the Covenant-breakers [Muḥammad-'Alí and his associates], which is none other than the tempting of Satan,* is far more deadly than that of the followers of Mírzá Yaḥyá . . .

One day when this servant and two other friends were in 'Abdu'l-Bahá's presence, He was talking in the same vein about Covenant-breakers . . . At one point I remembered an incident which happened in Ṭihrán and in order to support His arguments, I said: 'A new school has recently been opened in Ṭihrán and Hubbu'lláh, a son of the notorious Jamál-i-Burújirdí [father and son were both Covenant-breakers], was being considered for employment as a teacher. As soon as we heard this, the Hands of the Cause, two other friends and myself consulted together in a meeting and agreed to do everything in our power to prevent the appointment of Hubbu'lláh to this post. We sent a certain individual to persuade the school authorities not to appoint him . . .'

I had not yet finished my sentence when 'Abdu'l-Bahá interrupted me and instead of praising our action, said: 'Do you mean to say that you consulted together and decided to stop a Covenant-breaker earning a living? This is not the way to serve the Cause of God. In matters connected with one's livelihood there should be no differentiation between a believer and a Covenant-breaker. The loved ones of the Abhá Beauty must be the signs of the bounty of God among the people. They should, like the sun, illumine the world, and like the clouds of the spring season rain down upon everything. They must not look upon the capacity and worthiness of the individual' . . . 'Abdu'l-Bahá spoke in this vein to us for some time and I hung my head in shame![210]

In many of their Tablets Bahá'u'lláh and 'Abdu'l-Bahá exhorted the believers to show the utmost kindness to all, including their enemies, and to pray for them.

Whereas association with the peoples of the world is enjoined on the Bahá'ís, the Covenant-breakers are a legitimate exception. They are cast out of the community and shunned by the believers but to hate, oppose or confront them is against the teachings of Bahá'u'lláh. The story of Dr Yúnis Khán told above demonstrates that Bahá'ís are forbidden to take any measures designed to harm the Covenant-breakers or obstruct their personal work and activities. On the contrary, knowing that these people are misguided and ignorant of

* According to the Bahá'í teachings, there is no such being as Satan. Satan is a human being who is led by his ego to live a life of wickedness and ungodliness, Shoghi Effendi's secretary states on his behalf that 'devil or Satan is symbolic of evil and dark forces yielding to temptation' (From a letter written on behalf of Shoghi Effendi to an individual believer, 2 November 1938).

the truth, the believers should overlook and forgive their transgressions. Following in the footsteps of the Master, they are encouraged to feel the utmost compassion towards them in their hearts, for they are aware that unless these misguided souls change their ways, their plight will be disastrous and their end perilous. Since the Bahá'ís do not associate with Covenant-breakers, the only way they can help them is to pray that they may be guided to the pathway of truth. Indeed, a number of Covenant-breakers have recognized their folly, repented to the Centre of the Cause, been forgiven and have been welcomed back into the Bahá'í community. The prayer revealed in the Will and Testament and quoted in this chapter, in which 'Abdu'l-Bahá begs forgiveness for the Covenant-breakers who had inflicted untold sufferings upon Him for many years, demonstrates that although the Bahá'ís shun these sick souls, they do not bear antagonism or hatred towards them in their hearts.

It is helpful at this juncture to clarify the difference between Covenant-breakers and those who withdraw from the Faith of Bahá'u'lláh. There are always a small number of individuals who recognize Bahá'u'lláh as the Manifestation of God, embrace His Faith and even become active members of the community but later, for some reason, change their minds and withdraw from the Faith. Such individuals are not Covenant-breakers. The Bahá'ís will maintain friendly relationships with such people and respect their decision to withdraw their membership in the Faith. Bahá'u'lláh has enjoined upon His followers to associate with them in a spirit of love and fellowship.

There is another category of believers who become deprived of their administrative rights by the sanction, at the present time, of the National Spiritual Assemblies. This happens when an individual flagrantly breaks certain laws of Bahá'u'lláh which are related to social or administrative activities and by so doing brings disgrace upon the Faith. Although not Bahá'ís in good standing, these people are nevertheless part of the community and may, under certain conditions, regain their administrative rights.

'Abdu'l-Bahá has described Covenant-breaking as a contagious disease and therefore counselled the believers, for the sake of their own salvation and for the unity of the community, to sever their relationships with Covenant-breakers and to have no personal contact with them. The believers are also strongly discouraged from reading their propaganda, for their words can inject poison into the mind. When Mírzá Muḥammad-'Alí distributed his false propaganda against the Centre of the Covenant, the recipients in Persia who were loyal to the Faith used to return his communications to him sealed and unread. This is still a wise precaution today.

By their fidelity, courage and faith the believers during the ministries of 'Abdu'l-Bahá and Shoghi Effendi rallied around the Centre of the Cause, guarded the stronghold of the Faith, protected it from the onslaught of the Covenant-breakers and prevented them from spreading their venom among the believers. Thus they passed on to later generations a worldwide community whose unity is firmly established and the invincibility of whose rising institutions is fully demonstrated.

25
Teaching the Cause of God

13–14–WT O ye that stand fast in the Covenant! When the hour cometh that this wronged and broken-winged bird will have taken its flight unto the celestial Concourse, when it will have hastened to the Realm of the Unseen and its mortal frame will have been either lost or hidden neath the dust, it is incumbent upon the Afnán, that are steadfast in the Covenant of God, and have branched from the Tree of Holiness; the Hands, (pillars) of the Cause of God (the glory of the Lord rest upon them), and all the friends and loved ones, one and all to bestir themselves and arise with heart and soul and in one accord, to diffuse the sweet savours of God, to teach His Cause and to promote His Faith. It behoveth them not to rest for a moment, neither to seek repose. They must disperse themselves in every land, pass by every clime and travel throughout all regions. Bestirred, without rest and steadfast to the end they must raise in every land the triumphal cry 'O Thou the Glory of Glories!' (Yá Bahá'u'l-Abhá), must achieve renown in the world wherever they go, must burn brightly even as a candle in every meeting and must kindle the flame of Divine love in every assembly; that the light of truth may rise resplendent in the midmost heart of the world, that throughout the East and throughout the West a vast concourse may gather under the shadow of the Word of God, that the sweet savours of holiness may be diffused, that faces may shine radiantly, hearts be filled with the Divine spirit and souls be made heavenly.

In these days, the most important of all things is the guidance of the nations and peoples of the world. Teaching the Cause is of utmost importance for it is the head corner-stone of the foundation itself.

Thus a loving Master, in language at once tender, moving and forceful, exhorts His steadfast lovers of all ranks within the community to arise after His passing to teach the Cause – an act regarded as the most important and meritorious of all deeds in this Holy Dispensation.

Teaching, or 'diffusing the Divine Fragrances', was the first commandment enjoined by the Báb upon the Letters of the Living. Since then it has remained, and will continue to remain throughout the

Bahá'í era, the foremost obligation of every follower of the Blessed Beauty, who addressed the believers on the duty of teaching His Cause in the following words:

> Teach ye the Cause of God, O people of Bahá, for God hath prescribed unto every one the duty of proclaiming His Message, and regardeth it as the most meritorious of all deeds. Such a deed is acceptable only when he that teacheth the Cause is already a firm believer in God, the Supreme Protector, the Gracious, the Almighty. He hath, moreover, ordained that His Cause be taught through the power of men's utterance, and not through resort to violence. Thus hath His ordinance been sent down from the Kingdom of Him Who is the Most Exalted, the All-Wise.[211]

Bahá'u'lláh stressed the paramount importance of teaching His Cause in a Tablet to Jamál-i-Burújirdí,[212] telling him that if he were residing in the West of the world and learned that a person in the East was anxious to attain the knowledge of God and the recognition of His Manifestation, then it would be incumbent upon him, if he had the means, to travel to distant lands in order to bestow the water of life upon that enquirer.

To appreciate the significance of Bahá'u'lláh's utterance that teaching the Cause is 'the most meritorious of all deeds', let us turn to one of the basic laws of creation, namely, the love relationship between the Creator and the created. We observe in nature that the earth produces the mineral, vegetable and animal forms of life and therefore it may be regarded as the creator of all matter it produces. In this relationship, the love between the creator and the created is manifested by a force of attraction between the earth and every object that comes within its orbit. Thus the earth attracts everything to itself. One might say that the goal of every object is to reach and rest upon the surface of the earth. But if a barrier is placed between the object and the earth, this union cannot take place unless the barrier is removed.

The same law of attraction binds the Manifestation of God and the soul of man. There is a love relationship between Bahá'u'lláh and every human being but in most cases there are many manmade barriers between them – the veils mentioned by Bahá'u'lláh in the Kitáb-i-Íqán. They include pride in one's knowledge and background, attachment to the world and imitation of others in matters of religion and culture, to name but a few. The act of teaching is the removal of these barriers, one by one and with wisdom, so that the soul will be attracted to Bahá'u'lláh. The only person who can do this is a Bahá'í.

In the world of nature, when two opposite entities are attracted to each other, they unite and bring each other pleasure. This also happens between the Manifestation of God and the believer, one occupying the summit of glory and lordship and the other the depths of lowliness and servitude. When the soul recognizes Bahá'u'lláh and is drawn to Him, the attraction of the opposites brings pleasure to God as well as to the individual and there can be no reward more 'meritorious' for the Bahá'í teacher than being a source of pleasure to God.

Teaching the Cause is an act of devotion to God, as it brings pleasure to Him. In many of their Tablets, Bahá'u'lláh and 'Abdu'l-Bahá have stated that divine blessings will descend upon those who endeavour to teach the Cause and that the act of teaching itself becomes a magnet attracting the bounties of God to the soul. It is therefore important to appreciate that the primary purpose of teaching the Cause is not to increase the membership of the Bahá'í community, although this happens as a result. Rather, it is to enable a soul to draw near to Bahá'u'lláh and become enamoured of Him.

In a Tablet[213] Bahá'u'lláh discloses the pre-eminent position occupied in the sight of God by the act of teaching. He states that there are two things pleasing to God: the tears shed in fear of Him and the blood of the martyr spilled in His path. But since Bahá'u'lláh has advised His followers not to volunteer to give their lives, He has in this Tablet replaced the reward of martyrdom with teaching His Faith. Indeed, in another Tablet[214] Bahá'u'lláh explicitly states that in this Dispensation it is preferable to teach with wisdom than to give one's life.

In past Dispensations only a few privileged leaders of religion were engaged in teaching work but one of the greatest gifts that Bahá'u'lláh has bestowed upon His followers is to provide all believers, regardless of their abilities and accomplishments, the opportunity to become the recipients of God's bestowals as they teach His Cause – a duty He has enjoined on them all. He has written:

> God hath prescribed unto every one the duty of teaching His Cause. Whoever ariseth to discharge this duty, must needs, ere he proclaimeth His Message, adorn himself with the ornament of an upright and praiseworthy character, so that his words may attract the hearts of such as are receptive to his call. Without it, he can never hope to influence his hearers.[215]

This statement leaves no room for doubt that success in teaching depends upon the teacher having 'an upright and praiseworthy character', for Bahá'u'lláh says, 'Without it, he can never hope to influence his hearers.' The word 'never' is emphatic and rules out any other possibility. Similar statements are found in numerous other Tablets. 'Abdu'l-Bahá also writes:

> The aim is this: The intention of the teacher must be pure, his heart independent, his spirit attracted, his thought at peace, his resolution firm, his magnanimity exalted and in the love of God a shining torch. Should he become as such, his sanctified breath will even affect the rock; otherwise there will be no result whatsoever.[216]

The emphasis of the last sentence is repeated in other Tablets of 'Abdu'l-Bahá. Shoghi Effendi, too, has drawn our attention to this truth in many of his letters. To cite one celebrated passage:

> Not by the force of numbers, not by the mere exposition of a set of new and noble principles, not by an organized campaign of teaching – no matter how worldwide and elaborate in its character – not even by the staunchness of our faith or the exaltation of our enthusiasm, can we ultimately hope to vindicate in the eyes of a critical and sceptical age the supreme claim of the Abhá Revelation. One thing and only one thing will unfailingly and alone secure the undoubted triumph of this sacred Cause, namely, the extent to which our own inner life and private character mirror forth in their manifold aspects the splendour of those eternal principles proclaimed by Bahá'u'lláh.[217]

Here Shoghi Effendi leaves no alternative to this vital prerequisite for teaching, for he says (and let us note his double emphasis): 'One thing and only one thing will unfailingly and alone secure the undoubted triumph of this sacred Cause . . .'

Having discussed one of the most important prerequisites for teaching, let us now examine the work of teaching itself. There are no set methods or procedures, although we have been given certain principles and guidelines by the Author of the Faith and by 'Abdu'l-Bahá and Shoghi Effendi. These principles and guidelines are at variance with standards and methods current outside the Faith, where, generally, every expedient measure is used to influence people and convert them to various ideologies. The Cause of Bahá'u'lláh is founded on the truth of God's Revelation and truth cannot be clothed in false standards. It cannot employ the techniques of salesmanship, propaganda, expediency and compromise. The methods used in the commercial world to attract people to new ideas, such as extravagant and sensational publicity based on slogans, extreme statements and similar gimmicks, are all alien to the Cause of God.

In his teaching work a Bahá'í presents the message of Bahá'u'lláh as one would offer a gift to a king. Since his primary object in teaching is not to increase numbers but rather to bring a soul to its God, a Bahá'í ought to approach his fellow men with feelings of love and humility and, above all, take to them the transforming power of Bahá'u'lláh and nothing of himself. Indeed, if he tries to project himself by impressing upon the listener his knowledge and accomplishments and if he aims to establish the ascendancy of his arguments while teaching the Faith, then the power of Bahá'u'lláh cannot reach him.

Success in teaching depends on one's ability and readiness to draw on the power of Bahá'u'lláh, as was discussed in chapter 14. There is no alternative. If the believer does not open the way for Bahá'u'lláh through his love for Him, through living his life in accordance with His teachings and through teaching His Cause with devotion, Bahá'u'lláh's confirmations and assistance cannot reach the believer and he will fail in his service to Him. Those who rank foremost among Bahá'í teachers have always been conscious of the presence of Bahá'u'lláh at every stage of their teaching activities. Because of this consciousness they have been enabled to approach with genuine love and humility those who have been seeking the truth and have attracted them with the warmth of their faith and the creative power of the Word of God. It is this consciousness that has enabled them to radiate the glory of the new-born Faith of God, to demonstrate its truth, to promote its interests, to withstand the onslaught of its enemies and to win imperishable victories for their Lord.

In the third part of His Will and Testament 'Abdu'l-Bahá elaborates further on the subject of teaching the Cause:

> **53–WT Whosoever and whatsoever meeting becometh a hindrance to the diffusion of the Light of Faith, let the loved ones give them counsel and say: 'Of all the gifts of God the greatest is the gift of Teaching. It draweth unto us the Grace of God and is our first obligation. Of such a gift how can we deprive ourselves? Nay, our lives, our goods, our comforts, our rest, we offer them all as a sacrifice for the Abhá Beauty and teach the Cause of God.' Caution and prudence, however, must be observed even as recorded in the Book. The veil must in no wise be suddenly rent asunder. The Glory of Glories rest upon you.**

Throughout His ministry Bahá'u'lláh exhorted His followers to teach the Cause of God with great wisdom. He did not approve of teaching the public indiscriminately. He repeatedly advised the believers in

Persia, especially after the martyrdom of Badí',* that for their own safety and the protection of the Cause they should exercise care and prudence in their approach to people and not excite or antagonize them. In one of His Tablets Bahá'u'lláh counsels His followers:

> In this Day, We can neither approve the conduct of the fearful that seeketh to dissemble his faith, nor sanction the behaviour of the avowed believer that clamorously asserteth his allegiance to this Cause. Both should observe the dictates of wisdom, and strive diligently to serve the best interests of the Faith.[218]

To cite an example of wisdom in teaching, there is a Tablet of Bahá'u-'lláh[219] in which Fáris (the Christian Syrian who embraced the Faith in Alexandria)† is exhorted to teach with wisdom. Bahá'u'lláh counsels him not to disclose to people everything about the Cause at first but rather to teach them little by little until they are ready to absorb more. He likens this process to feeding infants who need to be given a little milk at a time until they grow in strength and are able to digest other food. This exhortation of Bahá'u'lláh is the basis of teaching the Cause of God. The principles involved are very similar to those employed by a schoolteacher in teaching his pupils. Before teaching the Cause to any person, it is important to know his background and capacity. The most successful teachers are those who, after familiarizing themselves with the beliefs and ideas of an individual, reveal the truths of the Faith gradually to him. What little they impart is the correct remedy and is so potent as to influence and stimulate the soul and enable it to take a step forward and become ready to absorb more.

Ḥájí Mírzá Ḥaydar-'Alí, the celebrated Bahá'í teacher, has left to posterity the following account of one of his memorable interviews with Bahá'u'lláh in 'Akká, in the course of which He spoke these words about teaching the Cause of God:‡

> 'The way to teach is to have a pleasing disposition and to deal with people in a spirit of loving-kindness. One must acknowledge whatever the other person says, even if it is vain imaginings, beliefs which are the result of blind imitation or absurd talk. One should avoid engaging in arguments or adducing proofs which bring out stubbornness and contention in the other person. This is because

---

* An illustrious youthful martyr of the Faith, whose exemplary sacrifice is described in Taherzadeh, *Revelation of Bahá'u'lláh*, vol. 3.

† See Taherzadeh, *Revelation of Bahá'u'lláh*, vol. 3, pp. 5–11.

‡ These are not the exact words of Bahá'u'lláh but convey the purport of His talk.

he finds himself defeated, and this will lead to his becoming more veiled from the truth and will add to his waywardness.

'The right way is to acknowledge the other person's statements and then present him with the alternative point of view and invite him to examine it to see whether it is true or false. Of course, when it is presented to him with courtesy, affection and loving-kindness, he will hear and will not be thinking in terms of defence, to find answers and look for proofs. He will acknowledge and admit the points. When the person realizes that the purpose behind discussions is not wrangling or the winning of arguments but rather to convey the truth and to reveal human qualities and divine perfections, he will of course show fairness. His inner eyes and ears and heart will open and, through the grace of God, he will become a new creation and will possess new eyes and new ears.'

Bahá'u'lláh spoke a great deal about the evils of controversial argument and aiming to become a winner in discussion. He then said, 'The Most Great Branch ['Abdu'l-Bahá] will listen to any absurd talk with such attentiveness that the person concerned believes that He is deriving enlightenment from him. However, little by little, and in a way that the person cannot realize, He bestows upon him a new vision and a new understanding.'[220]

The talks of 'Abdu'l-Bahá in the West provide the best example of wisdom in teaching. He addressed audiences who were almost alien to the history and genesis of the Faith and unfamiliar with the claims and the station of its founder. Yet He disclosed to them with simplicity and brevity only those essential truths which they were capable of understanding and which constituted the first stepping-stones for their eventual recognition of the stupendous message of Bahá'u'lláh. He clearly avoided at that early stage any elaboration on the many implications of the station of Bahá'u'lláh and His Revelation as well as the unfoldment of His laws and His World Order in the future. Instead, He bestowed upon everyone who had the capacity a measure of His all-embracing love, which animated and sustained those few who embraced the Faith in the West.

It is perhaps a temptation for a Bahá'í teacher, especially if he is a knowledgeable one, to pour out upon a seeker all his knowledge and bombard him with a series of profound utterances and lengthy discussions with the aim of proving the truth of his own arguments. When this happens, however, it blocks the way for the power of Bahá'u'lláh to reach the heart of the seeker and enlighten him with the light of faith.

As previously noted, a passage from the Will and Testament of 'Abdu'l-Bahá earnestly urges the believers to 'disperse themselves in every land, pass by every clime and travel throughout all regions'.

These words are reminiscent of a passage in the Tablet of Carmel in which Bahá'u'lláh makes this moving announcement:

> Oh, how I long to announce unto every spot on the surface of the earth, and to carry to each one of its cities, the glad-tidings of this Revelation – a Revelation to which the heart of Sinai hath been attracted, and in whose name the Burning Bush is calling: 'Unto God, the Lord of Lords, belong the kingdoms of earth and heaven.'[221]

From among all the writings of 'Abdu'l-Bahá, including His Tablets of the Divine Plan, which urge the believers to leave their homes and travel throughout the world for the purpose of diffusing the divine fragrances, the exhortations of 'Abdu'l-Bahá in the above passage of the Will and Testament penetrate the soul and are the most appealing to the heart. There can be no doubt that when 'Abdu'l-Bahá wrote these passages, He knew full well that souls would arise to fulfil His appeal. Years before, soon after the passing of Bahá'u'lláh, He had also addressed this theme in very moving language in the following Tablet, which was revealed for one of the Apostles of Bahá'u'lláh, Shaykh Káẓim-i-Samandar:*

> O phoenix of that immortal flame kindled in the sacred Tree! Bahá'u'lláh – may my life, my soul, my spirit be offered up as a sacrifice unto His lowly servants – hath, during His last days on earth, given the most emphatic promise that, through the outpourings of the grace of God and the aid and assistance vouchsafed from His Kingdom on high, souls will arise and holy beings appear who, as stars, would adorn the firmament of divine guidance; illumine the dayspring of loving-kindness and bounty; manifest the signs of the unity of God; shine with the light of sanctity and purity; receive their full measure of divine inspiration; raise high the sacred torch of faith; stand firm as the rock and immoveable as the mountain; and grow to become luminaries in the heavens of His Revelation, mighty channels of His grace, means for the bestowal of God's bountiful care, heralds calling forth the name of the One true God, and establishers of the world's supreme foundation.
>
> These shall labour ceaselessly, by day and by night, shall heed neither trials nor woe, shall suffer no respite in their efforts, shall seek no repose, shall disregard all ease and comfort, and, detached and unsullied, shall consecrate every fleeting moment of their lives to the diffusion of the divine fragrance and the exaltation of God's holy Word. Their faces will radiate heavenly gladness, and their

* For further information about him, see Taherzadeh, *Revelation of Bahá'u'lláh*, vol. 3, p. 88.

hearts be filled with joy. Their souls will be inspired, and their foundation stand secure. They shall scatter in the world, and travel throughout all regions. They shall raise their voices in every assembly, and adorn and revive every gathering. They shall speak in every tongue, and interpret every hidden meaning. They shall reveal the mysteries of the Kingdom, and manifest unto everyone the signs of God. They shall burn brightly even as a candle in the heart of every assembly, and beam forth as a star upon every horizon. The gentle breezes wafted from the garden of their hearts shall perfume and revive the souls of men, and the revelations of their minds, even as showers, will reinvigorate the peoples and nations of the world.

I am waiting, eagerly waiting for these holy ones to appear; and yet, how long will they delay their coming? My prayer and ardent supplication, at eventide and at dawn, is that these shining stars may soon shed their radiance upon the world, that their sacred countenances may be unveiled to mortal eyes, that the hosts of divine assistance may achieve their victory, and the billows of grace, rising from His oceans above, may flow upon all mankind. Pray ye also and supplicate unto Him that through the bountiful aid of the Ancient Beauty these souls may be unveiled to the eyes of the world.

The glory of God rest upon thee, and upon him whose face is illumined with that everlasting light that shineth from His Kingdom of Glory.[222]

Having encouraged the believers to arise after Him for the promotion of the Faith, 'Abdu'l-Bahá, in the following passage of the Will and Testament, invites them to follow His example of service to the Cause of Bahá'u'lláh:

14–WT This wronged servant has spent his days and nights in promoting the Cause and urging the peoples to service. He rested not a moment, till the fame of the Cause of God was noised abroad in the world and the celestial strains from the Abhá Kingdom roused the East and the West. The beloved of God must also follow the same example. This is the secret of faithfulness, this is the requirement of servitude to the Threshold of Bahá!

Finally, in the following passage of the Will and Testament, 'Abdu'l-Bahá urges the believers to follow the example of the disciples of Christ. This passage also serves to immortalize the memory of those who in an earlier Dispensation achieved memorable victories for the Cause of God.

15–WT The disciples of Christ forgot themselves and all earthly things, forsook all their cares and belongings, purged themselves of self and passion and with absolute detachment scattered far

and wide and engaged in calling the peoples of the world to the Divine Guidance, till at last they made the world another world, illumined the surface of the earth and even to their last hour proved self-sacrificing in the pathway of that Beloved One of God. Finally in various lands they suffered glorious martyrdom. Let them that are men of action follow in their footsteps!

Today a vast number of dedicated believers from all over the world, and of every conceivable background, have arisen with vigour and devotion to promote the Cause of God as Bahá'í pioneers and teachers. Indeed, with the rising of these detached and holy souls, the initial stage of the promise of Bahá'u'lláh has already been realized. The Faith of Bahá'u'lláh has now reached all parts of the world; through their self-sacrifice, their detachment and their faith, these men and women, drawing on the power of Bahá'u'lláh, have succeeded in erecting the framework of the divinely-ordained institutions of the Faith everywhere. The embryo of a new world order is now growing within the old and for this reason the world will never be the same again.

26

We Have Chosen 'the Greater' after 'the Most Great'

In the Kitáb-í-'Ahd, His Will and Testament, Bahá'u'lláh reveals these words.

> Verily God hath ordained the station of the Greater Branch [Muḥammad-'Alí] to be beneath that of the Most Great Branch ['Abdu'l-Bahá]. He is in truth the Ordainer, the All-Wise. We have chosen 'the Greater' after 'the Most Great,' as decreed by Him Who is the All-Knowing, the All-Informed.[223]

As we have already stated in chapter 3, a similar statement was made by Bahá'u'lláh in answer to a question by Mírzá 'Alí-Muḥammad, entitled Varqá. He wanted to know the identity of the person to whom all must turn as revealed in a verse of the Kitáb-i-Aqdas. Bahá'u'lláh intimated to him that the intended person was the Most Great Branch, and after Him, the Greater Branch.* The passage in which the Greater Branch is chosen 'after' the Most Great Branch, meaning that Mírzá Muḥammad-'Alí is to succeed 'Abdu'l-Bahá, brought about tests and misunderstandings for the believers, many of whom were astonished at this statement. These believers either knew Mírzá Muḥammad-'Alí personally or had read several condemnatory passages that Bahá'u'lláh had written about him. Both groups saw him as a perfidious person, deceitful, materialistic and avid for power – one who was related to Bahá'u'lláh physically but had no spiritual relationship with Him. These believers were deeply puzzled when they observed that Bahá'u'lláh had chosen such a person to succeed 'Abdu'l-Bahá.

Of course Bahá'u'lláh was very well aware of the reprehensible conduct in which Mírzá Muḥammad-'Alí had engaged from the early years of his life. We have discussed in chapter 15 how, when he was in his early teens, he claimed to share with Bahá'u'lláh the power of

* Ghuṣn-i-A'ẓam (the Most Great Branch) and Ghuṣn-i-Akbar (the Greater Branch) are titles which Bahá'u'lláh conferred upon His sons, 'Abdu'l-Bahá and Mírzá Muḥammad-'Alí respectively.

supreme infallibility and claimed to be, among other things, 'the sovereign ruler of all who are in heaven and on earth'. From Adrianople he dispatched to Persia some Arabic passages that he claimed were the words of God, thus creating tests and problems for some of the believers there. For this action he faced the wrath of Bahá'u'lláh, who chastised him with His own hands. He it was who, throughout his entire life, harboured implacable hatred in his heart towards 'Abdu'l-Bahá – a fact well known by the Holy Family, including Bahá'u'lláh.

About eight years before the ascension of Bahá'u'lláh, Mírzá Muḥammad-'Alí, encouraged by a number of his associates who later became Covenant-breakers, asked permission to leave the Holy Land to go sightseeing in India. Bahá'u'lláh told him that such a journey needed the approval of the Master. Mírzá Muḥammad-'Alí insisted so much on this issue that eventually 'Abdu'l-Bahá gave permission. Accompanied by a servant who lived in Port Said and volunteered to travel with him, Mírzá Muḥammad-'Alí departed for India in the year 1302 AH (1885). After spending a considerable time sightseeing there, he wished to return but Bahá'u'lláh was displeased with him and denied him permission to do so. Mírzá Muḥammad-'Alí then wrote to his mother who put pressure on 'Abdu'l-Bahá to intervene, with the result that he obtained Bahá'u'lláh's permission to return.

The second journey that Mírzá Muḥammad-'Alí made to India was for the purpose of transcribing some of the well-known Tablets of Bahá'u'lláh and printing them in one volume. As we have stated in chapter 16, he succeeded in printing a book known as *Kitáb-i-Mubín* but he deleted a passage which appeared to him to refer to the exalted nature of 'Abdu'l-Bahá's mission and instead substituted his own words. This occurred a year before Bahá'u'lláh's ascension and caused Him great sorrow.

It is a well-known fact that on numerous occasions Mírzá Muḥammad-'Alí, supported by his mother, committed acts that brought great displeasure to Bahá'u'lláh. In some of His Tablets He condemns him in strong terms, such as these:

> By God, the True One! Were We, for a single instant, to withhold from him the outpourings of Our Cause, he would wither, and would fall upon the dust.[224]

To such a person, Bahá'u'lláh in the Kitáb-i-'Ahd grants the right to succeed 'Abdu'l-Bahá. And indeed, Mírzá Muḥammad-'Alí publicly claimed this successorship both during the ministry of 'Abdu'l-Bahá and after His ascension. Referring to him, Shoghi Effendi states:

> He it was who had the impudence and temerity to tell 'Abdu'l-Bahá to His face that just as 'Umar had succeeded in usurping the successorship of the Prophet Muḥammad, he too, felt himself able to do the same. He it was who, obsessed by the fear that he might not survive 'Abdu'l-Bahá, had, the moment he had been assured by Him that all the honour he coveted would, in the course of time, be his, swiftly rejoined that he had no guarantee that he would outlive Him.[225]

In the light of these facts, we may ask ourselves two questions:

- Why did Bahá'u'lláh grant such an exalted station to so perfidious a person as Mírzá Muḥammad-'Alí?

- Why did the provision in Bahá'u'lláh's 'Book of the Covenant' for his successorship not materialize?

To resolve these puzzling questions, it is necessary to meditate on the nature of the Covenant of Bahá'u'lláh and try to discover its distinctive and challenging features.

The first question, concerning the appointment of such a disloyal person to so exalted a position, may be resolved through a careful examination of an essential feature of the Covenant of Bahá'u'lláh, namely, the non-interference of each party in the functions of the other. The two parties to this Covenant are not of equal station. After all, the station of Bahá'u'lláh is awe-inspiring and the believers are but humble servants. However, God in His justice gives His creatures the opportunity to carry out their duties without His interference; they have free will to behave as they please. Of course, He has full knowledge of how each individual will behave in discharging the obligations which the Covenant of Bahá'u'lláh has placed on him but He leaves the person free to play his part and He does not judge him before he commits an error. This is similar to the relationship between a teacher and pupil. In the course of teaching his students the teacher usually comes to know the ability and capacity of each one. Suppose that he finds one of his pupils to be inattentive to his work and negligent in his school duties. He may be certain that his pupil is going to fail his examinations but foreknowledge of that failure does not entitle the teacher to prevent the student from taking part. It is the student's prerogative to sit his examinations and no one has the right to deprive him of that privilege.

This analogy helps to clarify the statement about Mírzá Muḥammad-'Alí in the Kitáb-i-'Ahd. Bahá'u'lláh was fully aware of Mírzá Muḥammad-'Alí's shortcomings, yet, He decided that he should occupy a station next to that of 'Abdu'l-Bahá. God did not pronounce judgement on him before his rebellion against the Cause. Mírzá Muḥammad-'Alí was given the chance to mend his ways and take his rightful position within the Faith. However, he failed, as in a test, and perished spiritually.

Had Mírzá Muḥammad-'Alí remained a true and steadfast believer, had he lived a life of humility and self-effacement, had he devoted all his efforts to the promotion of the Cause and detached himself from earthly things and had he followed in the footsteps of the Master and emulated the one who was the supreme Exemplar of the teachings of Bahá'u'lláh, then who could have been more suited than he, a son of Bahá'u'lláh, to take over the reins of the Cause of God after 'Abdu'l-Bahá? But he did not fulfil any of these conditions and deprived himself of the bounties that might have been vouchsafed to him by Bahá'u'lláh.

Through his intense jealousy of 'Abdu'l-Bahá and his lack of spiritual qualities, Mírzá Muḥammad-'Alí sought throughout his life to undermine the position of 'Abdu'l-Bahá and usurp His God-given station as the Centre of the Covenant. During the lifetime of Bahá'u'lláh he was impotent to achieve the evil promptings of his heart because the overshadowing power of Bahá'u'lláh and His overwhelming authority frustrated his ambitions. But, as previously discussed, he rebelled against the Covenant immediately after the passing of Bahá'u'lláh and arose in opposition to 'Abdu'l-Bahá, its Centre.

In dealing with the question as to why the provision made by Bahá'u'lláh for Mírzá Muḥammad-'Alí to succeed 'Abdu'l-Bahá did not materialize, it is helpful to begin by looking at the many references Bahá'u'lláh makes in His Tablets to the creativity of His words. To cite an example:

> Every word that proceedeth out of the mouth of God is endowed with such potency as can instil new life into every human frame, if ye be of them that comprehend this truth. All the wondrous works ye behold in this world have been manifested through the operation of His supreme and most exalted Will, His wondrous and inflexible Purpose. Through the mere revelation of the word 'Fashioner', issuing forth from His lips and proclaiming His attribute to mankind, such power is released as can generate, through successive ages, all the manifold arts which the hands of man can produce. This, verily, is a certain truth. No sooner is this resplendent word uttered, than its animating energies, stirring within all created things, give birth to the means and instruments whereby such arts can be produced and perfected. All the wondrous achievements ye now witness are the direct consequences of the Revelation of this Name. In the days to come, ye will, verily, behold things of which ye have never heard before. Thus hath it

> been decreed in the Tablets of God, and none can comprehend it except them whose sight is sharp. In like manner, the moment the word expressing My attribute 'the Omniscient' issueth forth from My mouth, every created thing will, according to its capacity and limitations, be invested with the power to unfold the knowledge of the most marvellous sciences, and will be empowered to manifest them in the course of time at the bidding of Him Who is the Almighty, the All-Knowing. Know thou of a certainty that the Revelation of every other Name is accompanied by a similar manifestation of Divine power. Every single letter proceeding out of the mouth of God is indeed a mother letter, and every word uttered by Him Who is the Well Spring of Divine Revelation is a mother word, and His Tablet a Mother Tablet. Well is it with them that apprehend this truth.[226]

From this and other passages, we can be assured that owing to the creative power of the Word of God every event Bahá'u'lláh has foreshadowed in His Tablets has either taken place already or will come about in the future. Indeed, a careful study of His writings reveals that many of His promises have been fulfilled. However, there are exceptions to this, which are related to the subject of the Covenant. The appointment of Mírzá Muḥammad-'Alí in the Kitáb-i-'Ahd is one of these exceptions whereby Bahá'u'lláh's purpose, His implied wish, appeared not to materialize.

The main reason for the non-fulfilment of certain provisions of this momentous document is that this Covenant, like any other, is a reciprocal agreement between two parties. In this case, one party is Bahá'u'lláh and the other His followers. In general, the outcome of any agreement between two parties depends upon the manner in which each party fulfils his commitments. If one side fails to fulfil his obligations as set out in the contract, the other side will no longer be bound to honour his. For example, let us say that a landlord and a tenant draw up a lease. As long as the tenant pays his rent and meets his other responsibilities, the landlord has no reason to cancel the contract but if the former fails to discharge his liabilities, the latter will have no choice but to cancel the lease and possibly initiate eviction proceedings.

The Covenant of Bahá'u'lláh, as formulated in the Kitáb-i-'Ahd, also has two distinct sides. One side is the Almighty, who provides the spiritual energies for the achievement of His purpose and who rules over His creatures. The other side is His servants, the recipients of His grace, who abide by His bidding. This Covenant necessitates an interaction between the two parties. As in the analogy of the landlord and the tenant, if the followers of Bahá'u'lláh, the recipients of His grace, had faithfully carried out what was expected of them in this

Covenant, then every provision of the Kitáb-i-'Ahd would have been fulfilled and the plan of God, as ordained by Bahá'u'lláh, would have materialized. But they did not. The Covenant was broken by no less a person than Mírzá Muḥammad-'Alí himself, who rose up against the Centre of the Cause. Consequently, the plan of God as envisaged by Bahá'u'lláh was changed.

In His Will and Testament, 'Abdu'l-Bahá describes the many cases of 'deviation' from the Cause of God by Mírzá Muḥammad-'Alí and in unequivocal language proves that by his own actions he cut himself off from the tree of the Cause, changed into a dried branch and became the fulfilment of the following words of Bahá'u'lláh regarding him:

> He verily is one of My servants . . . Should he for a moment pass out from under the shadow of the Cause, he surely shall be brought to naught.[227]

The violation of the Covenant by Mírzá Muḥammad-'Alí and his many acts of infamy have been discussed in previous chapters.* Having disclosed his numerous transgressions to the believers, 'Abdu'l-Bahá in the following passages of the Will and Testament exhorts the believers to shun him:

> **39–WT In short, according to the explicit Divine Text the least transgression shall make of this man a fallen creature, and what transgression is more grievous than attempting to destroy the Divine Edifice, breaking the Covenant, erring from the Testament, falsifying the Holy Text, sowing the seeds of doubt, calumniating 'Abdu'l-Bahá, advancing claims for which God hath sent down no warrant, kindling mischief and striving to shed the very blood of 'Abdu'l-Bahá, and many other things whereof ye are all aware! It is thus evident that should this man succeed in bringing disruption into the Cause of God, he will utterly destroy and exterminate it. Beware lest ye approach this man, for to approach him is worse than approaching fire!**

And again:

> **11–WT In short, O ye beloved of the Lord! The Centre of Sedition, Mírzá Muḥammad 'Alí, in accordance with the decisive words of God and by reason of his boundless transgression, hath grievously fallen and been cut off from the Holy Tree. Verily, we wronged them not, but they have wronged themselves!**

---

* See chapters 12 to 24.

Thus, Mírzá Muḥammad-'Alí was cast out of the community of the Most Great Name. As in the analogy of the landlord and the tenant, the plan of God changed and 'Abdu'l-Bahá appointed Shoghi Effendi and the Universal House of Justice as His successors. We must bear in mind, however, that Bahá'u'lláh had ordained the Universal House of Justice in His writings. He states:

> The men of God's House of Justice have been charged with the affairs of the people. They, in truth, are the Trustees of God among His servants and the daysprings of authority in His countries.[228]

From another point of view, we may regard the appointment of Mírzá Muḥammad-'Alí as one of those cases by which God tests His servants. As we have already stated, many believers were tested either by this appointment or by the fact that the words of Bahá'u'lláh in the Kitáb-i-'Ahd were not fulfilled. Bahá'u'lláh explains in the Kitáb-i-Íqán that in every Dispensation certain acts or statements by the Manifestation of God have brought great tests to people, causing them to lose their faith altogether. Bahá'u'lláh gives several examples of this in His writings. Referring to these tests He states:

> . . . from time immemorial even unto eternity the Almighty hath tried, and will continue to try, His servants, so that light may be distinguished from darkness, truth from falsehood, right from wrong, guidance from error, happiness from misery, and roses from thorns. Even as He hath revealed: 'Do men think when they say "We believe" they shall be let alone and not be put to proof?' [Qur'án 29:2][229]

Returning to the story of Mírzá Muḥammad-'Alí, we note that during the last years of 'Abdu'l-Bahá's ministry the steadfast believers both in the East and the West were triumphant in their campaign to counteract the machinations of the Covenant-breakers. After years of fierce opposition against the Master, Mírzá Muḥammad-'Alí at last recognized his impotence to arrest the onward march of the Faith and retired to his den of ignominy and defeat. But as soon as 'Abdu'l-Bahá passed away he emerged into the open and audaciously attempted to seize the reins of the Cause of God and to establish himself as the successor of 'Abdu'l-Bahá. In order to do this, he gave the appearance of having changed his position of bitter enmity towards 'Abdu'l-Bahá into that of reconciliation.

The first thing he did was to appear at the gate of the Master's house, wanting to take part in a memorial meeting that was being held in His honour. A servant of the household told him to wait for permission. The Greatest Holy Leaf is reported to have sent a brief message to him:

> Our Beloved does not allow and does not like you to come in, and if you come in you will add to our sorrows.[230]

During the short period separating the ascension of the Master and the announcement of Shoghi Effendi's appointment, the perturbing thought uppermost in the minds of some of the believers was the position of the Arch-breaker of the Covenant, Mírzá Muḥammad-'Alí. Was he going to succeed 'Abdu'l-Bahá as laid down in the Kitáb-i-'Ahd, the Will and Testament of Bahá'u'lláh? Some were confused, wondering how the provisions of this momentous document could be allowed to come about when the very person who had assiduously tried to undermine the foundation of the Cause of God for almost 30 years was none other than Mírzá Muḥammad-'Alí himself. But the great majority of the believers knew that because of his deviation from the Faith, his appointment was null and void.

In the meantime, Mírzá Muḥammad-'Alí published far and wide his claim that according to the text of the Kitáb-i-'Ahd he was now 'Abdu'l-Bahá's successor. Not only did he publish this claim among the Persian Bahá'í community but he also declared in an Egyptian newspaper that he was the successor of Bahá'u'lláh. The Bahá'ís of Egypt responded to his statement by publishing a refutation of his claims in the same newspaper. The following account by Muhammad Said Adham, an Egyptian believer, describes the events which took place during those anxiety-filled days:

> A few days after this we had a telegram from the family of 'Abdu'l-Bahá, in reply to all cables sent from Egypt to Haifa, which read thus:
>
> 'The beauty of the Beloved disappeared and the hearts are melted by this great calamity. Our only hope is to raise the banner of the Covenant, and with all righteousness, unity and servitude we serve His sublime threshold.'
>
> A few days later the great violator addressed the Bahá'ís through the columns of the Arabic newspapers, calling upon them to follow him, according, as he stated, to the will of Bahá'u'lláh, pretending, in his call, that although he had been separated from his brother by God's destiny, yet the filial relationship and hearty sensations were strong in his heart, and he tried outwardly to show sorrow for the passing of 'Abdu'l-Bahá. One of his only two followers in Alexandria confirmed his call on a page of the same paper, but the House of Spirituality in Cairo replied and contested both statements, stating in effect that this violator is not recognized at all by the Bahá'ís, and since he has violated the Covenant of

Bahá'u'lláh for thirty years, he is not considered among the Bahá'ís, and has not the authority to speak in their behalf, for all the affairs of the Bahá'ís are now directed by the Houses of Spirituality, all over the world, whose members are elected and who will come under the control of the House of Justice, and they are the only representatives of the Bahá'ís. And this violator is not a Bahá'í in the true sense of the word and according to the dictates of Bahá'u'lláh. This reply was given especially for the benefit of the public, to give them correct information and to prove to them that the violators are not Bahá'ís and were cut off thirty years ago by their disobedience to the command of Bahá'u'lláh to turn, after His departure, to the Centre of the Covenant, 'Abdu'l-Bahá, and by their harmful actions to the Cause.

The reply produced the desired effect and we, individually, spread it among the inquirers and thus enlarged the circle of its influence.[231]

In the United States of America a public statement was issued by Shu'á'u'lláh, that son of the Arch-breaker of the Covenant who had been involved in the conspiracy to put 'Abdu'l-Bahá to death. In it he invited the American Bahá'ís to turn to his father, who, he claimed, was the legitimate successor of Bahá'u'lláh after 'Abdu'l-Bahá. His call was utterly ignored by the believers in the West.

In Persia, with the exception of a few Covenant-breakers, the Bahá'í community paid no attention to Muḥammad-'Alí's circular letters claiming successorship of 'Abdu'l-Bahá. The publication of the Will and Testament among the believers brought much comfort and consolation to their hearts; they realized that the Master had not abandoned them but rather had left the custodianship of the Cause of God in the hands of Shoghi Effendi, His eldest grandson, whom He appointed the Guardian of the Faith and the Interpreter of the holy writings.

27

The Appointment of Shoghi Effendi as the Guardian of the Cause

The announcement of the appointment of Shoghi Effendi as the Guardian of the Cause of God, about 40 days after the passing of the Master, brought much joy and a sense of relief to the believers who were concerned about the claims of Mírzá Muḥammad-'Alí. In the opening paragraphs of His Will and Testament, 'Abdu'l-Bahá pays great tribute to Bahá'u'lláh and then with loving and tender words, but without mentioning him by name, He lauds and glorifies the person of Shoghi Effendi:*

> **2–WT Salutation and praise, blessing and glory rest upon that primal branch of the Divine and Sacred Lote-Tree, grown out, blest, tender, verdant and flourishing from the Twin Holy Trees; the most wondrous, unique and priceless pearl that doth gleam from out the Twin surging seas . . .**

In this passage Shoghi Effendi is referred to by the word 'g͟huṣn', translated as 'branch'.† Bahá'u'lláh chose this Arabic word as a designation exclusively for His male descendants. 'The Divine and Sacred Lote-Tree' is a term which appears in many of the writings of Bahá'u'lláh and 'Abdu'l-Bahá, usually symbolizing the Manifestation of God. Shoghi Effendi is described as 'that primal branch . . . grown out . . . from the Twin Holy Trees . . . the priceless pearl that doth gleam from out the Twin surging seas'. The Twin Holy Trees and the Twin surging seas refer to the Báb and Bahá'u'lláh. The mother of Shoghi Effendi, Ḍíyá'íyyih K͟hánum, was the eldest daughter of 'Abdu'l-Bahá. His father, Mírzá Hádí S͟hírází, was a grandson of Ḥájí

---

* It becomes evident in a later passage of the Will and Testament that this is a reference to Shoghi Effendi.

† While there are no capital letters in Arabic or Persian, in English the word 'branch', the translation of 'g͟huṣn', is usually written with capital B. In the Will and Testament, however, it is not capitalized. The present author believes that since the word 'branch' referred to Shoghi Effendi, he made a point of not capitalizing it out of his deep sense of humility and self-effacement.

Abu'l-Qásim, a cousin of the mother of the Báb and a brother of the wife of the Báb. Thus Shoghi Effendi, descended from Bahá'u'lláh and related to the Báb, was an offshoot of the twin Manifestations of God.

'Abdu'l-Bahá extols Shoghi Effendi in matchless terms, as 'blest, tender, verdant and flourishing . . . the most wondrous, unique and priceless pearl'. Bearing in mind that when 'Abdu'l-Bahá wrote these words Shoghi Effendi was not yet ten years old, we can observe the superhuman foresight of the Master, who saw in that child such divine attributes as to appoint him the Guardian of the Cause of God and pay tribute to him in such laudatory terms.

In this paragraph, after Shoghi Effendi, the descendants of Bahá'u-'lláh and the Afnán – the relatives of the Báb and those of His wife – are addressed by 'Abdu'l-Bahá and He showers His blessings only upon those who have remained faithful to the Covenant, saying:

> **2–WT [Salutation and praise, blessing and glory rest] upon the offshoots of the Tree of Holiness, the twigs of the Celestial Tree, they that in the Day of the Great Dividing have stood fast and firm in the Covenant . . .**

The next people extolled by 'Abdu'l-Bahá for their outstanding services to the Faith are the Hands of the Cause of God:

> **2–WT [Salutation and praise, blessing and glory rest] upon the Hands (pillars) of the Cause of God that have diffused widely the Divine Fragrances, declared His Proofs, proclaimed His Faith, published abroad His Law, detached themselves from all things but Him, stood for righteousness in this world, and kindled the Fire of the Love of God in the very hearts and souls of His servants . . .**

This passage outlines the achievements of the Hands of the Cause as they carried out their exalted functions in the service of the Faith. At the time that 'Abdu'l-Bahá wrote His Will and Testament there were four Hands of the Cause who had been appointed by Bahá'u'lláh.*

Finally, 'Abdu'l-Bahá bestows His blessings upon those believers who are firm in the Covenant and who will follow Shoghi Effendi after His passing:

> **2–WT [Salutation and praise, blessing and glory rest] upon them that have believed, rested assured, stood steadfast in His Covenant and followed the Light that after my passing shineth**

* For detailed information about the life and activities of the Hands appointed by Bahá'u'lláh, see Taherzadeh, *Revelation of Bahá'u'lláh*, vol. 4.

from the Dayspring of Divine Guidance – for behold! he is the blest and sacred bough that hath branched out from the Twin Holy Trees. Well is it with him that seeketh the shelter of his shade that shadoweth all mankind.

'Abdu'l-Bahá excludes from these words of praise those who claim to believe in Bahá'u'lláh but are not firm in the Covenant. He also excludes those who may confess their belief in Bahá'u'lláh as the Author of the Faith and in 'Abdu'l-Bahá as the Centre of the Covenant but do not follow Shoghi Effendi, described here as the 'Light that . . . shineth from the Dayspring of Divine Guidance'.

Divine guidance was inherent within the person of Bahá'u'lláh. Through the institution of the Covenant it was conferred upon 'Abdu'l-Bahá, whose every word and deed during His ministry was divinely inspired. This process was continued in the ministry of Shoghi Effendi, as he inherited the same powers born of divine guidance.

In the above passage of the Will and Testament, 'Abdu'l-Bahá again identifies Shoghi Effendi as a branch of the Twin Holy Trees and makes a reference to 'the shelter of his shade that shadoweth all mankind'. One of the greatest achievements of Shoghi Effendi was the building of the Administrative Order, which is the nucleus of the World Order of Bahá'u'lláh. During the 36 years of his ministry he erected the institutions of this divine Order, designed by Bahá'u'lláh to act as channels to carry the world-vitalizing spirit of His Faith to humanity. These institutions are now established all over the world and are multiplying rapidly with the passage of time. In light of Shoghi Effendi's creation of a world-encircling network of divine institutions, we may not be wrong in concluding that indeed the shelter of his shade has overshadowed all mankind. But the influence that Shoghi Effendi has exerted on the ultimate establishment of a united world is not limited to his laying the foundations of the institutions of the Administrative Order. He has also left behind a vast number of divinely-guided instructions and counsels that will guide and sustain the Universal House of Justice in the discharge of its sacred duties until the end of this Dispensation.

In the following passage of the Will and Testament, 'Abdu'l-Bahá appoints Shoghi Effendi to succeed Him as the Guardian of the Cause of God:

16–WT O my loving friends! After the passing away of this wronged one, it is incumbent upon the Aghṣán (Branches), the Afnán (Twigs) of the Sacred Lote-Tree, the Hands (pillars) of the Cause of God and the loved ones of the Abhá Beauty to turn unto Shoghi Effendi – the youthful branch branched from the two hallowed and sacred Lote-Trees and the fruit grown from

> **the union of the two offshoots of the Tree of Holiness, – as he is the sign of God, the chosen branch, the guardian of the Cause of God, he unto whom all the Aghṣán, the Afnán, the Hands of the Cause of God and His loved ones must turn. He is the expounder of the words of God and after him will succeed the first-born of his lineal descendents** [sic].

If one were to summarize the Will and Testament of Bahá'u'lláh or of 'Abdu'l-Bahá in two words, those words would be 'turn unto'. 'Abdu'l-Bahá enjoins on believers of all ranks to 'turn unto' Shoghi Effendi. Again 'Abdu'l-Bahá states that Shoghi Effendi has branched from the Twin Holy Trees of Bahá'u'lláh and the Báb: He designates him as 'the guardian of the Cause of God' and empowers him to be 'the expounder of the words of God'.*

A statement of 'Abdu'l-Bahá exhorting the believers to turn to Shoghi Effendi in a spirit of utter obedience, as well as to the Universal House of Justice, is contained in a most challenging and thought-provoking passage found in paragraph 17 of the Will and Testament. Before reviewing this particular passage in the next chapter, it is helpful to study a brief account of the life of Shoghi Effendi during 'Abdu'l-Bahá's ministry and the many difficulties he encountered immediately after the passing of the Master.

As we have already stated, 'Abdu'l-Bahá describes Shoghi Effendi as 'the most wondrous, unique and priceless pearl that doth gleam from out the Twin surging seas . . . the blest and sacred bough that hath branched out from the Twin Holy Trees'. Knowing full well the glorious mission which the Almighty had destined for His first grandson, 'Abdu'l-Bahá extended to him from the time he was born a special measure of care and love and kept him under the wings of His protection. A few of those who had been admitted to the presence of Bahá'u'lláh and who were endowed with spiritual insight observed that the same relationship which existed between Bahá'u'lláh and 'Abdu'l-Bahá was also apparent between 'Abdu'l-Bahá and Shoghi Effendi. That deep sense of humility and utter nothingness which 'Abdu'l-Bahá manifested towards His Father, and which was reciprocated by Him through an outpouring of bounty and love, was likewise established between the young grandchild and his beloved Master. However, to avoid creating jealousy in the family, 'Abdu'l-Bahá was cautious of openly showing the intensity of His love for Shoghi Effendi. In spite of this, those believers who were endowed with discernment noticed

---

* We will discuss the question of Shoghi Effendi's successor, 'the first-born of his lineal descendants', later in this book.

this special relationship and had no doubt that the reins of the Cause of God would one day be placed in the hands of Shoghi Effendi.

Ḥájí Mírzá Ḥaydar-'Alí and Dr Yúnis Khán were among these enlightened believers. The famous poet and devoted promoter of the Cause 'Andalíb saw signs of the child's future glory as Shoghi Effendi lay in his cradle and he composed a most delightful lullaby, a song of praise and victory, for him. 'Abdu'l-Bahá conferred upon his first grandchild the name 'Shoghi' (one who longs) but commanded everyone to add the title 'Effendi'* after his name. He even told Shoghi Effendi's father not to call him merely 'Shoghi'. The Master Himself called him Shoghi Effendi when he was only a child and wrote this prayer which reveals His cherished hopes for the future of His first grandchild:

> . . . O God! This is a branch sprung from the tree of Thy mercy. Through Thy grace and bounty enable him to grow and through the showers of Thy generosity cause him to become a verdant, flourishing, blossoming and fruitful branch. Gladden the eyes of his parents, Thou Who giveth to whomsoever Thou willest, and bestow upon him the name Shoghi so that he may yearn for Thy Kingdom and soar into the realms of the unseen![232]

From his early childhood, Shoghi Effendi developed a passionate love for 'Abdu'l-Bahá. Their relationship was unlike that between any other grandchild and grandfather; it was a spiritual force, a heavenly power that linked Shoghi Effendi with his beloved Master. It was this degree of attachment and humble devotion that was reminiscent of 'Abdu'l-Bahá's own attitude towards Bahá'u'lláh. Mrs Ella Goodall Cooper, one of the distinguished believers of the West who attained the presence of 'Abdu'l-Bahá in 'Akká in 1899, recounted her impressions of Shoghi Effendi as a child when he came into a room in the house of 'Abdu'lláh Páshá to pay his respects to the Master. She writes:

> One day . . . I had joined the ladies of the Family in the room of the Greatest Holy Leaf for early morning tea, the beloved Master was sitting in His favourite corner of the divan where, through the window on His right, He could look over the ramparts and see the blue Mediterranean beyond. He was busy writing Tablets, and the quiet peace of the room was broken only by the bubble of the samovar, where one of the young maidservants, sitting on the floor before it, was brewing the tea.
>
> Presently the Master looked up from His writing with a smile, and requested Ziyyih Khanum to chant a prayer. As she finished, a small figure appeared in the open doorway, directly opposite

* 'Effendi' is a title given to men as a term of respect.

'Abdu'l-Bahá. Having dropped off his shoes he stepped into the room, with his eyes focused on the Master's face. 'Abdu'l-Bahá returned his gaze with such a look of loving welcome it seemed to beckon the small one to approach Him. Shoghi, that beautiful little boy, with his exquisite cameo face and his soulful appealing, dark eyes, walked slowly toward the divan, the Master drawing him as by an invisible thread, until he stood quite close in front of Him. As he paused there a moment 'Abdu'l-Bahá did not offer to embrace him but sat perfectly still, only nodding His head two or three times, slowly and impressively, as if to say – 'You see? This tie connecting us is not just that of a physical grandfather but something far deeper and more significant.' While we breathlessly watched to see what he would do, the little boy reached down and picking up the hem of 'Abdu'l-Bahá's robe he touched it reverently to his forehead, and kissed it, then gently replaced it, while never taking his eyes from the adored Master's face. The next moment he turned away, and scampered off to play, like any normal child . . . At that time he was 'Abdu'l-Bahá's only grandchild . . . and, naturally, he was of immense interest to the pilgrims.[233]

This attitude of humility and profound reverence towards the Master was one of the most outstanding features of Shoghi Effendi's personality throughout his entire life.

Shoghi Effendi grew up in the household of 'Abdu'l-Bahá under His care and protection but his childhood years were spent in 'Akká during the time when the Master and His family were incarcerated within the walls of the city and subjected to violent opposition by the Covenant-breakers. Great dangers surrounded the Holy Family. Thus Shoghi Effendi experienced, from the early years of his life, the venomous assaults launched against the Cause by the violators of the Covenant. When at one point the situation in 'Akká became too dangerous and unbearable, 'Abdu'l-Bahá sent Shoghi Effendi to Haifa with his nurse, where he lived until the Master was released from imprisonment and the Holy Family moved there permanently.

Concerning Shoghi Effendi's schooling Rúḥíyyih Kh̲ánum writes:

Shoghi Effendi entered the best school in Haifa, the *Collège des Frères*, conducted by the Jesuits. He told me he had been very unhappy there. Indeed, I gathered from him that he never was really happy in either school or university. In spite of his innately joyous nature, his sensitivity and his background – so different from that of others in every way – could not but set him apart and give rise to many a heart-ache; indeed, he was one of those people whose open and innocent hearts, keen minds and affectionate natures seem to combine to bring upon them more shocks and suffering in life than is the lot of most men. Because of his unhappiness in this school 'Abdu'l-Bahá decided to send him to Beirut

> where he attended another Catholic school as a boarder, and where he was equally unhappy. Learning of this in Haifa the family sent a trusted Bahá'í woman to rent a home for Shoghi Effendi in Beirut and take care of and wait on him. It was not long before she wrote to his father that he was very unhappy at school, would refuse to go to it sometimes for days, and was getting thin and run down. His father showed this letter to 'Abdu'l-Bahá Who then had arrangements made for Shoghi Effendi to enter the Syrian Protestant College, which had a school as well as a university, later known as the American College in Beirut, and which the Guardian entered when he finished what was then equivalent to the high school. Shoghi Effendi spent his vacations at home in Haifa, in the presence as often as possible of the grandfather he idolized and Whom it was the object of his life to serve. The entire course of Shoghi Effendi's studies was aimed by him at fitting himself to serve the Master, interpret for Him and translate His letters into English.[234]

Shoghi Effendi received his Bachelor of Arts degree from the University of Beirut in 1918. He was then able to return to Haifa and serve the Master, which he did uninterruptedly, day and night, with a devotion that knew no bounds. Not only did he serve as His secretary and the English translator of His Tablets, he also attended to many other duties, which he took upon himself in order to assist the Master in His manifold activities. He did this with characteristic sincerity, promptness and thoroughness, and brought great joy to the heart of the Master.

For a period of two years, until 1920, Shoghi Effendi was the constant companion of 'Abdu'l-Bahá. He accompanied his grandfather when He visited high-ranking government officials or religious dignitaries and he saw how the Master treated His friends and dealt with His enemies. In all these encounters, Shoghi Effendi observed the manner in which 'Abdu'l-Bahá conducted Himself, with that majesty and authority that were characteristic of His person. This period, which brought Shoghi Effendi so close to the Master and linked his heart to 'Abdu'l-Bahá's, was among the most fertile of his life. But this intimate association, in the course of which 'Abdu'l-Bahá bountifully endowed the future Guardian with special powers and capacities, irrevocably came to an end when it was decided that Shoghi Effendi should enter Oxford University in England to perfect his English, thus equipping himself to achieve his heart's desire to better translate the Tablets of 'Abdu'l-Bahá and other holy writings.

Shoghi Effendi left the Holy Land in the spring of 1920 and began his studies at Balliol College in the autumn of that year. During his short stay in Oxford – a little over one year – he concentrated all his energies on mastering the English language. But he could not complete his education, for the plan of God cut across his own plans in a most painful manner when 'Abdu'l-Bahá passed away.

The news of the ascension of 'Abdu'l-Bahá came to him as a shattering blow – so much so that when he was informed of it he collapsed. We read the following account by Rúḥíyyih Khánum in *The Priceless Pearl*:

> The address of Major Tudor Pole, in London, was often used as the distributing point for cables and letters to the Bahá'ís. Shoghi Effendi himself, whenever he went up to London, usually called there. On 29 November 1921 at 9.30 in the morning the following cable reached that office:
>
> Cyclometry London
> His Holiness 'Abdu'l-Bahá ascended Abhá Kingdom. Inform friends.
> Greatest Holy Leaf
>
> In notes he made of this terrible event and its immediate repercussions Tudor Pole records that he immediately notified the friends by wire, telephone and letter. I believe he must have telephoned Shoghi Effendi, asking him to come at once to his office, but not conveying to him at that distance a piece of news which he well knew might prove too much of a shock. However this may be, at about noon Shoghi Effendi reached London, went to 61 St James' [sic] Street (off Piccadilly and not far from Buckingham Palace) and was shown into the private office. Tudor Pole was not in the room at the moment but as Shoghi Effendi stood there his eye was caught by the name of 'Abdu'l-Bahá on the open cablegram lying on the desk and he read it. When Tudor Pole entered the room a moment later he found Shoghi Effendi in a state of collapse, dazed and bewildered by this catastrophic news. He was taken to the home of Miss Grand, one of the London believers, and put to bed there for a few days. Shoghi Effendi's sister Rouhangeze [sic] was studying in London and she, Lady Blomfield and others did all they could to comfort the heart-stricken youth.[235]

In a letter to a Bahá'í friend written a few days after the passing of the Master, Shoghi Effendi shares with him his thoughts about 'Abdu'l-Bahá and informs him of his plans:

> The terrible news has for some days so overwhelmed my body, my mind and my soul that I was laid for a couple of days in bed almost senseless, absent-minded and greatly agitated. Gradually His power revived me and breathed in me a confidence that I hope will henceforth guide me and inspire me in my humble work of service. The day had to come, but how sudden and unexpected. The fact

however that His Cause has created so many and such beautiful souls all over the world is a sure guarantee that it will live and prosper and ere long will compass the world! I am immediately starting for Haifa to receive the instructions He has left and have now made a supreme determination to dedicate my life to His service and by His aid to carry out His instructions all the days of my life.

The friends have insisted on my spending a day or two of rest in this place with Dr. Esslemont after the shock I have sustained and tomorrow I shall start back to London and thence to the Holy Land.

The stir which is now aroused in the Bahá'í world is an impetus to this Cause and will awaken every faithful soul to shoulder the responsibilities which the Master has now placed upon every one of us.

The Holy Land will remain the focal centre of the Bahá'í world; a new era will now come upon it. The Master in His great vision has consolidated His work and His spirit assures me that its results will soon be made manifest.

I am starting with Lady Blomfield for Haifa, and if we are delayed in London for our passage I shall then come and see you and tell you how marvellously the Master has designed His work after Him and what remarkable utterances He has pronounced with regard to the future of the Cause . . . With prayer and faith in His Cause, I am your well-wisher in His service,

Shoghi[236]

From Shoghi Effendi's other statements it is clear that although he knew that an envelope addressed to him by the Master was awaiting his return to the Holy Land, he had no knowledge at this time that he was appointed by 'Abdu'l-Bahá in His Will and Testament as the Guardian of the Faith, the Interpreter of the Word of God, and the one to whom all were bidden to turn. Such a heavy burden, so suddenly and unexpectedly laid upon his shoulders, came to him as a further shock no less agonizing than the earlier one caused by the news of 'Abdu'l-Bahá's passing.

Accompanied by his sister Rúḥangíz and by Lady Blomfield, Shoghi Effendi sailed from England on 16 December and arrived in Haifa on the 29th, one month after the passing of the Master. The agony of bereavement had taken its toll and Shoghi Effendi was physically a broken man. He was so frail that he had to be assisted up the steps of his home when he arrived. Grief-stricken by the absence of the Master, he was then confined to bed for a number of days.

The Will and Testament of 'Abdu'l-Bahá was awaiting the arrival of Shoghi Effendi to be opened. Concerning this, Rúḥíyyih Khánum writes:

> When 'Abdu'l-Bahá so unexpectedly and quietly passed away, after no serious illness, the distracted members of His family searched His papers to see if by chance He had left any instructions as to where He should be buried. Finding none, they entombed Him in the centre of the three rooms adjacent to the inner Shrine of the Báb. They discovered His Will – which consists of three Wills written at different times and forming one document – addressed to Shoghi Effendi. It now became the painful duty of Shoghi Effendi to hear what was in it; a few days after his arrival they read it to him. In order to understand even a little of the effect this had on him we must remember that he himself stated on more than one occasion, not only to me, but to others who were present at the table of the Western Pilgrim House, that he had had no foreknowledge of the existence of the Institution of Guardianship, least of all that he was appointed as Guardian; that the most he had expected was that perhaps, because he was the eldest grandson, 'Abdu'l-Bahá might have left instructions as to how the Universal House of Justice was to be elected and he might have been designated the one to see these were carried out and act as Convenor of the gathering which would elect it.[237]

The belief that the Universal House of Justice would come into being immediately after the passing of 'Abdu'l-Bahá was not uncommon among the Bahá'ís. Many of them thought this would happen and soon after Shoghi Effendi's appointment a few ambitious individuals such as Ávárih and Ahmad Sohrab[238] tried to insist that the House of Justice should be formed without delay. It is interesting to note that the Master, when in America, spoke to a few friends about the protection of the Faith and the role of the Universal House of Justice in securing it. Here is a summary translation of His words as recorded by Mírzá Maḥmúd-i-Zarqání, the faithful chronicler of His journeys to the West:

> I am bearing the discomforts of this journey with stop-overs so that the Cause of God may be protected from any breach. For I am still not sure about what is going to happen after me. If I could be sure, then I would sit comfortably in some corner, I would not leave the Holy Land and travel far away from the Most Holy Tomb. Once, after the martyrdom of the Báb, the Cause of God was dealt a hard blow through Yaḥyá. Again, after the ascension of the Blessed Beauty, it received another blow. And I fear that self-seeking persons may again disrupt the love and unity of the friends. If the time were right and the House of Justice were established, the House of Justice would protect the friends.[239]

The Master knew well that Covenant-breakers old and new would renew their onslaught against the Cause of God. From the way the institutions of the Faith have developed since the ascension of 'Abdu'l-Bahá, it can be seen that it was not timely then to establish the Universal House of Justice straight away. In His wisdom He knew that the Faith first needed a Guardian, whose purpose would be, on the one hand, to lay the foundation of the Administrative Order for future generations to build upon and, on the other, to wipe out the evils of Covenant-breaking in the Holy Land.

Although the Will and Testament of 'Abdu'l-Bahá was read out to Shoghi Effendi soon after his arrival in Haifa, it had to be formally presented to the members of the family and others in the Holy Land. On 3 January 1922, in the presence of nine persons, mainly senior members of 'Abdu'l-Bahá's family, and in Shoghi Effendi's absence, the Will and Testament was read aloud and its seal, signature and handwriting were shown to those present. Later, the Greatest Holy Leaf sent cables to Persia and America – the two major communities at that time – informing them that according to the Will and Testament of 'Abdu'l-Bahá, Shoghi Effendi had been appointed 'Guardian of the Cause of God'.

A major source of consolation and support for Shoghi Effendi from the time he returned to the Holy Land until the end of her earthly life in 1932 was the Greatest Holy Leaf, the adored sister of 'Abdu'l-Bahá. She, the most outstanding woman of the Bahá'í Dispensation, was a tower of strength for everyone. And now that the Master had gone to His heavenly abode, the burden of many responsibilities and, especially in the early days, the protection of the Guardian from the assaults of the Covenant-breakers, were placed upon her shoulders.

Rúḥíyyih Khánum writes:

> Immediately after these events Shoghi Effendi selected eight passages from the Will and circulated them among the Bahá'ís; only one of these referred to himself, was very brief and was quoted as follows: 'O ye the faithful loved ones of 'Abdu'l-Bahá! It is incumbent upon you to take the greatest care of Shoghi Effendi . . . For he is, after 'Abdu'l-Bahá, the guardian of the Cause of God, the Afnán, the Hands (pillars) of the Cause and the beloved of the Lord must obey him and turn unto him.' Of all the thundering and tremendous passages in the Will referring to himself, Shoghi Effendi chose the least astounding and provocative to first circulate among the Bahá'ís. Guided and guiding he was from the very beginning.[240]

28

The Guardian and the Universal House of Justice under the Protection of the Báb and Bahá'u'lláh

17–WT The sacred and youthful branch, the guardian of the Cause of God as well as the Universal House of Justice, to be universally elected and established, are both under the care and protection of the Abhá Beauty, under the shelter and unerring guidance of His Holiness, the Exalted One (may my life be offered up for them both). Whatsoever they decide is of God. Whoso obeyeth him not, neither obeyeth them, hath not obeyed God; whoso rebelleth against him and against them hath rebelled against God; whoso opposeth him hath opposed God; whoso contendeth with them hath contended with God; whoso disputeth with him hath disputed with God; whoso denieth him hath denied God; whoso disbelieveth in him hath disbelieved in God; whoso deviateth, separateth himself and turneth aside from him hath in truth deviated, separated himself and turned aside from God. May the wrath, the fierce indignation, the vengeance of God rest upon him! The mighty stronghold shall remain impregnable and safe through obedience to him who is the guardian of the Cause of God.

These words of the Master constitute the most momentous passage of the Will and Testament. As already stated, this document provides the means by which the believers are tested and of all that is in the Will and Testament, this passage creates the greatest test. Indeed, many souls who claimed to have recognized Bahá'u'lláh as the Supreme Manifestation of God, who had laboured in the promotion of His Cause and who were renowned for their deep knowledge of the writings of Bahá'u'lláh and 'Abdu'l-Bahá found themselves severely tested by this passage and consequently lost their faith altogether. This occurred because the faith of a believer and his steadfastness in the Covenant are determined by the extent to which he acknowledges the truth of the Master's words regarding the station of the Guardian and of the Universal House of Justice.

It is evident from this passage that the guidance and protection of Bahá'u'lláh and the Báb are conferred upon the Guardian and the Universal House of Justice, independently of each other. As 'Abdu'l-Bahá says, 'The guardian of the Cause of God as well as the Universal House of Justice . . . are both under the care and protection of the Abhá Beauty'. Further, in condemning those who oppose the two institutions, He refers to each separately, stating, 'whoso opposeth Him [the Guardian] hath opposed God; whoso contendeth with them [the Universal House of Justice] hath contended with God'. Neither in the above passage of the Will and Testament nor in any of 'Abdu'l-Bahá's Tablets can we find a single reference or allusion indicating that the guidance of Bahá'u'lláh would reach the Guardian and the House of Justice only if the two combined their functions and worked together.*

Having experienced bitter opposition by the Covenant-breakers, 'Abdu'l-Bahá aimed to protect the Guardian from the onslaught of the unfaithful. Thus, in language at once forceful and forbidding, in this passage He warns the believers of the consequences of opposition to him and to the House of Justice. He equates disobedience to Shoghi Effendi with disobedience to God. A careful study of the Master's words here makes it clear that there can be no justification for a believer to deny the infallibility conferred upon Shoghi Effendi or to arise against him. Although today some individuals question the validity of the pronouncements the Guardian left behind as divine guidance for generations yet unborn, it is obvious that such people ignore 'Abdu'l-Bahá's emphatic exhortations and act against His commandments.

While a few unfaithful persons rose up in opposition against Shoghi Effendi, the Bahá'í community as a whole, in both the East and the West, took to heart the Master's words and rallied around the Guardian with a devotion and love reminiscent of the days following the passing of Bahá'u'lláh, when the faithful turned in a spirit of utter dedication to 'Abdu'l-Bahá. During the ministry of the Guardian, the believers, through their passionate loyalty to him, their wholehearted belief in him as 'the sign of God on earth' and their faithful and enthusiastic obedience to his guidance, won memorable victories for the Cause of Bahá'u'lláh.

Because of his modesty and profound innate humility, Shoghi Effendi attributed the stupendous achievements of his 36–year ministry to the work of the believers but it is unquestionably clear that the enormous progress of the Faith was entirely due to his divinely

---

* For further discussion of this subject see chapter 36.

guided leadership. Indeed, it was he who nursed and reared the infant Faith of God until it reached the stage of adolescence. It was he who protected it from the attacks, the intrigues, the betrayals and the machinations of its adversaries and of the Covenant-breakers. It was he who fashioned the Bahá'í administration, who laid a broad and solid base for the establishment of its world order and erected the pillars that sustain and buttress the mighty edifice of the Universal House of Justice. It was he who brought the Faith into the limelight of recognition and world attention. It was he who, through his eloquent translations and original writings, immensely enriched Bahá'í literature and promoted its steady growth and dissemination. It was he who directed the construction of the House of Worship in Wilmette, built, embellished and enlarged the Bahá'í holy shrines and organized the Faith's international endowments. But the Guardian's most momentous feat was to organize and weld together the loosely knit, struggling, heterogeneous groups and elements that composed the Bahá'í world into a vast, vigorous, harmoniously functioning, international community. Its existence is something unique in the religious annals of humankind and constitutes the glory and the promise of the Bahá'í commonwealth of the future.

Had there been no appointed Guardian after 'Abdu'l-Bahá's passing, it is difficult to see how the Formative Period of the Faith would have unfolded and the glorious future of its Golden Age been assured. During this Formative Period the creative energies released through the Revelation of Bahá'u'lláh found incarnation in the rise of a world administrative order. Today its framework is being fashioned by the eager hands of Bahá'ís throughout the world in accordance with the Divine Plan, the instructions of the Guardian and the guidance flowing in great profusion from the Universal House of Justice.

The passing of the Master in November 1921 marks the termination of the Apostolic Age of our Faith and the opening of the Formative one. It, in turn, will culminate in the Golden Age, when the Most Great Peace and a new divine civilization based on the recognition of Bahá'u'lláh and the unity of mankind will be firmly established on this earth. The shape and pattern of this administrative order are outlined in the Will and Testament of 'Abdu'l-Bahá, in which He, among other things, nominates the Guardian, assigns his functions, makes provisions for the election of the Universal House of Justice and the creation of the institution of the Hands of the Cause and defines the scope and character of these institutions.

At the close of 'Abdu'l-Bahá's ministry there were well-established Bahá'í communities in Persia, the United States, India, Burma, Egypt, Iraq, France and England in which boards of consultation – rudimentary spiritual assemblies – were functioning. Groups of varying size also existed in Turkey, Canada, Russia, Austria, Italy, Holland, Hungary, Arabia, Switzerland, Tunisia, China, Japan, South Africa, Brazil and Australia. The construction of the first Bahá'í House of Worship in 'Ishqábád, Russia, had been completed, and the excavations for the House of Worship in Wilmette had begun. In the Holy Land the original mausoleum of the Báb had been built and an extensive property east of the Shrine acquired. The Eastern and the Western pilgrim houses had also been constructed.

The accession of Shoghi Effendi to the exalted office of Guardianship late in 1921 opened a new chapter in the history of the rise and establishment of Bahá'u'lláh's World Order. Bahá'í groups and communities at that time were still unorganized and most believers had their own crude ideas about the Faith and its outlook. They were still in a state of childhood and needed care and spiritual nourishment.

For no fewer than 15 years (1922–36) the Guardian set himself the herculean task of training and educating these diverse groups and elements in the art of administration and the Bahá'í way of life. He helped them both individually and collectively to attain maturity and spiritual consciousness by demonstrating the aim, the shape and the scope of Bahá'í administration. He harnessed the creative energies of these scattered groups into cohesive institutional forms and channels. And he created a broad and universal foundation for the world-embracing system of Bahá'í administration, delineating the features and functions of both local and national institutions.

The creation of local spiritual assemblies, together with the intensive preparation and instruction of diverse communities in matters of Bahá'í administration, went on so vigorously that four years after 'Abdu'l-Bahá's passing no fewer than five national spiritual assemblies came into being: the British Isles, India and Burma, Germany and Austria, Egypt, and the United States and Canada. A few years later three more national bodies were created: Iraq (1931), Iran (1934) and Australia and New Zealand (1934).

In 1927 the constitution and bylaws drawn up by the National Spiritual Assembly of the United States were universally adopted by the other national bodies. This was a vital step towards the unification of the Bahá'í world community and a necessary instrument for the legal incorporation of Bahá'í institutions, which began with the registration of the National Spiritual Assembly of the Bahá'ís of the United States and Canada in 1929. By this action the Assembly was given state protection and recognition and was empowered to hold property. Ever since, the process of incorporation of assemblies has continued steadily.*

At the time of the passing of 'Abdu'l-Bahá there was no adequate sense of community life among the believers. It was Shoghi Effendi who, through his eloquent translations of the writings of Bahá'u'lláh and 'Abdu'l-Bahá, through his own masterly writings,† through his guidance and direction of the affairs of local and national assemblies throughout the world and through his constant encouragement and perseverance, patiently and effectively unveiled the Faith of Bahá'u-'lláh to their eyes.

In the Heroic Age of the Faith the believers were so attracted to Bahá'u'lláh that they did not pay much attention to anything else. They were in love with Him and were completely intoxicated by the wine of His presence. But now was the time to build the new World Order and it was through Shoghi Effendi's endeavours and guidance that the vision of the Bahá'ís widened. They began to appreciate the Faith in a new light and many arose to build local and national institutions throughout the world.

From the early days of Shoghi Effendi's ministry the followers of the Most Great Name in the cradle of the Faith had been oppressed by the authorities and subjected to sporadic outbursts of persecution, resulting in the martyrdom of many. Shoghi Effendi turned his attention to the institutions of the Faith which, by then, were functioning throughout the length and breadth of that land. He gave them a special task that assumes a great importance in the Cause, namely, the implementation of some of the laws of the Kitáb-i-Aqdas, the 'warp and woof' of Bahá'u'lláh's World Order. He directed the spiritual assemblies in Persia to begin the enforcement of these laws within the Bahá'í community – laws which, although known to the believers in that land, had not previously been fully observed. In the course of his ministry, Shoghi Effendi elaborated a great deal on the application of these laws, elucidated many intricacies and details connected with them, urged the spiritual assemblies never to compromise when enforcing the laws and counselled them to uphold the standard of justice and impartiality in all cases. Thus he built up a great reservoir of knowledge and experience in this particular field, which will be of great value in the future.

---

* For further information about the development of the Administrative Order see Taherzadeh, *Covenant of Bahá'u'lláh*, chapter 26.

† For further information about the writings of Shoghi Effendi see Taherzadeh, *Covenant of Bahá'u'lláh*, chapter 27.

Another significant enterprise undertaken during the first 15 years of the Guardianship was the erection of the superstructure of the House of Worship in Wilmette and the completion of the exterior ornamentation of its dome. This unique achievement by the American Bahá'ís reflects the tenacity and spirit of dedication that enabled them to carry out this mighty task in spite of the unparalleled economic crisis prevailing at that time.

A vast expansion in the range of Bahá'í literature was a further outstanding step taken at this time. During the life of 'Abdu'l-Bahá only a few editions published in English, French, German, Turkish, Russian and Burmese had been available but by 1936 Bahá'í books and pamphlets were printed and circulated in no less than 29 additional languages. The Guardian's monumental renderings of the Word of Bahá'u'lláh into English and his own original works contributed immensely to the extension and enrichment of Bahá'í literature. Another brilliant achievement initiated a few years after the Master's passing was the biennial production of the volumes of *The Bahá'í World* and the publication of many books and pamphlets about the Faith in different languages.*

In the years following 'Abdu'l-Bahá's ascension teaching work received a greater impetus than ever before. Undismayed by the Master's sudden removal and spurred on by His brilliant example, Bahá'ís in both the East and the West arose to promote the expansion of the Faith. These teaching campaigns were at first intermittent and haphazard but gradually they became organized and systematic and the exploits and resourcefulness of the American friends in executing them are worthy of the highest admiration. Special reference should be made to the prodigious feats accomplished by Martha Root, 'the Pride of Bahá'í Teachers',[241] whose travels to teach the Faith continued for almost 20 years and carried her four times around the globe. Other international Bahá'í teachers who served during this period include Hyde and Clara Dunn, Keith Ransom-Kehler, May Maxwell and a host of others. Through their outstanding efforts no fewer than 30 sovereign countries were opened to the Faith during the first 15 years of the Guardianship. Some of the other noteworthy events that occurred between 1922 and 1936 include the following:

- The passing of the Greatest Holy Leaf, sister of 'Abdu'l-Bahá in July 1932

- The recognition of the independent status of the Faith in Egypt

* For further information see Taherzadeh, *Covenant of Bahá'u'lláh*, chapter 27.

- The seizure of Bahá'u'lláh's House in Baghdád, which led to the submission of a petition to the League of Nations
- The seizure of the Bahá'í House of Worship in Russia and dissolution of all Bahá'í institutions there
- The systematic institution of the 19 day feast
- The creation of the International Bahá'í Bureau in Geneva in 1925
- The growth of organized youth activities
- The acquisition of national centres in Iraq, Egypt, India and Persia
- The enlargement of Bahá'í endowments and properties in the Holy Land, United States and Persia.
- The acquisition of historic sites in Persia
- The establishment of permanent summer schools in the United States (Green Acre, Louhelen, Geyserville)
- Sporadic outbursts of persecution in Persia and the closing down of Bahá'í schools
- The transcription and documentation of all original Tablets of the Báb, Bahá'u'lláh and 'Abdu'l-Bahá
- The formation of the International Bahá'í Archives

The inauguration of the first Seven Year Plan was a turning point in the history of the Formative Period of the Faith, marking the fulfilment of the initial stage of the divine mandate 'Abdu'l-Bahá had issued to the American Bahá'ís in the Tablets of the Divine Plan. The outstanding feature of this remarkable period is the initiation of systematic and organized teaching activities, efficiently prosecuted under the direction of the Guardian. Before this, teaching work had been undertaken in a haphazard manner by individuals.

The Guardian launched the first Seven Year Plan (1937–44) in his message to the National Convention in the United States and Canada, saying:

> Would to God every State within American Republic and every Republic in American continent might ere termination of this

> glorious century embrace the light of the Faith of Bahá'u'lláh and establish structural basis of His World Order.[242]

The Plan was a supreme challenge to the American friends and its full significance made itself increasingly felt with every passing day. In it Shoghi Effendi introduced two basic strategies for expansion and consolidation, which have been pursued throughout the Bahá'í world ever since. One was the dispatch of a believer – a Bahá'í pioneer – to a territory where there were no Bahá'ís; there he or she engaged in teaching the Cause until enough people embraced the Faith to be able to establish a local spiritual assembly. The other was the systematic formation of spiritual assemblies in various localities of a country or region, resulting in the establishment of a specific number of assemblies by the end of the Plan.

By the time the Seven Year Plan was triumphantly completed in 1944, coinciding with the worldwide celebrations of the Centenary of the birth of the Faith, the number of local spiritual assemblies in the United States had almost doubled, the number of localities in which Bahá'ís lived had increased enormously and the nucleus of the institutions of the Faith had been established in every republic of Latin America. These tremendous achievements, together with the completion of the exterior ornamentation of the holiest House of Worship in the Bahá'í world, awakened the Bahá'ís of other lands to the pattern of systematic expansion and consolidation of the Faith – a pattern developed as a direct consequence of this first historic Plan, initiated by the Guardian of the Cause of God and executed by the followers of Bahá'u'lláh in the cradle of the Administrative Order of the Faith. Such a glorious triumph for the Cause created an upsurge of eagerness and dedication, of confidence and enthusiasm in the hearts of the believers in other lands. They, too, longed to scale loftier heights in service to the Cause of God.

As each national assembly reached the point of readiness the Guardian gave his approval and encouragement to the formulation of its national plan.* These plans were mainly designed to increase the number of local spiritual assemblies, to consolidate them as institutions and to multiply the number of Bahá'í centres within each assembly's boundaries – and beyond. The first to turn to the Guardian for a plan was the British community, which was given a Six Year Plan in 1944. Other plans followed within two to three years. Each had a certain duration and ended either in 1950, the hundredth anniversary

* For further information about various national plans and the Ten Year Crusade, see Taherzadeh, *Covenant of Bahá'u'lláh,* chapter 28, and *Bahá'í World* volumes.

of the Martyrdom of the Báb, or in 1953, the Holy Year,* the centenary of the birth of Bahá'u'lláh's revelation in the Síyáh-Chál of Ṭihrán.

Foremost among these was the second Seven Year Plan of the Bahá'ís of North America, the duration of which marks the second phase of the initial epoch of the Tablets of the Divine Plan. Major international goals incorporated into this Plan included the establishment of local spiritual assemblies in ten countries of Western Europe, the formation of three national assemblies in the Western hemisphere and the interior ornamentation of the Mashriqu'l-Adhkár in the United States. The goals of this Plan were accomplished by its end in 1953. Other national plans were the Indian Four and a Half Year Plan, which was followed by a Nineteen Month Plan; the Persian Forty-five Month Plan; the Australian Six Year Plan; the Iraqi Three Year Plan; the Egyptian Five Year Plan; the German Five Year Plan; the Canadian Five Year Plan, which could be regarded as the continuation of the Seven Year Plan of North America; and finally, the second British Two Year Plan, 'the Africa campaign', in which six national spiritual assemblies worked together for the establishment of the Faith on the continent of Africa. This latter Plan played a significant role in creating the pattern for future international cooperation and inter-assembly projects and was a prelude to the launching of later world-encircling Plans.

Apart from these Plans, which created an upsurge of activity among all the national Bahá'í communities and which inspired many believers to arise as pioneers and settle in goal towns or in virgin territories, other important developments at this time paved the way for the future unfoldment and rise of the Administrative Order of Bahá'u'lláh. Foremost among these were the appointment by Shoghi Effendi in 1951 of the first contingent of the Hands of the Cause of God, whose number was soon to be increased; the formation in the same year of the International Bahá'í Council, destined to evolve through successive stages into the Universal House of Justice; the participation of Bahá'í delegates with other non-governmental organizations at the United Nations; and the phenomenal growth of the Faith in Africa, the first continent to witness entry into the Faith in great numbers.

These far-reaching achievements, together with the triumphant conclusion of all national Plans, endowed the community of the Most Great Name with tremendous potentialities for the worldwide expansion and consolidation of the Faith. Through their pursuit of the goals of these Plans, the national communities acquired the vision and capacity to take part in the first international Plan.

* The Holy Year was from October 1952 to October 1953.

Shoghi Effendi launched the Ten Year World Crusade in 1953 and referred to it as the greatest spiritual crusade the world has ever witnessed. It marked both the opening of the third and final phase of the initial epoch of the Tablets of the Divine Plan and the inception of the Bahá'í International Community. It brought together the twelve existing national assemblies of the Bahá'í world to plant the banner of the Faith in all remaining virgin territories of the globe, to multiply the number of the local and national spiritual assemblies throughout the world and to accomplish many other goals.

When the Crusade's goals were announced, the followers of Bahá'u-'lláh in every land were staggered with the immensity of the tasks that confronted them. Nevertheless, by the end of the first year of the Plan alone they witnessed with gratitude, awe and wonder, that a hundred virgin territories had been opened to the Faith!

This prodigious expansion of the Cause in the initial phase of the Plan, which inspired an army of Bahá'í pioneers and teachers to rise to loftier heights of heroism and sacrifice and enabled them to accomplish all the major goals of the Plan in the following years, can only be attributed to one thing: the spirit of loyalty and devotion with which the Hands of the Cause of God and their Board Members, the national and local assemblies, the pioneers and the teachers turned to Shoghi Effendi, the Guardian of the Cause and the Sign of God on earth.

In the Holy Land, the process of building the World Centre of the Faith had originated with Bahá'u'lláh through the revelation of the Tablet of Carmel and was initiated by the hand of the Centre of His Covenant through the building of the original Mausoleum of the Báb. During the ministry of Shoghi Effendi this process gathered such momentum that by the end of his life the glory of Carmel, foretold by the Prophets of the past, had become manifest. The superstructure of the Shrine of the Báb, 'the Queen of Carmel', 'crowned in glowing gold, robed in shimmering white, girdled in emerald green', which enchanted 'every eye from air, sea, plain, and hill',[243] had been majestically raised. In its vicinity the monuments marking the resting places of the Greatest Holy Leaf, the Purest Branch and the mother and wife of 'Abdu'l-Bahá had been befittingly erected, forming the focal point of a series of buildings, situated around an arc, which are to constitute the international administrative centre of the Faith. The first in this series, the International Archives Building, within whose walls the most precious relics of the Central Figures of the Faith are preserved, had been constructed. The nine original terraces connecting the city of Haifa to the Shrine of the Báb had been completed and the gardens surrounding the Shrine and the adjoining buildings had been developed and embellished. The international endowments of the Faith stretching from the base to the summit of Mount Carmel, an area of over 350,000 square metres, had been acquired. A plot of land comprising approximately 36,000 square metres had, after tedious and prolonged negotiations, been purchased for the purpose of erecting a Mas͟hriqu'l-Ad͟hkár on Mount Carmel, to be located in 'close proximity to the Spot hallowed by the footsteps of Bahá'u'lláh, near the time-honoured Cave of Elijah, and associated with the revelation of the Tablet of Carmel, the Charter of the World Spiritual and Administrative Centres of the Faith on that mountain'.[244]

At Bahjí, the holiest spot in the Bahá'í world, around the Shrine of Bahá'u'lláh, within an area of approximately 160,000 square metres, beautiful gardens had been laid out. Within these gardens, where in the future a magnificent mausoleum over the Shrine of Bahá'u'lláh will be constructed, an outer sanctuary (termed the Ḥaram-i-Aqdas) designed to embrace this holy edifice had been created. The realization of such magnificent achievements in the Holy Land during the opening years of the Formative Age of the Faith, together with the detailed delineation of the blueprint for the future development of the World Centre of the Faith, will always be regarded as one of the noblest fruits associated with the ministry of Shoghi Effendi.*

As one surveys the progress of the Faith during the ministry of the Guardian, it becomes apparent that one of his great achievements was to bring about unity between the various elements that constituted the Bahá'í community in the early years of the Formative Age. When 'Abdu'l-Bahá passed away there was very little Bahá'í literature available in the West and the teachings of the Faith had not fully penetrated the hearts of the believers there. Consequently, one could find some very strange ideas about the Faith circulating among them. In Persia, the cradle of the Faith, the Bahá'ís were still identified as Bahá'ís from Muslim, Jewish or Zoroastrian backgrounds. Although there was unity of belief and thought concerning the station of Bahá'u-'lláh among the various sections of the community, the differences in their background, culture and social habits were discernible to all. For instance, Jewish Bahá'ís had their own meetings, distinct from the meetings held by Muslim Bahá'ís. The same was true of Zoroastrian Bahá'ís. Of course, on occasion the whole community worked together and held large gatherings. On Bahá'í holy days, for example, Bahá'ís of different religious backgrounds met together in a spirit of joy and unity. Nevertheless there were social barriers between these three groups in Persia. One of the great achievements of Shoghi Effendi

* For further information see Taherzadeh, *Covenant of Bahá'u'lláh,* chapter 29.

was to transform these differences into unity. Then, towards the end of his ministry, Shoghi Effendi brought together the Bahá'ís of the East and the West in a world-embracing fellowship – the international Bahá'í community.

By the time the Ten Year Crusade was launched in 1953, all the Bahá'ís were working together in a spirit of absolute unity and love under the guidance and leadership of Shoghi Effendi. Indeed, one of the Guardian's feats was the formation of a community spread throughout the world, consisting of peoples of every colour and former creed, of diversified backgrounds, young and old, educated and unlettered, tribal people and citizens of various cultures, speaking different languages and dialects, yet all united in one Faith, practising the same religious teachings, building the same Administrative Order and having one common purpose – the establishment of the oneness of mankind on this planet. Each local community with its local spiritual assembly was linked to a national assembly and through that institution to the World Centre of the Faith, described by Shoghi Effendi as the heart of the Bahá'í world. From this mighty heart the vivifying forces of the Revelation of Bahá'u'lláh flowed through the national and local institutions of the Faith to every believer, uniting and harmonizing their activities in the building of Bahá'u'lláh's embryonic institutions.

Shoghi Effendi placed everything that the Faith possessed in the proper perspective: its founders, laws, ordinances, teachings, principles and institutions. He enabled the believers to acquire a new conception of community life, of unity and solidarity. To appreciate this great achievement, let us use the following analogy. It is abundantly clear that the utterances of Bahá'u'lláh and 'Abdu'l-Bahá enshrine the truths of God's Revelation for this age. Each one of Bahá'u'lláh's teachings and ordinances resembles a piece of a colossal jigsaw puzzle. Each piece has a unique place in the overall scheme which, when assembled, produces a certain image intended by the makers. A person may be familiar with each piece but not until the whole set is assembled can he see the full picture emerge before his eyes. The same is true of the Revelation of Bahá'u'lláh. The scholars of the Faith and those who were well versed in the holy writings and the history of the Cause had full knowledge of the teachings and were able to appreciate the significance of His utterances as well as some of the events which were associated with them. But they did not have the vision to grasp fully the overall features of the Faith. At the close of 'Abdu'l-Bahá's ministry, the Bahá'ís were enamoured of Bahá'u'lláh but at the same time many had their own crude ideas about the Faith and its true status.

It was the Guardian who, through his writings, constructed a full image of the Faith for the Bahá'ís to see. He put together all the elements of truth enshrined in the utterances of Bahá'u'lláh, related them to each other, defined the verities of the Faith, explained their significance, clarified the stations of its Herald, its Author and the Centre of its Covenant, described the glorious destiny of its Administrative Order and portrayed the splendours of the Golden Age, during which the sovereignty of Bahá'u'lláh will be established throughout the world and His grandeur acclaimed by the generality of mankind. Thus the Guardian presented the Faith of Bahá'u'lláh to the Bahá'í community in its true perspective. This is one of his greatest gifts both to this generation and to those yet unborn.

29

Covenant-Breakers' Attacks on Shoghi Effendi

17–WT He that opposeth him hath opposed the True One, will make a breach in the Cause of God, will subvert His Word and will become a manifestation of the Centre of Sedition. Beware, beware, lest the days after the ascension (of Bahá'u'lláh) be repeated when the Centre of Sedition waxed haughty and rebellious and with Divine Unity for his excuse deprived himself and perturbed and poisoned others.

With the appointment of Shoghi Effendi as the Guardian of the Cause, the Bahá'í world embarked upon a new age. In a previous chapter* the Kitáb-i-'Ahd and the Will and Testament of 'Abdu'l-Bahá have been likened to an examination paper placed before students. Just as some pass and some fail the test, the followers of Bahá'u'lláh who came face to face with the Will and Testament of 'Abdu'l-Bahá were divided. The great majority remained faithful to the Covenant. However, some egotistical personalities failed the tests of the Covenant and were cast out, with the result that the community was purged.

In the passage quoted above 'Abdu'l-Bahá warns the believers not to allow the reprehensible accusations levelled against Him by the Covenant-breakers following Bahá'u'lláh's ascension to be repeated after His own passing. But, unfortunately, the forces of evil arrayed themselves against those of righteousness. The excuse of 'Divine Unity' mentioned in the above passage of the Will and Testament refers to slanderous accusations by the Covenant-breakers that 'Abdu'l-Bahá had claimed the station of divinity for Himself.†

The news of Shoghi Effendi's appointment as Guardian of the Cause of God was warmly greeted by the entire Bahá'í world. Nevertheless, there were some faithless individuals, motivated by their ambition to emerge as leaders of the community, who arose in

* See chapter 3.

† See chapter 13.

opposition to Shoghi Effendi and, despite all his efforts to save them, proved unrepentant and were consequently expelled from the community. After some time these egotistical personalities surfaced and launched their attacks.

There was another category of people who, although they did not openly oppose Shoghi Effendi in those early days, ultimately revealed their lack of faith in him as the Guardian of the Cause of God. These included most of the members of 'Abdu'l-Bahá's family. They failed to see Shoghi Effendi in the light of 'Abdu'l-Bahá's Will and Testament, which refers to him in terms such as the 'sign of God', the 'expounder of the words of God' and the 'Light that . . . shineth from the Dayspring of Divine Guidance'. These people contended that since Shoghi Effendi was only a youth, he ought to establish the House of Justice to assist him in his work. In later years, one by one, they rose up against him, violated the Covenant and were responsible for the greatest sufferings inflicted upon him during his ministry.

One of Bahá'u'lláh's titles is 'the Wronged One of the World' – a title that could well be applied to Shoghi Effendi too, for he silently suffered at the hands of those closest to him. Whereas Bahá'u'lláh's main enemies had been the divines of Islam and the despotic monarchs of Persia and Turkey, the primary adversaries of 'Abdu'l-Bahá and Shoghi Effendi were the Covenant-breakers. 'Abdu'l-Bahá, unlike Shoghi Effendi, did not always remain silent when sufferings were heaped upon him. In His writings and public appearances He disclosed the evil-doings of the Covenant-breakers and thus, to some extent, frustrated their wicked schemes. But Shoghi Effendi acted differently; he did not follow 'Abdu'l-Bahá's pattern of life as a public figure. He directed the affairs of the Cause and built the institutions of the Faith mainly through correspondence, privately enduring the onslaught of the Covenant-breakers with resignation and forbearance. Consequently, he suffered greatly.

Immediately upon Shoghi Effendi's return to the Holy Land after 'Abdu'l-Bahá's passing, opposition arose from the quarter of the old, established Covenant-breakers, especially Mírzá Muḥammad-'Alí, his brother and his associates. These unscrupulous men, who during the latter part of 'Abdu'l-Bahá's ministry had become demoralized, with no choice but to creep into the limbo of ignominy and defeat, raised their heads once again when they saw a youth of 25 years at the helm of the Faith. They thought they could wrest the leadership of the Bahá'í community from him – but soon discovered that they were gravely mistaken.

The Arch-breaker of the Covenant in the Holy Land and a few of his supporters in America and Persia actively tried to create division within the community. At the same time that Mírzá Muḥammad-'Alí was calling on the Bahá'ís to follow him as 'Abdu'l-Bahá's successor, he took ruthless action to seize custody of the Shrine of Bahá'u'lláh for himself. Rúḥíyyih Khánum describes this episode:

> Shortly after 'Abdu'l-Bahá's ascension, this disgruntled and perfidious half-brother had filed a claim, based on Islamic law (he who pretended he had still a right to be the successor of Bahá'u'lláh!), for a portion of the estate of 'Abdu'l-Bahá which he now claimed a right to as His brother. He had sent for his son, who had been living in America and agitating his father's claims there, to join him in this new and direct attack on the Master and His family. Not content with this exhibition of his true nature he applied to the civil authorities to turn over the custodianship of Bahá'u'lláh's Shrine to him on the grounds that he was 'Abdu'l-Bahá's lawful successor. The British authorities refused on the grounds that it appeared to be a religious issue; he then appealed to the Muslim religious head and asked the Mufti of Akka to take formal charge of Bahá'u'lláh's Shrine; this dignitary, however, said he did not see how he could do this as the Bahá'í teachings were not in conformity with Shariah law. All other avenues having failed he sent his younger brother, Badiullah, with some of their supporters, to visit the Shrine of Bahá'u'lláh where, on Tuesday, 30 January, they forcibly seized the keys of the Holy Tomb from the Bahá'í caretaker, thus asserting Muḥammad 'Alí's right to be the lawful custodian of his Father's resting-place. This unprincipled act created such a commotion in the Bahá'í Community that the Governor of Akka ordered the keys to be handed over to the authorities, posted guards at the Shrine, but went no further, refusing to return the keys to either party.[245]

Following Shoghi Effendi's arrival in Haifa, the shock of the announcement of his appointment as the Guardian of the Faith, coupled with the terrible ordeal of the passing of the Master, took their toll on his health. He was so crushed under the weight of bereavement that he could not even attend a memorial meeting for the Master which was held in His residence 40 days after His ascension. Three weeks later, the seizure of the sacred Shrine of Bahá'u'lláh by the Covenant-breakers came as a further blow.

The seizure of the keys of the Shrine by this bitterest enemy brought shock and sorrow to the tender and sensitive heart of Shoghi Effendi. Yet, despite his physical weakness, the evidence of divine guidance was apparent in his actions, which were characterized by a resolve and a wisdom that called to mind the wisdom of 'Abdu'l-Bahá and His penetrating foresight. While Shoghi Effendi's appeal to the government for the return of the keys was postponed by his absence from the Holy Land, which lasted about eight months, he continued to pursue this matter with great diligence until full rights of possession were restored to him by the authorities. Rúḥíyyih Khánum writes in some detail about this episode:

> The matter which concerned Shoghi Effendi most, however, was the Shrine of Bahá'u'lláh at Bahjí. The keys of the inner Tomb were still held by the authorities; the right of access to other parts of the Shrine was accorded Bahá'ís and Covenant-breakers alike; the Bahá'í custodian looked after it as before, and any decision seemed in a state of abeyance. Shoghi Effendi never rested until, through representations he made to the authorities, backed by insistent pressure from Bahá'ís all over the world, he succeeded in getting the custody of the Holy Tomb back into his own hands. On 7 February 1923 he wrote to Tudor Pole: 'I have had a long talk with Col. Symes and have fully explained to him the exact state of affairs, the unmistakable and overwhelming voice of all the Bahá'í Community and their unshakable determination to stand by the Will and Testament of 'Abdu'l-Bahá. Recently he sent a message to Muḥammad 'Alí requiring from him the sum of £108. for the expenses of the policeman, contending that he being the aggressor is liable to this expense. So far he has not complied with this request and I await future developments with deep anxiety.'
>
> The following day Shoghi Effendi received this telegram from his cousin, who was in Jerusalem:
>
> His Eminence Shoghi Effendi Rabbani, Haifa.
> Letter received immediate steps taken the final decision by the High Commissioner is in our favour the key is yours.[246]

Given his ill health and the weight of the custodianship of so mighty a Cause so suddenly placed upon his shoulders, the pressures which were building up around Shoghi Effendi were intolerable. In these circumstances he decided to leave the Holy Land for a period, during which he hoped to pray and commune with his Beloved in solitude, regain his strength and confidence, and return to the duties awaiting him at the World Centre. He announced his decision in a letter written in English to the Bahá'ís of the West and in a similar one in Persian to the Bahá'ís of the East:

> He is God!
>
> This servant, after that grievous event and great calamity – the ascension of His Holiness 'Abdu'l-Bahá to the Abhá Kingdom – has been so stricken with grief and pain and so entangled in the troubles (created) by the enemies of the Cause of God, that I consider my presence here, at such a time and in such an atmosphere, is not in accordance with the fulfilment of my important and sacred duties.

For this reason, unable to do otherwise, I have left for a time the affairs of the Cause, both at home and abroad, under the supervision of the Holy Family and the headship of the Greatest Holy Leaf – may my soul be a sacrifice to her – until, by the Grace of God, having gained health, strength, self-confidence and spiritual energy, and having taken into my hands, in accordance with my aim and desire, entirely and regularly the work of service, I shall attain to my utmost spiritual hope and aspiration.

The servant of His Threshold,
Shoghi[247]

Shoghi Effendi's absence from the Holy Land lasted only a few months. When he returned, he took the reins of the Cause of God in his hands and with great vigour and zeal directed its affairs uninterruptedly until the end of his life.

Opposition to the Guardian was not limited to Covenant-breakers residing in the Holy Land. Several believers raised their heads in violation of the Covenant in other parts of the world and began their onslaught against him from the early days of his ministry. One of the age-old factors which led certain believers to violate the Covenant of Bahá'u'lláh was their ambition and pride in wanting to become leaders of the community and to obtain positions of importance in the Cause. The truth, however, is that the Bahá'í community has no leaders as such and those who are elected or appointed to administrative office are expected to be servants of the Cause, manifesting self-effacement, humility and detachment from the things of this world. An inherent characteristic of the Faith of Bahá'u'lláh is that it does not harbour egotistical personalities. Its watchword is the servitude exemplified by 'Abdu'l-Bahá, whose supplication to God was to give Him 'to drink from the chalice of selflessness' and to make Him as 'dust' in the pathway of the loved ones of God.[248]

Considering these attributes of servitude that must govern the activities of the friends, it is not surprising to witness the eventual downfall of those who, either through their folly or their ambition and pride, tried with all their power to introduce into the Faith of Bahá'u'lláh the concepts of leadership and dominance and to create the cult of personality within its ranks. In their struggle for power these people brought about severe crises in the community; they violated the Covenant, rose up against Shoghi Effendi and, in the end, tragically destroyed themselves.

Soon after Shoghi Effendi assumed the office of the Guardianship and while there was widespread expectation among the Bahá'ís of the immediate establishment of the Universal House of Justice, some individuals longed to become members of that august institution. One such person in the East was 'Abdu'l-Ḥusayn, entitled by

'Abdu'l-Bahá 'Ávárih' (Wanderer). In the West it was Ahmad Sohrab. Both men were prominent teachers of the Faith, in Persia and North America respectively, and both had one thing in common: a passionate love of leadership.

Ávárih was a native of the village of Taft in the province of Yazd. Before he embraced the Faith he was a Muslim clergyman. Soon after becoming a follower of Bahá'u'lláh he was recognized by the believers to be a man of learning and knowledge and became renowned as one of the erudite teachers of the Faith. 'Abdu'l-Bahá, who was fully aware of the vices and corrupt practices of this man, did not prevent him from serving the Cause, and as long as he acted faithfully in relation to the Faith, He encouraged him, praised his work and wrote several Tablets in his honour. However, from the beginning of his involvement with the Bahá'í Faith, Ávárih displayed a pride and vanity that puzzled those Bahá'ís who were in close contact with him.

On 19 January 1922 Shoghi Effendi wrote a letter to the Persian believers stating that he would soon establish the Universal House of Justice. He then called a number of well-known believers to the Holy Land in March 1922 for consultation. Among these was Ávárih, who arrived late. Many of the believers, including Ávárih, thought that Shoghi Effendi should call for the election of the Universal House of Justice immediately. However, it became apparent to Shoghi Effendi that the election of that body had to wait until such time as local and national spiritual assemblies could be formed in various countries and were fully functioning. But Ávárih, dissatisfied with this decision, was still determined to press his point of view.

Following Ávárih's short stay in the Holy Land, he travelled to England in January 1923 and soon after he went to Egypt. During the few months that he remained in Cairo, he created dissension and disunity among the believers to such an extent that the Spiritual Assembly of Cairo complained to Shoghi Effendi. Thus he was invited to return to the Holy Land. Here he questioned the authenticity of the Will and Testament of 'Abdu'l-Bahá but was satisfied when shown the original copy in 'Abdu'l-Bahá's handwriting. He then met with the Greatest Holy Leaf and reiterated to her his opinion that Shoghi Effendi should be advised to call for the election of the Universal House of Justice. He is reported to have uttered a veiled threat that if his demand were not acted upon, he would have no choice but to arouse the Bahá'ís of Persia to rebel against the Guardian.

In the meantime, he wrote letters to the believers expressing his dissatisfaction with the way the affairs of the Cause were being conducted. Upon his arrival in Persia he began propagating his misconceived ideas aimed at creating division among the friends there, with the result that in May 1924 the Spiritual Assembly of

Ṭihrán sought guidance from the Guardian about to how to deal with Ávárih. The response was that the friends must be protected from his misguided intentions.

This clear violation of the Covenant isolated Ávárih from the believers. Even his wife left him and refused to associate with him. Soon he changed his tactics and wrote a series of letters to various members of 'Abdu'l-Bahá's family, saying that there had been misunderstandings and suggesting that if Shoghi Effendi were willing to arrange an annual income for him, he would alter his attitude and stop his activities against the Covenant of Bahá'u'lláh.

Covenant-breaking is a spiritual disease and those who are affected by it are victims of their own selfish ambitions. It is only through a real awakening of the soul and the recognition of his transgressions against God that a Covenant-breaker can find the urge to repent. When the repentant is sincere, God will forgive his past deeds and restore his spiritual health, and indeed, there were a number of Covenant-breakers who were forgiven in this way by 'Abdu'l-Bahá and Shoghi Effendi.

In the several letters Ávárih wrote asking for reinstatement, however, there was no expression of repentance, and when he received no positive response, he unveiled his satanic nature and wrote abusive letters to Shoghi Effendi, using offensive language and vowing to destroy the Faith of Bahá'u'lláh altogether. There was never among the Covenant-breakers during Shoghi Effendi's ministry a man so vile and hypocritical as he.

Covenant-breakers usually oppose the Centre of the Faith but most of them claim to be believers in Bahá'u'lláh. In this case, however, Ávárih rebelled against the Faith itself, in spite of the fact that he had spent more than two decades teaching the Cause of Bahá'u'lláh and had published voluminous writings declaring its truth and testifying to the authenticity of its Founder's message. He joined hands with the Muslim clergy and Christian missionaries in attacking the Faith in Persia. He disseminated far and wide a series of his despicable publications against the Faith. In foul language, he attacked every aspect of the Faith, misrepresented its aims, and uttered slanders about its Central Figures, whom he attacked in most distasteful terms. 'The volumes', Shoghi Effendi writes, 'which a shameless apostate composed and disseminated . . . in his brazen efforts not only to disrupt that Order [Administrative Order] but to undermine the very Faith which had conceived it, proved . . . abortive.'[249]

In one of his letters to the Bahá'ís of Persia, who had completely ignored the activities of this ignoble man, Shoghi Effendi referred to Ávárih as a dead body which the surging ocean of the Cause of God had cast upon its shores, thus cleansing itself of pollution. Shoghi

Effendi predicted that Ávárih would live to a very old age in order to see with his own eyes the progress of the Faith throughout the world. And, indeed, he did live to be about a hundred years of age and witness the rising prestige of the Faith, the inauguration of the Holy Year in 1953, the completion of the superstructure of the Shrine of the Báb, the launching of the Ten Year Crusade and the convocation of several international conferences at which a host of teachers and pioneers arose to carry the message of Bahá'u'lláh to many virgin territories and establish the institutions of His Faith all over the globe. In a cable of 16 December 1953 announcing the death of Ávárih, Shoghi Effendi referred to him as one who 'will be condemned by posterity as being the most shameless, vicious, relentless apostate in the annals of the Faith, who, through ceaseless vitriolic attacks recorded in voluminous writings and close alliance with its traditional enemies, assiduously schemed to blacken its name and subvert the foundations of its institutions'.[250]

The defection of Ávárih in Persia resulted in the expulsion from the Faith of a handful of unfaithful persons who were influenced by his propaganda. In the same way that all impurities are discharged at intervals from the body of man to keep it healthy, the process of the expulsion of the Covenant-breakers had a cleansing effect upon the Bahá'ís of Persia. It invigorated the community and gave it the extra stimulus necessary to expand and consolidate the institutions of its divinely ordained Administrative Order.

One of the people influenced by Ávárih was his close friend, the evil-minded Ḥasan-i-Níkú. A teacher of the Faith who had spent some time in India and who visited Shoghi Effendi in Haifa at the end of 1923, Ḥasan-i-Níkú was an ambitious man who looked for leadership in the Bahá'í community. When he did not find it he followed the same path as Ávárih. He published three volumes in which he viciously attacked the Faith and attributed appalling things to its Founders, totally misrepresenting its tenets in a language full of bitterness, hatred and falsehood. He was ignored by the believers and his hopes of discrediting the Faith and breaking up the solidarity of its adherents were frustrated.

Another notorious Covenant-breaker in Persia who became a close associate of Ávárih was Fayḍu'lláh Ṣubḥí, who had served as the Master's secretary for a number of years. A vacillating person, he had on more than one occasion rebelled against the institutions of the Faith and each time had repented, only to resume his opposition to the Cause. Although brought up in a Bahá'í family, he fell victim to the influence of Ávárih. His father tried hard to save him from spiritual extinction but he remained adamant and continued in his odious activities against the Cause, sustaining a prolonged campaign of shameful vilification not only against the Guardian but also against Bahá'u'lláh and 'Abdu'l-Bahá. At the height of his rebellion, he wrote a letter to Áyatu'lláh Burújirdí, a high-ranking Muslim cleric, in which he repented of having taken part in Bahá'í activities in his earlier days. The offensive language he used against Shoghi Effendi and the Universal House of Justice in this letter demonstrated the depraved character of this man, who remained in the abyss of ignominy and godlessness until the end of his life. All he left behind is the memory of his vile language and despicable conduct.

Notorious among the few Covenant-breakers outside Persia and the Holy Land was an Armenian by the name of Fá'iq who caused much agitation among the Egyptian Bahá'ís. He rebelled against Shoghi Effendi and tried to create an alternative organization to the Administrative Order – a 'Scientific Society', an experiment that ended in utter failure. After the friends dissociated themselves from him, he was left to his own devices and, deprived of the bounty of faith, died a Covenant-breaker.

Yet another Covenant-breaker was Falláḥ, a resident of Iskandarun, Turkey. He was a proud and arrogant man who misled a number of his relatives in that city and remained unrepentant until the end of his life.

These men were the ringleaders of the violators of the Covenant in the East but those who followed them were very few in number. As in the days of 'Abdu'l-Bahá, Covenant-breakers did not make any headway in Persia and the havoc they created in the early years of Shoghi Effendi's ministry was, within a short period of time, utterly eradicated.

The first to arise in opposition to Shoghi Effendi in the West was Ahmad Sohrab. He had been to the United States when he was a teenager to act as a servant and cook for Mírzá Abu'l-Faḍl, whose solitary habits caused the friends deep concern for his health. When Mírzá Abu'l-Faḍl left the United States in 1904, Ahmad was ordered by 'Abdu'l-Bahá to accompany him but he disobeyed and remained in the United States until 1912 when the Master took him back to the East, although he seemed loath to go. While in America, Ahmad became proficient in English and when the Master went to the United States he served Him as interpreter. From the beginning, however, Ahmad showed signs of insincerity and faithlessness and many times his behaviour caused 'Abdu'l-Bahá deep sorrow. But he remained with 'Abdu'l-Bahá throughout the journey and when he later went to Haifa he continued to serve Him as a secretary. The Master knew that Ahmad would rebel against the Centre of the Cause after His passing and had intimated this to one or two people who were close to Him.

Indeed, the Master's prediction was fulfilled. One of the believers, Mrs Nellie French, has recounted the reaction of Ahmad Sohrab when she communicated to him the contents of the Will and Testament of 'Abdu'l-Bahá. Intensely agitated, his face black, and pacing back and forth, he exclaimed: 'This cannot be. Shoghi Effendi knows nothing about the Cause. He was never with 'Abdu'l-Bahá as I have been. I am the one who should have been appointed.'[251]

By the time of 'Abdu'l-Bahá's passing, Ahmad had become well-known among the believers of the West. Having emerged as a prominent Bahá'í, he, like Ávárih, wanted the establishment of the Universal House of Justice immediately after the passing of 'Abdu'l-Bahá and opposed Shoghi Effendi's creation of local and national spiritual assemblies. With the help of a certain wealthy woman, Mrs Lewis Stuyvesant (Julie) Chanler, he formed an organization known as the New History Society and made a great deal of propaganda to recruit members. Using the name and teachings of the Faith to attract people to his cause, he clearly denounced Shoghi Effendi's directives for the building of the Administrative Order. He also created the 'Caravan of East and West', the chief activity of which was international correspondence.

Ahmad Sohrab, who was referred to by the believers as the 'Ávárih of the West', tried to create a new sect of his own based on the teachings of Bahá'u'lláh. He did not question the authenticity of the Will and Testament of 'Abdu'l-Bahá but maintained that Shoghi Effendi had erred in his function as the Guardian of the Faith. He made great efforts to penetrate the American Bahá'í community in order to undermine the foundation of the local and national spiritual assemblies and to establish himself in place of Shoghi Effendi but he utterly failed. The Bahá'ís remained faithful to the Covenant; they shunned him entirely and with the passage of time his hopes were dashed and his plans and activities bore no fruit whatsoever. At the height of Ahmad's endeavours, Shoghi Effendi through his secretary wrote the following to the American National Spiritual Assembly:

> In regard to the activities of Ahmad Sohrab, Shoghi Effendi has already stated that such attacks, however perfidious, do not justify the friends replying or taking any direct action against them. The attitude of the National Spiritual Assembly should be to ignore them entirely . . .[252]

Most Covenant-breakers engage in a common pattern of behaviour, at first claiming to be devoted and sincere Bahá'ís but later demonstrating by their actions that they are not. For instance, those who broke the Covenant during Shoghi Effendi's ministry declared their faith in Bahá'u'lláh and 'Abdu'l-Bahá in the early stages, but as time went on and they foresaw the bankruptcy of their position, they compromised and progressively distanced themselves from their earlier practices and assertions. In almost every case the new Covenant-breakers joined hands with the old, whom they had previously denounced. For example, Ahmad Sohrab at first did not have anything to do with Mírzá Muḥammad-'Alí and his associates, whom he regarded as enemies of 'Abdu'l-Bahá. But later when he noticed the ascendancy of the Cause of God, he forged links of friendship and cooperation with them. In fact, he even went so far as to denounce 'Abdu'l-Bahá, whom he used to regard in the early days of his rebellion as the Centre of the Covenant of Bahá'u'lláh and whose writings he used to quote in his public pronouncements.

In 1954, the year that witnessed the extraordinary expansion of the Faith as hundreds of Bahá'í pioneers settled in virgin territories of the globe, Ahmad Sohrab, incensed by the growth and consolidation of the institutions of the Cause worldwide, visited the Holy Land and went to the home of some of the old Covenant-breakers. Holding meetings there, he gave them his support and encouragement and created much agitation in the region.

Ahmad continued his shameful activities until the end of Shoghi Effendi's ministry but they produced no results. On the contrary, towards the end of his life, the movement which he had created and spent so much effort in promoting was near extinction and it disintegrated completely after his death in 1958. All endeavours exerted by this misguided man over several decades to undermine the Cause of God had quite the opposite effect: stimulating its growth. The message of Bahá'u'lláh reached the furthest corners of the earth and the institutions of His Faith were established in almost every country and territory of the globe.

Another person who rose up in opposition to Shoghi Effendi and to the establishment of the institutions of the Faith was Mrs Ruth White in the United States. A veteran believer, she had visited 'Abdu'l-Bahá in the Holy Land in 1920. She claimed that the Will and Testament of 'Abdu'l-Bahá was not authentic and created much agitation in the community by attacking the National Spiritual Assembly of the United States and Canada, whose establishment she considered to be against the teachings and wishes of 'Abdu'l-Bahá. For several years Mrs White persevered in her determination to prevent the establishment of the institutions of the Faith. One of her actions was to write a letter to the United States Postmaster General asking him, among other things, to prohibit the National Spiritual Assembly from 'using the United States mails to spread the falsehood that

Shoghi Effendi is the successor of 'Abdu'l-Bahá and the Guardian of the Bahá'í Cause'.[253]

Another of Mrs White's letters was addressed to the High Commissioner for Palestine. In it she completely misrepresented the position of Shoghi Effendi but the authorities in the Holy Land were well aware of the facts and did not heed her appeals.

Mrs White also wrote many letters to the National Spiritual Assembly of the Bahá'ís of the United States and Canada, as well as to some believers, vehemently objecting to the directives of Shoghi Effendi and the administration of the Cause through the local and national institutions. One of Mrs White's converts was Dr Herrigel, a founding member of the German Bahá'í community. He, too, rejected the authority of the Will and Testament and became numbered among the Covenant-breakers.

It is interesting to note that no one who has studied the Will and Testament of 'Abdu'l-Bahá, with the exception of Mrs White and a few others whom she influenced, has ever questioned its authenticity. Even other Covenant-breakers who rose up against Shoghi Effendi did not agree with her. Ahmad Sohrab and Ṣubḥí for example, who had both served 'Abdu'l-Bahá as His secretary, never questioned the authenticity of the Will. Neither did Muḥammad-'Alí, nor Badí'u'lláh nor other enemies who were looking for any excuse they could find to attack the Guardian of the Faith.

It must be remembered that the Will and Testament was in 'Abdu'l-Bahá's handwriting and bore His seal. These were very familiar to the Persian believers because 'Abdu'l-Bahá had written innumerable Tablets in His own hand and almost every Bahá'í family in Persia had received one or more of them. Thus, when the photostatic text of the Will and Testament was sent to Persia and elsewhere, it was easily acknowledged by everyone to be in the handwriting of 'Abdu'l-Bahá.

Another criterion for the Will's authenticity was 'Abdu'l-Bahá's unique style and mode of expression, with which the Persian friends were familiar. Indeed, anyone who is versed in the writings of the Faith in the original language can easily tell the difference between the writings of Bahá'u'lláh, 'Abdu'l-Bahá and Shoghi Effendi, as each has its own special tone and style.

The behaviour of those who rose up in opposition to Shoghi Effendi, such as Ruth White, Ahmad Sohrab and others, clearly demonstrates the truth of 'Abdu'l-Bahá's words, found in the following passages from the Will and Testament:

> **17–WT No doubt every vainglorious one that purposeth dissension and discord will not openly declare his evil purposes, nay rather, even as impure gold, will he seize upon divers measures**

and various pretexts that he may separate the gathering of the people of Bahá.

55–WT He that obeyeth him not, hath not obeyeth God; he that turneth away from him, hath turned away from God and he that denieth him, hath denied the True One. Beware lest anyone falsely interpret these words, and like unto them that have broken the Covenant after the Day of Ascension (of Bahá'u'lláh) advance a pretext, raise the standard of revolt, wax stubborn and open wide the door of false interpretation.

Each one of those who violated the Covenant and openly challenged the authority of the Guardian seized 'upon divers measures and various pretexts' to justify his or her position. Ávárih opened 'wide the door of false interpretation', maintaining that since Shoghi Effendi was only a youth, the House of Justice needed to be established immediately. Ahmad Sohrab's pretext was that Shoghi Effendi should not have engaged in building up the Administrative Order. Similarly, Mrs White was bitterly against the establishment of organizational institutions such as the national spiritual assembly, so she raised 'the standard of revolt' and contended that the Will and Testament of the Master was a forgery. Indeed, every other person who broke the Covenant justified his action through false interpretation of the writings, and as we have observed, the motivating force behind many of these violations of the Covenant was an intense ambition for leadership in the Bahá'í community.

Although the violators of the Covenant in the East and the West during Shoghi Effendi's ministry were few in number, their relentless attacks against the Faith during that entire period of his ministry were fierce. In spite of their persistent efforts to create a breach within the Bahá'í community, however, they did not succeed. The vast majority of believers remained firm in the Covenant, turned to Shoghi Effendi with great devotion and laboured to promote the Faith and establish its divinely ordained institutions throughout the world.

30

Rebellion of Shoghi Effendi's Relatives

While Shoghi Effendi endured many distressing afflictions at the hands of the enemies of the Faith and the Covenant-breakers in the East and the West, they pale into significance when compared with the pain and suffering inflicted upon him by the members of 'Abdu'l-Bahá's family who broke the Covenant and bitterly opposed him. The rebellion of these family members against Shoghi Effendi is reminiscent of the rebellion of Bahá'u'lláh's family after His ascension. As discussed elsewhere in this volume, it is usually those who are closest to the Manifestation of God or to His Chosen Ones who are in greatest danger of becoming Covenant-breakers.* Only those who are true servants of God, who are the embodiments of humility and utter nothingness, can survive spiritually and remain faithful in the holy and rarified atmosphere of Bahá'u'lláh's, 'Abdu'l-Bahá's or Shoghi Effendi's presence. Any trace of ambition or self-glorification which a believer may have in his personality can be fatal if he comes into frequent contact with the source of divine revelation because in that holy presence He shall 'accept naught but absolute virtue and deeds of stainless purity'.[254]

The history of the Faith has shown that many of those who were closest to Bahá'u'lláh fell from grace because of their insincerity and selfish interests. These people, however, could have remained faithful believers had they not served in His presence. A proud and egotistical person who serves the Cause of Bahá'u'lláh in his local community may create many unpleasant problems for himself and the other believers but these difficulties will not necessarily be the cause of the extinction of his faith. To give an analogy, a man who falls while standing on the ground may hurt himself but a fall will be fatal to a person flying high above the ground.

Most members of 'Abdu'l-Bahá's family were devoid of the spiritual qualities that distinguish men of God from the ungodly. Materialism had eaten into the core of their beings and 'Abdu'l-Bahá knew it. The high esteem in which they were held by the believers and the tokens

---

* For an explanation of this particular phenomena which relates to special tests surrounding the members of the family of Bahá'u'lláh or 'Abdu'l-Bahá see chapter 2.

of respect shown to them by Bahá'ís and non-Bahá'ís alike had made them haughty and vain instead of humble and lowly. 'Abdu'l-Bahá was not pleased with the spiritual development of His family and He often remarked on it.

From the early days of Shoghi Effendi's ministry, the old Covenant-breakers arose in opposition to him and tried to exploit the weaknesses of the members of 'Abdu'l-Bahá's family who lacked faith and were devoid of spiritual qualities. Among these instigators of dissension was Mírzá Muḥammad-'Alí, the Arch-breaker of the Covenant, who outlived the Master by 16 years and did everything in his power to extinguish the light of the Faith. He died in 1937 and all witnessed his tragic downfall.

The next in command, Mírzá Badí'u'lláh, the youngest son of Bahá'u'lláh, lived to an old age and died in 1950. He opposed Shoghi Effendi in every way he could. The Master knew that he would create great problems for the Cause and wrote these words about Mírzá Badí'u'lláh, warning the friends to shun his company:

> **41–WT My purpose is, however, to show that it is incumbent upon the friends that are fast and firm in the Covenant and Testament to be ever wakeful lest after this wronged one is gone this alert and active worker of mischief may cause disruption, privily sow the seeds of doubt and sedition and utterly root out the Cause of God. A thousand times shun his company. Take heed and be on your guard. Watch and examine; should anyone, openly or privily, have the least connection with him, cast him out from your midst, for he will surely cause disruption and mischief.**

It was Badí'u'lláh who, on the instructions of the Arch-breaker of the Covenant, seized the keys of the Shrine of Bahá'u'lláh from their custodian. It was he who complained to the British authorities, vehemently opposing the transfer of the remains of the Purest Branch to Mount Carmel. His acts of treachery, deceit and arrogance, perpetrated over almost 60 years, stained the annals of the Faith that his own father had founded.

Another unrepentant Covenant-breaker was the notorious Majdu'd-Dín, son of the faithful brother of Bahá'u'lláh, Áqáy-i-Kalím. He was an inveterate enemy of the Master and later of Shoghi Effendi. He lived to an old age and was one of those who succeeded in spreading the poison of Covenant-breaking among the family of 'Abdu'l-Bahá. He died in 1955, realizing the futility of his deeds and witnessing the triumph of the Cause on the global scale.

Ḥájí Siyyid 'Alí Afnán, a brief account of whose life appears in chapter 13, was yet another veteran Covenant-breaker. The members of his family were chiefly responsible for delivering the most painful blows to the person of Shoghi Effendi.

When Shoghi Effendi became the Guardian of the Faith, the family of the Master were expected to turn to him devotedly in a spirit of lowliness and humility, as true believers did. But of course this was not easy for his brothers, sisters and cousins to do. After all, Shoghi Effendi had grown up with them and they were his peers and next of kin. Although they acknowledged his appointment and outwardly showed their submissiveness to him, it was obvious from the very beginning that they were not sincere in their hearts.

During the first few years of the ministry of Shoghi Effendi his family remained outwardly loyal but the seed of rebellion and Covenant-breaking had been planted in their hearts, only needing time to germinate and bring forth the fruit of sedition and opposition. In direct contrast stood the Greatest Holy Leaf. Although she was the most venerable member of the Holy Family and the most outstanding woman in the Bahá'í era and had seen Shoghi Effendi grow up in the household of 'Abdu'l-Bahá, yet she turned to him in a spirit of devotion and humility. She did this because she believed the words of 'Abdu'l-Bahá that Shoghi Effendi was the Guardian of the Cause and the 'sign of God' on earth. In His Will and Testament 'Abdu'l-Bahá exhorts the believers 'to show their obedience, submissiveness and subordination unto the guardian of the Cause of God, to turn unto him and be lowly before him'.[255]

Shoghi Effendi's attitude towards the followers of Bahá'u'lláh who turned devotedly to him in the spirit of the Master's exhortation was absolute love and humility. Unlike some of the world leaders who show an air of superiority and authoritarianism to their subjects, Shoghi Effendi extended to all the believers, and especially to his relatives, the hand of fellowship and brotherhood. To the Western Bahá'ís he often signed himself 'Your true brother, Shoghi', and in his Persian letters, 'The servant of His ['Abdu'l-Bahá's] Threshold'.

Yet Shoghi Effendi's relatives did not respond with sincerity and faithfulness to his meekness and magnanimity. Knowing very well that most of the members of 'Abdu'l-Bahá's family were not able to turn to him as befitted his station as Guardian, Shoghi Effendi turned a blind eye to their aloofness and instead showed them extra warmth and encouragement. But he could see their insincerity from the very start, and although he looked upon them with a sin-covering eye, he suffered immensely. This suffering did not stem from the fact that they did not obey him personally but because the Will and Testament enjoined them to be obedient to the Guardian and he knew that as Guardian he would have to expel them from the Faith if they continued in this way.

For several years Shoghi Effendi called on the services of his close relatives in the work of the Faith in the Holy Land. His younger brother Ḥusayn and some of his cousins served him as secretaries. He bore with resignation and forbearance all of their deceitful and faithless actions and their disobedience to him as Guardian.

In the early years of the Guardianship, through the influence of the Greatest Holy Leaf, everyone in the household of 'Abdu'l-Bahá, even though insincere, rallied around Shoghi Effendi. The Greatest Holy Leaf acted as a shield for 'Abdu'l-Bahá's family, all of whom stood firm against the company of the old Covenant-breakers, who were the only people who publicly opposed the Cause and the person of the Guardian.

The passing of the Greatest Holy Leaf in 1932 caused untold sorrow to Shoghi Effendi and broke his heart forever. He built a befitting monument over her resting place in the vicinity of the Shrine of the Báb on Mount Carmel. With her passing, the great shield protecting the members of 'Abdu'l-Bahá's family was removed. Then, six years after Bahíyyih Khánum, in 1938, Munírih Khánum passed away. She and 'Abdu'l-Bahá had four surviving daughters; they were all married and between them had 13 children, of whom Shoghi Effendi was the eldest. The remaining 12, one by one, rebelled against him and were expelled from the Faith. The other members of the family were likewise disobedient to Shoghi Effendi; in some cases, he denounced them as Covenant-breakers and in others he remained silent about their status.

The eldest daughter of 'Abdu'l-Bahá was Ḍíyá'íyyih Khánum, who married Mírzá Hádí, an Afnán and a grandson of Ḥájí Mírzá Abu'l-Qásim, a brother of the wife of the Báb. This marriage brought forth three sons, Shoghi Effendi, Ḥusayn and Riáz, and two daughters, Rúḥangíz and Mehrangíz. Their family name was Rabbaní, a name given them by 'Abdu'l-Bahá.

Ṭúbá Khánum married Mírzá Muḥsin, an Afnán, a son of Ḥájí Mírzá Siyyid Ḥasan (the Great Afnán), the other brother of the wife of the Báb. They had three sons, Rúḥí, Suhayl and Fu'ád, and one daughter, Thurayyá. Their family name was Afnán.

Rúḥá Khánum married Mírzá Jalál, the son of the 'King of Martyrs'. They had two sons, Muníb and Ḥasan, and two daughters, Maryam and Zahrá. Their family name was Shahíd (Martyr).

Munavvar Khánum married Aḥmad Yazdí, the youngest son of Ḥájí 'Abdu'r-Raḥim-i-Qannád. They had no children.

Every member of the Master's family knew well that the old Covenant-breakers were all deadly enemies of the Master and of the Faith and were to be shunned as He had directed. They had not associated with them during the lifetime of 'Abdu'l-Bahá and they did not do so in the early years of Shoghi Effendi's ministry. It did not take very long, however, before secret ties were established between the old Covenant-breakers and certain members of the Master's family. As if a virus had attacked, the disease of Covenant-breaking spread and eventually infected all the surviving members of that noble family, sparing no one. This grievous downfall occurred because of their disobedience to the commandment to shun the Covenant-breakers. How clearly 'Abdu'l-Bahá admonishes the believers to avoid associating with them! In His Will and Testament, He thus enjoins:

> **38–WT And now, one of the greatest and most fundamental principles of the Cause of God is to shun and avoid entirely the Covenant-breakers, for they will utterly destroy the Cause of God, exterminate His Law and render of no account all efforts exerted in the past.**

And in another passage He repeats the same injunction:

> **52–WT Hence, the beloved of the Lord must entirely shun them, avoid them, foil their machinations and evil whisperings, guard the Law of God and His religion, engage one and all in diffusing widely the sweet savours of God and to the best of their endeavour proclaim His Teachings.**

It is clear, then, that the most obvious reason why the members of 'Abdu'l-Bahá's family failed to obey the Master was their lack of faith in Him and in His words.

'Abdu'l-Bahá wanted his family to turn to Shoghi Effendi in a spirit of devotion and servitude. In His Will and Testament He warned them in clear and unequivocal language that if they turned away from him, disobeyed him or contended with him, they had turned away, disobeyed and contended with God. Yet they chose to disregard the exhortations of the Master and rose up in open opposition against Shoghi Effendi.

The tragic spiritual extinction of the family of 'Abdu'l-Bahá, as its members fell, one by one, victim to the devouring flames of Covenant-breaking, left Shoghi Effendi entirely on his own. Over the years, his brothers and sisters, his several cousins, his aunts (the daughters of 'Abdu'l-Bahá) and other relatives were cut off from the tree of the Cause. As they rebelled against him, the Guardian tried his utmost to save them. He even refrained from disclosing their rebellion to the community for a considerable period of time. Instead he ignored their insults and endured their despicable conduct in silence until, at the end, he was left with no choice but to declare them Covenant-breakers and announce this to the Bahá'í world.*

Every one of these messages sent by Shoghi Effendi to the Bahá'í world at different times during his ministry was the consequence of many agonizing episodes of Covenant-breaking, acts of opposition, betrayal and open defiance by the members of the family of the Master. But far from weakening the fabric the Bahá'í community, the defection of these family members and that of some outstanding Bahá'ís who broke the Covenant strengthened and invigorated it. Through such a cleansing process the impurities are expelled from the body of the Cause.

As for the effect of the Covenant-breakers' rebellion, Shoghi Effendi wrote:

> We should also view as a blessing in disguise every storm of mischief with which they who apostatize their faith or claim to be its faithful exponents assail it from time to time. Instead of undermining the Faith, such assaults, both from within and from without, reinforce its foundations, and excite the intensity of its flame. Designed to becloud its radiance, they proclaim to all the world the exalted character of its precepts, the completeness of its unity, the uniqueness of its position, and the pervasiveness of its influence.[256]

In 1948 a fierce political upheaval erupted in the Holy Land. The State of Israel was founded, bringing an end to the British Mandate. War broke out between Arabs and Jews and a great many Arabs fled the country. During this period Shoghi Effendi remained in Haifa and, in the face of great dangers and severe difficulties, carried on his work as usual, including the building of the superstructure of the Shrine of the Báb. But the rest of the family, who were Covenant-breakers, allied themselves with the Arab community and fled the land. Among them were the family of Mírzá Jalál Shahíd, which included Rúḥá Khánum, the daughter of 'Abdu'l-Bahá; Ṭúbá Khánum, another daughter of 'Abdu'l-Bahá, and her son Rúḥí, his wife Zahrá and his brother; three cousins of Dr Faríd; and Nayyir Afnán, his wife Rúḥangíz (sister of Shoghi Effendi) and their children. Others who fled to Lebanon were Badí'u'lláh (next in command to the Arch-breaker of the Covenant) and his relatives, together with those Bahá'ís who were disloyal to Shoghi Effendi. As time went on these people, who were already cut off from the Holy Family by virtue

* For the text of these announcements and other details of Covenant-breaking by members of 'Abdu'l-Bahá's family and their expulsion from the Faith, see Taherzadeh, *Covenant of Bahá'u'lláh*, chapter 32.

of their association with the enemies of the Faith, integrated themselves into Islamic society.

Although the Cause of God benefits from the expulsion of unfaithful individuals who break the Covenant, the Centre of the Faith is the one who suffers most. In the case of Shoghi Effendi, this suffering was deepened by the fact that he was duty bound, by virtue of his position as Guardian of the Faith, to expel his closest loved ones. We cannot estimate the agony Shoghi Effendi must have undergone when he had to expel his brothers, sisters and aunts from the Faith.

Among those instrumental in raising up the spirit of Covenant-breaking, which had lain dormant within the hearts of most members of 'Abdu'l-Bahá's family during the early years of Shoghi Effendi's ministry, were the family of Siyyid 'Alí Afnán, an inveterate adversary of 'Abdu'l-Bahá.* Now his sons – the grandchildren of Bahá'u'lláh, all Covenant-breakers – inflicted the greatest injury upon the person of Shoghi Effendi.

Shoghi Effendi was dealt a great blow when Rúḥangíz, his eldest sister, married the second son of Siyyid 'Alí, Nayyir Afnán, who proved to be the greatest enemy of Shoghi Effendi throughout his ministry. This marriage created an unprecedented convulsion in the family and was followed by two similar marriages, one between the Covenant-breaker Ḥasan, another son of Siyyid 'Alí, and Mehrangíz, the younger sister of Shoghi Effendi, and the other between another son, Fayḍí, and Thurayyá, Shoghi Effendi's cousin. Shoghi Effendi refers to Nayyir as the 'pivot of machinations, connecting link between old and new Covenant-breakers'. He wrote: 'Time alone will reveal extent of havoc wreaked by this virus of violation injected, fostered over two decades in 'Abdu'l-Bahá's family.'[257]

These inroads made by the old Covenant-breakers into the family of 'Abdu'l-Bahá were fatal and soon most of its members became Covenant-breakers. Rúḥíyyih Khánum writes the following about the effect of the Covenant-breaking in the household of the Master:

> But the tale of defections such as these does not convey the true picture of what Covenant-breaking signified in the ministry of Shoghi Effendi. To understand that one must understand the old story of Cain and Abel, the story of family jealousies which, like a sombre thread in the fabric of history, runs through all its epochs and can be traced in all its events. Ever since the opposition of the younger brother of Bahá'u'lláh, Mírzá Yaḥyá, the poison of Covenant-breaking, which is opposition to the Centre of the Covenant, entered the Faith and remained. It is difficult for those who have neither experienced what this disease is, nor devoted any consider-

* See chapter 13.

> ation to the subject, to grasp the reality of the power for destruction it possesses. All the members of the family of Bahá'u'lláh grew up in the shadow of Covenant-breaking. The storms, separations, reconciliations, final sundering of ties, which are involved when a close, distinguished and often dear relative is dying spiritually of a spiritual disease, are inconceivable to one who has not experienced them . . .
>
> It looks simple on paper. But when year after year a house is torn by heart-breaking emotions, shaken by scenes that leave one's brain numb, one's nerves decimated and one's feelings in a turmoil, it is not simple, it is just plain hell. Before a patient lies on the operating table and the offending part is removed there is a long process of delay, of therapeutic effort to remedy the disease, of hope for recovery. So it is with Covenant-breaking; the taint is detected; warning, remonstrance, advice follow; it seems better; it breaks out again, worse than before; convulsive situations arise – repentance, forgiveness follow – and then all over again, the same thing, worse than before, recommences. With infinite variations this is what took place in the lifetimes of Bahá'u'lláh, 'Abdu'l-Bahá and Shoghi Effendi.[258]

In the following passage Rúḥíyyih K͟hánum shares her insights as to how the Centre of the Faith reacts when confronted with the unfaithful who rise in opposition to the Cause:

> Whereas we ordinary human beings react in one way, these extraordinary human beings react in an entirely different way. They are, in such matters – however great the difference in their own stations – entirely different from us. I used to wonder, in the early years of my life with the Guardian, why he got so terribly upset by these happenings, why he reacted so violently to them, why he would be prostrated from evidences of Covenant-breaking. Gradually I came to understand that such beings, so different from us, have some sort of mysterious built-in scales in their very souls; automatically they register the spiritual state of others, just as one side of a scale goes down instantly if you put something in it because of the imbalance this creates. We individual Bahá'ís are like the fish in the sea of the Cause, but these beings are like the sea itself, any alien element in the sea of the Cause, so to speak, with which, because of their nature, they are wholly identified, produces an automatic reaction on their part; the sea casts out its dead.[259]

The Covenant-breakers struggled continually to hurt Shoghi Effendi in whatever way they could. They attacked him from every direction and inflicted unbearable pain upon him, while he resisted their onslaught until they were vanquished one by one. In 1957, a few months before he passed away, he accomplished the task of removing once and for all the last traces of the Covenant-breakers' evil influence from the Holy Land. During his development of the gardens around the Mansion of Bahjí, he had made repeated efforts to secure from the government orders for demolition of the Covenant-breakers' houses around the Shrine of Bahá'u'lláh. The following is part of the cable Shoghi Effendi sent in June 1957 to the Bahá'í world when he achieved this goal.

> With feelings of profound joy, exultation and thankfulness, announce on morrow of sixty-fifth Anniversary of Ascension of Bahá'u'lláh, signal, epoch-making victory won over the ignoble band of breakers of His Covenant which, in the course of over six decades, has entrenched itself in the precincts of the Most Holy Shrine of the Bahá'í world, provoking through acts of overt hostility and ingenious machinations, in alliance with external enemies under three successive regimes, the wrath of the Lord of the Covenant Himself, incurring the malediction of the Concourse on high, and filling with inexpressible anguish the heart of 'Abdu'l-Bahá.
>
> The expropriation order issued by the Israeli government, mentioned in the recent Convention Message, related to the entire property owned by Covenant-breakers within the Ḥaram-i-Aqdas, recently contested by these same enemies through appeal to Israel's Supreme Court, now confirmed through adverse decision just announced by same Court, enabling the civil authorities to enforce the original decision and proceed with the eviction of the wretched remnants of the once redoubtable adversaries who, both within the Holy Land and beyond its confines, laboured so long and so assiduously to disrupt the foundations of the Faith, sap their loyalty and cause a permanent cleavage in the ranks of its supporters . . .
>
> The implementation of this order will, at long last, cleanse the Outer Sanctuary of the Qiblih of the Bahá'í world of the pollution staining the fair name of the Faith and pave the way for the adoption and execution of preliminary measures designed to herald the construction in future decades of the stately, befitting Mausoleum designed to enshrine the holiest dust the earth ever received into its bosom.[260]

Obtaining this expropriation order was Shoghi Effendi's last act in rooting out the nests of corruption and hatred that had plagued the holiest Shrine of the Bahá'í world for over six decades. During this time countless schemes had been devised against 'Abdu'l-Bahá and Shoghi Effendi by the Arch-breaker of the Covenant, his kinsmen and associates, and by enemies of the Faith. Today no trace of any of them remains in the areas surrounding the Shrine.

31

Turning to Shoghi Effendi

17–WT It is incumbent upon the members of the House of Justice, upon all the Aghsán, the Afnán, the Hands of the Cause of God to show their obedience, submissiveness and subordination unto the guardian of the Cause of God, to turn unto him and be lowly before him.

News of the appointment of Shoghi Effendi as the Guardian of the Faith was hailed by Bahá'ís all over the world who, as bidden by the Master in His Will and Testament, turned to Him with devotion and loyalty. This act endowed the community of the Most Great Name with tremendous potentialities for progress and bestowed upon the believers a fresh outpouring of divine bounties which, in turn, strengthened their faith. While a believer's faith depends upon the measure of his love for Bahá'u'lláh, that love cannot be realized unless the individual turns to the Guardian with devotion, humility and lowliness as exhorted by the Master in His Will and Testament. For how could one claim to love the Blessed Beauty while disregarding the authority of the very person who is infallibly guided by Bahá'u'lláh and is the Sign of God on earth?

Stories of the love and dedication which the believers in general, and the Hands of the Cause in particular, evinced towards Shoghi Effendi are numerous and heartwarming. In the East, the believers' enthusiasm knew no bounds. They carried out his instructions faithfully and, in many cases, suffered severe persecution in the accomplishment of various undertakings. Great numbers of Bahá'ís wrote to Shoghi Effendi and expressed their loyalty to him, while many with able pens expressed their deep love in verse and prose that were published within the community. Some had met Shoghi Effendi, knew him personally and had perceived even during his childhood that he would be the successor of 'Abdu'l-Bahá.

As mentioned in chapter 27, the famous Bahá'í poet 'Andalíb composed a delightful lullaby as Shoghi Effendi lay in his cradle, foretelling a glorious future for him. Another story of this kind of spiritual perceptiveness involves Dr Yúnis Khán, 'Abdu'l-Bahá's trusted secretary and translator for some years, who used to correspond with the believers in the West. Once he received a letter from an American believer saying that some of the friends had heard that the Master's successor had recently been born and asking him to confirm this. Dr Khán found it very difficult to mention this to 'Abdu'l-Bahá because he could not bear to think of the day when the Master would pass away, so he kept this matter to himself and was uncertain how to speak about it. Eventually he mustered his courage. Timorously and in a low voice, he asked the question. 'Abdu'l-Bahá responded affirmatively, saying, 'The triumph of the Cause is in his hands.'

Dr Khán knew who the child was and had previously had an experience of profound spiritual upliftment while visiting the infant Shoghi Effendi. Although he tried to put the matter out of his mind, as he believed it was unforgivable to pay attention to anyone except the Master during His lifetime, nevertheless he told Ḥájí Mírzá Ḥaydar-'Alí about the feelings he had experienced seeing Shoghi Effendi in his cradle – and discovered that the Ḥájí also had a similar experience. Thus, from the early days of Shoghi Effendi's life, the seed of love for him was planted in the hearts of a great many believers in the East. This is why his appointment as the Guardian of the Cause was greeted enthusiastically by the entire community of the Bahá'ís of Persia.

In the West the believers turned to Shoghi Effendi in obedience to the words of the Master but it took some time before they recognized him as a person endowed with God-given powers and virtues. As the believers met him and became enchanted with his personality, they recounted to the friends their stories of utter devotion to him, which in turn led the Bahá'ís of the West to acquire a deeper attachment to and love for him.

The following testimonials from some of the prominent believers, including the Hands of the Cause, demonstrate the extent of love and adoration felt for the Guardian by the believers in the West.

Mountfort Mills, an outstanding believer who served the Guardian ably and with great devotion, spoke to the friends on 22 April 1922, having met Shoghi Effendi a few months after the passing of 'Abdu'l-Bahá:

> . . . We met Shoghi Effendi, dressed entirely in black, a touching figure. Think of what he stands for today! All the complex problems of the great statesmen of the world are as child's play in comparison with the great problems of this youth, before whom are the problems of the entire world. He is a youth of twenty-six, left by the will of the Master as the Guardian of the Cause. No one

can form any conception of his difficulties, which are overwhelming.

We received his joyous, hearty hand grasp and our meeting was short. A bouquet was sent to our room in the form of a young tree filled with nectarines or tangerines. It was brought by Mr Fugeta. We awoke without any sense of sadness. That feeling was entirely gone. The Master is not gone. His Spirit is present with greater intensity and power, freed from bodily limitations. We can take it into our own hearts and reflect it in greater degrees. In the centre of this radiation stands this youth, Shoghi Effendi. The Spirit streams forth from this young man. He is indeed young in face, form and manner, yet his heart is the centre of the world today. The character and spirit divine scintillate from him today. He alone can today save the world and make true civilization. So humble, meek, selfless is he that it is touching to see him. His letters are a marvel. It is the great wisdom of God in granting us the countenance of this great central point of guidance to meet difficult problems. These problems, much like ours, come to him from all parts of the world. They are met and solved by him in the most informal way.[261]

In 1926 Hand of the Cause Mrs Keith Ransom-Kehler wrote:

The unique and outstanding figure in the world today is Shoghi Effendi. Unique, because the guardianship of this great Cause is in his hands and his humility, modesty, economy and self-effacement are monumental. Outstanding because he is the only person, we may safely say, who entrusted with the affairs of millions of souls, has but one thought and one mind – the speedy promulgation of peace and goodwill throughout the world. His personal life is absolutely and definitely sacrificed . . . The world, its politics, social relationships, economic situations, schemes, plans, aspirations, programmes, defects, successes, lie under his scrutiny like infusoria beneath a microscope.

. . . Shoghi Effendi is the Commander-in-chief of this great new army of faith and strength that is moving forth to vanquish the malevolent forces of life.[262]

And Hand of the Cause Dr Ugo Giachery left this account:

Of all the characteristics that Shoghi Effendi possessed, the one that I believe was at the very core of his personality and was deeply rooted in his soul was the immense faith he had, his complete reliance on the efficacy of Bahá'u'lláh's Revelation. He clung to His Teachings with a tenacity that cannot be likened to anything. His whole being was permeated with the power of the Revelation, and this is the reason that all who came near him or in contact with him felt so safe, so assured, so regenerated. For the same reason, scheming individuals who inclined towards evil-doing or deceit could not remain long in his presence and went away frightened, bewildered and chastened. During my years of association with Shoghi Effendi I experienced, over and over again, the power emanating from his belief, a power that removed difficulties, brought unexpected happy solutions and paved the way to better and greater achievements . . .

At this point I would like to illustrate still another of the spiritual virtues of Shoghi Effendi, which I had noticed before but which, during that vital conversation, became evident in all its strength and delicacy; namely, the capacity to separate himself as a man from Shoghi Effendi, the Guardian of the Cause of God. When he spoke of the labours, duties, plans, present and future, the inspiration, the decisions of the Guardian, he was so impersonal that one could have believed he was speaking of another person. This endeared him even more, because to find such a balance of humility and greatness, of objectivity and selflessness coupled with a fertile, creative and poetic mind is one of the rare happenings in thousands of years. I have used the word delicacy, because in all his thought and action there was no affectation or remote trace of pride or vainglory. An illuminating example of this is to be found in one of his masterly letters, The Dispensation of Bahá'u'lláh, in the section on the Administrative Order wherein is described the station of the Guardian . . .

Humility of a kind not yet known elsewhere was one of Shoghi Effendi's many unique virtues, a humility which came from the conviction that man's faculties are not self-created but are a precious trust from God, not to be displayed or used overbearingly or with vanity. And yet he emanated true pride and dignity, such a regal dignity that raised him far above any man I have yet met or known.

When conversing with him, one could strongly sense this feeling of humility, while his ample brow and penetrating eyes reflected an inner light born of faith, courage and determination. One could feel an awareness that was amazing and rendered one speechless.

Shoghi Effendi's selflessness was not only outstanding but exemplary. He never placed his personal interests or desires ahead of his functions as Guardian . . .

If one were to relate in detail the manifold aspects of the personality of Shoghi Effendi which like facets of a perfectly cut gem reflected the rays of divine light and inspiration, many volumes would not suffice. I firmly believe that psychologists will come to agree with the point of view that while human beings, generally, react in a voluntary or semi-voluntary way to circumstance, situations, inspiration and even to what may be considered illumination from the Divinity, Shoghi Effendi, like a sensitive instrument connected to the Source of all powers, reacted involuntarily, to the most imperceptible spiritual impulse which activated his organism, making him capable of executing and discharging all functions and responsibilities related to the Cause of God without the slightest probability of error.

This analysis, made at the very first meeting with him, explained to me clearly and conclusively the meaning of divine guidance and infallibility . . .[263]

Finally, a tribute was paid to Shoghi Effendi less than a year after his passing in an address delivered by Hand of the Cause Amelia Collins at the International Bahá'í Conference held in Frankfurt/Main, Germany, which she attended as the chosen representative of Shoghi Effendi. It provides ample testimony that the Hands of the Cause faithfully carried out the exhortations of the Master 'to show their obedience, submissiveness and subordination unto the guardian of the Cause of God, to turn unto him and be lowly before him'. Mrs Collins spoke as follows:

How can I ever find words to bring you what is in my heart about our beloved Guardian! I feel we must each so fill ourselves at this time with his spirit and his wishes that it will carry us through the next five years of the glorious Crusade he initiated and enable us to consummate his every hope and wish. This, the fulfilment of his own Plan, is the living memorial we must build in his memory.

When I first heard of the passing of 'Abdu'l-Bahá, I was a very young believer and after the provisions of His will became known, my whole heart and soul turned to that youthful Branch, appointed by Him to watch over and guide the Faith of Bahá'u'lláh. How I prayed that God would help me to make him happy!

In 1923 I first met our beloved Guardian in Haifa. He was just a young man then, full of determination to carry forward the great work entrusted to his care. He was so spontaneous, so trusting and loving and outgoing in the buoyancy of his beautiful heart. Through the years we all watched with wonder and ever-deepening devotion to him and appreciation of his God-given gifts, the unfoldment of Bahá'u'lláh's Divine Order which he built up so patiently and wisely all over the world. But, oh friends, at what great cost to himself!

In 1951, when the beloved Guardian called some of the friends to serve in Haifa, I began to learn of what he had passed through. His face was sad, one could see his very spirit had been heavily oppressed by the agony he went through for years during the period when the family pursued their own desires and finally abandoned the work of the Faith and their Guardian to go their own way. I can truthfully say that for a number of years we who served him at the World Centre seldom saw him smile, and very often he poured out to us his woes and confided some of the things he had passed through. I do not know in any great detail the day to day afflictions of Bahá'u'lláh and 'Abdu'l-Bahá, but sometimes

I wonder if they could have been any more heartbreaking than those of our beloved Shoghi Effendi.

The Guardian had a profound and innate humility. Whenever the Faith was involved, he was fiery in its defence, kinglike in the loftiness of his bearing, the authority with which he spoke. But as a human being he was self-effacing, would brush aside our adulation and praise, turn everything we wished to shower on him towards the central figures of our Faith. We all know this characteristic of his, how he would never allow any photographs to be taken of himself, or give any of himself, but invariably encouraged the friends to place the Master's picture in their rooms; how he would not allow anyone to have his clothes or personal things lest they be regarded as relics; how he disliked any signs of personal worship – though he could never control what was in our hearts for him!

The Master said: 'O ye the faithful loved ones of 'Abdu'l-Bahá! It is incumbent upon you to take the greatest care of Shoghi Effendi . . . that no dust of despondency and sorrow may stain his radiant nature . . .' Neither his family, nor the people of the world, nor I am afraid we Bahá'ís, protected that radiant heart of Shoghi Effendi.

After the years of sorrow and trial he went through with the family, after his final separation from them, there came a new joy and hope to our beloved Guardian. The rapid progress made in the attainment of so many of the goals of the World Crusade lifted him up. How can I ever describe to you his eyes when he would come over to the Pilgrim House and announce to us a new achievement; they sparkled with light and enthusiasm and his beautiful face would be all smiles. Often he would send over one of his maps and when it was spread out on the dining table, his finger, full of infinite strength, insistence and determination, would point out the new territory opened, the new Ḥaẓíratu'l-Quds purchased, the new language translated, as the case might be. I feel it would be no exaggeration to say that it was the progress of the Ten Year Plan that gave him the encouragement to go on working so hard, for he was very tired. More than once he said during the last year of his life, that his ministry had lasted longer than that of either Bahá'u'lláh or 'Abdu'l-Bahá, and complained of the crushing burden, but none of us could foresee it presaged his release, that he was burned out with thirty-six years of struggle, of constant work, of sorrow and self-sacrifice.

His conscientiousness was like a fire burning in him; from his earliest childhood he showed the sensitive, noble, painstaking qualities that characterized him, and grew stronger as he matured and throughout his Guardianship.

The friends should realize that Shoghi Effendi had no foreknowledge that he would be appointed the Successor of 'Abdu'l-Bahá. The shock of the Master's passing was followed by an even more terrible one – the shock of his own appointment as the 'Sign of God'. He grew in this supreme office, which we know was under the direct guidance of the Twin Manifestations of God, even as a tree grows to full maturity and bears goodly fruits, but at such cost to himself of sacrifice that no one will ever properly estimate.

Let us review for a moment, however briefly, some of the services Shoghi Effendi rendered the Faith of Bahá'u'lláh.

When 'Abdu'l-Bahá passed away, the Shrine of the Báb consisted of six rooms surrounded by a small piece of land. The Mansion of Bahjí and most of its lands were in the hands of the Covenant-breakers or their friends, except for the Holy Tomb itself, which covers a very small area, and two pilgrim houses, one rented. The Master Himself, though so widely loved and respected, was not known as the Head of an independent religion, but rather regarded as a Moslem notable and Holy Man. The young Guardian, freed by his very youthfulness, armed with the power conferred on him by his Grandfather, cut with one stroke the bonds still holding in appearance the Bahá'ís to Islam – he refused to go to the Mosque. Tender, sensitive, crushed with grief, fighting his own inner battle to be reconciled to the glory of the station so suddenly revealed to him, Shoghi Effendi began to do all the Master had hoped to accomplish and to carry into effect His Words when He hinted that after Him the veils would be rent asunder. The Perfect Exemplar, the loving and forgiving Father, had passed away and the Order of Bahá'u'lláh was now to take shape under the guidance of the Champion of Divine Justice.

With wistful eyes the blessed Master had gazed up at the Shine of the Báb and said that it was not possible to build the Shrine of the Báb, but God willing, it would be done. The Guardian first added three rooms during the early years of his ministry to make the building a nine-roomed edifice. In 1944, the model of the completed Shrine was unveiled on the occasion of the One Hundredth Anniversary of the Báb's Declaration; it had an arcade and a dome, both of which the Master had stated it should have. By 1953 it was all built. Year after year the Guardian increased the size of the Shrine gardens, himself laying out the design in its minutest detail. Patiently, persistently, he had the lands about it bought, designating each area, supervising each transaction, overcoming every obstacle. He got the Mansion of Bahá'u'lláh away from the arch Covenant-breaker, Muḥammad-'Alí, and turned it into a Museum and Holy Place; he had all the Bahá'í properties exempted from government and municipal taxes; he had the Bahá'í marriage recognized as legally binding; he secured first [from] the British and later, in a much stronger form, from the new State of Israel, recognition of the fact that this is a World Religion, whose Holy Places and whose World Centre are in Haifa and Acca, and that he as the Head of this Faith had a higher position than any other religious dignitary in the land.

He chose the design himself and erected the monuments over the resting places of the Greatest Holy Leaf, her mother and brother, and the wife of 'Abdu'l-Bahá. He likewise specified the International Archives building should be of the type and proportions which it is, approving himself every detail and often changing details until he got them the way he wanted them. He located its exact position on the ground, the size of its walls and stairs, the garden surrounding it. This building will house precious Bahá'í relics such as no previous religion has ever possessed. Shoghi Effendi, appealing direct to high government officials, secured Mazra'ih as a Holy Place for the Bahá'í pilgrims to visit, after it had been promised to other institutions when the Jewish State was formed. It was at his decision that the beautiful Temple site on Mt Carmel was purchased, in the spot 'Abdu'l-Bahá had wished; and from the World Centre streamed out the translations, the letters, the writings of the Guardian in a mighty flow, in exquisite language, full of power, accurate, profound, inspired.

The hand of the Guardian was a motivating force. Let there be no mistake that any glove ever did the work of that hand. The gloves were poor and unworthy instruments for the most part, well nigh useless judged by human standards. It was his hand in everything, from the littlest to the biggest thing, that grasped every work, initiated every enterprise, never relaxed, never relinquished its grip until the task was done. Many gloves frayed out on that powerful hand, fell apart, were of necessity cast aside, but the work of the Cause went on uninterrupted until the last night of his life!

The Administrative Order of the Faith, the provisions for which were laid down by Bahá'u'lláh Himself and amplified by 'Abdu'l-Bahá, Shoghi Effendi set out to build. When the Master passed away, there were few Spiritual Assemblies in the world, and only one national body functioning in a very rudimentary manner. The builder, however, had been provided by God; the Great Administrator, with an almost unique capacity for organization, with a wisdom vouchsafed from on High, with a world-encompassing vision, set about his task. Patiently, persistently, painstakingly, Shoghi Effendi reared strong national bodies. He brought into being the International Bahá'í Council – the embryonic Universal House of Justice. He kept the balance, the perfect balance, between a thing too loosely knit, too individualistic to function efficiently, and too much efficiency, too many rules and regulations, too much running into endless and unnecessary detail which is one of the great afflictions of present day civilization. When he had created the system and reared the machinery of the Bahá'í Administrative Order, he suddenly shifted the whole mechanism into gear; he called for the first Seven-Year Plan, the first step in the Promulgation of 'Abdu'l-Bahá's Divine Plan, which is the instrument for the spiritual conquest of the entire globe. Plan followed plan. The scattered diversified followers of the Faith began to take shape as the army of Bahá'u'lláh; guided by the National Spiritual Assemblies. The pioneers, the vanguard as he called them of this great host, began to march out and over the world until, at the half-way point of the mighty Crusade he had launched, Shoghi Effendi could look upon a united, strong, enthusiastic, world-wide community of believers, who had already achieved the major part of the tasks he had set for them.

What gifts he had, what gifts he gave: *Gleanings from the Writings of Bahá'u'lláh*, *The Dawn-Breakers – Nabíl's Narrative*, *The Kitáb-i-Íqán*, *The Hidden Words*, and the *Epistle to the Son of the Wolf*, translations of superlative style and power, making available the essence of Bahá'u'lláh's Message to the western world. What life he breathed into us through his own writings, beginning with his World Order letters – the *Goal of a New World Order*, the *Dispensation of Bahá'u'lláh*, followed by the *Unfoldment of World Civilization* (now *The World Order of Bahá'u'lláh*), *The Advent of Divine Justice*, *The Promised Day is Come*, works which were supplemented by dynamic cables and special messages. To such a long list of distinguished works was added the finest flower of his mind, his masterful review of the first one hundred years of the greatest Dispensation vouchsafed by God to man on this planet – *God Passes By*.

His was the vision which looked at the Cause as a whole, saw present and future as part of one mighty panorama. He not only collated the teachings, but, with a strong sense of history, assembled the most precious relics in the Bahá'í world into a religious archives such as no previous Faith has ever possessed. He saw to it that all the precious sites associated with the Báb and Bahá'u'lláh and the heroes and martyrs of this Cause were, whenever possible, purchased: the House where Bahá'u'lláh was born in Teheran, His father's house in Tákur, the Síyáh-Chál, where the first rays of His Divine Mission fell upon Him in the blackness of a dungeon, the House He occupied in Constantinople, and one of the Houses He occupied in Adrianople; the bleak fortress of Máh-Kú, where the Báb revealed the Bayán, His shop in Búshihr, and many other sites associated with Him and His companions. At Shoghi Effendi's instructions an exhaustive photographic record was made of hundreds of these spots associated with the Heroic Age of the Faith.

He encouraged the Persian believers to compile the histories of the early days of the Cause in their provinces, and laid upon the Persian National Spiritual Assembly the great responsibility of collecting and transcribing the Tablets of Bahá'u'lláh and 'Abdu'l-Bahá, thus preserving for posterity a truly priceless heritage.

He was truly the builder by nature; he completed the first Mashriqu'l-Adhkár in America, the great Mother Temple of the West, unique in having had its foundation stone laid by 'Abdu'l-Bahá Himself. He initiated, chose the designs, and set in motion the plans for the erection of the African, the European, the Australasian, the Teheran and the Holy Land Temples. He specified the sites for the National Ḥaẓíratu'l-Quds and the national endowments. He named the languages into which the literature of the Faith was to be translated, and personally encouraged the pioneers to go forth and fulfil 'Abdu'l-Bahá's plan.

Ah, but he did more than this! He made each believer feel that over him watched a just mind and a loving heart; that he had a part to play, was precious to the Faith, had duties to discharge, enjoyed privileges infinitely precious because he was a member of the Community of the Most Great Name. Let us never forget this, never lose sight of this! This oneness he made a reality, this staunch loyalty to our Faith he implanted in our hearts. His work in this world is done. Ours is not.

We are all, in a way, Shoghi Effendi's heirs. We have inherited his work. His plan is completely laid out. Ours is the task to fulfil it. We must, each of us, complete our share of the World Crusade. This is the memorial we must build to our beloved Shoghi Effendi.

Let us love him more now than ever before, and through the power of our love attract his love to us, and bring his blessing on our labours.

Let us not fail him, for he never failed us. Let us never forget him, for he never forgot us.[264]

In the third part of the Will and Testament 'Abdu'l-Bahá exhorts His loved ones to 'take the greatest care of Shoghi Effendi' and to turn to him.

54–5–WT O ye the faithful loved ones of 'Abdu'l-Bahá! It is incumbent upon you to take the greatest care of Shoghi Effendi, the twig that hath branched from and the fruit given forth by the two hallowed and Divine Lote-Trees, that no dust of despondency and sorrow may stain his radiant nature, that day by day he may wax greater in happiness, in joy and spirituality, and may grow to become even as a fruitful tree.

For he is, after 'Abdu'l-Bahá, the guardian of the Cause of God, the Afnán, the Hands (pillars) of the Cause and the beloved of the Lord must obey him and turn unto him.

For most of his ministry Shoghi Effendi suffered greatly at the hands of the old Covenant-breakers, the entire family of the Master and many so-called Bahá'ís who were not faithful to him. Far from the expectations of the Master that 'no dust of despondency and sorrow may stain his radiant nature', the sufferings inflicted on him by a band of godless men and women left their imprint on his radiant soul.

It was only through the loyalty of the majority of the friends and the Hands of the Cause who truly followed the exhortations of 'Abdu'l-Bahá and rallied around him with deepest love that Shoghi Effendi was able to sustain the heavy weight of responsibilities with which he was entrusted by the Master. Finally, towards the end of his life, through his guidance and encouragement, a host of itinerant teachers and pioneers won unprecedented victories in all the continents of the globe. The historic achievements in Africa and the spectacular progress during the first years of the Ten Year Crusade brought great joy to his heart.

32

Hands of the Cause of God

Since the inception of the Faith, the commandment to teach the Cause and proclaim the message of Bahá'u'lláh to the human race has been the cornerstone of the teachings and ordinances of the Cause of God. Bahá'u'lláh has enjoined every believer to teach His Faith, calling this act 'the most meritorious of all deeds'.[265] In Persia the friends carried out this vital duty in a spirit of unity and teamwork, with each person playing his part according to his ability. Not everyone was capable of speaking about religion and, in the absence of priests, the actual work of teaching, adducing proofs and confirming people was usually left to those who had the gift of knowledge and an understanding of religious subjects. Localities usually had a few knowledgeable believers, each known as *muballigh* (teacher). These souls were available to discuss the Faith in private meetings with people who had been contacted by individual Bahá'ís.

Often, teaching the Cause was carried out as team work. Many searched for receptive souls, attracted them to the Cause through prayer and perseverance and eventually prepared them to attend a meeting in which a *muballigh* would speak to them about the Faith. Others would offer their homes for such meetings and some rendered other services to make these meetings possible.

These teachers of the Cause usually had a deep understanding of the Faith and were well versed in the writings of Bahá'u'lláh and in the holy books of the past. Most of them were learned people but there were some very successful teachers who were illiterate or had very little education. While to be knowledgeable is a great advantage, teaching the Cause is not dependent upon academic knowledge. Rather, a teacher must have faith and be detached from earthly things.

The outstanding qualities possessed by most teachers of the Cause in those days were a deep understanding of the Faith, whether they were educated or not, and a passionate love for Bahá'u'lláh, which made them radiant souls. In the absence of any institutions of the Faith such as local and national spiritual assemblies in the days of Bahá'u'lláh and 'Abdu'l-Bahá, a *muballigh* would play a significant part in deepening the friends in the knowledge of the Faith and would encourage and help them to discharge their duties in the field of teaching.

As far back as 1881, Bahá'u'lláh in one of His Tablets[266] directed Ibn-i-Aṣdaq, in consultation with Mullá 'Alí-Akbar-i-Shahmírzádí* and another believer, to make arrangements for the appointment in every locality in Persia of a suitable resident Bahá'í teacher. He placed great emphasis on this matter and regarded it as supremely important. From the very early days, too, Bahá'u'lláh Himself directed a few outstanding and knowledgeable souls to travel continually throughout Persia and the neighbouring countries in the capacity of *muballigh* to teach the Faith in different towns and villages. Their main task was to speak to interested people in private meetings that were usually organized by local believers. These travelling teachers rendered an invaluable service: through their devotion, their knowledge, their spirituality and radiance they succeeded in helping the believers in their teaching work and brought a great many souls under the shadow of the Cause of God. This practice continued during the ministries of 'Abdu'l-Bahá and Shoghi Effendi. When the national institutions of the Faith were established in Persia, one of their important obligations was to ensure that in every locality there were some individuals who could function in the capacity of a *muballigh*.

Running parallel to the duty of teaching the Faith is the task of conducting the affairs of the community through the process of consultation, as ordained by Bahá'u'lláh in His teachings. Before the establishment of the institutions of the Faith, important decisions, whether concerned with the local community or an individual, were often made through consultation among a few teachers of the Faith and other older and experienced Bahá'ís. As we have already stated, the practice of naming certain individuals as *muballigh* continued during the ministries of 'Abdu'l-Bahá and Shoghi Effendi. When the local spiritual assemblies were constituted in Persia during the ministry of the Guardian, he advised that the spiritual assembly in its decision-making process pay special attention to the views of the *muballigh* in the area and try to act on his advice.

The appointment of the *muballigh* seems to have been a prelude to Bahá'u'lláh's appointment of the Hands of the Cause, whose functions were elaborated by 'Abdu'l-Bahá. The body of the Hands was later institutionalized during the ministry of the Guardian.

During the last few years of His life Bahá'u'lláh chose four of His devoted followers and designated them Hands of the Cause of God. They were Ḥájí Mullá 'Alí-Akbar-i-Shahmírzádí, known as Ḥájí

* Both were, some years later, appointed by Bahá'u'lláh as Hands of the Cause.

Á<u>kh</u>und; Mírzá Muḥammad-Taqí, known as Ibn-i-Abhar; Mírzá 'Alí-Muḥammad, known as Ibn-i-Aṣdaq; and Ḥájí Mírzá Ḥasan, surnamed Adíb. These appointments, so far as we know, did not take place at one time. Their names were not announced to the community, nor were their functions outlined in one special Tablet. With the exception of Mírzá Ḥasan-i-Adíb, who embraced the Faith about three years before the ascension of Bahá'u'lláh, the other three Hands of the Cause were long-standing believers. They were the recipients of many Tablets in which, over the years, He showered upon them His blessings, guided their steps, praised their work and exalted their station in glowing terms. In these Tablets He often referred to them as 'the Chosen Ones', 'the loved ones', 'the detached souls', 'the pure in spirit' and other similar designations.

Towards the end of His life Bahá'u'lláh revealed a Tablet to each of these four individuals, designating them 'Hands of the Cause of God'. As far as we can gather, the first time Bahá'u'lláh used the term 'Hand of the Cause' to refer to an individual with certain responsibilities was in a Tablet revealed in honour of Ibn-i-Aṣdaq on 19 Rajab 1304 (13 April 1887) and it is possible that the first three Hands of the Cause were appointed around the same time. Certainly there is a Tablet revealed in honour of Ibn-i-Abhar dated 24 Sha'bán 1306 (26 April 1889) which makes it clear that he had already been designated a Hand of the Cause. As yet, no definite date for the appointment of Ḥájí Mírzá Ḥasan-i-Adíb has been found. He was the last to be appointed, having become a believer around 1889.

For quite some time the believers did not appreciate the significance of the appellation 'Hand of the Cause' and the implications of designating certain individuals as such. One may think of two reasons for this. First, Bahá'u'lláh had often used the term 'Hands' in earlier Tablets without referring to any particular person; second, there was no apparent change in the activities of these souls after their appointment, since they continued to be engaged in promoting the Cause and assisting the believers in their many activities. For instance, Bahá'u'lláh confirms in a Tablet that from the early days of His arrival in 'Akká He had instructed Mullá 'Alí-Akbar to be engaged in the protection of the Cause. Gradually, however, as the years went by, the friends began to understand the functions and duties of the Hands of the Cause – particularly during the ministry of 'Abdu'l-Bahá, when He directed them to carry out certain duties as a body.

In His Will and Testament, 'Abdu'l-Bahá defines the duties of the Hands of the Cause in these words:

21–WT The obligations of the Hands of the Cause of God are to diffuse the Divine Fragrances, to edify the souls of men, to

> **promote learning, to improve the character of all men and to be, at all times and under all conditions, sanctified and detached from earthly things. They must manifest the fear of God by their conduct, their manners, their deeds and their words.**

To appreciate the function of the Hands of the Cause, it is helpful to examine some basic principles of life and creation. In a Tablet[267] revealed in honour of His Trustee, Ḥájí Abu'l-Ḥasan-i-Amín, Bahá'u-'lláh states that movement is caused by heat, and heat by the Word of God.* This is a profound statement, the first part of which is proved by science, the second taught by religion. Thus the pronouncement is not only valid physically but has deep spiritual significance, as religious enthusiasm and fervour are generated by the warmth of one's heart.

As in nature, when heat causes movement, so in spiritual life when the heart is warmed by the fire of the love of God the believer moves to action and arises to serve the Cause. In other words, when the love of Bahá'u'lláh enters the heart of a believer he will feel exhilarated and will be motivated to serve Him.

There are two potent factors that can ignite the fire of the love of God in a believer's heart. The first is the power of the Word of God, and the second is the influence that a true believer may, through close association, exert on the heart of another. So powerful is this influence that Bahá'u'lláh states in the Hidden Words:

> He that seeketh to commune with God, let him betake himself to the companionship of His loved ones; and he that desireth to hearken unto the word of God, let him give ear to the words of His chosen ones.[268]

This passage demonstrates the great contribution that the Hands of the Cause – who were highly exhilarated by the love of their Lord – made in enthusing and arousing the believers, thereby enabling them to draw nearer to Bahá'u'lláh. These devoted souls warmed the hearts of the friends by the fire of faith that burned brightly within them. To commune with these holy souls was to commune with God and to hear their words was to hear the Word of God.

We can see, therefore, the vital role which Bahá'u'lláh entrusted to the Hands of the Cause, who, by virtue of the fire which raged within their hearts, were able to ignite others. Of course this role is not limited to the Hands. Any believer who is aglow with the love of God can impart the fire of his faith to others and the history of the

* For more information on this topic see Taherzadeh, *Revelation of Bahá'u'lláh*, vol. 4, pp. 42–3.

Faith has recorded the names of many immortal teachers of the Cause who have been endowed with this quality.

The four Hands designated by Bahá'u'lláh held consultative meetings and were regarded in the community as occupying a position of spiritual leadership. It could be said that during the ministry of 'Abdu'l-Bahá these four created the nucleus of a sacred institution, since 'Abdu'l-Bahá did not appoint any Hands during His ministry but only named a few outstanding believers posthumously to that station. Of the first four Hands, Ibn-i-Aṣdaq lived long enough to serve the Guardian during the opening years of the Formative Age when the institution of the Hands of the Cause was further developed and consolidated to constitute one of the twin arms of the Administrative Order of Bahá'u'lláh.

In several of His Tablets Bahá'u'lláh pays tribute to the devotion and self-sacrifice of the Hands of the Cause, describes their main functions as the diffusion of the divine fragrances and the protection of His Cause, and prays that they may be assisted by the Almighty to serve His Faith, to guide and enthuse the believers and to be ready at all times to carry out His commandments. In a Tablet to Mullá 'Alí-Akbar[269] Bahá'u'lláh calls on the Hands to help the believers become aware of the laws and principles of the Faith and to exert every effort to carry them out. In a Tablet[270] He states that the Hands of His Cause circle around His Will and do not speak except by His leave. He declares that through them the standards of the oneness of God have been raised among people and the banners of holiness unfurled in all regions. Bahá'u'lláh further testifies that the inmates of the highest Paradise, the denizens of His Kingdom, and beyond them the Tongue of Grandeur, bestow upon them their blessings and salutations.

In another Tablet[271] Bahá'u'lláh states that God has appointed the Hands of His Cause as guards and custodians of the stronghold of His Faith to protect it from the onslaught of the unfaithful and the ignorant. He describes the Hands of the Cause as the lamps of guidance who stand guard at the entrance of His mighty edifice and prevent the ungodly from entering it. In several of His Tablets Bahá'u'lláh has revealed short prayers for the Hands of His Cause. One is found in the Lawḥ-i-Dunya and has been translated into English:

> Light and glory, greeting and praise be upon the Hands of His Cause, through whom the light of fortitude hath shone forth and the truth hath been established that the authority to choose rests with God, the Powerful, the Mighty, the Unconstrained, through whom the ocean of bounty hath surged and the fragrance of the gracious favours of God, the Lord of mankind, hath been diffused.

> We beseech Him – exalted is He – to shield them through the power of His hosts, to protect them through the potency of His dominion and to aid them through His indomitable strength which prevaileth over all created things. Sovereignty is God's, the Creator of the heavens and the Lord of the Kingdom of Names.[272]

These statements extolling the station of the Hands of the Cause and delineating their functions should not give rise to the erroneous view that the institution of the Hands, followed by that of the Counsellors appointed by the Universal House of Justice to carry on the main duties of the Hands in the future, is any kind of priesthood. The fact that Bahá'u'lláh has abolished priesthood is ample testimony that this is not the case and the following statement by the Universal House of Justice clarifies this point:

> It should be apparent to the friends that, as Bahá'u'lláh Himself both abolished the priesthood and instituted the body of the Hands of the Cause, the Hands cannot be confused with a priesthood. There are basic differences between a priesthood and Bahá'í institutions, such as the Hands of the Cause and the Continental Boards of Counsellors. A priesthood is usually a profession, has sacramental functions and confers upon the individual occupant of the ecclesiastical office jurisdiction over the believers. In the Bahá'í Faith, there is no profession in any of its institutions, there are no sacraments and no individual has a sacramental function. Jurisdiction over communities and individuals is not vested in individuals. Even in the matter of teaching, the friends must realize that although a Hand of the Cause or a member of the Continental Board of Counsellors or indeed any other believer may be deeply learned in the Teachings so that one naturally gives weight to his exposition of them, no one, apart from the Master and the Guardian, is authorized to interpret the Sacred Writings.[273]

During His lifetime Bahá'u'lláh directed the Hands to consult among themselves and with other believers on issues vital to the growth and development of the Bahá'í community. At a certain point in His ministry it seems that Bahá'u'lláh, wishing to emphasize the importance of consultation in resolving various issues, deliberately declined to give guidance when asked for it and instead urged the questioner to consult on the subject. For instance, Hand of the Cause Ibn-i-Abhar once sought guidance from Bahá'u'lláh as to where he should reside in Persia. The answer was that first he ought to consult with some souls who were well-assured and steadfast in the Faith and then act upon their advice.

It is apparent from these details that consultative meetings usually involved the Hands and different individuals they invited to take part, with discussions mainly centring on topics such as the propagation of the Faith and its protection. Such meetings were held long before the establishment of local and national spiritual assemblies. In fact, the consultative meetings of the first Hands evolved into the Spiritual Assembly of Ṭihrán, the first Assembly in the Bahá'í world.

Indeed, when in 1899 'Abdu'l-Bahá instructed the Hands of the Cause to establish the first elected Spiritual Assembly of the Bahá'ís of Ṭihrán, the details were left to the Hands. Unlike the present system, in which the whole Bahá'í community in a town takes part in the election of the Spiritual Assembly, the Hands invited a number of well known Bahá'ís of Ṭihrán to be the electors. These members of the community elected the Assembly members by secret ballot. The Hands were themselves permanent members who actually issued credential papers for all elected members and invited them to serve on the Assembly.

The four Hands appointed by Bahá'u'lláh exerted their utmost in serving their Lord. Through their supreme devotion to the Cause, their unswerving loyalty to the Covenant and their untiring labours in the promotion of the interests of the Faith, they left the legacy of their magnificent example for generations yet unborn to emulate throughout this Dispensation.

33

The Hands of the Cause during the Ministry of the Guardian

20–WT O friends! The Hands of the Cause of God must be nominated and appointed by the guardian of the Cause of God. All must be under his shadow and obey his command. Should any, within or without the company of the Hands of the Cause of God disobey and seek division, the wrath of God and His vengeance will be upon him, for he will have caused a breach in the true Faith of God.

At different times during his ministry Shoghi Effendi conferred the station of the Hands of the Cause posthumously upon certain outstanding servants of the Cause. Ten distinguished souls from different continents and backgrounds were thus honoured. Towards the end of his ministry he appointed living Hands of the Cause and directed them, step by step, to carry out various duties which he entrusted to them.

As we survey the life of Shoghi Effendi, it appears that although from the early days of his ministry he was in need of competent souls to assist him in his work, he could not find anyone with the necessary capacity and experience to undertake this important function. The only person who responded to his call for such service was the renowned Dr John Esslemont, who served the Guardian with the utmost devotion, zeal and enthusiasm. His untimely death in 1925 robbed Shoghi Effendi of one of his ablest assistants. Although the Guardian invited others to undertake a similar service, there were no suitable candidates available anywhere in the Bahá'í world.

There were few, if any, believers who had the vision and the experience needed to work with Shoghi Effendi in his efforts to build the foundations of the institutions of the Faith around the world. Although there were a number of outstanding scholars of the Faith in Persia who had studied all the holy writings available to them and were well versed in the history of the Faith as well as in the scriptures of older religions, it is highly unlikely that any of them had perceived the significance of the institutions of the Faith, the inevitability of their rise or the emergence of the Administrative Order of Bahá'u'lláh, the framework of His World Order for mankind. These learned Bahá'ís were fully conscious of the importance of the spiritual assemblies, which Bahá'u'lláh and 'Abdu'l-Bahá had emphasized, but probably none of them realized that the local spiritual assembly was destined to become the primary institution of the Administrative Order, about which very little was known at the time. Nor did anyone realize that the institutions of the Faith would become channels for the flow of the spiritual forces latent within the Revelation of Bahá'u'lláh.

It becomes clear now, only after the lapse of many decades, how little the early Bahá'ís understood the basic principles of Bahá'u'lláh's Administrative Order, the foundations of which Shoghi Effendi had begun to build. This is perhaps the main reason why Shoghi Effendi could not find a single believer who sufficiently understood the nature of the work which he had set himself to carry out and who was free to come to the Holy Land to assist him. Gradually, through the guidance of the Guardian, Bahá'ís the world over learned about the workings of the Administrative Order and acquired the capacity to serve befittingly on the institutions of the Faith. Shoghi Effendi waited for 30 years until, in 1951, he was able to appoint a number of dedicated souls to the exalted position of Hand of the Cause of God. Thus he fulfilled the command of 'Abdu'l-Bahá in this regard, as revealed in His Will and Testament. Apart from those whom he appointed posthumously, the Guardian named, at different times, 32 Hands of the Cause.

In the Will and Testament, 'Abdu'l-Bahá states that the Guardian must direct the activities of the Hands:

> **22–WT This body of the Hands of the Cause of God is under the direction of the guardian of the Cause of God. He must continually urge them to strive and endeavour to the utmost of their ability to diffuse the sweet savours of God, and to guide all the peoples of the world, for it is the light of Divine Guidance that causeth all the universe to be illumined. To disregard, though it be for a moment, this absolute command which is binding upon everyone, is in no wise permitted, that the existent world may become even as the Abhá Paradise, that the surface of the earth may become heavenly, that contention and conflict amidst peoples, kindreds, nations and governments may disappear, that all the dwellers on earth may become one people and one race, that the world may become even as one home.**

For six years the Guardian guided the Hands to carry out their sacred responsibilities. In his personal contact as well as in his communications, he laid down the principles on which the Hands were to act, described the details of their relationship with the national spiritual assemblies and the body of the believers and delineated the range and the scope of their functions. Shortly before he passed away he called on them to watch over and ensure the protection of the Cause and the Bahá'í community and introduced the body of the Hands as the 'Chief Stewards of Bahá'u'lláh's embryonic World Commonwealth'. Concerning the appointment of the first contingent of the Hands of the Cause, in his cablegram of 24 December 1951 the Guardian wrote:

> Hour now ripe to take long inevitably deferred step in conformity with provisions of 'Abdu'l-Bahá's Testament . . . through appointment of first contingent of Hands of Cause of God, twelve in number, equally allocated Holy Land, Asiatic, American, European continents. Initial step now taken regarded as preparatory full development of institution provided in 'Abdu'l-Bahá's Will, paralleled preliminary measure formation International Council destined to culminate in emergence of Universal House of Justice. Nascent institution forging fresh links binding rising World Centre of Faith to consolidating World Community of followers of Most Great Name, paving way to adoption supplementary measures calculated reinforce foundations structure of the Bahá'í Administrative Order.
>
> Nominated Hands comprise, Holy Land, Sutherland Maxwell, Mason Remey, Amelia Collins, President, Vice-President, International Bahá'í Council; cradle Faith, Valíyu'lláh Varqá, Ṭarázu'lláh Samandarí, 'Alí-Akbar Furútan; American continent, Horace Holley, Dorothy Baker, Leroy Ioas; European continent, George Townshend, Herman [sic] Grossmann, Ugo Giachery. Nine elevated to rank of Hand in three continents outside Holy Land advised remain present posts and continue discharge vital administrative, teaching duties pending assignment of specific functions as need arises. Urge all nine attend as my representatives all four forthcoming intercontinental conferences as well as discharge whatever responsibilities incumbent upon them at that time as elected representatives of national Bahá'í communities.[274]

In this message mention is made of the formation of the International Bahá'í Council. This appointed body was also created in 1951. Its membership included Rúḥíyyih Khánum, Mason Remey, Amelia Collins, Leroy Ioas and Ugo Giachery, who was designated as 'member-at-large'. Later its membership was increased to nine. Concerning this institution the Guardian wrote:

> Hail with thankful, joyous heart at long last the constitution of International Council which history will acclaim as the greatest

> event shedding lustre upon second Epoch of Formative Age of Bahá'í Dispensation potentially unsurpassed by any enterprise undertaken since inception of Administrative Order of Faith on morrow of 'Abdu'l-Bahá's Ascension, ranking second only to glorious immortal events associated with Ministries of the Three Central Figures of Faith . . .[275]

And concerning the functions of the International Council he wrote:

> Nascent Institution now created is invested with threefold function: first, to forge link with authorities of newly emerged State; second, to assist me to discharge responsibilities involved in erection of mighty superstructure of the Báb's Holy Shrine; third, to conduct negotiations related to matters of personal status with civil authorities.[276]

The International Bahá'í Council, working under the direction of Shoghi Effendi, rendered him valuable services by carrying out important tasks in the Holy Land, which resulted in the further strengthening of the World Centre of the Faith.

In his writings Shoghi Effendi attached great importance to the International Council, which was to evolve by stages into the Universal House of Justice. The first stage was the Council in its initial form as an appointed body. The second stage was its evolution into an elected body. This took place in 1961, during the Custodianship of the Hands of the Cause, when the national spiritual assemblies throughout the world elected a nine-member Council. The third stage was for the Council to be transformed into the International Bahá'í Court* in Israel, and the fourth stage was to be the establishment of the Universal House of Justice. The third stage did not materialize because after the passing of Shoghi Effendi, when the Hands of the Cause investigated the matter through legal channels, they found that the prerogatives and privileges that could legally be granted to a Bahá'í Court were inadequate and unbefitting the prestige of the Faith. The International Council ceased to exist with the election of the Universal House of Justice in 1963.

The presence of the Hands of the Cause and members of the International Bahá'í Council in the Holy Land who were engaged in rendering various forms of service to Shoghi Effendi unfortunately did not reduce his workload. On the contrary, it was increased. In the latter part of Shoghi Effendi's ministry the Bahá'í world had grown enormously and the local and national institutions of the Faith had

---

* In Islamic countries and in Israel there are religious courts legally recognized to administer matters in the context of religious law.

multiplied. The World Centre had also grown. The construction of the Shrine of the Báb, the terraces and the Archives Building, the beautification of the gardens in Haifa and Bahjí and the strengthening of ties with the government of Israel all brought in their wake heavier burdens to be borne by Shoghi Effendi in the last years of his ministry.

Rúḥíyyih Khánum describes the manner in which the Guardian directed the work of the International Bahá'í Council:

> In its functions the International Bahá'í Council acted as that Secretariat the Guardian, so many years earlier, had desired to establish; its members received their instructions from him individually, in the informal atmosphere of the dinners at the Pilgrim House table, and not formally as a body; its meetings were infrequent as all its members were kept constantly busy with the many tasks allotted to them by the Guardian himself. Skilfully Shoghi Effendi used this new institution to create in the minds of government and city officials the image of a body of an international character handling the administrative affairs at the World Centre. It was no concern of the public how much or how little that body had authority; we who were on it knew Shoghi Effendi was everything; the public, however, began to see an image which could evolve later into the Universal House of Justice.[277]

It is important to realize that whoever was given the privilege to work with the Guardian was never in a position to make a decision for him. It was he and he alone who directed the affairs of the Cause. Unlike world leaders who often authorize their subordinates to make decisions, 'Abdu'l-Bahá and Shoghi Effendi were the sole decision-makers because they alone were the recipients of divine guidance. Indeed, the writings of 'Abdu'l-Bahá and Shoghi Effendi are all products of that infallible guidance conferred upon them by the Author of the Faith Himself.

In a cablegram sent on 29 February 1952 the Guardian announced the appointment of seven new Hands of the Cause:

> Announce friends East and West, through National Assemblies, following nominations raising the number of the present Hands of the Cause of God to nineteen. Dominion Canada and United States, Fred Schopflocher and Corinne True, respectively. Cradle of Faith, Dhikru'lláh Khádem, Shu'á'u'lláh [sic] 'Alá'í. Germany, Africa, Australia, Adelbert Mühlschlegel, Músá Banání, Clara Dunn, respectively. Members august body invested in conformity with 'Abdu'l-Bahá's Testament, twofold sacred function, the propagation and preservation of the unity of the Faith of Bahá'u'lláh, and destined to assume individually in the course of time the direction of institutions paralleling those revolving around the Universal House of Justice, the supreme legislative body of the Bahá'í world,

are now recruited from all five continents of the globe and representative of the three principal world religions of mankind.[278]

Soon after this announcement William Sutherland Maxwell passed away. The Guardian appointed Mr Maxwell's illustrious daughter Rúḥíyyih Khánum a Hand of the Cause in his place and sent the following message to the Bahá'í world on 26 March 1952:

> With sorrowful heart announce through national assemblies that Hand of the Cause of Bahá'u'lláh, highly esteemed, dearly beloved Sutherland Maxwell, has been gathered into the glory of the Abhá Kingdom. His saintly life, extending well nigh four score years, enriched during the course of 'Abdu'l-Bahá's ministry by services in the Dominion of Canada, ennobled during Formative Age of Faith by decade of services in Holy Land, during darkest days of my life, doubly honoured through association with the crown of martyrdom won by May Maxwell and incomparable honour bestowed upon his daughter, attained consummation through his appointment as architect of the arcade and superstructure of the Báb's Sepulchre as well as elevation to the front rank of the Hands of the Cause of God. Advise all national assemblies to hold befitting memorial gatherings particularly in the Mashriqu'l-Adhkár in Wilmette and in the Ḥaẓíratu'l-Quds in Ṭihrán.
>
> Have instructed Hands of Cause in United States and Canada, Horace Holley and Fred Schopflocher, to attend as my representatives the funeral in Montreal. Moved to name after him the southern door of the Báb's Tomb as tribute to his services to second holiest Shrine of the Bahá'í world. The mantle of Hand of Cause now falls upon the shoulders of his distinguished daughter, Amatu'l-Bahá Rúḥíyyih, who has already rendered and is still rendering manifold no less meritorious self-sacrificing services at World Centre of Faith of Bahá'u'lláh.[279]

The next appointments were Jalál Kházeh, Paul Haney and 'Alí Muḥammad Varqá in 1953, 1954 and 1955 respectively. The latter was appointed Trustee of Ḥuqúqu'lláh and Hand of the Cause to succeed his father, Hand of the Cause Valíyu'lláh Varqá, who passed away in November 1955.

On the passing of George Townshend, Agnes Alexander was appointed a Hand of the Cause and the Guardian sent the following cablegram to the Bahá'í world on 27 March 1957:

> Inform Hands and national assemblies of the Bahá'í world of the passing into Abhá Kingdom of Hand of Cause George Townshend, indefatigable, highly talented, fearless defender of the Faith of Bahá'u'lláh.

> Agnes Alexander, distinguished pioneer of the Faith, elevated to rank of Hand of Cause. Confident her appointment will spiritually reinforce teaching campaign simultaneously conducted in north, south and heart of Pacific Ocean.[280]

A significant development in the unfoldment of the institution of the Hands of the Cause took place when the Guardian directed the Hands to appoint Auxiliary Boards in each continent of the globe to act as their deputies and advisers. He announced this decision in a cablegram on 6 April 1954. The following is the full text of that historic announcement:

> To all the Hands of the Cause and all National Assemblies of the Bahá'í World:
>
> Hail emergence of the unfoldment in the opening years of the second epoch of the formative age of the Bahá'í Dispensation of the august Institution foreshadowed by the Founder of the Faith and formally established in the Testament of the Centre of His Covenant, closely associated in provisions of the same Will with Institution of the Guardianship, destined to assume in the fullness of time, under the aegis of the Guardian, the dual sacred responsibility for protection and propagation of the Cause of Bahá'u'lláh.
>
> Desire to pay warm tribute to the services rendered severally and collectively by appointed hands at the World Centre of the Faith and in territories beyond its confines.
>
> Greatly value their support in the erection of the Báb's Sepulchre on Mt. Carmel; in reinforcing ties with the newly emerged State of Israel; in the extension of the International Endowments in the Holy Land; in the initiation of the preliminary measures for the establishment of the Bahá'í World Administrative Centre, as well as in their participation in four successive intercontinental Teaching Conferences; in their extensive travels in African territories, in North, Central and South America, in the European, Asiatic and Australian Continents.
>
> This newly constituted body, embarked on its mission with such auspicious circumstances, is now entering the second phase of its evolution signalized by forging of its ties with the National Spiritual Assemblies of the Bahá'í world for the purpose of lending them assistance in attaining the objectives of the Ten Year Plan.
>
> The hour is ripe for the fifteen Hands residing outside the Holy Land to proceed during Riḍván with the appointment, in each continent separately, from among the resident Bahá'ís of that Continent, of Auxiliary Boards, whose members, acting as deputies, assistants and advisers of the Hands, must increasingly lend their assistance for the promotion of the interests of the Ten Year Crusade.

Advise the Hands of the Asiatic, American and European Continents to convene in Ṭihrán, Wilmette and Frankfurt respectively for the purposes of consultation and nomination.

The Hands of the Cause of the African and Australian Continents must exercise their functions in Kampala and Sydney respectively.

The Auxiliary Boards of the American, European and African Continents must consist of nine members each, of the Asiatic and Australian continents of seven and two respectively.

The allocation of areas in each continent to the members of the Auxiliary Boards, as well as subsidiary matters regarding the development of the activities of the newly appointed bodies, and the manner of collaboration with the National Spiritual Assemblies in their respective Continents, is left to the discretion of the Hands.

All Boards must report and be responsible to the Hands charged with their appointment.

The Hands of each Continent in their turn must keep in close touch with, and report the result of the nominations and progress of the activities of the Boards to the National Assemblies in their respective continents, as well as to the four Hands residing in the Holy Land destined to act as liaison between themselves and the Guardian of the Faith.

Urge the initiation of five Continental Bahá'í Funds which, as they develop, will increasingly facilitate the discharge of the functions assigned to the Boards.

Transmitting five thousand pounds as my initial contribution to be equally divided among the five Continents.

Appeal to the twelve National Assemblies and individuals to insure a steady augmentation of these Funds through annual assignment in National Budgets and by individual contributions.

Advise transmit contributions to Varqá, Holley, Giachery, Banání and Dunn acting as Trustees of the Asiatic, American, European, African and Australian Funds respectively.

Fervently supplicating at the Holy Threshold for an unprecedented measure of blessings on this vital and indispensable organ of the embryonic and steadily unfolding Bahá'í Administrative Order, presaging the emergence of the World Order of Bahá'u'lláh which must pave the way for the establishment of the World Civilization destined to attain maturity in the course of successive Dispensations in the Five Thousand Century Bahá'í Cycle.[281]

In a passage of the Will and Testament previously quoted, 'Abdu'l-Bahá warns:

> Should any, within or without the company of the Hands of the Cause of God disobey and seek division, the wrath of God and His vengeance will be upon him, for he will have caused a breach in the true Faith of God.

We have already mentioned a number of individuals, including the close relatives of Shoghi Effendi, who rebelled against the Guardian and were cast out of the community as Covenant-breakers. However, during the lifetime of Shoghi Effendi none of the Hands showed the slightest sign of disobedience to him. On the contrary, they demonstrated the utmost faithfulness to the Guardian and left for posterity a supreme example of loyalty and utter obedience to his directives. After the passing of Shoghi Effendi, however, one of the Hands, Mason Remey,* rebelled against the Covenant and was cast out of the community by the decision of the Hands of the Cause.

One month before his passing, the Guardian sent a moving message to the followers of Bahá'u'lláh throughout the world and in it appointed eight additional Hands of the Cause. After enumerating the manifold victories achieved during the first five years of the World Crusade, the Guardian stated:

> So marvellous a progress, embracing so vast a field, achieved in so short a time, by so small a band of heroic souls, well deserves, at this juncture in the evolution of a decade-long Crusade, to be signallized by, and indeed necessitates, the announcement of yet another step in the progressive unfoldment of one of the cardinal and pivotal institutions ordained by Bahá'u'lláh, and confirmed in the Will and Testament of 'Abdu'l-Bahá, involving the designation of yet another contingent of the Hands of the Cause of God, raising thereby to thrice nine the total number of the Chief Stewards of Bahá'u'lláh's embryonic World Commonwealth, who have been invested by the unerring Pen of the Centre of His Covenant with the dual function of guarding over the security, and of insuring the propagation, of His Father's Faith.
>
> The eight now elevated to this exalted rank are: Enoch Olinga, William Sears, and John Robarts, in West and South Africa; Hasan Balyuzi and John Ferraby in the British Isles; Collis Featherstone and Rahmatu'lláh Muhájir, in the Pacific area; and Abu'l-Qásim Faizí in the Arabian Peninsula – a group chosen from four continents of the globe, and representing the Afnán, as well as the black and white races and whose members are derived from Christian, Muslim, Jewish and Pagan backgrounds.
>
> This latest addition to the band of the high-ranking officers of a fast evolving World Administrative Order, involving a further expansion of the august institution of the Hands of the Cause of God, calls for, in view of the recent assumption by them of their sacred responsibility as protectors of the Faith, the appointment by these same Hands, in each continent separately, of an additional Auxiliary Board, equal in membership to the existing one, and

---

* For further information about Mason Remey's violation of the Covenant see chapter 37.

> charged with the specific duty of watching over the security of the Faith, thereby complementing the function of the original Board, whose duty will henceforth be exclusively concerned with assisting the prosecution of the Ten-Year Plan.[282]

During the last six years of his ministry the Guardian showered his unfailing encouragement, loving guidance and inspiration upon the company of the Hands of the Cause and spurred them on to scale loftier heights of sacrifice and service in the promotion of the Cause. He addressed this last moving appeal to them a month before he passed away:

> I call upon each and every Hand of the Cause of God, previously or now appointed, upon the entire body of the believers participating in this Crusade, and, in particular, upon their elected representatives, the numbers of the various Regional and National Spiritual Assemblies in both the East and the West, and, even more emphatically, upon those privileged to convene and organize these history-making Conferences, to bestir themselves, and, according to their rank, capacity, function and resources, befittingly prepare themselves, during the short interval separating them from the opening of the first of these five Conferences, to meet the challenge, and seize the opportunities, of this auspicious hour, and insure, through a dazzling display of the qualities which must distinguish a worthy stewardship of the Faith of Bahá'u'lláh, the total and resounding success of these Conferences, dedicated to the glorification of His Name, and expressly convened for the purpose of accelerating the march of the institutions of His world-redeeming Order, and of hastening the establishment of His Kingdom in the hearts of men.[283]

34

The Hands in the Service of the Guardian

17–WT My object is to show that the Hands of the Cause of God must be ever watchful and so soon as they find anyone beginning to oppose and protest against the guardian of the Cause of God, cast him out from the congregation of the people of Bahá and in no wise accept any excuse from him. How often hath grievous error been disguised in the garb of truth, that it might sow the seeds of doubt in the hearts of men!

For 30 years of the Guardian's ministry there were no Hands of the Cause to carry out the directives of the Master or to take action against those who opposed him. Shoghi Effendi himself dealt with the Covenant-breakers and expelled them from the community of the Most Great Name. In so doing he went through a great deal of pain and anguish, especially since many of those he had to declare as Covenant-breakers were his closest relatives – aunts, cousins, brothers and sisters.

The appointment of the Hands of the Cause in 1951 created a shield between the Covenant-breakers and the Guardian. But the authority to expel the Covenant-breakers from the Faith was vested in the Guardian alone and he exercised this authority throughout his entire ministry. The investigation of the activities of those who appeared to oppose the Guardian and the assessment of their motives and pursuits were conducted by the Hands of the Cause but the decision to proclaim them as Covenant-breakers rested with the Guardian.

Today, in the absence of the Guardian, the expulsion of Covenant-breakers from the Faith takes place by the decision of the Hands of the Cause in the Holy Land, subject to the approval of the Universal House of Justice.

During the ministry of the Guardian, the Hands of the Cause serving on various continents of the world performed their duties as protectors of the Faith with great diligence and steadfastness. The four Hands who served as members of the International Bahá'í Council at the World Centre of the Faith made great efforts to counter the activities of the old Covenant-breakers but their actions were all closely guided by the Guardian. This is clearly seen in the following account from a biography of Hand of the Cause Leroy Ioas, who was the Secretary-General of the Council:

As the Hands of the Cause in the Holy Land visited with officials of the Government in the interests of the World Centre, as they met the press, as they greeted dignitaries from abroad, they were by their very presence a living demonstration of Bahá'í standards, practices, and attitudes. This was surely an important part of their teaching function.

Those Hands who were members of the International Bahá'í Council were immediately drawn into the protective aspect of their work, specifically as it related to the Covenant-breakers. They lived at the very centre of violation, where the enemies of the Faith could make common cause with the Covenant-breakers against the head of the Faith himself.

When Leroy arrived in Haifa, the Guardian was deeply preoccupied with such a matter, and it was causing him great concern. It involved a case brought against the Guardian by remnants of the Covenant-breakers in 'Akká. Starting with an insignificant incident it took on such dimensions that a deeper intent became evident on the part of those bringing suit, namely, to gain co-custodianship with the Guardian of the Shrine of Bahá'u'lláh, or to secure rooms for themselves in the Mansion of Bahjí, from which they had removed themselves so that the Guardian might repair the appalling deterioration that had occurred under their care. After its restoration the British High Commissioner had declared Bahjí a place of pilgrimage and not a personal residence, and the Guardian became its custodian. The court case is an example of the type of scheming with which Shoghi Effendi was forced to contend throughout his Guardianship.

The Guardian, ever intent on beautifying the surroundings of Bahá'u'lláh's Tomb, one day told the guard to tear down a dilapidated house of several rooms near the Tomb; the roof was falling in and the walls unstable. The Covenant-breakers living on the property of Bahjí, in a house leaning up against the Mansion, rushed to obtain an Order from the Haifa Court to halt the demolition because they had not been consulted and still held one-sixth of the deed to the Mansion. In fact the structure in question had been in Bahá'í hands since 1892 and in Shoghi Effendi's hands for more than twenty years.

Two of the Covenant-breakers and their lawyer met with Leroy, Mason Remey and the Guardian's lawyer with the intention of settling the question out of court. It was a fruitless meeting as sixty-year-old attacks on 'Abdu'l-Bahá were brought forward. So the case went to a hearing, scheduled to be held informally before a judge. After two ineffectual meetings with the judge, during which intense hostility was displayed on the part of the plaintiffs, the case was sent for a first hearing in Court.

Indicating the unchanging desire of the Covenant-breakers to humiliate the head of the Faith, they summoned Shoghi Effendi as a witness, an insulting act which caused the Guardian immense distress. 'His great suffering', Ugo Giachery recalled, 'was for the sacrilege being committed against this Institution of the Faith. It was so abhorrent to him that he felt physically ill, as if "a thousand scorpions had bitten him".'

The Guardian made the decision to appeal directly to the Government to lift the case out of the Civil Court and called Ugo Giachery from Rome to assist with the work that followed. The three Hands of the Cause called on the Attorney General, the Vice-Minister of Religions, and officials of the Foreign Office and the Prime Minister's Office. The result was that the Attorney-General on instructions of the Vice-Minister informed the president of the Haifa Court that in accordance with a 1924 law, the case in question was a religious matter and not to be tried by a Civil Court. It would appear that the Guardian's initiatives had concluded the case.

But the clever and hostile lawyer of the Covenant-breakers challenged the finding on a technicality and made an appeal to the Supreme Court of Israel, in effect putting themselves in an adversarial position to the State. The Hands of the Cause again went forth to a series of interviews, and Shoghi Effendi made a personal appeal to the Prime Minister. There was an immediate reaction. The Prime Minister's legal adviser called to his office the Vice-Minister of Religions, the two lawyers and those they represented. The Bahá'ís refused to meet further with the Covenant-breakers and waited in another room of the building. The opposing lawyer made repeated claims, conveyed by the Guardian's lawyers to the Hands of the Cause, all of them rejected categorically. Finally the Prime Minister's adviser told the plaintiffs that they could continue their appeal if they wished but they should understand that their fight was now with the Government of Israel and what it had the authority to do. At this point they dropped the appeal and the case, and the authorities issued authorization to demolish the ruins. The Guardian cabled the Bahá'í world of the successful conclusion to the painful case inspired by what he termed the 'blind, uncontrollable animosity' of the Covenant-breakers.

Within forty-eight hours the Guardian had levelled the house and sent over eight truckloads of plants and ornamental pieces to begin the beautification of the area. Leroy stayed in the Mansion to oversee the work. Within a week the Guardian had laid out a wide expanse of garden which appeared miraculously spread out before the eyes of the Bahá'ís in time for the commemoration of Bahá'u'lláh's Ascension. The case had frustrated the Guardian's intentions from December through mid-May . . .

Through this court case, occurring as it did shortly after the birth of the International Council, the Faith gained stature in the eyes of the most important government Ministries, as officials learned more of its history and purposes, dealt with its dignified emissaries, and noted its unified stand behind the head of the

Faith, even as the plaintiffs revealed themselves as vengeful and vindictive.[284]

The following account from the same biography describes the activities of the Hands of the Cause, under the guidance of the Guardian, to totally eradicate the influence of the Covenant-breakers at Bahjí. It also provides further details of an interesting episode briefly mentioned in chapter 30:

For more than sixty years, disaffected members of the family of 'Abdu'l-Bahá had lived on the property of Bahjí, step by step being pushed back and restricted in their freedom of movement. But never in his lifetime was the Guardian able to visit the Shrine of his great-grandfather without their presence and their viewing of his acts of devotion. Whatever he did there was done under their unfriendly gaze.

Five years earlier, as we have seen, the Covenant-breakers had brought legal suit against the Guardian. A major result of those efforts had been recognition by the State of Israel of the Guardian as sole Custodian of the Bahá'í Holy Places, and the 'irretrievable curtailment', in the words of Shoghi Effendi, 'of long-standing privileges extended to the Covenant-breakers during the course of six decades'.

'It was a very dramatic story', Leroy said some years later of the sequence of events which led to the final departure of the Covenant-breakers from Bahjí, 'and I remember when we started the process the Guardian said, "Do you think it can be done?" I said, Shoghi Effendi, if the Guardian wants it done, it can be done. I did not know what I was getting into! The Covenant-breakers had been there for sixty-five years desecrating that sacred place and the Guardian said, it will be a miracle to get them out.'

When Leroy was given this assignment, the Guardian said to him: 'Everything you have done up to now, including your work on the Shrine of the Báb, is as silver, whereas removing the Covenant-breakers from Bahjí, and securing the buildings and lands for the Faith, will be as gold.' It was to be the monumental victory which 'crowned the beloved Guardian's life and filled his heart with profound joy, exultation and thankfulness . . .'

The first step was taken on May 11, 1956 when lawyers representing the International Bahá'í Council applied for expropriation of the property owned by the Covenant-breakers within the Ḥaram-i-Aqdas, the outer Sanctuary of Bahá'u'lláh's Sepulchre, i.e. the consecrated grounds contiguous to the Shrine. This initiative was taken as a result of information Leroy gleaned from government officials responsible for questions of property ownership. The legal instrument was the Land Acquisition for Public Purposes Ordinance of 1943, permitting the Government to acquire land for purposes which it deemed public purposes, and to transfer that land to responsible authorities.

The Shrine and Mansion had been recognized as a Holy Place long years before by the Mandate authorities, a recognition confirmed by the Israeli Government in 1952. Its acquisition therefore on behalf of the Bahá'ís, so that it could be developed and maintained by them, was deemed by the Government to be a public purpose. (One of the arguments used by the Bahá'ís in urging expropriation was their intention to embellish and build on the Shrine of Bahá'u'lláh.) The Government issued an expropriation order which was published in the *Official Gazette* on December 20, 1956.

The expropriation order was immediately challenged by the Covenant-breakers, who appealed to the Supreme Court. They claimed that the expropriation (of their minimal shares of the property) constituted an interference in an internal dispute, an infringement of their spiritual and temporal rights, and discrimination against a minority group. The Bahá'ís appeared before the Court to answer what Leroy called 'many of their nasty attacks against the Guardian and the Faith'.

The case was heard by the Supreme Court in April of 1957 and judgement was given on May 31. The Court found against the Covenant-breakers, and in so doing found that the Government's purpose in acquiring the land was indeed a public purpose. The Court furthermore drew attention to the fact that the appellants had not contended the public purpose of the action and that the contentions which they had brought forward had no substance.

Following the judgement of the Supreme Court, the Bahá'ís proceeded with eviction orders against the Covenant-breakers. The Attorney General applied to the Haifa District Court for a dispossession order against them, but again they intervened, attempting to delay the court hearing. They were unsuccessful in this and judgement was given against them, resulting in orders that they quit the premises of Bahjí and relinquish whatever small holdings remained in their hands. The Supreme Court had set the amount of their recompense.

On June 3, Shoghi Effendi cabled the triumphant news that the expropriation order had been upheld, 'enabling the civil authorities to enforce the original decision and proceed with the eviction of the wretched remnants of the once redoubtable adversaries . . .'

Within three months, they were gone. The Ḥaram-i-Aqdas had been cleansed. The spiritual suffering inflicted on 'Abdu'l-Bahá and the Guardian by these enemies of the Faith had come to its end. Before leaving Haifa that summer, Shoghi Effendi had told Leroy that 'just as soon as we acquire this house of the Covenant-breakers we will tear it down', so the moment they were gone – in late August – he cabled the Guardian asking if this should be done. The Guardian replied: 'Postpone demolition until my return.' He wished to supervise the work himself.

Two months before his passing, Shoghi Effendi again cabled the Bahá'í world (September 6, 1957):

> ANNOUNCE TO HANDS AND ALL NATIONAL ASSEMBLIES THAT FOLLOWING LOSS OF THE APPEAL TO THE SUPREME COURT, THE GOVERNMENT EXPROPRIATION ORDER HAS BEEN IMPLEMENTED, RESULTING IN THE COMPLETE EVACUATION OF THE REMNANT OF COVENANT-BREAKERS AND THE TRANSFER OF ALL THEIR BELONGINGS FROM THE PRECINCTS OF THE MOST HOLY SHRINE, AND THE PURIFICATION, AFTER SIX LONG DECADES, OF THE HARAM-I-AQDAS FROM EVERY TRACE OF THEIR CONTAMINATION. MEASURES UNDER WAY TO EFFECT TRANSFER OF TITLE DEEDS OF THE EVACUATED PROPERTY TO THE TRIUMPHANT BAHAI COMMUNITY.

The legalities of the transfer took place in two stages. In October 1957 Leroy was able to cable the Guardian that the Bahá'ís had now acquired the properties, that 'they are ours'.

He left a memorandum of the second occasion, when the transfer was completed, here briefly noted:

> 'This morning I joined our lawyer at the Land Registry in connection with the transfer of the properties at Bahjí to the Israel branch of the United States National Spiritual Assembly. We had a conference to review the details of my signing on behalf of the National Assembly, Israel Branch, in view of the fact that His Eminence Shoghi Rabbani had passed away.
>
> 'It was demonstrated that the Power of Attorney which he had given me was not a Power of Attorney to act in his behalf, it was a Power of Attorney to act in behalf of the Israel Branch, and therefore his passing had no effect on the validity of my authority to sign. We likewise discussed the question of the local transfer tax of two per cent, inasmuch as I had brought from Jerusalem a letter waiving the government tax of four per cent. When it was learned that the property was definitely not within the city limits of 'Akká, it was stated that the two per cent would be waived.
>
> 'We then proceeded with the transfer of the property. The Official Deeds of Sale were signed before the transfer agent. Thus there is concluded the complete purification of the Shrine area and the Ḥaram-i-Aqdas.'

The historic day of the final transfer of properties was two days short of one month after the Guardian's passing, Monday, December 2, 1957. The Deeds for Bahjí – the Shrine, the Mansion, the house of the Covenant-breakers, and all small pieces of land which they held in 'Akká, were signed over to the Faith at 10:25 a.m. (It should be noted that until this date the Shrine itself was held by Covenant-breakers as part of their small percentage of property.) Leroy was signatory for the Bahá'ís with Ugo Giachery and Sylvia as witnesses. The property was put in the name of the Israel Branch of the National Spiritual Assembly of the Bahá'ís of the United States. After Leroy's death, Sylvia found the pen with which he had signed the documents, left in the page of his diary at the date of December 2, 1957. On leaving Haifa, she gave it to the International Archives.

On Sunday, December 15, demolition of the house of the Covenant-breakers was begun. The Hands of the Cause in Haifa and the members of the International Bahá'í Council went over to Bahjí and took pictures of the event; the demolition was completed one week later.[285]

A few months before the Guardian passed away he addressed a momentous message to the Hands of the Cause and the National Spiritual Assemblies. Sent in the form of a cablegram on 4 June 1957, this communication may be viewed as a mandate bequeathed by the Guardian to these two institutions of the Faith. In it he foreshadows 'dire contests destined to range the Army of Light against the forces of darkness', anticipates attacks on the Faith from within and without the community and offers guidance to both divinely ordained institutions about the means to counteract the forces of opposition and protect the Cause of God. The entire message reads as follows:

> Divinely appointed Institution of the Hands of the Cause, invested by virtue of the authority conferred by the Testament of the Centre of the Covenant with the twin functions of protecting and propagating the Faith of Bahá'u'lláh, now entering new phase in the process of the unfoldment of its sacred mission. To its newly assured responsibility to assist National Spiritual Assemblies of the Bahá'í world in the specific purpose of effectively prosecuting the World Spiritual Crusade, the primary obligation to watch over and insure protection to the Bahá'í world community, in close collaboration with these same National Assemblies, is now added.
>
> Recent events, the triumphant consummation of a series of historic enterprises, such as the construction of the superstructure of the Báb's Sepulchre, the dedication of the Mother Temple of the West, the world-wide celebrations of the Holy Year, the convocation of four Intercontinental Teaching Conferences launching the Ten Year Crusade, the unprecedented dispersal of its valiant prosecutors over the face of the globe, the extraordinary progress of the African and Pacific campaigns, the rise of the administrative order in the Arabian Peninsula in the heart of the Islámic world, the discomfiture of the powerful antagonists in the Cradle of the Faith, the erection of the International Archives, heralding the establishment of the seat of the World Administrative Order in the Holy Land, served to inflame the unquenchable animosity of its Muslim opponents and raised up a new set of adversaries in the Christian fold and roused internal enemies, old and new Covenant-breakers, to fresh attempts to arrest the march of the Cause of God,

misrepresent its purpose, disrupt its administrative institutions, dampen the zeal and sap the loyalty of its supporters.

Evidences of increasing hostility without, persistent machinations within, foreshadowing dire contests destined to range the Army of Light against the forces of darkness, both secular and religious, predicted in unequivocal language by 'Abdu'l-Bahá, necessitate in this crucial hour closer association of the Hands of the five continents and the bodies of the elected representatives of the national Bahá'í communities the world over for joint investigation of the nefarious activities of internal enemies and the adoption of wise, effective measures to counteract their treacherous schemes, protect the mass of the believers, and arrest the spread of their evil influence.

Call upon Hands and National Assemblies, each continent separately, to establish henceforth direct contact and deliberate, whenever feasible, as frequently as possible, to exchange reports to be submitted by their respective Auxiliary Boards and national committees, to exercise unrelaxing vigilance and carry out unflinchingly their sacred, inescapable duties. The security of our precious Faith, the preservation of the spiritual health of the Bahá'í communities, the vitality of the faith of its individual members, the proper functioning of its laboriously erected institutions, the fruition of its worldwide enterprises, the fulfilment of its ultimate destiny, all are directly dependent upon the befitting discharge of the weighty responsibilities now resting upon the members of these two institutions, occupying, with the Universal House of Justice, next to the Institution of the Guardianship, foremost rank in the divinely ordained administrative hierarchy of the World Order of Bahá'u'lláh.

Shoghi[286]

35

Successor to Shoghi Effendi

16–WT He [the Guardian] is the expounder of the words of God and after him will succeed the first-born of his lineal descendents [sic].

Shoghi Effendi passed away without issue and the intention of 'Abdu'l-Bahá that the first-born of Shoghi Effendi's lineal descendants would succeed him did not materialize. This event caused a crisis of faith for some believers who did not fully understand the workings of the Covenant.

These believers expected that whatever the Master wrote in His Will and Testament would come to pass. How could 'Abdu'l-Bahá, upon whom Bahá'u'lláh had conferred infallibility and endowed superhuman knowledge, make, in so important a document, a statement that could not be implemented, they asked. 'Abdu'l-Bahá further instructed the Guardian to appoint his successor during his lifetime, which the Guardian could not do. In the Will and Testament 'Abdu'l-Bahá states:

18–WT O ye beloved of the Lord! It is incumbent upon the guardian of the Cause of God to appoint in his own life-time him that shall become his successor, that differences may not arise after his passing.

How is it that 'Abdu'l-Bahá's conditions were not fulfilled? To resolve this perplexing question, we would do well, in the first instance, to recall that Bahá'u'lláh had invested 'Abdu'l-Bahá with divine knowledge and that although 'Abdu'l-Bahá was not a Manifestation of God, the powers of the Manifestation were conferred upon Him by Bahá'u-'lláh. This was proved during the 29 years of His ministry and the believers were witness that the utterances of 'Abdu'l-Bahá, like those of Bahá'u'lláh, were creative.

A great many believers who attained 'Abdu'l-Bahá's presence or maintained communication with Him realized that He was aware of what was hidden in the hearts of men. But since He had clothed Himself in the mantle of servitude, He seldom spoke about the spiritual powers vested in Him by Bahá'u'lláh. Occasionally, however, He opened the window of His heart to a few staunch believers and intimated to them the workings of the divine Spirit that animated the Centre of the Covenant of Bahá'u'lláh.

In an unpublished Tablet addressed to Bashír-i-Iláhí, a devoted believer and a trusted confidant residing in Shíráz, the Master revealed a glimpse of the heavenly powers conferred upon Him by Bahá'u'lláh.

In this Tablet 'Abdu'l-Bahá acknowledges the receipt of Bashír-i-Iláhí's letter and states that on the very day the letter was written in Shíráz 'Abdu'l-Bahá dictated to His secretary in 'Akká a response answering all his questions. He gives details. The letter written in Shíráz was dated the 9th of the month of Sha'bán; on that date the answer was issued by 'Abdu'l-Bahá and it took 12 days for the Tablet to be prepared and signed by Him. He explains that it usually took about 10 days between the time that He dictated the first draft to His secretary and the time He signed the Tablet. Thus the answer to the letter was sent from the Holy Land on the 21st of Sha'bán. However, the letter of the 9th of Sha'bán arrived in 'Akká on the 15th of the month of Ramaḍán, i.e. 24 days after 'Abdu'l-Bahá had dispatched His answer to Bashír-i-Iláhí.

'Abdu'l-Bahá says that this is enough proof of the power of the Covenant.

Another episode showing the Master's awareness of what is hidden in the innermost heart of people is the account of the conversion to the Faith of Mírzá Muḥammad-Ṣádiq, a talented graphic artist who lived in Ṭihrán and was extremely antagonistic to the Faith. He married his cousin, Gulsurkh Bagum, who some years later became a devoted believer. Whereas in earlier years the couple lived in great harmony, after Gulsurkh Bagum's conversion to the Faith there was nothing but turmoil in the household, which lasted for years.

Gulsurkh Bagum, who was later surnamed Fá'izih (she who has attained) by 'Abdu'l-Bahá, was aflame with the fire of the love of Bahá'u'lláh. So deep was her attachment to the Faith that in spite of opposition from her husband she emerged as a great teacher among the women and a tower of strength for the believers. Soon her activities became a legend in the land and the enemies of the Cause were intent upon taking her life. On one occasion, although she was wearing a veil over her face, the enemies recognized and attacked her in the street. Inflicting numerous blows on her body using sticks and other blunt implements, they were about to kill her on the spot when someone managed to rescue her. It took several months for her wounds and broken bones to heal and she lost sight in one eye. But instead of dampening her enthusiasm, her sufferings increased her ardour for teaching the Cause.

At home, Fá'izih encountered great opposition from her husband but she showed the utmost love and respect towards him. Many a time he would become so enraged as to raise his hand to beat her, but instead of resisting, Fá'izih would go forward with the aim of kissing the hand that was about to strike her because of her allegiance to the Faith. For many years Fá'izih tried to open the eyes of her husband to see the glory of the station of Bahá'u'lláh. She invited many outstanding Bahá'í teachers to her home in order to converse with him but he would reject every argument they put forward and deny every proof they adduced to establish the authenticity of the claims of Bahá'u'lláh.

The great Bahá'í teacher Ḥájí Mírzá Ḥaydar-'Alí describes his encounter with Mírzá Muḥammad-Ṣádiq. The following is a summary translation of this interview:

> The husband of Fá'izih Khánum was an obstinate and stubborn person who used to deny the truth which was presented to him . . . I spoke to him about the Faith for two hours. I found him to be angry and during this period the signs of malice and opposition were apparent from every limb of his body. He offered me tea in a special cup because he considered me to be an infidel and, therefore, a defiled person. In the course of my conversation with him, I quoted a verse of the Qur'án, and a tradition of Islam in support of my arguments. He angrily retorted that such a verse was not in the Qur'án and that I was uttering slander to the Prophet of Islam by attributing such a verse to the Holy Book. Of course I could have asked for a copy of the Book and shown him the verse in question but I knew in so doing he would feel defeated in argument and this would increase his animosity towards the Faith. Therefore in a loving spirit I said, 'I hope that God through His bounty may guide you to the truth.' I further suggested to him that he should try to find the verse in question in the Qur'án, as well as the tradition that I had quoted for him . . . I then requested permission to leave but he said that I could stay the night in his home because all he would have to do would be to wash and purify the dishes I ate from and wash the bedding after I left. I thanked him for the hospitality and left . . .
>
> The following day, Mírzá Ṣádiq searched the Qur'án, found the verse in question and became very ashamed and sorry for the way he had treated me. He then decided to seriously investigate the Cause but he continued to reject the proofs which the teachers of the Faith presented to him until he wrote to 'Abdu'l-Bahá.[287]

In his letter to 'Abdu'l-Bahá, Mírzá Ṣádiq asked certain questions, but instead of sending the letter to 'Abdu'l-Bahá, he kept it in a safe and locked it. He then placed a blank piece of paper in an envelope and asked his wife to send it to 'Abdu'l-Bahá. He assured his wife that if he received answers to his questions, he would acknowledge the truth of the Cause.

Upon receiving the envelope 'Abdu'l-Bahá immediately revealed a Tablet addressed to Mírzá Ṣádiq in which He answered all his questions. When he received the Tablet, Mírzá Ṣádiq was exhilarated beyond words that 'Abdu'l-Bahá had responded to his questions; he went to his wife, prostrated himself at her feet and begged forgiveness for all the opposition that he had shown towards her.

In a later Tablet 'Abdu'l-Bahá reminded Mírzá Ṣádiq that until this point no one had attempted to test a servant (i.e. 'Abdu'l-Bahá) by asking questions and receiving an answer. He reminded him that the same is true of a similar situation in the Qur'án. Having conveyed to him that it is not for man to test God, 'Abdu'l-Bahá mentioned that He has responded to his questions merely because of the wonderful services that his wife had rendered to the Cause. She suffered great persecution, remained steadfast in the face of severe opposition and demonstrated the staunchness of her faith. It was clear, 'Abdu'l-Bahá said, that her endeavours in the promotion of the Cause of God had not been in vain; rather, they would be rewarded in the Kingdom, were deeply appreciated by 'Abdu'l-Bahá and were praised by all. In this Tablet 'Abdu'l-Bahá invited the couple to undertake a pilgrimage to the Shrine of Bahá'u'lláh.

After visiting the Holy Shrines and the Master, both husband and wife returned home ablaze with the fire of love for the Master and played an especially important part in the promotion of the Covenant at a time when a few Covenant-breakers such as Jamál-i-Burújirdí were actively engaged in their efforts to mislead the believers in Persia.

The stories of Bas͟hír-i-Iláhí and Mírzá Muḥammad-Ṣádiq demonstrate the fact that the Centre of the Covenant of Bahá'u'lláh had been endowed with powers beyond mortal ken. On countless other occasions the Master, seeing future events, guided the believers both in their personal lives as well as on matters dealing with the Bahá'í community. Indeed, the perusal of His voluminous writings reveals the penetrating influence of His creative words, which inspired the hearts, revealed the innermost mysteries of God's creation and foreshadowed events stretching far into the future, many of which have already taken place.

No Second Guardian to Succeed Shoghi Effendi

'Abdu'l-Bahá states in His Will and Testament:

> **18–WT O ye beloved of the Lord! It is incumbent upon the guardian of the Cause of God to appoint in his own life-time him**

that shall become his successor, that differences may not arise after his passing. He that is appointed must manifest in himself detachment from all worldly things, must be the essence of purity, must show in himself the fear of God, knowledge, wisdom and learning. Thus, should the first-born of the guardian of the Cause of God not manifest in himself the truth of the words: – 'The child is the secret essence of its sire', that is, should he not inherit of the spiritual within him (the guardian of the Cause of God) and his glorious lineage not be matched with a goodly character, then must he, (the guardian of the Cause of God) choose another branch to succeed him.

The second part of the passage shows that 'Abdu'l-Bahá had anticipated the possibility that, even if the Guardian had a son, this son might not have the spiritual qualities to become his successor, and had authorized the Guardian in such a circumstance to 'choose another branch to succeed him'.

However, not only did Shoghi Effendi not have any children but all the Aghṣán* (Branches) mentioned in the above passage had violated the Covenant and had been cast out of the community. That the detailed conditions set out by 'Abdu'l-Bahá for the Guardian's appointment of his successor become inoperative remains a matter which each believer has to ponder in his own heart.

There is a profound wisdom hidden in this episode of successorship, namely, that God tests the believers in order to differentiate between the faithful and the unfaithful. After Shoghi Effendi passed away and the passages in the Will and Testament regarding a successor were not fulfilled, a number of believers were severely tested.

As stated in chapter 2, tests are an integral part of the Revelation of God. In every Dispensation He has tested His servants in various ways. Bahá'u'lláh speaks of this in many of His Tablets. For example, explaining the significance of symbolic terms recorded in heavenly Books of the past, Bahá'u'lláh states in the Kitáb-i-Íqán:

> Know verily that the purpose underlying all these symbolic terms and abstruse allusions, which emanate from the Revealers of God's holy Cause, hath been to test and prove the peoples of the world; that thereby the earth of the pure and illuminated hearts may be known from the perishable and barren soil. From time immemorial such hath been the way of God amidst His creatures, and to this testify the records of the sacred books.[288]

---

* Plural of Ghuṣn (Branch), an Arabic term used by Bahá'u'lláh to refer exclusively to His male descendants. Thus 'Abdu'l-Bahá was designated Ghuṣn-i-A'ẓam (the Most Great Branch). Shoghi Effendi is referred to by 'Abdu'l-Bahá as Ghuṣn-i-Mumtáz (the Chosen Branch).

In other passages in the same book Bahá'u'lláh elaborates further on the tests created by certain events in the lives of the Manifestations of old:

> But inasmuch as the divine Purpose hath decreed that the true should be known from the false, and the sun from the shadow, He hath, therefore, in every season sent down upon mankind the showers of tests from His realm of glory.
>
> ... For instance, consider Moses, son of 'Imrán, one of the exalted Prophets and Author of a divinely-revealed Book. Whilst passing, one day, through the market, in His early days, ere His ministry was proclaimed, He saw two men engaged in fighting. One of them asked the help of Moses against his opponent. Whereupon, Moses intervened and slew him. To this testifieth the record of the sacred Book [the Qur'án] ... While returning [from Midian,] Moses entered the holy vale, situate in the wilderness of Sinai, and there beheld the vision of the King of glory from the 'Tree that belongeth neither to the East nor to the West'. There He heard the soul-stirring Voice of the Spirit speaking from out of the kindled Fire, bidding Him to shed upon Pharaonic souls the light of divine guidance ...
>
> And now ponder in thy heart the commotion which God stirreth up. Reflect upon the strange and manifold trials with which He doth test His servants. Consider how He hath suddenly chosen from among His servants, and entrusted with the exalted mission of divine guidance Him Who was known as guilty of homicide, Who, Himself, had acknowledged His cruelty, and Who for well-nigh thirty years had, in the eyes of the world, been reared in the home of Pharaoh and been nourished at his table. Was not God, the omnipotent King, able to withhold the hand of Moses from murder, so that manslaughter should not be attributed unto Him, causing bewilderment and aversion among the people?[289]

Concerning the tests associated with the person of Jesus Christ, Bahá'u'lláh states:

> And now, meditate upon this most great convulsion, this grievous test. Notwithstanding all these things, God conferred upon that essence of the Spirit, Who was known amongst the people as fatherless, the glory of Prophethood, and made Him His testimony unto all that are in heaven and on earth.
>
> Behold how contrary are the ways of the Manifestations of God, as ordained by the King of creation, to the ways and desires of men![290]

There were many tests in the Islamic Dispensation. Bahá'u'lláh refers to one of them in the Kitáb-i-Íqán:

> And likewise, reflect upon the revealed verse concerning the 'Qiblih'.* When Muhammad [sic], the Sun of Prophethood, had fled from the day-spring of Baṭḥá [Mecca] unto Yat͟hrib [Medina], He continued to turn His face, while praying, unto Jerusalem, the holy city, until the time when the Jews began to utter unseemly words against Him – words which if mentioned would ill befit these pages and would weary the reader. Muḥammad strongly resented these words. Whilst, wrapt in meditation and wonder, He was gazing toward heaven, He heard the kindly Voice of Gabriel, saying: 'We behold Thee from above, turning Thy face to heaven; but We will have Thee turn to a Qiblih which shall please Thee.'† On a subsequent day, when the Prophet, together with His companions, was offering the noontide prayer, and had already performed two of the prescribed Rik'ats [prostrations], the Voice of Gabriel was heard again: 'Turn Thou Thy face towards the sacred Mosque [at Mecca].'‡ In the midst of that same prayer, Muḥammad suddenly turned His face away from Jerusalem and faced the Ka'bih. Whereupon, a profound dismay seized suddenly the companions of the Prophet. Their faith was shaken severely. So great was their alarm, that many of them, discontinuing their prayer, apostatized their faith. Verily, God caused not this turmoil but to test and prove His servants. Otherwise, He, the ideal King, could easily have left the Qiblih unchanged, and could have caused Jerusalem to remain the Point of Adoration unto His Dispensation, thereby withholding not from that holy city the distinction of acceptance which had been conferred upon it.[291]

In this Dispensation, too, there have been many causes for people to be tested. For example, the fact that Bahá'u'lláh had three wives at the same time has become a barrier for those who do not understand the circumstances and traditions of the time.** The faith of a number of the believers has also been tested by the laws of Bahá'u'lláh in the Kitáb-i-Aqdas. And above all, the terms of the Covenant as revealed in the Kitáb-i-'Ahd and the Will and Testament of 'Abdu'l-Bahá have provided severe tests for the believers. Such tests become barriers for those people whose vision does not extend beyond their own way of thinking. Only through an unbiased and earnest search for truth, conducted in a prayerful attitude, can these matters be clarified and many barriers preventing the individual from recognizing the truth be removed.

---

* The direction towards which the face must be turned when praying.

† Qur'án 2:144.

‡ Qur'án 2:149.

** For further details see chapter 2.

36

Shoghi Effendi's Statements about Future Guardians

Among the tests referred to in the previous chapter are three specific factors which puzzled some of the believers:

- Why Shoghi Effendi left no will
- What the significance was of the provision in 'Abdu'l-Bahá's Will and Testament requiring the nine Hands of the Cause to assent to the Guardian's appointment of his successor
- The statement in *The Dispensation of Bahá'u'lláh* about the inseparability of the institutions of the Guardianship and the Universal House of Justice

A thorough study of these items will make it clear how each one, while creating further tests for the believers, was divinely ordained and contributed significantly both to the unfoldment of the Administrative Order and to a better comprehension of the mysterious forces of the Covenant of Bahá'u'lláh.

It is important to bear in mind that a true understanding of these issues depends upon each believer deeply studying the holy writings in a prayerful attitude and examining the nature of the Covenant to discover the mysteries hidden in its innermost reality. To assist in this process, some explanation of these important issues is set down in the following pages.

In numerous letters Shoghi Effendi expounded in great detail the function of the Guardianship and the weighty responsibilities which the Master had placed upon that institution. In many instances he referred to future Guardians. Yet, at least towards the end of his life, Shoghi Effendi was fully aware that there was no one qualified to fill the position of Guardian after him and no one knew better than he that he had no offspring. Nevertheless, in 1954, three years before he passed away, Shoghi Effendi wrote about the administrative Seat of the Guardianship to be built on Mount Carmel.

If one takes these statements at their face value, one can be mystified about Shoghi Effendi's intentions. However, as we examine his relationship to the Master, the reason for such statements and the wisdom behind them become clear.

Throughout his ministry, the Guardian spoke and wrote in the context of the Will and Testament of 'Abdu'l-Bahá and acted in harmony with the Master's words. He never uttered a word to contradict or appear to contradict the statements of 'Abdu'l-Bahá in that important document. In His Will and Testament 'Abdu'l-Bahá categorically confirmed the position of the successors to Shoghi Effendi. In compliance with the Will and Testament, knowing that the Hand of God was involved, Shoghi Effendi remained, throughout his life, silent on the question of his own successor as Guardian.

The Question of Shoghi Effendi's Will

Soon after the passing of Shoghi Effendi the body of the Hands of the Cause of God, designated by him as the 'Chief Stewards of Bahá'u-'lláh's embryonic World Commonwealth',* informed the Bahá'í world that a thorough investigation revealed that Shoghi Effendi had not left a will.

As we look at the history of the unfoldment of the Covenant, we note that in the Kitáb-i-'Ahd Bahá'u'lláh appointed 'Abdu'l-Bahá as the Centre of His Covenant; in the Will and Testament 'Abdu'l-Bahá, in turn, appointed Shoghi Effendi as Guardian of the Faith. In both cases, the faithful knew where to turn. But Shoghi Effendi did not leave a will and this caused some to become perplexed. Indeed, Bahá'ís all over the world had taken it for granted that the Guardian would follow the same practice as Bahá'u'lláh and 'Abdu'l-Bahá and would appoint his successor.

That Shoghi Effendi did not write a will was due to the circumstances of his ministry and his life. He was a most meticulous person who never left anything to chance, especially in such a vital issue as writing a will and testament in which he was to appoint a successor.

One of Bahá'u'lláh's injunctions in the Kitáb-i-Aqdas is that every Bahá'í should write a will and testament and that foremost in it he should bear witness to the oneness of God in the Dayspring of His Revelation, Bahá'u'lláh. This confession of faith is to be a testimony for him in both this world and the next. A will also directs the distribution of wealth among one's heirs.

---

* See chapter 33.

Regarding the first requirement, Shoghi Effendi's letter entitled *The Dispensation of Bahá'u'lláh* is one of the finest declarations of faith ever written. Indeed, we may say that through writing this remarkable document, Shoghi Effendi fulfilled the requirement of the Kitáb-i-Aqdas. As to the second requirement for a will, which is the bequest of a person's wealth to his heirs, Shoghi Effendi did not have any worldly possessions and therefore had no need to distribute them. Thus from this perspective it can be said that Shoghi Effendi followed Bahá'u'lláh's injunction with regard to the writing of a will.

As to the appointment of a successor, the Master had stated in His Will and Testament that should the 'first-born' of the Guardian not inherit his spiritual qualities, he should appoint another Ghuṣn (Branch). As already noted, the word Ghuṣn was used by Bahá'u'lláh to signify His male descendants exclusively. Shoghi Effendi was not in a position to appoint a successor because he had no son and there was not a single Ghuṣn who was faithful to the Cause of God. Every one of the descendants of 'Abdu'l-Bahá had been declared a Covenant-breaker.

Not only was Shoghi Effendi unable to appoint a successor but he made no written statement of this situation. In this connection we must remember that Shoghi Effendi was the Interpreter of the Word of God. This allowed him to explain everything in the writings of Bahá'u'lláh and 'Abdu'l-Bahá and apply their teachings and commandments within the framework of the exigencies of the time. What Shoghi Effendi could not do, however, was to pronounce on subjects not recorded in the holy writings. These fell within the purview of the Universal House of Justice, which alone has the authority to legislate on matters not revealed by the pen of Bahá'u'lláh or 'Abdu'l-Bahá.

Since 'Abdu'l-Bahá's Will and Testament did not indicate the course to be taken should there be no Ghuṣn to succeed the Guardian, the resolution of this question did not fall within the domain of the Guardianship; it was the prerogative of the Universal House of Justice to find a solution. The authority of the House of Justice to legislate on matters which are not in the Book was primarily given by Bahá'u'lláh, as seen in the following passage:

> It is incumbent upon the Trustees of the House of Justice to take counsel together regarding those things which have not outwardly been revealed in the Book, and to enforce that which is agreeable to them. God will verily inspire them with whatsoever He willeth, and He, verily, is the Provider, the Omniscient.[292]

After the passing of Shoghi Effendi, the tests facing the believers were, in some respects, far greater than those that had descended upon the earlier believers as a result of the passing of Bahá'u'lláh or 'Abdu'l-Bahá. This time there was no will and testament; Shoghi Effendi was gone and the believers were left on their own. In spite of this, the institutions of the Administrative Order that were born of the Covenant and had been raised by Shoghi Effendi had been strengthened to such a point that practically the whole Bahá'í world community remained loyal to the Cause and its institutions. The believers of every land remained united as one soul in many bodies and for over two years after the passing of Shoghi Effendi there was no voice of dissent anywhere. All the believers turned to the Hands of the Cause of God and national and local spiritual assemblies declared their loyalty to them. There was never in the history of the Faith a time when the believers demonstrated such unity and solidarity and this in spite of the uncertainty created by the circumstances resulting from the passing of Shoghi Effendi. Indeed, this is the best proof of the indestructibility of the Covenant of Bahá'u'lláh.

As we shall see later, in April 1960 Charles Mason Remey, a Hand of the Cause of God, made a preposterous claim to be the second Guardian. He was eventually declared a Covenant-breaker and died in ignominy some years later.

The Authority of the Hands of the Cause to Assent to the Guardian's Choice of Successor

In the Will and Testament, 'Abdu'l-Bahá places the special responsibility of approving the choice of the Guardian upon the Hands of the Cause of God:

> **19–WT The Hands of the Cause of God must elect from their own number nine persons that shall at all times be occupied in the important services in the work of the guardian of the Cause of God. The election of these nine must be carried either unanimously or by majority from the company of the Hands of the Cause of God and these, whether unanimously or by a majority vote, must give their assent to the choice of the one whom the guardian of the Cause of God hath chosen as his successor. This assent must be given in such wise as the assenting and dissenting voices may not be distinguished (i.e., secret ballot).**

As previously noted, Shoghi Effendi did not appoint Hands of the Cause until 1951. After that date it was impossible for him to appoint someone to succeed him as the next Guardian. Therefore there was no occasion for him to implement 'Abdu'l-Bahá's instructions in this regard.

Indeed, the Hands, like the rest of the believers, did not know what would happen after Shoghi Effendi's passing. The general expectation was that the Guardian would live a long life and many thought that the question of successorship would be clarified by him later. But the Guardian unexpectedly passed away in 1957 at the age of 60 and from the time of his death until the Universal House of Justice made the following pronouncement, the question of a successor to Shoghi Effendi remained unresolved.

In October 1963, the Universal House of Justice wrote:

> After prayerful and careful study of the Holy Texts bearing upon the question of the appointment of the successor to Shoghi Effendi as Guardian of the Cause of God, and after prolonged consultation which included consideration of the views of the Hands of the Cause of God residing in the Holy Land, the Universal House of Justice finds that there is no way to appoint or legislate to make it possible to appoint a second Guardian to succeed Shoghi Effendi.[293]

The importance of this provision of 'Abdu'l-Bahá's Will was shown when Mason Remey made a claim to be the second Guardian. The Hands not only did not assent to his claim, they rejected it outright.

We now return to the final issue that seriously tested the faith of the believers:

The Inseparability of the Two Institutions of the Guardianship and the Universal House of Justice

When it became clear that there would be no Guardian to succeed Shoghi Effendi, a number of believers were troubled by the following statement by Shoghi Effendi in *The Dispensation of Bahá'u'lláh*:

> An attempt, I feel, should at the present juncture be made to explain the character and functions of the twin pillars that support this almighty Administrative Structure – the institutions of the Guardianship and of the Universal House of Justice . . .
>
> It should be stated, at the very outset, in clear and unambiguous language, that these twin institutions of the Administrative Order of Bahá'u'lláh should be regarded as divine in origin, essential in their functions and complementary in their aim and purpose. Their common, their fundamental object is to insure the continuity of that divinely-appointed authority which flows from the Source of our Faith, to safeguard the unity of its followers and to maintain the integrity and flexibility of its teachings. Acting in conjunction with each other these two inseparable institutions administer its affairs, coordinate its activities, promote its interests, execute

its laws and defend its subsidiary institutions. Severally, each operates within a clearly defined sphere of jurisdiction; each is equipped with its own attendant institutions – instruments designed for the effective discharge of its particular responsibilities and duties. Each exercises, within the limitations imposed upon it, its powers, its authority, its rights and prerogatives. These are neither contradictory, nor detract in the slightest degree from the position which each of these institutions occupies. Far from being incompatible or mutually destructive, they supplement each other's authority and functions, and are permanently and fundamentally united in their aims.

Divorced from the institution of the Guardianship the World Order of Bahá'u'lláh would be mutilated and permanently deprived of that hereditary principle which, as 'Abdu'l-Bahá has written, has been invariably upheld by the Law of God. 'In all the Divine Dispensations', He states, in a Tablet addressed to a follower of the Faith in Persia, 'the eldest son hath been given extraordinary distinctions. Even the station of prophethood hath been his birthright.' Without such an institution the integrity of the Faith would be imperilled, and the stability of the entire fabric would be gravely endangered. Its prestige would suffer, the means required to enable it to take a long, an uninterrupted view over a series of generations would be completely lacking, and the necessary guidance to define the sphere of the legislative action of its elected representatives would be totally withdrawn.

Severed from the no less essential institution of the Universal House of Justice this same System of the Will of 'Abdu'l-Bahá would be paralyzed in its action and would be powerless to fill in those gaps which the Author of the Kitáb-i-Aqdas has deliberately left in the body of His legislative and administrative ordinances.[294]

Shoghi Effendi's statement that 'divorced' from the institution of the Guardianship the World Order of Bahá'u'lláh would be 'mutilated' does not mean that without the Guardian the House of Justice would be ineffective. He is rather emphasizing the inseparability of the institutions; in other words, the two institutions are 'complementary' in their functions. In explaining this principle of inseparability, the Universal House of Justice wrote to an individual:

As you point out with many quotations, Shoghi Effendi repeatedly stressed the inseparability of these two institutions. Whereas he obviously envisaged their functioning together, it cannot logically be deduced from this that one is unable to function in the absence of the other. During the whole thirty-six years of his Guardianship Shoghi Effendi functioned without the Universal House of Justice. Now the Universal House of Justice must function without the Guardian, but the principle of inseparability remains. The Guardianship does not lose its significance nor position in the Order of

> Bahá'u'lláh merely because there is no living Guardian. We must guard against two extremes: one is to argue that because there is no Guardian all that was written about the Guardianship and its position in the Bahá'í World Order is a dead letter and was unimportant; the other is to be so overwhelmed by the significance of the Guardianship as to underestimate the strength of the Covenant, or to be tempted to compromise with the clear Texts in order to find somehow, in some way, a 'Guardian'.[295]

Indeed, if 'divorced from the institution of the Guardianship' means that the House of Justice without a Guardian is incapacitated, then we might ask, what about Shoghi Effendi functioning without the House of Justice? For he says that 'severed from the no less essential institution of the Universal House of Justice this same System . . . would be paralyzed'. But obviously that was not the case. Functioning without the institution of the House of Justice, Shoghi Effendi brought unprecedented victories to the Cause, as evidenced by the vitality of the institutions of the Cause, the phenomenal achievements of the Bahá'í community, and the spirit of joy, enthusiasm and self-sacrifice which animated its members during his ministry.

Thus, we observe that the words 'divorced from' and 'mutilated' are used in the above celebrated passage to indicate that the twin pillars of the Administrative Order, namely, the institutions of the Guardianship and the Universal House of Justice, are 'inseparable' even when one of them is absent.

That 'Abdu'l-Bahá in His Will and Testament made provision for a successor to Shoghi Effendi did not necessarily mean that there would be one. In this connection, the Universal House of Justice states:

> Future Guardians are clearly envisaged and referred to in the Writings, but there is nowhere any promise or guarantee that the line of Guardians would endure forever; on the contrary there are clear indications that the line could be broken. Yet, in spite of this, there is a repeated insistence in the Writings on the indestructibility of the Covenant and the immutability of God's Purpose for this Day.
>
> One of the most striking passages which envisage the possibility of such a break in the line of Guardians is in the Kitáb-i-Aqdas itself:
>
> > The endowments dedicated to charity revert to God, the Revealer of Signs. No one has the right to lay hold on them without leave from the Dawning-Place of Revelation. After Him the decision rests with the Aghṣán (Branches), and after them with the House of Justice – should it be established in

the world by then – so that they may use these endowments for the benefit of the Sites exalted in this Cause, and for that which they have been commanded by God, the Almighty, the All-Powerful. Otherwise the endowments should be referred to the people of Bahá, who speak not without His leave and who pass no judgement but in accordance with that which God has ordained in this Tablet, they who are the champions of victory betwixt heaven and earth, so that they may spend them on that which has been decreed in the Holy Book by God, the Mighty, the Bountiful.

The passing of Shoghi Effendi in 1957 precipitated the very situation provided for in this passage, in that the line of Aghṣán ended before the House of Justice had been elected. Although, as is seen, the ending of the line of Aghṣán at some stage was provided for, we must never underestimate the grievous loss that the Faith has suffered. God's purpose for mankind remains unchanged, however, and the mighty Covenant of Bahá'u'lláh remains impregnable.[296]

This is one passage in the Kitáb-i-Aqdas to which Shoghi Effendi refers in his *Dispensation of Bahá'u'lláh* when he writes 'the verses of the Kitáb-i-Aqdas the implications of which clearly anticipate the institution of the Guardianship'.[297]

In the verse cited above Bahá'u'lláh states: 'After Him [Bahá'u'lláh] the decision rests with the Aghṣán (Branches).' The word Aghṣán, being plural, indicates that there will be more than one Branch; in this case, two: 'Abdu'l-Bahá, the Most Great Branch, and Shoghi Effendi, the Chosen Branch. This foreshadows a break in the line of the Aghṣán as Bahá'u'lláh states, 'and after them with the House of Justice – should it be established in the world by then'. By 'the House of Justice' is meant the Universal House of Justice, for Bahá'u'lláh refers to it as a world institution.

When Shoghi Effendi passed away, there was no House of Justice. So it can be seen that the above passage in the Kitáb-i-Aqdas was prophetic, in that a period of more than five years separated the passing of Shoghi Effendi from the establishment of the Universal House of Justice, and the Hands of the Cause during this period – 'the people of Bahá who speak not without His leave' – fulfilled the last provision stated in the above text.

We can see, therefore, that the break in the line of Guardians, the custodianship of the Faith by the Hands of the Cause, and the subsequent establishment of the Universal House of Justice were vital developments that were known to Bahá'u'lláh and revealed by Him. The statement, 'The people of Bahá who speak not without His leave' is precisely applicable to the Hands of the Cause, because during the period of the custodianship the Hands of the Cause faithfully carried out the instructions of the Guardian. They did not introduce any innovations in the Faith, nor did they express their own opinions or exert undue influence on the future development of the Bahá'í community throughout the world.

As we meditate on the above passage from the Kitáb-i-Aqdas it becomes clear that the break in the line of the Guardians after Shoghi Effendi was not an unforeseen event. Having foreknowledge of this act, Bahá'u'lláh revealed the sequence of events leading to the establishment of the House of Justice.

Shoghi Effendi also, by implication, referred to the time when there would be no Guardian to direct the affairs of the Cause and the House of Justice would be the Head of the Faith. This reference is found in a letter he wrote to the British National Assembly in 1951, in which he paid the National Assembly a glowing tribute for its launching of the 'Africa Campaign'. This was a historic project in which, for the first time in the history of the Formative Age, four National Spiritual Assemblies in both hemispheres worked together under the direction of the British National Assembly with the aim of establishing the institutions of the Faith on the continent of Africa. Shoghi Effendi hailed this international cooperation as a befitting prelude to the formation of a future world-embracing Crusade in which all National Assemblies would take part. Two years later he launched the Ten Year Crusade.

In the 1951 letter Shoghi Effendi stated that after this Crusade, other international teaching plans would be launched by the Universal House of Justice. These are his words:

> On the success of this enterprise [Ten Year World Crusade], unprecedented in its scope, unique in its character and immense in its spiritual potentialities, must depend the initiation, at a later period in the Formative Age of the Faith, of undertakings embracing within their range all National Assemblies functioning throughout the Bahá'í World, undertakings constituting in themselves a prelude to the launching of world-wide enterprises destined to be embarked upon, in future epochs of that same age, by the Universal House of Justice, that will symbolize the unity and coordinate and unify the activities of these National Assemblies.[298]

Bearing in mind our discussions in this and previous chapters, it is clear that Shoghi Effendi, confident of the indestructibility of the Covenant and assured of divine guidance from the Author of the Faith and the Centre of the Covenant, remained silent on the question of his successor. He knew that the institutions of the Faith which he had reared with such hard work and sacrifice would be able to deal effectively with the situation after his passing, bringing into being the Universal House of Justice, one of the twin successors of Bahá'u'lláh and 'Abdu'l-Bahá and a divinely guided institution forever inseparable from the Guardianship.

37

The Chief Stewards, the Custodians

Shoghi Effendi passed away in the sixty-first year of his life on 4 November 1957, in London, half way through the Ten Year Crusade. His death, caused by a sudden heart attack in his sleep following Asian flu, came as a cruel blow to the Bahá'ís of the world and was yet another test of their steadfastness in the Covenant. This unexpected tragedy plunged the Bahá'í world into a state of utter grief and sorrow and shook the community of the Most Great Name to its foundations. The news flashed around the world in the following cable:

> Shoghi Effendi beloved of all hearts sacred trust given believers by Master passed away sudden heart attack in sleep following Asiatic flu. Urge believers remain steadfast cling institution Hands lovingly reared recently reinforced emphasized by beloved Guardian. Only oneness heart oneness purpose can befittingly testify loyalty all National Assemblies believers departed Guardian who sacrificed self utterly for service Faith.
>
> Rúḥíyyih[299]

Later, the news of the funeral was cabled to the Bahá'í world:

> Beloved all hearts precious Guardian Cause God passed peacefully away yesterday after Asiatic flu. Appeal Hands National Assemblies Auxiliary Boards shelter believers assist meet heartrending supreme test. Funeral our beloved Guardian Saturday London Hands Assembly Board members invited attend any press release should state meeting Hands shortly Haifa will make announcement to Bahá'í world regarding future plans. Urge hold memorial meetings Saturday.
>
> Rúḥíyyih[300]

These two cables were sent to the Bahá'í communities from the city of Haifa, based on a decision that all communications to the Bahá'í world should be issued from its World Centre.

The information that the Hands of the Cause were to meet in Haifa to 'arrange future plans' was welcomed by the Bahá'ís because the Hands had been appointed by the Guardian for the protection and propagation of the Faith and were its highest dignitaries. There were

27 Hands living when Shoghi Effendi passed away and nobody was more suited to advise the believers about the future development of the Cause and to consider the question of a successor to Shoghi Effendi. Almost the entire Bahá'í community expected that the will and testament of Shoghi Effendi would announce the appointment of his successor, as the wills of Bahá'u'lláh and 'Abdu'l-Bahá had done. For almost a month, the Bahá'ís of the world waited anxiously for news of this matter from the beloved and trusted Hands of the Cause but the news, when it finally came, was that the Guardian had left no will.

It is significant that five months before he passed away, Shoghi Effendi sent a cablegram to the Bahá'í world in which he conferred upon the Hands of the Cause the responsibility of protecting the Bahá'í community. In another message one month before his passing, he referred to the Hands as 'the Chief Stewards of Bahá'u'lláh's embryonic World Commonwealth'.* These two messages from Shoghi Effendi contained strong indications regarding the future destiny of the Cause and led the Bahá'í community to rally around the Hands after his passing. The first message, quoted in full in chapter 34, was sent on 4 June 1957.

Under the guidance and loving care of 'Abdu'l-Bahá the infant Faith of Bahá'u'lláh grew up protected from the onslaught of the Covenant-breakers and acquired greater strength and vitality. The message of Bahá'u'lláh reached the peoples both of the East and the West and, although not fully integrated, small Bahá'í communities sprang up in several countries of the world. Again, measures similar to those taken by Bahá'u'lláh were adopted by 'Abdu'l-Bahá when He appointed Shoghi Effendi as the Guardian to nurture the tender and flourishing Faith, which was still vulnerable to attacks from within and without the community.

During the 36 years of the Guardianship Shoghi Effendi built up the foundations of the institutions of the Administrative Order of Bahá'u'lláh, which were to act as channels for the outpouring of the spiritual energies latent in His Revelation. These institutions, which derive their authority from the Kitáb-i-Aqdas and from the Will and Testament of 'Abdu'l-Bahá, became bastions of protection for the Bahá'ís of the world. When Shoghi Effendi passed away, the Administrative Order was well established. By virtue of these institutions the Faith of Bahá'u'lláh had become impregnable and the body of the believers was united and harmonized. The forces of negation, which had attacked the Faith from within after the ascensions of Bahá'u'lláh and 'Abdu'l-Bahá and

* See chapter 33.

which had posed severe threats to its unity, were now impotent to penetrate the mighty stronghold of the Administrative Order that Shoghi Effendi had built up with meticulous care and with so much personal suffering. After the sudden passing of Shoghi Effendi, the Bahá'í community, having learned from the Hands of the Cause that Shoghi Effendi had left no will, was at first shaken and dismayed, but soon it recovered and organised itself to carry on the work without a Guardian. The following are excerpts from the first letter by the Hands of the Cause addressed to the Bahá'ís of the world on this issue:

> Beloved Friends:
>
> Nine days had not yet elapsed after the interment of the sacred remains of our beloved Guardian, Shoghi Effendi, in London, when the Hands of the Cause, to the number of twenty-six, assembled at the World Centre of the Faith, in our capacity as 'Chief Stewards of the embryonic World Commonwealth of Bahá'u'lláh', to consult together on the most tragic situation facing the Bahá'ís since the Ascension of 'Abdu'l-Bahá, and to take all necessary and appropriate measures to safeguard the highest interests of our Faith.
>
> On November 18th the Hands conducted a Memorial Meeting at Bahjí, in the Ḥaram-i-Aqdas surrounding the most sacred Shrine in the Bahá'í world, afterward entering the Holy Tomb itself and prostrating ourselves in utter humility at the Sacred Threshold.
>
> On the following morning, November 19th, nine Hands of the Cause, selected from the Holy Land, and the several continents of East and West, with Amatu'l-Bahá Rúḥíyyih K͟hánum, broke the seals placed upon the beloved Guardian's safe and desk and made careful examination of their precious contents. These same Hands, rejoining the other Hands assembled in the Mansion of Bahá'u'lláh at Bahjí, certified that Shoghi Effendi had left no Will and Testament. It was likewise certified that the beloved Guardian had left no heir. The Ag͟hṣán (branches) one and all are either dead or have been declared violators of the Covenant by the Guardian for their faithlessness to the Master's Will and Testament and their hostility to him named first Guardian in that sacred document.
>
> The first effect of the realization that no successor to Shoghi Effendi could have been appointed by him was to plunge the Hands of the Cause into the very abyss of despair. What must happen to the world community of his devoted followers if the Leader, the Inspirer, the Planner of all Bahá'í activities in all countries and islands of the seas could no longer fulfil his unique mission?
>
> From this dark abyss, however, contemplation of the Guardian's own life of complete sacrifice and his peerless services gradually redeemed our anguished hearts. Shoghi Effendi himself, we know, would have been the first to remind the Hands, and the widespread body of the believers, that the Dispensation of Bahá'u'lláh

has quickened those powers and resources of faith within mankind which will achieve the unity of the peoples and the triumph of His World Order. In this new light of understanding the company of the Hands could perceive with heightened gratitude the existence of those innumerable blessings which Shoghi Effendi had created and left as his true legacy to all Bahá'ís.

Has not the World Centre, with its sacred Shrines and institutions, been firmly established? Has not the Message been established in 254 countries and dependencies? Have not the National and Regional Spiritual Assemblies, forerunners of the Universal House of Justice, been implanted in twenty-six great areas of all continents? Has not the Guardian left us not only his incomparable translations, for English-reading Bahá'ís, of the Bahá'í sacred literature but also his own master works of interpretation which disclose to us the unshatterable edifice of an evolving Bahá'í Order and world community? Has not the Guardian, building upon the enduring foundation of the Master's Tablets of the Divine Plan, created the World Crusade to guide our work until 1963?

. . . Such reflections could but, in such a world-shattering experience as all Bahá'ís have this month endured, reveal to us how strongly Shoghi Effendi has laid the foundations of the World Order of Bahá'u'lláh through the appointment of Hands of the Cause and likewise the appointment of the International Bahá'í Council, the institution destined to evolve into the Universal House of Justice.

In our capacity of Chief Stewards of the embryonic World Commonwealth of Bahá'u'lláh, we Hands of the Cause have constituted a body of nine Hands to serve at the Bahá'í World Centre. This body of nine Hands will energetically deal with the protection of the Faith whenever attacks, whether from within or outside the Bahá'í community, are reported by Hands from their areas or by National or Regional Assemblies, or whether they arise within the Holy Land. Correspondence will likewise be maintained with the Hands of the Cause working in the several continents. This same body will correspond with National Assemblies on matters connected with the prosecution of the objectives of the Ten Year Plan. On matters involving administrative questions this same body will assist National Assemblies by citing those passages of the Bahá'í sacred literature which direct the Assemblies to a sound solution.

As to the International Bahá'í Council, appointed by the Guardian and heralded in his communications to the Bahá'í world, that body will in the course of time finally fulfil its purpose through the formation of the Universal House of Justice, that supreme body upon which infallibility, as the Master's Testament assures us, is divinely conferred: 'The source of all good and freed from all error.' . . .

Meanwhile the entire body of the Hands assembled by the nine Hands of the World Centre will decide when and how the International Bahá'í Council is to evolve through the successive stages outlined by the Guardian, culminating in the call to election of the Universal House of Justice by the membership of all National Spiritual Assemblies.

When that divinely ordained Body comes into existence, all the conditions of the Faith can be examined anew and the measures necessary for its future operation determined in consultation with the Hands of the Cause.[301]

The believers faithfully rallied around the Hands of the Cause, who now assumed the function of guiding the Bahá'í world. All National Spiritual Assemblies declared their loyalty to the Hands and turned to that institution with devotion. The nine Hands appointed to serve at the World Centre were referred to as 'Custodians of the Faith'. From the outset the Hands made it clear to the Bahá'ís that, unlike the Guardian and the Universal House of Justice, the Hands were not promised infallible guidance. The only way that they could carry out their responsibilities satisfactorily was to follow faithfully the provisions of the Ten Year Plan as delineated by the Guardian. In this way, there was no danger of misguiding the community.

The greatest achievement of the Hands in this period is that they did not deviate a hair's breadth from the teachings and guidance of Shoghi Effendi. For more than five years they held the reins of the Cause in their hands – a period that may be regarded as the most critical stage in the history of the Faith of Bahá'u'lláh. From the day the Faith was born until the passing of Shoghi Effendi divine protection had been vouchsafed to the community. For 113 years the infant Faith of Bahá'u'lláh had been nurtured by the infallible guidance of its Central Figures and its Guardian. Now it was entrusted to the care of a number of religious leaders, the Hands of the Cause, who did not have this promise of divine guidance.

It was a period fraught with dangers. In the same way that a newly built airplane is subjected to a series of rigorous tests in order to be sure that it works properly, the Covenant of Bahá'u'lláh was severely tried during these six years and found to be absolutely impregnable. The custodianship of the Hands was itself a proof of the invincibility of the Covenant, in that, unlike the leaders of former religions who introduced many man-made practices into the teachings of their Prophets, the Hands of the Cause did not add even a single dot to the Cause, nor did they introduce any innovation into the workings of its institutions. They guided the Bahá'í community strictly in accordance with the holy text and the writings of the Guardian. Their responses to questions from National Spiritual Assemblies and individuals were based on the holy writings and if they could not find the answer in the Tablets of Bahá'u'lláh or 'Abdu'l-Bahá or in the letters of Shoghi Effendi they strictly refrained from making any pronouncement. Such questions were left to be determined by the Universal House of Justice in the future.

The Hands acted with such loyalty that when they handed over the Cause of God, pure and unadulterated, to the elected body of the Universal House of Justice in 1963 the whole Bahá'í world acclaimed their devotion. This generation and those yet unborn owe the Hands of the Cause an immeasurable debt of gratitude. Through their faithfulness they took the Ark of the Covenant from the hands of the Guardian, steered it for over five years through treacherous waters, brought it safely to the shores of salvation and humbly delivered it into the hands of the Universal House of Justice.

This period witnessed the emergence of a new brand of Covenant-breakers, headed by Mason Remey, who had himself been appointed a Hand of the Cause of God by Shoghi Effendi and was one of the signatories of the first declaration of the Hands issued after the passing of Shoghi Effendi. In order to appreciate the genesis of this rebellion against the Covenant we must look back at the Bahá'í community as it was then.

At that time there were some believers who thought that the Faith must always have a Guardian. When it became clear that Shoghi Effendi had not appointed a successor, some Bahá'ís failed to appreciate the true significance of Shoghi Effendi's silence in this matter. Because they had not understood the spirit of the Covenant of Bahá'u'lláh, they insisted that a second Guardian must be created. Mason Remey, after a distinguished life of service, succumbed to both ambition and arrogance, which impelled him, without any word of instruction from Shoghi Effendi, to concoct the extraordinarily tortuous argument on which he based his claim to the Guardianship and assumed for himself the responsibility of guiding the Bahá'í world.

In His Will and Testament 'Abdu'l-Bahá extolled Shoghi Effendi as the 'sign of God', the 'chosen branch', the 'blest and sacred bough that hath branched out from the Twin Holy Trees', 'the most wondrous, unique and priceless pearl that doth gleam from out the Twin surging seas'. Such a being was created by God especially to be the Guardian of the Cause and his appointment was made by the Centre of the Covenant Himself. He was a descendant both of Bahá'u'lláh and of the family of the Báb. How could a few individuals who looked for leadership and sought power for their own selfish interests raise up a lesser man to the station of the Guardianship? In His Will and Testament, 'Abdu'l-Bahá laid down the conditions that Shoghi Effendi's successor must be either the 'first-born' of the Guardian or another Ghuṣn (male descendant of Bahá'u'lláh) and that the Hands of the Cause must give their assent to his choice. How could Mason Remey fulfil these conditions? It is interesting to note that, in a Tablet to the Hand of the Cause of God Mullá 'Alí-Akbar, 'Abdu'l-Bahá makes this important statement:

> . . . for 'Abdu'l-Bahá is in a tempest of dangers and infinitely abhors differences of opinion . . . Praise be to God, there are no grounds for differences.
>
> The Báb, the Exalted One, is the Morn of Truth, the splendour of Whose light shineth through all regions. He is also the Harbinger of the Most Great Light, the Abhá Luminary. The Blessed Beauty is the One promised by the sacred books of the past, the revelation of the Source of light that shone upon Mount Sinai, Whose fire glowed in the midst of the Burning Bush. We are, one and all, servants of Their threshold, and stand each as a lowly keeper at Their door.
>
> My purpose is this, that ere the expiration of a thousand years, no one has the right to utter a single word, even to claim the station of Guardianship. The Most Holy Book is the Book to which all peoples shall refer, and in it the Laws of God have been revealed. Laws not mentioned in the Book should be referred to the decision of the Universal House of Justice. There will be no grounds for difference . . . Beware, beware lest anyone create a rift or stir up sedition.[302]

After Mason Remey made his absurd claim, the Hands of the Cause in the Holy Land tried their utmost to bring him to his senses. But in his delusion he persisted on his errant course; consequently he and those few who followed him were declared to be Covenant-breakers. The Bahá'í community was once again purged by this process; the impurities that would have imposed dire afflictions upon the Faith, had they been allowed to remain within the fold, were cast out, resulting in the revitalization of the body of the Cause of God.

This episode of Covenant-breaking by Mason Remey was one of the flimsiest of all rebellions in the history of the Faith. It did not take very long before a number of those who had been misled by him realized their mistake, repented and returned to the community or withdrew from the Faith altogether. Mason Remey's efforts to form a following for himself failed miserably. Ultimately, he went so far as to deny the infallibility of Shoghi Effendi and to impute errors to 'Abdu'l-Bahá. After his death, serious rivalries broke out between his lieutenants, who claimed to be his successors. The divinely ordained instruments serving the Covenant of Bahá'u'lláh have been so strengthened today that the efforts of this group of Covenant-breakers have come to naught and the power of the Covenant has driven them into oblivion.

Those few who gathered around Mason Remey – and others who in recent times have taken his place – have tried to justify their rebellion against the Covenant. They misled themselves through their interpretation of the word 'branch' mentioned in the Will and Testament of 'Abdu'l-Bahá regarding a successor to Shoghi Effendi. They claimed that since Bahá'u'lláh referred to human beings as 'the fruits of one tree and the leaves of one branch', any believer was a branch who could succeed Shoghi Effendi. This assumption was made either through self-deception or ignorance – or perhaps both. The word Ghuṣn (branch), used by Bahá'u'lláh to refer to His male descendants, is Arabic; the term in the other passage is Persian and is a different word, never used by Bahá'u'lláh to refer to His male descendants. Both, however, have been translated into English as 'branch'.

Before Mason Remey's preposterous claim, the wisdom of the words of 'Abdu'l-Bahá in His Will and Testament that the Hands of the Cause 'must give their assent to the choice of the one whom the guardian of the Cause of God hath chosen as his successor' was not clear to some. But after Remey's defection, it became evident that this requirement was a means for the protection of the Cause of God. Far from assenting to the validity of his appointment as successor to Shoghi Effendi, the Hands were able unanimously to deny it.

Propelled by the forces of the Covenant, during the custodianship of the Hands of the Cause of God the Faith of Bahá'u'lláh advanced to such an extent as to eclipse the victories that had been won in preceding decades. The teaching work in five continents of the globe was intensified as the believers exerted themselves to win the goals of the Ten Year Crusade that the Guardian had formulated. Great numbers entered the Faith, especially in Africa, Latin America and Asia. Tens of thousands swelled the number of believers in the subcontinent of India when the Bahá'í community there experienced large scale entry by troops. The number of local spiritual assemblies, the bedrock upon which the national spiritual assemblies were established, vastly increased and more national spiritual assemblies were also formed during the remaining years of the Ten Year Crusade.

In 1961 the Hands of the Cause arranged for the election of the International Bahá'í Council, the forerunner of the Universal House of Justice. The electors were members of the national spiritual assemblies that were functioning at the time in the five continents of the globe. In this way the International Bahá'í Council, whose members had been appointed by the Guardian, was transformed into an elected body.

The call for the election of the Universal House of Justice was made by the Hands of the Cause in their message of 5 November 1961 to the Bahá'í world, from which the following excerpts are taken:

> With the erection in 1962 of twelve more future pillars* of that supreme legislative Body of the Bahá'í world, a firm foundation will have been laid for the election of 'that Universal House of Justice which', Shoghi Effendi stated, 'as its title implies, is to be the exponent and guardian of that Divine Justice which can alone ensure the security of, and establish the reign of law and order in, a strangely disordered world.'
>
> We are now able to envisage the steps that must still be taken before that 'Ark' referred to in Bahá'u'lláh's prophetic Tablet of Carmel shall come into being, an ark whose dwellers, the Guardian told us, 'are the men of the Supreme House of Justice which, in conformity with the exact provisions of the Will and Testament of the Centre of the Mighty Covenant, is the Body which should legislate on laws not explicitly revealed in the Text. In this Dispensation, these laws are destined to flow from this Holy Mountain, even as in the Mosaic Dispensation the law of God was promulgated from Zion.'
>
> The Chief Stewards of the Faith are therefore calling a Convention in the Holy Land for the election of the Universal House of Justice on the first, second and third days of Riḍván, 1963. The members of all National and Regional Spiritual Assemblies elected by the Bahá'ís in Riḍván, 1962, will, in conformity with the teachings, constitute the electoral body empowered to vote for this crowning unit of the embryonic World Order of Bahá'u'lláh, upon whose deliberations the unique bounty of receiving divine inspiration has been bestowed, and whose decisions are infallibly guided by both the Báb and Bahá'u'lláh.
>
> After long and conscientious consideration of the needs of the present hour and the writings of our dearly-loved Guardian, the following decision has been reached: All male voting members throughout the Bahá'í world are eligible for election to the Universal House of Justice. The Hands of the Cause do not limit the freedom of the electors. However, as they have been given the explicit duties of guarding over the security and ensuring the propagation of the Faith, they ask the electors to leave them free at this time to discharge their duties. When that supreme and infallible Body has been elected it will decide on all matters concerning its own membership.[303]

On 21 April 1963, exactly one hundred years after the declaration of Bahá'u'lláh in the Garden of Riḍván in Baghdád, the members of

---

* National spiritual assemblies. These twelve national spiritual assemblies (11 in Europe, one in Ceylon) brought the number of national spiritual assemblies in the world to 56.

56 national spiritual assemblies throughout the world took part in the election of the Universal House of Justice. The voting occurred in the home of 'Abdu'l-Bahá in Haifa, in a profoundly spiritual atmosphere. Thus the 'sailing of the Ark upon Mount Carmel', prophesied by Bahá'u'lláh, took place and the House of Justice came into being. It was a moment of relief and supreme joy for the members of the national spiritual assemblies and the Hands of the Cause to witness the birth of an institution which is to be the source of divine guidance until the end of this Dispensation. On this momentous occasion the Hands of the Cause sent the following message to the Bahá'í communities throughout the world:

> OCCASION WORLDWIDE CELEBRATIONS MOST GREAT JUBILEE COMMEMORATING CENTENARY ASCENSION BAHA'U'LLAH THRONE HIS SOVEREIGNTY WITH HEARTS OVERFLOWING GRATITUDE HIS UNFAILING PROTECTION OVERFLOWING BOUNTIES JOYOUSLY ANNOUNCE FRIENDS EAST WEST ELECTION SUPREME LEGISLATIVE BODY ORDAINED BY HIM IN HIS MOST HOLY BOOK PROMISED BY HIM RECEIVE HIS INFALLIBLE GUIDANCE STOP MEMBERS FIRST HISTORIC HOUSE JUSTICE DULY ELECTED BY DELEGATES COMPRISING MEMBERS FIFTYSIX NATIONAL ASSEMBLIES ARE CHARLES WOLCOTT ALI NAKHJAVANI BORRAH KAVELIN IAN SEMPLE LOTFULLAH HAKIM DAVID HOFMAN HUGH CHANCE AMOZ GIBSON HUSHMAND FATHEAZAM STOP TO JUBILATION ENTIRE BAHA'I WORLD VICTORIOUS COMPLETION BELOVED GUARDIAN'S UNIQUE CRUSADE NOW ADDED HUMBLE GRATITUDE PROFOUND THANKSGIVING FOLLOWERS BAHA'U'LLAH FOR ERECTION UNIVERSAL HOUSE JUSTICE AUGUST BODY TO WHOM ALL BELIEVERS MUST TURN WHOSE DESTINY IS TO GUIDE UNFOLDMENT HIS EMBRYONIC WORLD ORDER THROUGH ADMINISTRATIVE INSTITUTIONS PRESCRIBED BY BAHA'U'LLAH ELABORATED BY ABDU'L-BAHA LABORIOUSLY ERECTED BY SHOGHI EFFENDI AND ENSURE EARLY DAWN GOLDEN AGE FAITH WHEN THE WORD OF THE LORD WILL COVER THE EARTH AS THE WATERS COVER THE SEA STOP. . .[304]

38

The Universal House of Justice

Bahá'u'lláh ordained the institution of the Universal House of Justice as a channel of divine guidance and endowed it with infallibility. These are His words, as revealed in the Kalimát-i-Firdawsíyyih:

> It is incumbent upon the Trustees of the House of Justice to take counsel together regarding those things which have not outwardly been revealed in the Book, and to enforce that which is agreeable to them. God will verily inspire them with whatsoever He willeth, and He, verily, is the Provider, the Omniscient.[305]

Further, in the Tablet of Ishráqát, Bahá'u'lláh states:

> This passage, now written by the Pen of Glory, is accounted as part of the Most Holy Book: The men of God's House of Justice have been charged with the affairs of the people. They, in truth, are the Trustees of God among His servants and the daysprings of authority in His countries.
>
> O people of God! That which traineth the world is Justice, for it is upheld by two pillars, reward and punishment. These two pillars are the sources of life to the world. Inasmuch as for each day there is a new problem and for every problem an expedient solution, such affairs should be referred to the House of Justice that the members thereof may act according to the needs and requirements of the time. They that, for the sake of God, arise to serve His Cause, are the recipients of divine inspiration from the unseen Kingdom. It is incumbent upon all to be obedient unto them. All matters of State should be referred to the House of Justice, but acts of worship must be observed according to that which God hath revealed in His Book.[306]

In the same Tablet Bahá'u'lláh further enjoins the men of the House of Justice to train people and raise up the nations:

> It is incumbent upon the men of God's House of Justice to fix their gaze by day and by night upon that which hath shone forth from the Pen of Glory for the training of peoples, the upbuilding of nations, the protection of man and the safeguarding of his honour.[307]

These passages revealed by the Author of the Faith demonstrate that the Universal House of Justice derives its authority directly from Bahá'u'lláh Himself. There is also the promise of divine guidance which He vouchsafes unto that Body, for He says: 'God will verily inspire them with whatsoever He willeth . . .'[308]

The authority and infallibility which Bahá'u'lláh has conferred upon the Universal House of Justice have been further strengthened by the words of the Master in His Tablets, especially the following passages of His Will and Testament:

> **17–WT The sacred and youthful branch, the guardian of the Cause of God as well as the Universal House of Justice, to be universally elected and established, are both under the care and protection of the Abhá Beauty, under the shelter and unerring guidance of His Holiness, the Exalted One (may my life be offered up for them both). Whatsoever they decide is of God. Whoso obeyeth him not, neither obeyeth them, hath not obeyed God . . .**

And again He writes:

> **36–WT This is the foundation of the belief of the people of Bahá (may my life be offered up for them): 'His Holiness, the Exalted One (the Báb), is the Manifestation of the Unity and Oneness of God and the Forerunner of the Ancient Beauty. His Holiness the Abhá Beauty (may my life be a sacrifice for His steadfast friends) is the Supreme Manifestation of God and the Dayspring of His Most Divine Essence. All others are servants unto Him and do His bidding.' Unto the Most Holy Book every one must turn and all that is not expressly recorded therein must be referred to the Universal House of Justice. That which this body, whether unanimously or by a majority doth carry, that is verily the Truth and the Purpose of God Himself. Whoso doth deviate therefrom is verily of them that love discord, hath shown forth malice and turned away from the Lord of the Covenant.**

With the creation of the Universal House of Justice a new era opened in the history of the Bahá'í Faith. Divine guidance had been vouchsafed to the community for almost 113 years, first through the persons of the Manifestations of God, then through the chosen Centre of the Cause and the authorized interpreter of His words. But now, with the passing of Shoghi Effendi and the establishment of the Universal House of Justice, the vehicle of that guidance was changed from the channel of an individual, organically linked to the Manifestation of God, to an elected body of fallible members whose collective resolutions are guided by Bahá'u'lláh, who conferred infallibility upon the institution.

This provision of the continuity of divine guidance on matters which are within the prerogative of the House of Justice, and which are clearly defined to exclude any changes to the laws, the teachings and other provisions revealed in the Bahá'í scriptures, is unique in the history of religion. Never before has a Manifestation of God given authority to a council elected by universal suffrage to enact laws and administer the affairs of His religion with the assurance that it will be guided by God in its decisions. In this Dispensation, the Covenant of Bahá'u'lláh has provided mankind with the continuity of divine guidance on all problems that have caused differences, questions that are obscure, and matters that are not expressly recorded in the Book.

The manner of the election of the Universal House of Justice has been prescribed by 'Abdu'l-Bahá in His Will and Testament:

> **36–WT By this House is meant that Universal House of Justice which is to be elected from all countries, that is from those parts in the East and West where the loved ones are to be found, after the manner of the customary elections in Western countries such as those of England.**

The Universal House of Justice was instituted in 1963, when members of the national spiritual assemblies, in a prayerful attitude and in an atmosphere of intense spirituality and profound devotion, elected as members of this supreme institution nine souls from among the Bahá'ís of the world. The occasion is considered by the Bahá'ís to be, next to the appointment of Shoghi Effendi as the Guardian of the Faith, the most momentous event in the history of the Formative Age of the Faith. Even the manner of the election itself was befitting that institution described as the 'sole refuge of a tottering civilization'. The election of the Universal House of Justice now takes place every five years in the same atmosphere of spirituality and dedication.

Bahá'í elections are unlike any of the other forms of election currently practised in the various parts of the world. For a Bahá'í, it is an act of devotion to God to elect members of Bahá'í institutions. There are no candidates, no propaganda and no canvassing of any kind and the elections are conducted in a spirit of prayer and meditation. It is a sacred responsibility of the electorate to vote for those 'who can best combine the necessary qualities of unquestioned loyalty, of selfless devotion, of a well-trained mind, of recognized ability and mature experience'.[309] The act of voting in Bahá'í elections is free and secret; even the closest of relatives or friends do not consult together on their choice. To do so would be tantamount to breaking one of God's sacred spiritual commandments.

Every religion has spiritual and moral teachings. The Sermon on the Mount, for example, epitomizing the spiritual and moral teachings of Christ, has made a deep and abiding impression upon the followers of Jesus. Other religions have similar spiritual teachings. The passage of time does not usually affect the reverence with which the adherents view these teachings; for example, Muslims conscientiously carry out the law of daily prayer because they consider this teaching to be God's commandment and regard its violation as a sinful act.

Not until the advent of the Bahá'í Dispensation did a Manifestation of God include administrative principles among His spiritual teachings. Bahá'u'lláh has introduced an entirely new dimension; He has placed the spiritual and administrative principles on a par and so a violation of an administrative principle, such as electioneering, is as grave a betrayal of the Cause of Bahá'u'lláh as breaking a spiritual law. The purity, the integrity and incorruptibility of Bahá'í institutions are thereby preserved and the institutions themselves are protected from malpractice. Because the Universal House of Justice was ordained by Bahá'u'lláh as a channel of divine guidance and endowed by Him with infallibility, it should not be considered as merely the international administrative body of the Faith.

The question of infallibility has already been discussed in the Introduction. The Manifestations of God – in this day, the Báb and Bahá'u'lláh – are inherently possessed of supreme infallibility. In this they are analogous to the sun, which produces its own heat and light, and is thus independent of other sources of energy. But 'Abdu'l-Bahá, Shoghi Effendi and the Universal House of Justice are under the protection of Bahá'u'lláh, who conferred infallibility upon them. They are like the moon, in which light is not inherent but rather reflected by the sun. Their infallibility is validated in the writings of Bahá'u'lláh and 'Abdu'l-Bahá and specifically in Bahá'u'lláh's Kitáb-i-'Ahd (the Book of the Covenant) and the Will and Testament of 'Abdu'l-Bahá. The following are the words of 'Abdu'l-Bahá in this connection:

> To epitomize: essential infallibility belongs especially to the supreme Manifestations, and acquired infallibility is granted to every holy soul. For instance, the Universal House of Justice, if it be established under the necessary conditions – with members elected from all the people – that House of Justice will be under the protection and the unerring guidance of God. If that House of Justice shall decide unanimously, or by a majority, upon any question not mentioned in the Book, that decision and command will be guarded from mistake. Now the members of the House of Justice have not, individually, essential infallibility; but the body of the House of Justice is under the protection and the unerring guidance of God: this is called conferred infallibility.[310]

From study of the writings cited above, it becomes clear that it is an article of faith for a Bahá'í to believe in the authority and infallibility of the Universal House of Justice. An individual embraces the Faith of Bahá'u'lláh when he recognizes Him to be the Manifestation of God for this age. But this is only the beginning of the process of becoming a Bahá'í. The recognition of Bahá'u'lláh must be followed by an acknowledgement of the station of 'Abdu'l-Bahá as the Centre of the Covenant and Shoghi Effendi as the Guardian of the Faith and belief that their words and their interpretations of the holy writings are divinely guided and infallible. Similarly, a Bahá'í must believe that the Universal House of Justice is now the Head of the Faith and its supreme institution, that its pronouncements, legislation and general instructions are all derived from the unerring guidance of Bahá'u'lláh and the Báb, and, in the words of 'Abdu'l-Bahá, 'That which this body, whether unanimously or by a majority doth carry, that is verily the Truth and the Purpose of God Himself.'

It does not seem possible for a person who is not a Bahá'í to accept the House of Justice as 'the source of all good and freed from all error', nor is it possible to prove this statement to him scientifically. The only way that someone can become convinced of the authority and infallibility of the Universal House of Justice is to recognize Bahá'u'lláh as God's Messenger for this age. Then, as a matter of faith, he will be able to accept His assurances in this regard and become convinced of the truths enshrined in His words. As the believer grows in his faith and acquires greater depth in his understanding of the teachings of Bahá'u'lláh, he becomes progressively more assured that the Blessed Beauty 'shall guard it [the Universal House of Justice] from error and will protect it under the wing of His sanctity and infallibility'.

Remarking further on the protection which the Blessed Beauty provides for the Universal House of Justice, the Master states:

> Let it not be imagined that the House of Justice will take any decision according to its own concepts and opinions. God forbid! The Supreme House of Justice will take decisions and establish laws through the inspiration and confirmation of the Holy Spirit, because it is in the safekeeping and under the shelter and protection of the Ancient Beauty, and obedience to its decisions is a bounden and essential duty and an absolute obligation, and there is no escape for anyone.
>
> Say, O People: Verily the Supreme House of Justice is under the wings of your Lord, the Compassionate, the All-Merciful, that is under His protection, His care, and His shelter; for He has commanded the firm believers to obey that blessed, sanctified, and all-subduing body, whose sovereignty is divinely ordained and of

> the Kingdom of Heaven and whose laws are inspired and spiritual.[311]

Even a cursory review of the workings of the House of Justice since its establishment in 1963 makes it clear to a believer that the assurances given by 'Abdu'l-Bahá have all been fulfilled, that every directive issued by that body has been divinely inspired and that every plan it has devised and every act it has carried out have been blessed by Providence. Its achievements and victories, both at the World Centre of the Faith and around the world, and the progress it has made during the last three decades despite its modest resources, have been miraculous. In circumstances of crisis as well as triumph, the House of Justice has been enabled to steer the Bahá'í community on the course set for it by the hand of the Almighty. All these accomplishments are entirely due to the assistance and confirmations of Bahá'u'lláh, which have reached it continuously and guided every step it has taken in the execution of God's plan for mankind.

It is natural that the members of the House of Justice are always conscious of that outpouring of divine assistance; they know only too well that the decisions of the House are guided by Bahá'u'lláh. They have openly declared before their electors their sense of unworthiness to serve on that august institution but have confidently taken on the burden of such immense responsibility in the assurance of the protection, guidance and confirmations of Bahá'u'lláh that reach them during their deliberations.

One of the most important decisions made by the Universal House of Justice soon after its election was to clarify the issue of another Guardian to succeed Shoghi Effendi. As we have already stated in chapter 37, since 'Abdu'l-Bahá remained silent about how to deal with the situation in which there was no lineal descendant of Shoghi Effendi or another Ghuṣn to succeed him as the second Guardian, the question had to be resolved by the House of Justice and not the Guardian of the Faith. The following statement was issued on 6 October 1963:

> After prayerful and careful study of the Holy Texts bearing upon the question of the appointment of the successor to Shoghi Effendi as Guardian of the Cause of God, and after prolonged consultation which included consideration of the views of the Hands of the Cause of God residing in the Holy Land, the Universal House of Justice finds that there is no way to appoint or legislate to make it possible to appoint a second Guardian to succeed Shoghi Effendi.[312]

A similar statement was issued by the House of Justice concerning the Hands of the Cause of God:

> There is no way to appoint, or to legislate to make it possible to appoint, Hands of the Cause of God.
>
> Responsibility for decisions of matters of general policy affecting the institution of the Hands of the Cause, which was formerly exercised by the beloved Guardian, now devolves upon the Universal House of Justice as the supreme and central institution of the Faith to which all must turn.[313]

There were other issues that the House of Justice also had to resolve because the absence of a second Guardian created a situation for which Abdu'l-Bahá had left no guidance and for which no provision had been made. In other words, the holy writings did not deal with certain issues and therefore their resolution needed the legislation of the House of Justice. For example, among the buildings which Shoghi Effendi recommended to be constructed on a far-flung arc on Mount Carmel was the Seat of the institution of the Guardianship, as well as that of the Hands of the Cause. The House of Justice had to legislate to change these into the Centre for the Study of the Sacred Texts and the Seat of the International Teaching Centre.

To give another example of a situation about which there was no specific guidance, 'Abdu'l-Bahá in His Will and Testament states that the Guardian has the right to expel any member of the House of Justice who commits 'a sin injurious to the common weal'. But he does not say what should be done if there is no Guardian and so the House of Justice decided that this function should fall upon the Universal House of Justice itself.

In His Will and Testament, 'Abdu'l-Bahá describes some of the functions of the Universal House of Justice:

> **37–WT It is incumbent upon these members (of the Universal House of Justice) to gather in a certain place and deliberate upon all problems which have caused difference, questions that are obscure and matters that are not expressly recorded in the Book. Whatsoever they decide has the same effect as the Text itself. And inasmuch as this House of Justice hath power to enact laws that are not expressly recorded in the Book and bear upon daily transactions, so also it hath power to repeal the same. Thus for example, the House of Justice enacteth today a certain law and enforceth it, and a hundred years hence, circumstances having profoundly changed and the conditions having altered, another House of Justice will then have power, according to the exigencies of the time, to alter that law. This it can do because that law formeth no part of the Divine Explicit Text. The House of Justice is both the initiator and the abrogator of its own laws.**

25–WT And now, concerning the House of Justice which God hath ordained as the source of all good and freed from all error, it must be elected by universal suffrage, that is, by the believers. Its members must be manifestations of the fear of God and daysprings of knowledge and understanding, must be steadfast in God's faith and the well-wishers of all mankind. By this House is meant the Universal House of Justice, that is, in all countries a secondary House of Justice must be instituted, and these secondary Houses of Justice must elect the members of the Universal one. Unto this body all things must be referred. It enacteth all ordinances and regulations that are not to be found in the explicit Holy Text. By this body all the difficult problems are to be resolved and the guardian of the Cause of God is its sacred head and the distinguished member for life of that body. Should he not attend in person its deliberations, he must appoint one to represent him. Should any of the members commit a sin, injurious to the common weal, the guardian of the Cause of God hath at his own discretion the right to expel him . . .

In these two passages, 'Abdu'l-Bahá gives a wide range of authority to the House of Justice. It has to make decisions on the following:

- 'All problems which cause difference'
- 'Questions that are obscure'
- 'Matters that are not expressly recorded in the Book'
- 'Unto this body all things must be referred'
- 'It enacteth all ordinances and regulations that are not to be found in the explicit Holy Text'
- 'By this body all the difficult problems are to be resolved'

These, together with the exhortations of Bahá'u'lláh Himself, constitute a list of duties and functions which the Universal House of Justice must discharge. These functions exclude 'interpretation of the Holy Text', which is a special prerogative of 'Abdu'l-Bahá and Shoghi Effendi as authorized Interpreters of the Word of God. There is a vast difference between the interpretations of the Guardian and the elucidations of the House of Justice in the exercise of its function to 'deliberate upon all problems which have caused difference, questions that are obscure, and matters that are not expressly recorded in the Book'. The elucidation of the House of Justice originates from its legislative function. It offers guidance and elucidates what must be done in cases where there is some ambiguity in the interpretations of the Guardian or 'Abdu'l-Bahá. The legislation of the House of Justice is based on the elucidation of the issues involved and can be amended by the House of Justice when circumstances change, whereas the interpretations of the Guardian are statements of truth that cannot be changed.

As previously stated, an important feature of the functioning of the House of Justice is that it consults the writings of the Guardian when it begins the process of legislation or is about to make decisions on various issues. In this way, it ensures that its pronouncements are not in conflict with the meaning of the holy text as interpreted by the Guardian. Thus until the end of this Dispensation, there will be a meaningful interaction between the two pillars of the Administrative Order of Bahá'u'lláh, namely the institution of the Guardianship and the Universal House of Justice. Far from being divorced from each other, these two institutions will ensure their organic unity and will guarantee the sound development of the Bahá'í community through the integration of the interpretative and legislative functions of the Administrative Order.

In His Will and Testament 'Abdu'l-Bahá states:

> **25–WT . . . the guardian of the Cause of God is its [the Universal House of Justice] sacred head and the distinguished member for life of that body.**

While this situation did not materialize, we observe a great wisdom in 'Abdu'l-Bahá's appointment of the Guardian as the head of the House of Justice. The result was that the House of Justice decided not to have officers. In the House of Justice all members have equal responsibility; each one is a servant of Bahá'u'lláh.

The membership of the Universal House of Justice is confined to men, a position taken from the explicit writings of Bahá'u'lláh and therefore not subject to change through legislation of the House of Justice. The fact that the members of the House of Justice are men should not be regarded as a negation of the principle of the equality of men and women proclaimed by Bahá'u'lláh in His teachings. Concerning the equality of men and women, 'Abdu'l-Bahá states:

> And among the teachings of Bahá'u'lláh is the equality of women and men. The world of humanity has two wings – one is women and the other men. Not until both wings are equally developed can the bird fly. Should one wing remain weak, flight is impossible. Not until the world of women becomes equal to the world of men in the acquisition of virtues and perfections, can success and prosperity be attained as they ought to be.[314]

To appreciate this apparent contradiction, one should look at different aspects of equality. First, there is the equality of the spirit. We are told that although God has created men and women to be physically different, there is no difference between the soul of a man and the soul of a woman. Both have the same attributes of God and are created in His image and this is the most important aspect of equality. 'Abdu'l-Bahá states:

> Know thou, O handmaid, that in the sight of Bahá, women are accounted the same as men, and God hath created all humankind in His own image, and after His own likeness. That is, men and women alike are the revealers of His names and attributes, and from the spiritual viewpoint there is no difference between them. Whosoever draweth nearer to God, that one is the most favoured, whether man or woman. How many a handmaid, ardent and devoted, hath, within the sheltering shade of Bahá, proved superior to the men, and surpassed the famous of the earth.[315]

Another aspect of equality is that of rights and privileges. Here again 'Abdu'l-Bahá is unequivocal:

> In the Dispensation of Bahá'u'lláh, women are advancing side by side with the men. There is no area or instance where they will lag behind: they have equal rights with men, and will enter, in the future, into all branches of the administration of society. Such will be their elevation that, in every area of endeavour, they will occupy the highest levels in the human world.[316]

Equality, however, should not be confused with identity of function, as it is not always possible for women and men to perform identical functions.

Bahá'u'lláh, in creating the institution of the Universal House of Justice, has limited its membership to men. In a Tablet, 'Abdu'l-Bahá confirms this:

> According to the ordinances of the Faith of God, women are the equals of men in all rights save only that of membership on the Universal House of Justice, for, as hath been stated in the text of the Book, both the head and the members of the House of Justice must be men. However, in all other bodies, such as the Temple Construction Committee, the Teaching Committee, the Spiritual Assembly, and in charitable and scientific associations, women share equally in all rights with men.[317]

The wisdom of Bahá'u'lláh's injunction is not apparent today because we are too close to this nascent institution. However 'Abdu'l-Bahá has promised that the wisdom of this commandment of Bahá'u'lláh will become clear in the future:

> The House of Justice, however, according to the explicit text of the Law of God, is confined to men; this for a wisdom of the Lord God's, which will ere long be made manifest as clearly as the sun at high noon.[318]

The Guardian commented:

> The Bahá'ís should accept this statement of the Master in a spirit of deep faith, confident that there is a divine guidance and wisdom behind it which will be gradually unfolded to the eyes of the world.[319]

And the Universal House of Justice has made the following point:

> To the general premise that women and men have equality in the Faith, this, as often explained by 'Abdu'l-Bahá, is a fundamental principle deriving from Bahá'u'lláh and therefore His mention of the 'Men of Justice' in the Kitáb-i-Aqdas should be considered in light of that principle.[320]

The Seat of the Universal House of Justice is on Mount Carmel in Haifa, as foretold by Bahá'u'lláh in the Tablet of Carmel, the charter for the building of the World Centre of the Faith. In one of his letters to the Bahá'ís of the East, Shoghi Effendi elucidates some of the significances of the Tablet of Carmel and, in particular, the passage: 'Ere long will God sail His Ark upon Thee, and will manifest the people of Bahá who have been mentioned in the Book of Names.'[321]

> In this great Tablet [of Carmel] which unveils divine mysteries and heralds the establishment of two mighty, majestic and momentous undertakings – one of which is spiritual and the other administrative, both at the World Centre of the Faith – Bahá'u'lláh refers to an 'Ark', whose dwellers are the men of the Supreme House of Justice, which, in conformity with the exact provisions of the Will and Testament of the Centre of the Mighty Covenant, is the body which should lay down laws not explicitly revealed in the Text. In this Dispensation, these laws are destined to flow from this Holy Mountain, even as in the Mosaic Dispensation the law of God was promulgated from Zion. The 'sailing of the Ark' of His laws is a reference to the establishment of the Universal House of Justice, which is indeed the Seat of Legislation, one of the branches of the World Administrative Centre of the Bahá'ís on this Holy Mountain . . .[322]

In their writings Bahá'u'lláh and 'Abdu'l-Bahá counsel the Universal House of Justice to promote the best interests of mankind and to work for the betterment of the affairs of the world. In the Kitáb-i-Aqdas, Bahá'u'lláh thus reveals:

> O ye Men of Justice! Be ye, in the realm of God, shepherds unto His sheep and guard them from the ravening wolves that have appeared in disguise, even as ye would guard your own sons. Thus exhorteth you the Counsellor, the Faithful.[323]

In a Tablet, the Kalimát-i-Firdawsíyyih, Bahá'u'lláh addresses the members of the Universal House of Justice in these words:

> We exhort the men of the House of Justice and command them to ensure the protection and safeguarding of men, women and children. It is incumbent upon them to have the utmost regard for the interests of the people at all times and under all conditions. Blessed is the ruler who succoureth the captive, and the rich one who careth for the poor, and the just one who secureth from the wrong doer the rights of the downtrodden, and happy the trustee who observeth that which the Ordainer, the Ancient of Days hath prescribed unto him.[324]

And in the Tablet of Ishráqát He reveals:

> The progress of the world, the development of nations, the tranquillity of peoples, and the peace of all who dwell on earth are among the principles and ordinances of God. Religion bestoweth upon man the most precious of all gifts, offereth the cup of prosperity, imparteth eternal life, and showereth imperishable benefits upon mankind. It behoveth the chiefs and rulers of the world, and in particular the Trustees of God's House of Justice, to endeavour to the utmost of their power to safeguard its position, promote its interests and exalt its station in the eyes of the world. In like manner it is incumbent upon them to enquire into the conditions of their subjects and to acquaint themselves with the affairs and activities of the divers communities in their dominions. We call upon the manifestations of the power of God – the sovereigns and rulers on earth – to bestir themselves and do all in their power that haply they may banish discord from this world and illumine it with the light of concord.[325]

From the foregoing statements made by Bahá'u'lláh and the exhortations of 'Abdu'l-Bahá in His Will and Testament, it is clear that the Universal House of Justice is the protector of the Covenant of Bahá'u'lláh and the channel through which the forces of the Revelation of Bahá'u'lláh will flow to mankind. Through this august institution the unity of the Bahá'í community and the integrity of the Faith will be preserved. One of the causes of disunity in former Dispensations has been that the leaders of religion and men of learning have differed in their interpretations of the teachings of their faith and through their conflicting views they have created divisions within their communities. But in this Dispensation the door opening the way to allow such controversies is completely closed.

In the last passage of His Will and Testament 'Abdu'l-Bahá states:

> **55–WT To none is given the right to put forth his own opinion or express his particular conviction. All must seek guidance and turn unto the Centre of the Cause and the House of Justice. And he that turneth unto whatsoever else is indeed in grievous error.**
>
> **The Glory of Glories rest upon you!**

Bahá'ís give credence to the interpretations of 'Abdu'l-Bahá and Shoghi Effendi and consider them to be authentic and infallible, while any statement of an individual that is contrary to the spirit and form of the authorized interpretations of the Word of God is not acceptable. Furthermore, no pronouncements by the learned on various aspects of the Faith are considered valid unless sanctioned by the Universal House of Justice. The following commentary on the subject is from the pen of 'Abdu'l-Bahá:

> Briefly, this is the wisdom of referring the laws of society to the House of Justice. In the religion of Islám, similarly, not every ordinance was explicitly revealed; nay not a tenth part of a tenth part was included in the Text; although all matters of major importance were specifically referred to, there were undoubtedly thousands of laws which were unspecified. These were devised by the divines of a later age according to the laws of Islamic jurisprudence, and individual divines made conflicting deductions from the original revealed ordinances. All these were enforced. Today this process of deduction is the right of the body of the House of Justice, and the deductions and conclusions of individual learned men have no authority, unless they are endorsed by the House of Justice. The difference is precisely this, that from the conclusions and endorsements of the body of the House of Justice whose members are elected by and known to the worldwide Bahá'í community, no differences will arise; whereas the conclusions of individual divines and scholars would definitely lead to differences, and result in schism, division, and dispersion. The oneness of the Word would be destroyed, the unity of the Faith would disappear, and the edifice of the Faith of God would be shaken.[326]

This statement must not lead the reader to think that the hands of Bahá'í scholars are tied or that they are unable to undertake their own research and reach their own conclusions on matters connected with the Faith. On the contrary, every believer is free to read the writings and make his own interpretation, as long as he makes it clear that his views are his own and are not authoritative. The Universal House of Justice has clarified this subject:

> A clear distinction is made in our Faith between authoritative interpretation and the interpretation or understanding that each individual arrives at for himself from his study of its teachings. While the former is confined to the Guardian, the latter, according to the guidance given to us by the Guardian himself, should by no means be suppressed. In fact such individual interpretation is considered the fruit of man's rational power and conducive to a better understanding of the teachings, provided that no disputes or arguments arise among the friends and the individual himself understands and makes it clear that his views are merely his own. Individual interpretations continually change as one grows in comprehension of the teachings. As Shoghi Effendi explained: 'To deepen in the Cause means to read the writings of Bahá'u'lláh and the Master so thoroughly as to be able to give it to others in its pure form. There are many who have some superficial idea of what the Cause stands for. They, therefore, present it together with all sorts of ideas that are their own. As the Cause is still in its early days we must be most careful lest we fall into this error and injure the Movement we so much adore. There is no limit to the study of the Cause. The more we read the Writings, the more truths we can find in them and the more we will see that our previous notions were erroneous.' So, although individual insights can be enlightening and helpful, they can also be misleading. The friends must therefore learn to listen to the views of others without being overawed or allowing their faith to be shaken, and to express their own views without pressing them on their fellow Bahá'ís.[327]

In every Dispensation, the Manifestation of God has promulgated a number of teachings and ordinances that may be described as the framework of that religion. These teachings have been designed by God to bring about the advancement of those who have embraced them. They are always adapted to suit the condition of the people and are given according to their capacity. As a result of the application of these teachings in their lives, the members of a religious community develop higher levels of understanding. In the course of their progress they eventually reach a position where the teachings of their religion no longer adequately satisfy their spiritual and mental needs. When the teachings and laws of a religion become outdated, when they are no longer practicable in a new age, the followers have arrogated to themselves the right to amend or alter these teachings so that they will conform with new conditions prevailing at the time. But man has no right to interfere with the revealed teachings of God. Only a new Manifestation of God can abrogate the laws of a previous Dispensation and bring new laws for a new age. Otherwise, man's interference will cause the teachings of a religion to become adulterated.

Bahá'u'lláh envisaged – and this has already become evident – that in His Dispensation man will advance and progress at an unprecedented rate, needing new laws at every stage of his development. Therefore, He empowered the Universal House of Justice to enact secondary laws befitting the circumstances of the time, laws which can later be altered as conditions change. It must be noted, however, that the teachings, laws and ordinances revealed by Bahá'u'lláh Himself are unalterable until the advent of a future Manifestation of God, who will have the right to abrogate them. 'Abdu'l-Bahá states:

> Those matters of major importance which constitute the foundation of the Law of God are explicitly recorded in the Text, but subsidiary laws are left to the House of Justice. The wisdom of this is that the times never remain the same, for change is a necessary quality and an essential attribute of this world, and of time and place. Therefore the House of Justice will take action accordingly.[328]

A significant development since the establishment of the House of Justice is that the Covenant-breakers – especially those in the Holy Land – have been effectively thwarted in their plans and their fortunes have declined to the point of impotence.

Gone are the days after the ascension of Bahá'u'lláh, when an ignoble band of faithless men and women, including most members of His family and headed by no less a person than Bahá'u'lláh's son, Mírzá Muḥammad-'Alí, rose up against the Master with all their power and prestige and tried to wrest from Him the reins of the Cause of God, which had been entrusted to Him by His heavenly Father.

Gone are the days when some of the most erudite and outstanding teachers of the Faith, together with a number of influential men who ranked foremost in the community, rebelled against 'Abdu'l-Bahá, viciously attacked the newly born institution of the Covenant and caused grievous convulsions within the community of the Most Great Name.

Gone are the days when falsehoods and outrageous misrepresentations against the Centre of the Covenant by Mírzá Muḥammad-'Alí gained credibility among the people, both within and without this small and seemingly fragile community.

Gone are the days when the Master was maliciously accused in public by His unfaithful brothers of the most heinous crimes, causing alarm and apprehension within government circles in the Holy Land and further afield at the heart of the Ottoman Empire.

Gone are the days when, through his persistent machinations and intrigues, the Arch-breaker of the Covenant succeeded in poisoning the mind of the Sulṭán of Turkey to such an extent that he ordered 'Abdu'l-Bahá's incarceration within the walls of the prison city, an ordeal which He endured for eight years.

And gone are the days when the youthful Guardian of the Cause was subjected to untold sufferings at the hands of the members of 'Abdu'l-Bahá's family and the old Covenant-breakers, who, assisted by a number of erstwhile outstanding teachers of the Faith – then violators of the Covenant – opposed him for more than three decades.

Now, with the establishment of the Universal House of Justice, the situation is changed and the precious institution of the Covenant bequeathed by Bahá'u'lláh to His followers has been greatly fortified. Although there will always be some souls from among the followers who, from time to time, will rebel against the Cause of God and arise to break the Covenant, they will never be able to divide the Faith into sects and destroy the unity of its community. The truth of this can be seen in the history of the Faith. For almost one hundred years, desperate endeavours were made by various groups of Covenant-breakers who launched fierce onslaughts against the Cause of Bahá'u'lláh in order to bring about schism within its worldwide community. And despite all this, their efforts were in vain and they failed miserably in their objectives. Bahá'u'lláh has thus clearly proven that this is a 'day that shall not be followed by night'. [329]

In the Will and Testament 'Abdu'l-Bahá states:

> **25–WT This House of Justice enacteth the laws and the government enforceth them. The legislative body must reinforce the executive, the executive must aid and assist the legislative body so that through the close union and harmony of these two forces, the foundation of fairness and justice may become firm and strong, that all the regions of the world may become even as Paradise itself.**

This relationship between the Universal House of Justice and the governments, described by 'Abdu'l-Bahá, refers to the time when the authority of the Universal House of Justice will have been recognized by the nations of the world. At that time the legislature and the executive constituting the essential components of the World Order of Bahá'u'lláh will harmoniously interact. The supreme authority of the House of Justice, divinely conferred upon it, will be the guarantor of the unity of the nations and peoples of the world.

In response to a question about 'the government' stated in the passage of the Will and Testament cited above, Shoghi Effendi's secretary wrote on his behalf:

> By 'Government'. . . is meant the executive body which will enforce the laws when the Bahá'í Faith has reached the point when it is recognized and accepted entirely by any particular nation.[330]

And in another letter Shoghi Effendi stated:

> Not only will the present-day Spiritual Assemblies be styled differently in future, but they will be enabled also to add to their present functions those powers, duties, and prerogatives necessitated by the recognition of the Faith of Bahá'u'lláh, not merely as one of the recognized religious systems of the world, but as the State Religion of an independent and Sovereign Power. And as the Bahá'í Faith permeates the masses of the peoples of East and West, and its truth is embraced by the majority of the peoples of a number of the Sovereign States of the world, will the Universal House of Justice attain the plenitude of its power, and exercise, as the supreme organ of the Bahá'í Commonwealth, all the rights, the duties, and responsibilities incumbent upon the world's future super-state.[331]

Envisioning the mighty victories of the future, Shoghi Effendi foretells in his letters to the Persian believers that through the guidance of the Universal House of Justice the Cause of God will be exalted and the sovereignty of Bahá'u'lláh will be made manifest to the peoples of the world. The following passages are translated from one of these letters:

> The National Spiritual Assemblies, like unto pillars, will be gradually and firmly established in every country on the strong and fortified foundations of the Local Assemblies. On these pillars, the mighty edifice, the Universal House of Justice, will be erected, raising high its noble frame above the world of existence. The unity of the followers of Bahá'u'lláh will thus be realized and fulfilled from one end of the earth to the other . . . and the living waters of everlasting life will stream forth from that fountain-head of God's World Order upon all the warring nations and peoples of the world, to wash away the evils and iniquities of the realm of dust, and heal man's age-old ills and ailments . . .[332]

> Then will the Throne of Bahá'u'lláh's sovereignty be founded in the promised land and the scales of justice be raised on high. Then

will the banner of the independence of the Faith be unfurled, and His Most Great Law be unveiled and rivers of laws and ordinances stream forth from this snow-white spot with all-conquering power and awe-inspiring majesty, the like of which past ages have never seen. Then will appear the truth of what was revealed by the Tongue of Grandeur: 'Call out to Zion, O Carmel, and announce the joyful tidings: He that was hidden from mortal eyes is come! His all-conquering sovereignty is manifest; His all-encompassing splendour is revealed.' '. . . O Carmel . . . Well is it with him that circleth around thee, that proclaimeth the revelation of thy glory, and recounteth that which the bounty of the Lord, thy God, hath showered upon thee . . . Ere long will God sail His Ark upon thee, and will manifest the people of Bahá who have been mentioned in the Book of Names.'

Through it the pillars of the Faith on this earth will be firmly established and its hidden powers be revealed, its signs shine forth, its banners be unfurled and its light be shed upon all peoples.[333]

39

Ḥuqúqu'lláh, Obedience to Government, Supreme Tribunal

Ḥuqúqu'lláh

> **27–WT O friends of 'Abdu'l-Bahá! The Lord, as a sign of His infinite bounties, hath graciously favoured His servants by providing for a fixed money offering (Ḥuqúq), to be dutifully presented unto Him, though He, the True One, and His servants have been at all times independent of all created things, and God verily is the All-Possessing, exalted above the need of any gift from His creatures. This fixed money offering, however, causeth the people to become firm and steadfast and draweth Divine increase upon them. It is to be offered through the guardian of the Cause of God, that it may be expended for the diffusion of the Fragrances of God and the exaltation of His Word, for benevolent pursuits and for the common weal.**

In the Kitáb-i-Aqdas (the Most Holy Book), Bahá'u'lláh revealed the law of Ḥuqúqu'lláh (the Right of God). It applies to those whose possessions reach a certain value, beyond which they are bidden by God to pay 19 per cent of that value to the Centre of the Cause. In one of His Tablets, revealed in the words of His amanuensis, Bahá'u'lláh states that when the full text of the Kitáb-i-Aqdas was completed He did not order its release for some time because it contained the law of Ḥuqúq, which was given by God as a sign of His mercy and loving-kindness unto His servants. He explains that the reason for withholding the Book temporarily was His apprehension lest some of the believers might not carry out this commandment or might come to wrong conclusions. The mere contemplation of this, He says, is unworthy of the Day of God.

The very thought that some, in their immaturity, might have assumed that the Ḥuqúq was intended for Bahá'u'lláh's personal use must have been extremely painful to Him. The most cursory study of His life and teachings amply demonstrates that He constantly exhorted His followers to detach themselves from earthly possessions and not to place their affections on the things of this world. In His

Tablet to Napoleon III, Bahá'u'lláh admonishes the emperor in these words, which clearly demonstrate the worthlessness of this material world in His sight:

> Exultest thou over the treasures thou dost possess, knowing they shall perish? Rejoicest thou in that thou rulest a span of earth, when the whole world, in the estimation of the people of Bahá, is worth as much as the black in the eye of a dead ant?[334]

And in another Tablet He makes a similar statement:

> By the righteousness of God! The world, its vanities and its glory, and whatever delights it can offer, are all, in the sight of God, as worthless as, nay even more contemptible than, dust and ashes. Would that the hearts of men could comprehend it. Wash yourselves thoroughly, O people of Bahá, from the defilement of the world, and of all that pertaineth unto it.[335]

During the days of Bahá'u'lláh, the majority of the believers in Persia were poor and some were needy. But when Ḥájí Abu'l-Ḥasan-i-Amín* visited them, they had, through sacrifice, set aside small sums of money and were able to offer them to the Cause of God. It must be made clear that under Bahá'u'lláh's supervision the funds were spent for the promotion of the Cause and very little, if any, for His own expenses or those of His companions. The history of the life of Bahá'u'lláh bears ample testimony to this fact, for during most of the 40 years of His ministry He lived in the utmost poverty. There were days when a mere loaf of bread was not available to Him and the garments He wore were the only clothes He had. There were many occasions when He was in great need but He did not accept financial help from the friends. The last few years of His earthly life, although relatively more comfortable, were nevertheless greatly influenced by the austerity that had characterized His life from the days of the Síyáh-Chál in Ṭihrán, when all His possessions had been confiscated and He had been deprived of the means to support Himself and His family.

Desire for wealth is non-existent in the person of the Manifestation of God. He abides in a realm that is independent of all creation and He is detached from all earthly things. Bahá'u'lláh stated in many of His Tablets that this mortal world is only a handful of dust and as utter nothingness in His sight. In His Will and Testament, the Kitáb-i-'Ahd, He left us these exalted words:

* Trustee of Ḥuqúq appointed by Bahá'u'lláh. See Taherzadeh, *Revelation of Bahá'u'lláh,* vol. 3, chapter 4.

> Although the Realm of Glory hath none of the vanities of the world, yet within the treasury of trust and resignation We have bequeathed to Our heirs an excellent and priceless heritage. Earthly treasures We have not bequeathed, nor have We added such cares as they entail. By God! In earthly riches fear is hidden and peril is concealed. Consider ye and call to mind that which the All-Merciful hath revealed in the Qur'án: 'Woe betide every slanderer and defamer, him that layeth up riches and counteth them.' Fleeting are the riches of the world; all that perisheth and changeth is not, and hath never been, worthy of attention, except to a recognized measure.[336]

The same attitude of detachment from earthly things so permeated the souls of 'Abdu'l-Bahá and Shoghi Effendi, the two successive Centres of the Cause of Bahá'u'lláh, that it was against their nature to turn their affection to the things of this world. They both followed the example of Bahá'u'lláh and lived austere lives. Although they received large contributions from the friends, they authorized their spending strictly for the promotion of the Cause of God and did not have the slightest inclination to spend the funds for their own personal ends. Like Bahá'u'lláh, neither of them had any personal assets, whether monetary or of any other type.

When 'Abdu'l-Bahá travelled to the West to spread the Cause of Bahá'u'lláh and diffuse the divine fragrances in Europe and America, He had to use some of the funds which the Persian friends had contributed to Ḥájí Amín as Ḥuqúqu'lláh. But He observed such care in spending the absolute minimum for Himself that His companions sometimes felt concerned about the lack of comfort that often resulted.

The renowned chronicler of 'Abdu'l-Bahá's journeys to the West, Mírzá Maḥmúd-i-Zarqání, His devoted secretary and companion, has recorded in his diary (*Badáyi'u'l-Á͟thár*) that when 'Abdu'l-Bahá and His party were travelling across the United States, the train journey proved to be tiring – especially for 'Abdu'l-Bahá, who was nearly 70 years of age. Yet in spite of this, He frequently declined to pay the extra small sum of money for sleeping accommodation on the train. Instead He would sit up all night on the hard wooden seats and close His eyes to rest. But, as demonstrated on that journey, He opened His purse and generously placed coins of silver and gold in the palms of the poor and needy wherever He found them. How different are the ways of God and man!

During those same epoch-making journeys 'Abdu'l-Bahá demonstrated a magnanimity and detachment characteristic of God's chosen ones by declining with graciousness all offers of funds and gifts from friends and strangers. In his diary Mírzá Maḥmúd recounts a story of 'Abdu'l-Bahá when He was in New York shortly before His departure from the United States:

> 'Today some of the friends offered money to the Master but He would not accept it despite their pleading. Instead He told them, 'Distribute it among the poor on my behalf. It will be as though I have given it to them. But the most acceptable gift to me is the unity of the believers, service to the Cause of God, diffusion of the divine fragrances and adherence to the counsels of the Abhá Beauty.'
>
> The believers were saddened because He did not accept their gifts. However, since these were the last days of His visit and He was about to leave, the New York Bahá'ís collected several gifts for the women of the holy household and for the Greatest Holy Leaf.
>
> Some of the believers agreed among themselves to go to 'Abdu'l-Bahá and cling to His robe until He accepted their gifts. They came and begged He accept their offerings. The Master called them, saying:
>
>> I am most grateful for your services; in truth you have served me. You have extended hospitality. Night and day you have been ready to serve and to diffuse the divine fragrances. I shall never forget your services, for you have no purpose but the will of God and you desire no station but entry into the Kingdom of God. Now you have brought presents for the members of my family. They are most acceptable and excellent but better than all these are the gifts of the love of God which remain preserved in the treasuries of the heart. These gifts are evanescent but those are eternal; these jewels must be kept in boxes and vaults and they will eventually perish but those jewels remain in the treasuries of the heart and will remain throughout the world of God for eternity. Thus I will take to them your love, which is the greatest of all gifts. In our house they do not wear diamond rings nor do they keep rubies. That house is sanctified above such adornments.
>>
>> I, however, have accepted your gifts; but I entrust them to you for you to sell and send the proceeds to the fund for the Mas͟hriqu'l-Ad͟hkár in Chicago.
>
> When the friends continued to plead with Him, He said: 'I want to take from you a present which will endure in the eternal world and a jewel which belongs to the treasuries of the heart. This is better.'
>
> No matter how much the friends supplicated and pleaded, He would not accept their gifts and instead asked them all to contribute towards the Mas͟hriqu'l-Ad͟hkár fund. He did this everywhere He travelled.[337]

Returning to the subject of Ḥuqúqu'lláh, Bahá'u'lláh ordains this institution in the following passage of the Kitáb-i-Aqdas:

> Should anyone acquire one hundred mi<u>th</u>qáls* of gold, nineteen mi<u>th</u>qáls thereof are God's and to be rendered unto Him, the Fashioner of earth and heaven. Take heed, O people, lest ye deprive yourselves of so great a bounty. This We have commanded you, though We are well able to dispense with you and with all who are in the heavens and on earth; in it there are benefits and wisdoms beyond the ken of anyone but God, the Omniscient, the All-Informed. Say: By this means He hath desired to purify what ye possess and to enable you to draw nigh unto such stations as none can comprehend save those whom God hath willed. He, in truth, is the Beneficent, the Gracious, the Bountiful. O people! Deal not faithlessly with the Right of God, nor, without His leave, make free with its disposal. Thus hath His commandment been established in the holy Tablets, and in this exalted Book. He who dealeth faithlessly with God shall in justice meet with faithlessness himself; he, however, who acteth in accordance with God's bidding shall receive a blessing from the heaven of the bounty of his Lord, the Gracious, the Bestower, the Generous, the Ancient of Days. He, verily, hath willed for you that which is yet beyond your knowledge, but which shall be known to you when, after this fleeting life, your souls soar heavenwards and the trappings of your earthly joys are folded up. Thus admonisheth you He in Whose possession is the Guarded Tablet.[338]

> The minimum amount subject to Ḥuqúqu'lláh is reached when one's possessions are worth the number of Váḥid (19); that is, whenever one owneth 19 mi<u>th</u>qáls of gold, or acquireth possessions attaining this value, after having deducted therefrom the yearly expenses, the Ḥuqúq becometh applicable and its payment is obligatory.[339]

With regard to the application of the law of Ḥuqúqu'lláh, Shoghi Effendi has stated through his secretary:

> Regarding the Ḥuqúqu'lláh . . . this is applied to one's merchandise, property and income. After deducting the necessary expenses, whatever is left as profit, and is an addition to one's capital, such a sum is subject to Ḥuqúq. When one has paid Ḥuqúq once on a particular sum, that sum is no longer subject to Ḥuqúq, unless it should pass from one person to another. One's residence, and the household furnishings are exempt from Ḥuqúq . . . Ḥuqúqu'lláh is paid to the Centre of the Cause.[340]

---

* Each mi<u>th</u>qál is equal to 3.6416666 grams.

Bahá'u'lláh was very anxious that no one should ever feel forced to pay the Ḥuqúq. He instructed Ḥájí Abu'l-Ḥasan-i-Amín, the Trustee of the Ḥuqúq, and other eminent Bahá'ís not to accept money from anyone unless they were sure that the individual wished to give with the utmost joy and devotion. In many of His Tablets Bahá'u'lláh forbade the soliciting of Ḥuqúq by the Trustees, as seen in this part of a Tablet revealed in honour of His Trustee Ḥájí Amín:

> O Abu'l Ḥasan:
>
> May my Glory rest upon thee! Fix thy gaze upon the glory of the Cause. Speak forth that which will attract the hearts and the minds. To demand the Ḥuqúq is in no wise permissible. This command was revealed in the Book of God for various necessary matters ordained by God to be dependent upon material means. Therefore, if someone, with utmost pleasure and gladness, nay with insistence, wisheth to partake of this blessing, thou mayest accept. Otherwise, acceptance is not permissible.[341]

The concept that a portion of one's possessions is the right of God and belongs to Him may be better appreciated through observation of nature and examination of certain physical laws. As previously stated, laws that exist in the physical world are also present in the spiritual worlds of God and religious teachings are the spiritual counterparts of physical laws. The law of Ḥuqúqu'lláh, for example, finds its parallel in the growth of a tree, where the blossoms, the flowers and the fruits do not originate from the tree but are the hidden properties of the soil, which the tree brings out. Thus the entire substance of the tree comes from the earth, which produces the root, the trunk, the branches, the leaves and the fruits and provides all the nourishment for the tree's growth and fruition.

When the tree sheds its leaves upon the earth each year, it gives back to its creator, as a matter of course, a portion of its wealth. But the fallen leaves do not benefit the earth; they act as a fertilizer and therefore their benefit reverts to the tree itself. This physical process is similar to the effects of the law of Ḥuqúqu'lláh and, as Bahá'u'lláh has stated, 'The benefit of such deeds [payment of the Ḥuqúq] reverteth unto the individuals themselves.'[342]

During Bahá'u'lláh's ministry the law of Ḥuqúq was applicable only to a very small number of Bahá'ís. The great majority of the community members were poor and not liable to pay the Ḥuqúq. Often the Trustee of Bahá'u'lláh was unable to fully cover the expenses of the Bahá'í teachers and those in need. Of course, Ḥájí Amín, the Trustee, was not pleased about this. In one of His Tablets Bahá'u'lláh makes a sweet and humorous remark about His Trustee. He says:

> We must impose a fine upon Jináb-i-Amín! We have one treasurer and he is bankrupt! Gracious God, there is one treasury belonging to God and that is empty of funds. Indeed, by virtue of its exalted station, such a treasury ought to be freed and sanctified from earthly things and not be confused with the treasuries of the world.[343]

The law of Ḥuqúq was observed only by the Bahá'ís of the East until 1992, when the Universal House of Justice made it universally applicable. Before taking this step, the Universal House of Justice ensured that, over the period of a few years, the believers became fully familiar with the law and its application.

The Ḥuqúq should not be confused with the contributions of a believer to the International Funds. Although both are donated to the Centre of the Cause – today to the Universal House of Justice – there is a great difference between the two. In reality, the Ḥuqúq does not belong to the individual, as it is the right of God, whereas ordinary donations are given by the believer from his own resources and are motivated by a heartfelt desire to give of one's own substance for the promotion of the Cause of God.

Obedience to Government

> **28–9–WT O ye beloved of the Lord! It is incumbent upon you to be submissive to all monarchs that are just and to show your fidelity to every righteous king. Serve ye the sovereigns of the world with utmost truthfulness and loyalty. Show obedience unto them and be their well-wishers. Without their leave and permission do not meddle with political affairs, for disloyalty to the just sovereign is disloyalty to God Himself.**
>
> **This is my counsel and the commandment of God unto you. Well is it with them that act accordingly.**

One of the fundamental teachings of the Faith of Bahá'u'lláh is obedience to one's government, as seen in these words of Bahá'u'lláh revealed in the Tablet of Bis͟harát:

> In every country where any of this people reside, they must behave towards the government of that country with loyalty, honesty and truthfulness. This is that which hath been revealed at the behest of Him Who is the Ordainer, the Ancient of Days.[344]

In another Tablet Bahá'u'lláh writes:

> The one true God, exalted be His glory, hath bestowed the government of the earth upon the kings. To none is given the right to act

> in any manner that would run counter to the considered views of them who are in authority.[345]

In many of His Tablets 'Abdu'l-Bahá also exhorts the believers to be obedient and faithful to their governments, as the following passage reveals:

> Furthermore each and every one is required to show obedience, submission and loyalty towards his own government. Today no state in the world is in a condition of peace or tranquillity, for security and trust have vanished from among the people. Both the governed and the governors are alike in danger. The only group of people which today submitteth peacefully and loyally to the laws and ordinances of government and dealeth honestly and frankly with the people, is none other than this wronged community. For while all sects and races in Persia and Turkestan are absorbed in promoting their own interests and only obey their governments either with the hope of reward or from fear of punishment, the Bahá'ís are the well-wishers of the government, obedient to its laws and bearing love towards all peoples.
>
> Such obedience and submission is made incumbent and obligatory upon all by the clear Text of the Abhá Beauty. Therefore the believers, in obedience to the command of the True One, show the utmost sincerity and goodwill towards all nations; and should any soul act contrary to the laws of the government he would consider himself responsible before God, deserving divine wrath and chastisement for his sin and wrongdoing.[346]

Bahá'ís obey the government on those matters which do not violate the spiritual principles of their Faith. However, should any government require Bahá'ís to deny their Faith or take an action which would violate one its spiritual principles, they will refuse to obey, even if the penalty is death.

Supreme Tribunal

Speaking about the future state of affairs in the world, 'Abdu'l-Bahá in His Will and Testament, writes:

> **22–WT . . . that contention and conflict amidst peoples, kindreds, nations and governments may disappear, that all the dwellers on earth may become one people and one race, that the world may become even as one home. Should differences arise they shall be amicably and conclusively settled by the Supreme Tribunal, that shall include members from all the governments and peoples of the world.**

The establishment of a Supreme Tribunal is one of the teachings of Bahá'u'lláh. In a Tablet addressed to the Central Organization for a Durable Peace, in the Hague, 'Abdu'l-Bahá wrote in 1919:

> For example, the question of universal peace, about which Bahá'u-'lláh says that the Supreme Tribunal must be established: although the League of Nations has been brought into existence, yet it is incapable of establishing universal peace. But the Supreme Tribunal which Bahá'u'lláh has described will fulfil this sacred task with the utmost might and power. And His plan is this: that the national assemblies of each country and nation – that is to say parliaments – should elect two or three persons who are the choicest men of that nation, and are well informed concerning international laws and the relations between governments and aware of the essential needs of the world of humanity in this day. The number of these representatives should be in proportion to the number of inhabitants of that country. The election of these souls who are chosen by the national assembly, that is, the parliament, must be confirmed by the upper house, the congress and the cabinet and also by the president or monarch so these persons may be the elected ones of all the nation and the government. From among these people the members of the Supreme Tribunal will be elected, and all mankind will thus have a share therein, for every one of these delegates is fully representative of his nation. When the Supreme Tribunal gives a ruling on any international question, either unanimously or by majority rule, there will no longer be any pretext for the plaintiff or ground of objection for the defendant. In case any of the governments or nations, in the execution of the irrefutable decision of the Supreme Tribunal, be negligent or dilatory, the rest of the nations will rise up against it, because all the governments and nations of the world are the supporters of this Supreme Tribunal. Consider what a firm foundation this is! But by a limited and restricted League the purpose will not be realized as it ought and should. This is the truth about the situation, which has been stated . . .[347]

The Guardian further elaborates on this subject:

> Some form of a world Super-State must needs be evolved, in whose favour all the nations of the world will have willingly ceded every claim to make war, certain rights to impose taxation and all rights to maintain armaments, except for purposes of maintaining internal order within their respective dominions. Such a state will have to include within its orbit an International Executive adequate to enforce supreme and unchallengeable authority on every recalcitrant member of the commonwealth; a World Parliament whose members shall be elected by the people in their respective countries and whose election shall be confirmed by their respective govern-

ments; and a Supreme Tribunal whose judgement will have a binding effect even in such cases where the parties concerned did not voluntarily agree to submit their case to its consideration. A world community in which all economic barriers will have been permanently demolished and the interdependence of Capital and Labour definitely recognized; in which the clamour of religious fanaticism and strife will have been forever stilled; in which the flame of racial animosity will have been finally extinguished; in which a single code of international law – the product of the considered judgement of the world's federated representatives – shall have as its sanction the instant and coercive intervention of the combined forces of the federated units; and finally a world community in which the fury of a capricious and militant nationalism will have been transmuted into an abiding consciousness of world citizenship – such indeed, appears, in its broadest outline, the Order anticipated by Bahá'u'lláh, an Order that shall come to be regarded as the fairest fruit of a slowly maturing age.[348]

And in a letter written on behalf of Shoghi Effendi it is stated:

The Universal Court of Arbitration and the International Tribunal are the same. When the Bahá'í State will be established they will be merged in the Universal House of Justice.[349]

40

Steadfastness in the Covenant

The part that man has to play in the Covenant with his Creator is described by Bahá'u'lláh in the opening paragraph of the Kitáb-i-Aqdas:

> The first duty prescribed by God for His servants is the recognition of Him Who is the Dayspring of His Revelation and the Fountain of His laws, Who representeth the Godhead in both the Kingdom of His Cause and the world of creation. Whoso achieveth this duty hath attained unto all good; and whoso is deprived thereof hath gone astray, though he be the author of every righteous deed. It behoveth every one who reacheth this most sublime station, this summit of transcendent glory, to observe every ordinance of Him Who is the Desire of the world. These twin duties are inseparable. Neither is acceptable without the other. Thus hath it been decreed by Him Who is the Source of Divine inspiration.[350]

We see, then, that there are two requirements of man in this Covenant: to recognize the Manifestation of God as the source of all good and then to follow His commandments.

As previously stated, one of the most important commandments of Bahá'u'lláh is to turn to the Centre of His Covenant after Him. This injunction was revealed in both the Kitáb-i-Aqdas and the Kitáb-i-'Ahd.

Therefore, to a true Bahá'í who is steadfast in the Covenant, obedience to the utterances of 'Abdu'l-Bahá is obedience to God. As important as recognition of the station of Bahá'u'lláh and belief in Him are, they are not a sufficient guarantee of faith unless one remains loyal and steadfast in His Covenant. One of the distinguishing features of the Faith of Bahá'u'lláh is that He has not abandoned His followers to their own devices but has left in their midst a source of divine guidance to which they can turn. He conferred His divine powers and authority upon 'Abdu'l-Bahá and made a firm Covenant with the believers to follow and obey Him with absolute devotion and love. This Covenant was extended to include Shoghi Effendi and the Universal House of Justice. Faith in Bahá'u'lláh is, therefore, not a mere acknowledgement of His divine message but also involves obedience and faithfulness to those upon whom He conferred the mantle of infallibility.

The Kitáb-i-'Ahd and the Will and Testament of 'Abdu'l-Bahá may be summarized in two words: 'turn towards'. Bahá'u'lláh enjoined His followers to 'turn towards' 'Abdu'l-Bahá, after whose passing the believers had again to 'turn towards' Shoghi Effendi. Today they 'turn towards' the Universal House of Justice.

To emphasize this important feature of the Covenant, the following analogy may be helpful. An aircraft flies because its engines create a special condition that enables the machine to do so; without them the craft will not move. Similarly, belief in Bahá'u'lláh as the Supreme Manifestation of God in this age uplifts the soul and enables it to soar into the spiritual realms. A believer's faith in Bahá'u'lláh thus acts like the engine in the analogy. But a powerful engine, however necessary, cannot ensure the safety of an aircraft or its smooth landing at its destination. There is a need for the navigational signals which a modern aircraft receives from the control tower to determine its direction, height and speed, and the pilot obeys these instructions until the machine lands safely. Without these navigational aids and the pilot's readiness to follow them, there is every likelihood that a disaster will take place.

Similarly, faith in Bahá'u'lláh is not sufficient unto itself. The believer must faithfully obey the guidance he receives from the Centre of the Cause. If someone reaches the pinnacle of faith and certitude in the Revelation of Bahá'u'lláh but refuses to follow the guidance of Bahá'u'lláh, 'Abdu'l-Bahá, Shoghi Effendi or the Universal House of Justice, he cannot be considered a true believer.

Many people today frown upon the word 'obedience'. In present-day society, in which all moral and spiritual values are declining, the concept of obedience is often associated with dictatorship, tyranny, religious fanaticism and narrow-mindedness. This view is held by educated men and women who are otherwise open-minded and intelligent. These people come from all walks of life; some belong to religious movements with liberal leanings, while others may be humanists, agnostics or atheists. They have keenly observed the terrible consequences that blind obedience to various political regimes or religious hierarchies has engendered and they are fearful of any movement, whether religious or secular, that demands absolute obedience to its commandments. One can appreciate the honesty of these people and sympathize with their views, for they may have only experienced injustice and cruelty everywhere.

However, in his daily life a human being wholeheartedly obeys the directives of many individuals or institutions that speak with the voice of truth. He is willing to accept authority that appears credible and trustworthy. For instance, a motorist will unhesitatingly follow the signpost on a road until he reaches his destination. This blind following springs from his faith in the authority of the body that has set up the signposts. Similarly, a patient will willingly allow a surgeon to operate on a cancerous growth because he has faith in the doctor's diagnosis.

A similar response results from an individual's recognition of the truth of the Cause of God. Once he sees the teachings as credible, he will not find it difficult to obey them. And since man's part in the Covenant of God is obedience to God's teachings, it is clear that he cannot fulfil his obligation unless he recognizes the truth of His Revelation.

When the individual recognizes Bahá'u'lláh as the Manifestation of God, a spark of faith is ignited in his heart. At first a faint glimmer of light, this spark must be allowed to become a fire of ever-growing intensity for it is then that the believer will fall in love with Bahá'u'lláh. But how can a person who has just embraced this belief draw closer to Bahá'u'lláh, fan into flame the spark of his faith and increase his love for Him day by day?

A statement in Islam, which Bahá'u'lláh confirms and reiterates, says that 'Knowledge is a light which God casteth into the heart of whomsoever He willeth.' The assertion that the heart is the dawning-place of the knowledge of God may sound strange to some because it is commonly thought that the mind, rather than the heart, is the vehicle for acquiring knowledge. But faith and knowledge of God, like seeds, are planted first in the heart. It is only afterwards that the mind grasps the truth and begins to understand it. In the end it is the interaction of the two – the heart and the mind – that brings confirmation and certitude to the soul.

Although in some cases a believer's faith in Bahá'u'lláh may come to him intellectually, its intensification and growth day by day cannot continue purely through intellectual pursuits. And if a person's faith does not increase with the passage of time, it is like a child who is born but fails to grow. Such a person is very likely to feel a measure of doubt in his innermost heart concerning the Faith and may experience great conflicts in his mind, especially when he goes through tests. Although intellectually he may accept Bahá'u'lláh as a Manifestation of God and may even be well versed in His writings, he does not have that absolute certitude that endows a human being with spiritual qualities and confers upon him perpetual contentment, assurance and happiness.

The heart is the focal point of warmth and love. It is characteristic of the heart to fall in love with another but it is the individual who finds and chooses the object of that love. If he turns his affections to the material world, his heart will very easily become attached to it. But if he turns to God and spiritual things, then his heart can fall in love with his Creator, provided he fulfils one condition stated by Bahá'u'lláh:

> O Son of Being! Thy heart is My home; sanctify it for My descent. Thy spirit is My place of revelation; cleanse it for my Manifestation.[351]

How can one sanctify the heart? In another passage, Bahá'u'lláh explains:

> O Son of Dust! All that is in heaven and earth I have ordained for thee, except the human heart, which I have made the habitation of My beauty and glory; yet thou didst give My home and dwelling to another than Me; and whenever the manifestation of My holiness sought His own abode, a stranger found He there, and, homeless, hastened unto the sanctuary of the Beloved.[352]

And again:

> O My Friend in Word! Ponder awhile. Hast thou ever heard that friend and foe should abide in one heart? Cast out then the stranger, that the Friend may enter His home.[353]

To acquire faith, then, and to enable the revelation of God to shine within the heart, one must cast out the 'stranger', or man's attachment to this world, of which the most formidable and most harmful type is attachment to one's own self. It manifests itself mainly in pride in one's own knowledge and other accomplishments, such as rank and position. Love of one's self renders the individual opinionated, self-centred, proud and egotistical and, in fact, denudes him of spiritual qualities. Such a person has indeed harboured within his heart a great enemy, namely, the 'stranger' referred to by Bahá'u'lláh. Even if he becomes a Bahá'í, he will find it difficult to derive spiritual upliftment from the writings of Bahá'u'lláh because this attachment has become a barrier between himself and God.

To read the writings purely with the eye of intellect, while proudly regarding oneself as a being endowed with great qualities and accomplishments, undoubtedly closes the door to the bounties and confirmations of Bahá'u'lláh, and His words therefore cannot influence the heart. When a person truly recognizes Bahá'u'lláh as the Manifestation of God he becomes humble before Him and this is one of the main prerequisites for driving the 'stranger', step by step, out of one's heart. 'Humble thyself before Me, that I may graciously visit thee'[354] is Bahá'u'lláh's clear admonition to man:

> Blind thine eyes, that thou mayest behold My beauty; stop thine ears, that thou mayest hearken unto the sweet melody of My voice; empty thyself of all learning, that thou mayest partake of My knowledge; and sanctify thyself from riches, that thou mayest obtain a lasting share from the ocean of My eternal wealth.[355]

There is a beautiful Persian story in verse that elucidates this point quite vividly. It concerns a drop of rain falling down from the clouds. The drop knows itself to be the water of life, the most precious element that God had created, and so it is proud of itself. Boasting all the way down, it suddenly sees that it is falling into an ocean, whereupon it recognizes its own insignificance and exclaims: 'If this exists then what am I?' When the ocean hears this expression of humility it attracts the drop to itself and, as a reward, makes it a companion of the pearl.

The following portion of one of the obligatory prayers of Bahá'u-'lláh, though very brief, is reminiscent of the story of the drop and the ocean, and serves as a perfect confession of who we are:

> I bear witness, O my God, that thou has created me to know Thee and to worship Thee. I testify, at this moment, to my powerlessness and to Thy might, to my poverty and to Thy wealth.[356]

The daily recital of any of the three obligatory prayers can act as a mighty weapon in the spiritual battle against one's own self, a battle that every believer must fight in order to subdue his greatest enemy and drive the 'stranger' away. The recital of the obligatory prayer, which is enjoined upon every believer by Bahá'u'lláh and constitutes one of the most sacred rites of the Faith, is a major factor in enabling a soul to recognize its own impotence in relation to its Creator and to acknowledge its own shortcomings.

The saying of obligatory prayers, along with the daily recitation of the holy writings as ordained by Bahá'u'lláh in the Kitáb-i-Aqdas and a deeper study of the Revelation of Bahá'u'lláh, will enable the believer to gain a glimpse of the majesty and grandeur of the Blessed Beauty. Like the drop when it sees the ocean, he will become humble and self-effacing. The 'stranger' will be driven out and the heart will be filled with the spirit of God's Faith.

The following prayer revealed by a caring Master for His devoted lovers is a fitting conclusion to this book.

> **12–WT O God, my God! Shield Thy trusted servants from the evils of self and passion, protect them with the watchful eye of Thy loving kindness from all rancour, hate and envy, shelter them in the impregnable stronghold of Thy care and, safe from**

the darts of doubtfulness, make them the manifestations of Thy glorious Signs, illumine their faces with the effulgent rays shed from the Dayspring of Thy Divine Unity, gladden their hearts with the verses revealed from Thy Holy Kingdom, strengthen their loins by Thy all-swaying power that cometh from Thy Realm of Glory. Thou art the All-Bountiful, the Protector, the Almighty, the Gracious!

Appendix 1

The Administrative Order, by Shoghi Effendi

A word should now be said regarding the theory on which this Administrative Order is based and the principle that must govern the operation of its chief institutions. It would be utterly misleading to attempt a comparison between this unique, this divinely-conceived Order and any of the diverse systems which the minds of men, at various periods of their history, have contrived for the government of human institutions. Such an attempt would in itself betray a lack of complete appreciation of the excellence of the handiwork of its great Author. How could it be otherwise when we remember that this Order constitutes the very pattern of that divine civilization which the almighty Law of Bahá'u'lláh is designed to establish upon earth? The divers and ever-shifting systems of human polity, whether past or present, whether originating in the East or in the West, offer no adequate criterion wherewith to estimate the potency of its hidden virtues or to appraise the solidity of its foundations.

The Bahá'í Commonwealth of the future, of which this vast Administrative Order is the sole framework, is, both in theory and practice, not only unique in the entire history of political institutions, but can find no parallel in the annals of any of the world's recognized religious systems. No form of democratic government; no system of autocracy or of dictatorship, whether monarchical or republican; no intermediary scheme of a purely aristocratic order; nor even any of the recognized types of theocracy, whether it be the Hebrew Commonwealth, or the various Christian ecclesiastical organizations, or the Imamate or the Caliphate in Islám – none of these can be identified or be said to conform with the Administrative Order which the master-hand of its perfect Architect has fashioned.

This new-born Administrative Order incorporates within its structure certain elements which are to be found in each of the three recognized forms of secular government, without being in any sense a mere replica of any one of them, and without introducing within its machinery any of the objectionable features which they inherently possess. It blends and harmonizes, as no government fashioned by mortal hands has as yet accomplished, the salutary truths which each of these systems undoubtedly contains without vitiating the integrity of those God-given verities on which it is ultimately founded.

The Administrative Order of the Faith of Bahá'u'lláh must in no wise be regarded as purely democratic in character inasmuch as the basic assumption which requires all democracies to depend fundamentally upon getting their mandate from the people is altogether lacking in this Dispensation. In the conduct of the administrative affairs of the Faith, in the enactment of the legislation necessary to supplement the laws of the Kitáb-i-Aqdas, the members of the Universal House of Justice, it should be borne in mind, are not, as Bahá'u'lláh's utterances clearly imply, responsible to those whom they represent, nor are they allowed to be governed by the feelings, the general opinion, and even the convictions of the mass of the faithful, or of those who directly elect them. They are to follow, in a prayerful attitude, the dictates and promptings of their conscience. They may, indeed they must, acquaint themselves with the conditions prevailing among the community, must weigh dispassionately in their minds the merits of any case presented for their consideration, but must reserve for themselves the right of an unfettered decision. 'God will verily inspire them with whatsoever He willeth,' is Bahá'u'lláh's incontrovertible assurance. They, and not the body of those who either directly or indirectly elect them, have thus been made the recipients of the divine guidance which is at once the life-blood and ultimate safeguard of this Revelation. Moreover, he who symbolizes the hereditary principle in this Dispensation has been made the interpreter of the words of its Author, and ceases consequently, by virtue of the actual authority vested in him, to be the figurehead invariably associated with the prevailing systems of constitutional monarchies.

Nor can the Bahá'í Administrative Order be dismissed as a hard and rigid system of unmitigated autocracy or as an idle imitation of any form of absolutistic ecclesiastical government, whether it be the Papacy, the Imamate or any other similar institution, for the obvious reason that upon the international elected representatives of the followers of Bahá'u'lláh has been conferred the exclusive right of legislating on matters not expressly revealed in the Bahá'í writings. Neither the Guardian of the Faith nor any institution apart from the International House of Justice can ever usurp this vital and essential power or encroach upon that sacred right. The abolition of professional priesthood with its accompanying sacraments of baptism, of communion and of confession of sins, the laws requiring the election by universal suffrage of all local, national, and international Houses of Justice, the total absence of episcopal authority with its attendant privileges, corruptions and bureaucratic tendencies, are further evidences of the non-autocratic character of the Bahá'í Administrative Order and of its inclination to democratic methods in the administration of its affairs.

Nor is this Order identified with the name of Bahá'u'lláh to be confused with any system of purely aristocratic government in view of the fact that it upholds, on the one hand, the hereditary principle and entrusts the Guardian of the Faith with the obligation of interpreting its teachings, and provides, on the other, for the free and direct election from among the mass of the faithful of the body that constitutes its highest legislative organ.

Whereas this Administrative Order cannot be said to have been modelled after any of these recognized systems of government, it nevertheless embodies, reconciles and assimilates within its framework such wholesome elements as are to be found in each one of them. The hereditary authority which the Guardian is called upon to exercise, the vital and essential functions which the Universal House of Justice discharges, the specific provisions requiring its democratic election by the representatives of the faithful – these combine to demonstrate the truth that this divinely revealed Order, which can never be identified with any of the standard types of government referred to by Aristotle in his works, embodies and blends with the spiritual verities on which it is based the beneficent elements which are to be found in each one of them. The admitted evils inherent in each of these systems being rigidly and permanently excluded, this unique Order, however long it may endure and however extensive its ramifications, cannot ever degenerate into any form of despotism, of oligarchy, or of demagogy which must sooner or later corrupt the machinery of all man-made and essentially defective political institutions.

Dearly-beloved friends! Significant as are the origins of this mighty administrative structure, and however unique its features, the happenings that may be said to have heralded its birth and signalized the initial stage of its evolution seem no less remarkable. How striking, how edifying the contrast between the process of slow and steady consolidation that characterizes the growth of its infant strength and the devastating onrush of the forces of disintegration that are assailing the outworn institutions, both religious and secular, of present-day society!

The vitality which the organic institutions of this great, this ever-expanding Order so strongly exhibit; the obstacles which the high courage, the undaunted resolution of its administrators have already surmounted; the fire of an unquenchable enthusiasm that glows with undiminished fervour in the hearts of its itinerant teachers; the heights of self-sacrifice which its champion-builders are now attaining; the breadth of vision, the confident hope, the creative joy, the inward peace, the uncompromising integrity, the exemplary discipline, the unyielding unity and solidarity which its stalwart defenders manifest; the degree to which its moving Spirit has shown itself capable of assimilating the diversified elements within its pale, of cleansing them of all forms of prejudice and of fusing them with its own structure – these are evidences of a power which a disillusioned and sadly shaken society can ill afford to ignore.

Compare these splendid manifestations of the spirit animating this vibrant body of the Faith of Bahá'u'lláh with the cries and agony, the follies and vanities, the bitterness and prejudices, the wickedness and divisions of an ailing and chaotic world. Witness the fear that torments its leaders and paralyzes the action of its blind and bewildered statesmen. How fierce the hatreds, how false the ambitions, how petty the pursuits, how deep-rooted the suspicions of its peoples! How disquieting the lawlessness, the corruption, the unbelief that are eating into the vitals of a tottering civilization!

Might not this process of steady deterioration which is insidiously invading so many departments of human activity and thought be regarded as a necessary accompaniment to the rise of this almighty Arm of Bahá'u'lláh? Might we not look upon the momentous happenings which, in the course of the past twenty years, have so deeply agitated every continent of the earth, as ominous signs simultaneously proclaiming the agonies of a disintegrating civilization and the birthpangs of that World Order – that Ark of human salvation – that must needs arise upon its ruins?

The catastrophic fall of mighty monarchies and empires in the European continent, allusions to some of which may be found in the prophecies of Bahá'u'lláh; the decline that has set in, and is still continuing, in the fortunes of the Shí'ih hierarchy in His own native land; the fall of the Qájár dynasty, the traditional enemy of His Faith; the overthrow of the Sultanate and the Caliphate, the sustaining pillars of Sunní Islám, to which the destruction of Jerusalem in the latter part of the first century of the Christian era offers a striking parallel; the wave of secularization which is invading the Muḥammadan ecclesiastical institutions in Egypt and sapping the loyalty of its staunchest supporters; the humiliating blows that have afflicted some of the most powerful Churches of Christendom in Russia, in Western Europe and Central America; the dissemination of those subversive doctrines that are undermining the foundations and overthrowing the structure of seemingly impregnable strongholds in the political and social spheres of human activity; the signs of an impending catastrophe, strangely reminiscent of the Fall of the Roman Empire in the West, which threatens to engulf the whole structure of present-day civilization – all witness to the tumult which the birth of this mighty Organ of the Religion of Bahá'u'lláh has cast into the world – a tumult which will grow in scope and in intensity as the implications of this constantly evolving Scheme are more fully understood and its ramifications more widely extended over the surface of the globe.

A word more in conclusion. The rise and establishment of this Administrative Order – the shell that shields and enshrines so precious a gem – constitutes the hall-mark of this second and formative age of the Bahá'í era. It will come to be regarded, as it recedes farther and farther from our eyes, as the chief agency empowered to usher in the concluding phase, the consummation of this glorious Dispensation.

Let no one, while this System is still in its infancy, misconceive its character, belittle its significance or misrepresent its purpose. The bedrock on which this Administrative Order is founded is God's immutable Purpose for mankind in this day. The Source from which it derives its inspiration is no one less than Bahá'u'lláh Himself. Its shield and defender are the embattled hosts of the Abhá Kingdom. Its seed is the blood of no less than twenty thousand martyrs who have offered up their lives that it may be born and flourish. The axis round which its institutions revolve are the authentic provisions of the Will and Testament of 'Abdu'l-Bahá. Its guiding principles are the truths which He Who is the unerring Interpreter of the teachings of our Faith has so clearly enunciated in His public addresses throughout the West. The laws that govern its operation and limit its functions are those which have been expressly ordained in the Kitáb-i-Aqdas. The seat round which its spiritual, its humanitarian and administrative activities will cluster are the Mashriqu'l-Adhkár and its Dependencies. The pillars that sustain its authority and buttress its structure are the twin institutions of the Guardianship and of the Universal House of Justice. The central, the underlying aim which animates it is the establishment of the New World Order as adumbrated by Bahá'u'lláh. The methods it employs, the standard it inculcates, incline it to neither East nor West, neither Jew nor Gentile, neither rich nor poor, neither white nor coloured. Its watchword is the unification of the human race; its standard the 'Most Great Peace'; its consummation the advent of that golden millennium – the Day when the kingdoms of this world shall have become the Kingdom of God Himself, the Kingdom of Bahá'u'lláh.

Shoghi [357]

Appendix 2

The Constitution of the Universal House of Justice

DECLARATION OF TRUST

IN THE NAME OF GOD, THE ONE, THE INCOMPARABLE, THE ALL-POWERFUL, THE ALL-KNOWING, THE ALL-WISE.

The light that is shed from the heaven of bounty, and the benediction that shineth from the dawning-place of the will of God, the Lord of the Kingdom of Names, rest upon Him Who is the Supreme Mediator, the Most Exalted Pen, Him Whom God hath made the dawning-place of His most excellent names and the dayspring of His most exalted attributes. Through Him the light of unity hath shone forth above the horizon of the world, and the law of oneness hath been revealed amidst the nations, who, with radiant faces, have turned towards the Supreme Horizon, and acknowledged that which the Tongue of Utterance hath spoken in the Kingdom of His knowledge: 'Earth and heaven, glory and dominion, are God's, the Omnipotent, the Almighty, the Lord of grace abounding!'

* * *

With joyous and thankful hearts we testify to the abundance of God's Mercy, to the perfection of His Justice and to the fulfilment of His Ancient Promise.

Bahá'u'lláh, the Revealer of God's Word in this Day, the Source of Authority, the Fountainhead of Justice, the Creator of a new World Order, the Establisher of the Most Great Peace, the Inspirer and Founder of a world civilization, the Judge, the Lawgiver, the Unifier and Redeemer of all mankind, has proclaimed the advent of God's Kingdom on earth, has formulated its laws and ordinances, enunciated its principles, and ordained its institutions. To direct and canalize the forces released by His Revelation He instituted His Covenant, whose power has preserved the integrity of His Faith, maintained its unity and stimulated its world-wide expansion throughout the successive ministries of 'Abdu'l-Bahá and Shoghi Effendi. It continues to fulfil its life-giving purpose through the agency of the Universal

House of Justice whose fundamental object, as one of the twin successors of Bahá'u'lláh and 'Abdu'l-Bahá, is to ensure the continuity of that divinely-appointed authority which flows from the Source of the Faith, to safeguard the unity of its followers, and to maintain the integrity and flexibility of its teachings.

The fundamental purpose animating the Faith of God and His Religion, declares Bahá'u'lláh, *is to safeguard the interests and promote the unity of the human race, and to foster the spirit of love and fellowship amongst men. Suffer it not to become a source of dissension and discord, of hate and enmity. This is the straight Path, the fixed and immovable foundation. Whatsoever is raised on this foundation, the changes and chances of the world can never impair its strength, nor will the revolution of countless centuries undermine its structure.*

Unto the Most Holy Book, 'Abdu'l-Bahá declares in His Will and Testament, *every one must turn, and all that is not expressly recorded therein must be referred to the Universal House of Justice.*

The provenance, the authority, the duties, the sphere of action of the Universal House of Justice all derive from the revealed Word of Bahá'u'lláh which, together with the interpretations and expositions of the Centre of the Covenant and of the Guardian of the Cause – who, after 'Abdu'l-Bahá, is the sole authority in the interpretation of Bahá'í Scripture – constitute the binding terms of reference of the Universal House of Justice and are its bedrock foundation. The authority of these Texts is absolute and immutable until such time as Almighty God shall reveal His new Manifestation to Whom will belong all authority and power.

There being no successor to Shoghi Effendi as Guardian of the Cause of God, the Universal House of Justice is the Head of the Faith and its supreme institution, to which all must turn, and on it rests the ultimate responsibility for ensuring the unity and progress of the Cause of God. Further, there devolve upon it the duties of directing and coordinating the work of the Hands of the Cause, of ensuring the continuing discharge of the functions of protection and propagation vested in that institution, and of providing for the receipt and disbursement of the Ḥuqúqu'lláh.

Among the powers and duties with which the Universal House of Justice has been invested are:

> To ensure the preservation of the Sacred Texts and to safeguard their inviolability; to analyse, classify, and coordinate the Writings; and to defend and protect the Cause of God and emancipate it from the fetters of repression and persecution;
>
> To advance the interests of the Faith of God; to proclaim, propagate and teach its Message; to expand and consolidate the

institutions of its Administrative Order; to usher in the World Order of Bahá'u'lláh; to promote the attainment of those spiritual qualities which should characterize Bahá'í life individually and collectively; to do its utmost for the realization of greater cordiality and comity amongst the nations and for the attainment of universal peace; and to foster that which is conducive to the enlightenment and illumination of the souls of men and the advancement and betterment of the world;

To enact laws and ordinances not expressly recorded in the Sacred Texts; to abrogate, according to the changes and requirements of the time, its own enactments; to deliberate and decide upon all problems which have caused difference; to elucidate questions that are obscure; to safeguard the personal rights, freedom and initiative of individuals; and to give attention to the preservation of human honour, to the development of countries and the stability of states;

To promulgate and apply the laws and principles of the Faith; to safeguard and enforce that rectitude of conduct which the Law of God enjoins; to preserve and develop the Spiritual and Administrative Centre of the Bahá'í Faith, permanently fixed in the twin cities of 'Akká and Haifa; to administer the affairs of the Bahá'í community throughout the world; to guide, organize, coordinate and unify its activities; to found institutions; to be responsible for ensuring that no body or institution within the Cause abuse its privileges or decline in the exercise of its rights and prerogatives; and to provide for the receipt, disposition, administration and safeguarding of the funds, endowments and other properties that are entrusted to its care;

To adjudicate disputes falling within its purview; to give judgement in cases of violation of the laws of the Faith and to pronounce sanctions for such violations; to provide for the enforcement of its decisions; to provide for the arbitration and settlement of disputes arising between peoples; and to be the exponent and guardian of that Divine Justice which can alone ensure the security of, and establish the reign of law and order in, the world.

The members of the Universal House of Justice, designated by Bahá'u'lláh 'the Men of Justice', 'the people of Bahá who have been mentioned in the Book of Names', 'the Trustees of God amongst His servants and the daysprings of authority in His countries', shall in the discharge of their responsibilities ever bear in mind the following standards set forth by Shoghi Effendi, the Guardian of the Cause of God:

In the conduct of the administrative affairs of the Faith, in the enactment of the legislation necessary to supplement the laws of the Kitáb-i-Aqdas, the members of the Universal House of Justice, it should be borne in mind, are not, as Bahá'u'lláh's utterances clearly imply, responsible to those whom they represent, nor are they allowed to be governed by the feelings, the general opinion, and even the convictions of the mass of the faithful, or of those who directly elect them. They are to follow, in a prayerful attitude, the dictates and promptings of their conscience. They may, indeed they must, acquaint themselves with the conditions prevailing among the community, must weigh dispassionately in their minds the merits of any case presented for their consideration, but must reserve for themselves the right of an unfettered decision. '*God will verily inspire them with whatsoever He willeth*', is Bahá'u'lláh's incontrovertible assurance. They, and not the body of those who either directly or indirectly elect them, have thus been made the recipients of the divine guidance which is at once the life-blood and ultimate safeguard of this Revelation.

The Universal House of Justice was first elected on the first day of the Festival of Riḍván in the one hundred and twentieth year of the Bahá'í Era,* when the members of the National Spiritual Assemblies, in accordance with the provisions of the Will and Testament of 'Abdu'l-Bahá, and in response to the summons of the Hands of the Cause of God, the Chief Stewards of Bahá'u'lláh's embryonic World Commonwealth, brought into being this 'crowning glory' of the administrative institutions of Bahá'u'lláh, the very 'nucleus and forerunner' of His World Order. Now, therefore, in obedience to the Command of God and with entire reliance upon Him, we, the members of the Universal House of Justice, set our hands and its seal to this Declaration of Trust which, together with the By-Laws hereto appended, form the Constitution of the Universal House of Justice.

Hugh E. Chance
Hushmand Fatheazam
Amoz E. Gibson
David Hofman
H. Borrah Kavelin
Ali Nakhjavani
David S. Ruhe
Ian C. Semple
Charles Wolcott

Signed in the City of Haifa on the fourth day of the month of Qawl in the one hundred and twenty-ninth year of the Bahá'í Era, corresponding to the twenty-sixth day of the month of November in the year 1972 according to the Gregorian calendar.

* 21 April 1963 AD

Preamble

The Universal House of Justice is the supreme institution of an Administrative Order whose salient features, whose authority and whose principles of operation are clearly enunciated in the Sacred Writings of the Bahá'í Faith and their authorized interpretations. This Administrative Order consists, on the one hand, of a series of elected councils, universal, secondary and local, in which are vested legislative, executive and judicial powers over the Bahá'í community and, on the other, of eminent and devoted believers appointed for the specific purposes of protecting and propagating the Faith of Bahá'u'lláh under the guidance of the Head of that Faith.

This Administrative Order is the nucleus and pattern of the World Order adumbrated by Bahá'u'lláh. In the course of its divinely propelled organic growth its institutions will expand, putting forth auxiliary branches and developing subordinate agencies, multiplying their activities and diversifying their functions, in consonance with the principles and purposes revealed by Bahá'u'lláh for the progress of the human race.

I. Membership in the Bahá'í Community

The Bahá'í Community shall consist of all persons recognized by the Universal House of Justice as possessing the qualifications of Bahá'í faith and practice.

1. In order to be eligible to vote and hold elective office, a Bahá'í must have attained the age of twenty-one years.

2. The rights, privileges and duties of individual Bahá'ís are as set forth in the Writings of Bahá'u'lláh, 'Abdu'l-Bahá and Shoghi Effendi and as laid down by the Universal House of Justice.

II. Local Spiritual Assemblies

Whenever in any locality the number of Bahá'ís resident therein who have attained the age of twenty-one exceeds nine, these shall on the First Day of Riḍván convene and elect a local administrative body of nine members to be known as the Spiritual Assembly of the Bahá'ís of that locality. Every such Spiritual Assembly shall be elected annually thereafter upon each successive First Day of Riḍván. The members shall hold office for the term of one year or until their successors are elected. When, however, the number of Bahá'ís as aforesaid in any locality is exactly nine, these shall on the First Day of Riḍván constitute themselves the Local Spiritual Assembly by joint declaration.

1. The general powers and duties of a Local Spiritual Assembly are as set forth in the Writings of Bahá'u'lláh, 'Abdu'l-Bahá and Shoghi Effendi and as laid down by the Universal House of Justice.

2. A Local Spiritual Assembly shall exercise full jurisdiction over all Bahá'í activities and affairs within its locality, subject to the provisions of the Local Bahá'í Constitution.*

3. The area of jurisdiction of a Local Spiritual Assembly shall be decided by the National Spiritual Assembly in accordance with the principle laid down for each country by the Universal House of Justice.

III. National Spiritual Assemblies

Whenever it is decided by the Universal House of Justice to form in any country or region a National Spiritual Assembly, the voting members of the Bahá'í community of that country or region shall, in a manner and at a time to be decided by the Universal House of Justice, elect their delegates to their National Convention. These delegates shall, in turn, elect in the manner provided in the National Bahá'í Constitution† a body of nine members to be known as the National Spiritual Assembly of the Bahá'ís of that country or region. The members shall continue in office for a period of one year or until their successors shall be elected.

1. The general powers and duties of a National Spiritual Assembly are as set forth in the Writings of 'Abdu'l-Bahá and Shoghi Effendi and as laid down by the Universal House of Justice.

2. The National Spiritual Assembly shall have exclusive jurisdiction and authority over all the activities and affairs of the Bahá'í Faith throughout its area. It shall endeavour to stimulate, unify and coordinate the manifold activities of the Local Spiritual Assemblies and of individual Bahá'ís in its area and by all possible means assist them to

---

* By-Laws of a Local Spiritual Assembly

† Declaration of Trust and By-Laws of a National Spiritual Assembly

promote the oneness of mankind. It shall furthermore represent its national Bahá'í community in relation to other national Bahá'í communities and to the Universal House of Justice.

3. The area of jurisdiction of a National Spiritual Assembly shall be as defined by the Universal House of Justice.

4. The principal business of the National Convention shall be consultation on Bahá'í activities, plans and policies and the election of the members of the National Spiritual Assembly, as set forth in the National Bahá'í Constitution.

(a) If in any year the National Spiritual Assembly shall consider that it is impracticable or unwise to hold the National Convention, the said Assembly shall provide ways and means by which the annual election and the other essential business of the Convention may be conducted.

(b) Vacancies in the membership of the National Spiritual Assembly shall be filled by a vote of the delegates composing the Convention which elected the Assembly, the ballot to be taken by correspondence or in any other manner decided by the National Spiritual Assembly.

IV. Obligations of Members of Spiritual Assemblies

Among the most outstanding and sacred duties incumbent upon those who have been called upon to initiate, direct and coordinate the affairs of the Cause of God as members of its Spiritual Assemblies are: to win by every means in their power the confidence and affection of those whom it is their privilege to serve; to investigate and acquaint themselves with the considered views, the prevailing sentiments and the personal convictions of those whose welfare it is their solemn obligation to promote; to purge their deliberations and the general conduct of their affairs of self-contained aloofness, the suspicion of secrecy, the stifling atmosphere of dictatorial assertiveness and of every word and deed that may savour of partiality, self-centredness and prejudice; and while retaining the sacred right of final decision in their hands, to invite discussion, ventilate grievances, welcome advice and foster the sense of interdependence and co-partnership, of understanding and mutual confidence between themselves and all other Bahá'ís.

V. The Universal House of Justice

The Universal House of Justice shall consist of nine men who have been elected from the Bahá'í community in the manner hereinafter provided.

1. Election

The members of the Universal House of Justice shall be elected by secret ballot by the members of all National Spiritual Assemblies at a meeting to be known as the International Bahá'í Convention.

(a) An election of the Universal House of Justice shall be held once every five years unless otherwise decided by the Universal House of Justice, and those elected shall continue in office until such time as their successors shall be elected and the first meeting of these successors is duly held.

(b) Upon receiving the call to Convention each National Spiritual Assembly shall submit to the Universal House of Justice a list of the names of its members. The recognition and seating of the delegates to the International Convention shall be vested in the Universal House of Justice.

(c) The principal business of the International Convention shall be to elect the members of the Universal House of Justice, to deliberate on the affairs of the Bahá'í Cause throughout the world, and to make recommendations and suggestions for the consideration of the Universal House of Justice.

(d) The sessions of the International Convention shall be conducted in such manner as the Universal House of Justice shall from time to time decide.

(e) The Universal House of Justice shall provide a procedure whereby those delegates who are unable to be present in person at the International Convention shall cast their ballots for the election of the members of the Universal House of Justice.

(f) If at the time of an election the Universal House of Justice shall consider that it is impracticable or unwise to hold the International Convention it shall determine how the election shall take place.

(g) On the day of the election the ballots of all voters shall be scrutinized and counted and the result certified by tellers appointed in accordance with the instructions of the Universal House of Justice.

(h) If a member of a National Spiritual Assembly who has voted by mail ceases to be a member of that National Spiritual Assembly between the time of casting his ballot and the date of the counting of the ballots, his ballot shall nevertheless remain valid unless in the interval his successor shall have been elected and the ballot of such successor shall have been received by the tellers.

(i) In case by reason of a tie vote or votes the full membership of the Universal House of Justice is not determined on the first ballot, then one or more additional ballots shall be held on the persons tied until all members are elected. The electors in the case of additional ballots shall be the members of National Spiritual Assemblies in office at the time each subsequent vote is taken.

2. Vacancies in Membership

A vacancy in the membership of the Universal House of Justice will occur upon the death of a member or in the following cases:

(a) Should any member of the Universal House of Justice commit a sin injurious to the common weal, he may be dismissed from membership by the Universal House of Justice.

(b) The Universal House of Justice may at its discretion declare a vacancy with respect to any member who in its judgement is unable to fulfil the functions of membership.

(c) A member may relinquish his membership on the Universal House of Justice only with the approval of the Universal House of Justice.

3. By-Election

If a vacancy in the membership of the Universal House of Justice occurs, the Universal House of Justice shall call a by-election at the earliest possible date unless such date, in the judgement of the

Universal House of Justice, falls too close to the date of a regular election of the entire membership, in which case the Universal House of Justice may, at its discretion, defer the filling of the vacancy to the time of the regular election. If a by-election is held, the voters shall be the members of the National Spiritual Assemblies in office at the time of the by-election.

4. Meetings

(a) After the election of the Universal House of Justice the first meeting shall be called by the member elected by the highest number of votes or, in his absence or other incapacity, by the member elected by the next highest number of votes or, in case two or more members have received the same highest number of votes, then by the member selected by lot from among those members. Subsequent meetings shall be called in the manner decided by the Universal House of Justice.

(b) The Universal House of Justice has no officers. It shall provide for the conduct of its meetings and shall organize its activities in such manner as it shall from time to time decide.

(c) The business of the Universal House of Justice shall be conducted by the full membership in consultation, except that the Universal House of Justice may from time to time provide for quorums of less than the full membership for specified classes of business.

5. Signature

The signature of the Universal House of Justice shall be the words 'The Universal House of Justice' or in Persian 'Baytu'l-'Adl-i-A'ẓam' written by hand by any one of its members upon authority of the Universal House of Justice, to which shall be affixed in each case the Seal of the Universal House of Justice.

6. Records

The Universal House of Justice shall provide for the recording and verification of its decisions in such manner as it shall, from time to time, judge necessary.

VI. Bahá'í Elections

In order to preserve the spiritual character and purpose of Bahá'í elections the practices of nomination or electioneering, or any other procedure or activity detrimental to that character and purpose shall be eschewed. A silent and prayerful atmosphere shall prevail during the election so that each elector may vote for none but those whom prayer and reflection inspire him to uphold.

1. All Bahá'í elections, except elections of officers of Local and National Spiritual Assemblies and committees, shall be by plurality vote taken by secret ballot.

2. Election of the officers of a Spiritual Assembly or committee shall be by majority vote of the Assembly or committee taken by secret ballot.

3. In case by reason of a tie vote or votes the full membership of an elected body is not determined on the first ballot, then one or more additional ballots shall be taken on the persons tied until all members are elected.

4. The duties and rights of a Bahá'í elector may not be assigned nor may they be exercised by proxy.

VII. The Right of Review

The Universal House of Justice has the right to review any decision or action of any Spiritual Assembly, National or Local, and to approve, modify or reverse such decision or action. The Universal House of Justice also has the right to intervene in any matter in which a Spiritual Assembly is failing to take action or to reach a decision and, at its discretion, to require that action be taken, or itself to take action directly in the matter.

VIII. Appeals

The right of appeal exists in the circumstances, and shall be exercised according to the procedures, outlined below:

1. (a) Any member of a local Bahá'í community may appeal from a decision of his Local Spiritual Assembly to the National Spiritual Assembly which shall determine whether it shall take jurisdiction of the matter or refer it back to the Local Spiritual Assembly for

reconsideration. If such an appeal concerns the membership of a person in the Bahá'í community, the National Spiritual Assembly is obliged to take jurisdiction of and decide the case.

(b) Any Bahá'í may appeal from a decision of his National Spiritual Assembly to the Universal House of Justice which shall determine whether it shall take jurisdiction of the matter or leave it within the final jurisdiction of the National Spiritual Assembly.

(c) If any differences arise between two or more Local Spiritual Assemblies and if these Assemblies are unable to resolve them, any one such Assembly may bring the matter to the National Spiritual Assembly which shall thereupon take jurisdiction of the case. If the decision of the National Spiritual Assembly thereon is unsatisfactory to any of the Assemblies concerned, or if a Local Spiritual Assembly at any time has reason to believe that actions of its National Spiritual Assembly are affecting adversely the welfare and unity of that Local Assembly's community, it shall, in either case, after seeking to compose its difference of opinion with the National Spiritual Assembly, have the right to appeal to the Universal House of Justice, which shall determine whether it shall take jurisdiction of the matter or leave it within the final jurisdiction of the National Spiritual Assembly.

2. An appellant, whether institution or individual, shall in the first instance make appeal to the Assembly whose decision is questioned, either for reconsideration of the case by that Assembly or for submission to a higher body. In the latter case the Assembly is in duty bound to submit the appeal together with full particulars of the matter. If an Assembly refuses to submit the appeal, or fails to do so within a reasonable time, the appellant may take the case directly to the higher authority.

X. The Boards of Counsellors

The institution of the Boards of Counsellors was brought into being by the Universal House of Justice to extend into the future the specific functions of protection and propagation conferred upon the Hands of the Cause of God. The members of these boards are appointed by the Universal House of Justice.

1. The term of office of a Counsellor, the number of Counsellors on each Board, and the boundaries of the zone in which each Board of Counsellors shall operate, shall be decided by the Universal House of Justice.

2. A Counsellor functions as such only within his zone and should he move his residence out of the zone for which he is appointed he automatically relinquishes his appointment.

3. The rank and specific duties of a Counsellor render him ineligible for service on local or national administrative bodies. If elected to the Universal House of Justice he ceases to be a Counsellor.

X. The Auxiliary Boards

In each zone there shall be two Auxiliary Boards, one for the protection and one for the propagation of the Faith, the numbers of whose members shall be set by the Universal House of Justice. The members of these Auxiliary Boards shall serve under the direction of the Continental Boards of Counsellors and shall act as their deputies, assistants and advisers.

1. The members of the Auxiliary Boards shall be appointed from among the believers of that zone by the Continental Board of Counsellors.

2. Each Auxiliary Board member shall be allotted a specific area in which to serve and, unless specifically deputized by the Counsellors, shall not function as a member of the Auxiliary Board outside that area.

3. An Auxiliary Board member is eligible for any elective office but if elected to an administrative post on a national or local level must decide whether to retain membership on the Board or accept the administrative post, since he may not serve in both capacities at the same time. If elected to the Universal House of Justice he ceases to be a member of the Auxiliary Board.

XI. Amendment

This Constitution may be amended by decision of the Universal House of Justice when the full membership is present.

Appendix 3

Guide to Paragraphs in the Will and Testament

The following guide, which is presented in two sections, provides an easy reference linking passages of the Will and Testament to chapters of this book. In the first section, the paragraphs of the Will and Testament are listed in order and show in which chapters of *The Child of the Covenant* they are discussed. In the second section, the order is reversed, with the chapters of *The Child of the Covenant* appearing in order and indicating which paragraphs of the Will and Testament are covered in each chapter. The Will and Testament consists of 56 paragraphs. These are shown here as 1–WT up to 55–WT. The subject matter in each paragraph is discussed in one or more chapters of the book.

Will & Testament Paragraphs	**Opening lines of paragraph of Will and Testament**	**Chapters in *Child of the Covenant***
1 – WT	All-Praise to Him who, by the Shield of His Covenant . . .	4
2 – WT	Salutation and praise, blessing and glory rest upon . . .	27
3 – WT	O ye beloved of the Lord! The greatest of all things . . .	5, 6, 7, 8
4 – WT	And still another of His trials was the hostility . . .	9, 10, 11
5 – WT	O ye that stand fast and firm in the Covenant!	12, 13, 14, 15, 21, 22, 24
6 – WT	What deviation can be greater than breaking the Covenant . . .	16, 17, 18, 19, 20, 21
7 – WT	A few months ago, in concert with others . . .	22
8 – WT	According to the direct and sacred command of God . . .	22
9 – WT	In like manner, the focal Centre of Hate . . .	21
10 – WT	O God, my God! Thou seest this wronged servant of Thine . . .	22, 24

Will & Testament Paragraphs	Opening lines of paragraph of Will and Testament	Chapters in *Child of the Covenant*
11 – WT	In short, O ye beloved of the Lord!	26
12 – WT	O God, my God! Shield Thy trusted servant from the evils . . .	40
13 – WT	O ye that stand fast in the Covenant. When the hour cometh . . .	25
14 – WT	In these days, the most important of all things is the guidance . . .	25
15 – WT	The disciples of Christ forgot themselves and all earthly things . . .	25
16 – WT	O my loving friends! After the passing away of this wronged one . . .	27, 35
17 – WT	The sacred and youthful branch, the guardian of the Cause of God . . .	13, 28, 29, 31,
18 – WT	O ye beloved of the Lord! It is incumbent upon the guardian . . .	35
19 – WT	The Hands of the Cause of God must elect from their own number . . .	36
20 – WT	O friends! The Hands of the Cause of God must be nominated . . .	33
21 – WT	The obligations of the Hands of the Cause of God are to diffuse . . .	32
22 – WT	This body of the Hands of the Cause of God is under the direction . . .	33, 39
23 – WT	O ye beloved of the Lord! In this sacred Dispensation, conflict . . .	24
24 – WT	Wherefore, O my loving friends! Consort with all the peoples . . .	24
25 – WT	And now, concerning the House of Justice which God hath ordained . . .	38
26 – WT	O Lord, my God! Assist thy loved ones to be firm in Thy Faith . . .	–
27 – WT	O friends of ‘Abdu’l-Bahá! The Lord, as a sign of His infinite bounties . . .	39
28 – WT	O ye beloved of the Lord! It is incumbent upon you to be submissive . . .	39
29 – WT	This is my counsel and the commandment of God unto you.	39
30 – WT	O my Lord, my heart’s desire, Thou Whom I ever invoke . . .	22

Will & Testament Paragraphs	**Opening lines of paragraph of Will and Testament**	**Chapters in *Child of the Covenant***
31 – WT	Yet now Thou seest them, O Lord, my God!	23
32 – WT	Adversities have waxed still more severe as they rose . . .	12, 16, 22, 23
33 – WT	Lord! Thou seest all things weeping me and my kindred rejoicing . . .	22
34 – WT	I call upon Thee, O Lord my God! with my tongue . . .	23
35 – WT	Thou art the Powerful . . .	23
36 – WT	O dearly beloved friends! I am now in very great danger . . .	23, 24, 38
37 – WT	It is incumbent upon these members . . .	38
38 – WT	And now, one of the greatest and most fundamental principles . . .	16, 24, 30
39 – WT	In short, according to the explicit Divine Text . . .	26
40 – WT	Gracious God! After Mírzá Badí'u'lláh had declared . . .	16
41 – WT	My purpose is, however, to show that it is incumbent . . .	30
42 – WT	O ye beloved of the Lord! Strive with all your heart . . .	24
43 – WT	O God, my God! I call Thee, Thy Prophets . . .	24
44 – WT	O my God! my Beloved, my heart's Desire! Thou knowest . . .	22
45 – WT	Thou seest, O my God! how my long-suffering . . .	22
46 – WT	Lord! My cup of woe runneth over . . .	22
47 – WT	Thou art, verily, the Merciful . . .	22
48 – WT	O ye the true, the sincere, the faithful friends . . .	21
49 – WT	When, in all parts of the earth, the enemies of God . . .	12
50 – WT	Thereupon the loved ones of the Lord arose . . .	22
51 – WT	And as they lost their cause, grew hopeless . . .	22
52 – WT	Hence, the beloved of the Lord must entirely shun them . . .	24, 30
53 – WT	Whosoever and whatsoever meeting becometh a hindrance . . .	25
54 – WT	O ye the faithful loved ones of 'Abdu'l-Bahá.	31
55 – WT	For he is, after 'Abdu'l-Bahá, the guardian of the Cause . . .	29, 31, 38

Chapters in *Child of the Covenant*	Chapter Titles	Paragraphs in Will and Testament
1	Prerequisites for the Study of the Covenant of Bahá'u'lláh	–
2	The Family of Bahá'u'lláh	–
3	Tests of Faith	–
4	The Covenant, A Shield for the Protection of the Faith	1
5	The Greatest of All Things	3
6	The Suffering of the Báb and Bahá'u'lláh	3
7	Bahá'u'lláh's Retirement to the Mountains of Kurdistan	3
8	Bahá'u'lláh's Exiles	3
9	Mírzá Yaḥyá	4
10	The Breaker of the Covenant of the Báb	4
11	Open Rebellion of Mírzá Yaḥyá	4
12	The Arch-Breaker of the Covenant of Bahá'u'lláh	5, 32, 49
13	Attacks on the Centre of the Covenant	5, 17
14	Confirmations of Bahá'u'lláh Bestow Victory	5
15	Mírzá Muḥammad-Alí Claims Partnership with Bahá'u'lláh	5
16	Deviations of Mírzá Muḥammad-'Alí (1)	6, 32, 38, 40
17	Deviations of Mírzá Muḥammad-'Alí (2)	6
18	Deviations of Mírzá Muḥammad-'Alí (3)	6
19	Deviations of Mírzá Muḥammad-'Alí (4)	6
20	Deviations of Mírzá Muḥammad-'Alí (5)	6
21	Decreeing the Death of 'Abdu'l-Bahá	5, 6, 9, 48
22	Covenant-Breakers Petition Government against 'Abdu'l-Bahá	5, 7, 8, 10, 30, 32, 33, 45, 46, 47, 50
23	'Abdu'l-Bahá's Greatness Transcends His Suffering	31, 32, 34, 35, 36
24	Dissociation with Covenant-Breakers	6, 31, 32, 34, 35, 36, 38, 40
25	Teaching the Cause of God	13, 14, 15, 53
26	We Have Chosen 'the Greater' after 'the Most Great'	11, 39
27	The Appointment of Shoghi Effendi as the Guardian of the Cause	2, 16

Chapters in ***Child of the Covenant***	**Chapter Titles**	**Paragraphs in Will and Testament**
28	The Guardian and the Universal House of Justice under the Protection of the Báb and Bahá'u'lláh	17
29	Covenant-Breakers' Attacks on Shoghi Effendi	17, 55
30	Rebellion of Shoghi Effendi's Relatives	38, 41, 52
31	Turning to Shoghi Effendi	17, 54, 55
32	Hands of the Cause of God	21
33	The Hands of the Cause during the Ministry of the Guardian	20, 22
34	The Hands in the Service of the Guardian	17
35	Successor to Shoghi Effendi	16, 18
36	Shoghi Effendi's Statements about Future Guardians	19
37	The Chief Stewards, the Custodians	–
38	The Universal House of Justice	17, 25, 36, 37, 55
39	Ḥuqúqu'lláh, Obedience to Government, Supreme Tribunal	22, 27, 28, 29
40	Steadfastness in the Covenant	12

Bibliography

'Abdu'l-Bahá. *Memorials of the Faithful*. Wilmette, Ill.: Bahá'í Publishing Trust, 1971.

— *Risáliy-i-Ayyám-i-Tis'ah*.

— *Selections from the Writings of 'Abdu'l-Bahá*. Haifa: Bahá'í World Centre, 1978.

— *Some Answered Questions*. Wilmette, Ill.: Bahá'í Publishing Trust, 1981.

— *Tablets of the Divine Plan*. Wilmette, Ill.: Bahá'í Publishing Trust, 1977.

— *The Will and Testament of 'Abdu'l-Bahá*. Wilmette, Ill.: Bahá'í Publishing Trust, 1971.

The Báb. *Persian Bayán*.

— *Selections from the Writings of the Báb*. Haifa: Bahá'í World Centre, 1976.

Bahá'í Prayers: A Selections of Prayers revealed by Bahá'u'lláh, the Báb and 'Abdu'l-Bahá. Wilmette, Ill.: Bahá'í Publishing Trust, 1991.

Bahá'í World, The. vol. 13. Haifa: The Universal House of Justice, 1970.

Bahá'u'lláh. *Amr va Khalq*.

— *Epistle to the Son of the Wolf*. Wilmette, Ill.: Bahá'í Publishing Trust, 1988.

— *Gleanings from the Writings of Bahá'u'lláh*. Wilmette, Ill.: Bahá'í Publishing Trust, 1983.

— *The Hidden Words*. Wilmette, Ill.: Bahá'í Publishing Trust, 1990.

— *Iqtidárát*.

— *The Kitáb-i-Aqdas*. Haifa: Bahá'í World Centre, 1992.

— *Kitáb-i-Íqán*. Wilmette, Ill.: Bahá'í Publishing Trust, 1989.

— *Majmú'iy-i-Alwáh*.

— *Mu'assisy-i-Ayádíy-i-Amru'lláh*.

— *Tablets of Bahá'u'lláh revealed after the Kitáb-i-Aqdas*. Haifa: Bahá'í World Centre, 1978.

Balyuzi, H. M. *'Abdu'l-Bahá*. Oxford: George Ronald, 1971.

— *Bahá'u'lláh, The King of Glory*. Oxford: George Ronald, 1980.

Blomfield, Lady [Sara Louise]. *The Chosen Highway*. Wilmette, Ill.: Bahá'í Publishing Trust, 1967.

Chapman, Anita Ioas. *Leroy Ioas: Hand of the Cause of God*. Oxford: George Ronald, 1998.

Collins, Amelia. *A Tribute to Shoghi Effendi*. Wilmette, Ill.: Bahá'í Publishing Trust.

Compilation of Compilations, The. Prepared by the Universal House of Justice 1963-1990. 2 vols. [Sydney]: Bahá'í Publications Australia, 1991.

Fáḍil-i-Mazandaráni. *Asráru'l-Á<u>th</u>ár*.

Fáḍil-i-Yazdí, *Manáhiju'l-Aḥkám*.

Giachery, Ugo. *Shoghi Effendi: Recollections*. Oxford: George Ronald, 1973.

Ḥaydar-'Alí, *Bihjatu'ṣ-Ṣudúr*.

Ḥuqúqu'lláh. Compiled by the Research Department of the Universal House of Justice. Oakham: Bahá'í Publishing Trust, rev. edn. 1989.

<u>Kh</u>áṭirát-i-Afnán.

Lights of Guidance: A Bahá'í Reference File. Compiled by Helen Hornby. New Delhi: Bahá'í Publishing Trust, 2nd edn. 1988.

Maḥmúd-i-Zarqání. *Maḥmúd's Diary*. Oxford: George Ronald, 1998.

Má'idiy-i-Ásmání. Compiled from the Writings by 'Abdu'l-Ḥamid-i-I<u>sh</u>ráq <u>Kh</u>ávarí, New Delhi: Bahá'í Publishing Trust, 1984.

The Ministry of the Custodians, 1957-1963: An Account of the Stewardship of the Hands of the Cause. Haifa: Bahá'í World Centre, 1992.

Nabíl-i-A'ẓam. *The Dawn-Breakers: Nabíl's Narrative of the Early Days of the Bahá'í Revelation*. Wilmette, Ill.: Bahá'í Publishing Trust, 1970.

Rabbaní, Rúḥíyyih. *The Priceless Pearl*. London: Bahá'í Publishing Trust, 1969.

Raḥíq-i-Ma<u>kh</u>túm.

Shoghi Effendi. *The Advent of Divine Justice*. Wilmette, Ill.: Bahá'í Publishing Trust, 1990.

— *Bahá'í Administration*. Wilmette, Ill.: Bahá'í Publishing Trust, 1968.

— *Citadel of Faith: Messages to America 1947-1957*. Wilmette, Ill.: Bahá'í Publishing Trust, 1965.

— *God Passes By*. Wilmette, Ill.: Bahá'í Publishing Trust, rev. edn. 1974.

— *Messages to America*. Wilmette, Ill.: Bahá'í Publishing Trust, 1947.

— *Messages to the Bahá'í World*. Wilmette, Ill.: Bahá'í Publishing Trust, 1971.

— *The Promised Day is Come*. Wilmette, Ill.: Bahá'í Publishing Trust, rev. edn. 1980.

— *The Unfolding Destiny of the British Bahá'í Community: The Messages of the Guardian of the Bahá'í Faith to the Bahá'ís of the British Isles*. London: Bahá'í Publishing Trust, 1981.

— *The World Order of Bahá'u'lláh*. Wilmette, Ill.: Bahá'í Publishing Trust, 1991.

Star of the West. Rpt. Oxford: George Ronald, 1984.

Taherzadeh, Adib. *The Covenant of Bahá'u'lláh*. Oxford: George Ronald, 1992.

— *The Revelation of Bahá'u'lláh*, vol. 1. Oxford: George Ronald, 1974.

— *The Revelation of Bahá'u'lláh*, vol. 2. Oxford: George Ronald, 1977.

— *The Revelation of Bahá'u'lláh*, vol. 3. Oxford: George Ronald, 1983.

— *The Revelation of Bahá'u'lláh*, vol. 4. Oxford: George Ronald, 1987.

The Universal House of Justice. *Messages from the Universal House of Justice 1968-1973*. Wilmette, Ill.: Bahá'í Publishing Trust, 1976.

— *Wellspring of Guidance*. Wilmette, Ill.: Bahá'í Publishing Trust, 1976.

Yúnis Khán. *Kháṭirát-i-Nuh-Ṣáliḥ*.

References

A Note from the Publisher

1. Shoghi Effendi, *World Order*, p. 144.

Preface

2. ibid.
3. Shoghi Effendi, *God Passes By*, p. 328.
4. Shoghi Effendi, *Bahá'í Administration*, p. 90.
5. From a letter written on behalf of Shoghi Effendi to an individual believer, 25 March 1930, quoted in *Compilation*, vol. 1, p. 366.

Introduction

6. Matt. 16:18.
7. Bahá'u'lláh, quoted in Shoghi Effendi, *God Passes By*, p. 245.
8. For more information on the manner of revelation of Tablets, see Taherzadeh, *Revelation of Bahá'u'lláh*, vol. 1, pp. 23–4.
9. Shoghi Effendi, *World Order*, p. 134.
10. See Taherzadeh, *Revelation of Bahá'u'lláh*, vol. 4, pp. 143, 149–53.
11. Bahá'u'lláh, in Shoghi Effendi, *World Order*, p. 135.
12. *Máidiy-i-Ásmání*, vol. 5, pp. 98–9.
13. Shoghi Effendi, *World Order*, p. 98.
14. 'Abdu'l-Bahá, *Will and Testament*, p. 15.
15. Shoghi Effendi, *World Order*, p. 8.
16. Shoghi Effendi quoted in *Wellspring of Guidance*, pp. 54–5.
17. Shoghi Effendi, *World Order*, p. 144.
18. Shoghi Effendi, *God Passes By*, p. 328.
19. Shoghi Effendi, *World Order*, p. 4.
20. ibid. pp. 19–20.
21. Shoghi Effendi, *God Passes By*, p. 324.

Chapter 1

22. Bahá'u'lláh, quoted in Shoghi Effendi, *Advent of Divine Justice*, p. 77.
23. ibid.
24. ibid.
25. ibid.
26. ibid. p. 78.
27. *Iqtidárát*, p. 85.
28. Shoghi Effendi, *World Order*, p. 100.
29. Bahá'u'lláh, *Kitáb-i-Aqdas*, para. 173.
30. Bahá'u'lláh, *Kitáb-i-Íqán*, p. 3.
31. ibid. p. 211.

Chapter 2

32. Bahá'u'lláh, quoted in Shoghi Effendi, *Promised Day is Come*, pp. 40–1.
33. See 'Abdu'l-Bahá, *Memorials of the Faithful*, p. 95.
34. See Taherzadeh, *Revelation of Bahá'u'lláh*, vol. 2.
35. Blomfield, *Chosen Highway*, pp. 39–40.
36. Shoghi Effendi, *God Passes By*, p. 188.
37. Bahá'u'lláh, in Shoghi Effendi, *God Passes By*, p. 148.
38. There is a further reference to him to chapter 13.
39. Shoghi Effendi, *Messages to the Bahá'í World*, p. 24.

Chapter 3

40. Bahá'u'lláh, *Kitáb-i-Aqdas*, para. 121.
41. ibid. para. 174.
42. Quoted by Fáḍil-i-Yazdí in his *Manáhiju'l-Aḥkám*, vol. 2, p. 657.
43. 'Abdu'l-Bahá, quoted in Rabbaní, *Priceless Pearl*, p. 1.
44. ibid. p. 2.
45. Shoghi Effendi, *Bahá'í Administration*, p. 90.
46. Bahá'u'lláh, *Hidden Words*, Arabic no. 4.
47. The full text of this Tablet, with an explanation of its significance, is given in Taherzadeh, *Revelation of Bahá'u'lláh*, vol. 1, chapter 14.
48. Bahá'u'lláh, in *Bahá'í Prayers*, pp. 223–4.
49. 'Abdu'l-Bahá, *Selections*, p. 87.

Chapter 4

50. Bahá'u'lláh, *Tablets*, p. 221.
51. Bahá'u'lláh, *Kitáb-i-Íqán*, p. 144.
52. ibid. p. 153.
53. Bahá'u'lláh, quoted in Shoghi Effendi, *God Passes By*, p. 245.
54. Shoghi Effendi, *Citadel of Faith*, p. 131.
55. Bahá'u'lláh, *Kitáb-i-Aqdas*, para. 173.
56. Bahá'u'lláh, Tablet of Aḥmad, *Bahá'í Prayers*, p. 211.
57. Ḥaydar-'Alí, *Bihjatu'ṣ-Ṣudúr*, pp. 337–8.

Chapter 5

58. Bahá'u'lláh, *Gleanings*, p. 9.
59. *Má'idiy-i-Ásma'ní*, vol. 9, p. 128.
60. Bahá'u'lláh, *Gleanings*, pp. 100–1.
61. Bahá'u'lláh, quoted in Shoghi Effendi, *God Passes By*, p. 190.
62. ibid.
63. From an unpublished compilation, Iranian National Bahá'í Archives, no. 18, p. 41.
64. *Gleanings*, p. 287.
65. ibid. p. 272.
66. As an example, see the message of Shoghi Effendi dated 4 June 1957, 'Call to Hands of the Cause and National Assemblies', in Shoghi Effendi, *Messages to the Bahá'í World*, pp. 122-3.
67. Bahá'u'lláh, *Gleanings*, pp. 329–30.

Chapter 6

68. The Báb, *Selections*, p. 59.
69. Shoghi Effendi, *God Passes By*, p. 52–4.
70. Bahá'u'lláh, quoted in Nabíl, *Dawn-Breakers*, pp. 583–4.
71. Nabíl, ibid. pp. 368–75.
72. Bahá'u'lláh, *Epistle to the Son of the Wolf*, p. 22.
73. Quoted in Blomfield, *Chosen Highway*, p. 45.
74. Bahá'u'lláh, quoted in Shoghi Effendi, *God Passes By*, p. 109.

Chapter 7

75. ibid. p. 117.
76. ibid. pp. 118–20.
77. Shoghi Effendi, *God Passes By*, p. 120.

Chapter 8

78. Bahá'u'lláh, quoted in Shoghi Effendi, *God Passes By*, p. 133.
79. Quoted in ibid. pp. 147–8.
80. Bahá'u'lláh, quoted in ibid. p. 149.
81. 'Abdu'l-Bahá, *Risáliy-i-Ayyám-i-Tis'ah*, p. 330.
82. Bahá'u'lláh, *Gleanings*, p. 35.
83. Shoghi Effendi, *God Passes By*, p. 155.
84. ibid. p. 156.
85. ibid. p. 157.
86. ibid. pp. 159–61.
87. Bahá'u'lláh, quoted in ibid. p. 161.
88. ibid.
89. ibid. pp. 161–2.
90. ibid. pp. 170–1.
91. ibid. pp. 180–2.
92. Bahá'u'lláh, quoted in ibid. p. 185.
93. Bahá'u'lláh, *Gleanings*, p. 345.
94. Bahá'u'lláh, quoted in Shoghi Effendi, *God Passes By,* p. 184.
95. 'Abdu'l-Bahá, *Asráru'l-Áthár*, vol. 4. p. 349.
96. Persian ambassador, quoted in ibid. p. 186.
97. Bahá'u'lláh, quoted in ibid.
98. Bahá'u'lláh, *Gleanings*, p. 203.
99. ibid. p. 148.

Chapter 9

100. Nabíl, *Dawn-Breakers*, p. 433.
101. Bahá'u'lláh, quoted in ibid. p. 583.
102. Bahá'u'lláh, *Kitáb-i-Aqdas*, para. 184.
103. Ḥaydar-'Alí, *Bihjatu'ṣ-Ṣudúr*, pp. 22–4.
104. The Báb, *Selections*, p. 149.
105. The Báb, quoted in Shoghi Effendi, *World Order*, p. 100.
106. ibid.
107. ibid.
108. The Báb, *Selections*, p. 3.
109. The Báb, quoted in Bahá'u'lláh, *Epistle to the Son of the Wolf*, p. 171.

110. ibid. p. 154.
111. ibid. p. 158.
112. The Báb, *Selections*, p. 98.
113. The Báb, quoted in Bahá'u'lláh, *Epistle to the Son of the Wolf*, pp. 142–3.
114. The Báb, *Selections*, p. 157.
115. ibid. p. 131.
116. ibid. p. 155.
117. The Báb, *Persian Bayán*, III, 7.
118. ibid. III, 15.
119. The Báb, quoted in Shoghi Effendi, *God Passes By*, p. 25.
120. The Báb, quoted in Bahá'u'lláh, *Epistle to the Son of the Wolf*, pp. 154–5.
121. ibid. p. 152.
122. ibid. p. 174.
123. The Báb, *Selections*, p. 104.
124. ibid. p. 100.
125. The Báb, quoted in Bahá'u'lláh, *Epistle to the Son of the Wolf*, p. 151.
126. ibid. p. 141.
127. ibid.
128. ibid. p. 152.
129. The Báb, quoted in Shoghi Effendi, *God Passes By*, p. 29.
130. The Báb, *Selections*, p. 85.
131. The Báb, quoted in Bahá'u'lláh, *Epistle to the Son of the Wolf*, p. 153.

Chapter 10
132. Shoghi Effendi, *God Passes By*, p. 164.
133. Bahá'u'lláh, *Kitáb-i-Íqán*, p. 248.
134. Shoghi Effendi, *God Passes By*, pp. 112–13.
135. ibid. p. 117.
136. Bahá'u'lláh, *Kitáb-i-Aqdas*, para. 2.
137. Nabíl, quoted in Shoghi Effendi, *God Passes By*, p. 113.
138. Bahá'u'lláh, quoted in ibid. p. 115.
139. Greatest Holy Leaf, quoted in Blomfield, *Chosen Highway*, pp. 50–2.
140. Bahá'u'lláh, *Epistle to the Son of the Wolf*, pp. 176–7.
141. ibid. p. 173.
142. ibid. p. 22.
143. 'Abdu'l-Bahá, quoted in Shoghi Effendi, *God Passes By*, p. 133.
144. 'Abdu'l-Bahá, quoted in Balyuzi, *King of Glory*, pp. 183–4.
145. Bahá'u'lláh, *Epistle to the Son of the Wolf*, p. 168.

Chapter 11
146. Shoghi Effendi, *God Passes By*, pp. 165–6.
147. Quoted in ibid. p. 167.
148. Quoted in ibid. p. 167.
149. Ḥaydar-'Alí, *Bihjatu'ṣ-Sudúr*, p. 76.
150. Shoghi Effendi, *God Passes By*, pp. 167–8.
151. ibid. pp. 168–9.

152. Ḥaydar-'Alí, *Bihjatu'ṣ-Sudúr*, pp. 77–8.
153. 2 Thess. 2:3, 4, 8.

Chapter 12

154. Ḥaydar-'Alí, *Bihjatu'ṣ-Ṣudúr*, pp. 326–31.
155. ibid. p. 323.
156. Yúnis Khán, *Kháṭirát-i-Nuh-Ṣáliḥ*, pp. 51–2.

Chapter 13

157. *Kháṭirát-i-Afnán*, pp. 165–6.
158. Ḥaydar-'Alí, *Bihjatu'ṣ-Ṣudúr*, p. 328.
159. Yúnis Khán, *Kháṭirát-i-Nuh-i-Ṣáliḥ*, pp. 59–60.
160. ibid. pp. 40–3.
161. *Má'idiy-i-Ásmání*, vol. 5, pp. 98–9.

Chapter 14

162. Bahá'u'lláh, *Hidden Words*, Arabic no. 5.
163. ibid. Arabic no. 42.
164. Bahá'u'lláh, *Bahá'í Prayers*, p. 71.
165. Bahá'u'lláh, *Kitáb-i-Aqdas*, para. 53.
166. Bahá'u'lláh, Lawḥ-i-Ṭibb (Tablet of Medicine) in *Majmú'iy-i-Alwáḥ*.
167. Bahá'u'lláh, *Gleanings*, p. 280.
168. 'Abdu'l-Bahá, in *Compilation*, vol. 2, p. 211.
169. From a letter of Shoghi Effendi to an individual believer, 28 March 1953, in ibid. p. 223.
170. Shoghi Effendi, *God Passes By*, pp. 256–8.
171. ibid. pp. 260–1.
172. Yúnis Khán, *Kháṭirát-i-Nuh-i-Sálih*, pp. 63–6.
173. ibid. pp. 259–65.
174. ibid. pp. 570–3.

Chapter 15

175. *Raḥíq-i-Makhtúm*, vol. 2, p. 850.
176. Bahá'u'lláh, quoted in Shoghi Effendi, *God Passes By*, p. 242.
177. *Má'idiy-i-Ásmání*, vol. 8, p. 40.
178. Bahá'u'lláh, quoted in Shoghi Effendi, *God Passes By*, p. 251.
179. As an example, see chapter 12, the story of Ḥájí Muḥammad Ṭáhir-i-Málmírí's first meeting with Mírzá Muḥammad-'Alí.

Chapter 16

180. Bahá'u'lláh, *Gleanings*, p. 285.

Chapter 17

181. Ḥaydar-'Alí, *Bihjatu'ṣ-Sudúr*, pp. 334–5.
182. Yúnis Khán, *Kháṭirát-i-Nuh-i-Sálih*, p. 216.
183. ibid. pp. 250–6.
184. Memoirs of Ḥájí 'Alí Yazdí.

Chapter 18
185. Bahá'u'lláh, *Tablets*, p. 222.
186. ibid. p. 219.
187. Quoted in Balyuzi, *'Abdu'l-Bahá*, pp. 271–2.
188. Quoted in Browne, *Materials*, p. 171.

Chapter 19
189. Yúnis Khán, *Kháṭirát-i-Nuh-i-Sálih*, pp. 309–10.
190. ibid. pp. 313–15.
191. Owen, *My Perilous Life in Palestine*, pp. 230–5.

Chapter 20
192. Yúnis Khán, *Kháṭirát-i-Nuh-Ṣáliḥ*, pp. 45–7.
193. 'Abdu'l-Bahá, quoted in Shoghi Effendi, *God Passes By*, pp. 275–6.
194. Yúnis Khán, *Kháṭirát-i-Nuh-Ṣáliḥ*, pp. 174–5.

Chapter 21
195. Bahá'u'lláh, *Kitáb-i-Aqdas*, para. 37.

Chapter 22
196. Translation of Fáḍil-i-Mazandarání, *Asraru'l-Áthár*, pp. 361–3.

Chapter 23
197. 'Abdu'l-Bahá, *Selections*, pp. 216–22.
198. Quoted in Bahá'u'lláh, *Kitáb-i-Íqán*, p. 67.
199. Shoghi Effendi, *World Order*, pp. 131–4.
200. Bahá'u'lláh, quoted in ibid. p. 135.
201. ibid.
202. ibid.
203. ibid. pp. 135–6.
204. Bahá'u'lláh, *Tablets*, pp. 227–8.
205. Ḥaydar-'Alí, *Bihjatu'ṣ-Sudúr*, pp. 251–2.

Chapter 24
206. 'Abdu'l-Bahá, in *Star of the West*, vol. 12, no. 14, p. 233.
207. ibid.
208. 'Abdu'l-Bahá, *Will and Testament*, para. 38.
209. 'Abdu'l-Bahá, *Selections*, pp. 210–11.
210. Yúnis Khán, *Kháṭirát-i-Nuh-i-Ṣáliḥ*, pp. 357–8.

Chapter 25
211. Bahá'u'lláh, *Gleanings*, p. 278.
212. *Má'idiy-i-Ásmání*, vol. 4, p. 47.
213. ibid. pp. 123–4.
214. ibid. vol. 1, p. 69.
215. Bahá'u'lláh, *Gleanings*, p. 335.
216. 'Abdu'l-Bahá, *Tablets of the Divine Plan*, p. 51.
217. Shoghi Effendi, *Bahá'í Administration*, p. 66.
218. Bahá'u'lláh, *Gleanings*, p. 343.

219. Bahá'u'lláh, *Amr va Khalq*, vol. 3, p. 121.
220. Ḥaydar-'Alí, *Bihjatu'ṣ-Ṣudúr*, p. 257.
221. Bahá'u'lláh, *Gleanings*, p. 16.
222. 'Abdu'l-Bahá, *Selections*, pp. 251–2.

Chapter 26

223. Bahá'u'lláh, *Tablets*, p. 222.
224. Bahá'u'lláh, quoted in Shoghi Effendi, *God Passes By*, p. 251.
225. ibid. p. 249.
226. Bahá'u'lláh, *Gleanings*, pp. 141–2.
227. Bahá'u'lláh, quoted in Shoghi Effendi, *God Passes By*, p. 251.
228. Bahá'u'lláh, *Tablets*, p. 128.
229. Bahá'u'lláh, *Kitáb-i-Íqán*, pp. 8–9.
230. Quoted in *Star of the West*, vol. 12, no. 19, p. 303.
231. ibid. pp. 294–5.

Chapter 27

232. 'Abdu'l-Bahá, quoted in Rabbaní, *Priceless Pearl*, p. 5.
233. Cooper, quoted in ibid. pp. 5–6.
234. ibid. p. 17.
235. ibid. p. 39.
236. Quoted in ibid. pp. 40–1.
237. ibid. pp. 42–3.
238. See chapter 29.
239. Maḥmúd-i-Zarqání, *Maḥmúd's Diary*, p. 268.
240. Rabbaní, *Priceless Pearl*, p. 48.

Chapter 28

241. Shoghi Effendi, *God Passes By*, p. 386.
242. Message of Shoghi Effendi to the 1936 American Convention, in Shoghi Effendi, *Messages to America*, p. 6.
243. Letter of Shoghi Effendi, October 1953, in Shoghi Effendi, *Messages to the Bahá'í World*, p. 169.
244. Letter of Shoghi Effendi, April 1954, in ibid. p. 63.

Chapter 29

245. Rabbaní, *Priceless Pearl*, pp. 53–4.
246. ibid. pp. 70–1.
247. Shoghi Effendi, quoted in ibid. p. 57.
248. 'Abdu'l-Bahá, *Selections*, p. 320.
249. Shoghi Effendi, *God Passes By*, p. 327.
250. Shoghi Effendi, *Messages to the Bahá'í World*, p. 53.
251. Letter from Nellie French to Albert Windust, 20 April 1948.
252. From a letter written on behalf of Shoghi Effendi to the National Spiritual Assembly of the United States and Canada, *Bahá'í News*, May 1934.
253. Quoted in Rabbaní, *Priceless Pearl*, p. 119.

Chapter 30
254. Bahá'u'lláh, *Hidden Words*, Persian no. 69.
255. 'Abdu'l-Bahá, *Will and Testament*, para. 17.
256. Shoghi Effendi, quoted in Rabbaní, *Priceless Pearl*, pp. 120–1.
257. Cablegram of Shoghi Effendi, 5 April 1952, in Shoghi Effendi, *Messages to the Bahá'í World*, pp. 24–5.
258. Rabbaní, *Priceless Pearl*, pp. 121–2.
259. ibid. pp. 122–3.
260. Cablegram from Shoghi Effendi, 3 June 1957, in Shoghi Effendi, *Messages to the Bahá'í World*, pp. 120–2.

Chapter 31
261. Mills, quoted in Giachery, *Shoghi Effendi*, p. 189.
262. Ransom-Kehler, in ibid. pp. 192–3.
263. Giachery, in ibid. pp. 16–20.
264. Collins, *A Tribute to Shoghi Effendi*.

Chapter 32
265. Bahá'u'lláh, *Gleanings*, p. 278.
266. Unpublished compilation, Iran National Bahá'í Archives, no. 27, p. 281.
267. Bahá'u'lláh, *Iqtidárát*, p. 249.
268. Bahá'u'lláh, *Hidden Words*, Persian no. 56.
269. Unpublished compilation, Iran National Bahá'í Archives, no. 15, p. 385.
270. Bahá'u'lláh, *Mu'assisy-i-Ayádíy-i-Amru'lláh*, p. 11.
271. ibid. p. 12.
272. Bahá'u'lláh, *Tablets*, p. 83.
273. From a letter of the Universal House of Justice to a National Spiritual Assembly, 19 May 1969.

Chapter 33
274. Cablegram from Shoghi Effendi, 24 December 1951, in Shoghi Effendi, *Messages to the Bahá'í World*, p. 20.
275. Cablegram from Shoghi Effendi, 9 January 1951, in ibid. p. 8.
276. ibid. p. 7.
277. Rabbaní, *Priceless Pearl*, p. 253.
278. Cablegram from Shoghi Effendi, 29 February 1952, in Shoghi Effendi, *Messages to the Bahá'í World*, pp. 20–1.
279. Cablegram from Shoghi Effendi, 26 March 1952 in ibid. pp. 132–3.
280. Cablegram from Shoghi Effendi, 27 March 1957, in ibid. p. 174.
281. Cablegram from Shoghi Effendi, 6 April 1954, in ibid. pp. 58–60.
282. Letter of Shoghi Effendi, October 1957, in ibid. pp. 127–8.
283. ibid. p. 130.

Chapter 34
284. Chapman, *Leroy Ioas*, pp. 187–90.
285. ibid. pp. 193–7.

286. Cablegram from Shoghi Effendi, 4 June 1957, in Shoghi Effendi, *Messages to the Bahá'í World*, pp. 122–3.

Chapter 35

287. Ḥaydar-'Alí, *Bihjatu'ṣ-Ṣudúr*, pp. 441–3.
288. Bahá'u'lláh, *Kitáb-i-Íqán*, p. 49.
289. ibid. pp. 53–6.
290. ibid. p. 57.
291. ibid. pp. 49–51.

Chapter 36

292. Bahá'u'lláh, *Tablets*, p. 68.
293. The Universal House of Justice, *Wellspring of Guidance*, p. 11.
294. Shoghi Effendi, *World Order of Bahá'u'lláh*, pp. 147–8.
295. The Universal House of Justice, *Wellspring of Guidance*, pp. 86–7.
296. The Universal House of Justice, *Messages from the Universal House of Justice*, pp. 40–1.
297. Shoghi Effendi, *World Order*, p. 147.
298. Shoghi Effendi, *Unfolding Destiny*, p. 261.

Chapter 37

299. Rabbaní, *Priceless Pearl*, p. 447.
300. ibid.
301. 'Proclamation by the Hands of the Cause to the Bahá'ís of East and West', 25 November 1957, in *Bahá'í World*, vol. 13, pp. 341–3.
302. 'Abdu'l-Bahá, quoted in Universal House of Justice, *Wellspring of Guidance*, p. 47.
303. Conclave Message 1961, in *Ministry of the Custodians*, pp. 321–2.
304. Cablegram from the Hands of the Cause, 21 April 1963, in ibid. pp. 425–6.

Chapter 38

305. Bahá'u'lláh, *Tablets*, p. 68.
306. ibid. pp. 128–9.
307. ibid. p. 125.
308. ibid. p. 68.
309. Shoghi Effendi, *Bahá'í Administration*, p. 88.
310. 'Abdu'l-Bahá, *Some Answered Questions*, pp. 172–3.
311. 'Abdu'l-Bahá, quoted in the Universal House of Justice, *Wellspring of Guidance*, pp. 84–5.
312. The Universal House of Justice, *Wellspring of Guidance*, p. 11.
313. ibid. p. 41.
314. 'Abdu'l-Bahá, *Selections*, p. 302.
315. ibid. pp. 79–80.
316. 'Abdu'l-Bahá, in *Compilation*, vol. 1, p. 416.
317. Tablet of 'Abdu'l-Bahá to Corinne True, translated by the Bahá'í World Centre, 1977. The original translation was made by Ameen Farid on 29 July 1909.
318. 'Abdu'l-Bahá, *Selections*, p. 80.

319. From a letter written on behalf of Shoghi Effendi to an individual believer, 28 July 1936, in *Compilation*, vol. 2, p. 369.
320. From a letter written on behalf of the Universal House of Justice to an individual believer, 29 June 1976 in ibid. p. 371.
321. Bahá'u'lláh, *Tablets*, p. 5.
322. Letter written by Shoghi Effendi to the Bahá'ís of the East, Naw-Rúz 111–1954, in *Compilation*, vol. 1, pp. 341–2.
323. Bahá'u'lláh, *Kitáb-i-Aqdas*, para. 52.
324. Bahá'u'lláh, *Tablets*, pp. 69–70.
325. ibid. pp. 129–30.
326. 'Abdu'l-Bahá, quoted in Introduction to *Kitáb-i-Aqdas*, p. 5.
327. From a letter of the Universal House of Justice to an individual believer, 27 May 1966, in *Compilation*, vol. 1, p. 358.
328. 'Abdu'l-Bahá, quoted in the Universal House of Justice, *Wellspring of Guidance*, p. 84.
329. Bahá'u'lláh, in Shoghi Effendi, *God Passes By*, p. 245.
330. From letter written on behalf of Shoghi Effendi to an individual believer, 18 April 1941, in *Lights of Guidance*, no. 1604, p. 483.
331. Shoghi Effendi, *World Order*, pp. 6–7.
332. Letter of Shoghi Effendi to the Bahá'ís of Persia, 27 November 1929, translated from the Persian in *Compilation*, vol. 1, p. 333.
333. Letter of Shoghi Effendi to the Bahá'ís of Persia, 27 November 1929, translated from the Arabic in ibid. pp. 333–4.

Chapter 39

334. Bahá'u'lláh, *Epistle to the Son of the Wolf*, p. 56.
335. Bahá'u'lláh, quoted in Shoghi Effendi, *Advent of Divine Justice*, pp. 30–1.
336. Bahá'u'lláh, *Tablets*, p. 219.
337. Maḥmúd-i-Zarqání, *Maḥmúd's Diary*, pp. 414–15.
338. Bahá'u'lláh, *Kitáb-i-Aqdas*, para. 97.
339. Bahá'u'lláh, in *Ḥuqúqu'lláh*, no. 18.
340. From a letter written on behalf of Shoghi Effendi, 4 April–3 May 1927, in ibid. no. 80.
341. Bahá'u'lláh, in ibid. no. 9.
342. ibid. no. 27.
343. Unpublished, Iran National Bahá'í Archives, no. 27, pp. 206–7.
344. Bahá'u'lláh, *Tablets*, pp. 22–3.
345. Bahá'u'lláh, *Gleanings*, p. 241.
346. 'Abdu'l-Bahá, *Selections*, pp. 293.
347. ibid. pp. 306–7.
348. Shoghi Effendi, *World Order*, pp. 40–1.
349. From a letter written on behalf of Shoghi Effendi to an individual believer, 17 June 1933.

Chapter 40

350. Bahá'u'lláh, *Kitáb-i-Aqdas*, para. 1.
351. Bahá'u'lláh, *Hidden Words*, Arabic no. 59.
352. ibid. Persian no. 27.

353. ibid. Persian no. 26.
354. ibid. Arabic no. 42.
355. ibid. Persian no. 11.
356. Bahá'u'lláh, in *Bahá'í Prayers*, p. 4.

Appendix 1

357. Shoghi Effendi, *World Order*, pp. 152–7.

Index

This index is alphabetized word for word; thus *Sám Khán* precedes *Ṣamadíyyih*. Connecting letters -i- and y-i- are ignored; 'in', 'of', 'on' 'and', 'for' and the' in entries are ignored.

Lightning Source UK Ltd.
Milton Keynes UK
UKOW020352220212

187722UK00001B/46/A

9 780853 984399